Czech (& Central European) Yearbook of Arbitration®

Czech (& Central European) Yearbook of Arbitration®

Volume IX

2019

Recognition and Enforcement of Arbitral Awards

Editors

Alexander J. Bělohlávek
Professor
at the VŠB TU
in Ostrava
Czech Republic

Naděžda Rozehnalová
Professor
at the Masaryk University
in Brno
Czech Republic

Questions About This Publication

www.czechyearbook.org; www.lexlata.pro; editor@lexlata.pro

LEX LATA

Printed in the EU.
ISBN/EAN: 978-90-829824-0-4
ISSN: 2157-9490

Lex Lata B.V.
Mauritskade 45-B
2514 HG – THE HAGUE
The Netherlands

The title Czech (& Central European) Yearbook of Arbitration®
as well as the logo appearing on the cover are protected by EU
trademark law.

Typeset by Lex Lata B.V.

Address for correspondence & manuscripts

Czech (& Central European) Yearbook of Arbitration®

Jana Zajíce 32, Praha 7, 170 00, Czech Republic

editor@lexlata.pro

Editorial support:

Tereza Tolarová, Jan Šamlot, Lenka Němečková, Karel Nohava, Kim Mašek

Impressum

Institutions Participating in the CYArb® Project

Academic Institutions

University of West Bohemia in Pilsen, Czech Republic
Faculty of Law, Department of International Law
& Department of Constitutional Law
Západočeská univerzita v Plzni, Právnická fakulta
Katedra mezinárodního práva & Katedra ústavního práva

Masaryk University in Brno, Czech Republic
Faculty of Law, Department of International and European Law
Masarykova univerzita v Brně, Právnická fakulta
Katedra mezinárodního a evropského práva

Pavol Jozef Šafárik University in Košice, Slovakia
Faculty of Law, Department of Commercial Law and Business
Law
Právnická fakulta UPJŠ, Košice, Slovensko
Katedra obchodného a hospodárskeho práva

VŠB – TU Ostrava, Czech Republic
Faculty of Economics, Department of Law
VŠB – TU Ostrava, Ekonomická fakulta Katedra práva

Institute of State and Law of the Academy of Sciences of the Czech Republic, v.v.i.
Ústav státu a práva Akademie věd ČR, v.v.i.

Institute of State and Law, Slovak Academy of Sciences, Slovakia
Ústav štátu a práva Bratislava, Slovenská akadémia vied, Slovensko

Non-academic Institutions Participating in the CYArb® Project

International Arbitral Centre of the Austrian Federal Economic Chamber
Wiener Internationaler Schiedsgericht (VIAC), Vienna

Court of International Commercial Arbitration attached to the Chamber of Commerce and Industry of Romania
Curtea de Arbitraj Comercial Internaţional de pe lângă Camera de Comerţ şi Industrie a României, Bucharest

Arbitration Court attached to the Hungarian Chamber of Commerce and Industry
A Magyar Kereskedelmi és Iparkamara mellett szervezett Választottbíróság, Budapest

Arbitration Court attached to the Economic Chamber of the Czech Republic and Agricultural Chamber of the Czech Republic
Rozhodčí soud při Hospodářské komoře České republiky a Agrární komoře České republiky, Prague

International Arbitration Court of the Czech Commodity Exchange, Prague, Czech Republic
Mezinárodní rozhodčí soud při Českomoravské komoditní burze (Prague, Czech Republic)

ICC National Committee Czech Republic
ICC Národní výbor Česká republika

The Court of Arbitration at the Polish Chamber of Commerce in Warsaw
Sąd Arbitrażowy przy Krajowej Izbie Gospodarczej w Warszawie

Proofreading and translation support provided by:
SPĚVÁČEK překladatelská agentura s.r.o., Prague, Czech Republic and Pamela Lewis, USA.

Contents

CASE LAW

Czech Republic

Poland

BOOK REVIEWS

NEWS & REPORTS

BIBLIOGRAPHY, CURRENT EVENTS, CYIL & CYArb® PRESENTATIONS, IMPORTANT WEB SITES

Alexander J. Bělohlávek

All contributions in this book are subject to academic review.

List of Abbreviations

1923 Geneva Protocol	Protocol on Arbitration Clauses signed in Geneva on 24 September 1923
1927 Geneva Convention	Convention on the Execution of Foreign Arbitral Awards signed in Geneva on 26 September 1927
1961 Geneva Convention	European Convention on International Commercial Arbitration signed in Geneva on 21 April 1961
ADR	Alternative Dispute Resolution
AUT	Austria
BIT	Bilateral Investment Treaty
Brussels I Regulation	Regulation (EU) No 1215/2012 of the European Parliament and of the Council of 12 December 2012 on jurisdiction and the recognition and enforcement of judgments in civil and commercial matters
CCP	Polish Code of Civil Procedure
CDC	Cartel Damage Claims
CETA	The Comprehensive Economic and Trade Agreement
CJEU	Court of Justice of the European Union
COMI	Centre of Main Interest
COMMISA	Corporación Mexicana De Mantenimiento Integral
Constitutional Court RF	Constitutional Court of the Russian Federation
ČR	Česká republika (Czech republic)
DEU	Deutschland (Germany)
Directive	Directive on Alternative Dispute Resolution in Consumer Cases
EC	The European Community
EC Treaty	Energy Charter Treaty signed in Lisbon on 17 December 1994
ECHR	European Court of Human Rights
ECJ	European Court of Justice
EEA	European Economic Area
EEC	European Economic Community
EGPC	Société Egyptian General Petroleum

	Corporation
EU	European Union
FCIArb	Fellow of the Chartered Institute of Arbitration
Global Panel	Global Enforcement and Recognition Panel
HLV Report	The Heidelberg-Luxembourg-Vienna Report
ICAC	International Commercial Arbitration Court at the Chamber of Commerce of Trade and Industry of the Russian Federation
ICC	International Chamber of Commerce
ICCA	International Congress and Convention Association
ICCt	The International Criminal Court
ICSID	International Centre for Settlement of Investment Disputes
INSOL-Europe	International Association of Restructuring, Insolvency & Bankruptcy Professionals
ISDS	Investor-state dispute settlement
KBC	Karaha Bodas Company
KKO	Korkein oikeus (The Supreme Court of Finland)
LCIA	London Court of International Arbitration
NATCAS	Société National Gas Company
New York Convention	Convention on the Recognition and Enforcement of Foreign Arbitral Awards signed in New York on 10 June 1958
OHADA	Organisation for the Harmonization in Africa of Business Law
OTV	Omnium de Traitement et de Valorisation
Pertamina	Persusahaan Pertambangan Minyak Dan Gas Bumi Negara
PIL	Private International Law
PPP	Public-private partnership
RAA	Russian Arbitration Association
RIMA	Russian Institute of Modern Arbitration
SCC	Stockholm Chamber of Commerce
Swiss PILA	Swiss International Private Law
TEU	Treaty on European Union
TFEU	Treaty on the Functioning of the European Union
U.A.E.	United Arab Emirates
UK	United Kingdom

UN	United Nations
UNCITRAL	United Nations Commission on International Trade Law
UNCITRAL Model Law	The UNCITRAL Model Law on International Commercial Arbitration adopted in 1985
US	United States of America
VIAC	Vienna International Arbitral Centre
WJA	The World Jurist Association
ZBP	Polish Bank Association
ZPO	Zivilprozessordnung

Articles

Petr Dobiáš

The Recognition and Enforcement of Arbitral Awards Set Aside in the Country of Origin

Key words:
arbitration | enforcement | recognition

Abstract *| In the legal theory and practice disputes are arising related to Article V of the Convention on the Recognition and Enforcement of Foreign Arbitral Awards, ratified in New York in 1958. Foreign arbitral award annulled in the country of origin may be enforced in the Czech Republic in exceptional cases on the basis of a decision of a Czech court of general jurisdiction. Such a case could typically be the enforcement of an arbitral award in accordance with Article V of the New York Convention, which was annulled in the country of origin for being contrary to public policy but is not contrary to public policy in terms of Czech law.*

| | |

JUDr. Petr Dobiáš, Ph.D., MCIArb currently holds the position of Senior Lecturer at CEVRO INSTITUT in Prague. In his research activities, he primarily focuses on international arbitration, international insurance law and European private international law including contract law, in particular, under the Rome I Regulation. Petr Dobiáš is the author of the monograph Selected Issues of the International Insurance Law in Consideration of the Resolution of Insurance Disputes in Arbitration Proceedings, co-author of the Commentary on Obligations arising of the Juridical Acts in Civil Code and author of numerous other scientific publications. He also acts as an arbitrator.
E-mail: petr.dobias@vsci.cz

Czech (& Central European) Yearbook of Arbitration®

I.   Introduction

1.01. This article is devoted to a comparative analysis of the legislation and case law pertaining to the recognition and enforcement of arbitral awards annulled in their country of origin. Disputes arising in legal theory and practice relate mainly to ambiguous drafting of Article V(1)(e) of the Convention on the Recognition and Enforcement of Foreign Arbitral Awards, ratified in New York in 1958 New York Convention.[1] According to this Convention

> recognition and enforcement of the award *may* be refused, upon a petition submitted by the party against whom it is invoked, only if that party furnishes to the competent authority of the country where the recognition and enforcement is sought, proof that the award has not yet become binding on the parties, or has been annulled or suspended by a competent authority of the country in which, or under the law of which, that award was made.

1.02. A major dispute in legal theory as well as in practice is the use of the non-mandatory word *may* instead of the mandatory word *must* in Article V(1)(e) of the New York Convention. Some foreign courts of general jurisdiction adopted the stance that they can recognise and permit the enforcement of an arbitral award, even if this award was annulled by the competent court of general jurisdiction in the jurisdiction where the arbitral proceedings are held. A consequence then of the above-mentioned stance taken by some foreign courts of general jurisdiction is that a situation arises whereby the recognition and enforcement of an arbitral award may be denied in one country under the New York Convention, the enforcement of which cannot be permitted as a result of its suspension in the country of origin. Conversely, in another state the same award will be recognised, and its enforcement permitted. Article VII(1)[2] of the New York Convention further provides for the application of provisions that are more favourable from the viewpoint of the recognition and enforcement of arbitral awards. The New York Convention thus expressly enables a party to the dispute to refer to provisions of the national law of a certain signatory

---

[1]   UN Convention on the Recognition and Enforcement of Foreign Arbitral Awards, United Nations Conference on International Commercial Arbitration (adopted 10 June 1958, entered into force 7 June 1959) 330 UNTS 38.

[2]   Reyadh Seyadi is of the opinion that Article VII(1) of the New York Convention does not permit neglecting the grounds for refusing to recognise and enforce foreign arbitral awards set out in Article V of this Convention and thus giving domestic law preference over international law [Reyadh Seyadi, *Enforcement of Arbitral Awards Annulled by the Court of the Seat*, 84(2) ARBITRATION 128, 140 (2018)].

country, if their application from the aspect of the recognition and enforcement of arbitral awards is more favourable.

1.03. If we are to take a stance on the question of the recognition and enforcement of arbitral awards annulled in the country of origin, then we must evaluate the law applicable in arbitral proceedings. This includes multilateral and bilateral international treaties and the legislation contained in the legal systems of the individual signatory countries of the New York Convention. We must evaluate such law and policy in connection with the decision-making practice of the courts of general jurisdiction in the signatory countries of the New York Convention.

II. Recognition and Enforcement of Arbitral Awards Annulled in the Country of Origin in the Case Law of French Courts

II.1. Pabalk Ticaret v. Norsolor

1.04. In its decision in the *Norsolor*[3] case, France's Court of Cassation (*Cour de Cassation*), had already taken the stance that the suspension of an arbitral award in the country of origin need not necessarily lead to the refusal to recognise and enforce an arbitral award in France under Article V(1)(e) of the New York Convention. This is because the relevant provisions of the French Civil Procedure Code,[4] which may be applied in accordance with the provisions of Article VII(1) of the New York Convention cited above, do not contain a regulation that would generally not allow the recognition and enforcement of arbitral awards annulled by a court of general jurisdiction in the country of origin.[5] In reference to this ruling, Professor Georgios C. Petrochilos notes that the Court of Cassation took a proactive approach, as it is clear from the wording of Article VII(1) that

---

[3] Cour de Cassation *Pabalk Ticaret* v. *Norsolor* of 9 October 1984, appeal number 83-11355, Bulletin 1984 I No. 248, Yearbook Commercial Arbitration XI (1986) et. 484 et seq.

[4] This ruling ensues from the French Civil Procedure Code, Articles 1501 to 1507, in wording effective as of 14 May 1981. This conclusion generally applies under Article 1526 in conjunction with Article 1520 even following the amendment implemented under Decree No. 2011-48 issued by the French Ministry of Justice on 13 January 2011, as under Article 1526 'the judge assigned to the matter may stay or set conditions for enforcement of an award where enforcement could severely prejudice the rights of one of the parties'.

[5] For the decision in the *Norsolor* case, compare ALAN REDFERN, MARTIN HUNTER, NIGEL BLACKNABY, CONSTANTINE PARTASIDES, LAW AND PRACTICE OF INTERNATIONAL COMMERCIAL ARBITRATION, London: Sweet and Maxwell Ltd. 556-557 (2004). This conclusion was also confirmed in the decision handed down by the Paris Court of Appeal in *Société Egyptian General Petroleum Corporation (EGPC)* v. *Société National Gas Company (NATCAS)* of 24 November 2011, case no. 10/16525, which was however annulled by the decision of the Court of Cassation of 26 June 2013, appeal no. 12-16224.

it concerns the right of the party to the dispute to propose the application of legislation that is more favourable for it.[6]

II.2. Hilmarton v. Omnium de Traitement et de Valorisation

1.05. In the *Hilmarton* case, one of the key questions was an assessment of the relationship between the public policy reservation[7] in two countries in connection with the recognition and enforcement of an arbitral award under the New York Convention. Hilmarton Ltd. initiated the launch of arbitral proceedings under the ICC Rules of Arbitration in Geneva. In its arbitral award,[8] the arbitral tribunal stated that the provisions of Algerian law guaranteeing observance of the principles of fair trade (healthy and fair commercial practices) and the fight against corruption create general principles that must be observed in all jurisdictions, including the Swiss legal system. In its ruling, the arbitral tribunal found that the contract[9] between Hilmarton Ltd. and Omnium de Traitement et de Valorisation (OTV) was in breach of the above-mentioned principles and dismissed the action on the grounds of the nullity of the contract between Hilmarton Ltd. and OTV.

1.06. The arbitral award in the *Hilmarton* case was annulled upon a petition of Hilmarton Ltd. by the Swiss Court of Appeal (*Cour de Justice*) on 17 November 1989 and this decision was confirmed by the Swiss Supreme Court (*Tribunal Fédéral*) on 17 April 1990.[10] The Court of Appeal (Cour de Justice) based its decision on the established case law of the Swiss Supreme Court, according to which a contract is not in breach of the law and, for this reason, null and void only because it allows the contracting parties to undertake activities prohibited by local law. The Swiss Court of Appeal further ruled that, under Swiss law, illicit, and therefore null and void, is only a breach of the provisions of Swiss law. In its decision, the Swiss Supreme Court arrived at the conclusion that a breach of a provision of foreign legislation pertaining to a public policy reservation may have relevance for assessing the validity of a contract only if the acceptance of its breach could result in a simultaneous

---

[6] Georgios C. Petrochilos, *Enforcing Awards annulled in their country of origin under the New York Convention*, 48(4) I. C. L. Q. 856, 865 (1999).

[7] For a definition of the term public policy, compare ALEXANDER J. BĚLOHLÁVEK, ACT ON ARBITRAL PROCEEDINGS AND ON THE ENFORCEMENT OF ARBITRAL AWARDS, Prague: C. H. Beck 1380 (2nd edition 2012).

[8] Final award in case no. 5622 of 1988, Yearbook Commercial Arbitration XIX (1994) et. 105 et seq.

[9] In the case at hand this concerned an agency contract which, upon careful analysis of its content, the arbitral tribunal designated as contradicting good morals and international public policy.

[10] Both decisions published in Yearbook Commercial Arbitration XIX (1994) et. 214 et seq.

disruption in the common good and Swiss public policy. The provision of foreign legislation that was breached must further protect such individual and common interests that, according to general opinion, are vitally important, and at the same time must concern legal values which, from a moral viewpoint, outweigh the interest in protecting the freedom of contract.

1.07.   OTV sought permission for the enforcement in France of the aforementioned arbitral award. The enforcement of the arbitral award was permitted by the Paris Court of First Instance (*Tribunal de grande instance de Paris*) on 26 February 1990 and this decision was confirmed by the Paris Court of Appeal (*Cour d'Appel de Paris*) on 19 December 1991.[11] In the opinion of the Paris Court of Appeal, the French regulation of arbitral proceedings in international trade does not oblige French courts to take into account the suspension of a decision made in a foreign legal system, and thus permitting the enforcement of an arbitral award that was annulled under the national legislation of another country is not in conflict with Article 1502(2) of the French Civil Procedure Code.[12] The aforementioned decision was upheld by the French Court of Cassation,[13] which in its decision ruled that the arbitral award made in Switzerland

---

[11]   Court of Appeal case no. 90-16778. Yearbook Commercial Arbitration XIX (1994) et. 655 et seq. Claudia Alfons noted in regards to the Court of Appeal decision that the court arrived at the conclusion that Article V(1)(e) of the New York Convention is mandatory, but does not apply because the law in the State where the order for the enforcement of the arbitral award was proposed permits the enforcement of the award in such a case [CLAUDIA ALFONS, RECOGNITION AND ENFORCEMENT OF ANNULLED FOREIGN ARBITRAL AWARDS: AN ANALYSIS OF THE LEGAL FRAMEWORK AND ITS INTERPRETATION IN CASE LAW AND LITERATURE, Frankfurt: Petr Lang 87 (2010)]. Volker Nienaber takes the view that Article V(1) of the French language version has a mistake, which came about during the translation process, and this provision of the New York Convention is not mandatory [VOLKER NIENABER, DIE ANERKENNUNG UND VOLLSTRECKUNG IM SITZSTAAT AUFGEHOBENER SCHIEDSSPRÜCHE, Frankfurt: Petr Lang 122 (2002)]. Nevertheless, Franz T. Schwarz and Christian W. Konrad state that the words 'may', 'can' and 'must' also appear in turn in case law of the Austrian Supreme Court of Justice in several various decisions where Article V of the New York Convention is employed [FRANZ T. SCHWARZ AND CHRISTIAN W. KONRAD: THE VIENNA RULES, A COMMENTARY ON INTERNATIONAL ARBITRATION IN AUSTRIA, Alphen aan den Rijn: Wolters Kluwer 72 (2009)].

[12]   Under the version valid at the time the decision was handed down, Article 1502(2) of the French Civil Procedure Code allowed an appeal to be filed against a decision permitting the recognition or enforcement of an arbitral award solely in the following cases:

A. If the arbitrator has rendered their decision in the case even in the absence of an arbitral agreement or on the basis of an arbitral agreement that is invalid or that has expired;

B. If the arbitral tribunal was irregularly constituted or the sole arbitrator irregularly appointed;

C. If the arbitrator has not rendered their decision in accordance with the mission conferred upon them;

D. If the right to due process has not been respected;

E. If the recognition and enforcement of an arbitral award is contrary to international public policy (*ordre public*).

The valid Article 1514 of the French Civil Procedure Code allowed states: 'An arbitral award shall be recognised or enforced in France if the party relying on it can prove its existence and if such recognition and enforcement is not manifestly contrary to international public policy.'

[13]   Decision of 23 March 1994, appeal no. 92-15137, Bulletin 1994 I No. 104 et. 79, Yearbook Commercial Arbitration XX (1995) et. 663 et seq. The fact that the Court of Cassation is an advocate of the delocalisation theory can also be documented by the controversial decision of 29 June 2007 in *Société PT Putrabali*

was an international arbitral award. It was therefore not incorporated into the legal system of the country, and thus remained in existence even though it was annulled and its recognition was not contrary to international public policy.[14] In the period following the issue of the first arbitral award in the case, the dispute was re-submitted for a new hearing in arbitral proceedings in Switzerland, with a new second arbitral award subsequently issued, this time in favour of Hilmarton Ltd. In its decision of 22 September 1993,[15] the Court of First Instance (*Tribunal de Grande Instance*) in Nanterre approved the enforcement of the second arbitral award, whilst at the same time approving the enforcement of the decision of the Swiss Supreme Court (*Tribunal Fédéral*), by which the first arbitral award was annulled. The decision of the Court of First Instance (*Tribunal de Grande Instance*) in Nanterre was subsequently upheld by the decision of the Court of Appeal in Versailles (*Cour d'Appel Versailles*) on 29 June 1995.[16] The court upheld it on the grounds that the concept of international public policy in France did not preclude the recognition of a foreign arbitral award issued after the preceding arbitral award, the enforcement of which was permitted in France but subsequently annulled in the country of origin. In that situation, the Court of Cassation annulled, by its decision of 10 December 1997,[17] both of the decisions handed down by the Court of Appeal in Versailles and ruled that decisions concerning the same case between identical parties establishes an obstacle in France for the recognition of court decisions and arbitral awards made abroad, which are inconsistent with them.

Adyamulia v. *SA Rena Holdings*, in which the court arrived at the conclusion that there is no reason to deny the recognition and enforcement of an arbitral award which was annulled in the country of origin by a court of general jurisdiction, even if a new arbitral award was subsequently issued in the same case.

[14] Albert Jan van den Berg states that in 1958 it was generally accepted that the award which had been set aside in the country of origin ceases to legally exist [Albert Jan van den Berg, *Should the Setting Aside of the Arbitral Award be Abolished?* 29(2) ICSID Review 263, 266 (2014)].

[15] Yearbook Commercial Arbitration XX (1995) et. 194 et seq.

[16] Decision of the Court of Appeal in Versailles no. 315 and 316, Yearbook Commercial Arbitration XXI (1996) et. 524 et seq.

[17] Decision of 10 June 1993, appeal no. 95-18402 and 95-18403 (joined cases), Bulletin 1997 I No. 195 et. 130, Yearbook Commercial Arbitration XXII (1997) et. 696 et seq.

III. Recognition and Enforcement of Arbitral Awards Annulled in the Country of Origin in the Case Law of the United States of America

III.1. Chromalloy Aeroservices, Inc. v. The Arab Republic of Egypt

1.08.   In the *Chromalloy* case, the enforcement of an arbitral award was permitted in the same case by the Paris Court of First Instance. This decision was upheld in its decision of 14 January 1997[18] by the Paris Court of Appeal (*Cour d'Appel de Paris*). It was subsequently also permitted in the United States of America by the United States Federal Court for the District of Columbia.[19]

1.09.   In its decision, the United States Federal Court for the District of Columbia stated that the court of general jurisdiction must (compare Article 201 of the Federal Arbitration Act)[20] recognise and permit the enforcement of an arbitral award if it does not find at least one of the grounds for refusing to recognise or permit the enforcement of arbitral awards under Article V of the New York Convention. In the legal opinion of the United States Federal Court for the District of Columbia, a court of general jurisdiction may, at its discretion, refuse to recognise or permit the enforcement of an arbitral award in accordance with Article V(1) of the New York Convention. In its decision, the United States Federal Court for the District of Columbia used as a basis the mandatory provisions of Article VII of the New York Convention, which allowed it to apply the provisions of the Federal Arbitration Act to a decision on permitting the enforcement of an arbitral award issued in Egypt, which was annulled by the Court of Appeal in Cairo. According to Part 1 (General Provisions), Article 10 of the Federal Arbitration Act, arbitral awards may be annulled only in a very limited circle of cases,[21] such as the issue of an arbitral award under the influence of fraud, bribery of the arbitrators or if the arbitrators exceed the powers conferred upon them. In accordance with the relevant jurisdiction[22] of the courts of general jurisdiction

---

[18]   Compare the decision in *The Arab Republic of Egypt* v. Chromalloy Aeroservices, Inc. (US), case no. 95/23025, Yearbook Commercial Arbitration XXII (1997) et. 691 et seq.

[19]   Decision of 31 June 1996, Civil No. 94-2339 (JLG), 939 F. Supp. 907 (D.D.C. 1996), Yearbook Commercial Arbitration XXII (1997) et. 1001 et seq.

[20]   The United States Arbitration Act (Title 9 U.S.C. Article 1 et seq.) per the wording valid as of 15 November 1990.

[21]   Albert Jan van den Berg designates this procedure of the court in the application of the Federal Arbitration Act as generous [Albert Jan van den Berg, *Enforcement of Annulled Awards?* 9(2) The ICC International Court of Arbitration Bulletin 15, 18 (1998)].

[22]   With regard to this compare Yearbook Commercial Arbitration XXII (1997), et. 1005.

in the United States of America, an arbitral award can also be annulled if it is in clear conflict with, or displays a manifest disregard for, the law. Such clear conflict with the law occurs, for example, in the situation where the arbitrator understands the legislation and can interpret it correctly, but instead chooses to ignore it. The United States Federal Court for the District of Columbia arrived at the conclusion that Egypt had denied its commitment to respect the results of the arbitral proceedings (as, in the arbitration clause, the parties explicitly ruled out the possibility of appealing against the arbitration finding or another remedy), and thus recognition of the decision of the Court of Appeal in Cairo is contrary to the policy of the United States of America promoting arbitral proceedings. The United States Federal Court for the District of Columbia further arrived at the conclusion that the arbitral award made by the arbitral tribunal was valid under the legislation of the United States of America and granted the petition for recognition and enforcement of arbitral award.

III.2.   Baker Marine Ltd. v. Chevron Ltd. et al.

1.10.   In *Baker Marine Ltd.* v. *Chevron Ltd. Et al.*[23] the Second Circuit of the United States Court of Appeals permitted the enforcement of the arbitral award, which was annulled by the court of general jurisdiction at the place of the arbitral proceedings. They did so because the appellant did not provide an adequate reason for refusing to recognize the decision of Nigerian courts of general jurisdiction. The Second Circuit of the United States Court of Appeals justified its verdict by stating that unlike the applicant in the *Chromalloy* case, *Baker Marine Ltd.* Is not a domestic legal entity and does not seek recognition from the onset for the recognition of the arbitral award in the United States of America. In addition, the defendants did not breach any obligation by filing an appeal against the arbitral award in Nigeria. Thus, the recognition of Nigerian court decisions in this case is not contrary to public policy in the United States of America.

---

[23]   Decision of 12 August 1999, Nos. 97-9615, 97-9617, 191 F.3d 194 (2d Cir 1999), Yearbook Commercial Arbitration XXIV (1999) et. 909 et seq.

III.3.   Martin I. Spier v. Calzaturificio Tecnica S.p.A

1.11.   In *Martin I. Spier* v. *Calzaturificio Tecnica S.p.A.*,[24] the United States District Court for the Southern District of New York refused to follow the decision in the Chromalloy case. Their reasoning was that the appellant had not waived the right to appeal against the arbitral award and did not provide any adequate reason for refusing to recognise the decisions of the Italian courts of general jurisdictions. The arbitral award was suspended by the competent Italian courts under Article V(1) (c) of the New York Convention, because the arbitrators had exceeded the powers conferred to them. The United States District Court for the Southern District of New York declared as irrelevant the argument concerning the waiving of the right to an appeal, as the Italian Civil Procedure Code did not at that time allow the waiving of the right to file a petition for the annulment of the arbitral award in the cases referred to in Article 829. The United States District Court for the Southern District of New York further ruled that the party applying for the enforcement of an arbitral award to be permitted cannot demand the application of the domestic legislation of the United States of America via Article VII(2) of the New York Convention. This is because as in the decision in the *Baker Marine* case, Spier and Tecnica agreed in another country that their disputes would be resolved in this other country, and the applicable international treaties make no reference to the legislation of the United States of America. There was nothing to indicate that the parties had selected the legislation of the United States of America governing arbitral proceedings as the governing law in the event of a contract dispute arising.

III.4.   Karaha Bodas Company L.L.C.
v. Persusahaan Pertambangan Minyak Dan
Gas Bumi Negara a.k.a. Pertamina (US)

1.12.   The enforcement of the arbitral award was granted by the decision of the United States District Court for the Southern District of Texas in the United States of America, and this decision was upheld by the Fifth Circuit of the United States Court of Appeals.[25]

---

[24]   Decisions of 22 October and 29 November 1999, No. 86 Civ. 3447 (CSH), 71 F. Supp. 2d 279, 288 (S.D.N.Y. 1999), Yearbook Commercial Arbitration XXV (2000) et. 1042 et seq.
[25]   Decision of the United States District Court for the Southern District of Texas, Houston Division, of 26 April 2002, 22 July 2002 and 17 April 2003, Civil Action No. H 01-0634 and the Fifth Circuit of the United States Court of Appeals of 18 June 2003, No. 02-20550, Yearbook Commercial Arbitration XXVIII (2003) et. 908 et seq. Decision of the Fifth Circuit of the United States Court of Appeals of 23 March 2004, Nos. 02-20042, 03-20602, extract from Yearbook Commercial Arbitration XXIX (2004) et. 1262 et seq.

The decisions of the courts of general jurisdiction in the United States of America are based on the following arguments. Courts of general jurisdiction with so-called *primary jurisdiction* are usually the courts of general jurisdiction at the place where the arbitral proceedings are held.[26] Only these may apply their national law when considering a petition to annul an arbitral award. Courts of general jurisdiction with so-called *secondary jurisdiction* may refuse to grant the enforcement of an arbitral award only on the grounds set out in Article V of the New York Convention. The decision of the Indonesian court of general jurisdiction on the annulment of the arbitral award thus has no influence on the decision of the United States District Court for the Southern District of Texas, because the Indonesian court did not have *primary jurisdiction*. The United States District Court for the Southern District of Texas further ruled that, under the New York Convention, courts of general jurisdiction have the discretional power to permit the enforcement of an arbitral award even if proceedings had been instigated for its annulment in the country of origin. Furthermore, they ruled that the court of general jurisdiction in the United States of America had the discretional power to grant the enforcement of an arbitral award, regardless of its annulment in another country.

III.5. Termorio SAESP v. Electranta SP

1.13. As in the *Chromalloy* case, this case was also decided on 17 March 2006 by the United States Federal Court for the District of Columbia,[27] but it denied the recognition and enforcement of the arbitral award annulled in Columbia. The first difference from the facts of the *Chromalloy* case consists of the fact that in the *Termorio* v. *Electranta* case, no arrangement was concluded between the parties to the dispute about a party to the dispute waiving its right to file an appeal against an arbitral award. In addition, a party to the dispute in these proceedings was not a party from the United States of America, and thus in this case there is no interest in the application of the legal system of the United States of America. The decision was upheld by the United States Court of Appeals,[28] which stated that the decision

---

[26] Difference between 'primary and secondary jurisdiction' analysed in detail by Burton S. De Witt [Burton S. De Witt, *A Judgment Without Merits: The Recognition and Enforcement of Foreign Judgments Confirming, Recognizing, or Enforcing Arbitral Awards*, 50(3) TEX. INT'L L.J. 495, 512 (2015)].
[27] Decision of the United States Federal Court for the District of Columbia of 17 March 2006, 421 F. Supp. 2d 87, 99 (D.D.C. 2006).
[28] Decision of the District of Columbia Circuit of the United States Court of Appeals of 25 May 2007, No. 06-7058, 487 F.3d 928, 938 (D. C. Cir 2007).

of the court of first instance was, for the stated reason, not in contradiction to the decision in the *Chromalloy* case.

III.6. Corporación Mexicana De Mantenimiento Integral v. Pemex-Exploración Y Producción

1.14. In the case in question, an arbitral award was rendered based on an arbitration clause in an action filed by the company Corporación Mexicana De Mantenimiento Integral (COMMISA). This granted a monetary claim in a dispute with the Pemex-Exploración Y Producción (company acting on behalf of the Mexican government). In the meantime, Mexico approved legislation that had retroactive effects and established the exclusive jurisdiction of the Mexican Tax and Administrative Court in similar cases. In addition, Pemex-Exploración Y Producción filed a petition with the Mexican court for the annulment of the arbitral award, which was successful. At the same time, COMMISA filed a petition in the United States of America for the confirmation of the arbitral award to the United States District Court for the Southern District of New York[29] under the Panama Convention.[30] The United States District Court for the Southern District of New York arrived at the conclusion that the annulment of the arbitral award was contrary to 'the basic notions of justice in that it applied a law that was not in existence at the time the parties' contract was formed and left COMMISA without an apparent ability to litigate its claims' and that the acceptance of the retroactive effect of the Mexican legislation would prevent Pemex from exercising its claims. The Second Circuit of the United States Court of Appeals[31] confirmed this decision and in the grounds to its decision stated that the principle of comity obliges American courts to respect a decision to annul an arbitral award if it is not contrary to public policy. The decision of the Mexican court on the annulment of the arbitral award was contrary to public policy, because it denied the applicant the possibility of filing an action in arbitral proceedings and to exercise its claims.

---

[29] *Corporación Mexicana De Mantenimiento Integral* v. *Pemex-Exploración Y Producción*, No. 10 Civ. 206 (AKH), 962 F. Supp. 2d 642 (Southern District, New York 2013).
[30] Inter-American Convention on International Commercial Arbitration (adopted 30 January 1975, entered into force on 16 June 1976) 1438 UNTS 245.
[31] No. 13-4022 1, 27 (2d Cir. 2016).

III.7. Thai-Lao Lignite Co Ltd. and Hongsa Lignite v. Government of the LPDR

1.15. In a recent decision, the Second Circuit of the Court of Appeal[32] arrived at the conclusion that if an arbitral award was annulled by a court which has primary jurisdiction, after an American court confirmed such an arbitral award, the American court should apply Article 60(b)(5) of the Federal Rules of Civil Procedure, according to which 'a court may relieve a party from final judgment if the judgement has been satisfied, released, or discharged'.[33] In accordance with the decisions handed down in *Termorio* v. *Electranta*[34] and *COMISSA* v. *Pemex*,[35] however, it must be investigated whether the decision of the court with primary jurisdiction complies with the 'fundamental notions of what is decent and just in the United States.'

IV. Recognition and Enforcement of Arbitral Awards Annulled in the Country of Origin in the Case Law of the Austria

IV.1. Kajo-Erzeugnisse Essenzen GmbH v. DO Zdravilisce Radenska

1.16. In *Kajo-Erzeugnisse Essenzen GmbH* v. DO Zdravilisce Radenska,[36] the Austrian Supreme Court of Justice came to the legal opinion that under Article IX of the European Convention on International Commercial Arbitration of 1961 (European Convention),[37] the annulment of an arbitral award in the country of origin due to a breach of domestic public policy does not constitute grounds for refusing the enforcement of an arbitral award in other signatory countries where public policy is not violated by this arbitral award. With regard to the relationship between Article V(1)(e) of the New York Convention and Article IX(1) of the European Convention, the Supreme Court adopted the stance that the purpose of Article IX(2) in conjunction

---

[32] The decision of the Second Circuit of the Court of Appeal of 20 July 2017 *Thai-Lao Lignite (Thailand) Co.* v. *Government of the Lao People's Democratic Republic* 864 F.3d 172 (2d Cir. 2017), which upheld decision no. 10-cv-5256 (KMW), 997 F. Supp. 2d 214 (S.D.N.Y, 2014).

[33] *Thai-Lao Lignite (Thailand) Co.* v. *Government of the Lao People's Democratic Republic* 864 F.3d 172, 175 (2d Cir. 2017).

[34] Decision of the District of Columbia Circuit of the United States Court of Appeals of 25 May 2007, No. 06-7058, 487 F.3d 928, 938 (D. C. Cir 2007).

[35] *Corporación Mexicana De Mantenimiento Integral* v. *Pemex-Exploración Y Producción* 832 F.3d 92, 106 (2d Cir. 2014).

[36] Decision of 20 October 1993 and 23 February 1998, Yearbook Commercial Arbitration XXIV (1999) et. 919 et seq.

[37] European Convention on International Commercial Arbitration (adopted on 21 April 1961, entered into force 7 January 1964) 484 UNTS 349.

with Article IX(1) of the European Convention is to restrict the application of Article V(1)(e) of the New York Convention if the given country is a signatory of both of the aforementioned conventions.[38] The Supreme Court further ruled that the application of the aforementioned provisions of international conventions, in conjunction with Section 81(3) of the Austrian Enforcement Act (*Exekutionsordnung*)[39] may only be considered if the enforcement of the arbitral award was in clear conflict with the domestic legislation. Under no circumstances may the arbitral award be reviewed from a factual or legal point of view. A review from the aspect of a public policy reservation must be used with maximum restraint The Supreme Court thus took a very restrictive approach allowing the application of a public policy reservation only in the case that granting the enforcement of an arbitral award would violate the fundamental values of the Austrian legal system and EU law.

V. Recognition and Enforcement of Arbitral Awards Annulled in the country of origin in the case law of the Federal Republic of Germany

V.1. Decision of the Court of Appeal in Rostock of 28 October 1999

1.17. In the Federal Republic of Germany, the Higher Regional Court in Rostock ruled[40] to reject a petition for granting the enforcement of an arbitral award which was annulled by the court of general jurisdiction at the place of the arbitral proceedings, even though the decision on the annulment of the arbitral award had yet to take legal force. The decision of the Higher Regional Court in Rostock is an illustrative example of the application of Section 1061(3) of the German Civil Procedure Code (ZPO), which confers to courts of general jurisdiction the power to decide, upon a petition submitted by an interested party, on the annulment of a declaration of enforceability (*exequatur*), if the arbitral award was subsequently (i.e. after it was declared enforceable) annulled by the competent foreign authority. According to the decision of the Higher Regional Court in

---

[38] In comparing the differing approach in French case law, it should be mentioned that France is also a signatory of the New York Convention (ratified 26 June 1959) and the European Convention (ratified 16 December 1966). Cf. Higher Regional Court of Munich of 13 February 1995, file reference 17 U 6591/93.

[39] Act No. 79/1896 of the Federal Collection of Acts, on Enforcement and Securing Proceedings, as amended. Section 81(3) of the Austrian Enforcement Act was repealed with effect from 1 January 2017.

[40] Higher Regional Court Rostock of 28 October 1999, file reference 1 Sch 3/99, Yearbook Commercial Arbitration XXV (2000) et. 717 f.

Rostock, a decision on the declaration of enforceability can be issued if the arbitral award became legally binding under the law applicable for the arbitral award, i.e. that an appeal cannot be filed against it to another arbitral tribunal or court of general jurisdiction. This aspect must be reviewed by the court of general jurisdiction *ex officio*. The arbitral award ceases to be binding if annulled by a competent court of general jurisdiction or by the appellate arbitral tribunal, and thus its recognition must be refused under Article V(1)(e) of the New York Convention. The Federal Court of Justice reacted to the aforementioned court decision in its resolution of 22 February 2001. In its follow-up decision, the Federal Court of Justice ruled that a decision on the validity or annulment of an arbitral award issued in the country of origin may be taken into account by the filing of an infringement complaint within the meaning of Section 1065(1) of the ZPO against a decision on the denial of a permission to enforce a decision. Having said that, in general, new facts cannot be taken into account at this stage of the proceedings on the recognition of the arbitral award.[41]

1.18. If the arbitral award has yet to become binding in the country of origin or has been annulled, its recognition in the relevant country should be denied in accordance with Article V(1)(e) of the New York Convention. If a petition for the annulment of the arbitral award was filed in the country of origin, the proceedings on recognition of the arbitral proceedings may be suspended in accordance with the provisions of Article VI of the New York Convention. In view of the aforementioned court decision, it can therefore be concluded that the arbitral award, which was annulled in the country of origin, is highly unlikely to be enforced and recognised in the Federal Republic of Germany.

V.2. Decision of the Higher Regional Court in Munich of 30 July 2012

1.19. Under a resolution of the Higher Regional Court in Munich,[42] the recognition and enforcement of an arbitral award annulled by Ukrainian courts was denied for being contrary to public policy and the lack of jurisdiction of the arbitration court. In its decision on the appeal against the cited resolution of the Higher Regional Court in Munich, the Federal Court of Justice[43] arrived

---

[41] Cf. Federal Court of Justice of 22 February 2001, file reference III ZB 71/99, Neue Juristische Wochenschrift (2001) et. 1730; WM (2001) et. 971.
[42] Higher Regional Court Munich of 30 July 2012, file reference 34 Sch 18/10.
[43] Federal Court of Justice 23 April 2013, file reference III ZB 59/12. This decision is considered controversial by Stefan Kröll [ARBITRATION IN GERMANY, THE MODEL LAW IN PRACTICE Alphen aan den Rijn: Wolters Kluwer 485 (Karl-Heinz Böckstiegel, Stefan Michael Kröll, Patricia Nacimiento ed.,

at the conclusion that if reciprocity is established between the signatory countries of the New York Convention and the European Convention, it is not necessary to examine whether the decision on the annulment of the arbitral award was correct in the terms of the ground for annulment of the arbitral award and whether it could be enforced in the Federal Republic of Germany. For the sake of completeness, it must be noted that according to the case law of the German courts, they may suspend the proceedings on the enforcement of the decision, if it can be assumed that the proceedings on the annulment of the arbitral award in the country of origin will be successful.[44]

VI. Recognition and Enforcement of Arbitral Awards Annulled in the Country of Origin in the Case Law of the Hong Kong

VI.1. Karaha Bodas Company L.L.C. v. Persusahaan Pertambangan Minyak Dan Gas Bumi Negara a.k.a. Pertamina (HK)

1.20. In *Karaha Bodas Company L.L.C. v. Persusahaan Pertambangan Minyak Dan Gas Bumi Negara a.k.a. Pertamina* et. al, contracts were concluded between Karaha Bodas (KBC) and Persusahann Pertambangan Minyak Dan Gas Bumi Negara (Pertamina) (a Joint Operations Contract) and between KBC, Pertamina and Perusahaan Listruik Negara[45] (an Energy Sales Contract). Both of these contracts were subject to Indonesian legislation and contained arbitration clauses stating that any disputes would be settled in arbitral proceedings under the UNCITRAL Rules of Arbitration[46] in Switzerland. In 1998, KBC initiated the launch of arbitral proceedings against Pertamina and in 2000 the arbitral tribunal issued an arbitral award in favour of KBC. Pertamina subsequently sought the annulment of the arbitral award in Switzerland. However, the petition of Pertamina for

---

2015)]. On the contrary, Gottfried Hammer gives arguments in support of this decision, because Section 1061 of the ZPO assumes that an arbitral award was duly issued abroad, given that this condition cannot be met if the arbitral award was annulled in the country of origin (GOTTFRIED HAMMER, ÜBERPRÜFUNG VON SCHIEDSVERFAHREN IN GERMANY DURCH STAATLICHE GERICHTE IN DEUTSCHLAND, Munich: C. H. Beck 146 (2018).

[44] Higher Regional Court in Schleswig of 16 June 2008, file reference 16 Sch 02/07. In these proceedings, the German court arrived at the conclusion that it is not precluded from declaring the enforceability of an arbitral award, if a decision was issued in the country of origin in which a petition for the annulment of the arbitral award was rejected, even though this decision has yet to take legal force.

[45] In the case in question, Pertamina and Perusahaan Listruik Negara were entities owned by the Indonesian state.

[46] Resolution 31/98 of the General Assembly of 15 December 1976 (Arbitration Rules of the United Nations Commission on International Trade Law).

the annulment of the arbitral award was rejected by the Swiss Supreme Court (*Tribunal Fédéral*) in 2001 for procedural reasons. In 2002 Pertamina filed a petition with Indonesia's Central Jakarta District Court for the launch of proceedings on the annulment of the aforementioned arbitral award and the issue of a court order preventing KBC in the enforcement of the arbitral award anywhere in the world. Both petitions were later granted.

1.21.   The Court of First Instance of Hong Kong, in its decision in *KBC v. Pertamina*,[47] arrived at the conclusion that the fact that the court of general jurisdiction in Indonesia annulled the arbitral award under its domestic legislation has no influence on the proceedings before the Court of First Instance of Hong Kong, because in the case in question the *lex arbitri* is clearly Swiss law, since the place of the arbitral proceedings was Switzerland. Additionally, during the course of the arbitral proceedings, the parties to the dispute referred in their arguments to the provisions of the Swiss procedural law regulations. It is important to note that Article 44(2)(f) of the Hong Kong Arbitration Ordinance[48] contains a provision identical to Article V(1)(e) of the New York Convention. The Court of First Instance of Hong Kong rejected the argumentation employed by Pertamina that the claim of the award was contrary to public policy under Article V(2)(b) of the New York Convention in conjunction with Article 44(3) of the Hong Kong Arbitration Ordinance. The Court of First Instance of Hong Kong therefore confirmed the permission to enforce the arbitral award.

VII.   Conclusion

1.22.   The question of the enforcement of arbitral awards annulled in the country of origin is a fundamental question vis-a-vis the existence or absence of the extraterritorial effect of a decision to annul an arbitral award in the country of its enforcement. Nevertheless, Article V of the New York Convention is not mandatory and gives national courts discretionary power. The

---

[47]   Court of First Instance, In the High Court of the Hong Kong Special Administrative Region, *Karaha Bodas Company LLC (KBC)* v. Persusahaan Pertambangan Minyak Dan Gas Bumi Negara (Pertamina), decisions of 20 December 2002 and 27 March 2003, Construction and Arbitral Proceedings No. 28 of 2002 publ. in [2003] 2 HKLRD 381 and Yearbook Commercial Arbitration XXVIII (2003) et. 752 et seq.

[48]   The new Hong Kong Arbitration Ordinance (Cap. 609) dates back to 2011 and was last amended on 1 February 2018.

grounds for the annulment of an arbitral award are limited by Article IX of the European Convention.[49]

1.23. As demonstrated by the decision in the *Hilmarton* case, the enforcement of arbitral awards which were annulled may result in the issuing of mutually contradictory arbitral awards concerning the same disputed issues between the same parties. Such a situation is undoubtedly contrary to the principle of legal certainty of the parties and not only of them. It can lead to competitive enforcement of the arbitral award between the parties. With the exception of some of the aforementioned court decisions, the national courts tend to reject petitions for the enforcement of annulled arbitral awards.

1.24. It must be pointed out that under Article V(1)(e) of the New York Convention, an arbitral award may only be annulled by the competent authority of the country in which or under whose legal system it was issued.

1.25. Furthermore, it should be noted that the winning party still has an arbitral award that can be enforced in another country if the arbitral award is annulled. The possibility of permitting the enforcement of an arbitral award annulled in another country will probably depend on the reason for its annulment.

1.26. If the arbitral award was annulled for the reason of being contrary to public policy, it would be possible to find another country on which public policy is not based on the same moral values.[50] In the event of a breach of the right to a fair trial, if, for example, a party did not have the opportunity to attend a hearing before the arbitral tribunal, it would not be possible to enforce such an arbitral award anywhere, because the principle of a fair trial is internationally recognized.[51] In this regard, Professor Jan Paulsson takes the view that a reason for not respecting a court decision on the annulment of an arbitral award may also

---

[49]   In regard to the regulation and decision-making practice of courts in the area of the recognition and enforcement of foreign arbitral awards in the Czech Republic, compare Alexander Bělohlávek, *Interpretation and Application of the New York Convention in Czech Republic*, in RECOGNITION AND ENFORCEMENT OF FOREIGN ARBITRAL AWARDS, THE INTERPRETATION AND APPLICATION OF THE NEW YORK CONVENTION BY NATIONAL COURTS, Cham: Springer 263, 263 (George A. Bermann ed., 2017).

[50]   Compare for example the narrow concept of public policy in the United States of America in *Karaha Bodas Company L.L.C. (KBC)* v. Pertamina, et al.

[51]   Christopher Koch within this context suggests, that 'it would be useful if the courts in enforcement jurisdictions would lead the way in determining in their decisions what standards pertaining to the annulment of awards are internationally acceptable and what are not.' Christopher Koch, *Enforcing Awards annulled in their country of origin under the New York Convention*, 26(2) JOURNAL OF INTERNATIONAL ARBITRATION 267, 292 (2009).

be that: 'unusual or unacceptable annulments are destructive of legitimate and increasingly settled expectations.'[52]

1.27. A possible solution to the issue of recognition and enforcement of arbitral awards annulled in the country of origin could be the adoption of a delocalisation theory,[53] which does away with a dual system of controlling arbitral awards by the law in force at the place of the arbitral proceedings (*lex arbitri*) and then by the competent authority at the place where the arbitral award is to be enforced. Delocalisation theory recommends that control of an arbitral award should be entrusted solely to the competent authority of the country in which a petition is filed for recognition and enforcement.[54] But this solution appears inappropriate from the point of view of current legal practice, as was demonstrated by Article 1717(3) of the Belgian Judicial Code.[55] This provision established mandatory delocalisation in international arbitration, but was subsequently amended.

1.28. No known cases of the enforcement of arbitral awards annulled in the country of origin can be found in the case law of Czech courts of general jurisdiction. On the topic of the enforcement of arbitral awards annulled in the country of origin, Czech legal scholarship expresses itself largely at only a general level. Professor Alexander Bělohlávek is of the view that Czech legislation contained in Section 121(a) and (b) of Act No. 91/2012 Coll., on Private International Law (PIL) does not allow the enforcement of arbitral awards annulled in the country of origin.[56] In the view of this author, it is important to realise that

---

[52] Jan Paulsson, *Enforcing Arbitral Awards Notwithstanding Local Standard Annulments*, 9(1) The ICC International Court of Arbitration Bulletin 14, 28 (1998). This also relates to the question of public confidence in the arbitral proceedings and in the decision-making practice of state courts, which decide on the recognition and enforcement of arbitral awards annulled in the country of origin. More closely on this point see Christopher R. Drahozal, *Enforcing Vacated International Arbitral Awards: An Economic Approach*, 11(4) AM. REV. INT'L ARB. 451, 458 (2000).

[53] With regard to this compare PHILIPPE FOUCHARD, L'ARBITRAGE COMMERCIAL INTERNATIONAL, Paris: Dalloz, 22 (1965), Jan Paulsson: *Arbitration Unbound: Award Detached from the Law of its Country of Origin*, 30(2) I.C.L.Q. 358 (1981) and Jan Paulsson, *Delocalisation of International Commercial Arbitration: When and Why Matters*, 32(1) I.C.L.Q. 53 (1983).

[54] For the sake of completeness, we must mention the theoretical concept that the court of the country whose legal system has been elected by the parties shall have the exclusive jurisdiction to decide on an annulment of the arbitral award. In the event that this court does annul the arbitral award, this should prevent its recognition and enforcement anywhere in the world [Kenneth R. Davis, *Unconventional Wisdom: A New Look at Articles V and VII of the Convention on the Recognition and Enforcement of Foreign Arbitral Awards*, 37(1) TEX. INT'L L.J. 43, 63 (2002)].

[55] On 28 June 2013 the new Belgian law of 24 June 2013 amending Part 6 of the Judicial Code (Code Judiciare of 10 October 1967, as amended) on arbitration was published and entered into force on 1 September 2013.

[56] The same opinion is shared by Petr Dobiáš [Petr Dobiáš, *The Recognition and Enforcement of the Arbitral Awards Set Aside in the Country of Origin According the Relevant Case Law of Foreign State Courts*, 146(3) LAWYER 325, 336 (2007)] and Zdeňka Tesařová [Zdeňka Tesařová, *Recognition and Enforcement of Foreign Arbitral Awards in the Context of the New York Convention and Czech Legislation*, (17)10 TAX AND LAW IN PRACTICE 34, 41 (2012)]. According to Section 121 of the PIL: 'The recognition or enforcement of a foreign arbitral award **will be refused**, if the foreign arbitral award:

the Czech Republic is a signatory of the New York Convention as well as of the European Convention, and therefore it will only rarely be possible to apply Section 121(a) and (b) of the PIL. This is because Section 2 of the PIL and Article 10 of the Constitution of the Czech Republic[57] provide for the priority application of international conventions in the event of their collision with domestic legislation. Thus, at the current time, when 159 signatory countries are bound by the New York Convention, application of Section 121(a) and (b) of the PIL is more in the realm of theory. Professor Alexander Bělohlávek concedes the possibility of the recognition and enforcement of an arbitral award annulled in the state of origin, if Article IX(1) of the European Convention or the legal regulation contained in some of the conventions on legal assistance are applied. The said question was also addressed in an article by Karel Střelec,[58] who deals with a legal analysis of Article V of the New York Convention and Article IX(1) of the European Convention and concludes that every case must be considered individually.

1.29.   Thus, in relation to the Czech legislation, it can be summarised that a foreign arbitral award annulled in the country of origin may only be enforced in exceptional cases on the basis a decision of the Czech court of general jurisdiction. Such a case could typically be the enforcement of an arbitral award in accordance with Article V of the New York Convention, which was annulled in the country of origin for being contrary to public policy but is not contrary to public policy in terms of Czech law. Article 5(3)(g) of the hypothetical draft of a new convention on the international recognition and enforcement of arbitral agreements and awards of 2008,[59] written by Professor Albert Jan van den Berg, who is also one of the co-authors of the New York Convention, addresses the still-current issue of a denial of the recognition and enforcement of arbitral awards annulled by the court of general jurisdiction in the country of origin. The draft prescribes that the enforcement of such an award must be denied if one of the grounds for denial of an arbitral award is

a) is not final and conclusive or enforceable in accordance with the body of laws of the country in which it was published,

b) has been annulled in the state in which it was issued or according to whose body of laws it has been issued.'

[57]   Constitutional Act No. 1/1993 Coll., as amended.
[58]   Compare Karel Střelec, *On the Possibility of Recognising and Enforcing a Foreign Arbitral Award*, (11)3 BULLETIN ADVOKACIE 34, 34 (2004).
[59]   Albert Jan van den Berg (Text of Draft Convention, 29 May 2008) Hypothetical Draft Convention on the International Enforcement of Arbitral Agreements and Awards, available at: www.arbitration-icca.org/media/0/12133674097980/hypothetical_draft_convention_ajbrev06.pdf (accessed on 21 July 2018).

present under Article 5(3)(a) to (e) of the draft.[60] The proposal, following the model of Article IX of the European Convention on International Commercial Arbitration of 1961, thus excludes denial of the enforcement of an arbitral award annulled solely because of the application of a local public policy reservation. On the other hand, a breach of an international public policy reservation constitutes grounds for denial of an arbitral award's enforcement even without a petition. The principle to be applied anew shall be that, except for denying the enforcement of an arbitral award annulled in the country of origin and an award that is contrary to international public policy, objections must be invoked during the arbitral proceedings or they cannot be considered.[61] The discretionary power of courts of general jurisdiction in the matter of denying the enforcement of an arbitral award is preserved solely in relation to the denial of arbitral awards where proceedings are underway in the country of origin on a petition for the annulment of the arbitral award. This is especially true given that the duty to lodge a security deposit may, at the petition of a party, be newly imposed upon both the petitioner as well as the respondent.

| | |

Summaries

DEU [*Anerkennung und Vollstreckung von im Ursprungsland aufgehobenen Schiedssprüchen*]
Gemäß Artikel V des New Yorker Übereinkommens aus dem Jahr 1958 dürfen die allgemeinen Gerichte die Anerkennung und Vollstreckung von Schiedssprüchen nur aus den in ihm aufgeführten Gründen verweigern. An der Entscheidungspraxis von Gerichten in verschiedenen Staaten lässt sich das unterschiedliche Herantreten an die Anwendung dieser Bestimmung in denjenigen Fällen ablesen, in denen die Anerkennung und Vollstreckung eines ausländischen Schiedsspruchs, der im Ursprungsland aufgehoben wurde,

---

[60]   Emannuel Gaillard considers the proposed amendment to the convention to be insufficient in view of the protectionist efforts of State courts in proceedings on the annulment of an arbitral award Emannuel Gallard, *The Urgency of Not Revising the New York Convention*, in 50 YEARS OF THE NEW YORK CONVENTION, Alphen aan den Rijn: Kluwer Law International, 695, 695 (Albert Jan van den Berg ed., 2009). The opposite opinion, in favour of the solution contained in Article 5(3)(g) of the Draft, is supported by Carolyn B. Lamm (Carolyn B. Lamm, *Comments on the Proposal to Amend the New York Convention*, in 50 YEARS OF THE NEW YORK CONVENTION, Alphen aan den Rijn: Kluwer Law International, 697, 705 (Albert Jan van den Berg ed., 2009).
[61]   Compare Section 33 of Czech Act No. 216/1994 Coll., on Arbitral Proceedings and on the Enforcement of Arbitral Awards.

beantragt wird. In einigen Staaten weigern sich die Gerichte, derartige Schiedssprüche zu vollstrecken, während die Gerichte anderer Staaten deren Anerkennung und Vollstreckung zulassen. Ein möglicher Ausweg aus der Situation wäre die Verabschiedung eines neuen Übereinkommens über die Anerkennung und Vollstreckung ausländischer Schiedssprüche oder eines Nachtrags zum bestehenden New Yorker Übereinkommen von 1958.

CZE [*Uznání a výkon rozhodčích nálezů zrušených v zemi původu*] *Podle čl. V Newyorské úmluvy z roku 1958 může obecný soud odepřít uznání a výkon rozhodčího nálezu pouze z důvodů v tomto ustanovení uvedených. V rozhodnutích soudů z různých států se liší přístup k aplikaci tohoto ustanovení v případě, že je navrhováno uznání a výkon cizího rozhodčího nálezu zrušeného ve státě jeho původu. Soudy v některých státech odmítají takové rozhodčí nálezy vykonat, zatímco soudy v jiných státech jejich uznání a výkon připouštějí. Řešením této situace by mohlo být přijetí nové úmluvy o uznání a výkonu cizích rozhodčích nálezů, nebo dodatku k Newyorské úmluvě z roku 1958.*

| | |

POL [*Uznawanie i wykonywanie orzeczeń arbitrażowych uchylonych w kraju pochodzenia*] *Zgodnie z art. V Konwencji nowojorskiej z 1958 roku sąd powszechny może odmówić uznania i wykonania orzeczenia arbitrażowego wyłącznie z przyczyn przewidzianych przez postanowienia wspomnianego artykułu. W teorii i praktyce prawa brak zgodności opinii odnośnie tego, czy może zostać uznane i wykonane orzeczenie arbitrażowe uchylone w kraju pochodzenia.*

FRA [*La reconnaissance et l'exécution des sentences arbitrales annulées dans le pays d'origine*] *Conformément à l'article V de la Convention de New York de 1958, une juridiction nationale ne peut refuser la reconnaissance et l'exécution d'une sentence arbitrale que pour les raisons mentionnées dans cette disposition. L'opinion de la doctrine et de la jurisprudence est partagée quant à la possibilité de reconnaître une sentence arbitrale annulée dans le pays d'origine.*

Czech (& Central European) Yearbook of Arbitration®

RUS [*Признание и приведение в исполнение арбитражных решений, отмененных в государстве, где они были вынесены*]

Согласно статье V Нью-Йоркской конвенции 1958 года, суд общей юрисдикции может отказать в признании и приведении в исполнение арбитражного решения исключительно по причинам, указанным в данном положении. В правовой теории и практике отсутствует единое мнение относительно признания и приведения в исполнение арбитражного решения, отмененного в государстве, где оно было вынесено.

ESP [*Reconocimiento y ejecución de laudos arbitrales anulados en el país de origen*]

De acuerdo con el artículo V de la Convención de Nueva York del año 1958, el tribunal ordinario puede negarse a reconocer y ejecutar el laudo arbitral solo por motivos recogidos en dicha disposición. Ni en la teoría ni en la práctica del Derecho existe una opinión unánime sobre si el laudo arbitral anulado en el Estado de origen puede ser reconocido y ejecutado.

| | |

Bibliography

CLAUDIA ALFONS, RECOGNITION AND ENFORCEMENT OF ANNULLED FOREIGN ARBITRAL AWARDS: AN ANALYSIS OF THE LEGAL FRAMEWORK AND ITS INTERPRETATION IN CASE LAW AND LITERATURE, Frankfurt: Petr Lang (2010).

Albert Jan van den Berg, *Enforcement of Annulled Awards?* 9(2) The ICC International Court of Arbitration Bulletin (1998).

Albert Jan van den Berg, *Should the Setting Aside of the Arbitral Award be Abolished?* 29(2) ICSID Review (2014).

ALEXANDER J. BĚLOHLÁVEK, ACT ON ARBITRAL PROCEEDINGS AND ON THE ENFORCEMENT OF ARBITRAL AWARDS, Prague: C. H. Beck (2nd edition 2012).

RECOGNITION AND ENFORCEMENT OF FOREIGN ARBITRAL AWARDS, THE INTERPRETATION AND APPLICATION OF THE NEW YORK CONVENTION BY NATIONAL COURTS, Cham: Springer (George A. Bermann ed., 2017).

ARBITRATION IN GERMANY, THE MODEL LAW IN PRACTICE, Alphen aan den Rijn: Wolters Kluwer (Karl-Heinz Böckstiegel, Stefan Michael Kröll, Patricia Nacimiento ed., 2015).

Kenneth R. Davis, *Unconventional Wisdom: A New Look at Articles V and VII of the Convention on the Recognition and Enforcement of Foreign Arbitral Awards*, 37(1) TEX. INT'L L.J. (2002).

Petr Dobiáš, *The Recognition and Enforcement of the Arbitral Awards Set Aside in the Country of Origin According the Relevant Case Law of Foreign State Courts*, 146(3) LAWYER (2007).

Christopher R. Drahozal, *Enforcing Vacated International Arbitral Awards: An Economic Approach*, 11(4) AM. REV. INT'L ARB. (2000).

PHILIPPE FOUCHARD, L'ARBITRAGE COMMERCIAL INTERNATIONAL, Paris: Dalloz (1965).

Emannuel Gallard, *The Urgency of Not Revising the New York Convention*, in 50 YEARS OF THE NEW YORK CONVENTION, Alphen aan den Rijn: Kluwer Law International (Albert Jan van den Berg ed., 2009).

GOTTFRIED HAMMER, ÜBERPRÜFUNG VON SCHIEDSVERFAHREN IN GERMANY DURCH STAATLICHE GERICHTE IN DEUTSCHLAND, Munich: C. H. Beck (2018).

Christopher Koch, *Enforcing Awards annulled in their country of origin under the New York Convention*, 26(2) JOURNAL OF INTERNATIONAL ARBITRATION (2009).

Carolyn B. Lamm, *Comments on the Proposal to Amend the New York Convention*, in 50 YEARS OF THE NEW YORK CONVENTION, Alphen aan den Rijn: Kluwer Law International (Albert Jan van den Berg ed., 2009).

VOLKER NIENABER, DIE ANERKENNUNG UND VOLLSTRECKUNG IM SITZSTAAT AUFGEHOBENER SCHIEDSSPRÜCHE, Frankfurt: Petr Lang (2002).

Jan Paulsson: *Arbitration Unbound: Award Detached from the Law of its Country of Origin*, 30(2) I.C.L.Q. (1981).

Jan Paulsson, *Delocalisation of International Commercial Arbitration: When and Why Matters*, 32(1) I.C.L.Q. (1983).

Jan Paulsson, *Enforcing Arbitral Awards Notwithstanding Local Standard Annulments*, 9(1) The ICC International Court of Arbitration Bulletin (1998).

Georgios C. Petrochilos, *Enforcing Awards annulled in their country of origin under the New York Convention*, 48(4) I. C. L. Q. (1999).

ALAN REDFERN, MARTIN HUNTER, NIGEL BLACKNABY, CONSTANTINE PARTASIDES, LAW AND PRACTICE OF INTERNATIONAL COMMERCIAL ARBITRATION, London: Sweet and Maxwell Ltd. (2004).

FRANZ T. SCHWARZ AND CHRISTIAN W. KONRAD: THE VIENNA RULES, A COMMENTARY ON INTERNATIONAL ARBITRATION IN AUSTRIA, Alphen aan den Rijn: Wolters Kluwer (2009).

Reyadh Seyadi, *Enforcement of Arbitral Awards Annulled by the Court of the Seat*, 84(2) Arbitration (2018).

Karel Střelec, *On the Possibility of Recognising and Enforcing a Foreign Arbitral Award*, (11)3 Bulletin advokacie (2004).

Zdeňka Tesařová, *Recognition and Enforcement of Foreign Arbitral Awards in the Context of the New York Convention and Czech Legislation*, (17)10 TAX AND LAW IN PRACTICE (2012).

Burton S. De Witt, *A Judgment Without Merits: The Recognition and Enforcement of Foreign Judgments Confirming, Recognizing, or Enforcing Arbitral Awards*, 50(3) TEX. INT'L L.J. (2015).

Alexander J. Bělohlávek

ORCID iD 0000-0001-5310-5269
https://orcid.org/0000-0001-5310-5269

Arbitration Versus Insolvency Proceedings from the Perspective of EU Law

Key Words:
administrator | anationality | arbitration agreement | autonomy | bankruptcy | Brussels Ibis Regulation | Center of Main Interest | certainty | COMI | common law | conflict-of-laws | Czech law | ECJ | Elektrim SA | enforcement | enforceability | English law | escape clause | EU | EU law | forum selection | choice-of-court | choice-of-law | in favorem validitatis | insolvency | insolvency proceedings | jurisdiction | legal certainty | lex arbitri | lex causae | lex concursus | lex fori concursus | lex personae | lex processuali | liquidator | New-York Convention | Kompetenz-Kompetenz | opening of insolvency proceedings | permanent arbitral institution | place of arbitration[1] | pending lawsuit | Polish law | predictability | procedural capacity | procedural economy | recognition | Regulation (EC) 1346/2000 | Regulation (EU) 2015/848 | Rome I Regulation | satisfaction of creditors | seat of arbitration[2] | supranationalization | Syska v. Vivendi | validity of arbitration agreement | Swiss law | West Tankers Inc.

Abstract | *The influence of insolvency proceedings to a pending arbitration seated in another country has been a sensitive topic for many years. The core issue is if and how fair the arbitrators have been to reflect or incorporate insolvency proceedings pending in another country. The meanings have significantly changed in the course of the past two or three decades, since for some twenty or thirty years the basic principle has been that insolvency proceedings pending in another country have no exterritorial effect. Scholarly doctrine has changed mainly due to EU law reining in arbitrators as much as possible. One example is Article 18 of the Regulation (EU) 2015/848 applicable to insolvency proceedings commenced after June 2017. This provision binds arbitrators to apply domestic effects on pending insolvency proceedings in force in the country of the seat of the arbitral tribunal, and also if the party of the arbitration is bankrupt in another EU country. This regulation is applicable within the EU common market (excepting Denmark). However this provision is disputable*

Alexander J. Bělohlávek, Univ. Professor, Prof. zw., Dr. iur., Mgr., Dipl. Ing. oec (MB), prof. hon., Dr. h. c. Lawyer (Managing Partner of Law Offices Bělohlávek), Dept. of Law, Faculty of Economics, Ostrava, Czech Republic; Faculty of Law and Administration Collegium Humanum University (Poland), Dept. of Int. law, Faculty of law, West Bohemia University, Pilsen, Czech Republic, Dept. of Int. and European Law, Faculty of Law, Masaryk University, Brno, Czech Republic (visiting). Vice-President of the

---

[1]   See also „seat of arbitration".
[2]   See also „place of arbitration".

for many reasons. In fact, non-failure to reflect of insolvency proceedings pending in another country to a party of arbitration may also have effects on the recognition and enforcement of arbitral awards. Finally, the development of rules in countries beyond the EU common market is significant, as for instance in Switzerland.

| | |
| | |

International Arbitration Court at the Czech Commodity Exchange, Arbitrator in Prague, Paris (ICC), Vienna (VIAC), Moscow, Vilnius, Warsaw, Minsk, Almaty, Kiev, Bucharest, Ljubljana, Sofia, Kuala Lumpur, Harbin (China), Shenzhen (China) etc., Arbitrator pursuant to UNCITRAL Rules. Member of ASA, DIS, ArbAut etc. Immediately past president of the WJA – the World Jurist Association, Washington D.C./USA. E-mail: office@ablegal.cz

I.   The General Conflict of Interest Between Arbitration and Insolvency Proceedings

2.01.   The determination of the jurisdiction to hear and resolve disputes belongs among the most critical issues encountered by arbitrators, and appears with seemingly ever-increasing frequency. The arbitrators' jurisdiction or, as applicable, the possibility to conduct arbitration must be examined not only whenever the validity, or the subject-matter or personal scope of the arbitration agreement is contested, but also if any insolvency proceedings[3] are opened and conducted against one of the parties in terms of the applicable *lex concursus*.

2.02.   This situation involves a conflict between two principles. The first is the contractual autonomy that gives the parties the right to exclude the jurisdiction of courts and submit their particular dispute or disputes arising from their legal relationship to arbitrators in a procedure that is not bound by strict procedural rules, as opposed to litigation in court. The parties may therefore express their will and choose a dispute resolution method that is more appropriate in view of the circumstances of their particular relationship. They may either choose the possibility of applying a whole range of procedural rules, plus a review of the delivered

---

[3]   Specific law may stipulate that the effects associated with the existence of insolvency proceedings are not connected with the opening of such proceedings, the definition of which also differs in the individual legal systems but, for instance, with the moment at which the debtor's insolvency is ascertained, with the decision on the method of resolving the insolvency, whether in the form of bankruptcy (i.e. liquidation, which results in the discontinuation of the debtor's activity), or through restructuring, etc. These issues have been subject to a thorough analysis of the CJ EU in relation to Council Regulation (EC) No. 1346/2000 of 29 May 2000, on insolvency proceedings. Published in OJ L 160 of 30 June 2000, et. 0001–0018, as amended; EurLex: 32000R1346 ('Regulation 1346/2000'). This moment is irrelevant from the perspective of the subject matter of this article, despite the fact that the arbitrators must consider it in their assessment of the particular situation; conversely, principal importance must be attributed to the contents of such effects on pending proceedings, or the possibility to open any proceedings to which the debtor should be a party.

decision, or the informality, flexibility and usually greater expediency primarily offered by international arbitration. Conversely, insolvency proceedings, as collective proceedings, are characterized by a substantial degree of centralization and endeavor to maximize the assets of the debtor and their proportionate distribution among creditors. In other words, insolvency proceedings aim to ensure that as many disputes as possible concerning the debtor's assets are resolved uniformly (in the same manner) by the competent authority. At the same time, the process of identifying, gathering and distributing the debtor's assets should be as transparent and effective as possible, and all creditors should enjoy equal standing. This basic definition justifies the conclusion that the desired objective cannot be accomplished through individual agreements of the debtor and the individual creditors regarding the method of resolving their disputes, but only in public proceedings, in which the State and governmental authorities are usually deemed the only authorities appropriate for conducting such proceedings and balancing the (logically) opposing interests of the debtor and the individual creditors.

2.03.   One fundamental principle of insolvency proceedings is the equal standing and treatment of the creditors. Insolvency law prohibits any differentiation among creditors in terms of the means and possibility of legal protection against a debtor that would be afforded to selected creditors while denied to the others. Such a situation can result in more advantages and higher satisfaction for those creditors whose claim against the debtor's insolvency estate was not subject to the resolution method envisaged by the *lex concursus* (law applicable to insolvency proceedings), but through other means, such as arbitration. Naturally, each national *lex concursus* contains different rules. However, insolvency proceedings are based on the presumption that claims against the debtor's insolvency estate cannot be asserted individually as of a certain point of time, such as the opening of the insolvency proceedings, the declaration of the debtor's insolvency, or a decision on the resolution of the debtor's insolvency, but only and exclusively through insolvency proceedings. Such proceedings also duly incorporate the equal treatment of creditors and factor in the economic perspective – a higher number of individual disputes may substantially burden the debtor's insolvency estate. At the same time, the rising costs of international arbitration have been subject to increasing criticism. If the premise is accepted that insolvency proceedings concerning one of the parties do not and cannot influence the possibility to open and conduct arbitration, it could easily happen that the respective creditor will have the opportunity to get an enforceable decision,[4] and at the same time, the creditor will draw substantial funds from the debtor's insolvency estate which should be equally distributed among creditors in terms of the *lex fori concursus*. Such ramifications arising from the exclusion of arbitration from the application of the consequences connected with the existence of insolvency proceedings are considered unacceptable by legislators. Consequently, the *lex fori concursus* contains provisions dealing with said issues and addresses the effects of insolvency proceedings on the possibility to resolve the debtor's disputes with third parties. At the same time, professionals and legal practitioners vary in their opinions on the degree to which arbitrators are bound by such provisions of the *lex fori concursus* in decisions regarding their own jurisdiction and are obliged to have regard for such provisions in their assessment of the requirements for conducting arbitration.

2.04. Arbitration is based on the principle of giving precedence to the autonomy of the parties or, as applicable, their agreement on the method of resolving their dispute, regardless of the parties' situation when the dispute arises. Put another way, arbitration involves excluding the jurisdiction of courts and submitting parties' disputes to arbitrators as private-law entities. Moreover, based on the generally accepted *Kompetenz-Kompetenz* principle, only arbitrators are primarily entitled to make decisions regarding their jurisdiction. To assess the fulfillment of the procedural requirements, the arbitrators are indeed obliged to do so of their own volition at any time during the proceedings. The underlying idea is that if the parties have expressed their will to resolve their dispute before arbitrators in a valid arbitration agreement, and at the same time, the subject matter of the dispute can be submitted to arbitrators as private-law entities, the expressed will of the parties ought to be honored, without any interference by the State that would ultimately enable the suspension of the arbitrability of the dispute under certain circumstances.

2.05. Conversely, insolvency proceedings tend to suspend general rules governing the determination of the forum competent to resolve disputes, whether such rules are incorporated in civil procedural law or agreed by the parties, and give precedence

---

[4] I have intentionally left aside any considerations as to whether and to what extent the debtor is *de facto* disadvantaged, in view of the necessarily costs spent, by the necessity itself of defending their rights in arbitration, which may also result in the recognition of claims made by the creditors that could otherwise be contested.

to centralized insolvency proceedings based on the principle of protecting all creditors, who are all treated equally. Centralized insolvency proceedings then determine the requirements for conducting any proceedings affecting the debtor's insolvency estate, including the determination of the forum competent to conduct such proceedings. But the creditors are not the only protected group; the uniform method of settling the debtor's liabilities with final effect is a necessary prerequisite for any potential plans for reorganization, and if possible, the further existence and functioning of the debtor, apart from the partial or full satisfaction of creditors. This objective could not be accomplished if a category of disputes existed with a direct or indirect impact on the debtor's insolvency estate, or if any such proceedings were conducted autonomously, completed outside the bounds of insolvency proceedings.

2.06.　The essential prerequisites for the due conduct of insolvency proceedings include, on the one hand, the uniform resolution of any claims made against the debtor's insolvency estate with maximum regard for the estate, and on the other hand, the liquidator's possibility to assess whether it appears appropriate or desirable to continue the proceedings in which the debtor asserts claims against third parties. The first objective is usually accomplished through the obligation of third parties to assert their claims in the insolvency proceedings using the prescribed form. If any of the claims are contested, all such disputes are submitted to one and the same forum – primarily within the framework of incidental disputes resolved by the insolvency court. In the latter case, the *lex concursus* often allows the liquidator to choose whether any pending proceedings against third parties will continue. These approaches (arbitration v insolvency proceedings) are frequently in conflict with one another, because the two types of proceedings represent opposite approaches to dispute resolution.[5]

2.07.　Insolvency laws and regulations set forth the consequences that insolvency has for a significant number of specific problems that are, analogically to litigation, also more and more frequently subject to assessment in arbitral proceedings. In view of the above, the party against whom the insolvency proceedings are opened often pleads, considering the party's status, a lack of jurisdiction of the arbitrators to hear and resolve the dispute, arguing that the dispute ought primarily to be resolved in

---

[5]　See also the decision in *United States Lines Inc*, 197 F.3d 631, 640 (2d Cir. 1999): '...a conflict of near polar extremes: bankruptcy policy exerts an inexorable pull towards centralization, while arbitration policy advocates a decentralized approach towards dispute resolution.'

insolvency proceedings. Such procedural defense is often initiated by the liquidator, the insolvency court, creditors or even the debtor themself. Objections are usually targeted at the debtor's capacity to be a party to arbitration. The principle of fair process is often invoked,[6] as well as the objection of public policy in terms of a preference for the interests of insolvency proceedings as collective proceedings – as opposed to arbitration as individual proceedings.[7] One may often encounter arguments concerning the validity of the arbitration agreement – some jurisdictions stipulate that the opening of insolvency proceedings (or, as applicable, any corresponding relevant moment, which may differ in the individual *leges fori concursus*) cancels the arbitration agreement, suspending its effects in the broadest sense, and consequently, disenables the commencement and conduct of arbitral proceedings against the debtor on the basis of the arbitration agreement. In other words, the conclusion is that the arbitrators, in any and all circumstances, are obliged to factor in and proceed in compliance with the *lex fori concursus*.

2.08.   Although it might *prima facie* appear that it is necessary to consider the above-described effects of insolvency proceedings in arbitration, it is by no means a universally accepted approach. On the contrary, international arbitration is characterized by a diversity of approaches based on the principle of the absolute autonomy of arbitration and the associated independence of arbitration from any national law. The premise is that arbitration and the arbitral proceedings cannot be prejudiced by the existence of any insolvency proceedings affecting one of the parties.[8] Such an approach is especially typical for doctrines founded on the exclusively contractual basis of arbitration and its independence from any legal system, even to the degree of the anationality of arbitration. Advocates of these opinions (lacking, for instance, any application in our domestic jurisdiction) argue that as soon as the parties submit their dispute to the arbitrators

---

[6]   Compare also Domitille Baizeau, *Arbitration and Insolvency: Issues of Applicable Law*, NEW DEVELOPMENTS IN INTERNATIONAL COMMERCIAL ARBITRATION, ZÜRICH/BASEL/GENEVA: SCHULTHESS 97 (Christian Müller, Antonio Rigozzi eds., 2009).

[7]   Compare Alexander Bělohlávek, *Impact of Insolvency of a Party on Pending Arbitration Proceedings in Czech Republic, England and Switzerland and Other Countries*, 1 YEARBOOK ON INTERNATIONAL ARBITRATION. ANTVERPEN / BERLIN / COPENHAGEN / WIEN / GRAZ: EAP (EUROPEAN ACADEMIC PRESS) / NEUER WISSENSCHAFTLICHER VERLAG 145–166 (Marianne Roth, Michael Geistlinger eds., 2010).

[8]   Compare also STEFAN M. KRÖLL, ARBITRATION AND INSOLVENCY PROCEEDINGS – SELECTED PROBLEMS, Pervasive Problems in International Arbitration, KLI 357–376 (Loukas A. Mistelis, Julian D. M. Lew eds., 2006); José Rosell, Prager Harvey, *International Arbitration and Bankruptcy: United States, France and the ICC*, 18(4) JOURNAL OF INTERNATIONAL ARBITRATION 417–434 (2001), see especially et. 426–427; Fernando Mantilla-Serrano, *International Arbitration and Insolvency Proceedings*, 11(1) ARBITRATION INTERNATIONAL 51–74 (1995), and a number of sources and legal opinions quoted therein.

based on their private-law contract, the arbitrators assume exclusive liability for further progress in the proceedings, without being bound by any laws or regulations. This doctrine therefore allows the arbitrators to choose any procedure that they deem appropriate, while being bound only by the agreement of the parties to the dispute. Consequently, it is up to the arbitrators alone as to whether and to what extent they factor in the existence and effects of any insolvency proceedings. The author refuses any such opinions advocating the existence of the anational nature of arbitration,[9] which is not bound by any individual legal system and which is based exclusively on the generally accepted principles of international arbitration. Such an approach suppresses the significance of the place of arbitration, which the author considers to be the most important factor influencing arbitration and the arbitral procedure through the *lex arbitri*, including the importance of the choice of the place of arbitration. At the same time, it is one of the main criteria on the basis of which the parties enter into their arbitration agreement. The possibility to influence the arbitral procedure, delimited via the contents of the applicable *lex arbitri*, belongs to, is often quoted as, and undoubtedly constitutes one of the main advantages of arbitration. The *lex arbitri*, inter alia, sets forth the requirements of and conditions for the validity of the arbitration agreement. The practice of international arbitration is not unfamiliar with and, indeed, frequently employs an 'escape clause', which stipulates that it is perfectly possible to conduct arbitration in a particular case if the arbitration agreement complies, at least, with the requirements imposed on the form and contents thereof by the law applicable in the place of arbitration (*lex arbitri*). The determination of the basic limits and guarantees of the elementary procedural rights and principles of fair process within which arbitration is conducted can by no means be opposed to the general characteristics of arbitration. These include both contractual autonomy and the principle of security in business transactions. The latter involves honoring the existence and contents of the arbitration agreement entered into by the parties in relation to a particular legal relationship

---

[9]   The anationality or delocalization of the proceedings, as applicable, is often mentioned in a broader procedural context. See also Radim Polčák, *Delokalizovaná jurisdikce a možnosti argumentace extenzivního výkladu § 87 písm. b) OSŘ [Title in Translation: Delocalized Jurisdiction and Possibility to Argue Using Broad Interpretation of Section 87(b) of the CCP]*, 5(1) JURISPRUDENCE, 9–11 (2004); Zdeněk Kapitán, *Volba sudiště v soukromoprávních vztazích s mezinárodním prvkem. [Title in Translation: Choice of Forum in Private-Law Relationships with International Dimension]*, 12(1) ČASOPIS PRO PRÁVNÍ VĚDU A PRAXI 18–26 (2004).

existing between them as regards the resolution of the dispute that has arisen from the relationship.

2.09.   Last, but not least, it is necessary to point out that the issue of the mandatory application of a foreign *lex concursus* could also be connected to the issue of whether, and to what extent, the decision can be recognized, whereby the insolvency proceedings are opened, or, as applicable, whereby insolvency is declared in the place of arbitration (i.e. seat of arbitration),[10] and consequently, whether the general principles of private international law require that its effects be honored. In this connection, one may refer to one of the first arbitral awards dealing with these issues and rendered in proceedings at the ICC International Court of Arbitration (ICC Case 6057),[11] in which the arbitrators assessed the significance of insolvency proceedings opened in France in view of the possibility to conduct arbitration if the place of arbitration is in a different State. The arbitral tribunal concluded that because the decision opening the insolvency proceedings had not been recognized in the State of the place of arbitration, the arbitral tribunal was not bound by the decision and the effects thereof, or by the insolvency laws and regulations of the debtor's country (*lex fori concursus*).

2.10.   In view of the above, are the arbitrators obliged to have regard to the opening of insolvency proceedings affecting the assets of any of the parties in the decision that they come to with respect to their own jurisdiction? Which country's laws should be considered? The answer to these questions is not always straightforward. The respective issue can be defined and perceived as follows: whether the arbitrators' jurisdiction established by the arbitration agreement entered into by the debtor remains unaffected by the insolvency proceedings, or whether the possibility to hear and resolve the given dispute will be resolved according to the rules/law regulating the effects of insolvency proceedings on the possibility to conduct and resolve disputes to which the debtor is a party (*lex concursus*). The solution to this issue often principally depends on the *lex*

---

[10]   Naděžda Rozehnalová, *Určení fóra a jeho význam pro spory s mezinárodním prvkem, [Title in Translation: Determination of the Forum and Its Importance for Disputes with an International Dimension]*, 1(4) BULLETIN ADVOKACIE 8–16 (2005); Naděžda Rozehnalová, *Určení fóra a jeho význam pro spory s mezinárodním prvkem, [Title in Translation: Determination of the Forum and Its Importance for Disputes with an International Dimension]*, 2(5) BULLETIN ADVOKACIE 12–17 (2005); David Sehnálek, *Sudiště v elektronickém rozhodčím řízení, [Title in Translation: Venue in Electronic Arbitration]*, 12(4) ČASOPIS PRO PRÁVNÍ VĚDU A PRAXI 313–317 (2004); Alexander Bělohlávek, *Místo konání rozhodčího řízení, [Title in Translation: Place of Arbitration]*, 3 PRÁVNÍ ZPRAVODAJ 13–15 (2004).

[11]   Collection of ICC Awards 1991-1995, *Recueil des sentences arbitrales de la CCI*, PARIS/NEW YORK/ THE HAGUE/LONDON/BOSTON: ICC PUBLISHING S.A./KLUWER LAW INTERNATIONAL 487 (Jean-Jacques Arnaldez, Yves Derains, Dominique Hascher eds., 1997).

arbitri, which determines the scope of application and the effects of the applicable law, including the possibility of preserving arbitrability on the basis and in consequence of the application of *lex arbitri.* A simplified summary of this approach is that the arbitrators must have regard to the effects of the insolvency proceedings, but only to the extent to which the effects are not suspended and/or superseded in consequence of the *lex arbitri.*

II. General EU Approach and Legislation

2.11. Legal theory is not unified with respect to whether arbitrators are bound by EU law. Nonetheless, it is necessary to accept that EU law forms part of the national laws of the individual Member States, and as such must be applied.

2.12. The influence of insolvency proceedings on arbitration has primarily been considered according to Regulation 1346/2000.[12] Specifically, Article 4(2)(e) and (f) of Regulation 1346/2000[13] stipulated that the law of the State of the opening of the main insolvency proceedings shall determine, inter alia, the effects of insolvency proceedings[14] on current contracts to which the debtor is party, as well as the effects of the insolvency proceedings on proceedings brought by individual creditors, with the exception of lawsuits pending. The effects of insolvency proceedings on a lawsuit pending concerning an asset or a right of which the debtor has been divested were governed, in terms of Article 15 of Regulation 1346/2000,[15] by the law of the Member State in which that lawsuit is pending. Although Regulation 1346/2000 explicitly refers to lawsuits, practicing lawyers in most Member States usually agree that those rules had to be analogically applied to arbitration as well, despite the fact that some arbitrators have been inclined to accept the premise of absolute preference for the will of the parties, in that the opening of insolvency proceedings affecting the assets of one of the parties should not in any manner affect the chosen dispute resolution method and the validity of the arbitration agreement.

2.13. However, the conclusion regarding the applicability of Regulation 1346/2000 in the assessment of the requirements for

---

[12] For the purposes of this article, the author mostly refers to the rules incorporated in Regulation 1346/2000, which was valid and effective for proceedings opened before 26 June 2017. On that day, Regulation 1346/2000 was replaced by a new EU law, which contains no material changes that would affect the conclusions formulated in this article. Consequently, any and all conclusions formulated herein shall also apply to the interpretation of Regulation (EU) 2015/848 of the European Parliament and of the Council ('Regulation 2015/848').

[13] Compare Article 7(2)(e) and (f) of Regulation 2015/848.

[14] Insolvency proceedings according to the wording of Regulation 2015/848.

[15] Compare Article 18 of Regulation 2015/848.

conducting arbitration can be inferred not only from the expert interpretations of the Regulation,[16] but also accepted by the case law of several Member States. It is true that the theoretical interpretation is primarily based on private-law interpretation report, which, from the formal perspective, does not represent any official source that would be binding with respect to the manner of applying the law. However, this particular source was fully used and significantly considered in the interpretation of Regulation 1346/2000 by practicing lawyers due to its factual acceptance. The necessity of applying Regulation 1346/2000 in arbitration has been especially advocated by French courts;[17] the same conclusion has, however, also been confirmed by English courts – see, for instance, the decision of Justice Clark of 2 October 2008 in *Syska* v. *Vivendi SA*,[18] which was subsequently upheld by the court of appeal.[19] The decision delivered in proceedings before the Arbitration Court at the Economic Chamber of the Czech Republic and the Agricultural Chamber of the Czech Republic on 15 January 2008 was probably the first decision of arbitrators in which the arbitrators applied EU law in terms of Article 15 of Regulation 1346/2000 to the assessment of procedural requirements, i.e. including the consequences of the existence of insolvency proceedings involving one of the parties to the arbitration conducted by the arbitrators.[20]

2.14. This author is of the opinion that the conclusion itself regarding the applicability of the EU insolvency law to arbitration is not a problem. (see the detailed analysis below). Priority (in this particular case) of collective insolvency proceedings

---

[16] See MIGUEL VIRGÓS, FRANCISCO GARCIMARTÍN, THE EUROPEAN INSOLVENCY REGULATION: LAW AND PRACTICE, KLI 142 (2004)., and elsewhere in that publication (cit.):
[...] Regulation does not make any express reference to the effects of the insolvency proceedings on lawsuits pending before arbitral tribunals in Member States. Arbitration is not excluded from the general effects of *lex concursus* under Art. 4, and the literal wording of Art. 15 is broad enough to include arbitration in the exception it provides to the application of that law. Arbitration proceedings are equivalent substitutes to ordinary legal proceedings in all Member States, and there is no substantive or procedural reason justifying a different solution.

[17] See also the decision of the French *Cour de cassation* (France) of 3 April 2001 in *Lamy Lutti* v. *J. Whihelm*. The decision was also annotated and commented on by Fouchard, Ph. in: Revue de l'arbitrage, 2003, et. 219 et seq., but primarily et. 220-221, where the author of the annotation presumes that Regulation 1346/2000 also applies to arbitration.
[18] Neutral citation [2008] EWHC 2155 (Comm); [2009] Bus. L.R. 367. The approach of Great Britain (England and Wales) or, as applicable, their courts and arbitrators in proceedings with the place (seat) of the proceedings in England may often be relatively questionable. This also applies to the English doctrine, which certainly cannot be deemed unanimous.
[19] Court of Appeal (Civil Division) of 9 July 2009 in *Syska* v. *Vivendi Universal SA et al.*, neutral citation [2009] EWCA Civ 677; [2009] Bus. L.R. 1494.
[20] Decision in Rsp 135/2006. The anonymous decision was also annotated and analyzed in: Alexander Bělohlávek, *Impact of Insolvency of a Party on Pending Arbitration Proceedings in Czech Republic, England and Switzerland and Other Countries*, 1 YEARBOOK ON INTERNATIONAL ARBITRATION. ANTVERPEN / BERLIN / COPENHAGEN / WIEN / GRAZ: EAP (EUROPEAN ACADEMIC PRESS) / NEUER WISSENSCHAFTLICHER VERLAG 145–166 (Marianne Roth, Michael Geistlinger eds., 2010).

over arbitration is the necessary result of the very nature of collective proceedings, which excludes individual agreements with individual creditors regarding the method of resolving disputes affecting the debtor's insolvency estate. One also may not ignore the practical implications – international arbitration would be endowed with a substantially specific nature different from any and all other agreements concerning dispute resolution methods. There is no doubt that, once the insolvency proceedings have been opened, the exclusion of the effects of insolvency proceedings may not be invoked *vis-à-vis* any existing choice-of-court agreements. No academic has argued that by entering into a choice-of-court agreement (whether according to the rules of private international law or pursuant to Regulation 1215/2012)[21] the parties expressed their unambiguous will to exclude the effects of insolvency law on the agreed method of resolving their dispute, including the exclusion of the jurisdiction of the insolvency court.

2.15.   This example illustrates the fact that the argument relating to the necessity of honoring the parties' contractual autonomy cannot stand, because it would mean that any and all agreements entered into by the debtor would have to be honored. But the insolvency proceedings are distinguished by the fact that, at a particular moment, the steps taken by the debtor before the insolvency proceedings are opened are subject to review, and the effects of such steps may be suspended directly by the law or upon assessment by the liquidator and/or the insolvency court. The general premise underlying the theory stipulates that no subsequent acts of the debtor may stand if they were contrary to the principles and objective of the insolvency proceedings and ultimately disrupted the equal standing of the individual creditors. In view of the above, a higher number of pending international arbitrations would probably be in conflict with the requirement of conducting the insolvency proceedings in a manner that would preserve the debtor's insolvency estate to the maximum extent and secure maximum proportionate satisfaction of the creditors.

2.16.   Contractual autonomy enabling the parties to exclude the jurisdiction of civil courts and agree that their dispute shall be heard and resolved in proceedings before private entities/arbitrators, and the scope of such autonomy is and must be completely independent from the nature of the

---

[21]   Regulation (EU) No. 1215/2012 of the European Parliament and of the Council of 12 December 2012 on jurisdiction and the recognition and enforcement of judgments in civil and commercial matters ('Brussels I bis Regulation').

Czech (& Central European) Yearbook of Arbitration®

legal relationship or obligation for which the jurisdiction of arbitrators has been agreed, as well as any other circumstances concerning the resolution of the given dispute. If the arbitrators' obligation to factor in the effects of insolvency proceedings depended on whether the arbitration is international, where an international dimension is, logically, also involved in the insolvency proceedings or domestic, it would generate entirely unjustifiable differences. Moreover, unjustified differences would also arise between purely domestic arbitrations. If we accept the abovementioned definition of the international dimension of insolvency proceedings, the arbitrators could, in otherwise purely domestic arbitration, refuse the effects of the insolvency proceedings prescribed by the *lex concursus*, arguing that (for instance) a single foreign claim requires that one has regard not only to the national *lex concursus*, but also to EU law, represented by Regulation 1346/2000.[22] Such an approach involves a principal loss of legal certainty, because the determination of whether or not the effects of insolvency proceedings will be considered would depend on random circumstances, which, or some of which, may be completely independent of the will of the parties.

2.17.   Although the above might suggest that the author agrees with the rules regulating the effects of insolvency proceedings on arbitration, as defined by the EU law, the opposite is the case. The author agrees that the prerequisites for conducting arbitration must also be assessed in arbitral proceedings with respect to the potential existence of insolvency proceedings affecting the parties; nonetheless, this should by no means be done through the explicit rules in Regulation 2015/848. The author considers such an approach inappropriate on at least two levels. Firstly, these issues should in no case be regulated by the EU law and ought to be reserved for the *lex arbitri*, which is capable of securing an effective solution thereof without denying the parties their contractual autonomy, which forms the basis of the greatest number of objections against the currently applicable EU law. Besides, these rules must also be deemed unfortunate from the perspective of the contents thereof. The rule that sets forth the impact of the effects of insolvency proceedings on arbitration is analogically based on the effects of insolvency proceedings on litigation. Lawmakers therefore considered arbitration a certain kind of litigation, without any regard for its specific features, which have the result that the effects of insolvency proceedings

---

[22]   In view of the explicit extension of the material scope of Regulation 2015/848, as analyzed below, in this place the author is intentionally only referring to Regulation 1346/2000.

cannot be assessed formulaically in arbitration, and the current law may lead to substantial problems in application.

2.18. As concerns the first issue, the EU law is based on the principle that EU laws do not generally apply to arbitration or, as applicable, that issues connected with arbitration are excluded from the scope of EU laws. In this connection, one may invoke Regulation (EC) No. 593/2008 of the European Parliament and of the Council of 17 June 2008, on the law applicable to contractual obligations (the 'Rome I Regulation'),[23] but especially the Brussels I bis Regulation.

2.19. Indeed, the Brussels I Regulation already excluded arbitration from its scope.[24] It is true, however, that the scope to which the application of this law to arbitration is excluded has been extensively discussed. This was the reason for the obvious endeavor to develop the definition of the relationship between litigation and its EC (later EU) regulation, on the one hand, and arbitration on the other hand.[25] In view of the sensitive nature of the given issue, the legislator did not directly amend the Brussels I Regulation, but chose to incorporate the corresponding interpretation in the Recitals of the (new) Brussels I bis Regulation.[26] Consequently, the fact that the EU law does not apply to arbitration should be interpreted as meaning that the courts of the Member States are entitled to consider the existence of the arbitration agreement, including its validity, effectiveness, scope, or its ability to have the envisaged effects,

---

[23] According to its Article 1(2)(e), the Rome I Regulation shall not apply, inter alia, to arbitration agreements and choice-of-court agreements. This appears appropriate, especially in view of the unambiguous connection of such agreements of the parties to the place of proceedings, the intensity of which differs exclusively in connection with the public nature of proceedings before civil courts and the private nature of arbitral proceedings. The private nature does not *a priori* exclude the choice of law applicable to the arbitration agreement; conversely, the premise is that the parties have the right to choose the law applicable to their arbitration agreement. Despite its procedural consequences, an arbitration agreement cannot be deemed a purely procedural contract. It is an instrument of substantive law (at least in *civil law*), and consequently, it cannot be excluded from the scope of the Rome I Regulation solely on the basis of the nature thereof, even though the first step would have to be the classification of the parties' agreement to submit their dispute to arbitrators for resolution as a substantive-law and procedural agreement. However, it has been duly considered that the conditions for entering into and the essential requirements of an arbitration agreement are set forth in the *lex arbitri*, which, inter alia, explicitly provides for any restrictions and limits to the choice of law for the arbitration agreement in connection with the procedural status of the particular arbitration. In view of the fact that the respective issues are fully regulated by the *lex arbitri*, there is no reason to harmonize the respective rules by the EU. The freedom to choose the procedural status and the law applicable to the arbitration agreement is one of the reasons for choosing arbitration as a dispute resolution method. Any attempt at a unification of the applicable conflict-of-laws rules could interfere with the autonomy of arbitration.
[24] Article 1(2)(d) of the Brussels I Regulation.
[25] Especially as a reaction to the decision of the CJEU in C-185/07, *Allianz SpA*, formerly *Riunione Adriatica di Sicurtà SpA, Generali Assicurazioni Generali SpA v. West Tankers Inc.*, in which the court came to the conclusion that the recognition of an anti-suit injunction, whereby a particular person was prohibited from filing a motion to open proceedings with the courts of another Member State, or to continue any such proceedings, because of the fact that such proceedings are contrary to an agreement on arbitration, is incompatible with the Brussels I Regulation.
[26] Recital 12 to the Brussels I bis Regulation.

relating to the dispute initiated in the courts. In compliance with the applicable law (provided that the existence of the arbitration agreement is established), the courts can refer the parties to the agreed arbitration. However, court decisions concerning the declaration of the validity, effectiveness or other issues concerning the submitted arbitration agreement cannot be the subject of recognition and enforcement in other Member States pursuant to the procedure under Article 36 et seq. of the Brussels I bis Regulation. Conversely, if the court concludes that the submitted arbitration agreement is not valid, effective or capable of being applied, the corresponding decision may be recognized and enforced in other Member States. However, this instrument is without prejudice to the courts' power to decide on the enforcement of arbitral awards in terms of the New York Convention on the Recognition and Enforcement of Foreign Arbitral Awards (1958),[27] the priority application of which has been incorporated into the law. This ensures that the court making the decision on the enforcement of an arbitral award will not be bound by a court decision of a different Member State on the invalidity, ineffectiveness or ineligibility of the arbitration agreement, and will be authorized to independently assess the issue of whether the presented arbitral award constitutes a final and binding decision in terms of the New York Convention (1958). Indeed, no other solution is possible, or otherwise the application of the New York Convention (1958) and the possibility of the recognition and enforcement of the issued arbitral award would be excluded in advance. Instead, the assessment of the enforceability of arbitral awards in the Member States would *de facto* (through the assessment of the validity of the arbitration agreement) be transferred to national law, on the basis of which subjective arbitrability (meaning the existence of the parties' agreement on the exclusion of the jurisdiction of civil courts and the submission of their disputes to arbitrators) would be assessed according to criteria different from the international interpretation of international agreements. Other proceedings concerning completed arbitration were explicitly excluded from the scope of the Brussels I Regulation, namely disputes concerning the constitution of the tribunal/appointment of arbitrators, their powers, issues relating to the conduct of arbitration, or any of its other aspects, or petitions or decisions

---

[27] Convention on the Recognition and Enforcement of Foreign Arbitral Awards of 10 June 1958, promulgated in the Czech Republic by Decree of the Minister of Foreign Affairs No. 74/1959 Coll.

concerning the annulment, review, appeal, recognition or enforcement of an arbitral award.

2.20. Besides, it is necessary to point out that the EU has until now endeavored to adhere to the principle of compatibility and a uniform approach to certain issues, especially as concerns any issues connected with the choice of the applicable law and of the forum competent to hear and resolve a dispute.[28] There are indeed no reasonable grounds to abandon the long-standing principle of non-interference in arbitration, but rather keep the applicable rules of the *lex arbitri* and unify the effects of insolvency proceedings on arbitration by the EU law.

III. The Approach of Regulation 2015/848 to the Relationship Between Arbitration and Insolvency Proceedings

2.21. As concerns the material aspects of the issue, the rules incorporated in Regulation 1346/2000[29] have also been adopted by Regulation 2015/848. To avoid any doubts as to whether the effects of insolvency proceedings on other pending proceedings also apply to arbitration, Article 18 of Regulation 2015/848 explicitly stipulates that the provision also applies to arbitral proceedings, which may principally be considered the only difference to Article 15 of Regulation 1346/2000 as concerns the material scope of the law. Indeed, the same conclusion must analogically be inferred in relation to Article 7 of Regulation 2015/848.[30] Specifically, it must also apply to the determination of the law applicable to contracts entered into by the debtor and the effects of insolvency proceedings on proceedings other than those that fall within Article 18 of Regulation 2015/848.[31] Consequently, the opening of insolvency proceedings must be reflected in the arbitral proceedings, and such insolvency

---

[28] In this connection, see also Recital 7 to the Rome I Regulation, which explicitly stipulates that rules regulating the applicable law and rules for the determination of court jurisdiction should be based on the same principles (cit): 'The substantive scope and the provisions of this Regulation should be consistent with Council Regulation (EC) No 44/2001 of 22 December 2000 on jurisdiction and the recognition and enforcement of judgments in civil and commercial matters (Brussels I) and Regulation (EC) No 864/2007 of the European Parliament and of the Council of 11 July 2007 on the law applicable to non-contractual obligations (Rome II).'

[29] Article 15 of Regulation 1346/2000.

[30] Compare Article 4 of Regulation 1346/2000.

[31] Compare Article 15 of Regulation 2015/848.

Article 18 of Regulation 2015/848 (cit.): 'Effects of insolvency proceedings on pending lawsuits or arbitral proceedings - The effects of insolvency proceedings on a pending lawsuit or pending arbitral proceedings concerning an asset or a right which forms part of a debtor's insolvency estate shall be governed solely by the law of the Member State in which that lawsuit is pending or in which the arbitral tribunal has its seat.'

Article 15 of Regulation 1346/2000 (cit.): 'Effects of insolvency proceedings on lawsuits pending - The effects of insolvency proceedings on a lawsuit pending concerning an asset or a right of which the debtor has been divested shall be governed solely by the law of the Member State in which that lawsuit is pending.'

proceedings have consequences for the existence of procedural requirements. The arbitrators should also address this issue in order to eliminate the risk of the potential annulment of their arbitral award in case the decision opening the insolvency proceedings can be recognized in the place where the enforcement is sought, or, as applicable, if it has a universal effect. The latter situation might involve the principles underlying both Regulation 1346/2000 and Regulation 2015/848,[32] or if the above specified *lex concursus* can be deemed a mandatory provision (*ius cogens*) or even overriding mandatory provision, or part of public policy (*ordre public*), as applicable. Article V of the New York Convention (1958) affords the courts of the State in which the recognition of a foreign arbitral award is sought the possibility to refuse the recognition and enforcement of the decision in such cases. Related to this, Recital 73 of Regulation 2015/848 explicitly confirms that national rules on the recognition and enforcement of arbitral awards are not affected, which also applies if the national laws refer to the application of the law of international origin (New York Convention [1958]).

2.22.   Consequently, the arbitrators may easily fail to consider the existence of insolvency proceedings, and the issued arbitral award will not be recognizable and enforceable in other countries, especially in the State of the place of arbitration, even if the arbitration otherwise fully complied with the requirements and rules of the *lex arbitri,* and even if any and all principles of fair process were observed. One may also envisage that, due to the existence of insolvency proceedings, enforcement will also be refused in the State where the arbitral award was issued, which could be a State different from the State of the place of arbitration, although such situations happen only rarely these days. This may have significant ramifications for the creditor, especially if the debtor's assets are subject to insolvency proceedings.

2.23.   The creditor is running a relatively low risk if they commence the arbitration, but also duly lodges their claim in insolvency proceedings. This is because the *lex concursus* usually draws a distinction between two situations. In the first, the creditor lodges a claim, the existence of which was already verified in the finding proceedings and the claim is enforceable (which, at least, renders the possibility to contest the claim in insolvency proceedings *more complicated*). In the second, the creditor

---

[32]   Domitille Baizeau, *Arbitration and Insolvency: Issues of Applicable Law,* NEW DEVELOPMENTS IN INTERNATIONAL COMMERCIAL ARBITRATION, ZÜRICH/BASEL/GENEVA: SCHULTHESS 97 (Christian Müller, Antonio Rigozzi eds., 2009).

lodges their claim that has not yet been subject to resolution between the parties, and the existence and amount of the claim is based on allegations presented by the creditor. The creditor is facing the risk that the liquidator or, as applicable, the authority competent to resolve any potential subsequent incidental dispute in terms of the *lex fori concursus* arrives at a conclusion opposite to the arbitrators' conclusion, and satisfaction of the claim in insolvency proceedings will be impossible. But the creditor will still have an opportunity to prove the existence of the claim in incidental proceedings. If the creditor relied on the enforceability of an award rendered in arbitration, they have practically no opportunity to enforce the creditor's claims, because the issued arbitral award will be unenforceable, but at the same time, the creditor will not be able to assert the claim in any new proceedings.[33]

2.24. The arbitrators should proceed so as to ensure that any decisions they issue are enforceable. Naturally, this does not mean that the arbitrators are under the obligation to make any active inquiries, or take into consideration in which State the enforcement of their future arbitral award might be sought, and adjust the arbitral proceedings accordingly. The arbitrators are especially prohibited, on the basis of such considerations, from tailoring the interpretation and application of the law chosen by the parties for their legal relationship as the applicable law, to the law applicable in the expected place of enforcement. However, if it is clear that the arbitrators' conduct, which, moreover, has no basis in any agreement of the parties or the *lex arbitri*, will obviously result in an unenforceable future arbitral award, the arbitrators' procedure must be considered incorrect and contrary to their obligations. Such obligations also include the making of a decision that determines with certainty the parties' mutual rights and obligations and ensures that the parties will be able to enforce the rights awarded by the decision, whether in the form of individual enforcement, or in (collective) insolvency proceedings, or in any other manner approved by the law. The rules will always apply, whether or not the arbitrators ought to have regard to the EU law or whether or not the EU law applies

---

[33] This is true subject to the requirement that the *lex fori concursus* allows the separate satisfaction of a claim after the insolvency proceedings are terminated. From the practical perspective, it is also necessary to realize that, based on the *lex concursus*, this is mostly just a theoretical possibility of the subsequent satisfaction of claims that have not been lodged in the insolvency proceedings, considering the limitation of actions, as well as the fact that there are usually no assets after the end of insolvency proceedings from which any claims could be satisfied.

to the respective insolvency proceedings. Consequently, it is necessary to apply only the national *lex concursus.*

2.25. As concerns the EU law, however, the obligation to factor in the effect of the opening of insolvency proceedings and, consequently, the application of the relevant provisions of the *lex concursus* is primarily based on the automatic recognition of decisions opening insolvency proceedings in terms of Regulation 2015/848 (similarly to Regulation 1346/2000). If this principle were ignored, the courts might refuse the recognition and enforcement of arbitral awards on grounds of the reservation of *ordre public*, specifically in view of the principles on which the recognition of insolvency proceedings opened in a different Member State are based. The reason is that Recital 66 of Regulation 2015/848[34] stipulates that Regulation 2015/848 should set out, for the matters covered by it, uniform rules on conflict of laws of the Member States which replace, within their scope of application, national rules of private international law of the Member States.[35] The general universal effect of a decision opening the insolvency proceedings is incorporated in Article 20 of Regulation 2015/848.[36]

2.26. A contrary interpretation, i.e. that the relevant provisions of Regulation 2015/848, primarily represented by Articles 7 and 18 of Regulation 2015/848,[37] do not apply to arbitration, would have undesirable consequences – the EU law would be deprived of its purpose and its main effects, because it is based on the principle of universality. Moreover, its objective is to create a mechanism of automatic and universal application of the effects of all insolvency proceedings in all EU Member States (except Denmark) in compliance with the law under and on the basis of which the decision opening the insolvency proceedings was rendered. If, under such circumstances, the arbitrators *ignored* the provisions of the insolvency law of another EU Member State that would otherwise apply pursuant to the conflict-of-laws rules incorporated in Regulation 2015/848, their approach could constitute grounds for the refusal of the recognition and enforcement of their arbitral award, as indicated above, for being contrary to *public policy*, especially and primarily with respect to this possibility as incorporated in Article V of the New York Convention (1958).

2.27. It is necessary to bear in mind that the desired objective of arbitral proceedings is a decision that would constitute a proper

---

[34]   Compare Recital 23 to Regulation 1346/2000.
[35]   Compare also Recital 22 to Regulation 2015/848.
[36]   Compare Article 16 of Regulation 1346/2000.
[37]   Compare Article 4 of Regulation 1346/2000 and Article 15 of Regulation 1346/2000.

basis for enforcement (sometimes known as an execution title), on the basis of which the successful party would be able to enforce the claims awarded to them. This is by no means intended to mean that the arbitrators could and should assess the case and/or otherwise proceed contrary to the applicable law. The reverse side of the principle governing arbitration, contractual freedom, is the parties' responsibility for their own decisions and the consequences thereof, including proper consideration of the choice of the applicable law, place of arbitration, procedural rules, all in connection with the place of the potential, or even anticipated enforcement of the arbitral award. The parties should therefore properly assess any and all of these aspects and the potential consequences of the provisions contained in their arbitration agreement for the enforceability of the arbitral award in a place other than the place where the arbitral award is rendered. But the opposite approach would be similarly inappropriate, i.e. allowing the arbitrators to entirely disregard the issue of the enforceability of the arbitral award rendered by them and to deliver an arbitral award that could from the very beginning indicate that its enforcement will most probably be refused. This is by no means intended to suggest that the arbitrators should conduct the proceedings contrary to the applicable law and/or tailor the interpretation to the circumstances of the likely place of enforcement of the arbitral award. At the same time, the arbitrators are not allowed to intentionally proceed contrary to the law to which they are obliged to have regard and thereby give rise to grounds for the refusal of the arbitral award. This very situation might occur, though, if the arbitrators entirely failed to acknowledge the consequences of the insolvency status of a party to the arbitration and gave unilateral preference to the conclusion that arbitral proceedings cannot, or even must not, be prejudiced by the opening of insolvency proceedings against one of the parties, and that the effects of properly initiated insolvency proceedings should not and cannot be considered.

2.28. Should the consequences arising from the *lex fori concursus* be considered in arbitration? Without prejudice to the conclusions resulting from such a consideration, the answer must be yes. However, the degree to which the rule represented by Article 18 of Regulation 2015/848[38] is in fact an appropriate solution and whether the differences between litigation and arbitration have not been erased is unclear. The rule incorporated in Article 18 of Regulation 2015/848, however imperfect, has a rationale

---

[38] Compare Article 15 of Regulation 1346/2000.

in litigation; the rules and sometimes even the principles of litigation differ from one EU Member State to another, and such proceedings are subject to sovereign national laws. If the courts were obliged to apply the laws of another/foreign jurisdiction to pending proceedings, it would ultimately result in an unacceptable violation of independence and sovereignty. Hence, the choice of the law of the Member State in which the respective litigation is conducted as the law applicable to the effects of insolvency proceedings is, at least, relatively logical, considering the principle of sovereignty. The author is of the opinion, though, that there is no such logic with respect to arbitration.

2.29. It is necessary to point out that at the early stages of the legislative process, Regulation 1346/2000 became one of the most controversial laws ever adopted in the territory of the European Communities, and its wording is the result of numerous political compromises. Moreover, the issue of the effects that the opening of insolvency proceedings has on other pending proceedings must be classified as a procedural issue, and it would run contrary to the principle of State sovereignty to require that the court of any particular State apply the procedural laws of a foreign State to the proceedings pending in the former court, even if the laws form part of the *lex concursus*. Indeed, the fact that the effects that the opening of insolvency proceedings have on other pending proceedings is a procedural issue, and that these rules fall within the domain of sovereign procedural laws of the Member States is confirmed by the very concept of Article 18 of Regulation 2015/848.[39] As a matter of fact, one of the premises already underlying the adoption of Regulation 1346/2000[40] was the fact that Regulation 2015/848 (Regulation 1346/2000) would under no circumstances endeavor to unify the national *leges concursus* and the rules applicable in the territory of the Member States, and that due respect would be paid in this regard to the differences between national laws. On the contrary, the only purpose of the EU insolvency law is to facilitate the access of foreign creditors to insolvency proceedings and the possibility to file claims in insolvency proceedings conducted abroad, as well as the mutual recognition of decisions connected with the insolvency proceedings.[41] The transfer from Regulation

---

[39] The same applies to Article 15 of Regulation 1346/2000.

[40] The same has been preserved in relation to Article 18 of Regulation 2015/848.

[41] See Recital 11, in which the said fact and the differing interests of the individual states were duly acknowledged, and which states as follows (cit): 'This Regulation acknowledges the fact that as a result of widely differing substantive laws it is not practical to introduce insolvency proceedings with universal scope in the entire Community. The application without exception of the law of the State of opening of proceedings would, against this background, frequently lead to difficulties.'

1346/2000 to the adoption of the regime of Regulation 2015/848 has not been accompanied with any change in the standpoint of the individual Member States that would enable a material resolution of the contested issues. It is still only a compromise that reflects the individual States' political interests more than anything else, and no change has been made to the law on the basis of any broader conceptual considerations where the application of Regulation 1346/2000 proved difficult. This relatively unfortunate approach is also manifested in the additions incorporated in Regulation 2015/848, which basically represent a codification of the conclusions articulated by the ECJ/CJ EU in the interpretation of Regulation 1346/2000, rather than a novel solution based on the experience with the application of Regulation 1346/2000.

2.30. Considering the above, it is therefore clear why the courts apply their own *lex concursus* in relation to pending litigation, and not the law of the State in which the debtor's center of main interests (COMI) is located, as the main conflict-of-laws criterion for the determination of international jurisdiction for conducting the main insolvency proceedings and for determining the *lex fori concursus primariae*. However, any and all considerations concerning State sovereignty may be dismissed in the case of arbitration, and there are even reasons for the application of the *lex fori concursus*.

IV. Grounds for the Preferential Application of *Lex Fori Concursus* in Arbitration, as Opposed to *Lex Arbitri*

2.31. Apparently, the most important reason for applying the *lex fori concursus,* and not the *lex arbitri,* on the effects of the opening of insolvency proceedings is the equal treatment of creditors. As mentioned above, the insolvency laws in the individual States exhibit significant differences. The effects of the opening of insolvency proceedings on other pending proceedings could therefore range from a prohibition to conduct any other proceedings outside the framework of the insolvency proceedings, and the resulting need to terminate such proceedings, to an obligation to suspend such proceedings, to the possibility of permitting the proceedings to continue restricted by the requirement that a decision rendered in such proceedings cannot be submitted for enforcement, for instance.[42] Depending

---

[42] One may infer that Article 18 of Regulation 2015/848 or, as applicable, Article 15 of Regulation 1346/2000 ought to be construed as only regulating procedural aspects, i.e. the law of the Member State in which the arbitration is pending determines whether the proceedings should be continued or discontinued

on the place where the proceedings are held, the individual creditors could therefore have different standing, because some of them will be allowed to continue the pending proceedings, whereas other creditors will be denied such a possibility, which is in direct conflict with the objectives of Regulation 2015/848[43] and the principle of the uniform settlement of all of the debtor's liabilities.

2.32. We may also invoke the issue of procedural economy and effectiveness, which should also, and primarily, apply to arbitration. If we apply the law of the place of arbitration, there is a real risk that the result will be of no further use to the parties. If the law of the place of arbitration allows the arbitration to continue after the opening of insolvency proceedings, whereas the *lex fori concursus* stipulates that the opening of insolvency proceedings entails the obligation to terminate, interrupt or otherwise suspend the arbitration, or even invalidates or cancels the arbitration agreement, it is possible that the result of such other proceedings will not be recognized in the place of the insolvency proceedings, or will not even be able to serve the creditor as evidence proving the creditor's claim. Yet, the approaches of the individual countries differ in this respect as well. One may invoke, for instance, the decision of the French *Cour de Cassation* concerning the consequences of insolvency proceedings opened in France against a party to pending international arbitration.[44] The court has held that the principle of interrupting pending proceedings constitutes part of national and international public policy, and ruled that the arbitral tribunal acted contrary to public policy if the tribunal ordered the debtor to pay damages, instead of merely ascertaining and calculating such damage and losses without explicitly imposing an obligation to pay the damages. The respective decision indicates that the court primarily considered as contrary to public policy the failure to interrupt that part of the proceedings in which the arbitrators imposed an obligation to the detriment of the insolvency estate, i.e. to the detriment of the creditors of the debtor whose assets have been subject to the opened insolvency proceedings. Despite this, the court did not limit the arbitrators by making a decision on the existence of the execution title and the amount of damage. We may *a contrario* conclude that the arbitration might not be contrary to *ordre public* if the arbitral award focuses exclusively on the title underlying the claim.

(suspended or terminated).

[43] The same applied under Regulation 1346/2000.

[44] Judgment of the *Cour de Cassation civ 1er*, Case No. 08-10281 of 06 May 2009.

Conversely, the Czech Insolvency Act stipulates that as soon as the debtor's insolvency is ascertained, all pending proceedings (including arbitration) are automatically suspended, and the arbitrators would therefore be prohibited from issuing any decision, even a decision on the basis of the creditor's claim.

2.33. Under certain circumstances, the entire arbitration (including the hearing of the claim within the framework thereof) could therefore become useless to the parties, and its conclusions unusable, which is in direct conflict with all of the principles on which arbitration is based. These consequences can be exacerbated by the fact that if the arbitration continues without due regard for the effects of the opening of insolvency proceedings, a party different from the debtor may ultimately be deprived of the possibility to assert their rights in the State in which the insolvency proceedings are conducted. This applies especially if the arbitration continues. The arbitral award will not be recognized and enforced in the State of the insolvency proceedings, and in the meantime, the legal possibility to *(re)* assert such rights in the State of the insolvency proceedings using the means envisaged and provided by the *lex fori concursus* will expire, due to the expiration of time limits.

2.34. Other issues to be considered are the issues of legal certainty and predictability. In their assessment of the risks involved in a potential insolvency, the parties will instinctively and quite correctly examine the *lex fori concursus* in the COMI, rather than the *lex fori concursus* in the potential place of arbitration, which is generally chosen on the basis of criteria completely different from the standard and the contents of the *lex concursus*. Even if the parties approached the negotiations regarding the transfer of the jurisdiction to hear their disputes to arbitrators with maximum responsibility and expertise, it is necessary to point out that an agreement on the place of arbitration does not represent an essential component of the arbitration agreement. Indeed, the parties may not have any influence on the place where the arbitration will be held, and consequently, what effects the opening of insolvency proceedings will have.[45] This holds true despite the fact that the parties incorporate an agreement

---

[45] See also Article 17 of Act No. 216/1994 Coll., on Arbitration and Enforcement of Arbitral Awards. For an example, see also Article 18(1) of the ICC (International Chamber of Commerce) Rules of Arbitration. One cannot argue that a rule stipulating that the place of arbitration is not determined on the basis of the parties' will, but by a third party, is an exceptional and uncommon rule in the practice of international arbitration. This is true whether it is derived from an arbitral institution for the benefit of which the arbitration agreement was entered into, or whether it was determined directly by the arbitrators called upon to hear and resolve the dispute. This applies despite the fact that the international practice adheres to a clear recommendation that, in order to secure legal certainty, the parties should agree on the place of arbitration, and if possible, should incorporate such an agreement in their arbitration agreement.

on the place of arbitration in their arbitration agreements more and more frequently, because they are more knowledgeable about arbitration.

2.35.   More or less all of the abovementioned objections can also be raised in relation to litigation. However, it is necessary to have regard for the interests of the individual Member States in the preservation of their sovereignty, which is reflected, inter alia, in the principle of procedural sovereignty. As mentioned above, arbitration does not require any consideration of this particular aspect, and there is no obstacle to a reference to the *lex fori concursus* in any given case.

2.36.   The argument concerning the equal standing of creditors applies regardless of whether the proceedings held in a State different from the State where the insolvency proceeding are pending is a litigation or an arbitration. The same holds true for the risk of the non-recognition of the decision in the place where the insolvency proceedings are held. As concerns *legal certainty*, the Brussels I bis Regulation provides for alternative court jurisdiction in a number of cases, and consequently, the parties may, again, be unaware of the forum that will hear their dispute until the moment a lawsuit is filed. However, it is necessary to consider the fact that the issue of legal uncertainty in arbitration manifests itself much more significantly. The conflict-of-laws criteria for the determination of court jurisdiction in litigation are characteristic for and based on the principle that the rules for the determination of jurisdiction should be highly predictable and should primarily be derived from the place/residence of the respondent, unless the subject matter of the dispute or the contractual freedom of the parties authorize the use of a different connection. The tendency to connect the forum to the parties and/or the subject matter of the dispute is thus clear. Conversely, the main criterion for the choice of the place of arbitration is usually the *lex arbitri*. The choice of the place of international arbitration is commonly influenced by the place's reputation as a place with a positive approach to arbitration. The place need not have any relation to the parties and the subject matter of the dispute. It can be a neutral place. From this perspective, and considering the independence of arbitration from the law of the place of arbitration, there is no reason to apply the local *lex concursus*.

V. The Scope of Rules Affected by Article 18 of Regulation 2015/848 (Article 15 of Regulation 1346/2000)

2.37. If we conclude that arbitrators should have regard to and apply Regulation 2015/848, it is necessary to inquire into the material scope of Article 18 of Regulation 2015/848,[46] because the words 'effects of insolvency proceedings on pending lawsuits [or arbitral proceedings]'[47] can be perceived in a number of different ways. The first option is an interpretation of the provision as a rule regulating the consequences of the opening of insolvency proceedings for the arbitration agreement negotiated between the parties.

V.1. The Effects of the Opening of Insolvency Proceedings on the Validity of the Arbitration Agreement

2.38. If the rule incorporated in Article 18 of Regulation 2015/848 were to be construed as a rule regulating the consequences of the opening of insolvency proceedings for the arbitration agreement and the validity thereof, the Article would be deprived of its procedural nature, which appears universally accepted. At the same time, it would mean a substantial simplification of the issue of whether the arbitrators are obliged to have regard to this effect, because the existence of a valid arbitration agreement is directly connected with the issue of the subjective arbitrability of the dispute and is a necessary prerequisite for conducting the arbitral proceedings. The issue of arbitrability in the sense of the existence of a valid agreement of the parties regarding the exclusion of the jurisdiction of courts and the submission of a defined category of disputes to independent arbitrators for hearing and resolution is an issue that the arbitrators are obliged to examine. According to the doctrines applicable in certain States, such an examination must be performed at each individual moment of the proceedings.[48] The absence of any such an agreement automatically entails the termination of the arbitration. Hence, we may even go so far as to conclude that any corresponding rules that would specially address and explicitly

---

[46] The same applies with respect to Article 15 of Regulation 1346/2000, even though Article 15 of Regulation 1346/2000 did not cover arbitration or at least not explicitly.

[47] Article 15 of Regulation 1346/2000, contrary to Article 18 of Regulation 2015/848, contained no explicit reference to *arbitral proceedings*. The issue of the material impact of the rule on arbitration has been the subject matter of a number of discussions and controversies.

[48] In the Czech Republic, for instance, this is true at each moment of the proceedings where arbitrability is perceived as a procedural requirement'. Conversely, Polish doctrine demands that the procedural requirements be fulfilled at least at the moment when the proceedings are opened.

regulate the influence of the opening of insolvency proceedings on the validity and/or effectiveness of the arbitration agreement would become a quasi-component of the *lex arbitri* (albeit formally incorporated in a different law), and would have to be considered on that basis alone.

2.39. But there are other reasons for dismissing this theory. If Article 18 of Regulation 2015/848 (Article 15 of Regulation 1346/2000) were to be interpreted in terms of the validity of the arbitration agreement, the provision would be duplicated. The conflict-of-laws rule on the basis of which the applicable law is determined, which regulates the influence of the opening of insolvency proceedings on contracts entered into by the debtor, is incorporated in Article 7(2)(e) of Regulation 2015/848.[49] Although the arbitration agreement is not a typical substantive-law agreement to which this provision should primarily apply, there is no reason to exclude the arbitration agreement from the scope thereof. The author believes that the arbitration agreement is primarily a substantive-law agreement, despite the fact that it has effects in procedure whenever a dispute arises and arbitration is initiated.[50] This applies in spite of the fact

---

[49]   Compare Article 4(2)(e) of Regulation 1346/2000.

[50]   For more details, see Alexander Bělohlávek, *The definition of procedural agreements and the importance to define the contractual nature of the arbitration clause in international arbitration*, 2 YEARBOOK ON INTERNATIONAL ARBITRATION. ANTVERPEN/COPENHAGEN/ZURICH/WIEN: INTERSENTIA/ NEUER WISSENSCHAFTLICHER VERLAG 21–50 (Marianne Roth, Michael Geistlinger eds., 2012); or Alexander Bělohlávek, *Procesní smlouvy a kvalifikace rozhodčích a prorogačních smluv: aplikace hmotněprávní úpravy na smlouvy s procesním účinkem pro futuro, [Title in Translation: Procedural Agreements and Qualification of Arbitration Agreements and Choice-Of-Forum Agreements: Application of Substantive Laws to Agreements with Procedural Effects Pro Futuro]*, 151(9) PRÁVNÍK, PRAGUE/CZECH REPUBLIC: ÚSTAV STÁTU A PRÁVA AKADEMIE VĚD ČR V.V.I. [INSTITUTE OF STATE AND LAW, ACADEMY OF SCIENCE CZECH REPUBLIC V.V.I.] 389–418 (2012); Alexander Bělohlávek, Tomáš Pezl, *Aplikace procesních předpisů na rozhodčí řízení, [Title in Translation: Application of Procedural Laws to Arbitration]*, 16(2) PRÁVNÍ RÁDCE 16–24 (2008). But cf. also Vilém Steiner, *K teoretické koncepci rozhodčí smlouvy v mezinárodní arbitráži, [Title in Translation: Regarding the Theoretical Concept of the Arbitration Agreement in International Arbitration]*, 1 PRÁVNÍK 908-909 (1971); ACHIM AHRENDT, DER ZUSTÄNDIKEITSSTREIT IM SCHIEDVERFAHREN, Tübingen: Max Planck Institut für ausländisches und Internationales Privatrecht 30 (1996); *Hledik, M.* Povaha rozhodčí smlouvy. [Title in Translation: Nature of Arbitration Agreement]. Master's thesis successfully defended at the Department of International and European Law, Faculty of Law, Masaryk University in Brno, 2008. Available online in the information system of the Faculty of Law, MU, available at: http://is.muni.cz/th/125255/pravf_m/Diplomova_prace_-_Martin_ Hledik.txt (accessed on 28 January 2019).
Procedural agreements can be interpreted as agreements that are exclusively procedural in nature, especially agreements on procedure, or agreements regarding evidence. These differences have been correctly pointed out by, inter alia, Gonsorčíková, M.' Právně teoretické aspekty procesní smlouvy jako nástroje upravujícího rozhodčí řízení. [Title in Translation: Legal Theoretical Aspects of Procedural Contract as Instrument Regulating Arbitration]. iPrávník, 12 June 2006, section: civil procedure, available at: http://www.ipravnik. cz/cz/clanky/civilni-proces/art_3708/pravne-teoreticke-aspekty... (accessed on 21 June 2011). However, Gonsorčíková classifies arbitration and choice-of-court agreements in the second category, i.e. agreements with purely procedural effects. In this connection, we would probably recommend a more cautious approach. These are contracts that establish jurisdiction, if we base our conclusions on the typically continental civil law tradition, according to which jurisdiction is the domain of procedural law and usually constitutes one of the procedural requirements. I believe that Gonsorčíková errs in that she makes no distinction between arbitration/choice-of-court agreements and understandings entered into in the course of a particular dispute, although she apparently is aware of these differences. This is the reason why the differentiation of

that the arbitration agreement is a condition and prerequisite for the arbitrators' jurisdiction, and according to the classical concept of civil law (as opposed to common law), jurisdiction is a procedural, not a substantive-law category. Moreover, a conflict-of-laws rule connecting the validity and effects of executed contracts (including arbitration agreements) to the *lex fori concursus* is more logical – especially because the *lex arbitri*, which would be referred to in Article 18 of Regulation 2015/848 and Article 15 of Regulation 1346/2000, is not a law that would automatically be applicable to the arbitration agreement. Despite the fact that this difference is often ignored even by professionals, the *lex arbitri* as the law governing the prerequisites and the course of arbitration must be strictly differentiated from the law applicable to the arbitration agreement, and both these legal systems must, naturally, be differentiated from the substantive law applicable to the legal relationship between the parties (*lex causae*). Hence, the parties are theoretically entirely free to choose that their arbitration agreement shall be governed by a law completely different from the *lex arbitri*, and similarly independent from the *lex causae*. It is also necessary to bear in mind that the *lex arbitri* is not the automatically applicable law, even if the parties fail to choose the law applicable to their arbitration agreement. However, the principle of the separability of the arbitration agreement from the main agreement does not rule out the possibility that the specific circumstances of the case will support the conclusion of the integrity and indivisibility of the contractual documentation, including the arbitration agreement (in the form of an arbitration clause), and that the law applicable to the parties' legal relationship (*lex causae*) will be deemed to be the law applicable to the arbitration agreement. Consequently, even if the application of the *lex arbitri* is not entirely excluded, it is not the primary law to be considered, especially if the arbitration

---

the individual types and kinds of procedural contracts is so important, and why such differentiation is the *conditio sine qua non* for further examination of the nature and effects of procedural contracts, including the determination of the law applicable to these contracts and the manner of application thereof.

However, one may also come across the opinion that the nature of the arbitration agreement is a matter of differing conceptual interpretations. Some experts maintain that the nature of arbitration agreements is not important and has no significant implications for practice. See also KVĚTOSLAV RŮŽIČKA, ROZHODČÍ ŘÍZENÍ PŘED ROZHODČÍM SOUDEM PŘI HOSPODÁŘSKÉ KOMOŘE ČR A AGRÁRNÍ KOMOŘE ČR, [TITLE IN TRANSLATION: ARBITRATION BEFORE ARBITRATION COURT AT ECONOMIC CHAMBER OF CZECH REPUBLIC AND AGRICULTURAL CHAMBER OF THE CZECH REPUBLIC.] Plzeň: Aleš Čeněk 38 (2005). (cit.:) 'Discussions about the legal nature of the arbitration agreement can be reflected in the relevant laws on arbitration; they do not, however, affect legal practice in any significant manner'; see also EMMANUEL GAILLARD, JOHN SAVAGE, FOUCHARD GAILLARD GOLDMAN ON INTERNATIONAL COMMERCIAL ARBITRATION, DenHaag: Kluwer Law International 221 (1999). But the insolvency proceedings show how important the issue is and the application of the Insolvency Regulations is a typical example thereof.

agreement was entered into separately and it contains no explicit or implicit choice of applicable law. The importance of the *lex arbitri* in relation to the arbitration agreement inheres much more in the escape clauses.[51] These preserve arbitrability in those cases where the arbitration agreement is invalid according to the law applicable to the agreement, but it suffices to establish the jurisdiction of the arbitrators, and to hold the arbitral proceedings if the arbitration agreement meets the requirements of the *lex arbitri*.[52]

2.40. Moreover, the connection to the *lex fori concursus* also complies with the above-described principles of insolvency proceedings, the objectives of which obviously do not include an intention to cause each of the arbitration agreements entered into by the debtor to have a different destiny depending on the selected place of arbitration. Naturally, the issue is also related to procedural economy – it would be significantly onerous and costly even for the liquidator if they had to separately assess each individual contract according to foreign law. It would be equally onerous if they had to individually address the consequences of such a consideration for the future of the contract with each individual contract partner. We may therefore conclude that if the *lex fori concursus* explicitly sets forth the effects of the opening of insolvency proceedings on the arbitration agreements to which the debtor is a party (whether through any autonomous regulation or on the basis of a general rule applicable to all contracts or a category of contracts), the arbitrators should have regard to that aspect (without prejudice to the outcome of their considerations), but not on the basis of applying Article 18 of

---

[51] In the theory of many countries (cf. also in the English-speaking countries or *Ausweichklausel* in Germany) the escape clause represents a theological reduction, also taken over by the normative terminology in several countries. From the terminological perspective, however, it represents a certain internal conflict, which ignores the functional and methodological scope of the purpose of the law. Cf. also THOMAS HIRSE, DIE AUSWEICHKLAUSEL IM INTERNATIONALEN PRIVATRECHT, Tübingen: Mohr Siebeck 433 (2006); cf. also NADĚŽDA ROZEHNALOVÁ, INSTITUTY MEZINÁRODNÍHO PRÁVA SOUKROMÉHO. [TITLE IN TRANSLATION: INSTRUMENTS OF PRIVATE INTERNATIONAL LAW], Prague: Wolters Kluwer ČR, (1st ed., 2016); Krzysztof J. Pelc, *Seeking Escape: The Use of Escape Clauses in International Trade Agreements*, 53 INTERNATIONAL STUDIES QUARTERLY 349–368 (2009); Mostafa Beshkar, *Arbitration and Renegotiation in Trade Agreements*, JOURNAL OF LAW, ECONOMICS, AND ORGANIZATION ADVANCE ACCESS 1–34 (2016); Alexander Bělohlávek, *Substantive Law Applicable to the Merits in Arbitration*, 8(2/30) ROMANIAN REVIEW OF ARBITRATION – REVISTA ROMÂNĂ DE ARBITRAJ 1–16 (2014); NEIL ANDREWS, ARBITRATION AND CONTRACT LAW: COMMON LAW PERSPECTIVES, Springer 19 (2016).; JEAN-FRANCOIS POUDRET, SEBASTIEN BESSON, COMPARATIVE LAW OF INTERNATIONAL ARBITRATION, Sweet & Maxwell 155 (2007).

[52] Indeed, this fact alone clearly indicates that both the theory and the practice strictly distinguish the *lex arbitri* from the law applicable to the arbitration agreement, and do not consider the *lex arbitri* to be the law primarily governing the arbitration agreement. Hence, these categories may in no case be considered identical, which is especially evident in the application of the EU insolvency law in the case of the opening of insolvency proceedings on pending arbitration.

Regulation 2015/848, but in compliance with Article 7(2)(e) of Regulation 2015/848.[53]

2.41. However, the consequences of the application of these provisions will remain very limited. In this particular case, the influence of the *lex arbitri* can be observed, which may ultimately modify, or even suspend the effects of the *lex fori concursus*. The general principle requiring maximum respect for the contractual autonomy of the parties in international arbitration and the broadest interpretation in favor of preserving arbitrability is often expressed as a rule that stipulates that arbitrability is sufficiently proven if the arbitration agreement is valid under at least one of the potentially applicable legal systems. A typical example of such a rule can be found in the Swiss Private International Law Act, Chapter 12, which provides for international arbitration held on the territory of Switzerland. Article 178 of the said Swiss Private International Law Act stipulates that an arbitration agreement is deemed valid if it complies either with (i) the law chosen by the parties, (ii) the law applicable to the subject matter of the dispute, or (iii) Swiss law. In other words, the fact that the arbitration agreement is invalid or ineffective under the law applicable[54] to the arbitration agreement need not automatically mean that arbitration could not be held in Switzerland on the basis thereof. It is fully sufficient if the arbitration agreement meets the criteria imposed on such an instrument by Swiss law. This rule is by no means exceptional in jurisdictions that are traditionally arbitration-friendly; such provisions preserve arbitrability to the broadest possible extent.[55]

2.42. An analogous approach, must also be adopted if the *lex fori concursus* declares the arbitration agreement invalid. Such an approach allows, in compliance with the rules of the *lex arbitri*, the establishment of subjective arbitrability on the basis of more alternative legal systems. The reason it must be adopted is that we cannot infer that the rules of the *lex fori concursus* would not be taken into consideration under such circumstances.

---

[53] Compare Article 15 of Regulation 1346/2000 or, as applicable, Article 4(2) of Regulation 1346/2000. Article 15 of Regulation 1346/2000, as opposed to Article 18 of Regulation 2015/848, contains no explicit reference to arbitration. However, the author believes that the explicit broadening of the material scope of Article 18 of Regulation 2015/848 compared to the previous law was more likely a codification of the majority opinions on the interpretation of the material scope of Article 15 of Regulation 1346/2000 in relation to arbitration, at least in the civil law environment.

[54] See the first criterion mentioned, i.e. the law chosen by the parties. In the absence of a choice of law, and if the arbitration agreement is executed in the form of an arbitration clause incorporated in the main contract, the law applicable to the merits of the case is often deemed to be the law applicable to the arbitration agreement. Naturally, this does not exclude the possible conclusion that, even in this case, the arbitration agreement shall be governed by a law different from the *lex causae* of the main contract.

[55] The reference to Swiss law is in this case used exclusively as the most commonly invoked example of an escape clause relating to the validity of the arbitration agreement, although Switzerland is, naturally, not bound by EU law, including Regulation 2015/848 or Regulation 1346/2000, as applicable.

Undeniably, the opening of insolvency proceedings could, in theory, render the arbitration agreement invalid, although such a result is rather unique in the global context. But the possibility to hold arbitration is inferred using the alternative connection in terms of the *lex arbitri*. Hence, it is necessary to distinguish between the arbitrators having regard to the *lex fori concursus*, and the fact that the rules could, under certain circumstances, be outweighed by the *lex arbitri*, which enables the establishment of the arbitrators' jurisdiction by an alternative method. Consequently, the invalidity of the arbitration agreement could be remedied if the *lex arbitri* allows for such a remedy and determines substitute criteria for holding arbitration. From the perspective of the application of these rules, the reason why the arbitration agreement fails to comply with the law otherwise applicable to the agreement is entirely irrelevant. Arbitrability can be established by a substitute method if the arbitration agreement fails to meet the formal and/or material requirements of the applicable law, but also if the arbitration agreement is rendered invalid by the opening of insolvency proceedings, while it would not be prejudiced by the opening of insolvency proceedings in the place of arbitration. The result is the same, but the possibility to hold arbitration based on an escape clause incorporated in the *lex arbitri* cannot be considered identical to a situation when the arbitrators entirely ignore the existence of insolvency proceedings.

2.43.   The latter case – as described above – involves the real risk that the outcome of the arbitration will not be recognized and the arbitral award will be unenforceable if the award was rendered in a situation where the arbitrators, for instance, entirely ignored the issue of procedural requirements in connection with insolvency proceedings opened by one of the parties; the former case, conversely, should not entail any such risk. The reason is that the conclusion regarding the possibility to hold the arbitration was articulated after the effects of the insolvency proceedings, as well as the subsequent rules of the *lex arbitri* being duly considered. One may therefore argue that the conclusion regarding the existence of the requirements for holding the arbitration is based on a thorough examination thereof and the application of the relevant law. From this perspective, the procedure adopted by the arbitrators and the final outcome of the arbitration cannot be objected to, despite the fact that the framework of the insolvency proceedings was *de facto* exceeded, or, as the case may be, the application of the *lex concursus* failed to achieve a result in the given case that would comply with that law, and differences may have occurred among the individual creditors.

2.44. We may therefore conclude that as concerns the validity of the executed arbitration agreement, Article 18 of Regulation 2015/848[56] cannot be interpreted in terms of an explicit cancellation of such validity. Firstly, Regulation 2015/848[57] contains separate rules in this regard. Secondly, and most importantly, it would be a most ineffective provision in this regard, which would fail to accomplish the envisaged effect. For one thing, each arbitration agreement would be subject to a different legal system, which, moreover, does not comply with the law that could primarily be considered as the law applicable to the arbitration agreement in light of the doctrines of international arbitration. Additionally, the envisaged objective would only be achieved to a significantly limited extent. The reason is that modern laws on international arbitration mostly offer an alternative connection on the basis of which arbitrability can be established, whereby the rules governing insolvency proceedings are often eliminated. But in view of the contractual autonomy of the parties, this result is acceptable, and properly considers the interests of both arbitral and insolvency proceedings. Moreover, the parties may, to some extent, influence the result. I am not saying that it would be necessary to apply the national laws of the place of arbitration that do not form part of the *lex arbitri*; conversely, the parties may be expected to have paid attention to the regulation of such issues in the *lex arbitri* when they were entering into the arbitration agreement. Whether, and under what circumstances, the arbitration agreement entered into by the parties holds up in light of the *lex arbitri* will logically belong among the main issues coming into play in the parties' considerations when selecting the place of arbitration.

2.45. However, the above conclusions concerning the potential mitigation or direct suspension of the effects of the *lex fori concursus* on the validity of the arbitration agreement can by no means be interpreted as suggesting that the insolvency proceedings have no or only limited influence on arbitration; it is exactly the opposite, and it may often be a very complicated issue in practice. Moreover, the potential influence of the opening of insolvency proceedings on the arbitration agreement under the *lex fori concursus* constitutes merely one aspect whereby the arbitration could be affected by the opening of

---

[56] Compare Article 15 of Regulation 1346/2000, here despite the absence of any explicit reference to arbitration.
[57] The same applies to Regulation 1346/2000.

insolvency proceedings. At the same time, this aspect should be resolved exclusively through the application of the *lex arbitri,* which governs the issue of whether or not the invalidity of the arbitration agreement according to the *lex fori concursus* can be remedied (by applying the *lex arbitri*), or whether it entails an absolute lack of subjective arbitrability, which means that the arbitrators lack jurisdiction and, consequently, no arbitration may be held as a result thereof.

V.2. The Influence of Opening of Insolvency Proceedings on the Procedural Capacity of the Debtor

2.46. Another possibility is to interpret Article 18 of Regulation 2015/848[58] as a reference to the procedural capacity of the debtor, i.e. by reference to the debtor's ability to be a party to litigation or arbitration. But the author believes that this interpretation also cannot be deemed correct. In this connection, we may, for instance, refer to the ruling of the Swiss Federal Supreme Court in the *Vivendi* case, which will be analyzed in greater detail below.[59] This decision has been accepted by legal professionals only with major misgivings, and has been subjected to debates by experts even in Switzerland itself, the outcomes of which have not always been positive. We may only speculate as to the degree to which this particular criticism has contributed to its subsequent scholarly correction. Besides, we must not forget that it is a decision rendered by an authority of a non-EU Member State, which is not bound by Regulation 2015/848 or Regulation 1346/2000, as applicable.

2.47. The opening of insolvency proceedings usually has no effect on the legal personality or even procedural capacity of a party to litigation/arbitration. Indeed, this would be contrary to the structure and purpose of insolvency proceedings, which aim to settle the rights and obligations of the debtor. This would be impossible to implement if the legal personality of the debtor were limited in any manner or even entirely absent. It is necessary to accept as a premise that insolvency proceedings usually entail a restriction or extinguishment of the debtor's right to make free dispositions with their assets. But such measures are usually adopted only in order to preserve the debtor's insolvency estate

---

[58]   Despite the explicit reference to arbitration, principally also according to Article 15 of Regulation 1346/2000.

[59]   Also in spite of the fact that Switzerland, a non-EU Member State, is naturally not bound by the Insolvency Regulation. However, the Swiss case law represents an important example of a possible interpretation, which need not be void of logic even as concerns the interpretation of the Insolvency Regulation within the scope of its territorial applicability.

and protect creditors by preventing the debtor from making dispositions with their property contrary to the interests of the creditors and to the detriment of the debtor's insolvency estate. The power to act on behalf of the debtor and, as applicable, the insolvency estate itself are therefore partially or entirely transferred to a court-appointed liquidator, depending on the diversity of the *leges fori concursus* in the individual States. Any interpretation suggesting that these measures result in the debtor being divested of their procedural capacity, or even legal personality in general, would be contrary to the generally accepted rule that a properly appointed liquidator of the debtor is authorized to act on the debtor's behalf, and sue or be sued as the debtor's agent, or act directly in the name of the insolvency estate. It is irrelevant whether, according to the applicable national law, the liquidator merely acts on behalf of the debtor or represents the debtor. It is not significant whether the powers of the statutory authority, or even the debtor's insolvency estate, transfer to the liquidator, who acts in their own name, though for the benefit of the insolvency estate, which is separated from the liquidator's other assets. Consequently, it is also irrelevant whether the *lex fori concursus* contains different rules after such a decision for the substantive-law capacity of the debtor to perform juridical acts and for the debtor's procedural capacity, or whether, conversely, the *lex fori concursus* prescribes the same concept for these two different levels in which the debtor's personality is manifested.

2.48.   The fact that the authority to act, whether in the substantive-law or procedural sense, transfers to a different person such as the liquidator appointed or, depending on the national laws, confirmed/approved by the insolvency court, this transfer may not be connected with any restriction of legal personality. The fact that the debtor is mostly unable to influence the choice of the liquidator and that the liquidator has a varying status, depending on the particular *lex concursus,* is without prejudice to the above conclusion. Consequently, the liquidator cannot be perceived as a person completely different from the debtor. It is irrelevant that, in terms of the *lex concursus*, the liquidator may – again depending on the varying concepts of national insolvency laws – act in their own name in certain proceedings. This does not mean, however, that the debtor would be deprived of their capacity to act independently in the debtor's own name. Indeed, it is possible to come across such *leges concursus* according to which the debtor may themselves insist that the proceedings continue, should the liquidator decide, having considered all of the circumstances and the potential benefit for the insolvency estate, to exercise the liquidator's powers and discontinue the proceedings.

2.49. Moreover, if the procedural capacity of the debtor were indeed limited, it would be impossible for the debtor to be a party to any proceedings conducted within the framework of and in connection with the insolvency proceedings, whether such proceedings concern incidental disputes (disputes concerning the existence of the lodged claims or disputes, whereby a third party claims part of the insolvency estate arguing that the third party, and not the debtor, is the rightful owner thereof), or any other disputes. Similarly, the debtor alone, and independent of the liquidator, is usually authorized to perform selected acts and, for instance, lodge procedural motions in insolvency proceedings, including the possibility to raise objections against the liquidator and the steps they have taken. However, if we concluded that the effects of insolvency proceedings on pending litigation or arbitration must be interpreted as meaning the debtor's procedural capacity, the capacity to be a party to such proceedings, or the debtor's general capacity to legally perform relevant juridical acts, we could only come to the conclusion that the proceedings regarding incidental and other disputes could not be conducted within the framework of the insolvency proceedings. This conclusion applies regardless of the selected method of resolving the debtor's insolvency, i.e. regardless of whether the debtor's activity should be preserved and restructured, or whether the objective of the insolvency proceedings is the settlement of the debtor's liabilities and subsequent liquidation of the debtor. According to a number of national insolvency laws, the debtor is also not deprived of their legal personality at the moment when the liquidator takes steps to terminate the debtor's existence (also known as resolution of the insolvency by liquidation). The debtor ceases to exist under the law and, consequently, loses their legal personality only as a result of and after the termination of the insolvency proceedings and on the basis of the completed liquidation. In other words, the debtor's dissolution as a juridical person (in this case, we logically refer to juridical persons) is the consequence of the insolvency proceedings, not an effect connected with the opening of insolvency proceedings.

2.50. Finally, the ability to be a party to proceedings is a necessary requirement for conducting such proceedings, including arbitration. This is a general principle that applies to any type of proceedings and stipulates that, where there is no party or a legal successor, there are no proceedings. In this regard, it is not possible to remedy the absence of personality in any manner, and it principally constitutes an obstacle to the proceedings that cannot be eliminated. In this case as well, the arbitrators, similarly to judges in courts, are obliged to proceed of their own volition and examine whether the parties have procedural capacity. If the arbitrators concluded that this was not the case, they are obliged to terminate the proceedings. Even the arbitrators are obliged to examine at their own behest whether the debtor has the necessary procedural capacity. Hence, if the *lex fori concursus* restricted the procedural capacity of the debtor in any manner, the consequences associated therewith would have to be factored in, regardless of Article 18 of Regulation 2015/848.[60] This case thus also represents a rather general rule, and it is principally irrelevant why the party was deprived of its procedural capacity. The arbitrators' approach, as well as the termination of the proceedings as the only possible outcome, is the same whether the procedural capacity expires as a result of the opening of insolvency proceedings or otherwise.

2.51. Moreover, it is a generally accepted principle of private international law that legal personality is examined pursuant to a single legal system, namely the law applicable to the person's personal status. Hence, legal personality should not depend on any particular juridical act, and situations should be avoided in which the person would have the personality necessary for selected juridical acts and could be a party to certain proceedings, while they would lack such capacity in other cases, for instance, in connection with arbitration.[61] It is therefore hardly imaginable that, in consequence of the opening of insolvency proceedings, the debtor would be deprived of their procedural capacity in relation to arbitration, whereas such capacity remains fully preserved in relation to other acts and the possibility to participate in other proceedings. Such a situation, though unlikely, must be distinguished from a situation in which the *lex fori concursus* restricts the debtor's possibility to act as a party to arbitration in consequence of a potential statement declaring any and all arbitration agreements entered into by the debtor invalid.

---

[60]   Article 15 of Regulation 1346/2000.

[61]   The above is a general conclusion. Specific situations in which the capacity to perform certain acts is limited, for instance, for juveniles or in consequence of a mental disorder, are beyond the scope of this article.

V.3. The Influence of the Opening of Insolvency Proceedings on Arbitral Procedure

2.52. The last possible interpretation of Article 18 of Regulation 2015/848 (Article 15 of Regulation 1346/2000), which the author himself considers correct, is the emphasis on the procedural aspect, that is the fact that it is a rule concerning the effects of insolvency on pending litigation or arbitration. This approach complies with the linguistic, systematic and teleological interpretation of the provision. Hence, the essence of the provision inheres in the influence of insolvency proceedings on other pending proceedings, their interruption, termination or any other specific form of suspension, depending on the applicable procedural law/rules. This interpretation is also consistent with the purpose and objectives of insolvency proceedings, which are based on the principle that any and all claims against the creditor ought to be settled in insolvency proceedings, not by means of any individually opened litigation or arbitration. If a dispute arises regarding the validity of a claim made by a creditor, the insolvency court has the power to conduct any incidental disputes. Hearing claims before other forums therefore becomes unnecessary. Analogous rules have been adopted by several countries, such as in English law,[62] Czech law,[63] the Swiss Federal Act on Enforcement of Claims and Insolvency,[64] as well as the Austrian Insolvency Code,[65] and the corresponding rules in the French Commercial Code.[66] As regards the opposite situation, i.e. the debtor has a claim against a third party, the *lex fori concursus* delimits the corresponding powers of the liquidator,

---

[62] Insolvency Act of 1986, Section 130(2) (approximate translation, cit.): 'When a winding-up order has been made or a provisional liquidator [cf. liquidator] has been appointed, no action or proceeding shall be proceeded with or commenced against the company or its property, except by leave of the court and subject to such terms as the court may impose.'

[63] See Section 263(1) (cit.:) 'Unless provided otherwise in this Act, on the date the bankruptcy is declared, the judicial, administrative or other proceedings concerning the rights and obligations relating to the estate or to be satisfied from the estate, to which the debtor is a party, shall be suspended.'

[64] Swiss Federal Act on Enforcement of Claims and Insolvency of April 11, 1889, Section 207 (approximate translation, cit.):

> 1. All civil proceedings shall be suspended to which the debtor is a party and which concern the existence of the estate; this does not apply to emergency proceedings. The proceedings may be commenced in the time period of ten days after the second meeting of creditors, and the collective bankruptcy proceedings not earlier than 20 days after the Collocation is resumed. 2. Under the same conditions, administrative procedures shall be suspended. 3. In the course of suspension, the limitation periods shall be suspended. 4. This provision does not apply to compensation claims regarding slander and personal injury or family law proceedings.

[65] Austrian Bankruptcy Code (*Konkursordnung*, RGBl. No. 337/1914), Section 6(1) (approximate translation, cit.): 'Actions to enforce claims against assets forming part of the insolvency estate cannot be brought or continued once insolvency proceedings have been commenced.'

[66] The French Commercial Code stipulates in Section L622-21 (approximate translation, cit.): 'A decision on the opening of insolvency proceedings suspends or prevents any action on behalf of all creditors whose claims are aimed at forcing the debtor to pay a sum of money or terminating a contract for the failure to pay a sum of money.'

including whether and how the liquidator is entitled to enforce these claims in separate proceedings, and what the procedural consequences are for any pending proceedings if the liquidator concludes that such separate proceedings are ineffective and will not ultimately contribute to the greater satisfaction of the creditors. The assessment of the measures taken by the debtor in the past, including any proceedings initiated by the debtor, belongs among the usual competences of the liquidator. But in order for the liquidator to be able to responsibly assess whether the continuation of the proceedings is desirable, the *lex fori concursus* often interrupts or otherwise suspends, at least temporarily, such proceedings conducted before a third party. The liquidator subsequently announces whether or not the liquidator wishes to continue the proceedings, or, as applicable, whether the liquidator has any influence on the continuation or the debtor's steps in such proceedings, depending on the *lex fori concursus*.

2.53. However, one must again distinguish between proceedings pending at the moment of the opening the insolvency proceedings or at any other moment with which the *lex concursus* connects the relevant procedural effects, on the one hand, and proceedings that are yet to be opened in the future, on the other hand. The former situation is addressed by Article 18 of Regulation 2015/848 (Article 15 of Regulation 1346/2000), and the applicable law would be the law of the place where the proceedings are conducted *(lex processuali)*, i.e. the *lex arbitri* in the case of arbitration. As concerns proceedings other than pending proceedings opened by the individual creditors, Article 7(2)(f) of Regulation 2015/848 (Article 4(2)(f) of Regulation 1346/2000) – which incorporates the conflict-of-laws rule referring to the *lex fori concursus* – must be considered in arbitration as well. This division is logical, because as mentioned above, the grounds for giving precedence to the law of the place where the proceedings are actually conducted are closely connected to the principle of State sovereignty and to the Member States' endeavor to retain full control over all aspects of the insolvency proceedings. From this perspective, it would be unacceptable for the EU law to prescribe for the Member States an obligation to apply a foreign *lex concursus* in relation to any proceedings conducted in the respective Member State's territory. There is no such problem as concerns future proceedings, because the liquidator decides, in accordance with the powers vested in them by the *lex fori concursus*, whether or not the liquidator will open any proceedings against a third party. Considering the fact that there is no conflict with any other legal system, i.e. there is no prior conduct of the debtor that the liquidator would be bound by or obliged to follow, it is logical that the powers entrusted to the liquidator in this regard, including the proceedings that the liquidator may open and in which forum, are governed by the *lex fori concursus*.

2.54. There was a legislative mistake made during the drafting of Regulation 2015/848, which may be important from a practical perspective. Article 18 of Regulation 2015/848 explicitly refers to 'pending lawsuit or pending arbitral proceedings'. Article 7(2)(f) of Regulation 2015/848 only refers to 'pending lawsuits'. A systematic interpretation, however, does not allow any conclusion other than that the provision also includes arbitration.[67] If the EU legislation deemed it necessary to explicitly emphasize this difference in Article 18 of Regulation 2015/848, there is no reason why the same distinction should not be reflected in Article 7(2)(f) of Regulation 2015/848. This inconsistency has already appeared in the proposal for Regulation 2015/848.[68] The author believes that the legislators have merely overlooked the inconsistency, and it is rather doubtful how necessary the addition actually was. Although some language versions of Regulation 1346/2000 employed the word 'lawsuit,' where the requirement appears legitimate for an unambiguous inclusion of arbitration as a dispute resolution method to which the said provision also applies, the English and German versions used terms that can be interpreted more broadly, namely 'lawsuit' and 'Rechtsstreit' which translates as a legal dispute in the procedural sense. In this place, we could refer generally to legal proceedings without the term necessarily denoting litigation or civil proceedings within the meaning of the applicable procedural law. Indeed, this was probably the reason why the interpretation was principally uncontroversially also applied to arbitration.

2.55. Although it makes no sense from a practical perspective (especially because the reference is always made to one and the same conflict-of-laws rule), it is equally possible that the disproportion is intentional, if one considers the report on the

---

[67] One of the reasons being that, in the opposite case, and if the literal wording of Regulation 2015/848 should be applied, that the provisions only apply to the proceedings explicitly mentioned, then the effects of the opening of insolvency proceedings on arbitration would be governed both by the *lex arbitri* (on the basis of Article 18) and by the *lex fori concursus* (according to Article 7(2)(f)). This is naturally impossible.

[68] Proposal for a Regulation [2015/848] prepared by the European Commission of 12 December 2012 (European Commission Proposal for a Regulation of the European Parliament and of the Council Amending Council Regulation (EC), No. 1346/2000 on Insolvency Proceeding). [CELEX: 52012PC0744], available at: http://www.europarl.europa.eu/RegData/docs_autres_institutions/commission_europeenne/com/2012/0744/COM_COM%282012%290744_EN.pdf (accessed on 28 January 2019)

application/functioning of Regulation 1346/2000 of 9 January 2013, administered and managed by Professors Burkhard Hess, Paul Oberhammer and Thomas Pfeiffer (the HLV Report).[69] This Report, inter alia, addressed the proposal of the International Association of Restructuring, Insolvency & Bankruptcy Professionals (INSOL-Europe) to supplement Article 4(2)(f) of Regulation 1346/2000 with a reference to arbitration. However logical this conclusion is and in compliance with the systematic interpretation and purpose of the law, the authors of the HLV Report have unequivocally refused the proposal. The interesting thing in this connection is not the fact itself, but their reasons for such approach. The authors have presented no material or legal arguments that would justify their conclusion. The HLV Report suggests beyond any doubt that the opinion of its authors was the result of exclusively political considerations. They specifically argued that if the proposed amendment were implemented, it would most likely give rise to an extensive and useless discussion regarding the law applicable to the effects of insolvency proceedings on the arbitration agreement,[70] which would ultimately open the controversial issue of the general status of arbitration.

2.56.   The author of this article believes that this approach is a typical example of the approach adopted by the EU with respect to any issues that could, albeit potentially, appear controversial. Instead of a material discussion and a search for a suitable resolution, the EU apparently, and consistently with its past approaches, endeavors to ignore any problems, hoping that they will just go away, or adopts a resolution that none of the parties considers materially correct or beneficial (and which in most instances transpires to be a source of further problems in future), but which enables the rules to be acceptable from a political perspective. Unfortunately, this deferment of problems contributes to the negative perception of the EU and its activities by the public, and sometimes results in principal problems in the application of EU laws, where each Member State often interprets this political compromise, devoid of any substance, in

---

[69]   The Heidelberg-Luxembourg-Vienna Report on the Application of Regulation No. 1346/2000/EC on Insolvency Proceedings (External Evaluation JUST/2011/JCIV/PR/0049/A4) (*External Evaluation of Regulation No. 1346/2000/EC on Insolvency Proceedings*) prepared by Institute of Foreign and International Private and Business Law, Ruprecht-Karls-Universität Heidelberg [DEU] and the Institute for Civil Procedure, Universität Wien [AUT]. Also referred to as the *'Heidelberg – Vienna Report'*, *'Heidelberg – Luxemburg – Vienna Report'* etc. in legal resources and literature. Also cited as Hess, B., Oberhammer, P. et Pfeiffer, Th. et al. External Evaluation of Regulation No. 1346/2000/EC on Insolvency Proceedings, et. 453. Available at: http://ec.europa.eu/justice/civil/files/evaluation_insolvency_en.pdf (accessed on 28 January 2019)

[70]   Here specifically in relation to the issue of whether Article 4(2)(e) of Regulation 1346/2000 applies in relation to the arbitration agreement.

line with its own interests, subsequently construed in a manner far from the required autonomous interpretation.

2.57. It is necessary to strictly distinguish between the individual aspects of arbitration that can be affected by the opening of insolvency proceedings, in consequence of which, according to the author, one may not limit the application of insolvency proceedings to a single provision to which any and all such aspects would be subordinated. Regardless of this, the approach adopted by the authors of the HLV Report is inconsistent and illogical, even within the limits of their own reasoning.

2.58. The reason is that it is more than clear that regardless of the addition to Article 4(2)(f) of Regulation 1346/2000 (Article 7(2) (f) of Regulation 2015/848) – or lack thereof – the provision must also be applied in relation to arbitration. Article 18 of Regulation 2015/848 (Article 15 of Regulation 1346/2000) and the effects are limited to pending proceedings concerning the assets or rights belonging to the debtor's insolvency estate. However, the opening of insolvency proceedings also affects other proceedings, which need not explicitly concern the debtor's insolvency estate. One may also not dismiss the possibility to open proceedings in the future. The only viable conclusion is that Article 7(2)(f) of Regulation 2015/848 (Article 4(2)(f) of Regulation 1346/2000) must apply in relation to such proceedings. The opposite conclusion would leave no conflict-of-laws criterion that could be applied in relation to these proceedings. Moreover, the premises are unclear on the basis of which the authors of the HLV Report arrived at their conclusion, i.e. that Article 15 of Regulation 1346/2000 will give rise to no discussion regarding the relationship between arbitration and insolvency proceedings, whereas the addition of entirely identical text to Article 4(2)(f) of Regulation 1346/2000 would allegedly create unacceptable controversy.

2.59. In addition, the author of this article is of the opinion that the reference that the authors make in the HLV Report to the decision in C 294/02 of March 17, 2005 is not pertinent. The case concerned an application under Article 238 EC brought on 12 August 2002 by the Commission against (i) AMI Semiconductor Belgium BVBA, (ii) A-Consult EDV-Beratungsgesellschaft mbH (in liquidation), (iii) Intracom SA Hellenic Telecommunications & Electronic Industry, (iv) ISION Sales + Services GmbH & Co. KG (in liquidation), (v) Euram-Kamino GmbH, (vi) HSH Nordbank AG, and (vii) InterTeam GmbH (in liquidation). Before the application was lodged, insolvency proceedings were opened

Czech (& Central European) Yearbook of Arbitration®

against several of the above respondents.[71] The jurisdiction of the ECJ was established on the basis of an agreement designated as an arbitration clause,[72] which was agreed by and between the parties in terms of Article 238 EC. It is clear that the law employs the term arbitration clause,[73] and it is not, an incorrect translation of one of the language versions. Nonetheless, the proceedings at the ECJ clearly cannot be deemed arbitration in the traditional meaning with respect to which the issue of the effects of insolvency proceedings is addressed. Moreover, the author assumes that the shift in meaning could have theoretically occurred right at the beginning, when the EC Treaty was being entered into, when one might imagine that the legislature was primarily working with the French language version, which was subsequently translated into other language versions.

2.60.   This is because the French version of the EC Treaty employs the words *clause compromissoire*, which may indeed be translated as an arbitration clause, but the current trend is to use the more modern *convention d'arbitrage*[74] or *clause d'arbitrage.* Consequently, the words *clause compromissoire* in the EC Treaty might have been originally intended to mean an agreement on a kind of conciliation. But the subsequent translations used a translation that employed the words 'arbitration clause,' even though it is clear that the ECJ, while an authority competent to hear and resolve disputes, still conducts court proceedings, not arbitration in the sense of proceedings before private-law entities chosen by the parties. Hence, the agreement in the respective case was rather a certain kind of a choice-of-court agreement entered into on the basis of a special authorization by the authorities of the Communities (currently the EU). An arbitration clause and a choice-of-court agreement must be

---

[71]   The author does not consider it important to provide any detailed description of the circumstances and the subject matter of the proceedings here, because the intention is only to demonstrate that the decision cannot apply to the respective issues.
[72]   The said agreement read as follows (cit.): 'The Court of First Instance of the European Communities, and in the case of appeal, the Court of Justice of the European Communities shall have exclusive jurisdiction in any dispute between the Commission and the contractors concerning the validity, application and interpretation of this contract.'
[73]   Czech version: '*Soudní dvůr má pravomoc rozhodovat na základě rozhodčí doložky obsažené ve veřejnoprávní nebo v soukromoprávní smlouvě uzavřené Společenstvím nebo jeho jménem.*'
English version: 'The Court of Justice shall have jurisdiction to give judgment pursuant to any arbitration clause contained in a contract concluded by or on behalf of the Community, whether that contract be governed by public or private law.'
German version: '*Der Gerichtshof ist für Entscheidungen aufgrund einer Schiedsklausel zuständig, die in einem von der Gemeinschaft oder für ihre Rechnung abgeschlossenen öffentlich-rechtlichen oder privatrechtlichen Vertrag enthalten ist.*'
French version: '*La Cour de justice est compétente pour statuer en vertu d'une clause compromissoire contenue dans un contrat de droit public ou de droit privé passé par la Communauté ou pour son compte.*'
[74]   See also the terminology used in the ICC Rules of Arbitration (Rules of the International Chamber of Commerce) in the 2012 version.

strictly distinguished from one another. In any case, the respective proceedings must be deemed a kind of court proceeding, and must also be perceived as such in the application of Regulation 2015/848, or, as applicable, Regulation 1346/2000. Hence, the reference to Case C 294/02 of 17 March 2005 was an obvious mistake made during the drafting of the HLV Report.

2.61. Apart from the above, it is also necessary to consider the special nature of the proceedings before the Court of Justice, governed by special procedural rules, as a result of the very nature of this entity. The rules are not tied to any particular place of proceedings, but to a particular authority before which the proceedings are held. Consequently, if paragraph 67 of the ECJ ruling in Case C-294/02 of 17 March 2005 stipulates that the issue of how ECJ jurisdiction is to be exercised *vis-à-vis* a party against which insolvency proceedings have been instituted shall be assessed in light of the procedural law applicable in the Court of Justice, it must be interpreted as a reference to the procedural rules that the Court of Justice must comply with. It is not as an expression of any specific conflict-of-laws rule, let alone a conflict-of-laws rule that would apply to the respective agreement, whether designated as a choice-of-court or arbitration agreement. In this connection, one may invoke the immediately following paragraph (paragraph 68 of the ruling), in which the ECJ states as follows (cit.):

> [G]iven that neither the Statute of the Court of Justice nor its Rules of Procedure contain any specific provisions concerning the treatment of applications brought against parties against which insolvency proceedings have been commenced, it is necessary to deduce what rules are applicable from the principles common to the procedural laws of the Member States in this area.

2.62. It is clear that the ECJ does not refer to the *lex fori concursus* or the procedural law of the place of the proceedings. Conversely, the ECJ has created a special *ad hoc* conflict-of-laws rule (known as principles common to the laws of the individual Member States) that reflects the specific status of the Court of Justice. Again, it appears inappropriate, regardless of the nature of the proceedings, to deduce any rules of a general nature from this specific situation. Additionally, it is by no means questioned and has been reflected in both Article 15 of Regulation 1346/2000 and finally also in Article 18 of Regulation 2015/848 that it is necessary to apply in any pending proceedings the procedural rules that are binding on the forum, which are invoked by the authors of the HLV Report. The principle of State sovereignty indeed allows no other conflict-of-laws rule. But it is a completely different question whether this conflict-of-laws rule is also appropriate in relation to arbitration. Although the author argues that this is not the case, and that, in view of the differences between arbitration and litigation, it would be possible to determine an autonomous conflict-of-laws criterion, this is not the subject of criticism here.

VI. The Consequences of the Opening of Insolvency Proceedings for the Validity of Arbitration Agreements and Choice-of-court Agreements in Light of the Report Evaluating Application of Regulation 1346/2000 with Recommendations for New EU Insolvency Law (HLV Report)

2.63. The controversy and principal mistake that the authors of the HLV Report make is their failure to distinguish between the individual aspects of other proceedings that could be affected by the opening of insolvency proceedings. Exclusively procedural aspects in terms of the suspension of any pending proceedings are undoubtedly governed by the rules of the *lex fori*, as provided for in Article 18 of Regulation 2015/848 (Article 15 of Regulation 1346/2000). However, the suspension of proceedings may never be confused with other aspects,[75] including the validity of an arbitration or choice-of-court agreement, which, indeed, has not even been subject to any examination in the given case. This also renders the conclusion incorrect in which the authors of the HLV Report argue that the ECJ ruling in Case C-294/02 of 17 March 2005 actually stipulated conflict-of-laws criteria for the effects of the opening of insolvency proceedings on an agreement establishing the jurisdiction of the Court of Justice

---

[75] See paragraphs 59 to 61 of the ECJ decision in Case No. C-294/02 of 17 March 2005, which deal with the loss of procedural capacity of one of the defendant companies, which was correctly assessed separately. In particular, the provisions read as follows (cit.):

> [...] the action is inadmissible to the extent to which it relates to InterTeam because the latter was removed from the commercial register on 8 November 2001, that is to say nine months before the Commission lodged its application, and consequently InterTeam had lost its legal capacity by that date. As the Advocate General states in point 67 of her Opinion, an action against a company is inadmissible if, when the action is brought, that company had neither legal capacity nor standing to be a party to legal proceedings. The applicable law in that connection is that governing the incorporation of the company in question, which in this case is German law (see Case 81/87 Daily Mail and General Trust [1988] ECR 5483, paragraph 19, and Case C-208/00 Überseering [2002] ECR I-9919, paragraph 81). It is common ground that under German law a limited liability company ('GmbH'), such as InterTeam, loses its capacity to be a party to legal proceedings as a result of being dissolved, which necessarily involves its removal from the commercial register following a finding that it has no assets. De-registration thus creates a presumption that there are no assets. [...].

to hear the case. The inadmissibility of a lawsuit lodged with respect to entities against which insolvency proceedings were opened was not based on the conclusion that an agreement on the jurisdiction of the Court of Justice became invalid or ineffective after the opening of the insolvency proceedings. The conclusion was that the insolvency courts have exclusive jurisdiction to hear claims made against the insolvency debtors. The HLV Report argues that such claims logically concern the debtor's insolvency estate, and hearing such claims in a different regime would favor the Commission as a creditor if the case could be handled in proceedings conducted before a specially agreed forum. The Report authors have specifically stated that, according to most procedural laws of the Member States, creditors may not enforce their claims in court separately against a person that is subject to insolvency proceedings. The creditors are in such a case obliged to observe the applicable procedures, and if they fail to adhere to such rules, their lawsuit is inadmissible. Invoking the opinion of the Advocate General, the authors argued that the objective of Regulation 1346/2000 (currently Regulation 2015/848) is to secure the effective and proper coordination of insolvency proceedings in the individual Member States, and thereby ensure equal distribution of the existing assets among all creditors. The Commission would be unjustifiably privileged to the detriment of the other creditors if it were allowed to assert its claims in proceedings conducted before any individually agreed forum, while no such proceedings are allowed before the national courts (according to a strict application of the *lex fori concursus*).[76]

2.64.   This decision, on the one hand, invokes the principles of insolvency proceedings that are common to the procedural laws of the Member States, and on the other hand, applies the applicable rules of the *lex fori concursus*. Aside from this internal inconsistency, it is clear that the reason for holding the lawsuit inadmissible in the part in which it related to the defendants against whom insolvency proceedings were opened was the finding that the respective claim could only be heard by the competent insolvency court. The entire ruling makes no mention of anything from which we could infer that a choice-

---

[76]   Reference is made to the German Insolvency Code (*Insolvenzordnung*) of 5 October 1994 (BGBl. 1994 I, et. 2.866), Section 87, according to which creditors may assert their claims against a company only in compliance with the laws on insolvency proceedings. The law thus replaces proper lawsuits regulated under the rules of civil procedure, and any proceedings opened directly against the debtor company or against the liquidator are prohibited. Another reference is made to Article 6(1) of the Austrian Bankruptcy Code, RGBl. No. 337/1914 – *Konkursordnung*, which prohibits the opening or continuation of any proceedings concerning a dispute aimed at the exercise of rights to assets that comprise the insolvent company's bankruptcy estate after the insolvency proceedings were opened.

Czech (& Central European) Yearbook of Arbitration®

of-court agreement between the parties was rendered null and void or ineffective as a consequence of the opening of insolvency proceedings. Such an agreement would necessarily outline how the parties clearly expressed their will to exclude the jurisdiction of national courts and establish the jurisdiction of the ECJ for any potential disputes between the parties.

2.65.   The above categories have no proceedings opened and conducted on the basis of the agreement and where the insolvency proceedings actually have effects on the agreement of the parties, including an arbitration clause. They must be distinguished from the obligation to examine the agreement's applicability in a particular case. The fact that any particular proceedings cannot be held due to the delimitation of the subject of the proceedings or any other circumstance does not automatically mean that no proceedings may be held. If the *lex fori concursus* prescribes the exclusive jurisdiction of the insolvency court for any particular type of proceedings, one cannot infer that the law thereby cancels an agreement of the parties due to a particular forum being authorized to hear their dispute. Insolvency proceedings could be said to have effects on an arbitration agreement if the *lex fori concursus* stipulates that the opening of insolvency proceedings renders the arbitration agreement invalid, and no proceedings may be opened on the basis thereof. Paradoxically (and without the author being aware of any actual existence of a *lex concursus* with these particular contents), such rules need not be accompanied by any other measures. One may imagine a situation where the legislature may theoretically desire to make sure that the debtor's disputes are not submitted to arbitration, and consequently, the legislature declares all arbitration agreements invalid. At the same time, however, the legislature will not consider it necessary to provide for any further limitations applicable to the handling of disputes that do not fall within the exclusive jurisdiction of the insolvency courts. Consequently, the applicable rules determining court jurisdiction will be used. In such cases, and only in such cases, one may legitimately refer to the effects of insolvency proceedings on an arbitration agreement.

2.66.   The opinion presented by the authors of the HLV Report, according to which the ruling in Case C-294/02 proves that the law applicable to the effects of insolvency proceedings on arbitration agreements is the law of the place of arbitration, has no support whatsoever in the text of the ruling. Moreover, as the entire HLV Report indicates, this conflict-of-laws criterion cannot be considered very well chosen. The validity and effectiveness of a particular legal relationship was unambiguously resolved in Article 4(2)I of Regulation 1346/2000, and the same holds true for Article 7(2)(e) of Regulation 2015/848. Hence, there is no reason to exclude issues concerning the arbitration agreement from the scope of the provision. This conclusion applies notwithstanding the unquestionable procedural connotations of the arbitration agreement. The determination of a different applicable law for each arbitration agreement that the debtor might have entered into would be contrary to the underlying principle of legal certainty. Moreover, and as mentioned above, the HLV Report does not clearly indicate whether the distinction between Article 18 of Regulation 2015/848 (Article 15 of Regulation 1346/2000) and Article 7(2)(f) of Regulation 2015/848 (Article 4(2)(f) of Regulation 1346/2000) should also be preserved in relation to arbitration agreements, or, as applicable, whether the criterion of the place of arbitration ought to apply with respect to all arbitral proceedings, or indeed whether the authors of the HLV Report support the introduction of a brand new conflict-of-laws criterion.

VII. The Significance of *Lex Arbitri* in the Context of Insolvency Proceedings Across Borders

2.67.   The above paragraphs are not intended to undermine the significance of the *lex arbitri*; quite the opposite. But it does appear unnecessary in the given context. The first problem lies in those proceedings which were not yet opened at the moment of the opening of the insolvency proceedings (or, as applicable, the decision on the method of resolving insolvency, or at the moment of any other procedural fact or event relating to the insolvency proceedings under the *lex arbitri*), in which the place of arbitration may be unclear. Considering the principal importance accompanying the choice of the place of arbitration in such a case, one would have to expect that both parties would attempt to influence the choice, to an extent that would have to be classified as prohibited. Moreover, it is not true that the *lex arbitri* would be eliminated if the conflict-of-laws criterion of the *lex fori concursus* were applied. The author considers the mutual interaction of these laws very important. As described above in detail, the *lex arbitri* mostly anticipates a potential confrontation with arbitration agreements governed by a foreign law that defines the conditions that must be fulfilled in order for the arbitration to take place, regardless of the how the respective issue is provided for under the law applicable to the arbitration agreement.[77] Similarly, the *lex arbitri* may stipulate auxiliary criteria and a possibility to preserve the subjective arbitrability of the dispute. This could occur if the arbitration agreement exhibits any deficiencies in light of the law applicable to the agreement ultimately resulting in the invalidity of the agreement, while the requirements for holding arbitration were fulfilled on the basis of the *lex arbitri* or any other criteria determining this law. The author is not of the opinion that it is necessary, or even desirable, that the EU law address this issue beyond that scope and *de facto* change the conditions of the *lex arbitri* in relation to the assessment of arbitration agreements.

2.68.   Considering all of the circumstances, the author considers the arguments relating to the conflict-of-laws criteria for the determination of the effects of insolvency proceedings on arbitration materially incorrect. But the approach of the authors of the HLV Report to the matter as a whole is even more important – instead of an open professional discussion regarding the issues that could potentially be deemed controversial, there is an endeavor to disguise the existence of any differing opinions with the intention of keeping the text on the general level, which cannot stand any closer scrutiny and can be expected to result in problems with interpretation and inconsistent case law. This approach also explains why the interaction of insolvency proceedings and arbitration is entirely ignored in all preparatory documents concerning Regulation 2015/848.

VIII. The Powers of the Liquidator in Relation to Arbitration under EU Law

2.69.   Article 7(2)(c) of Regulation 2015/848 (Article 4(2)(c) of Regulation 1346/2000) also stipulates that the *lex fori concursus* shall also determine the powers of the liquidator. These powers must include the scope of the liquidator's entitlement to open proceedings and enforce claims against third parties, including the determination of whether the liquidator remains bound by an arbitration agreement concerning a claim asserted by the debtor. In other words, the issue is whether the liquidator is entitled to commence arbitration or whether the claims asserted by the liquidator are subject to any special court jurisdiction. The opening of any proceedings exceeding the scope of the powers entrusted to the liquidator by the *lex fori concursus* clearly constitutes a lack of essential procedural requirements, which the arbitrators are bound to address of their own volition.

---

[77]   Typically, the issue is objective arbitrability. It is considered inadmissible to conduct arbitration in a case where the hearing before arbitrators is prohibited by the *lex arbitri*.

However, this situation does not concern the application of Article 18 of Regulation 2015/848 (Article 15 of Regulation 1346/2000), but the determination of the scope within which the liquidator is authorized to act in the name of the debtor or as the debtor's agent, or as the case may be, the determination of the proceedings which the liquidator may open.

2.70. In practice, these rules are intertwined with the above-analyzed issue of the validity of the arbitration agreement, because if the *lex fori concursus* generally declares arbitration agreements entered into by the debtor null and void, this particular effect of the opening of insolvency proceedings is naturally also binding on the liquidator. However, an interesting situation may occur depending on how the *lex fori concursus* (applicable under Article 7(2)(c) of Regulation 2015/848 or, as the case may be, under Article 4(2)(f) of Regulation 1346/2000) defines the powers of the liquidator. Consider a situation where, at the opening and conduct of any proceedings (including arbitration), no limitations are set *vis-à-vis* third parties, and at the same time, the *lex arbitri* contains provisions preserving arbitrability if the otherwise invalid arbitration agreement meets the conditions of the *lex arbitri*.[78] In this case, the liquidator will likely avail themselves of this opportunity and open the arbitral proceedings, regardless of the *lex fori concursus*. Such measures, if adopted by the liquidator, cannot be deemed contrary to and exceeding the liquidator's powers. Conversely, if the *lex fori concursus* (apart from the limitation of the validity/effectiveness of arbitration agreements) explicitly limits the type of proceedings that the liquidator may open and the forum before which such proceedings may be conducted, one may deduce that the arbitrators ought to refuse the opening of any arbitration. The argument for doing so is that even if the arbitration agreement can be held valid with reference to the *lex arbitri*, the statement of claim was lodged by a person without the authority to do so, or as applicable, the particular case may only be heard and resolved before a different forum which is endowed with exclusive jurisdiction. If the arbitrators decided to ignore the effects of insolvency proceedings and heard the case anyway, the recognition and enforcement of that decision in the place of the insolvency proceedings would be seriously jeopardized for this very failure to honor the *lex fori concursus*. Moreover, the opening of such proceedings would represent

---

[78] Insolvency proceedings in the place of arbitration do not affect the arbitration agreement, especially the validity and effectiveness. In other words, they do not affect the possibility to initiate arbitration on the basis of the arbitration agreement.

a major risk for the liquidator, who is strictly bound by the rules of the *lex fori concursus,* and any breach thereof exposes the liquidator to the risk of sanctions, or at least disciplinary measures imposed by the authority supervising liquidators under the *lex fori concursus.* One may also not exclude general liability and the obligation to pay damages consisting of, for instance, the costs expended on the arbitration whose opening was prohibited, and of which the liquidator could and should have been aware.

IX. The Subject Matter of Arbitration in Relation to Insolvency Proceedings Conducted Against a Party to Proceedings

2.71.   The aforementioned criteria are by no means the only aspect that the arbitrators are obliged to address in disputes relating to insolvency proceedings against a party to the dispute. The same importance must also be attributed to the subject matter of the arbitration. However, this situation may again turn out to be complicated and ambiguous. As Article 18 of Regulation 2015/848 (Article 15 of Regulation 1346/2000) indicates, it is necessary to factor in the influence of the *lex fori concursus* on all proceedings concerning the assets or rights belonging to the insolvency estate. In this connection, it would be incorrect to limit the material scope of Article 18 of Regulation 2015/848 (Article 15 of Regulation 1346/2000) to financial claims made against the debtor. A dispute that concerns the insolvency estate might also be a dispute over the ownership of a particular asset registered in the insolvency estate, such as whether the asset belongs to the debtor or to a third party. This category of disputes similarly encompasses the abovementioned claims made against third parties. However, such disputes require a consideration of the procedural consequences of the opening of insolvency proceedings, which are referred to in Article 18 of Regulation 2015/848 (Article 15 of Regulation 1346/2000), i.e. the potential effects in the form of the *suspension* or termination of such proceedings. Nonetheless, the *suspension* need not be permanent or absolute, because the *lex concursus* usually allows the liquidator to decide on the further progress of the proceedings, and to assess whether the continuation of the proceedings benefits the creditors and the insolvency estate, or whether the effects of the suspension connected with the opening of insolvency proceedings should continue. But this already concerns the powers and considerations of the liquidator, which is a factor that does not fall under the *lex arbitri*, but under the scope of the liquidator's powers and the manner of exercising such powers in terms of the *lex fori concursus*, as previously discussed. The author insists that these two aspects must be strictly distinguished from one another. The reason is that it would run counter to the principles of insolvency proceedings if the liquidator were limited in the discharge of their office by the *lex fori concursus* applicable in the place of the arbitral proceedings that, for instance, would not grant them the power to demand the reopening of the case. However, it appears similarly inappropriate for the liquidator to be able to invoke, referring to the *lex arbitri*, powers that do not belong to them under the *lex fori concursus*. Leaving aside the issue of State sovereignty, if the powers of the liquidator performing their activity within the territory of a particular State and its jurisdictional sovereignty were defined by a law adopted by authorities of a different State, it would again violate one of the fundamental principles of insolvency proceedings, namely the equal standing and treatment of creditors. The reason is that the liquidator would have 'new' powers defined by the *lex arbitri* and could exercise them only with respect to a particular small group of claims. It would not matter whether the *lex arbitri* ultimately discriminated against or benefited such creditors.

2.72.   Moreover, the classification of the subject matter of the proceedings and its connection to insolvency proceedings is not straightforward, because it is necessary to assess two levels here that might at first sight overlap. Firstly, it is necessary to ask whether the case allows any proceedings to take place at all. The reason is that the *lex fori concursus* does not usually allow the debtor's creditors to assert their claims through individual proceedings, including arbitration. They are obliged to do so by filing an application specifying their claim in the insolvency proceedings where the claim is subject to review. If the creditor refuses to accept the liquidator's standpoint, the dispute is resolved on the basis of an incidental lawsuit lodged within the framework of the insolvency proceedings. In no case, however, may the decision on the claim be rendered by a forum other than the court determined in compliance with the *lex fori concursus*. This restriction is also binding on the arbitrators, who may not hold arbitration in a case falling within the exclusive powers of the insolvency court or any other forum determined by the *lex fori concursus*. Consequently, the arbitrators are also bound by the *lex fori concursus* with respect to the delimitation of the proceedings that can be conducted exclusively before a court determined according to the *lex fori concursus*. At the general level, this will always refer to the claims of creditors against the debtor, claims for the release of assets which, in the liquidator's opinion, belong to the insolvency estate, and finally disputes arising from the conduct of the insolvency proceedings. If the arbitrators failed to have regard to the exclusive jurisdiction of the insolvency court, they would again be running a real risk of delivering a decision that would be unenforceable under the *lex fori concursus*. Whereas financial claims raised against the debtor give rise to no doubts as concerns the essence of the claim and its impact on the insolvency estate, we may also come across cases which may not be so straightforward. The same holds true for claims relating to the release of assets from the debtor's insolvency estate.

2.73. This includes, for example, motions for determination filed by third parties, the purpose of which is to make certain and determine whether the third party has a specific claim against the debtor that falls within the exclusive competence of the insolvency court. This is a typical example of a motion that ultimately affects the creditor's claim for proportionate satisfaction from the insolvency estate. Another situation may occur if a third party files a motion for determination that aims to prevent the liquidator from asserting an alleged claim of the debtor against the third party and demanding performance of the claim toward the insolvency estate. Such cases require a very individual approach and assessment of whether the order of a potential arbitral award would directly determine whether the debtor has a claim against the third party, and whether the third party is obliged to provide the corresponding performance to the insolvency estate. If this were indeed the case, it would be necessary to conclude that the claim affects the debtor's insolvency estate. It is possible to deduce, under such circumstances, that the arbitrators are bound by Article 18 of Regulation 2015/848 (Article 15 of Regulation 1346/2000) in any proceedings that are already pending and must therefore honor the effects of the opening of insolvency proceedings according to the *lex arbitri,* or, as applicable, that they are bound by the liquidator's decision as to whether or not the proceedings shall continue. If a third party intended to file such a statement of claim only after the insolvency proceedings were opened, the arbitrators would, conversely, be bound to examine whether and subject to what conditions such a statement of claim is admissible under the *lex fori concursus.*

2.74. But there are also motions for determination, whose influence on the insolvency estate is so indirect that they can be classified as entirely unrelated to the insolvency proceedings, and consequently, outside the scope of the effects of the *lex fori concursus.* Such motions include, for instance, a motion that aims to determine whether or not a particular document that is the subject of dispute between the parties is binding upon them. Such expert assessments are frequent in the resolution of the origin of technical problems arising in connection with the legal relationship between the parties. If the document has no direct financial consequences for any of the parties, and specifically if it does not determine whether a third party is entitled to proportionate performance from the insolvency estate, or whether, conversely, the third party is obliged to provide performance to the insolvency estate, it is possible to commence arbitration without any other limitations. It would be a manifestly disproportionate interference with the contractual autonomy of the parties if the opening of insolvency proceedings rendered it impossible to submit to arbitration any matter that could constitute a preliminary issue in the assessment of the mutual financial claims of the parties, though not the only preliminary issue and by far not determinative for the mutual claims of the parties. This occurs primarily in those cases where the parties' dispute concerns not only the nature of the respective document, but also its interpretation and consequences. In other words, one may only speak of any influence on the debtor's insolvency estate if the decision (expected in the arbitral or any other proceedings) is supposed to unequivocally stipulate (directly or indirectly) an obligation to pay a particular amount or provide any particular performance, or any other method of property settlement between the parties. Conversely, consider proceedings that are focused solely on an issue that is only one of two or more preliminary issues, although it should or could also be discussed in proceedings regarding a property claim relating to the debtor's insolvency estate, and the assessment of which in their mutual connections determines the legitimacy of the property claim. In such a case, one may infer that the proceedings belong to the category of proceedings that may be conducted outside the insolvency proceedings. This would of course need to be in compliance with the general rules for the determination of the jurisdiction of the forum designated to resolve the dispute or, as applicable, in compliance with the parties' agreement on dispute resolution.

2.75. From the perspective of insolvency law, nothing should principally prevent arbitration concerning, for example, the nature of a document or any other motion for determination with only an indirect impact on the parties' assets from taking place, because the corresponding statement of claim (request for arbitration) cannot be subsumed under the scope of Article 18 of Regulation 2015/848 (Article 15 of Regulation 1346/2000), or, as applicable, such arbitration does not even constitute proceedings whereby the claimant demands performance from the debtor's insolvency estate. It is also not possible to argue that there is a theoretical possibility of a motion for performance that could be filed by the liquidator and in which the nature of the respective document or any other issue raised in the motion for determination, as applicable, would have to be resolved as a preliminary issue. The third party is in such a case not obliged to wait, whether or not and when the liquidator asserts the claim. The opening of insolvency proceedings cannot be interpreted as preventing third parties from opening proceedings regarding motions that are not directly related to the debtor's insolvency estate.

2.76. However, it is necessary to examine, as a procedural requirement, whether the liquidator is bound by the agreed arbitration agreement and whether the debtor's procedural capacity has been limited. Another category of motions that could, in theory, be discussed by the arbitrators outside the insolvency proceedings are motions concerning the existence (or the validity of the termination, as applicable) of the parties' legal relationship if such a termination occurred before the opening of the insolvency proceedings. The property basis of such disputes and the associated existence of objective arbitrability are in such cases usually deduced by international practice, and the existence of a contract connected with a particular financial performance has an impact on the assets of the parties.

2.77. We may also adduce examples of other proceedings that could be opened regardless of insolvency proceedings, but which are not subject to the effects of the opening of insolvency proceedings. In those cases, the obstacle of the opening of insolvency proceedings consists in the general lack of objective arbitrability. However, we may trace the criteria in such cases on the basis of which the independence from arbitration must be assessed. This applies, for instance, to a motion whereby the debtor is requested to abstain from a particular activity, unless the request involves the requirement to provide financial performance – the latter requirement would have to be claimed in the insolvency proceedings as a separate claim. Again, the third party is not bound by the mandatory rules of the *lex fori concursus,* which stipulate the exclusive jurisdiction of the insolvency court or any other forum called upon to hear and resolve claims affecting the debtor's insolvency estate. The third party may, for instance, open proceedings before a forum determined in compliance with a choice-of-court agreement entered into between the debtor and the third party. The criteria for the assessment of the connection between the subject matter of the proceedings and the insolvency proceedings and the influence thereof on the debtor's insolvency estate ought to be identical, regardless of whether the issue is examined by the arbitrators or by a forum other than the court called upon to hear and resolve disputes relating to insolvency proceedings and/or the debtor's insolvency estate in terms of the *lex fori concursus.*

X. The Necessary Connection Between the Subject Matter of Arbitral Proceedings and Insolvency Proceedings

2.78.   The opening of insolvency proceedings requires that the arbitrators examine whether the arbitration they are to hold can be classified as proceedings in terms of Article 3(1) of Regulation 2015/848 (Article 3(1) of Regulation 1346/2000), because this provision must be interpreted as meaning that the Member State with jurisdiction to open the insolvency proceedings also has jurisdiction to resolve any related disputes.[79] It has been argued that such a concentration of the decision-making power in the courts of a single State fully complies with the objectives of Regulation 1346/2000 (also applies to Regulation 2015/848), and will ensure more effective proceedings and the limitation of forum shopping, which is a generally negative phenomenon in connection with insolvency proceedings. The reason is that an intentional transfer of the power to open and conduct proceedings relating to the debtor's insolvency into a State with rules more favorable to the debtor may ultimately harm the creditors and reduce their satisfaction from the insolvency estate. Whereas the choice of the forum, including the transfer of the power to hear and resolve the case to arbitrators in relation to disputes arising from a particular legal relationship by a

---

[79]   See also Recital 5 to Regulation 2015/848 or, as applicable, Recital 6 to Regulation 1346/2000.

voluntary agreement of the parties must be viewed positively in light of the principle of contractual autonomy, forum shopping of the debtor in insolvency proceedings is unacceptable for the very fact that it is the debtor's unilateral act, evading the consequences of the their financial situation and the obligation to secure at least partial payment or settlement of the debtor's commitments.

2.79.   This general conclusion must also be applied to arbitration, which can be held if, and only if, the courts of the State in which the debtor's main interests are concentrated (COMI) and where the main insolvency proceedings were opened, are not vested with exclusive jurisdiction in terms of Article 3 of Regulation 2015/848 (Article 3 of Regulation 1346/2000). It has also been firmly established that Article 32(1) of Regulation 2015/848, or, as applicable, the second subparagraph of Article 25(1) of Regulation 1346/2000,[80] cannot be interpreted as a denial of jurisdiction vested in the courts of the State competent to open the insolvency proceedings, but only as a means of respecting national rules. This is true whether these are the general civil procedure rules or any special insolvency procedure rules which determine the court with territorial and subject-matter jurisdiction authorized to conduct the given proceedings. However, this court need not necessarily be identical to the court that opened the insolvency proceedings. Nonetheless, it is still necessary to take as the basis the criterion of a connection with insolvency proceedings. Unless such a connection exists, the general rules for the determination of court jurisdiction apply, including the obligation to honor a properly executed arbitration agreement. Hence, the arbitrators may conduct such proceedings without any restriction, or, as applicable, the opening of insolvency proceedings or the decision on insolvency or the method of resolving the insolvency (depending on the particular rules of the *lex fori concursus*) have no bearing on the possibility to hold the arbitration. Naturally, the reverse of this *independence* of arbitration from insolvency proceedings is the fact that the outcome of such proceedings is not automatically applicable in the insolvency proceedings, i.e. the rules governing the automatic recognition of decisions relating to insolvency proceedings are not automatically applicable to it. Hence, if a party wishes to have the given decision considered in the insolvency proceedings, for instance, as a binding decision concerning one

---

[80]   A reference to decisions that result directly from or that are closely related to the insolvency proceedings, although made by a different court.

of the preliminary issues influencing the claim of the person that was lodged in the insolvency proceedings, it is necessary to proceed in compliance with the New York Convention of 1958. Clearly, if the subject matter of the arbitration were a case directly related to the insolvency proceedings, where the jurisdiction of the forum authorized to hear and resolve the case is prescribed by mandatory provisions, one may expect that the recognition and enforcement of the respective decision of the arbitrators would be refused, invoking their failure to honor the exclusive jurisdiction under the *lex fori concursus*.

2.80. The connection between the subject matter of the proceedings and the insolvency proceedings has also been analyzed by the ECJ/CJ EU repeatedly and in great detail, as this particular connection is crucial for the assessment of whether or not it is necessary to honor the exclusive jurisdiction of the courts of the State in which the insolvency proceedings were opened, or whether the case can be submitted to a different forum whose jurisdiction has been determined by private international law, or to arbitration. The ECJ has articulated a clear conclusion that the material perspective prevails over the formal approach where the latter is based on the presumption that claims concerning the debtor are automatically governed by the *lex fori concursus* of the respective Member State. Consequently, it is necessary to examine the material connections between the subject matter of the proceedings and the insolvency proceedings. This approach is nothing new, and can be traced back to the Judgment of the ECJ of 12 February 2009 in C-339/07.[81] The dispute in this case revolved around the issue of whether or not the courts of the Member State on the territory of which the insolvency proceedings were opened would have international jurisdiction under Regulation 1346/2000 with respect to an action in the context of insolvency to set a transaction aside that was brought by the liquidator against a person whose registered office was in another Member State.[82] The case did not concern the issue of whether the applicable provisions of the German Insolvency Act could be applied,[83] but in which court the liquidator could exercise their powers if a claim was to be made

---

[81]   ECJ Judgment, Case C-339/07 of 12 February 2009, in *Christopher Seagon, in his capacity as liquidator with respect to the assets of Frick Teppichboden Supermärkte GmbH* v. *Deko Marty Belgium NV.*

[82]   The case concerned an action brought under Section 129 et seq. of the German Insolvency Code (*Insolvenzordnung*), which provides the liquidator with the power to challenge juridical acts that the debtor had performed before the opening of the insolvency proceedings and which ultimately disadvantage the creditors.

[83]   The case concerned insolvency proceedings conducted on the territory of the Federal Republic of Germany against a German legal entity as the debtor. Hence, the applicability of the German rules on insolvency proceedings has not been questioned.

against a foreign entity. In short, the question was whether an action to set a transaction aside lodged by the liquidator constituted a case falling within the international jurisdiction determined according to Article 3(1) of Regulation 1346/2000,[84] or whether the general rules applied in this particular case for the determination of the jurisdiction to open civil proceedings with an international dimension in the E. In other words, the issue was to what extent the insolvency proceedings in this case influence the jurisdiction of an otherwise competent forum (specifically a civil court or arbitrators) to hear and resolve the case. Invoking its former case law,[85] the European Court of Justice (ECJ) concluded that the action constituted an action related to and resulting from insolvency proceedings.

2.81. However, the decision of the ECJ in C-339/07 can by no means be interpreted as demanding that individual proceedings to which the debtor, or a properly appointed liquidator, is a party have to be classified as proceedings related to pending insolvency proceedings if the former is initiated after the insolvency proceedings were opened. General rules for the assessment of the relationship between other actions and the insolvency proceedings were articulated, inter alia, in the decision of the CJ EU of 4 September 2014 in C-157/13,[86] in which the CJ EU held that the decisive criterion to identify the area within which an action falls is not the procedural context, but the legal basis of the subject matter of the proceedings. The Court ruled that according to that approach, it must be determined whether the right or the obligation which respects the basis of the action finds its source in the common rules of civil and commercial law, or in the derogating rules specific to insolvency proceedings. The case involved the examination of the international jurisdiction of courts of the State in which the insolvency proceedings were opened to hear an action lodged by the liquidator against a third party with respect to a claim arising from a commercial legal relationship of the debtor and the third party-respondent. The Court ruled in the said case that if the insolvency proceedings had not been opened or, as applicable, if the debtor had done so and asserted its claim before the opening thereof, that action could have been brought by the debtor itself. In that situation, the action would have been

---

[84] By analogy now Article 3(1) of Regulation 2015/848.

[85] Compare ECJ Judgment, Case C-133/78 of 22 February 1979, in *Henri Gourdain* v. *Franz Nadler*. This case concerned an action under Article 99 of French Act No. 67-563 (the basic statute on which modern French insolvency law is based), which allows the liquidator to assert liability claims against the officers or representatives of an insolvent company.

[86] Judgment of the CJ EU, Case C-157/13 of 4 September 2014, in *Nickel & Goeldner Spedition GmbH* v. *'Kintra' UAB*.

governed by the rules on court jurisdiction applicable in civil or commercial matters. The CJ EU held that, from this perspective, it was immaterial that the action in the insolvency proceedings was no longer an action that would directly benefit the debtor, but, conversely, that the liquidator acted for the benefit of the debtor's creditors, and any potentially awarded amount would become part of the debtor's insolvency estate and would be used for the proportionate satisfaction of the creditors in compliance with the applicable rules of the *lex fori concursus*.

2.82. Conversely, if we return to Case C-339/07, it is clear that the possibility of an action to set a transaction aside is based solely on the provisions of the *lex fori concursus*, this power is vested in the liquidator, and the debtor themselves cannot file such an action against a third party. Hence, the fulfillment of the requirements for opening insolvency proceedings and the associated possibility to oppose the debtor's prior acts as being incompatible with the objectives of insolvency proceedings are the necessary prerequisite for the possibility to open such proceedings, and there can be no doubt about the mutual interconnection between these proceedings. Under these circumstances, it is necessary to honor the exclusive jurisdiction of the competent courts of the State in which the insolvency proceedings were opened to hear and resolve the case.

2.83. We can therefore conclude that the words 'proceedings relating to and resulting from insolvency proceedings' cannot be construed too broadly. Conversely, it is necessary to apply the principles underlying the Brussels I bis Regulation.[87] The EU legislature's intent in connection with the Brussels I bis Regulation was to introduce the broadest possible definition of the term 'civil and commercial matters,' and thereby secure general applicability for these rules, unless any of the exceptions applies in which special international jurisdiction is stipulated differently for precisely defined cases.[88] The Insolvency Regulation represents one such exception. Apart from the abovementioned case, we may also

---

[87] Or, as applicable, any other rules of [European] private international law. These rules apply not only *vis-à-vis* the Member States, which are bound by the Brussels I bis Regulation, but if the subject matter of the proceedings has no relation to insolvency proceedings, one may imagine the application of the Convention on jurisdiction and the recognition and enforcement of judgments in civil and commercial matters of 30 October 2007, published in the Official Journal of the European Union L 339 of 21 December 2007 (the '2007 Lugano Convention') in relation to Switzerland, Norway and Iceland, or the application of national rules of private international law or a bilateral legal assistance treaty that also includes rules determining international court jurisdiction *vis-à-vis* third countries which are not bound by any multilateral international treaty in this regard.

[88] These conclusions already applied at the time when the Brussels I Regulation was in effect (cf. Recital 7 to the Brussels I Regulation, as well as Recital 10 to the Brussels I bis Regulation).

invoke the ECJ ruling in Case C-292/08 of 10 September 2009,[89] in which the Court concluded that an action for the adoption of protective measures regarding several machines located on the premises of the debtor's company (on the territory of a Member State where the insolvency proceedings were opened) was not directly connected with the insolvency proceedings. This proposal was based on a reservation of title agreed in the purchase contract entered into by and between the debtor and the claimant, who invoked the reservation of title.[90]

2.84. Similarly, the EU case law has held that an action to set a transaction aside lodged in a Member State by the sole creditor of a company against which insolvency proceedings were opened in another Member State is not related to the insolvency proceedings. Rather, the action was based on the right to sue a third party for a claim that had been contractually assigned to the claimant by the liquidator for consideration, and the scope of the liquidator's rights is therefore limited.[91] However, it is necessary to point out that this case concerned the assignment of a claim based on the liquidator's right to challenge the juridical acts of the debtor in terms of Section 129 et seq. of the German Insolvency Code,[92] i.e. a claim that can only be brought by the liquidator and solely for the purpose of protecting the interests of the creditors. At the same time, German law allows the assignment of the right to file an action to set a transaction aside, on condition that the assignment was provided in exchange for an equivalent consideration benefiting the creditors. The CJ EU has held in this connection that the exercise of the acquired right by the assignee is subject to rules different from the rules applicable to the insolvency proceedings. The CJ EU has reasoned that while the liquidator, is principally obliged to act in the interests of the creditors, the assignee is free to decide whether or not they will enforce the acquired claim. Moreover, the CJ EU has argued that the termination of the insolvency proceedings has no impact on the exercise of the right to file an

---

[89]   ECJ Judgment, Case C-292/08 of 10 September 2009, in *German Graphics Graphische Maschinen GmbH* v. *Alice van der Schee (as the liquidator for Holland Binding BV)*.
[90]   Considering the subject matter of this article, I only refer in this connection to the conclusion regarding the mutual connections between existing insolvency proceedings and an action pending, regardless of the fact that the considerations entertained by the CJEU were more complex with respect to the determination of jurisdiction, because it was also necessary to have regard to the specific provisions of Article 7(1) of Regulation 1346/2000 (cf. Article 10(1) of Regulation 2015/848). However, the court also concluded in this case that the action, as filed by the claimant, did not fall within the exception under Article 1(2)(b) of the Brussels I Regulation (cf. Article 1(2)(b) of the Brussels I bis Regulation).
[91]   Judgment of the CJ EU (First Chamber), Case C-213/10 of 19 April 2012, in *F-Tex SIA* v. *Lietuvos-Anglijos UAB 'Jadecloud-Vilma'*.
[92]   Concerning these rules, cf. also Judgment of the ECJ in Case C-339/07 of 12 February 2009, in *Christopher Seagon, in his capacity as liquidator with respect to the assets of Frick Teppichboden Supermärkte GmbH* v. *Deko Marty Belgium NV.*

action to set aside a transaction by the assignee. This conclusion was apparently based on the presumption that as soon as the claim is transferred from the liquidator's power to the domain of a third party, the connection with insolvency proceedings is severed. Conversely, one may conclude that if a third party was assigned a claim based on the liquidator's right to challenge the juridical acts of the debtor, and they failed to pay the agreed amount to the debtor's insolvency estate, the special exclusive jurisdiction of the courts determined on the basis of the *lex fori concursus* would continue to apply.

2.85.   Although there may appear cases in practice that can be considered controversial,[93] (to say the least) – see the abovementioned ruling in C-213/10,[94] in which the respective claim would not arise at all if the insolvency proceedings did not exist – one may conclude that the fundamental criterion, at the general level, is the assessment of whether the respective proceedings could be initiated even if the insolvency proceedings had not been opened. If the answer is yes, it is possible to infer that the claim is a civil-law claim, in which case the forum competent to hear and resolve the case will be determined on the basis of general conflict-of-laws criteria. Only if the answer to the question were no, and if it were clear that the respective proceedings could never be initiated if no insolvency proceedings had been opened in relation to the debtor, one could deduce a connection between the subject matter of such proceedings and the insolvency proceedings and thus the exclusive jurisdiction of the courts in terms of Article 3 of Regulation 2015/848.[95]

XI.   The Influence of Insolvency Proceedings on Arbitration in the Case Law of Courts

2.86.   The series of decisions in the *Vivendi* case is probably the most notorious ruling analyzing the issue of the influence that the opening of insolvency proceedings in one State has on arbitrations in another State. The English courts dismissed all objections raised by the debtor, the Polish company Elektrim SA regarding the jurisdiction of arbitrators and the impossibility to hold arbitration in England. They concluded that if the main insolvency proceedings were opened pursuant to Article 3 of

---

[93]   See the aforementioned ruling in C-213/10, in which the respective claim would not arise at all if the insolvency proceedings did not exist. Judgment of the CJ EU (First Chamber), Case C-213/10 of 19 April 2012, in *F-Tex SIA* v. *Lietuvos-Anglijos UAB 'Jadecloud-Vilma'*.

[94]   Judgment of the CJ EU (First Chamber), Case C-213/10 of April 19, 2012, in *F-Tex SIA* v. *Lietuvos-Anglijos UAB "'Jadecloud-Vilma'"*.

[95]   Compare Article 3 of Regulation 1346/2000 by analogy.

Regulation 1346/2000[96] in Poland, whereas the arbitration had already been pending in England at that time, the effects of the insolvency proceedings on the pending arbitration or, as applicable, the possibility to conduct the arbitration, were governed by English law (as the *lex arbitri* of the pending arbitration), not Polish law (here as the *lex fori concursus*). The English courts have therefore concluded that it is necessary to apply Article 4(2)(f) of Regulation 1346/2000[97] in conjunction with Article 15 of Regulation 1346/2000 and apply English law as the law of the Member State in which the arbitration is held. Based on the application of this law, both the trial court and the court of appeal in England ruled that the arbitrators had jurisdiction to hear the case. It is necessary to emphasize that the decisions by no means denied the necessity of considering the fact that insolvency proceedings were opened in Poland. However, the English courts, by invoking Regulation 1346/2000 (currently Regulation 2015/848), concluded that the law applicable to the assessment of the effects of the opening of insolvency proceedings on pending arbitration was not the *lex fori concursus*, but the *lex arbitri*.

2.87.   The decision of the English courts was also substantially influenced by the understanding of certain legal concepts in the common law system, compared to the continental legal systems. This is a general problem afflicting the interpretation and application of EU laws, which is by no means connected to the conflict of insolvency proceedings with other proceedings, or, as applicable, the effects that the opening of insolvency proceedings has on the possibility to conduct other proceedings. The assessment of the effects that the opening of insolvency proceedings has on other proceedings requires that we properly distinguish between procedural aspects and substantive-law aspects. The procedural effects under the continental system can include the interruption or termination or other specific forms of suspending pending arbitration or any other proceedings or, as applicable, any issues relating to further progress of the proceedings and any measures that may be necessary with respect to the debtor's restricted right to make dispositions with their assets and the potential transfer of certain powers to the liquidator. Conversely, the common law system tends to describe these issues as questions of fact.

---

[96]   By analogy now Article 3 of Regulation 2015/848.
[97]   By analogy now pursuant to Article 7(2)(f) of Regulation 2015/848 in conjunction with Article 18 of Regulation 2015/848, although Article 18 of Regulation 2015/848, contrary to Article 15 of Regulation 1346/2000, also contains an explicit reference to arbitration, which is indeed the topic of the detailed analysis in this article.

The effects of the opening of insolvency proceedings on the validity of an arbitration agreement, which is perceived as a substantive-law issue in the continental system, has procedural connotations in the common law system. These differences also contribute to a different perception of these issues by the courts of the individual States and a different assessment of a factually and legally analogous situation, even in those cases in which the courts of both states do not deny, or even recognize, the necessity of applying the EU law represented by Article 15 of Regulation 1346/2000 (Article 18 of Regulation 2015/848).

2.88. A completely different approach to identical issues, and also in connection with the *Vivendi* case, has been adopted by the Swiss courts, where, conversely, the Polish debtor succeeded with its objections. However, it is necessary to emphasize that even though the case law of the Swiss courts may *prima facie* appear as unimportant for the interpretation of Regulation 1346/2000, and currently, of course, Regulation 2015/848,[98] because it is case law developed by courts of a non-EU Member State, these decisions in particular and their comparison to the approaches adopted by the EU Member States may serve as the basis for a very clear demonstration of the interpretation of the EU insolvency law. Moreover, we may demonstrate it in comparison with the effects of one and the same insolvency proceedings, namely insolvency proceedings conducted in an EU Member State. The Swiss case law also shows, and again in comparison with the influence of the EU law, the development of the international doctrine regarding the existence or absence of exterritorial, cross-border effects of the decision to open insolvency proceedings in the sense of general private international law.

2.89. Regarding the decision in the *Vivendi* case *(Elektrim SA)*, the Swiss Federal Supreme Court delivered its ruling in Case No. 4A_428/2008 on 31 March 2009, which has for a very long time become the subject of many scholarly discussions. Despite the fact that the criticism of this decision may appear legitimate, especially from the perspective of the principles of arbitration, it is more than appropriate to distinguish between the doctrinal principles that arise from the *Vivendi* case and their application in the given case. The legal conclusions of the Swiss ruling are not controversial. Indeed, they are based on the necessity of the mutual interaction of the *lex fori concursus*, and the *lex*

---

[98] The author is not aware of any decision of the Swiss courts dealing with Regulation 2015/848. Naturally, it has to be pointed out in this regard that Switzerland is not bound by the EU Regulations, although a *reasoning* referring to a connection to the EU law is not so uncommon in connection with cross-border issues between Switzerland and an EU Member State.

arbitri, which may at the same time limit some of the effects of the insolvency law, as the necessity of mutual assessment of both laws was analyzed above. Rather, what is controversial about the decision is its assessment of the findings of fact and the implemented interpretation of the relevant provisions of Polish insolvency law. The Swiss court by no means questioned the principle of *favor validatis*,[99] which stipulates that it is fully sufficient if, even though insolvency proceedings are opened, the validity of the arbitration agreement is preserved under Swiss law, regardless of the fact that it is declared invalid by the *lex fori concursus*. This long-established doctrine remains intact even after the decision in the *Vivendi* case, and indeed, the doctrine, as well as the validity thereof, are being explicitly referred to. In other words, if the contents of the Polish *lex concursus* were evaluated *exclusively* in terms of the arbitration agreement being declared invalid, there would be no doubts about the application of the *lex arbitri* (Article 178(2) of the Swiss Private International Law Act) and the possibility to conduct arbitration.

2.90.   However, the Swiss court strictly distinguished between the validity of the arbitration agreement itself and the procedural capacity of the debtor against whom the insolvency proceedings were conducted, i.e. the debtor's ability to be a party to arbitration. Hence, the impossibility to conduct the arbitration was not deduced with regard to the existence of a valid arbitration agreement, but with respect to the discovered lack of procedural capacity, which, according to the Swiss court, resulted from the Polish *lex fori concursus*. However, this particular issue is the most controversial in the entire decision, because it is unclear which specific findings were the basis for such conclusions and how the Polish law differs from other analogous rules that form part of the *lex fori concursus*. Naturally, the decision is not silent on the issue. It is clear that the court employed doctrinal interpretations presented in an expert report submitted by leading academics with respect to the interpretation of the Polish *lex concursus*. But there is an absence of any explicit statement in the particular law concerning procedural capacity, and the fact that this principal decision is based on an expert report, according to which the law ought simply to be interpreted in a particular manner.

2.91.   However, one may also not exclude the possibility of a shift in meaning caused by the potentially imprecise use of terminology in translations, where the issue of legal personality and the

---

[99]   Compare Article 178(2) of the Swiss Private International Law Act.

Czech (& Central European) Yearbook of Arbitration®

potential limitation of certain acts (which may not automatically be classified as a loss of legal personality) may, in this regard, be the source of many inconsistencies and much confusion in interpretation. From this perspective, the crucial question is how the issue of the capacity of being a party to arbitration was perceived by (i) the authors of the expert report, (ii) the arbitrators making an assessment within the framework of the *Kompetenz-Kompetenz* principle, and subsequently (iii) the Swiss court. Specifically, the question is whether the limitation of the capacity to be a party relates generally to any proceedings, or whether it was limited exclusively to arbitration, as well as how the Polish debtor proceeded in the exercise of its rights if the debtor lacked procedural capacity. The status of the liquidator and their authorization to act also became more important in this regard. But it is again necessary to point out that the transfer to the liquidator of the authorization to act cannot automatically be interpreted as the simultaneous loss of the debtor's legal personality.

2.92. Indeed, principles analogous to those described above were the basis for a decision of an arbitral tribunal in arbitration conducted in the Czech Republic, which also ruled in the case of the *Vivendi* Group,[100] long before the issue was addressed by the Swiss Federal Supreme Court. The difference was that the arbitral tribunal that delivered the decision in the Czech Republic arrived at these conclusions on the basis of the distinction under Article 15 of Regulation 1346/2000, which the arbitrators assessed as an exclusively procedural provision, contrary to the applicable substantive-law rules of the Polish law, as the *lex fori concursus primariae*. In other words, the opening of insolvency proceedings under the latter law had the result of extinguishing the arbitration agreement.[101]

2.93. As concerns the validity of the arbitration agreement, the Swiss court thus did not question the fact that the *lex fori concursus* may influence the validity of the arbitration agreement. However, it also held that it is immaterial whether or not the arbitration agreement is invalid under the *lex fori concursus*, because the *lex arbitri* stipulates that the possibility to conduct

[100] Resolution of the Arbitration Court at the Economic Chamber of the Czech Republic and Agricultural Chamber of the Czech Republic, Case No. Rsp 135/2006 of 15 January 2008. This decision is also annotated and analyzed in detail in: Alexander Bělohlávek, *Impact of Insolvency of a Party on Pending Arbitration Proceedings in Czech Republic, England and Switzerland and Other Countries*, 1 YEARBOOK ON INTERNATIONAL ARBITRATION. ANTVERPEN / BERLIN / COPENHAGEN / WIEN / GRAZ: EAP (EUROPEAN ACADEMIC PRESS) / NEUER WISSENSCHAFTLICHER VERLAG 145–166 (Marianne Roth, Michael Geistlinger eds., 2010).
[101] This provision has been replaced with a new Polish law, which no longer prescribes the cancellation of the arbitration agreement as a consequence of the opening of insolvency proceedings.

arbitration is preserved, in the sense of the preservation of the validity of the arbitration agreement following the application of Article 178(2) of the Swiss Private International Law Act.[102] This is due to the fact that the Swiss rules on insolvency proceedings do not connect such effects with the opening of insolvency proceedings, and consequently, the rules to be applied are the rules favoring the validity of the arbitration agreement. Hence, the Swiss court did not hold that the *lex fori concursus* should be entirely disregarded, but that it is necessary to interpret its effects globally in conjunction with the rules of the *lex arbitri*. Compared to the Czech arbitrators in Rsp 135/2006, the Swiss court could not even consider Article 15 of Regulation 1346/2000. Conversely, the arbitrators in the arbitration conducted in the Czech Republic in Rsp 135/2006 could not employ the principle of *in favorem validitatis* of the arbitration agreement, because the principle is not incorporated in the rules of the *lex arbitri*, which were binding on the arbitrators.

2.94.   However, the Swiss court in the *Vivendi* case also held that the opening of insolvency proceedings could also affect the debtor's procedural capacity and the debtor's capacity to be a party to arbitration. The Swiss court held that in such a case the general conflict-of-laws criteria of private international law shall apply, i.e. the legal personality of a juridical person is, pursuant to Article 154(1) in conjunction with Article 155(c) of the Swiss Private International Law Act, assessed according to the law under which it was formed and incorporated.

2.95.   This particular difference between a simple lack of validity of the arbitration agreement and the impact on the legal personality of the given entity, i.e. dissolution, was analyzed in another Swiss decision delivered after the *Vivendi* case. This was the decision of the Swiss Federal Supreme Court in Case No. 4A_50/2012 of 16 October 2012, which addressed the issue of the influence of insolvency law on the possibility to hold arbitration in connection with a Portuguese debtor. Whereas the court in the *Vivendi* case concluded that Article 142 of the Polish Insolvency Act deprived the debtor of the legal personality and therefore the procedural capacity necessary for the debtor's participation in arbitration,[103] analogous Portuguese law only affects the

---

[102]   Approximate translation (cit.): 'Apart from the above, an arbitration agreement is valid if it complies with (i) the law chosen by the parties, or (ii) the law governing the subject matter of the dispute, especially the main contract, or (iii) Swiss law.'

[103]   Conversely, the arbitral tribunal in the Czech Republic, which had also delivered a prior decision in Case No. Rsp 135/2006, based its decision on the extinguishment of the arbitration agreement as a substantive-law instrument under the substantive rules of the *lex fori concursus primariae* (Polish law). The arbitral tribunal had to apply this both in connection with Article 4(2)(f) of Regulation 1346/2000 (currently cf. Article 7(2)(f) of Regulation 2015/848), and in consequence of the classification of Article 15 of Regulation

validity of the arbitration agreement, not the legal personality of the debtor, who is therefore not prevented from participating in arbitration. However, the Swiss court again refrained from applying Portuguese substantive law as the *lex fori concursus primariae* or, as applicable, applied the law with the reservation that its effects are overridden by the Swiss *lex arbitri*. They did this firstly, because Switzerland is not an EU Member State, and consequently, it is not bound by Regulation 1346/2000 (presently Regulation 2015/848), and secondly, because the court was obliged under the *lex arbitri* to have regard to the principle *in favorem validitatis* of the arbitration agreement in terms of the Swiss *lex arbitri*. Generally, the Swiss court concluded in the case of the Portuguese debtor that if the limitation of the debtor's legal status exclusively concerns the debtor's capacity to be a party to arbitration (within the meaning of the validity and effects of any acts whereby the future debtor agreed with the exclusion of the jurisdiction of courts and the transfer to arbitrators), but the debtor's general legal personality/procedural capacity remains intact, such limitations are irrelevant in relation to the possibility to hold arbitration in Switzerland. In other words, the incapacity to be a party to proceedings cannot be tied exclusively to arbitration. It is only if the debtor were

---

1346/2000 as a procedural, not a substantive-law rule. The extinguishment of the arbitration agreement is the consequence of applying substantive law. If the arbitral tribunal held that the extinguishment of the arbitration agreement or, as applicable, the effects of insolvency proceedings on other (in this case arbitral) proceedings according to the Polish *lex fori concursus* is a matter of procedural law, it would, conversely, have to apply, in compliance with Article 15 of Regulation 1346/2000, Czech procedural law as the law of the place of arbitration. This is significant because Czech law only provides for the suspension of arbitration, not the extinguishment of the arbitration agreement. The Czech arbitral tribunal did not suspend the arbitration, but rather it terminated it conclusively. Although the Polish subject as a party to these Czech proceedings had premises on the territory of the Czech Republic, there were no secondary insolvency proceedings pending in the Czech Republic at the time of the decision issued in the Czech arbitration.

The law applicable in the case was Article 142 of the Polish Insolvency Act, which has in the meantime been replaced by a new law.

As concerns the applicability of Regulation 1346/2000, the Czech arbitral tribunal had no doubts and considered Regulation 1346/2000 directly applicable (i.e. part of the legal system to which the tribunal must have regard). The tribunal also applied the principle of the automatic recognition of the decision to open insolvency proceedings in all other Member States from the moment the decision took effect in the State which opened the proceedings. Hence, this is the first documented case in which the arbitrators directly applied Regulation 1346/2000 in proceedings conducted in an EU Member State as the place of arbitration. The recognition implies, as an integral part thereof, a due regard for the effects that the opening of insolvency proceedings has according to the *lex concursus*. It has been held that if the arbitral tribunal failed to honor the automatic recognition of the decision opening the insolvency proceedings, arguing that the tribunal is not bound by this law, which would in effect limit the category of persons and entities to which the given law applies, the rules incorporated in Articles 16 and 17 of Regulation 1346/2000 (now Articles 19 and 20 of Regulation 2015/848) would become irrelevant. The reason is that the EU legislature clearly intended to ensure the immediate recognition of the decision to open, conduct and terminate insolvency proceedings within the scope of the Insolvency Regulation, and any decisions made in direct connection therewith, without the decision being subject to any review in other Member States. Hence, automatic recognition must be interpreted as meaning that the effects resulting from insolvency proceedings according to the law of the State in which the proceedings were opened have a broader scope and cover other Member States. Such law is based on the principle of mutual trust, while, at the same time, any grounds for a refusal to recognize the effects should be limited to the necessary minimum.

also not capable of being a party to civil proceedings would the arbitrators be obliged to have regard to such effects. Moreover, the above comparison of the approach adopted by Swiss courts, English courts, the French courts (though not in the case of the *Vivendi* Group), and indeed, also the approach opted for by the arbitrators in the arbitration conducted in the Czech Republic, confirms the fundamental importance of the place of proceedings, as stated in the introduction, as the law that, under certain circumstances, is capable of supplementing or modifying the effects of the *lex fori concursus*. Consequently, there is no doubt at a general level that the *lex fori concursus* and any effects associated therewith cannot be ignored, even if it is always necessary to simultaneously consider the *lex arbitri*.

2.96.   The ability to be a party to proceedings and the associated legal personality in light of the case law is generally assessed as the entity's ability to have rights and obligations. The criteria considered by the Swiss court in its examination of the debtor's legal personality in Case No. 4A_50/2012 and on the basis of which the court concluded that such legal personality exists, include the fact that (i) Portuguese insolvency law allows any pending proceedings to continue, (ii) the debtor's procedural capacity to be a party to civil litigation remains intact, (iii) the debtor may continue their activities, (iv) where the capacity to perform juridical acts is limited, it is transferred to the liquidator. The Swiss court had regard to the principle according to which the very basis of the debtor's personality must be affected. A simple limitation of the possibility to perform a particular act, which, moreover, may transfer to an appointed liquidator, is not enough.

XII.   The Scope and Manner of Application of Article 18 of Regulation 2015/848, or, as Applicable, Article 15 of Regulation 1346/2000, to Arbitral Proceedings

2.97.   Although the decisions may *prima facie* appear different, it is not possible to argue that the decision in the *Vivendi* case was overruled by the subsequent decision concerning the Portuguese debtor. Quite the opposite; the latter supplements the former and provides a broadening and clarifying interpretation. The criteria that have been set in this case are still relevant and could be important for the proper understanding of the direction that the arbitrators could, or even should, follow in their assessment of the possibility to hold arbitration where one of the parties to the arbitration is insolvent. Paradoxically, these principles, articulated by the courts of a country that is not an EU Member State, are also applicable within the scope of application of Regulation 1346/2000 and Regulation 2015/848. The reason is that the scope of the effects of insolvency proceedings and the application of the EU insolvency law must be based on identical, or at least analogous criteria, regardless of the explicit broadening of the rule under Article 18 of Regulation 2015/848 in comparison to Article 15 of Regulation 1346/2000.

2.98.   The legal personality/procedural capacity of each party to arbitration is clearly one of the preconditions for holding such arbitration. If the opening of insolvency proceedings results in a loss or restriction of such legal personality, it is not possible to hear the case before arbitrators. Conversely, the procedural requirements in terms of the *lex arbitri* must always be examined, regardless of the reason for a potential lack thereof. This constitutes an absolute obstacle that prevents the arbitral proceedings from being held, and the arbitrators are not allowed to factor in the circumstances underlying the absence of the procedural requirements. In view of the above, the *lex fori concursus* is only one of many reasons that could theoretically result in the procedural requirements not being fulfilled. It is similarly necessary to address the existence of a valid arbitration agreement. However, as demonstrated above, the *lex fori concursus* must be interpreted in conjunction with the *lex arbitri,* and one must examine whether the latter is perhaps based on the preservation of arbitrability in those cases where the dispute ceases to be arbitrable on the basis of the otherwise applicable law. The corresponding rule in this case is also usually defined generally, without any specific connection to insolvency proceedings. The escape clause, or, as applicable, *in favorem validitatis,* thus applies in all cases, without any examination of the circumstances that render the existing arbitration agreement establishing arbitrability invalid or of the deficiencies thereof, as the case may be. The potential procedural consequences of the opening of insolvency proceedings consisting in the termination, suspension or any other procedural consequence relating to pending arbitration are a different matter. Whereas arbitrators in the European Union will be obliged to have regard to this fact under Article 18 of Regulation 2018/848 (Article 15 of Regulation 1346/2000), despite the fact that they will apply the otherwise corresponding rules of the *lex arbitri,* one may imagine that the practice will differ outside the scope of Regulation 2015/848 (Regulation

1346/2000), depending on whether or not, and to what extent, the decision opening insolvency proceedings can be recognized in the place of arbitration. We may therefore conclude that it is by no means a settled issue, and that it will definitely be the subject matter of further important decisions in the future.

2.99. The problem does not really inhere in the conclusion according to which the arbitrators must have regard to the opening of insolvency proceedings in relation to one of the parties, and address the consequences therefor for pending proceedings according to the *lex fori concursus*. The important, if not principal, issue is the interpretation itself, and the classification of the corresponding rules of the *lex fori concursus*. As demonstrated above, one may principally arrive at two completely different outcomes regarding the effects of the opening of insolvency proceedings, depending on the interpretation of the particular rules of the *lex fori concursus*. Completely different effects may already occur, depending on whether the rules of the *lex fori concursus* will be perceived as procedural or substantive-law (in terms of the approach of the legal principles embraced by the forum in the place of proceedings). Only the solution to this issue will determine which conflict-of-laws rules will apply, i.e. Article 7(2)(e), Article 7(2)(f) or Article 18 of Regulation 2015/848 (or, as applicable, Article 4(2)(e), Article 4(2)(f) or Article 15 of Regulation 1346/2000). Naturally, a problem may arise if the doctrinal approaches conflict between the place of proceedings affected by the opening of insolvency proceedings, and the place where the outcome of such proceedings is subsequently to be recognized and/or enforced. The court making a decision on the recognition and/or enforcement of the decision might, in theory, ignore the differences, and may consider the classification prevailing in the place of the proceedings incorrect (contrary to the fundamental principles of the law represented by the Insolvency Regulation), and consequently, deny the recognition and/or enforcement of the decision.

2.100. Such situations should not occur, because the courts ought to be principally bound by the manner whereby the law was applied in the place where the proceedings were held, and the decision issued whose recognition and enforcement is sought. This must naturally include the classification and doctrinal interpretation relating to the individual legal instruments. In this connection, it is necessary to apply and honor the principal of State sovereignty, because the court in the place of the proceedings must not be forced to apply and be bound to proceed according to a foreign interpretation of the respective legal rules applicable in the place of the potential recognition and enforcement. Indeed, such an approach would also be impossible from the practical perspective as the place of the future recognition/enforcement need not be known in advance. Depending on the nature of the subject matter of the proceedings, its recognition or enforcement may potentially be sought in a third country different from the place of the insolvency proceedings. As a matter of course, the court should appropriately establish/verify such information in compliance with the general principles of private international law. But regardless of this, one cannot absolutely exclude the possibility that the court in the place where the enforcement/recognition is sought need not be aware of the different doctrinal approach, and may consider the different result a principally incorrect application of the applicable conflict-of-laws rules. A consequence of this is that the effects of the opening of insolvency proceedings on other proceedings were subject to the wrong legal system. This might, in theory, constitute grounds for a refusal to enforce such a decision, especially if the proceedings could not be conducted in the place where the recognition/enforcement is sought on the basis of a doctrinal interpretation.

2.101. Hence, if the EU legislator's aim was to lay down uniform rules for the conflict-of-laws rules of the individual States that replace the States' own private international law rules, one may conclude that the Insolvency Regulation meets the formal aspects of this requirement. However, it is unclear to what extent Regulation 2015/848 will be uniformly applied in the individual States and within the scope of their legal systems as regards the effects of the opening of insolvency proceedings on other proceedings. Apart from the doctrinal differences, one may also not dismiss the principal differences that may arise on the basis of the interpretation of the applicable law determined under the EU law. The risks associated with the interpretation of foreign law were demonstrated by way of the example of the Swiss decision in the *Vivendi* case and its controversial interpretation of the Polish *lex fori concursus*, which ultimately resulted in the controversy accompanying the decision, and has made the decision the subject of professional, often turbulent discussions.

2.102. Considering all the imaginable combinations of the application of the *lex fori concursus* and *lex arbitri*, as indicated above, it is entirely impossible to reach any universally valid conclusions that could lay the basis for the determination of the effects that the opening of insolvency proceedings always has on other proceedings. This is true regardless of any other circumstances attending such other proceedings, especially as concerns the place of the proceedings and the valid local law. Quite the opposite, because despite the effort to secure predictability and unify the conflict-of-laws rules, which cannot be denied to Regulation 2015/848 or Regulation 1346/2000, the result will remain substantially unpredictable and dependent on the individual circumstances of the given case. This applies *a fortiori* in arbitration, because the *lex arbitri* must be generally perceived as more variable than litigation and forcing the arbitrators to have regard to other circumstances.

XIII. Article 18 of Regulation 2015/848 and Changes *Vis-à-vis* Article 15 of Regulation 1346/2010

XIII.1. Preparatory Works and Assessment of Application of Article 15 of Regulation 1346/2000 in Relation to Arbitration

2.103. Article 15 of Regulation 1346/2000 contained no explicit reference to arbitration, and the fact that the provision should also apply to arbitration was inferred using a systematic interpretation of the law. In this connection, it is necessary to point out that this conclusion was generally deemed somewhat controversial. Nonetheless, the application of the provision to arbitration was (at least in the Czech Republic) principally accepted. The question arises, then, whether the modification implemented in Article 18 of Regulation 2015/848, compared to Article 15 of Regulation 1346/2000, had any specific meaning, or whether it merely represented the codification of a principle that more or less worked in practice, leaving aside the more noticeable controversies, especially in the common law countries.

2.104. This author is definitely inclined towards the theory that the modification was a codification of the interpretation of Article 15 of Regulation 1346/2000, because there is principally no material reason for a conclusion that the EU legislator intended to make any changes to the existing law. This can be inferred, inter alia, from the fact that the preparatory documents concerning Regulation 2015/848 contain no special commentary on the issue and no special explanation that would suggest what changes should be made compared to the situation represented by Regulation 1346/2000. The HLV Report, one of the background materials for the drafting of the new law, also provides indirect confirmation of these conclusions, because it states that no principal problems with the application of Article 15 of Regulation 1346/2000 were mentioned in any of the national reports. No legal issues arose that would require a modification of the existing rules, let alone any brand new rules in relation to any controversial topic. If any aspects of the respective rules are mentioned that merit any attention, they include practical problems. For instance, the Lithuanian national report mentions the issue of the exchange of information about the effects associated with the opening of insolvency proceedings in the individual Member States, so that the competent authorities of other Member States could properly apply such effects in compliance with the Insolvency Regulation. In the case of Lithuania, this specifically concerned proceedings in which the enforcement of certain decisions was sought after the insolvency proceedings were opened. In this connection, the HLV Report concludes that this is a pure question of fact, not a legal problem that would require any further legislative solution. Hence, if – in theory – any problems arose in the application of the respective rules (Article 15 of Regulation 1346/2000), the HLV Report argues that they cannot be attributed to the unwillingness of the Member States to accept the effects of the opening of insolvency proceedings in another Member State,[104] but to the potential lack of information regarding the precise nature, scope and consequences of such effects.[105] One may generally agree with the opinion that practical issues relating to the application of the Insolvency Regulation should not be resolved through other administrative measures. One must indeed admit that insufficient knowledge concerning the *leges fori concursus* in other Member States instead concerns (at least according to the Lithuanian report) proceedings before authorities other than courts. If this is the case, we may *a contrario* infer that courts possess the relevant information, or, as applicable, are able to acquire such information in compliance with the procedure envisaged by private international law. Such circumstances allow the conclusion that the given problem could be solved and that measures at the national level would appear sufficient.

2.105. Arbitrators, as private entities, have no access to the means available to State authorities, including measures relating to legal

---

[104] Obviously this also concerns the effects on other proceedings.

[105] The Lithuanian Report mentions that bailiffs complain about their lack of information with regard to the effects that a foreign insolvency proceeding brings about in relation to individual enforcement proceedings in Lithuania. Yet, according to the Lithuanian Report, this is a factual rather than a legal problem. It is not doubtful that Lithuanian authorities respect the legal effects of an insolvency proceeding in another Member State. The problem is rather a lack of information as to what these effects are.

assistance, and primarily the possibility to address competent authorities in order to gather information about foreign law. However, this fact can in no case be viewed as negative. It is necessary to accept as a fact that arbitration is held within the limits of objective and subjective arbitrability, on the basis of a voluntary agreement of the parties incorporated in their arbitration agreement. The parties assume increased liability for the protection of their rights and interests, and are obliged to propose, themselves and in time, any procedural measures, make statements and support them with corresponding evidence, so that their rights and legitimate interests are duly considered. The parties' increased liability may be perceived as the reverse of their extensive contractual autonomy, characteristic of arbitration.

2.106. Consequently, the *lex arbitri* provides the parties to arbitration with the possibility to exert active influence on the course of the proceedings, whether in the form of the parties' agreement on procedure (the possibility of which is usually incorporated in the *lex arbitri*), or in the form of a broad opportunity to propose evidence in order to support the parties' allegations. On the other hand these rights of the parties are balanced by their increase in liability in terms of their obligation to state the facts of the case and meet their burden of proof. It is by no means unusual in international arbitration that the arbitrators' factual and legal assessment of the case is based exclusively on the allegations and evidence presented by the parties, without taking into consideration any other facts (doctrines, case law, etc.), unless explicitly invoked by any of the parties. This approach is typical for France.

2.107. From the perspective of arbitration and in view of the above, it is necessary to consider the issue of access to information regarding the effects of the opening of insolvency proceedings on other proceedings in terms of the *lex fori concursus* (in those cases where the *lex fori concursus* is to be applied on the basis of Article 18 of Regulation 2015/848, formerly Article 15 of Regulation 1346/2000) to be an issue of civil and other proceedings, the conduct of which is regulated and guaranteed by the State. It is usually the parties who must state that insolvency proceedings were opened against one of them, and submit the applicable rules of the *lex fori concursus* or any other rules defining the effects of the opening of insolvency proceedings on arbitration. Naturally, this does not negate the obligation of the arbitrators to examine the existence of the procedural requirements (at least as concerns the continental procedural approach of *civil law*; the approach to this issue adopted by common law is usually the opposite) as elaborated on above, primarily with respect to the legal personality of the parties and the validity of the arbitration agreement. It has been consistently held that arbitrators are not generally obliged to examine in the arbitral proceedings the legal personality of the parties or other persons or entities participating in the proceedings or persons or entities who are the subject or object of the proceedings and/or who are otherwise involved Any and all claims or counterclaims in this regard, as applicable, are usually reserved for the parties. Arbitrators are not bound by the investigative principle. Consequently, if any of the parties intend to invoke the opening of insolvency proceedings, which influences the possibility to hold arbitration regardless of the reason/manner, that party should point out the fact and support it with corresponding evidence, including the contents and the existence of foreign law, the application of which the party invokes. Such a procedure is by no means unusual. In practice, the parties often submit very extensive expert reports, which frequently form the basic material for the arbitrators' decision (see the *Vivendi* case) in order to provide evidence of foreign law, at least in international arbitration. This aspect of Article 18 of Regulation 2015/848, or previously Article 15 of Regulation 1346/2000, should therefore cause no major problems in practice.

2.108. Another issue analyzed by the HLV Report is the classification issue, i.e. the specification of the category of other proceedings that fall within the scope of Article 18 of Regulation 2015/848, or formerly Article 15 of Regulation 1346/2000, as applicable. The Netherlands have raised this issue in relation to preliminary/interim injunctions. Again, no reasons were found (at least in the HLV Report) for any new legislative measures, and the entire text resembles a kind of a marginal note. But nobody denies the fact that issues concerning classification may sometimes arise.

2.109. Consider the situation dealt with in *MG Probud Gdynia*.[106] In that case, the Court held that Regulation 1346/2000 must be interpreted as meaning that after the main insolvency proceedings have been opened in a Member State, the competent authorities of another Member State in which no secondary insolvency proceedings have been opened, are required to recognize and enforce all judgments relating to the

---

[106] Judgment of the CJ EU, Case C-444/07 of 21 January 2010, in *MG Probud Gdynia sp. z o.o.*, where the request for a preliminary ruling was made by *Sąd Rejonowy Gdańsk-Północ w Gdańsku*. Official Journal C 283, 24 November 2007. EUR-Lex: 62007CJ0444, CELEX: 62007CJ0444.

main insolvency proceedings. Therefore, they are not entitled to order, pursuant to the legislation of that other Member State, enforcement measures relating to the assets of the debtor declared insolvent that are situated on its territory when the legislation of the State of the opening of proceedings does not so permit. It has been argued that because of the universal effect that all main insolvency proceedings must be accorded, the insolvency proceedings opened in a Member State encompass all of the debtor's assets, including those situated in another Member State, and the *lex fori concursus* determines not only the opening of insolvency proceedings, but also their course and closure. The Court has held that, on that basis, the *lex fori concursus* is required to govern the treatment of assets situated in other Member States and the effects of the insolvency proceedings on the measures to which those assets are liable to be subject. This author agrees and identifies with the conclusion that no classification issues that may in theory arise with respect to certain types of proceedings constitute grounds for the introduction of any new rules and the determination of other special conflict-of-laws criteria.

2.110. This issue is very broad, and despite maximum efforts, it would probably be impossible to have regard for any and all potential proceedings that could be affected by Article 18 of Regulation 2015/848 (Article 15 of Regulation 1346/2000). Moreover, it is necessary to consider the fact that the classification problem mostly does not include the type of proceeding. The important thing is its particular contents, so that one may assess whether and to what extent the proceedings are directly related to and based on the insolvency proceedings in terms of Article 3(1) of Regulation 2015/848 or, as applicable, Article 3(1) of Regulation 1346/2000 (which fall within the jurisdiction of the courts in the place of the insolvency proceedings), or any proceedings that directly or indirectly concern the debtor's insolvency estate and which must be subject to the application of Article 18 of Regulation 2015/848, or formerly Article 15 of Regulation 1346/2000, as applicable. The variety itself of the situations that may arise renders it reasonable to leave this issue up to the individual assessment of the forum competent to hear and resolve the case. This forum should also consider which category the proceedings fall into and which law is the law applicable to the effects of the insolvency proceedings in view of the above. To summarize, the parties themselves should make and substantiate, duly and in time, any statements concerning the classification of the dispute and the specification of which effects of the insolvency proceedings and on the basis of which legal system ought to be considered. The guidelines that have in the meantime been provided by extensive case law may be deemed sufficient. It is to be expected, in this connection, that the number of cases will continue to grow,[107] and the scope of application of Article 15 of Regulation 1346/2000, or today rather Article 18 of Regulation 2015/848, will gradually be refined.

2.111. The last issue mentioned by the HLV Report is indeed the relationship between insolvency proceedings and arbitration, with reference to the proceedings in the *Vivendi* case. Despite the fact that the different results reached by the courts in England and Switzerland were duly reflected, the authors have voiced an opinion that the applicability of Article 15 of Regulation 1346/2000 in arbitration may already be inferred by analogy from the original text of the law, without the need for any changes and other legislative measures. The authors have referred to academic literature,[108] as well as national reports from Poland, Spain and Great Britain, arguing that their opinion is the prevailing opinion, which has not been contested by the majority. From this perspective, the HLV Report has arrived at a unanimous conclusion that no immediate legislative measures are necessary, because the existing law provides a sufficient basis for including arbitration in the scope of application of Article 15 of Regulation 1346/2000. Despite the above, and in order to eliminate any doubts, the HLV Report has recommended modifying Article 15 of Regulation 1346/2000 (which was ultimately implemented) and supplementing the wording of the provision with the following words:

'[...] on pending lawsuits *or arbitral proceedings*'.

---

[107] One may invoke a recent request for a preliminary ruling lodged on 12 May 2017 by the Portuguese Supremo Tribunal de Justiçave věci Virgílio Tarragó da Silveira v. *Massa Insolvente da Espírito Santo Financial Group, SA*. The case is administered by the CJ EU under No. C-250/17, and the question referred for a preliminary ruling concerns the issue of whether the rule incorporated in Article 15 of Regulation 1346/2000 (now Article 18 of Regulation 2015/848) must (should) be interpreted to the effect that its scope includes a lawsuit pending before a Member State seeking an order that a debtor pay a monetary sum due under a contract for the provision of services, and pay monetary damages for failure to comply with that obligation. All of this was considered while bearing in mind that: (i) the debtor was declared insolvent in proceedings opened in another Member State; and (ii) the declaration of insolvency applies to all of the debtor's assets. Considering the date of the request for a preliminary ruling, no further information is available concerning the resolution of the case.

[108] THOMAS PFEIFFER, FESTSCHRIFT FÜR JOBST WELLENSIEK 821–832 (2011); in favor of direct application, e.g. Mankowski, P. in: ZIP, 2010, et. 2478.

XIII.2.The Impact of Expanded Law Compared to Article 15 of Regulation 1346/2000 on the Future Application Practice Concerning Article 18 of Regulation 2015/848 in Relation to Arbitration

2.112. It might appear at first sight that Regulation 2015/848 has not introduced any modifications concerning the issue, and the perception thus has not changed. If we accept as the basis the lone issue of the applicability of the Insolvency Regulation in arbitration, we may agree with this conclusion. Unfortunately, the HLV Report opens an issue that may have a major influence on the mutual interaction between insolvency proceedings and arbitration in the future, without any sign in the drafting of Regulation 2015/848, and unfortunately, without any significant attention paid to the issue in the drafting of Regulation 2015/848. Although the HLV Report considers the necessity of due regard for Article 18 of Regulation 2015/848 (Article 15 of Regulation 1346/2000) in arbitration to be clear and resolved for any future application of the EU insolvency law, the authors admit that certain opinions exist that do not consider the issue to be so clear-cut. The authors refer to the national reports from Romania, France and Latvia. The reports from France and Latvia invoke their national law. However, the principal reference is the reference to the national report from Austria, which stipulates that Article 4(2)(e) of Regulation 1346/2000[109] cannot be interpreted as a provision relating to arbitration agreements. The authors of the HLV Report agree with this conclusion.

2.113. The author of this article, however, cannot agree with such an interpretation. The inclusion of the note in the text concerning Article 15 of Regulation 1346/2000 seems to indicate that the rule contained cannot apply in conjunction with Article 4(2)(e) of Regulation 1346/2000.[110] The note asserts that the effects of insolvency proceedings on arbitration can be defined by the former or by the latter, but not by both simultaneously. The author of this article is of the opinion that nothing can be further from the truth. As thoroughly analyzed above, Article 15 of Regulation 1346/2000 or, as the case may be, the currently applicable Article 18 of Regulation 2015/848, in its present wording, governs the procedural aspects of other proceedings that (may) conflict with insolvency proceedings. The procedural

---

[109] This provision stipulates that the *lex fori concursus* applies as the governing law to the effects of insolvency proceedings on pending contracts entered into by the debtor. Cf. Article 7(2)(e) of Regulation 2015/848.

[110] Article 7(2)(e) of Regulation 2015/848.

aspects of an arbitration agreement cannot be contested, because such an agreement primarily affords the parties a broad opportunity to agree on the rules governing the conduct of the arbitral proceedings. Nonetheless, in the continental-law system, the issue of the validity of an arbitration agreement can hardly be deemed a procedural effect of insolvency proceedings *stricto sensu* at which the provision is directed.[111]

XIV. The Importance of Place or Seat of Arbitration

2.114. The validity of an arbitration agreement must be distinguished from, inter alia, the obligation to suspend the proceedings or adopt any other procedural measures. As repeatedly emphasized, the reference to the *lex arbitri* cannot be deemed ideal with relation to an arbitration agreement. *Lex arbitri* in the procedural sense must be strictly distinguished from the law applicable to the arbitration agreement. Conversely, as concerns arbitration clauses, an arbitration agreement is, unless the parties agree otherwise, deemed to be governed by the law applicable to the contractual relationship itself between the parties. As concerns litigation, EU law requires that the forum determined on the basis of conflict-of-laws criteria exhibit a connection to the parties and/or the subject matter of the proceedings. Conversely, the nature of the place of arbitration is completely different. It by no means aims to secure that arbitration is held in a place that is deemed suitable from the perspective of litigation. On the contrary, the possibility to choose the place of arbitration belongs to the fundamental characteristic features of this dispute resolution method, and its significance inheres in the possibility to procure the application of the procedural rules of the *lex arbitri* that the parties deem appropriate for the resolution of their dispute. Consequently, the main criterion for the choice of the place of arbitration usually consists of the corresponding procedural rules, on the basis of and in compliance with which the arbitration will be held. It is not unusual and is, indeed, commonplace in international

---

[111] The HLV Report itself tends to support this interpretation, because it states with respect to Article 15 of Regulation 1346/2000 that no serious problems arise in the context thereof, as most national *leges fori concursus* provide for a priority of collective insolvency proceedings over individual resolution of the debtor's disputes. This is regardless of the fact that the individual rules exhibit major differences in this regard, such as the suspension or termination of such individual proceedings, the transfer of the jurisdiction to resolve such disputes to the insolvency court, or the prohibition of enforcement of decisions made outside the insolvency proceedings.

arbitration that the place of arbitration has nothing in common with the merits of the dispute, as such.

2.115. Besides, it has to be noted that the choice of the place of arbitration does not, in the majority of cases, belong to the essential requirements of an arbitration agreement. For instance, in arbitral proceedings before the ICC (International Chamber of Commerce) International Court of Arbitration, whose rules and practice are considered the global benchmark of arbitration practice worldwide, this particular arbitral tribunal is entitled to determine the place of arbitration in the absence of the parties' agreement. This power raises no problems under normal circumstances, but it might become controversial in relation to the effects of insolvency proceedings. Under such circumstances, the ICC International Court of Arbitration could *de facto* decide, through the determination of the place of arbitration, whether or not the arbitration agreement remains valid. This analogically applies to most permanent arbitral institutions and their rules, as well as to *ad hoc* arbitral proceedings. However infrequent in practice, we cannot rule out the possibility that the statement of claim will be lodged shortly before the insolvency proceedings are opened.

2.116. Finally, one may also invoke the already voiced argument that the conflict-of-laws criterion of the place where other proceedings are held ought to be used as rarely as possible, because it dilutes the effects of insolvency proceedings and indirectly results in a situation in which the individual creditors will be treated differently, depending on the place of the other proceedings.

2.117. Indeed, the author is of the opinion that the HLV Report fails to properly factor in the purpose of the rule of the *lex concursus* regarding the lack of validity of the arbitration agreement, which primarily aims to make sure that no future arbitrations are opened on the basis of the arbitration agreements entered into by the debtor. The issue of pending proceedings is usually resolved through the specific procedural measures described above. Should the effects on pending proceedings in terms of Article 18 of Regulation 2015/848 (Article 15 of Regulation 1346/2000) also include the issue of the validity of the arbitration agreement, it would be necessary to address the potential conflict of the applicable rules governing these two categories and determine the validity and effectiveness of the arbitration agreement and procedure in pending proceedings separately. This could, for instance, include a situation in which the liquidator may, on one hand, avail themselves of the opportunity to request, under certain circumstances, the continuation of the proceedings, and, on the other hand, that option would be denied to the liquidator, because the *lex fori concursus* would prohibit any arbitrations on the basis of the executed arbitration agreements. If the authors of the HLV Report based their conclusions on the premise that the recognized priority of collective proceedings will suspend any pending proceedings concerning the debtor's insolvency estate, regardless of the particular method thereof,[112] it appears unnecessary to subsume the issue of the validity/effectiveness of the arbitration agreement under Article 18 of Regulation 2015/848 (Article 15 of Regulation 1346/2000). Irrespective of the resolution thereof, it would be necessary to honor the procedural effects of the opening of insolvency proceedings described above. The arbitration would be suspended, whether or not the corresponding rules still considered the arbitration agreement valid.

2.118. The effects of the opening of insolvency proceedings could, in theory, only apply to the validity of the arbitration agreement if the legal system of the place of arbitration contained no other rules in the procedural sense, the proceedings were not suspended, and no pending proceedings were affected by the insolvency proceedings. But the author is not aware of any *lex concursus* in which this issue would be entirely absent.

2.119. Hence, it is unclear how the validity of the arbitration agreement should be considered under Article 18 of Regulation 2015/848 (Article 15 of Regulation 1346/2000), as the authors of the HLV Report suggest. The *lex arbitri* mostly contains a mechanism whereby these rules can be aligned with the *lex fori concursus*. This mutual interaction appears more appropriate with respect to the validity of the arbitration agreement, compared to a solution according to which the rules of the *lex fori concursus* would be entirely disregarded, and the conflict-of-laws rules determined as applicable only the rules of the *lex arbitri*.

2.120. One may imagine, from a purely theoretical perspective, that – in relation to the proceedings governed by these rules – the validity of the arbitration agreement will or may be assessed in terms of Article 7(2)(f) of Regulation 2015/848 (Article 4(2) (f) of Regulation 1346/2000). The reason is that most of the reservations mentioned in relation to the subsuming of this issue under Article 18 of Regulation 2015/848 (Article 15 of Regulation 1346/2000) shall not apply in this case, especially as concerns the possibility to open new proceedings in the future. However, such considerations have no practical application. The conflict-of-laws rules incorporated in Article 7(2)(e) of

112   The author considers such presumption reasonable.

Regulation 2015/848 (Article 4(2)(e) of Regulation 1346/2000) and Article 7(2)(f) of Regulation 2015/848 (Article 4(2)(f) of Regulation 1346/2000) refer to one and the same legal system, namely the *lex fori concursus*. The validity of the arbitration agreement will always be assessed on the basis of the *lex fori concursus*, regardless of which of the abovementioned provisions will formally govern. At the same time, this interpretation fails to explain the inclusion of the respective subject in the part of the HLV Report that concerns Article 15 of Regulation 1346/2000, which suggests that the authors of the HLV Report believe that these very rules should play at least some role in the assessment of the validity of the arbitration agreement. Unfortunately, the arguments are not elaborated on and, apart from the general statement that the subsuming of the issue of the validity of an arbitration agreement under a particular provision of the Insolvency Regulation is controversial, the HLV Report fails to reveal the actual opinion of the authors of the HLV Report and the grounds for the alleged controversy.

2.121. Purely for the sake of completeness, it seems appropriate to emphasize that the conclusions made by the English courts in the *Vivendi* case cannot form the necessary basis for the purposes of Regulation 2015/848. The English courts have ruled that arbitration could be held in England, despite the objection that Polish *lex concursus* rendered the arbitration agreement invalid. However, these conclusions cannot be interpreted as a confirmation of the *lex arbitri* as the legal system in compliance with which the effects of the opening of insolvency proceedings on the arbitration agreement must be assessed. The reason is that the decision must be viewed in the context of the different perception of the validity and effectiveness of an arbitration agreement in the continental law system and in the common law system. Continental law perceives these issues as issues of substantive law. Conversely, the influence of the opening of insolvency proceedings on the validity of an arbitration agreement will be classified as a procedural issue. Consequently, if the courts applied the *lex arbitri*, such a procedure would be fully in compliance with the interpretation of Article 15 of Regulation 1346/2000 (Article 18 of Regulation 2015/848), according to which the *lex arbitri* governs the effects concerning the procedural aspects of arbitration. The continental system would not allow such a conclusion, and the validity of the arbitration agreement would have to be classified as an issue of substantive law.

XV.   The Manner of Application of Article 18 of Regulation 2015/848

XV.1.   The Mechanical Expansion of the Scope of Provision Without Due Regard for its Specific Features of Arbitration and Instruments

2.122. Although the wording of Article 18 of Regulation 2015/848 may *prima facie* appear entirely clear and unambiguous, the interpretation thereof suffers from major difficulties. The problem is that the EU legislature drafted the provision mechanically, simply inserting the words 'or arbitral proceedings,' and failed to duly consider whether any and all conclusions articulated with respect to proceedings conducted in courts or other State authorities can be applied to arbitration in the given context. But arbitration cannot be perceived as a mere choice of arbitrators as private-law subjects to hear and resolve a case, as opposed to a hearing and resolution of the case before State authorities. The different essence of certain instruments is the reason why the parties choose this dispute resolution mechanism, and must also be considered in connection with the interaction of insolvency proceedings and arbitration.

XV.2.   The Place in Which the Arbitral Tribunal Has its Seat

2.123. One may start with the definition of the place in which the arbitral tribunal has its seat. Whereas the interpretation of the seat of a civil court only requires the general definition of the term,[113] the place of arbitration has an autonomous meaning. Hence, it is necessary to address the issue of whether this interpretation will stand in the context of Article 18 of Regulation 2015/848, and how much the interpretation of this rule must be adjusted to the term 'place of arbitration.'

2.124. Strictly speaking, arbitration does not use the term 'seat of the arbitral tribunal,' but 'place of arbitration.' Alternatively, one may come across the terms, 'forum'[114] or 'seat of arbitration.' To put it simply, the place of arbitration can be characterized as a place where the arbitration is held in the legal sense, i.e. the term refers to the legal domicile of the respective arbitration. The terminology regarding this term is not entirely united.

---

[113]   Hence, it means the place where the respective court is physically located.

[114]   However, 'forum' is sometimes strictly refused by some academics and practitioners in connection with arbitration. They argue that forum is a term reserved solely for a public-law *forum*.

For instance, some authors attempt to distinguish the 'seat' of arbitration from 'place' of arbitration. The former is supposed to mean the legal determination of the arbitration, whereas the latter is perceived as the place of the actual hearing of the dispute or the actual place where the arbitral proceedings are held.[115] Nonetheless, even those authors who attempt to find a clear distinction admit that the terminology is used rather confusingly in practice. Consequently, the use of any of the terms is usually accepted. However, this also means that any interpretation thereof must be performed individually and with due regard for the context in which the term was used. The words used in Article 18 of Regulation 2015/848 merely demonstrate the mistaken and inaccurate use of terminology, and the EU legislature had no intention of coming up with an autonomous expression applicable in relation to Regulation 2015/848. If this were not the case and the EU legislature attributed any special meaning to the term 'place in which the arbitral tribunal has its seat,' the author would expect that this fact would at least be pointed out, and the legislature would provide guidelines for the interpretation of the term. This has not happened, and, indeed, any and all available materials suggest that the new law did not aim to introduce any new rules and/or doctrinal interpretations. The new law merely desired to strengthen procedural certainty by emphasizing that Article 18 of Regulation 2015/848 also applies to arbitration.

2.125. Moreover, the place or seat of arbitration is substantially dependent on the will of the parties or on the autonomous determination of the arbitrators or a permanent arbitral institution. The reason is that the international practice does not interpret the term 'seat of the arbitral tribunal' as a seat of [any] permanent arbitral institution,[116] but as a seat or place of the particular arbitral proceedings. Such a place may be, and

---

[115]   Compare ALAN REDFERN, MARTIN HUNTER, NIGEL BLACKABY, CONSTANTINE PARTASIDES, LAW AND PRACTICE OF INTERNATIONAL COMMERCIAL ARBITRATION, London: Sweet & Maxwell 270 (2004).

[116]   In the individual language versions: English:'... or in which the arbitral tribunal has its seat;' Bulgarian: ' ...в която се намира арбитражния съд;' Czech: ' ... ve kterém má sídlo rozhodčí soud;' Danish:' ... eller hvor voldgiftsretten har sit sæde;' Estonian: „...on pooleli või kus asub vahekohus;' Finnish:' ... jossa oikeudenkäynti tai välimiesmenettely on vireillä;' French: ' ... ou dans lequel le tribunal arbitral a son siège;' Croatian: '... ili u kojoj je mjesto arbitraže;' Irish: ' ... agus leis an dlí sin amháin;' Italian: ' ... ha sede il collegio arbitrale;' Lithuanian: ' ... yra arbitražo teismo buveinė, teisė;' Latvian: ' ... kurā notiek minētā tiesvedība vai kur atrodas šķīrējtiesa található;' Maltese: ' ...iż-żmien tal-ftuh ta' proċedimenti;' German: ' ...in dem das Schiedsgericht belegen ist;' Dutch: ' ... of het scheidsgerecht zijn zetel heeft;' Polish: „... lub w którym ma siedzibę organ polubowny;' Portuguese:' ... ou em que o Tribunal arbitral tem a sua sede;' Romanian:' ... sau în care se instanţa de arbitraj îşi are sediul;' Greek:' ... στο οποίο εκκρεμεί η δίκη ή εδρεύει το διαιτητικό δικαστήριο;' Slovak: ' ... alebo v ktorom má rozhodcovský súd svoje sídlo;' Slovene:' ... ali v kateri je sedež arbitražnega sodišča;' Spanish: ' ... el que tenga su sede el tribunal arbitral;' Swedish: '... eller där skiljedomstolen har sitt säte.'

presently often is, rather virtual. If any arbitration other than *ad hoc* arbitration is conducted at any permanent arbitral institution, the seat of the institution principally plays no role from the perspective of the *lex arbitri*. Consequently, the standards of international arbitration do not prohibit the parties from a Member State to agree on a place of arbitration ('arbitral tribunal' according to the international terminology commonly recognized at present) outside the EU. For instance, it is by no means exceptional and is indeed very common that parties to a dispute submitted to arbitration who come from EU Member States agree that the place (seat) of arbitration, i.e. the seat of the particular dispute, will be Switzerland, as a non-EU Member State.

2.126. It is a different matter whether, and to what extent, the EU legislature was aware of all the consequences of using that term and the potential problems associated with the interpretation thereof. The author has à priori no doubts about the fact that the term used in that provision must be interpreted as meaning the place of particular arbitral proceedings, as understood by the arbitration law. Nevertheless, it is necessary, primarily in view of the EU legislature's tendency to see arbitration merely as *quasi* litigation, which exhibits no principal differences from litigation, to add at least a brief analysis regarding the use of the term 'seat of the arbitral tribunal' employed in several language versions. Despite the fact that arbitration is generally characterized as proceedings conducted before arbitrators as specific private-law subjects, one may not ignore the existence of arbitral tribunals or arbitral institutions that mostly provide the arbitrators with administrative services and support relating to the arbitral proceedings.[117] It is then logical to ask whether Article 18 of Regulation 2015/848 is in the case of such institutionalized arbitration perhaps targeted at the seat of the respective arbitral institutions, instead of the place of the particular arbitral proceedings. However, such an interpretation would have no statutory basis in the *lex arbitri* of the overwhelming majority of the EU Member States, because most of those countries lack any basis in their law for permanent arbitral institutions. The seat of the arbitral tribunal or, as applicable, seat of arbitration is exclusively the domiciliation of the particular dispute in a particular legal system, i.e. its subsuming under a particular

---

[117] The concept of permanent arbitral institutions as special institutions established by law or on the basis of a special statue, such as in terms of Section 13 of Act No. 216/1994 Coll., as amended, is rather an exception in international practice, and is more common in certain countries of Central and Eastern Europe.

lex arbitri as a result of the expression of will of the parties or expression of the arbitrators' autonomy.

2.127. Hence, the interpretation according to which the term would refer to the seat of a permanent arbitral institution would be contrary to the understanding of the place of arbitration, as generally accepted in the doctrine of international arbitration. On the other hand, however, one must take into consideration the possibility, which appears highly probable, that the EU legislature was completely unaware of the difference and the special concept of the term 'seat of arbitration', and considered it to be the seat of the arbitral institution administering the said dispute, here in the sense of a conflict-of-laws criterion that should be factored in. It is necessary to bear in mind that some countries make a distinction, even a terminological one, between a 'forum', as the arbitral tribunal appointed to hear and resolve the dispute, and an 'arbitral tribunal', as the institution providing administrative services necessary to conduct the arbitration. Indeed, most countries have already abandoned the designation of such institutions as arbitral tribunals/arbitration courts, and tend to exclusively use the term 'arbitral institution.' In view of the bad experience in these countries with *ad hoc* arbitration, the difference is also accentuated by the general public, which perceives an arbitral tribunal as a guarantee of a certain standard, which, moreover, may also be provided by the State.[118] If the wording of Article 18 of Regulation 2015/848 contains a reference to an *arbitral tribunal* in the language versions applying to these particular countries, as opposed to the place of arbitration, a major problem could arise with respect to the interpretation of the term.

2.128. However, comparing the individual language versions, one may conclude that the problem only inheres in an inaccuracy connected with unsettled terminology. The main language versions refer to the arbitral tribunal (natural persons who hear and resolve a particular dispute), not any arbitral institution. The absolutely clear and unambiguous version in this regard is the English version, which employs the term 'arbitral tribunal', as opposed to 'arbitral institution' or 'arbitration court.'[119] Similarly, the French language version is based on the term *'le*

---

[118] For instance, an arbitral institution in the Czech Republic may only be established by the law (Section 13(1) of Act No. 216/1994 Coll., on Arbitration and Enforcement of Arbitral Awards, as amended), and no other entities are allowed to use any designation that would create the impression that they are an arbitral institution in terms of that provision, even if they provide administrative services in connection with *ad hoc* arbitration.

[119] Although one needs to be careful with respect to the last of the terms mentioned above, because an arbitration court may exceptionally appear in linguistically unsettled environments in the sense of an arbitral tribunal.

tribunal arbitral, not *'cour de l'arbitrage,'* which could be used if the text were supposed to refer to an arbitral institution, not a particular arbitral tribunal, in the sense of a domiciliation of a particular dispute within the framework of a particular *lex arbitri*. Finally, one may also invoke the German language version, in which the term *'Schiedsgericht'* is interpreted strictly in the sense of a particular arbitral tribunal or sole arbitrator hearing and resolving a particular dispute, despite the fact that a literal translation contains a reference to a court. Where the German language refers to an arbitration court, the terms used are *'Institut'* or *'Institution,'* as applicable.

2.129. Considering the above, the author is of the opinion that Article 18 of Regulation 2015/848 is clearly targeted at the place of a particular arbitration, as perceived in the context of arbitration, i.e. a place in which a particular dispute is legally domiciled. Moreover, it is necessary to point out that arbitration practice strictly distinguishes the place of arbitration from the seat of the particular arbitral institution, and the latter has essentially no significance from the legal perspective. For instance, if the arbitration is conducted at the ICC International Court of Arbitration, nobody would argue that Paris, France should be regarded as the place of the arbitration, because of the actual seat of this arbitral institution. The sole criterion in this regard is the place of the arbitration determined according to Article 18 of the ICC Rules of Arbitration (ICC Rules).[120] It makes no difference that some cases exceptionally refer to the seat of the arbitral tribunal as a subsidiary criterion applicable if the parties fail to agree on the place of arbitration, or, as applicable, if their arbitration agreement contains no agreement in this regard. Hence, we cannot infer that the seat of the respective arbitral institution would have any principal importance in the sense of the place of arbitration. But even these cases are based on the principle of contractual autonomy enjoyed by the parties to the arbitration. The seat of the arbitral institution as an auxiliary criterion is applied (exceptionally in international practice) only if the parties fail to agree on the place of arbitration.

2.130. The place of arbitration is, indeed, very important from the procedural perspective, and it merits closer attention. This is because the choice of the place influences the course of the arbitral proceedings from the procedural perspective and affects many issues, from arbitrability and the applicable procedural

---

[120] Cit.: 1 'The place of the arbitration shall be fixed by the Court, unless agreed upon by the parties. 2 The arbitral tribunal may, after consultation with the parties, conduct hearings and meetings at any location it considers appropriate, unless otherwise agreed by the parties. 3 The arbitral tribunal may deliberate at any location it considers appropriate.'

rules, to the possibilities and the range of reasons that allow a party to seek the annulment of the arbitral award, or the jurisdiction of the courts in the exercise of their subsidiary and control function *vis-à-vis* arbitration. In view of this fact, there are fewer and fewer cases in international arbitration where the parties fail to designate the place of arbitration in their arbitration agreement and let this issue be resolved according to the applicable procedural rules, whether statutory rules or rules of the individual arbitral institutions.

2.131. In connection with the determination of the place of arbitration, one may invoke the traditional principles of arbitration, namely the extensive contractual autonomy and especially the weaker connection between the place of arbitration and the arbitration, as such, and its subject matter. This is an area where the principal difference between litigation and arbitration becomes visible. Litigation is governed by the principle of *lex fori*, i.e. the courts as State authorities always proceed on the basis of their own procedural rules, and strictly apply the principle of territoriality. The determination of the international jurisdiction of courts includes an assessment of the relationship between the subject matter of the proceedings and the parties (factual, personal and territorial relationship), on the one hand, and the territory of the said State, on the other hand. Conversely, arbitration affords maximum freedom to the parties to choose the rules governing the course of the proceedings (*lex arbitri*), which is manifested by the choice of the place of arbitration. Consequently, it is not only possible, but in fact fairly common that the parties or the subject matter of the proceedings have no connection to the chosen place of arbitration, and the place of the particular arbitration is completely neutral *vis-à-vis* the parties and the subject matter of disputes.

2.132. This approach to the place of arbitration is based on the *seat theory* (also known as localization theory), which is founded on the presumption that the place in which the arbitration takes place must always be fixed from the legal perspective, and which connects the arbitration to a particular legal system. The traditional theories identify the chosen place of arbitration with the legal system applicable in that place. It is entirely irrelevant whether the place of arbitration was determined by the agreement of the parties, or whether it was determined by a person or entity competent to do so (typically the arbitrators or a permanent arbitral institution). One may even argue, from this perspective, that the place of arbitration cannot be perceived as a geographic category. It is a connection of the chosen place of arbitration with the law applicable to the arbitral procedure, applicable in the place where the place of the arbitration is formally and legally located.

2.133. As indicated above, this possibility to influence the procedural rules usually means that the parties are interested in the explicit determination of the procedural rules, on the basis of which the arbitration will be conducted. Hence, the number of cases in which the parties delegate the determination of the place of arbitration to a third party has dropped. Conversely, there are opinions that argue that the issue of the place of arbitration is losing its principal significance for the parties from the procedural perspective, because the individual national *leges arbitri* are gradually converging. A certain harmonization of the individual legal systems is an undoubted fact. Nonetheless, the author believes that we are still miles away from a situation in which the place of a particular arbitration, as perceived by the international practice and international terminology, entirely loses its meaning and the parties consider it irrelevant in which jurisdiction their arbitration is formally conducted.[121] Practitioners are familiar with situations in which the arbitration agreement contains no explicit agreement of the parties regarding the place of arbitration, and merely determines the manner whereby the place shall be determined after the arbitration is opened. Such an agreement is only possible if the parties remain equal. For instance, it is permitted to leave the choice up to the claimant. The statement of claim/request for arbitration may, in theory, be lodged and the arbitration may be opened by any of the parties. Consequently, one cannot conclude that any of the parties was deprived of the possibility to influence the place of arbitration in advance because it is impossible to predict which party will have the right to choose the place of arbitration. In view of this, it is argued that such an agreement breaches no procedural rights of any of the parties.

2.134. However, such agreements will have to be assessed individually in the course of the arbitral proceedings, at least from the perspective of the principles of insolvency proceedings, which require, on the one hand, that the debtor is not allowed to evade their obligations by fictitious acts, and on the other hand, that the individual creditors are prevented from gaining any advantages to the detriment of the debtor's insolvency estate

---

[121] The approach of the individual States to arbitration still exhibits certain differences, which may also appear in the scope of the parties' autonomy afforded to the parties in relation to the possibility to influence the course of the proceedings. Similarly, the scope and the manner of the exercise of the State's control functions in relation to arbitration, or, as applicable, the general tendency itself of the States to intervene in arbitration, may also be important.

and the other creditors. Nonetheless, such principles should be balanced out by the respect for the contractual autonomy of the parties that was expressed before the arbitration commenced. The scope of contractual freedom in relation to arbitration after the insolvency proceedings are initiated will be governed by the *lex fori concursus*.

2.135. At the same time, international arbitration typically involves the interaction of two or more legal systems, and the place of arbitration influences only one of them, namely the *lex arbitri*. But the procedural rules of the *lex arbitri* must be distinguished from the substantive law applicable to the merits of the dispute, as well as the law applicable to the arbitration agreement, and in exceptional cases, the law applicable to arbitrability, although the law applicable to arbitrability is in the overwhelming majority of cases identical to the *lex arbitri*. Consequently, as we have repeatedly mentioned above, there is no reason to subsume the effects of insolvency proceedings on existing arbitration agreements under the *lex arbitri* and apply the *lex arbitri* to such effects. Hence, the relation of the *lex arbitri* to arbitration is, for the most part, indirect, which also needs to be considered in the determination of the conflict-of-laws criteria. The legal and formal nature of the *lex arbitri* is, inter alia, manifested by the fact that the proceedings may actually take place in a completely different place. This primarily applies to hearings, the taking of evidence, as well as other procedural measures. Frequently, these are performed in a place completely different from the place of any particular arbitration as the localization instrument that subjects this or that arbitration to a particular *lex arbitri*. As described above, this is often completely different from the seat of the permanent arbitral institution administering the dispute, let alone the *ad hoc* arbitrations held outside the realm of any permanent arbitral institution. It is also quite common that the arbitrators meet and debate elsewhere. The parties may even agree that the place of arbitration shall not be the place where the arbitral award will be made.[122] Indeed, whereas *leges arbitri* commonly refer to the place [seat] of a particular arbitration, the New York Convention (1958) classifies a foreign arbitral award

---

[122] However, in the absence of any such agreement between the parties, the place of arbitration is deemed to coincide with the place where the arbitral award is made. This conclusion applies regardless of the place where the members of the arbitral tribunal agreed on the arbitral award and the place where it was signed. At the same time, the determination of the place where the arbitral award is made may be crucial from the perspective of its subsequent enforcement. But some lawyers also attribute more importance to the place where the arbitral award is signed. The importance of this place would arise especially if it were clear that the formal place of arbitration is only fictitious and was chosen by the parties only for the purposes of evading the law.

according to the place where it was made, not the place [seat] of the arbitral tribunal (= place [seat] of the particular arbitration).

2.136. However, the place where the arbitral proceedings are actually conducted may become important if it is determined neither by agreement of the parties, nor by a third entity in such manner as envisaged by the applicable rules. In its decision of 23 March 2003 in Case No. 6 Sch 02/99, the High Regional Court in Düsseldorf ruled that, under such circumstances, the place of arbitration must be determined on the basis of the actual place where the case was heard. If these criteria also fail to provide a clear answer, the decisive place is the place of the last hearing.

2.137. Conversely, the proponents of the anational theory of arbitration advocate an approach that completely undermines the significance of the place of arbitration. Their approach is based on the presumption that international arbitration would be substantially simpler if the arbitration were delocalized from the State in the territory of which it is held, and if the underlying basis consisted exclusively in the agreement of the parties. The author does not share these tendencies towards the supranationalization of arbitration, not only for doctrinal reasons, but also for purely practical reasons. The *lex arbitri* de facto still exists and would exist even if the arbitration were conducted without a single reference to such law, only on the basis of the general principles of arbitration. The application of the *lex arbitri* may become necessary in practice, typically in relation to the interaction with State authorities in situations when the corresponding measures exceed the powers entrusted to the arbitrators, such as certain injunctions, etc.

2.138. All of these criteria will also have to be considered in the determination of the place in which the arbitral tribunal has its seat in terms of Article 18 of Regulation 2015/848. If the basis for further developments is a certain separation of the place of arbitration from its factual circumstances, and if it is perceived in the abovementioned sense as a choice of such procedural law by the parties that best corresponds to their needs, various problems might obviously arise in practice that will concern the scope of application of Article 18 of Regulation 2015/848. Consequently, this provision may in such cases become principally inapplicable to arbitration.

2.139. The only interpretation of Article 18 of Regulation 2015/848 acceptable for the practice appears to be the interpretation that the place where the arbitral tribunal has its seat will be, in terms of the wording of this provision, the place of arbitration. This is true no matter how the parties may exclude by their expression of will and thereby eliminate the effects of the application of Article 18 of Regulation 2015/848 on arbitration. Indeed, such interpretation is probably closest to the interpretation embraced by common law, but is not quite compatible with the objectives of Regulation 2015/848. Hence, one cannot rule out the possibility that this apparent inconsistency in Regulation 2015/848, which probably stems from the EU legislators' ignorance of the fundamental instruments of arbitration, could only be remedied in any future amendment of the EU Insolvency Regulation.

XVI. The Subjective Scope of the Application of Article 18 of Regulation 2015/848 in Relation to Arbitration in a Member State Where Parties Have No Relevant Relation to Any EU Member State

2.140. As mentioned above, the choice of the place of arbitration is generally at the discretion of the parties. It may therefore easily happen that arbitration will be conducted on the territory of a Member State, and the parties to the arbitration will, conversely, have no relevant relationship to any Member State. In such a case, the respective provision cannot apply, because the application of the law presumes the existence of insolvency proceedings that could affect other pending proceedings. Logically, only insolvency proceedings conducted under Regulation 2015/848 may have such effects. One of the fundamental principles of Regulation 2015/848 is the principle according to which this law can only be applied if the center of the debtor's main interests (COMI) is located on the territory of a Member State (other than Denmark[123]). Only the COMI is relevant, and if it is situated outside the defined territory, it is not possible to proceed pursuant to Regulation 2015/848, even if the respective party had its registered office or assets belonging to the insolvency estate in the territory of a Member State.

2.141. If the insolvency proceedings concerning one of the parties are governed by a different law, consideration thereof requires the application of general principles of private international law and an assessment of whether and to what extent such insolvency proceedings can be recognized in the place of arbitration.

---

[123] See Recital 88 to Regulation 2015/848, according to which (cit.): 'In accordance with Articles 1 and 2 of Protocol No 22 on the position of Denmark annexed to the Treaty on European Union and the Treaty on the Functioning of the European Union, Denmark is not taking part in the adoption of this Regulation and is not bound by it or subject to its application.'

However, the division mentioned above must also apply in this case, i.e. the arbitral tribunal will have to deal at least with the issue of the legal personality of the parties and the validity of the arbitration agreement. Save for procedural capacity, which is under any circumstances assessed according to the *lex personae* of the respective person, it will always be necessary to examine whether any conflict-of-laws criteria exist that could be applied. If the insolvency proceedings can be recognized in the place of arbitration, but no particular law exists that could be used, the author maintains that the reasonable arrangement of relationships is best accomplished by having regard to the *lex fori concursus*.

2.142. Naturally, a contrary situation may also occur. This would be where there are persons or entities from EU Member States, one of whom is or will be subject to insolvency proceedings falling within the scope of Regulation 2015/848. Such persons then enter into an arbitration agreement on the basis of which arbitration will be held with its place located outside the territorial scope of Regulation 2015/848. The delimitation of the territorial scope of Regulation 2015/848 allows no conclusion other than that the respective law will not be applied under such circumstances. This conclusion is based on entirely general principles, according to which no law can be applied outside its territorial scope. Even if the general principles of private international law were disregarded, this conclusion could be deduced from the text itself of Article 18 of Regulation 2015/848, which explicitly refers to the law of the Member State in which that lawsuit is pending or in which the arbitral tribunal has its seat. The scope of the respective provision is explicitly limited to other proceedings that are held in a place covered by the territorial scope of Regulation 2015/848. Naturally, this does not exclude the possibility that if it is possible to recognize the insolvency proceedings in the agreed place of arbitration, the effects of the insolvency proceedings should be considered on the basis of the application of private international law.

2.143. This fact can also be deemed one of the reasons why the conflict-of-laws criterion referring to the *lex arbitri* appears controversial – it would clearly result in a fragmentation of the applicable law, and in exceptions to the principle of the uniform treatment of all creditors.

| | |

Summaries

FRA [*La procédure d'arbitrage vs. la procédure d'insolvabilité au vu du droit de l'UE*]

L'incidence d'une procédure d'insolvabilité sur une procédure d'arbitrage ouverte dans un autre État représente depuis bien des années un sujet très sensible. La question fondamentale est de savoir si et dans quelle mesure les arbitres sont tenus de prendre en compte la procédure d'insolvabilité en cours dans un autre pays. Les opinions en la matière ont profondément changé au cours des dernières décennies : en effet, il y a vingt ou trente ans, on considérait généralement qu'une procédure d'insolvabilité menée dans un autre État n'avait pas d'effets extraterritoriaux. Depuis, la doctrine a été exposée à l'influence du droit de l'UE, qui tend à imposer la législation européenne, autant que faire se peut, dans les procédures d'arbitrage. À titre d'exemple, l'article 18 de la directive (UE) 2015/848 est applicable aux procédures d'insolvabilité ouvertes à partir de juin 2017. En vertu de cette disposition, les arbitres sont tenus d'appliquer la loi du siège du tribunal arbitral aux procédures d'insolvabilité en cours, et ce même lorsqu'une partie à une telle procédure est en faillite dans un autre pays membre de l'UE ; ce règlement concerne l'ensemble du marché unique de l'UE à l'exception du Danemark. Il s'agit, à bien des égards, d'une disposition très discutable. La prise en compte ou non d'une procédure d'insolvabilité ouverte dans un autre État lors d'une procédure d'arbitrage peut en principe affecter la reconnaissance et l'exécution de la sentence arbitrale. L'évolution en la matière en dehors du marché unique, par exemple en Suisse, n'est pas non plus sans intérêt.

CZE [*Rozhodčí řízení versus insolvenční řízení z pohledu práva EU*]

Vliv insolvenčního řízení na zahájené rozhodčí řízení se sídlem v jiném státě je velmi citlivou otázkou po řadu let. Základním problémem je, zda a jak dalece musí rozhodci zohlednit insolvenční řízení zahájené v jiné zemi. Názory se zásadně změnily v průběhu posledních dvou, resp. tří desetiletí, neboť základním principem ještě před dvaceti nebo třiceti lety bylo, že insolvenční řízení vedená v jiném státě nemají žádný exteritoriální účinek. Doktrína se změnila především z důvodu práva EU, které se snaží co nejvíce vázat rozhodce evropským právem. Jedním z příkladů je článek 18 nařízení (EU) 2015/848, které se použije na insolvenční řízení zahájená od června 2017. Toto ustanovení zavazuje rozhodce, aby použili tuzemské účinky na zahájená insolvenční řízení platná ve státě sídle (místa) rozhodčího řízení také v případě, že strana takového rozhodčího řízení je v úpadku v jiné členské zemi EU; toto nařízení se použije na jednotném trhu EU (s výjimkou Dánska). Nicméně toto ustanovení je velmi diskutabilní z mnoha důvodů. Zohlednění (nezohlednění) insolvenčního řízení zahájeného v jiném státě na stranu rozhodčího řízení může v zásadě mít vliv i na uznání a výkon rozhodčích nálezů. Významný je však i vývoj v této oblasti mimo jednotný trh EU, jako například ve Švýcarsku.

| | |

POL   [*Postępowanie arbitrażowe a postępowanie upadłościowe w świetle prawa UE*]
Eksterytorialne skutki postępowania upadłościowego dla postępowania arbitrażowego z miejscem postępowania w innym państwie to kwestia nad wyraz wrażliwa. W myśl Rozporządzenia (UE) 2015/848 sędziowie rozjemczy muszą uwzględnić postępowanie upadłościowe wszczęte w innym państwie członkowskim UE. Przedmiotowe regulacje jednak są bardzo sporne. Ponadto w krajach poza UE doktryna tematu w dynamiczny sposób rozwija się.

DEU   [*Spannungsfeld zwischen Schiedsverfahren und Insolvenzverfahren aus Sicht des EU-Rechts*]
Die exterritoriale Wirkung von Insolvenzverfahren auf Schiedsverfahren, deren Verfahrensort in einem anderen Staat liegt, ist eine überaus heikle Sache. Nach der Verordnung (EU) 2015/848 müssen die Schiedsrichter ein in einem anderen EU-Mitgliedsstaat eröffnetes Insolvenzverfahren berücksichtigen. Diese Regelung ist jedoch höchst umstritten. Auch in Drittstaaten außerhalb der EU haben zu diesem Problemkreis wichtige doktrinäre Entwicklungen stattgefunden.

RUS   [*Арбитраж против производства по делу о несостоятельности в свете законодательства ЕС*]
Весьма деликатным вопросом является экстерриториальное действие производства по делу о несостоятельности на арбитраж с местом проведения в другом государстве. Регламент (ЕС) 2015/848 предусматривает, что арбитры должны принимать во внимание производство по делу о несостоятельности, возбужденное в другом государстве-члене ЕС. Однако данное регулирование очень спорное. Доктрина по данному

вопросу значительно развивается и в других государствах, не входящих в ЕС.

ESP [*Procedimiento arbitral contra procedimiento de insolvencia desde el punto de vista del Derecho de la UE*]
Los efectos extraterritoriales del procedimiento de insolvencia en el procedimiento arbitral con el centro en otro Estado constituyen un asunto sumamente delicado. El Reglamento (UE) 2015/848 establece que los árbitros deben tener en cuenta el procedimiento de insolvencia abierto en otro Estado miembro de la UE. No obstante, dicha legislación es más que discutible. Además, la doctrina que aborda este tema se viene desarrollando de manera considerable también en Estados no miembros de la UE.

Bibliography

ACHIM AHRENDT, DER ZUSTÄNDIKEITSSTREIT IM SCHIEDVERFAHREN, Tübingen: Max Planck Institut für ausländisches und Internationales Privatrecht (1996).

NEIL ANDREWS, ARBITRATION AND CONTRACT LAW: COMMON LAW PERSPECTIVES, Springer (2016).

Domitille Baizeau, *Arbitration and Insolvency: Issues of Applicable Law*, NEW DEVELOPMENTS IN INTERNATIONAL COMMERCIAL ARBITRATION, Zürich/Basel/Geneva: Schulthess (Christian Müller, Antonio Rigozzi eds., 2009).

Mostafa Beshkar, *Arbitration and Renegotiation in Trade Agreements*, JOURNAL OF LAW, ECONOMICS, AND ORGANIZATION ADVANCE ACCESS (2016).

Alexander Bělohlávek, *Impact of Insolvency of a Party on Pending Arbitration Proceedings in Czech Republic, England and Switzerland and Other Countries*, 1 YEARBOOK ON INTERNATIONAL ARBITRATION. Antverpen / Berlin / Copenhagen / Wien / Graz: EAP (European Academic Press) / Neuer Wissenschaftlicher Verlag (Marianne Roth, Michael Geistlinger eds., 2010).

Alexander Bělohlávek, *Místo konání rozhodčího řízení, [Title in Translation: Place of Arbitration]*, 3 PRÁVNÍ ZPRAVODAJ (2004).

Alexander Bělohávek, *Procesní smlouvy a kvalifikace rozhodčích a prorogačních smluv: aplikace hmotněprávní úpravy na smlouvy s procesním účinkem pro futuro, [Title in Translation: Procedural Agreements and Qualification of Arbitration Agreements and Choice-Of-Forum Agreements: Application of Substantive Laws to Agreements* with *Procedural Effects Pro Futuro]*, 151(9) PRÁVNÍK, PRAGUE/ CZECH REPUBLIC: ÚSTAV STÁTU A PRÁVA AKADEMIE VĚD ČR V.V.I. [INSTITUTE OF STATE AND LAW, ACADEMY OF SCIENCE CZECH REPUBLIC V.V.I.] (2012).

Alexander Bělohlávek, *Substantive Law Applicable to the Merits in Arbitration*, 8(2/30) ROMANIAN REVIEW OF ARBITRATION – REVISTA ROMÂNÂ DE ARBITRAJ (2014).

Alexander Bělohlávek, *The definition of procedural agreements and the importance to define the contractual nature of the arbitration clause in international arbitration*, 2 YEARBOOK ON INTERNATIONAL ARBITRATION. ANTVERPEN/COPENHAGEN/ZURICH/WIEN: INTERSENTIA/NEUER WISSENSCHAFTLICHER VERLAG (Marianne Roth, Michael Geistlinger eds., 2012).

Alexander Bělohlávek, Tomáš Pezl, *Aplikace procesních předpisů na rozhodčí řízení*, *[Title in Translation: Application of Procedural Laws to Arbitration]*, 16(2) PRÁVNÍ RÁDCE (2008).

Collection of ICC Awards 1991-1995, *Recueil des sentences arbitrales de la CCI*, PARIS /NEW YORK/THE HAGUE/LONDON/BOSTON: ICC PUBLISHING S.A./KLUWER LAW INTERNATIONAL (Jean-Jacques Arnaldez, Yves Derains, Dominique Hascher eds., 1997).

EMMANUEL GAILLARD, JOHN SAVAGE, FOUCHARD GAILLARD GOLDMAN ON INTERNATIONAL COMMERCIAL ARBITRATION, Haag: Kluwer Law International (1999).

THOMAS HIRSE, DIE AUSWEICHKLAUSEL IM INTERNATIONALEN PRIVATRECHT, Tübingen: Mohr Siebeck (2006).

Zdeněk Kapitán, *Volba sudiště v soukromoprávních vztazích s mezinárodním prvkem*. *[Title in Translation: Choice of Forum in Private-Law Relationships with International Dimension]*, 12(1) ČASOPIS PRO PRÁVNÍ VĚDU A PRAXI (2004).

STEFAN M. KRÖLL, ARBITRATION AND INSOLVENCY PROCEEDINGS – SELECTED PROBLEMS, Pervasive Problems in International Arbitration, KLI (Loukas A. Mistelis, Julian D. M. Lew eds., 2006).

Fernando Mantilla-Serrano, *International Arbitration and Insolvency Proceedings*, 11(1) ARBITRATION INTERNATIONAL (1995).

Krzysztof J. Pelc, *Seeking Escape: The Use of Escape Clauses in International Trade Agreements*, 53 INTERNATIONAL STUDIES QUARTERLY (2009).

THOMAS PFEIFFER, FESTSCHRIFT FÜR JOBST WELLENSIEK (2011).

Radim Polčák, *Delokalizovaná jurisdikce a možnosti argumentace extenzivního výkladu § 87 písm. b) OSŘ [Title in Translation: Delocalized Jurisdiction and Possibility to Argue Using Broad Interpretation of Section 87(b) of the CCP]*, 5(1) JURISPRUDENCE (2004).

JEAN-FRANCOIS POUDRET, SEBASTIEN BESSON, COMPARATIVE LAW OF INTERNATIONAL ARBITRATION, Sweet & Maxwell (2007).

ALAN REDFERN, MARTIN HUNTER, NIGEL BLACKABY, CONSTANTINE PARTASIDES, LAW AND PRACTICE OF INTERNATIONAL COMMERCIAL ARBITRATION, London: Sweet & Maxwell (2004).

José Rosell, Prager Harvey, *International Arbitration and Bankruptcy: United States, France and the ICC*, 18(4) JOURNAL OF INTERNATIONAL ARBITRATION (2001).

NADĚŽDA ROZEHNALOVÁ, INSTITUTY MEZINÁRODNÍHO PRÁVA SOUKROMÉHO. [TITLE IN TRANSLATION: INSTRUMENTS OF PRIVATE INTERNATIONAL LAW], Prague: Wolters Kluwer ČR (1st ed., 2016).

Naděžda Rozehnalová, *Určení fóra a jeho význam pro spory s mezinárodním prvkem, [Title in Translation: Determination of the Forum and Its Importance for Disputes with an International Dimension]*, 1(4) BULLETIN ADVOKACIE (2005).

Naděžda Rozehnalová, *Určení fóra a jeho význam pro spory s mezinárodním prvkem, [Title in Translation: Determination of the Forum and Its Importance for Disputes with an International Dimension]*, 2(5) BULLETIN ADVOKACIE (2005).

KVĚTOSLAV RŮŽIČKA, ROZHODČÍ ŘÍZENÍ PŘED ROZHODČÍM SOUDEM PŘI HOSPODÁŘSKÉ KOMOŘE ČR A AGRÁRNÍ KOMOŘE ČR, [TITLE IN TRANSLATION: ARBITRATION BEFORE ARBITRATION COURT AT ECONOMIC CHAMBER OF CZECH REPUBLIC AND AGRICULTURAL CHAMBER OF THE CZECH REPUBLIC.] Plzeň: Aleš Čeněk (2005).

David Sehnálek, *Sudiště v elektronickém rozhodčím řízení, [Title in Translation: Venue in Electronic Arbitration]*, 12(4) ČASOPIS PRO PRÁVNÍ VĚDU A PRAXI (2004).

Vilém Steiner, *K teoretické koncepci rozhodčí smlouvy v mezinárodní arbitráži, [Title in Translation: Regarding the Theoretical Concept of the Arbitration Agreement in International Arbitration]*, 1 PRÁVNÍK (1971).

MIGUEL VIRGÓS, FRANCISCO GARCIMARTÍN, THE EUROPEAN INSOLVENCY REGULATION: LAW AND PRACTICE, KLI (2004).

Czech (& Central European) Yearbook of Arbitration®

Elena Zucconi Galli Fonseca |
Carlo Rasia

Recognition and Enforcement of an Annulled Foreign Award

Key Words:
Arbitral awards |
enforcement | *recognition* |
annulled award | *New York*
Convention | *foreign award*
| *the seat of arbitration* |
Geneva Convention |
recognition proceeding | *stay*
of enforcement

Abstract | *The international practice of the institute of arbitration leads to the possibility of recognizing and executing an annulled award. Modern approaches must allow the foreign award to be released from the provisions of the legal systems of the State of the seat of the arbitration. Because of the difference between grounds for setting aside and for refusal of the foreign award, the most invasive challenging controls in the State where the arbitration is settled must not limit the circulation and thus the effects of arbitral awards. According to this, the choice of the seat cannot prevent the award from being directly enforced in the legal system of destination. Control must be minimalist. The judge of the State where the arbitral award is enforced must prevent enforcement only in the most serious or manifest cases of breaches of generally accepted principles, thus avoiding reviewing the merits of the dispute settled via arbitration.*

| | |

Elena Zucconi Galli Fonseca is a full professor of Civil Procedural Law. She teaches Civil Procedural Law and International and Domestic Arbitration Law at the Alma Mater Studiorum-University of Bologna, School of Law. She has written more than seventy books, articles and essays. Her research interests include arbitration, with particular reference to the arbitral convention, arbitration and company law, arbitral awards; *res iudicata*, objective and subjective limits, connections between rights and collateral estoppel. Among her books are *La convenzione arbitrale rituale nei confronti dei terzi* (The Arbitral Convention and Third Persons) Milan, 2006 and *Pregiudizialità e rinvio. Contributo allo studio dei limiti soggettivi dell'accertamento* (Contribute to the Doctrine of Res Judicata and Third Persons), Bologna, 2011. She is a member of the Italian Association of Civil Procedure Law, and of the International Association of Procedural Law. She also practices civil and commercial law in Bologna. Her address is: Università di Bologna, Scuola di giurisprudenza, via Zamboni n. 22,

Czech (& Central European) Yearbook of Arbitration®

Czech (& Central European) Yearbook of Arbitration®

I. The Circulation of the Foreign Award[1]

3.01. In light of a contemporary tendency towards geographical delocalization of jurisdiction in a globalized world, the parties to a dispute are free to place that dispute almost anywhere, even if that place does not correspond to the one where the facts are carried out or where the effects of the award will be enforced. This applies in particular to arbitration.[2]

3.02. The arbitration award remains a product of the will of the parties and therefore by its nature does not assume, as happens for a State judgment, an exclusive link with the judicial system of the State of the seat of the arbitration.[3]

3.03. Therefore, there is a break in the objective link between the dispute and the private judge called to decide it.

3.04. Nevertheless, the parties must base the arbitration in a certain judicial system (the seat of arbitration), submitting, as a consequence, to the rules of the means of control that that judicial system provides.

3.05. The seat of arbitration plays such a central role in the practice of arbitration, since in many cases it is considered the equivalent of the 'forum' in the State solution, to determine the same nationality of the arbitration.[4]

3.06. It is the location of the seat that makes it possible to distinguish between domestic and foreign arbitration.

Bologna, Italy.
E-mail: elena.
zucconigallifonseca@
unibo.it

Carlo Rasia is a professor in charge of Civil Procedural Law at the School of Law of the Alma Mater Studiorum-University of Bologna, where he also teaches Domestic and International Arbitration Law. His main research areas are focused on European Procedural Law and on National and International Arbitration. Among his works is the book *Tutela giudiziale europea e arbitrato* (European judicial protection and arbitration), Bologna, 2010, for which he won the 2015 'Mauro Cappelletti Prize' to a young proceduralist for the best procedural book from the International Association of Procedural Law, and the book *La crisi della motivazione nel processo civile* (The crisis of reasons for judgment in civil trial), Bologna, 2016. He is a member of the Italian Association of Civil Procedure Law. He also practices civil and commercial law in Bologna. His address is: Università di Bologna, Scuola di giurisprudenza, via Zamboni n. 22, Bologna, Italy.
E-mail: carlo.rasia@unibo.it

---

[1] Sections 1, 2, 3 and 6 were authored by Carlo Rasia while sections 4 and 5 were written by Elena Zucconi Galli Fonseca.

[2] Paolo Biavati, Giurisdizione civile, territorio e ordinamento aperto, Milano: Giuffré 151 and 271 (1997).

[3] Paolo Biavati, *Arbitrato internazionale, in* Arbitrati speciali, Bologna: Zanichelli 577 (Federico Carpi ed., 2016).

[4] About recognition and enforcement of a foreign award, see Carlo Rasia, *Subarticles 839 e 840 c.p.c.*, Commentario breve al codice di procedura civile, Milano: Kluwer 3139 ff. (Federico Carpi, Michele Taruffo eds., 2018): Elena Zucconi Galli Fonseca, Diritto dell'arbitrato, Bologna: Bononia University Press 497 (2016); Mauro Bove, *Il riconoscimento del lodo straniero tra Convenzione di New York e codice di procedura civile*, Rivista dell'arbitrato 21 (2006); Mauro Rubino-Sammartano, International Arbitration. Law and Practice, New York: Juris 1367 ff. (2014); Piero Bernardini, *Riconoscimento ed esecuzione dei lodi in Italia*, Rivista dell'arbitrato 429 (2010); Laura Salvaneschi, Arbitrato, Bologna: Zanichelli 984 (2014).

With the latter concept we indicate those arbitrations that are settled in a State other than that of the place of origin and that require a special procedure for the enforcement within them of the settlement rendered by arbitrators.

3.07. Therefore, the foreign award can produce effects within a different State only to the extent that it recognizes or enforces such an award.

3.08. It is important to distinguish between recognition and enforcement of the foreign award.

3.09. 'Recognition' means the attribution to the award of legal effectiveness within a given legal system by a State that does not consider it as a domestic award. Conversely, 'enforcement' means the attribution to the award of the particular effectiveness consisting in the ability to allow the recourse to the means provided for by the law to enforce the award or to achieve any other effects.[5]

3.10. The conditions of recognition and enforcement being similar, we will not make a distinction between them in this article.

3.11. The recognition and enforcement of foreign awards is governed principally by the New York Convention of 10 June 1958, which allows the parties of an arbitration established in a contracting State (or even a non-Contracting State, in States that have reciprocity) to obtain the circulation of the award in all the other Contracting States of the Convention.[6]

II.   The Notion of Foreign Award

3.12. In order to establish whether there can be enforcement abroad of an award, it is first necessary to understand what is meant by an 'arbitral award' according to the New York Convention.

3.13. To this end, it is necessary to identify the law applicable to this notion. In this regard there are several divergent opinions:[7] these refer to (i) the *'lex fori'*, that is the law of the State where recognition and enforcement are sought;[8] (ii) the law of the State of origin of the decision;[9] (iii) an autonomous definition specific to the Convention and inferred from its purpose and its

---

[5]   For example, to publicize the decision itself, in the case that, in consideration of its subject matter, there is a need to proceed to transcription on public registers.

[6]   Article X, 1958 New York Convention.

[7]   In general, amongst scholars, see GARY BORN, INTERNATIONAL COMMERCIAL ARBITRATION, Alphen aan den Rijn: Kluwer Law International 3394 ff. (2014); NIGEL BLACKABY, CONSTANTINE PARTASIDES, ALAN REDFERN, AND MARTIN HUNTER, REDFERN AND HUNTER ON INTERNATIONAL ARBITRATION, Oxford: Oxford University Press Sections 11.01 ff. (2015).

[8]   FOUCHARD, GAILLARD, GOLDMAN, ON INTERNATIONAL COMMERCIAL ARBITRATION, The Hague: Kluwer Law International Section 1668 (Emmanuel Gaillard, John Savage eds., 1999).

[9]   ALBERT JAN VAN DEN BERG, THE NEW YORK ARBITRATION CONVENTION OF 1958, Deventer: Kluwer 46 (1981); FERRUCCIO AULETTA, *L'efficacia in Italia dei lodi stranieri, in* DIRITTO DELL'ARBITRATO, Torino: Giappichelli 544 (Giovanni Verde ed., 2005).

structure, that is to say a uniform notion drawn up on the basis of common principles that can be deduced from international conventions and which is independent of individual State rights.[10]

3.14. We prefer to follow a pragmatic approach to the problem. This allows the use of more than one of the aforementioned criteria, but it assigns a decisive and coordinating role to the third. This is because, where applicable, international conventions prevail over national law, in order to achieve a uniformity of solutions in the different States.[11]

3.15. In any case, this criterion held that a judge is not bound by the qualification given by the arbitrators to their awards.

3.16. In this perspective, and on the base of the discipline established by the New York Convention, it must be assumed that there are three constituent elements of the notion of 'award.'

3.17. First of all, the award must have been pronounced in the context of a proceeding based on the voluntary agreement of the parties to submit to arbitration any dispute which might arise between them in the future or which have already arisen.[12] This excludes the decisions pronounced by arbitrators whose power comes from the law, also known as mandatory arbitrations.[13]

3.18. Secondly, the arbitration proceeding is aimed at resolving a legal dispute, current or potential, between the parties,[14] with the consequence that several types of cases must be excluded from the list of enforceable awards. These include cases where a third party is responsible for determining the subject matter of the contract, the amount of price, or more elements (in the Italian system, *arbitraggi*), and settlement agreements concluded during an arbitration proceeding, unless the settlement has been 'incorporated' in the award (also known as 'agreed or consent awards').[15]

3.19. Thirdly, the award must have the character of definitiveness. In other words, it must contain a ruling no longer changeable by the arbitration panel that issued it.[16] According this criterion, the

[10] Antonio Briguglio, L'arbitrato estero, Padova: Cedam 78 (1999); Andrea Atteritano, L'enforcement delle sentenze arbitrali nel commercio internazionale, Milano: Giuffré 21 (2009).

[11] Jean-François Poudret, Sébastien Besson, Comparative Law of International Arbitration, London: Sweet & Maxwell Section 878 (2007).

[12] Article I paragraph 2 and Article II of the New York Convention.

[13] Luigi Fumagalli, Sub Article 839 c.p.c., in Legge 5 gennaio 1994, n. 25, Padova: Cedam 264 (Giuseppe Tarzia, Riccardo Luzzatto, Edoardo F. Ricci eds., 1995); Serge Lazareff, L'arbitrage forcé, Cahiers de l'arbitrage 14 (2006).

[14] Albert Jan Van Den Berg, Consolidated Commentary in New York Convention, Yearbook Commercial Arbitration 219 (2003).

[15] Yaraslau Kryvoi, Dmitry Davydenko, Consent awards in International Arbitration: From Settlement to Enforcement, Brooklyn Journal of International Law 827 (2015).

[16] See Jean-François Poudret, Sébastien Besson, *supra* note 11, at 883.

judgments that resolve one or more of the questions submitted to the arbitrators, even without exhausting the mandate assigned to them, can be qualified as awards, such as:

    i)   provisional or interim awards, which are decisions that aim to safeguard the rights of the parties while there is a pending procedure without being susceptible to review of the final award;

    ii)   partial awards that definitively decide one or more controversial issues without exhausting the subject matter of the dispute; and

    iii)   awards that decide on preliminary rulings (for example, on the jurisdiction of the arbitrators).

3.20.   On the other hand, the procedural orders of the arbitrators are not enforceable.

3.21.   In general, the provisional measures are not recognizable, because of their non-definitive nature.[17]

3.22.   The main criterion to identify the nationality of the award is that of the seat of arbitration. This setting is confirmed by Article 1, paragraph 1, of the New York Convention, which regulates the recognition of both the awards rendered in the territory of a State other than those in which recognition and enforcement are required, and awards not considered as domestic by the requested State. From this point of view, each legal system establishes nationality criteria for the awards.[18]

III.   The Non-Recognition of the Suspended or Annulled Award

3.23.   According to the provisions of Article 840, paragraph 3, n° 5 of the Italian Civil Procedure Code, the recognition and execution of a foreign award in Italy are refused if the same 'has been declared null or stayed by a competent authority of the State, or pursuant to the law of the State where it has been rendered.'

3.24.   The provision reproduces, almost literally, Article V, paragraph 1, e) of the 1958 New York Convention, according to which recognition and enforcement of the award may be refused, at the request of the party against whom it is invoked, if that party furnishes proof the award 'has been set aside or suspended by

---

[17]   Even if there are some legal systems that equate the provisional measures with awards, as in the Dutch legal system (see Article 1051 of the Netherlands Code of Procedure). See Gary Born, *supra* note 7, at 2934.

[18]   For example, in the Italian system, an award is Italian if the arbitration has its seat in Italian territory (Article 816 Code of Civil Procedure).

the competent authority of the country in which, or under the law of which, that was made'.

3.25. The purpose of the provision is to avoid awards which may circulate in other States, even though they have lost their effectiveness in the legal system where they were seated, due to serious flaws.[19]

3.26. The first reference is obviously to the State of the seat of arbitration.

3.27. The second reference is a hypothesis of 'delocalization' of arbitration. This is an arbitration which, although having its seat in a determined State, is then based in the law system of another State by the will of the parties. For example, this would be from the referral of a foreign law as the law regulating the procedure. This second hypothesis is difficult to carry out in practice as it supposes that the law system of the seat admits an integral 'referral' to a foreign system, even in derogation from its own mandatory rules.[20]

3.28. According Article V, it does not prevent enforcement, on the other hand, of any annulment of the award by the judge of a State other than that of the seat of arbitration or pursuant to the law of the State where the award has been rendered.[21]

3.29. The *'ratio legis'* is based on the assumption that the judgment of suspension or annulment has already been pronounced, since the mere pendency of the setting aside proceeding is not enough. This is true even when, according to the applicable procedural law, this automatically suspends the enforceability of the award. Instead, it is not required that the judgment, of annulment or suspension of the award, has already become final.[22]

3.30. It is debatable whether for the judge of the State *ad quem*, there is a duty to deny the recognition or enforcement of a foreign award which is the subject of a suspended or annulled judgment, or whether it can nevertheless pronounce the exequatur upon the outcome of a review of the foreign judgment.

3.31. This applies in general, except among the States that joined the 1961 Geneva Convention (such as Italy), in respect of which the annulment of the award by the State of origin is a ground for refusal of recognition and enforcement in another State only if it is founded on one of the cases listed by Article IX of that convention. These are the same grounds for resisting recognition and enforcement as provided by Article V, paragraph 1, of the New York Convention with the exception of the grounds of

---

[19] In Italian literature, see Antonio Briguglio, *supra* note 10, at 219; Carlo Rasia, *supra* note 4, at 3147.

[20] Jean-François Poudret, Sébastien Besson, *supra* note 11, Section at 922.

[21] Albert Jan Van Den Berg, *supra* note 9, at 20.

[22] Antonio Briguglio, *supra* note 10, at 220.

refusal of Article V, paragraph 2 (discussing in-arbitrability and public policy). Therefore, the setting based on a violation of internal public order according to the law of the seat does not justify the rejection of the recognition and enforcement according to the European Convention.[23]

3.32. Article V, e), of the 1958 New York Convention does not operate, according to Article VII of the Convention, when in the requested State there are more favorable provisions of national law to the circulation of the award. This includes those that in some juridical systems simply do not include this ground of refusal of recognition (for example, Article 1520 of the French Code of Civil Procedure) or those that limit it to the case of cancellation measures and not also to the case of suspension of the award (Article 1076, paragraph 1, e) in the Netherlands Code of procedure), provisions that case law has held to prevail over the discipline of the New York Convention.[24]

3.33. In Italy, the text of the Article 840, paragraph 3°, of the Code of Civil Procedure ('the recognition or the enforcement... are refused') seems to prevent the recognition of the foreign annulled award.

3.34. Most Italian scholars believe that the recognition and enforcement of the award must be rejected.[25] In this context, a group of scholars, considering that the fate of the recognition of the judgment is ancillary to that of the award, believe that the possible annulment in the original legal system of the foreign award previously recognized will cause the loss of effectiveness of the exequatur already granted.[26]

3.35. Furthermore, Italian case law established that in cases of partial annulment of the foreign award, there is no foreseeable possibility of recognizing the enforceability of only the non-annulled parts of the award, as Article 840 (which reproduces Article V(e) of the New York Convention) does not distinguish between total or partial annulment.[27]

3.36. Other scholars admit the recognition and the enforcement of the foreign award when the annulment in the State of origin

---

[23] The Geneva Convention is an additional instrument, which is not applicable in cases of more favorable domestic rules of the Member States.

[24] In France, a series of judgment of the Supreme Court confirmed the possibility to recognize and enforce an award in France which had been set aside or suspended abroad. The starting point was Cour de cassation, 9 October 1984, *Pabalk c. Norsolor*, REVUE DE L'ARBITRAGE 431 (1985).

[25] Antonio Briguglio, *supra* note 10, at 218; Salvaneschi, *supra* note 4, at 1033-1034. The authors criticized the theory of recognition of an annulled or suspended award in the original legal system, as they considered that it entails a risk of contrast between *res judicata* and does not respect the alleged willingness of the parties to place the arbitration in a certain legal system.

[26] Paolo Biavati, *Subarticle 839 and 840, in* ARBITRATO, Bologna: Zanichelli 1088 (Federico Carpi ed., 2016).

[27] Corte di Cassazione, 7 September 2015, n. 17712.

is not based on annulment grounds that are internationally recognized and substantially coincident with the grounds for refusal provided for by the New York Convention in Article V.[28]

3.37. In our opinion, the international institution of arbitration leads to the possibility of recognizing and executing an annulled award.

3.38. The most modern approach, from the perspective of a juridical globalized world, must allow the foreign award to be released from the provisions of the legal systems of the State of the seat. Having said that, there is a difference between grounds for setting aside and grounds for refusal of the foreign award. Precisely for this reason, the most invasive challenging controls in the State where the arbitration is settled must not limit the circulation and thus the effectiveness (the *effet utile*) of the awards.

3.39. We therefore believe that the choice of the seat with its control means cannot prevent the award from being directly enforced in the legal system of destination.

3.40. It is clear that this control must be minimalist or the judge of the State *ad quem* must prevent the enforcement to the most serious or manifest cases of breaches of principles generally accepted, without invading the field of a substantial revision of the arbitration dispute.

IV. Recognition Proceedings in the Italian System and Stay of Enforcement

3.41. Italian legislation outlines a proceeding similar to the Italian injunction procedure: a first phase, which takes place *inaudita altera parte*, and a second optional phase, on the request of the respondent.[29]

3.42. The party of the arbitration process, or their successor, files an application for the recognition of the award, before the President of the Court of Appeal in the district where the defendant resides, that is to say the other party of the arbitral proceedings, or their successor, against whom they intend to execute the award.

3.43. In the case of residence abroad, the jurisdiction belongs to the President of the Court of Appeal of Rome. If there are several parties, the claimant can file the application only against the party concerned in the enforcement of the award. This is possible

---

[28] Luca Radicati di Brozolo, *I rimedi contro le interferenze statali con l'arbitrato internazionale*, RIVISTA DELL'ARBITRATO 15 (2015).

[29] This is more widely reported in Elena Zucconi Galli Fonseca, *supra* note 4, at 505. On the proceeding, see Paolo Biavati, *supra* note 26; Ferruccio Auletta, *supra* note 9; Antonio Briguglio, *supra* note 10; Andrea Atteritano, *supra* note 10.

only when that part of the award, referred to the respondent, is divisible with respect to the others.

3.44. An original or certified copy of the award, as well as the arbitration agreement, also an original or certified copy, must accompany the application.

3.45. Because of the different tone of Article 839 of the Code of Civil Procedure, with respect to the 1958 New York Convention, doubts were raised both with regard to the necessity that the award and the arbitral agreement must be formally authenticated,[30] and about the necessity of production of the aforementioned documents with the application.[31]

3.46. The President then issues a motivated decree that can accept or reject the application.

3.47. In both cases, opposition can be filed within thirty days from the communication of the decree, which rejects the application, while, in the case of acceptance, from its service.

3.48. If the judge only partially accepts the enforcement, both parties will be entitled to the opposition.

3.49. Therefore, in the case of rejection, the request cannot be filed a second time (at least when the reason of rejection is on the merits), and, in order to avoid *res judicata*, the claimant is obliged to propose an opposition.

3.50. In the case of acceptance, on the other hand, the opposition can be filed by the respondent. Consider what happens if, hypothetically, an award that condemns Tom and Dick to pay a certain sum in solidarity with Harry, but the recognition decree is only opposed by Tom, even though it had been serviced to both of them. Can Dick take advantage of the judgment by which the Court of Appeal refuses recognition by reforming the decree? The answer is negative, because the decree of acceptance, in the absence of opposition, is binding against Dick.

3.51. The interpreters are in favor of a third party's intervention in the procedure, as well as the possibility of challenging the final decision with a specific means, known as the Third-Party Challenge of an arbitral award.

3.52. There is also the case where the application for annulment or the request for suspension of the effectiveness of the award has not been decided yet by a judge of the country of origin. In this case, according to Article 840 of the Code of Civil Procedure, the Italian judge may suspend the proceeding before them, in order to evaluate the outcome of the foreign proceeding, and

---

[30] In a positive sense Corte di Cassazione, 8 October 2008, n. 24856.
[31] In a positive sense Corte di Cassazione, 23 July 2009, n. 17291.

arranging, if necessary, suitable guarantees in favor of the instant party.

3.53. Recall that the judge can choose to continue the proceedings before them, and they could thus pronounce the exequatur, while the award is annulled in the country of origin.

3.54. In this case, as Article 840 of the Code of Civil Procedure prevents the recognition of the award, many authors believe that the enforcement should be immediately canceled, or it could at least be challenged by a specific means called 'revocation'.

3.55. In our opinion, in line with what has been said above, the fate of enforcement will depend on the grounds for annulment of the award in the country of origin, which could be different from the grounds for refusal of the foreign award. In this case, the effectiveness of the exequatur provision cannot be excluded.

V. The Enforcement of the Award Recognized by the Court

3.56. The enforcement of the award proceeds from the publication of the judgment with which, in the opposition, the enforcement is granted.

3.57. On the other hand, it is unclear whether the enforcement decree is provisionally enforceable, pending the term for filing the opposition, or during the opposition proceedings.

3.58. We propose, even with all the doubts of the case, for the positive solution,[32] provided that the opponent can request suspension in analogical application of Article 649 of the Italian Code of Civil Procedure, a provision applicable in injunction procedure.

3.59. It seems to us that there are some arguments in favor of this thesis. One example is the reference, contained in Article 840, to Articles 645 ff, of the Code of Civil Procedure, including Article 649. Another is the rule contained in the New York Convention according to which the conditions for recognition and enforcement of foreign awards must be no more burdensome than those for internal awards.

3.60. However, there are divergent theses. Some scholars deny the automatic enforceability, allowing the claimant to request interim measures that preserve their right during opposition.[33]

3.61. This thesis is based on the provision of Article 840, paragraph 4. As we said before, this provision indicates that if the award has been declared null or suspended in the country of origin, the

---

[32]   See *amplius* Elena Zucconi Galli Fonseca, *L'esecutorietà del lodo straniero in pendenza di opposizione*, Rivista dell'arbitrato 347 (1997). See also Fumagalli, *supra* note 13, at 258 and 262.

[33]   Court of Appeal of Milan, 17 July 1995, Corriere Giuridico 706 (1997), with note of Claudio Consolo, *Sulla provvisoria esecutorietà del lodo straniero tra Article 840 c.p.c. e Convenzione di New York.*

judge can suspend the opposition, arranging suitable guarantees, if necessary. The authors deduce that the first decree does not produce provisional efficacy.

3.62. According to other interpreters, it would be possible to ask for an express declaration of provisional enforceability of the foreign award, pending the term for the opposition based on Article 642 of the Code of Civil Procedure, however not referred to in Article 840, or, in any case, during the opposition proceedings pursuant to Article 648 of the Code of Civil Procedure.[34]

3.63. Regardless, the request for an interim measure, both before and during the proceeding, is always possible, when there are the conditions provided by the Law and the Italian judge does not lack jurisdiction.

3.64. There is a problem of jurisdiction in the hypothesis of an interim request *ante causam*, between the Court of first instance of the place where the measure has to be enforced and the Court of Appeal in charge of the enforcement procedure. Probably the second option is the correct one, given the subject-matter of the recognition proceeding of the arbitration award in Italy.

VI. Concluding Remarks

3.65. Arbitration allows the will of the parties, much better than the identification of a certain jurisdiction, to achieve the targets of delocalization of the dispute.

3.66. To delocalize does not mean to escape from a system of rules, and therefore from a law system. It means the parties can choose to which system to belong. In this way, they subtract themselves from any relationship with the place to which that law system is physically linked.

3.67. Arbitration does not escape this logic. The parties can place the legal relationships in the system they prefer. What can never happen, however, is that the arbitration is totally untied by any sort of legal system, because it is necessary to have a legal system on which to stand to guarantee effective protections.

3.68. Therefore, the foreign award is an award linked to a certain foreign law system and it is effective in the State of origin before the State of enforcement.

3.69. This does not mean that the State of origin, through its own means of challenge, can be an obstacle to the existence and validity of the award. From this point of view, the challenging of the award in front of the judge represents a failure of the arbitration model. Therefore, in order to promote the existence

---

[34] Antonio Briguglio, *Subarticle 840*, *in* La nuova disciplina dell'arbitrato, Milano: Giuffrè 282 (Antonio Briguglio, Elio Fazzalari, Roberto Marengo eds., 1994).

of the award and, in particular, its circulation (a principle that emerges from the New York Convention), it is necessary to avoid creating automatic obstacles to the recognition of the award, as happened in Italy, when the award has been annulled in the State of origin, through a distorted reading of the Article V(e) of the New York Convention.

3.70. In fact, it should not be forgotten that the national judge only acts formally as an official of the internal law system but in substance, is a spokesperson for an internationally oriented supra-system.

| | |

Summaries

FRA [*La reconnaissance et l'exécution d'une sentence arbitrale étrangère annulée*]

La pratique internationale de l'Institut d'arbitrage admet la possibilité de reconnaître et d'exécuter une sentence arbitrale annulée.

Les approches modernes en la matière doivent permettre d'affranchir la sentence arbitrale étrangère des exigences du système législatif de l'État du for. Compte tenu des différences entre les motifs d'annulation et les motifs de rejet d'une sentence arbitrale étrangère, les mesures de réexamen mises en œuvre par l'État où la procédure d'arbitrage a eu lieu, ne doivent restreindre ni la circulation, ni les effets de la sentence.

Partant, le choix du for ne doit pas empêcher l'exécution de la sentence arbitrale sous le système législatif du lieu de destination. Le contrôle doit rester minimaliste. Le juge de l'État d'exécution ne peut empêcher l'exécution que dans les cas les plus graves ou les plus manifestes de violation des principes généralement reconnus, afin d'éviter le réexamen quant au fond du litige qui fait l'objet de la procédure d'arbitrage.

CZE [*Uznání a výkon cizího rozhodčího nálezu, který byl zrušen*]

Mezinárodní praxe institutu pro rozhodčí řízení vede k možnosti uznání a výkonu zrušeného rozhodčího nálezu.

Moderní přístupy musí umožňovat, aby byl cizí rozhodčí nález vyvázán z působnosti ustanovení právního řádu státu sídla rozhodčího řízení. Vzhledem k rozdílu mezi důvody pro zrušení a pro odmítnutí cizího rozhodčího nálezu nesmí nejvíce invazivní přezkumné kontroly ve státě, kde je rozhodčí řízení urovnáno, omezovat oběh, a tudíž ani účinky rozhodčích nálezů.

Na základě tohoto předpokladu nemůže volba sídla rozhodčího řízení bránit tomu, aby byl rozhodčí nález v právním řádu místa určení přímo vykonán. Kontrola musí být minimalistická. Soudce státu výkonu rozhodčího nálezu musí bránit výkonu jen v těch nejvážnějších či nejzjevnějších případech porušení obecně přijímaných zásad, aby se tak vyhnul věcnému přezkumu sporu projednávaného v rozhodčím řízení.

| | |

POL [*Uznawanie i wykonywanie zagranicznych uchylonych orzeczeń arbitrażowych*]

Nowoczesne podejście powinno umożliwiać wyłączenia zagranicznego orzeczenia arbitrażowego z zakresu postanowień prawa kraju siedziby postępowania arbitrażowego. Ze względu na różnice w przesłankach uchylenia i przesłankach oddalenia zagranicznego orzeczenia arbitrażowego nie powinno dochodzić do sytuacji, kiedy najbardziej inwazyjne systemy apelacyjne w państwie, w którym rozstrzygnięto arbitraż, ograniczają obieg, a tym samym skutki orzeczeń arbitrażowych. Zgodnie z tym założeniem wybór siedziby postępowania arbitrażowego nie może uniemożliwiać bezpośredniego wykonania orzeczenia arbitrażowego w porządku prawnym miejsca przeznaczenia.

DEU [*Anerkennung und Vollstreckung eines ausländischen Schiedsspruchs, welcher aufgehoben wurde*]

Moderne Ansätze müssen es ermöglichen, den ausländischen Schiedsspruch aus dem Geltungsbereich der Vorschriften der Rechtsordnung desjenigen Staates herauszulösen, in dem der Sitz des Schiedsverfahrens lag. Angesichts des Unterschieds zwischen den Gründen für die Aufhebung eines ausländischen Schiedsspruchs einerseits und den Gründen für eine Nichtanerkennung eines solchen Schiedsspruchs andererseits darf es nicht dazu kommen, dass von den Prüfungsmechanismen des Staats, in dem das Schiedsverfahren abgewickelt werden soll, gerade diejenigen, die besonders 'invasiv' sind, den Verkehr und damit die Wirkungen von Schiedssprüchen einschränken. Ausgehend von dieser Prämisse darf die Wahl des Sitzes eines Schiedsverfahrens einer direkten Vollstreckung des Schiedsspruchs innerhalb der Rechtsordnung des Bestimmungsorts nicht entgegenstehen.

Czech (& Central European) Yearbook of Arbitration®

RUS [*Признание и приведение в исполнение отмененного иностранного арбитражного решения*]

Современные подходы должны позволять, чтобы иностранное арбитражное решение было исключено из сферы действия положений законодательства государства, в котором находится место проведения арбитража. Учитывая разницу между причинами для отказа и причинами для отмены иностранного арбитражного решения, самые инвазивные процедуры пересмотра в государстве, в котором арбитражное разбирательство улаживается, не должны ограничивать ход, а, следовательно, и действие арбитражного решения. Исходя из этого предположения, выбор места проведения арбитража не может препятствовать прямому приведению в исполнение арбитражного решения в правовой системе места назначения.

ESP [*Reconocimiento y ejecución del laudo arbitral extranjero anulado*]

Los enfoques modernos deben facilitar que el laudo arbitral extranjero sea excluido del ámbito de aplicación del ordenamiento jurídico del Estado donde se encuentra la sede del procedimiento arbitral. Dada la diferencia entre los motivos para la anulación y los motivos para el no reconocimiento del laudo arbitral extranjero, los exámenes de revisión más invasivos realizados en el Estado donde se dirime el procedimiento arbitral no tienen que restringir la circulación y, por consiguiente, tampoco los efectos de los laudos arbitrales. Partiendo de esta premisa, la elección de la sede del procedimiento arbitral no puede impedir que el laudo arbitral sea ejecutado directamente en el ordenamiento jurídico del destino.

| | |

Bibliography

ANDREA ATTERITANO, L'ENFORCEMENT DELLE SENTENZE ARBITRALI NEL COMMERCIO INTERNAZIONALE, Milano: Giuffré (2009).

FERRUCCIO AULETTA, *L'efficacia in Italia dei lodi stranieri, in* DIRITTO DELL'ARBITRATO, Torino: Giappichelli (Giovanni Verde ed., 2005).

ALBERT JAN VAN DEN BERG, *Consolidated Commentary in New York Convention*, YEARBOOK COMMERCIAL ARBITRATION (2003).

ALBERT JAN VAN DEN BERG, THE NEW YORK ARBITRATION CONVENTION OF 1958, Deventer: Kluwer (1981).

Piero Bernardini, *Riconoscimento ed esecuzione dei lodi in Italia*, Rivista dell'arbitrato 429 (2010).

Paolo Biavati, *Subarticle 839 and 840*, *in* Arbitrato, Bologna: Zanichelli (Federico Carpi ed., 2016).

Paolo Biavati, *Arbitrato internazionale*, *in* Arbitrati speciali, Bologna: Zanichelli (Federico Carpi ed., 2016).

Paolo Biavati, Giurisdizione civile, territorio e ordinamento aperto, Milano: Giuffré (1997).

Nigel Blackaby, Constantine Partasides, Alan Redfern, and Martin Hunter, Redfern and Hunter on International Arbitration, Oxford: Oxford University Press (2015).

Gary Born, International Commercial Arbitration, Alphen aan den Rijn: Kluwer Law International (2014).

Mauro Bove, *Il riconoscimento del lodo straniero tra Convenzione di New York e codice di procedura civile*, Rivista dell'arbitrato (2006).

Antonio Briguglio, *Sub article 840*, *in* La nuova disciplina dell'arbitrato, Milano: Giuffrè (Antonio Briguglio, Elio Fazzalari, Roberto Marengo eds., 1994).

Antonio Briguglio, L'arbitrato estero, Padova: Cedam (1999).

Luca Radicati di Brozolo, *I rimedi contro le interferenze statali con l'arbitrato internazionale*, Rivista dell'arbitrato (2015).

Luigi Fumagalli, *Sub Article 839 c.p.c.*, *in* Legge 5 gennaio 1994, n. 25, Padova: Cedam (Giuseppe Tarzia, Riccardo Luzzatto, Edoardo F. Ricci eds., 1995).

Fouchard, Gaillard, Goldman, On International Commercial Arbitration, The Hague: Kluwer Law International Section 1668 (Emmanuel Gaillard, John Savage eds., 1999).

Yaraslau Kryvoi, Dmitry Davydenko, *Consent awards in International Arbitration: From Settlement to Enforcement*, Brooklyn Journal of International Law (2015).

Serge Lazareff, *L'arbitrage forcé*, Cahiers de l'arbitrage (2006).

Jean- François Poudret, Sébastien Besson, Comparative Law of International Arbitration, London: Sweet & Maxwell Section (2007).

Carlo Rasia, *Sub Articles 839 e 840 c.p.c.*, Commentario breve al codice di procedura civile, Milano: Kluwer (Federico Carpi, Michele Taruffo eds., 2018).

Laura Salvaneschi, Arbitrato, Bologna: Zanichelli (2014).

Mauro Rubino-Sammartano, International Arbitration. Law and Practice, New York: Juris (2014).

Elena Zucconi Galli Fonseca, Diritto dell'arbitrato, Bologna: Bononia University Press (2016).

Elena Zucconi Galli Fonseca, *L'esecutorietà del lodo straniero in pendenza di opposizione*, Rivista dell'arbitrato (1997).

Josep Maria Julià

Recognition and Enforcement of Annulled Foreign Arbitral Awards

Key words:
Annulment | arbitral award | double exequatur | enforcement | New York Convention

Czech (& Central European) Yearbook of Arbitration®

Abstract | *This article examines how different jurisdictions have handled the question of enforcement of annulled foreign arbitral awards. This matter is also analysed in connection with the objectives of the New York Convention, and considers the significance of the seat of arbitration and territorial sovereignty, the legal effects of foreign arbitral awards, the scope of discretion under Article V.1 of the Convention, the presumed intention of the parties and the need to maintain some review over the award. Although the New York Convention includes preferences for and against the enforcement of annulled awards, States should record their option within the boundaries of the New York Convention and legislate accordingly. Strictly prohibiting the enforcement of annulled awards bears some risks but a more liberal approach also requires a guarantee of review of international standards during proceedings for recognition and enforcement of foreign arbitral awards.*

Josep Maria Julià founded *Delegaltessen*, a legal boutique for businesses, after leading the litigation and arbitration department of an international firm in Spain for several years. His professional practice mainly focuses on the resolution of disputes as counsel and arbitrator, corporate and commercial law, acquisitions, private equity, competition law and EU law. He advises clients in different sectors, with a special focus on technology, media and communications. E-mail: jmjulia@ delegaltessen.biz

| | |

I.   Introduction

4.01. The question of whether arbitral awards that have been annulled at the seat of arbitration can be recognised and enforced in another State has been the subject of much controversy for decades since the *Norsolor* arbitral award was recognised in France in 1984.[1] Recent developments, such as the worldwide attempts to enforce the arbitral awards in the *Yukos* saga[2] or the still-uncertain impact of the *Achmea* judgment[3] on many arbitration awards under bilateral investment treaties between EU Member States or under the EC Treaty, have revived awareness regarding the feasibility and adequacy of enforcing annulled foreign arbitral awards. A brief review of the treatment of such annulled awards in several jurisdictions, together with an analysis of the possible interpretations of the New York Convention, may shed some new light on the subject.

II.   Enforcement of Annulled Arbitral Awards in Certain Jurisdictions

4.02. We have reviewed some key cases to show how different jurisdictions have tackled the enforcement of annulled foreign awards. The different arguments provided to support or deny such enforcement confirm that there is no uniform international response to this question nor to the application or interpretation of the relevant provisions of the New York Convention.

II.1.   France

4.03. In the pioneering *Norsolor* case,[4] the French *Cour de Cassation* recognised an ICC arbitral award that had been annulled in Austria on the basis of the application of more favourable French legislation in accordance with Article VII of the New York Convention. Under former Article 1502 of French Code of Civil Procedure,[5] the annulment of a foreign arbitral award in the jurisdiction of the seat of arbitration was not one of the grounds for refusing enforcement. The same legal grounds for enforcement were used in 1994 by the *Cour de Cassation* in the

---

[1]   *Pabalk Ticaret Limited Sirketi* v. *Norsolor, S.A.*, French *Cour de Cassation*, Civil Chamber 1, 9 October 1984, 83-11.355.

[2]   *Yukos Capital S.a.r.l.* v. *OJSC Yuganskneftegaz*, four arbitration awards issued in Moscow on 19 September 2006 under the rules of ICAC; *Hulley Enterprises Limited* v. *The Russian Federation*, UNCITRAL, Hague Permanent Court of Arbitration, Case Nº. AA 226; *Yukos Universal Limited* v. *The Russian Federation*, UNCITRAL, Hague Permanent Court of Arbitration, Case N. AA 227 and *Veteran Petroleum Limited* v. *The Russian Federation*, UNCITRAL, Hague Permanent Court of Arbitration, Case N. AA 228.

[3]   ECJ Judgment of 6 March 2018, C-284/16, *Slowakische Republik* v. *Achmea BV*, ECLI:EU:C:2018:158.

[4]   *Supra* note 1.

[5]   Current Article 1520 of French Code of Civil Procedure.

Hilmarton case to confirm the enforcement of an arbitral award annulled in Switzerland, where the court declared that such international arbitration award was not incorporated in the Swiss legal system. Thus, it was existent despite being set-aside by Swiss courts, and its recognition in France was not contrary to international public policy.[6]

4.04. The Court of Appeal of Paris followed the same reasoning in the *Chromalloy* case in 1997.[7] In the *Bechtel* case in 2005, where the New York Convention did not apply, the Court of Appeal of Paris still applied the more favourable French system and considered that annulment decisions, like exequatur decisions, have no international effect as they only concern sovereignty over a specific territory.[8]

4.05. By allowing the enforcement of an arbitral award that was set aside in England, the *Putrabali* case in 2007, served the *Cour de Cassation* to go beyond *Hilmarton* and declare that an international arbitration award, which is not anchored in any national legal system, is in itself an international judicial decision.[9]

II.2. The United States

4.06. Before exequatur in France, the *Chromalloy* award was recognised in the United States (US).[10] Even if Article VII of the New York Convention was applied, the District Court for the District of Columbia also took into account that the word 'may' in Article V.1.(e) of the New York Convention was intended to give discretionary power to the court of enforcement and that recognition of annulment in Egypt would be contrary to US public policy in favour of final and binding arbitration.

4.07. Subsequent decisions cast doubt on such a favourable position on enforcement. In the refusal to enforce an award annulled in Nigeria in the *Baker Marine* case, the Court of Appeals of the 2nd Circuit gave more weight to international comity, the absence of adequate reasons to use its discretion to disregard the annulment and the risk of forum shopping for enforcement by beneficiaries of annulled awards.[11] The reasoning in *Baker*

---

[6]   *Société Hilmarton Ltd* v. *Société Omnium de traitement et de valorisation (OTV)*, French Cour de Cassation, Civil Chamber 1, 23 March1994, 92-15137.

[7]   *République arabe d'Egypte* v. *Société Chromalloy Aero Services*, Paris Court of Appeal, Chamber 1 Section C, 14 January 1997, 95-23025.

[8]   *DGAC Dubaï* v. *International Bechtel Co.*, *Paris Court of Appeal*, Chamber 1 Section C, 29 September 2005, 2004-07635.

[9]   *PT Putrabali Adyamulia* v. *Rena Holding*, French Cour de Cassation, Civil Chamber 1, 29 June 2007, 05-18053.

[10]   *Chromalloy Aeroservices* v. *Arab Republic of Egypt*, 939 F. Supp. 907 (D.D.C. 1996).

[11]   *Baker Marine (Nig.) Ltd.* v. *Chevron (Nig.) Ltd.*, 191 F. 3d 194 (2nd Cir. 1999).

Marine was also followed to deny enforcement of an award annulled in Italy in the *Spier* case[12] and another in Colombia in the *Termorio* case.[13] Apart from reading *Baker Marine* to prevent a review of the foreign annulment decision in the absence of extraordinary circumstances, *Termorio* respected the reasoning in the *Karaha Bodas* cases,[14] which interpreted that the New York Convention distinguishes between a primary jurisdiction of the State at the seat of arbitration and other secondary jurisdictions in the States of enforcement.

4.08. In the *Commisa* case,[15] the Court of Appeal of the 2nd Circuit spelt out the extraordinary circumstances that justified disregard of the annulment decision: the violation of basic notions of justice. The retroactive application of law that deprived the beneficiary of the award of any remedy justified the enforcement of the foreign award in the US despite its annulment in Mexico. By refusing to enforce in the US a Malaysian award that had been annulled in Malaysia but enforced in England, the *Thai-Lao Lignite* case confirmed the restrictive review of foreign annulment decisions. Such review was limited to offences of public policy or fundamental notions of justice, and took into consideration the existence of available remedy and the absence of suspicious involvement by the State against due process.[16] Although the refusal to recognise annulment decisions in secondary jurisdictions other than the seat of arbitration had already been established by the *2004 Karaha Bodas* case on the annulment of a Swiss award in Indonesia and by the *Castillo Bozo* case on the annulment of a US award in Venezuela,[17] *Thai-Lao Lignite* complemented them with the heavier weight of annulment decisions at the primary jurisdiction over enforcement decisions in other secondary jurisdictions.[18] The Court of Appeals of the District of Columbia also confirmed in the *Getma* case the high standard for extraordinary review of annulment decisions at the seat of arbitration by refusing to enforce an OHADA award annulled in Guinea.[19]

[12] *Spier v Calzaturificio Tecnica, S.p.A.*, 71 F.Supp.2d 279 (S.D.N.Y. 1999).
[13] *Termorio S.a. E.s.p. and Leaseco Group, Llc v. Electranta S.p., et al.*, 487 F.3d 928 (D.C. Cir. 2007).
[14] *Karaha Bodas Company, L.l.c.,v. Perusahaan Pertambangan Minyak Dan Gas Bumi Negara*, 335 F.3d 357 (5th Cir. 2003) and *Karaha Bodas Co., L.l.c. v. Perusahaan Pertambangan Minyak Dan Gas Bumi Negara*, 364 F.3d 274 (5th Cir. 2004).
[15] *Corporación Mexicana de Mantenimiento Integral v. Pemex-Exploración*, No. 13-4022 (2d Cir. 2016).
[16] *Thai-Lao Lignite (Thailand) Co., Ltd. v. Government of the Lao People's Democratic Republic*, No. 14-597 (2nd Cir. 2017), at 34 and 44.
[17] *Supra* note 14 and *Juan Jose Castillo Bozo v. Leopoldo Castillo Bozo and Gabriel Castillo Bozo*, 12-CV-24174-Williams (S.D. Fla. 2013).
[18] *Thai-Lao Lignite (Thailand) Co., Ltd. v. Government of the Lao People's Democratic Republic*, No. 14-597 (2nd Cir. 2017), at 34 and 44.
[19] *Getma International v. Republic of Guinea*, No. 16-7087 (D.C. Cir. 2017).

II.3. England

4.09. The English Supreme Court in the *Dallah* case anticipated the eventual use of discretion under the New York Convention to enforce a foreign award if the applicable law that declared the arbitration invalid was contrary to the sense of justice.[20] The decision of the English High Court on some preliminary issues concerning the enforcement in England of the four arbitral awards annulled in Russia in the *Yukos* saga[21] clarified the conditions for the recognition of a foreign annulment decision.[22] Referring to the Court of Appeal in the *Dallah* case,[23] the High Court considered that recognition of the annulment decision requires compliance with the ordinary principles for the recognition of foreign judgments.[24] Although the High Court assumed that the choice of seat of arbitration implied acceptance of the supervisory jurisdiction at the seat and that the annulment decision in such jurisdiction would normally be decisive,[25] it contested recognition of the annulment decision if it was contrary to public policy or if it was obtained by fraud or in breach of rules of natural justice.[26] In any event, the High Court denied the application of the *ex nihilo nihil fit* principle to annulled foreign arbitral awards.[27]

4.10. Even if the reasoning in *Yukos* was confirmed, the High Court in the *Maximov* case refused to enforce an ICAC arbitration annulled in Russia and stressed the high hurdle or heavy burden to establish not only that the annulment decision was wrong but that it was so perverse that it could not have been arrived at in good faith or otherwise than by bias.[28]

II.4. The Netherlands

4.11. The Court of Appeal of Amsterdam recognised the four arbitral awards annulled in Russia in the *Yukos* case because the annulment decision was the result of a partial and dependent procedure.[29] The recognition of an annulment decision was

---

[20] *Dallah Real Estate and Tourism Holding Company* v. *The Ministry of Religious Affairs, Government of Pakistan*, [2010] UKSC 46 (3 November 2010), at 53.
[21] *Supra* note 2.
[22] *Yukos Capital Sarl* v. *OJSC Rosneft Oil Company*, [2014] EWHC 2188 (Comm) (3 July 2014).
[23] *Dallah Real Estate and Tourism Holding Company* v. *The Ministry of Religious Affairs*, Government of Pakistan, [2009] EWCA Civ 755 (20 July 2009).
[24] *Supra* note 22, paragraph 16.
[25] *Supra* note 22, paragraphs 11 and 20.
[26] *Supra* note 22, paragraphs 12 and 13.
[27] *Supra* note 22, paragraph 22.
[28] *Nikolay Viktorovich Maximov* v. *Open Joint Stock Company 'Novolipetsky Metallurgichesky Kombinat'*, [2017] EWHC 1911 (Comm) (27 July 2017), paragraphs 2 and 53.
[29] *Yukos Capital S.à.r.l.* v. *OAO Rosneft*, Court of Appeal of Amsterdam, 28 April 2009, 200.005.269/01.

dependent on the rules for the recognition of foreign judgments, which required review of the jurisdiction of the foreign court, due process and non-contradiction of public policy. The judgment of the Court of Appeal was confirmed by the Supreme Court.[30]

4.12. Some authors have criticised the light burden imposed in the *Yukos* case to prove the breach of due process.[31] Despite confirmation of the possibility to refuse recognition of foreign annulment for grounds that are contrary to Dutch rules for recognition of foreign judgments, the Supreme Court in the *Maximov* case took a more stringent approach when verifying the breach of due process and refused to enforce the arbitral award annulled in Russia.[32]

II.5.   Germany

4.13. The Rostock Court of Appeal in 1999 refused to enforce an arbitral award of the Maritime Arbitration Commission at the Chamber of Commerce and Industry in Moscow that had been annulled in Russia by the Moscow Court of Appeal. The Rostock Court of Appeal applied Article V.1.(e) of the New York Convention and declared that an award was no longer binding when it had been set aside by a competent court.[33] By the time the case reached the Federal Court of Justice, the Russian Supreme Court had reversed the annulment decision and thus the Federal Court of Justice concluded that there were no longer grounds to refuse enforcement under Article V.1.(e).[34]

4.14. In spite of a request to ignore annulment due to the existence of a dictatorship and the undue influence on the court of annulment, in 2007 the Dresden Court of Appeal refused to enforce an arbitral award annulled in Belarus in accordance with Article V.1.(e) because the annulment resulted from grounds covered by Article IX.1 of the 1961 Geneva Convention. Even if the existing case law and the prevailing opinion seems to support refusal to enforce annulled awards, some scholars have suggested that Article 328 of the German Code of Civil Procedure would prevent the recognition of annulment decisions that result from

---

[30]   *OAO Rosneft* v. *Yukos Capital S.à.r.l.*, Supreme Court of The Netherlands, 25 June 2010, 09/02566.
[31]   Albert Jan van den Berg, *Enforcement of Arbitral Awards Annulled in Russia*, 27 (2) JOURNAL OF INTERNATIONAL ARBITRATION, 179 (2010), at 180; and Vesna Lazić-Smoljanić, *Enforcing annulled arbitral awards: a comparison of approaches in the United States and in The Netherlands*, 39 (1) ZBORNIK PRAVNOG FAKULTETA SVEUČILIŠTA U RIJECI, 215 (2018), at 226.
[32]   *Nikolai Viktorovich Maximov* v. *OJSC Novolipetsky Metallurgichesky Kombinat*, Supreme Court of The Netherlands, 24 November 2017, 16/05686.
[33]   Judgment of the Court of Appeal of Rostock, 28 October 1999, 1 Sch 03/99.
[34]   Judgment of German Federal Court of Justice, 22 February 2001, III ZB 71/99.

a violation of the right to be heard or of fundamental principles of German law.[35]

II.6. Spain

4.15. There are no cases in Spain in which an annulled foreign award has been recognised. However, there have been several cases where Spanish courts have been requested exequatur of foreign awards pending annulment. In such cases, the majority of recent judgments granted exequatur of the foreign arbitral award without prejudice to the subsequent eventual request of suspension of enforcement or even reversal of enforcement if annulment was confirmed. Such cases include exequatur of ICC awards pending annulment in France,[36] an award pending annulment in Italy,[37] a VIAC award pending annulment in Austria[38] and an award of the Chamber of Commerce of Bogotá pending annulment in Colombia.[39] Nevertheless, Spanish courts seem to take for granted that a foreign annulment decision would be respected if such was the final outcome of the pending proceedings and, in such case, they would even assume the *ex nihil nihilo fit* principle.[40]

4.16. Such a clear stance against suspending exequatur pending annulment proceedings, which may be understandable to avoid delays and frivolous challenges, yields in the presence of a foreign decision that expressly suspends effects of the award pending annulment. This occurred with the refusal of exequatur of an Argentinean award whose effects had been suspended in Argentina during annulment proceedings.[41] The prevailing opinion among authors also supports the view that the direct application of the New York Convention imposed by Spanish

---

[35] Peter Schlosser cited in William W. Park, *What is to be done with annulled awards?*, in ARBITRATION OF INTERNATIONAL BUSINESS DISPUTES, Chapter II.C.1, 351, 354, Oxford (ed 2012), at 353; and in Vesna Lazić-Smoljanić , *Enforcing annulled arbitral awards: a comparison of approaches in the United States and in The Netherlands*, 39 (1) ZBORNIK PRAVNOG FAKULTETA SVEUČILIŠTA U RIJECI, 215 (2018), at 217.

[36] Resolution of the Judge of First Instance and Instruction of Rubí (Barcelona), 11 June 2007, JUR\2010\96143, and resolution of the High Court of Justice of Catalonia, 15 May 2014, JUR\2014\196691.

[37] Resolution of the High Court of Justice of Andalusia, 29 July 2015, AC\2016\236.

[38] Resolution of the High Court of Justice of Catalonia, 15 December 2016, RJ\2016\6432.

[39] Resolution of the High Court of Justice of Madrid, 23 January 2018, AC\2018\138.

[40] Nothing comes from nothing.

[41] Resolution of Section 10 of the Provincial Court of Madrid, 22 December 2009, JUR\2010\68021.

Czech (& Central European) Yearbook of Arbitration®

Arbitration Law does not allow Spanish courts to recognise annulled foreign arbitral awards.[42]

4.17. The rule of *favor arbitrii* in Article 9.6 of Spanish Arbitration Law favours the validity of an arbitration agreement and arbitrability in international arbitration. Such rule expressly applies to foreign arbitral awards.[43] If we were to accept the prevailing opinion this rule would be devoid of effect because Spanish courts would not be entitled to grant exequatur under the New York Convention when the foreign award had been annulled for grounds of invalidity of the arbitration agreement or non-arbitrability of the dispute. As explained below, Spanish courts taking a more favourable stance to enforcing annulled foreign arbitral award in specific cases cannot be completely ruled out in the future.

II.7. Other jurisdictions

4.18. An award set aside in Algeria was enforced in Belgium in the *Sonatrach* case, but enforcement was based on the absence of opposition grounds under Belgian domestic law rather than the application of the New York Convention.[44]

4.19. In the *Commisa* case, the Court of Appeal of Luxembourg rejected the exequatur of the annulled Mexican award, denying the existence of a more favourable domestic law, discretion or grounds of public order that would allow the review of the Mexican annulment decision based on the interpretation of Mexican law.[45]

4.20. The Swiss Federal Court held that the enforcement of a foreign arbitral award should be refused if the award had been declared null and void or annulled in the country where it was rendered.[46]

4.21. No annulled awards have been enforced in Canada, but in some cases in which annulment proceedings were pending,

---

[42]   Francisco J. Garcimartín & Sara Sánchez, *Sobre el reconocimiento en España de laudos arbitrales extranjeros anulados o suspendidos en el estado de origen*, 8 (1) CUADERNOS DE DERECHO TRANSNACIONAL, 111 (2016); Javier Díez-Hochleitner & Iván Heredia, *Exequátur en España de laudos anulados y suspendidos en el estado de origen*, 13 SPAIN ARBITRATION REVIEW, 93 (2012); Jesús Remón, *La anulación del laudo: el marco general, el pacto de exclusión y el orden público*, 1 SPAIN ARBITRATION REVIEW, 115 (2008); Miguel Virgós, *Arbitraje comercial internacional y convenio de Nueva York de 1958*, 2 LA LEY, 1682 (2007).

[43]   According to Article 9.6 of the Spanish Arbitration Law, arbitration agreements in international arbitration are valid and a dispute arbitrable if arbitration complies with the requirements of the *lex arbitrii* chosen by the parties, the law applicable to the merits or Spanish law. Article 1.2 of the Spanish Arbitration Law establishes that Article 9.6 applies to foreign arbitral awards.

[44]   *Sonatrach* v. *Ford, Bacon and Davis Inc.*, Court of First Instance of Brussels, 6 December 1988, XV Y.B. COM. ARB. 370 (1990).

[45]   *Pemex-Exploración* v. *Corporación Mexicana de Mantenimiento Integral*, Court of Appeal of Luxembourg, 8th Chamber, 27 April 2017.

[46]   *A SA (Switzerland)* v. *B Co Ltd (British Virgin Islands), C SA (Ecuador)*, Swiss Federal Court, 8 December 2003, 834 YB Com. Arb. XXIX (2004).

the suspension of enforcement was granted subject to security being provided.[47]

4.22. Notwithstanding the absence of cases in Singapore, in the *PT First Media* case the Court of Appeal hinted that, irrespective of the debatable discretion in Article V of the New York Convention, it would recognise the *erga omnes* effect of the foreign annulment decision and conclude that there was no award to enforce.[48]

4.23. The notice of the Chinese Supreme People's Court on the implementation of China's accession to the New York Convention provides that the annulment of an award at the seat of arbitration is a mandatory ground for refusing enforcement of such an award.[49]

II.8. The 1961 Geneva Convention

4.24. Even if they have not adopted an interpretation of the New York Convention favourable to enforcement of foreign annulled awards, Article IX of the 1961 Geneva Convention imposes on Contracting States the recognition of foreign arbitral awards that have been annulled for reasons other than the grounds in Article V.1.(a) to (d) of the New York Convention. Such could be the case if the foreign award had been annulled at the seat for reasons of arbitrability or public policy. The importance of the 1961 Geneva Convention should not be disregarded because it has been ratified by thirty-one States, including Russia, many other Eastern European States and non-European States such as Cuba and Burkina Faso.[50] The application of the 1961 Geneva Convention requires an arbitration agreement between two parties resident in different Contracting States but even in such a case, courts occasionally do not apply the Convention in the absence of a request to do so by the parties[51] or for lack

---

[47] *Schreter* v. *Gasmac Inc.*, Ontario Court of Justice General Division, 13 February 1992, 89 DLR (4th) 365 (1992); *Europcar Italia S.p.A.* v. *Alba Tours International Inc.*, Ontario Court of Justice General Division, 21 January 1997, OJ 133, 23 OTC 376 (1997); *Powerex Corp.* V. *Alcan Inc.*, Supreme Court of British Columbia, 30 June 2004, BCSC 876 (2004); *Dalimpex Ltd.* v. *Janicki*, Ontario Court of Appeal, 30 May 2003, 228 DLR (4th) 179 (2003).

[48] *PT First Media TBK* v. *Astro Nusantara International BV*, Court of Appeal of Singapore, 31 October 2013, 1 SLR 372 (2014).

[49] Notice of the Supreme People's Court on Implementing the Convention on the Recognition and Enforcement of Foreign Arbitral Awards Acceded to by China, 10 April 1987, Fa (Jing) Fa (1987) No. 5.

[50] The 1961 Geneva Convention has been ratified by Albania, Austria, Azerbaijan, Belarus, Belgium, Bosnia and Herzegovina, Bulgaria, Burkina Faso, Croatia, Cuba, Czech Republic, Denmark, France, Germany, Hungary, Italy, Kazakhstan, Latvia, Luxembourg, Montenegro, Poland, Republic of Moldova, Romania, Russian Federation, Serbia, Slovakia, Slovenia, Spain, The former Yugoslav Republic of Macedonia, Turkey and Ukraine.

[51] *Supra* note 33.

of information on the grounds for annulment at the seat of arbitration.[52]

III. Interpretation of the New York Convention

4.25. The different treatment of foreign annulled awards in each jurisdiction and the diverse arguments to support or object to their enforcement run parallel to the doctrinal debate surrounding the interpretation of the New York Convention and the adequacy of the diverse solutions adopted in each country. Some issues, such as the application of international treaties like the 1961 Geneva Convention or national legislation that are more favourable to exequatur in accordance with Article VII.1 of the New York Convention, may be less controversial but still raise some questions of adequacy.

III.1. Objectives of the New York Convention

4.26. At a risk of over-simplifying matters, a back-to-basics approach could help disentangle an elevated but convoluted discussion. The Title and Articles I.1 and III of the New York Convention clearly suggest, or rather affirm, that the Convention is about recognition and enforcement of foreign arbitral awards, not about recognition and enforcement of foreign judgments on arbitral awards, whether on annulment, exequatur or other matters. References to the annulment or suspension of foreign awards in Articles V.1.(e) or VI are made merely in connection with the implementation at the jurisdiction of the enforcement of the powers to recognise or enforce arbitral awards, not judgments. Unlike Article IV for awards, there is no specific provision imposing requirements of authenticity or language to foreign annulment decisions. The rule in favour of enforcement in Article VII is also restricted to arbitral awards.

4.27. The purpose of the Convention is not to harmonise the treatment of an arbitral award in different jurisdictions, as praiseworthy a goal as this may be. The mere acceptance in Article V that there are grounds to refuse enforcement assumes that there will be cases in which a foreign arbitral award, which is valid and effective at the jurisdiction of the seat, is not so in another jurisdiction, most probably because even equally-defined annulment grounds are also subject to diverging interpretations

---

[52] Resolution of the Judge of First Instance and Instruction of Rubí (Barcelona), 11 June 2007, JUR\2010\96143.

in many countries.[53] This is often the case but does not seem to disconcert any scholar as long as the refusal falls within the scope of Article V. The very application of Article VII is based on the existence of a divergence and the solution is to favour enforcement rather than downplay it to a common position.[54] True uniformisation would require changing the New York Convention, which is hardly achievable or desirable outside international areas with a genuinely integrated legal system. In addition, it would probably result in the removal of exequatur at enforcement like the system for recognition of judgments within the EU. Eliminating double exequatur by removing the exequatur at the seat and the focus in Article III on the law and procedures at the enforcement jurisdiction are two clear indicators that the Convention aimed for more modest goals than uniformisation. Moreover, recognising foreign judgments which reject a request for annulment would be required for consistency of uniformisation, which clearly contradicts the terms of Article V.

4.28.   In the absence of uniformity, Article V.1 contains a lowest common denominator that is consistent with the objective to favour enforcement of the arbitral award reflected in the prohibition of more onerous conditions in Article III or the application of more favourable treaties or legislation in Article VII. The alleged risk of forum shopping for favourable enforcement[55] is unlikely to be significant because the choice of place of enforcement is mainly driven by the location of sizeable assets.[56] It is much easier for parties to make an initial choice or change the seat of arbitration than to move their assets irrespective of their business needs. Furthermore, a forum shopping aligned with the express objective of the Convention to favour enforcement of the award is hardly reprehensible. On the contrary, if annulment at the seat were always to be respected, there could be a perverse forum shopping for seats that would hinder subsequent enforcement and countries with bizarre annulment grounds would be given an international passport to impose their eccentricity beyond their borders.

4.29.   Although Article VII.2 of the Convention already leaves little room for speculation, there is consensus that one of the objectives of the Convention is to eliminate the requirement of

---

[53]   Emmanuel Gaillard, *The Enforcement of Awards Set Aside in the Country of Origin*, 14 (1) ICSID REVIEW, 16 (1999), at 16.

[54]   Jan Paulsson, *Enforcing arbitral awards notwithstanding a local standard annulment (LSA)*, 9 (1) THE ICC INTERNATIONAL COURT OF ARBITRATION BULLETIN, 14 (1998), at 29.

[55]   Jesús Remón, *La anulación del laudo: el marco general, el pacto de exclusión y el orden público*, 1 SPAIN ARBITRATION REVIEW, 115 (2008), at 118.

[56]   *Supra* note 53, at 40.

double exequatur imposed by the 1923 Geneva Protocol and the 1924 Geneva Convention.[57] Due to their limited nature, which normally does not allow a substantive review of the merits, annulment decisions are equivalent to an exequatur based on validity and enforcement rather than a substantive judgment. For this reason, some authors criticise that recognition of the annulment decision at the seat equates to re-introducing double exequatur through the back door contrary to the admitted goal of the Convention.[58] Other authors who are against the enforcement of annulled awards are opposed to applying the rules of judgment recognition to the annulment decision,[59] a paradoxical admission of the non-substantive nature of such annulment decisions that would justify exclusion of their extraterritorial effect.

III.2. Seat, Territory and International Comity

4.30. The theory that the New York Convention assigns a leading role to the jurisdiction of the seat of arbitration is supported by many jurisdictions and scholars.[60] However, Article V.1.(a) of the Convention links validity to the law chosen by the parties and makes no reference to the seat while Article V.1.(d) on the appointment of arbitrators and procedure only applies the law of the seat in the absence of an agreement by the parties. The law of the seat is not the only reference in Article V.1.(e) and it shares honours with the law under which the award was rendered, that is, the *lex arbitrii* which the parties may have chosen. The choice of an arbitration law other than the seat of arbitration may be rare but not unknown. In the *Satyam* case, the Supreme Court of India assumed jurisdiction over annulment of an LCIA arbitration in London on the basis that Indian law was the law of arbitration implicitly chosen by the parties by their choice of

---

[57] Albert Jan van den Berg, *The New York Convention of 1958: An Overview*, ICCA website (2003), at 17; Jan Paulsson, *supra* note 54, at 18; Matthew D. Slater, *On Annulled Arbitral Awards and the Death of Chromalloy*, 25 (2) ARBITRATION INTERNATIONAL, 271 (2009), at 276; Philippe Pinsolle, *The Status of Vacated Awards in France: the Cour de Cassation Decision in Putrabali*, 24 (2) ARBITRATION INTERNATIONAL, 277 (2008), at 288; *Yusuf Ahmed Alghanim & Sons, W.l.l. v. Toys 'r' Us, Inc.*, 126 F.3d 15 (2nd Cir. 1997); resolution of Spanish Supreme Court, 10 December 2002, JUR\2003\720; resolution of Spanish Supreme Court, 20 July 2004, RJ\2004\5817.

[58] Philippe Pinsolle, *The Status of Vacated Awards in France: the Cour de Cassation Decision in Putrabali*, 24 (2) ARBITRATION INTERNATIONAL, 277 (2008), at 290.

[59] Vesna Lazić-Smoljanić, *Enforcing annulled arbitral awards: a comparison of approaches in the United States and in The Netherlands*, 39 (1) ZBORNIK PRAVNOG FAKULTETA SVEUČILIŠTA U RIJECI, 215 (2018), at 228.

[60] *Supra* note 14; Albert Jan van den Berg, *Supra* note 31 at 182; Javier Díez-Hochleitner & Iván Heredia, *Supra* note 42, at 100; Maria Slobodchikova, *Enforcement of Annulled Arbitral Awards in the United States: Discretion to Confirm an Arbitral Award Constrained by Principles of Comity*, in 40 UNDER 40 INTERNATIONAL ARBITRATION, Madrid, Dykinson, 469 (C. González Bueno ed. 2018), at 477.

substantive law.[61] A similar situation might arise in jurisdictions that recognise such implied choices, such as in England in the *Sulamerica* or *Arsanovia* cases.[62] The most important task of the seat of arbitration in the New York Convention is not to allocate primary or secondary jurisdictions, but rather to ensure the ancestral principle of territorial sovereignty. Once the seat of arbitration outside the territory of a State determines the application of the Convention according to Article I.1, Article III ensures that any enforcement in the territory of a State is consistent with the rules of enforcement in such territory.

Article V.1 restricts the principle of territorial sovereignty not for reasons of recognition of a primary jurisdiction at the seat or international uniformisation but to achieve the declared goal of the convention: to favour enforcement of foreign arbitral awards. In view of the diverse outlook in international arbitration, the logic of Article V.1.(e) fits as a piece of *real politik* to leave open the possibility to maintain some remnants of the then existing regime. In fact, the option to recognise an extraterritorial effect to the annulment decision implies a limited revival of the double exequatur.[63] Yet many jurisdictions opt for it for the sake of international comity, either by recognition of a major part of the jurisdiction of the seat in the supervision of the award or by mere application of rules for recognition of foreign judgments.[64] The problem with such a policy is that those States still wish to keep some safeguard in the form of a final due-process check. Ultimately, by reviewing the international adequacy of foreign jurisdictions, such States risk denting the very same international comity that they intended to respect. Thus, it may be wiser to stick to good old territorial sovereignty, decide what you are going to enforce in your territory and, avoiding the censure of other jurisdictions, just ignore foreign annulment decisions.

III.3. Discretion and the Discrete Authority of Foreign Arbitral Awards

4.31. The wording of Article V of the New York Convention in various languages has raised much controversy.[65] Given the wording of

---

[61] *Venture Global Engineering v. Satyam Computer Services Ltd,* Civ. App. No. 309 of 2008 (Sup. Ct of India, 10 January 2008).

[62] *Sulamerica Cia Nacional de Seguros SA & Ors v. Enesa Engenharia SA & Ors,* [2012] EWCA Civ 638 (16 May 2012); *Arsanovia Ltd & Ors v. Cruz City 1Mauritius Holdings,* [2012] EWHC 3702 (Comm) (20 December 2012).

[63] *Supra* note 53, at 33.

[64] *Supra* sections II.2, II.3 and II.4.

[65] Albert Jan van den Berg, *supra* note 31, at 190; Jan Paulsson, *May or Must Under the New York Convention: An Exercise in Syntax and Linguistics,* 14 (2) ARBITRATION INTERNATIONAL, 227 (1998).

all the versions, the absence of uniformisation and consistency with the application of more favourable rules in Article VII.1, it seems difficult to deny that discretion is granted in Article V. The question is who holds such discretionary power. Some authors argue that such discretion is given to States,[66] which would be confirmed by the different wording in Article VI where the competent authority is the subject of the active voice of 'may adjourn' and allowed to consider propriety. The problem is that many countries have incorporated the New York Convention merely by reference in their laws, thus wasting an opportunity to clarify whether their judges have any discretion to decide on the legal grounds of V.1 or, in particular, on Article V.1.(e).[67] It would be desirable for countries to clarify in their legislation whether Article V.1.(e) is a ground for refusal to enforce foreign arbitral awards and, if so, whether judges are given any discretion or directions as to how to exercise such discretion.

4.32. The option of countries such as France to exclude annulment at the seat as a ground to refuse enforcement has been criticised.[68] Although the recognition of the international arbitration award as an international judicial decision without a link to any jurisdiction in the *Putrabali* case may be difficult to accept,[69] in practice such universal recognition is not floating in the void of international space but results from the international obligations undertaken by each country under Articles II and III of the New York Convention. The starting point is the recognition of the award and thereafter each country may decide the legal grounds to refuse enforcement in its territory within the limits of Article V. The apparent risk of contradiction is not relevant because uniformisation is not the name of the game. There is no contradiction in enforcement in one country and refusal to enforce in another country. Two different sovereign territories are affected and inconsistency could be explained by the different interpretation of the very same legal grounds or by a more favourable attitude to enforcement in one country. The uncertainty or risk of contradiction within the same country is solved by the ordinary application of the *res judicata* principle as in the *Hilmarton* case.[70]

---

[66] Francisco J. Garcimartín & Sara Sánchez, *supra* note 42, at 121;

[67] Section 1061.1 of German Code of Civil Procedure or Article 46.2 of Spanish Arbitration Law.

[68] Albert Jan van den Berg, *supra* note 31, at 194; Miguel Virgós, *supra* note 42.

[69] *Supra* note 9.

[70] *Société Omnium de traitement et de valorisation (OTV)* v. *Société Hilmarton Ltd*, French Cour de Cassation, Civil Chamber 1, 10 June 1997, 95-18402 95-18403; *supra* note 53, at 24.

III.4. Intention of the Parties and Review of the Arbitral Award

4.33. In order to oppose enforcement of foreign annulled awards, many authors give significant weight to the express choice of *lex arbitrii* by the parties or to their implied choice by selecting the seat.[71] It is rare that parties make an express choice of arbitration law. If they do and in the absence of any contradictory choice, the jurisdiction of enforcement can still take into account such a choice in the evaluation of grounds for refusal under Articles V.1.(a) and V.1.(d) of the New York Convention. If no express choice is made, the choice of seat may not be sufficient evidence of agreement to the annulment procedures. Both Article V.1.(a) and V.1.(d) give precedence to the choice of the parties, which may have chosen institutional arbitral rules that waive any right to challenge the award. In any event, in countries where waiving annulment is not an option and part of public policy, it is doubtful that the parties have made any relevant choice.[72] Practice shows that choice of seat of arbitration is mostly a question of convenience, frequently in search of a neutral venue with little or no intervention of jurisdiction. It does not seem fair to punish parties for their ignorance of the peculiarities of the seat unless it is crystal clear that they wanted to avail of the annulment action at the seat, in which case an enforcement jurisdiction could still consider any foreign annulment decision in taking its decision under Articles V.1.(a) or V.1.(d).

4.34. The enforcement of foreign annulled awards has also been criticised for ignoring the implied intention of parties to have the possibility of limited ulterior review of the award by jurisdiction.[73] This legitimate concern should not hinder enforcement of annulled awards. Firstly, the New York Convention does not prevent any annulment procedure at the seat and, at the most, it may only limit its extraterritorial effect in other countries.[74] Secondly, the Convention does not exclude review at the jurisdiction of enforcement. The catalogue of grounds for refusal in Articles V.1 and V.2 seem sufficient to ease the most significant fears of any party. It is true that the scope of review or the interpretation of such legal grounds may be different in each country but, in the absence of uniformisation,

[71] Matthew D. Slater, *supra* note 57, at 291; Javier Díez-Hochleitner & Iván Heredia, *supra* note 42, at 101; Maria Slobodchikova, *supra* note 60, at 477.
[72] *Supra* note 53, at 44.
[73] Matthew D. Slater, *supra* note 57, at 283; Maria Slobodchikova, *supra* note 60, at 478.
[74] José Carlos Fernández Rozas, *El arbitraje comercial internacional entre la autonomía, la anacionalidad y la deslocalización*, LVII REVISTA ESPAÑOLA DE DERECHO INTERNACIONAL, 605 (2005), at 637.

Czech (& Central European) Yearbook of Arbitration®

the system ensures that the country of enforcement may afford a reasonable protection to the parties in the exequatur procedure.

IV.   Conclusion

4.35.   There is no international uniform treatment of enforcement of foreign annulled awards. The New York Convention embraces all possible alternatives: mandatory or discretionary refusal to enforce annulled foreign arbitral awards or enforcement of such awards. In order to avoid the open nature of the Convention, it is desirable that countries adopt legislation to establish the legal grounds for refusal to enforce foreign arbitral awards within the boundaries of Article V, to decide if foreign annulment is one of such grounds, whether courts are given any discretion in such a case and what circumstances should be considered if such discretion is granted.

4.36.   If a country opts for refusal to enforce foreign annulled awards, it must take into account the danger of importing certain peculiar grounds for annulment and the risk of international tension if exequatur involves passing judgment on the standards of foreign jurisdictions. If a country decides to ignore foreign annulment decisions, it should ensure that the exequatur procedure provides reasonable protection to parties according to international standards. Despite criticism and rarity, this second route aligns with the objective of the New York Convention to favour enforcement of international arbitral awards without encroaching on the traditional principle of territorial sovereignty.

| | |

Summaries

FRA   [*La reconnaissance et l'exécution des sentences arbitrales étrangères annulées*]
Le présent article se propose de réfléchir sur l'attitude des différents États vis-à-vis de l'exécution des sentences arbitrales étrangères annulées. Cette question est analysée, entre autres, à la lumière des finalités de la Convention de New York. L'auteur examine le rôle du siège du tribunal arbitral, le problème de la souveraineté territoriale, les effets juridiques des sentences arbitrales étrangères, les limites du pouvoir d'appréciation quant à l'article V, paragraphe 1, de la Convention de New York, l'intention présumée des parties, ainsi que la nécessité de

préserver la possibilité de réexamen de la sentence arbitrale. La Convention de New York propose des arguments en faveur de l'exécution des sentences arbitrales annulées tout comme des arguments contraires ; les États devraient ainsi adopter des textes juridiques qui restent dans les limites de cette convention. Une interdiction absolue de l'exécution des sentences arbitrales annulées implique des risques, alors qu'une approche plus libérale exige que soit garanti le respect des normes internationales dans le cadre des procédures de reconnaissance et d'exécution des sentences arbitrales.

CZE [*Uznání a výkon cizích rozhodčích nálezů, které byly zrušeny*]
Tento článek se zabývá pojednáním o tom, jak se různé státy (jurisdikce) vypořádaly s otázkou výkonu cizích rozhodčích nálezů, které byly zrušeny. Tato otázka je rovněž analyzována v souvislosti s účelem Newyorské úmluvy, přičemž autor se zabývá významem sídla rozhodčího řízení a územní svrchovaností, právními účinky cizích rozhodčích nálezů, rozsahem uvážení dle čl. V.1 Newyorské úmluvy, předpokládaným úmyslem stran a potřebou zachovat možnost přezkumu rozhodčího nálezu. Přestože Newyorská úmluva obsahuje preference pro i proti výkonu zrušených rozhodčích nálezů, měly by státy volit v rámci mezi Newyorské úmluvy a přijímat právní předpisy tomu odpovídajícím způsobem. Přísný zákaz výkonu zrušených rozhodčích nálezů s sebou nese určitá rizika, avšak liberálnější přístup rovněž vyžaduje záruku přezkumu mezinárodních standardů v rámci řízení o uznání a výkonu cizích rozhodčích nálezů.

| | |

POL [*Uznawanie i wykonywanie zagranicznych orzeczeń arbitrażowych, które zostały uchylone*]
Artykuł omawia podejście różnych państw (jurysdykcji) do kwestii wykonywania zagranicznych orzeczeń arbitrażowych, które zostały uchylone. Problematyka jest analizowana także w świetle celów Konwencji nowojorskiej, przy czym autor rozważa, na ile znacząca jest siedziba postępowania arbitrażowego i suwerenność terytorialna, skutki prawne zagranicznych orzeczeń arbitrażowych, zakres uwzględniania w myśl art. V.1 Konwencji nowojorskiej, zakładaną intencję stron i potrzebę zachowania możliwości ponownego rozpatrzenia orzeczenia.

Czech (& Central European) Yearbook of Arbitration®

Czech (& Central European) Yearbook of Arbitration®

DEU [*Anerkennung und Vollstreckung ausländischer, bereits aufgehobener Schiedssprüche*]

Dieser Beitrag handelt ab, wie sich verschiedene Staaten (Rechtsordnungen) mit der Frage der Vollstreckung aufgehobener ausländischer Schiedssprüche auseinandergesetzt haben. Diese Frage wird zugleich im Kontext des beabsichtigten Zwecks des New Yorker Übereinkommens analysiert; dabei befasst sich der Autor mit der Relevanz des Sitzes des Schiedsverfahrens und der Gebietshoheit, den Rechtswirkungen ausländischer Schiedssprüche, dem von Art. V.1 des New Yorker Übereinkommens gezogenen Ermessungsspielraum, dem unterstellten Parteiwillen und dem Bedürfnis, die Möglichkeit einer richterlichen Prüfung von Schiedssprüchen aufrechtzuerhalten.

RUS [*Признание и приведение в исполнение отмененных иностранных арбитражных решений*]

В данной статье говорится о том, как некоторые государства (юрисдикции) справляются с вопросом приведения в исполнение отмененных иностранных арбитражных решений. Этот вопрос также анализируется в контексте цели Нью-Йоркской конвенции, причем автор рассматривает важность места проведения арбитража и территориального суверенитета, правовые действия иностранных арбитражных решений, объем рассмотрения согласно статье V.1 Нью-Йоркской конвенции, предполагаемое намерение сторон и потребность сохранить возможность пересмотра арбитражного решения.

ESP [*Reconocimiento y Ejecución de Laudos Arbitrales Extranjeros Anulados*]

Este artículo examina el tratamiento en diferentes jurisdicciones de la ejecución de laudos extranjeros anulados. Asimismo analiza la cuestión en relación con los objetivos del Convenio de Nueva york, valorando la relevancia de la sede del arbitraje y la soberanía territorial, la autoridad de los laudos extranjeros, el alcance discrecional del artículo V.1 de la Convención, la supuesta intención de las partes y la necesidad de mantener cierta supervisión del laudo.

| | |

Bibliography

Albert Jan van den Berg, *The New York Convention of 1958: An Overview*, ICCA website (2003).

Albert Jan van den Berg, *Enforcement of Arbitral Awards Annulled in Russia*, 27 (2) JOURNAL OF INTERNATIONAL ARBITRATION, 179 (2010).

Jennifer Cabrera, Dante Figueroa & Herfried Wöss, *The administrative contract, non-arbitrability, and the recognition and execution of awards annulled in the country of origin: the case of Commisa v Pemex*, 32 ARBITRATION INTERNATIONAL, 125 (2016).

Javier Díez-Hochleitner & Iván Heredia, *Exequátur en España de laudos anulados y suspendidos en el estado de origen*, 13 SPAIN ARBITRATION REVIEW, 93 (2012).

Emmanuel Gaillard, *The Enforcement of Awards Set Aside in the Country of Origin*, 14 (1) ICSID REVIEW, 16 (1999).

Francisco J. Garcimartín & Sara Sánchez, *Sobre el reconocimiento en España de laudos arbitrales extranjeros anulados o suspendidos en el estado de origen*, 8 (1) CUADERNOS DE DERECHO TRANSNACIONAL, 111 (2016).

Francisco González de Cossío, *Enforcement of annulled awards: towards a better analytical approach*, 32 ARBITRATION INTERNATIONAL, 17 (2016).

Vesna Lazić-Smoljanić, *Enforcing annulled arbitral awards: a comparison of approaches in the United States and in The Netherlands*, 39 (1) ZBORNIK PRAVNOG FAKULTETA SVEUČILIŠTA U RIJECI, 215 (2018).

Fernando Mantilla-Serrano, *La Convención de Nueva York y los Derechos Nacionales: a propósito de la ejecución de los laudos anulados en su país de origen*, 2 (2) ARBITRAJE, 468 (2009).

William W. Park, *What is to be done with annulled awards?*, in ARBITRATION OF INTERNATIONAL BUSINESS DISPUTES, Chapter II.C.1, 351, 354, Oxford (ed. 2012).

Jan Paulsson, *Enforcing arbitral awards notwithstanding a local standard annulment (LSA)*, 9 (1) THE ICC INTERNATIONAL COURT OF ARBITRATION BULLETIN, 14 (1998).

Jan Paulsson, *May or Must Under the New York Convention: An Exercise in Syntax and Linguistics*, 14 (2) ARBITRATION INTERNATIONAL, 227 (1998).

César Pereira & Luísa Quintão, *Reconocimiento de laudos arbitrales extranjeros anulados: una perspectiva latinoamericana*, 7 LIMA ARBITRATION, 181 (2016-2017).

Álvaro López de Argumedo Piñeiro & Katherine Menéndez, *La intervención judicial en el arbitraje: análisis de jurisprudencia española reciente*, 8 SPAIN ARBITRATION REVIEW, 53 (2010).

Philippe Pinsolle, *The Status of Vacated Awards in France: the Cour de Cassation Decision in Putrabali*, 24 (2) ARBITRATION INTERNATIONAL, 277 (2008).

Luca G. Radicati di Brozolo, *The fate of awards annulled at the seat in light of Thai-Lao Lignite*, TRANSNATIONAL NOTES, March 19, 2014.

Jesús Remón, *La anulación del laudo: el marco general, el pacto de exclusión y el orden público*, 1 SPAIN ARBITRATION REVIEW, 115 (2008).

José Carlos Fernández Rozas, *El arbitraje comercial internacional entre la autonomía, la anacionalidad y la deslocalización*, LVII REVISTA ESPAÑOLA DE DERECHO INTERNACIONAL, 605 (2005).

Kwadwo Sarkodie & Joseph Otoo, *Getma v Republic of Guinea— implications for African arbitration*, 33 ARBITRATION INTERNATIONAL, 167 (2017).

Matthew D. Slater, *On Annulled Arbitral Awards and the Death of Chromalloy*, 25 (2) ARBITRATION INTERNATIONAL, 271 (2009).

Maria Slobodchikova, *Enforcement of Annulled Arbitral Awards in the United States: Discretion to Confirm an Arbitral Award Constrained by Principles of Comity*, in 40 UNDER 40 INTERNATIONAL ARBITRATION, Madrid, Dykinson, 469 (C. González Bueno ed. 2018).

Miguel Virgós, *Arbitraje comercial internacional y convenio de Nueva York de 1958*, 2 LA LEY, 1682 (2007).

Magdalena Krzemińska | Marek Malciak

New Ground for the Refusal of Recognition or Enforcement of an Arbitral Award in Consumer Cases

Key words:
Recognition or enforcement
of arbitral awards | civil
procedure | domestic law |
EU Directive on Consumer
ADR | consumer protection

Abstract | This paper discusses the new ground for the refusal of recognition or enforcement of arbitral awards in consumer cases established in Article 1214(3)(3) of the Polish Code of Civil Procedure. The regulation was introduced on 10 January 2017 as a result of the implementation of Article 11 of the EU Directive on Consumer ADR. The aim of this paper is to explain the relevance of the new regulation, and its influence on the arbitration proceedings and on the system of control of the arbitral award by State courts in domestic post-arbitration proceedings. The authors analyse the manner in which the Directive`s provisions have been implemented into Polish law. In particular, by trying to assess the scope of application of both the Directive`s provisions and the new provisions of the Polish Code of Civil Procedure as well. The discussed ground for the refusal of recognition or enforcement of arbitral awards rendered in disputes with consumer participation has not been further discussed in the Polish judicature and doctrine thus far. However, this regulation may significantly remodel the resolution of disputes between consumers and traders decided in consumer arbitration and the recognition or enforcement of arbitral awards issued in these types of cases.

| | |

Magdalena Krzemińska is an attorney-at-law and senior associate at the Polish law firm Kubas Kos Gałkowski. She collaborates with the court and arbitral proceedings desk and the real estate desk. She provided comprehensive legal assistance for domestic and foreign clients from such sectors as: construction, telecommunication or banking. Her experience includes, among others, international arbitration in the area of multimillion BIT investment disputes in the scope of protection of investments in the real estate sector.
Email: magdalena.krzeminska@kkg.pl

Marek Malciak is an attorney-at-law and senior associate at the Polish law firm Kubas Kos Gałkowski. His practice focuses mainly on litigation and ADR, with particular emphasis on cases stemming from civil law, commercial companies law, corporate disputes as well as unfair competition law. He represented in court proceedings and advised domestic and foreign clients in numerous complex disputes combining different areas of law he specializes in.
E-mail: marek.malciak@kkg.pl

I.   Preliminary Remarks

5.01.   The Act of 23 September 2016 on the Out of Court Resolution of Consumer Disputes[1] introduced into Article 1214 (3) (3) of the Polish Code of Civil Procedure ('CCP') a new ground for the refusal of recognition or enforcement of awards rendered by arbitral tribunals which shall apply to arbitral tribunal awards rendered in disputes between consumers and traders. The regulation implements Directive 2013/11/EU of the European Parliament and of the Council of 21 May 2013 on alternative dispute resolution for consumer disputes and amending Regulation (EC) No 2006/2004 and Directive 2009/22/EC (Directive on ADR in consumer cases)[2] ('Directive') into the Polish legal order.

5.02.   The Directive was drafted against the backdrop of a pan-European trend oriented towards the protection of a consumer as a weaker party to a legal relationship. According to its assumptions, an effective consumer protection policy contributes to the good functioning of the European market and its effective development. In consequence, ensuring a high consumer protection level constitutes one of the main goals of public orders of the European Union and its Member States. This goal is accomplished on multiple levels.[3] One of them is an attempt at creating a system guaranteeing consumers effective access to Alternative Dispute Resolution (ADR) methods, and thus facilitating an easier method of pursuing claims. Solutions stemming from the Directive are to constitute an essential step in this direction and contribute to the increasing popularity of ADR in consumer disputes. Its fundamental goal is to create a European network of entities offering ADR services (the so-called ADR entities) in the scope of consumer disputes and to provide EU consumers with the right to submit a dispute with a trader regarding a sales or service contract to such an entity. The ADR entities network is to consist of recognised and impartial out-of-court institutions, established on a durable basis, and listed in registers kept by Member States' competent

---

[1]   (Journal of Laws 2016, pos. 123). The Act came into force on 10 January 2017.

[2]   (Journal of Laws L 165 of 18.06.2013, et. 63-79).

[3]   Cf. among others Council Directive 85/374/EEC of 25 July 1985 on the approximation of the laws, regulations and administrative provisions of the Member States concerning liability for defective products (Journal of Laws L 210 of 7 August 1985, et. 29—33); Council Directive 93/13/EEC of 5 April 1993 on unfair terms in consumer contracts (Official Journal of the European Communities, L 95, 21 April 1993, et. 29—34); Directive 1999/44/EC of the European Parliament and of the Council of 25 May 1999 on certain aspects of the sale of consumer goods and associated guarantees (Journal of Laws L 171 of 7 June 1999, et. 12—16); Directive 2011/83/EU of the European Parliament and of the Council of 25 October 2011 on consumer rights, amending Council Directive 93/13/EEC and Directive 1999/44/EC of the European Parliament and of the Council and repealing Council Directive 85/577/EEC and Directive 97/7/EC of the European Parliament and of the Council Text with EEA relevance (Journal of Laws L 304 of 22 November 2011, et. 64—88).

authorities, offering dispute resolution in the frames of ADR. The need for introducing solutions of this type for the purpose of consumer dispute resolution is, in particular, connected with the increasing importance of e-commerce (Internet), including cross-border trading in the frames of the EU. This phenomenon forces a review of traditional rights protection instruments used previously and the introduction of adjusted mechanisms for pursuing claims in consumer transactions in all Member States.

II. Principle of Legality and Its Implementation Into Polish Law

5.03.   The Directive introduces a number of solutions, catering to the different methods for out-of-court resolution of consumer disputes.[4] The principle of legality expressed in the Directive's Article 11 is of fundamental significance in the scope of ADR proceedings aimed at resolving a dispute by imposing a solution (which includes proceedings before arbitral tribunals).[5] Referring to provisions adopted in Regulation (EC) No 593/2008 of the European Parliament and of the Council of 17 June 2008 on the law applicable to contractual obligations (Rome I)[6] and in the Convention on the law applicable to contractual obligations opened for signature in Rome on 19 June 1980 (Rome Convention),[7] this principle requires the Member States to guarantee that a resolution imposed onto a consumer and rendered by an ADR entity shall not result in the consumer being

---

[4]   In this scope the Directive identifies three types of ADR proceedings: 1) procedures where the ADR entity brings the parties together with the aim of facilitating an amicable solution, 2) procedures where the ADR entity proposes a solution; 3) procedures where the ADR entity imposes a solution; the Directive does not rule out an intermediate form of proceedings combining two or more such procedures (Cf. Recital 21 of the Directive).

[5]   'Article 11 Legality
     1. Member States shall ensure that in ADR procedures which aim at resolving the dispute by imposing a solution on the consumer:
     (a) in a situation where there is no conflict of laws, the solution imposed shall not result in the consumer being deprived of the protection afforded to him by the provisions that cannot be derogated from by agreement by virtue of the law of the Member State where the consumer and the trader are habitually resident;
     (b) in a situation involving a conflict of laws, where the law applicable to the sales or service contract is determined in accordance with Article 6(1) and (2) of Regulation (EC) No 593/2008, the solution imposed by the ADR entity shall not result in the consumer being deprived of the protection afforded to him by the provisions that cannot be derogated from by agreement by virtue of the law of the Member State in which he is habitually resident;
     (c) in a situation involving a conflict of laws, where the law applicable to the sales or service contract is determined in accordance with Article 5(1) to (3) of the Rome Convention of 19 June 1980 on the law applicable to contractual obligations, the solution imposed by the ADR entity shall not result in the consumer being deprived of the protection afforded to him by the mandatory rules of the law of the Member State in which he is habitually resident.
     2. For the purposes of this Article, 'habitual residence' shall be determined in accordance with Regulation (EC) No 593/2008.'

[6]   (Journal of Laws L 177 of 4.7.2008, et. 6—16).

[7]   (Journal of Laws C 169 of 8.7.2005, et. 10—22).

deprived of the protection afforded to him by the provisions of the law of the Member State where the consumer is habitually resident and which cannot be derogated from by agreement (mandatory provisions).[8]

5.04. One of the tools intended to guarantee the effectiveness of Article 11 of the Directive in the Polish law is the introduction of a new ground for the refusal of recognition or enforcement of an arbitral award into Article 1214(3) CCP. Pursuant to the new Article 1214(3)(3) CCP 'The [state] court shall refuse to recognise or enforce of a judgment of an arbitral tribunal or a settlement reached before an arbitral tribunal if a ruling of an arbitral tribunal or a settlement concluded before an arbitral tribunal deprives a consumer of the protection afforded to them by the mandatory provisions of the law applicable to the agreement to which the consumer is a party, and where the applicable law is a law selected by the parties - the protection afforded to the consumer by the mandatory provisions of the law which would be applicable should no law have been selected.'

5.05. In connection to the transposition of the Directive into Polish law, an analogical solution was introduced in Article 1206(2)(3) CCP providing a new ground for setting aside an arbitral award.[9] Simultaneously, the implementing Act of 23 September 2016 also added a new Article 1194(3) CCP pertaining to observance of protection afforded to consumer by the mandatory provisions of the law where an arbitral tribunal settles a dispute in accordance with the general rules of law or rules of equity.[10] The abovementioned provisions are intended to jointly implement the rule of legality into Polish law.[11]

5.06. It is worth emphasising that according to the new Polish regulation, an arbitral award may be verified from the perspective of the consumer's interest only at the stage following the issuance of such an award – in post-arbitral proceedings

---

[8] Compare also Recital 44 of the Directive.

[9] Article 1206 paragraph 2 CCP: 'Moreover, a judgment of an arbitration court shall be set aside if the court determines that:
1) the dispute cannot be settled by an arbitration court according to this Act,
2) a judgment of an arbitration court is contrary to the basic principles of the legal order of the Republic of Poland (the public order clause),
3) a ruling of an arbitration court deprives a consumer of the protection afforded to them by the mandatory provisions of the law applicable to the agreement to which the consumer is a party, and where the applicable law is a law selected by the parties - the protection afforded to the consumer by the mandatory provisions of the law which would be applicable should no law have been selected.'

[10] Article 1194 paragraph 3 CCP: 'In the case of disputes arising from an agreement a party to which is a consumer, the settlement of a dispute in accordance with the general rules of law or rules of equity shall not lead to depriving the consumer of the protection afforded to them by the mandatory provisions of the law applicable to the given relationship.'

[11] Compare Correlation Table, available at: https://legislacja.rcl.gov.pl/docs//2/12283400/12342485/1234 2486/dokument222681.pdf, et. 19 (accessed on 25 September 2018).

conducted before a State court. Where any of the parties initiates post-arbitral proceedings, the new ground for the refusal of recognition or enforcement of an arbitral award introduced in Article 1214(3)(3) CCP (similarly as the ground for setting such an award aside provided for in Article 1206(2)(3) CCP) is taken into consideration by the State court ex officio.

5.07.   The question arises whether such a solution guarantees the actual effectiveness of the goal stemming from the Directive. This question requires a thorough analysis reaching far beyond the scope of this paper. It is only worth indicating here that the implementation model adopted by the Polish legislator stirs certain doubts. Specifically, it does not create a mechanism allowing for the effective detection of all cases where an arbitral award may infringe upon consumer's interests protected by the Directive. The State court shall be entitled and, at the same time, obligated to verify an award rendered in arbitral proceedings (or a settlement concluded before an arbitral tribunal) through the prism of appropriate provisions granting the consumer protection, in principle, only in a situation in which this award is not complied with voluntarily and, in consequence, the need arises for it to be recognised or enforced by the State court (or where a motion to set aside thereof is lodged). Meanwhile, oftentimes even if parties do not approve of the settlement stemming from an arbitral award, they do not decide to initiate post-arbitral proceedings. A decision to not attempt to set aside an arbitral award may be (and frequently is) motivated by, e.g. cost-related considerations or the intention to quickly put an end to the dispute. This rationale is relevant in relation to consumer disputes as well (moreover, consumers by assumption do not possess the full or at least sufficient knowledge that would allow them to autonomously, without resorting to an assistance of a lawyer, assess whether they should comply with the rendered award or whether such an award may be contested before a State court due to its defective nature) which creates a situation where the solution provided by the Polish legislator cannot provide a full guarantee of eliminating all awards which are defective in terms of Article 11 of the Directive, from legal transactions.

5.08.   The substantiation of the Act of 23 September 2016 provides only a brief and basic explanation for the introduction of the new regulations into the Code of Civil Procedure (addressing only the change introduced by Article 1194(3) CCP).[12] The

---

[12]   Compare Sejm paper no. 630, act draft substantiation, et. 29, available in Polish at: http://www.sejm. gov.pl/sejm8.nsf/druk.xsp?no. =630 (accessed on 25 September 2018).

changes were discussed in a somewhat more detailed manner in assumptions for a draft of the implementing act which were submitted by the Office of Competition and Consumer Protection.[13] This document, however, does not address the specificity of the adopted solution and consequences stemming from its introduction either. So far, the issue of the application of Article 1214(3)(3) CCP has neither been commented on in case law,[14] nor has it been comprehensively discussed in literature, whereas the changes introduced by virtue of this regulation are worth discussing.

III. The Significance of Article 1214(3)(3) CCP and the Impact of the New Regulation on Arbitral and Post-arbitral Proceedings

III.1. Scope of the Regulation

5.09. In the new Article 1214(3)(3) CCP, the Polish legislator pointed to two situations where a State court shall be forced to refuse the recognition or enforcement of an arbitral award. Firstly, when the ruling being verified deprives a consumer of the protection afforded to them by the mandatory provisions of the law applicable to the agreement to which the consumer is a party. Secondly, in a situation in which the applicable law is a law selected by the parties – the ruling deprives the consumer of the protection afforded thereto by the mandatory provisions of the law which would be applicable should no law have been selected.

5.10. Despite departing from the literal wording of Article 11 of the Directive, the Polish regulation may be applied in situations predicted by the European legislator – both where it is necessary to rule on a dispute of an exclusively domestic nature and in the case of a cross-border dispute, but also in a situation in which parties selected an applicable law. Yet, at the same time, it seems that the implementing Act of 23 September 2016 introduced solutions that to a large degree, reach far beyond the scope

---

[13] Compare Assumptions of the Office of Competition and Consumer Protection to the Act on Out of Court Settlement of Consumer Disputes, September 2014, et. 70-71, available in Polish at: http://legislacja. rcl.gov.pl/docs//1/241375/241376/241377/dokument125933.pdf; (accessed on 25 September 2018).

[14] As on the date of submitting this paper for publication (25 September 2018) the databases which the Authors hereof are familiar with did not contain a single ruling where the settlement was based on Article 1214(3)(3) CCP or that would refer to the meaning of this provision.

required by the Directive which is of fundamental significance for the entire consumer arbitration system in Poland.

5.11.   This is because the scope of application of the Directive has been narrowed down to domestic or cross-border disputes related to contractual obligations stemming from sales contracts[15] or service contracts[16] between traders established in the European Union and consumers residing in the European Union (see: Article 2(1) of the Directive).[17] At the same time, due to the fact that the fundamental principle of ADR proceedings in consumer disputes is the initiation of this procedure by a motion filed by a consumer – proceedings initiated by traders against consumers have been directly excluded from the scope of the Directive's application (see: Article 2(2)(g) of the Directive). Moreover, ADR proceedings by assumption encompass proceedings pending before ADR entities included in national lists of such entities. In turn, other out-of-court proceedings, including those conducted on the grounds of the procedure put in place ad hoc for the needs of a single dispute between a consumer and a trader, have been excluded from under the notion of ADR proceedings (see: Article 4(1)(g) of the Directive and Recital 20 of the Directive).

5.12.   The Polish regulation does not provide for these types of restrictions. It being located in the provisions of Title V of the Code of Civil Procedure regarding arbitral tribunals allows one to hold that the legislator did not intend to restrict the application of Article 1214(3)(3) CCP only to the cases specified under the Directive. Hence, it may not be ruled out that the added regulation shall be deemed applicable not only to arbitral awards rendered in arbitral proceedings before ADR entities which the Directive explicitly mentions.[18] One cannot simply rule out its application to rulings rendered by entities

---

[15]   Pursuant to Article 4(1)(c) of the Directive, 'sales contract' means any contract under which the trader transfers or undertakes to transfer the ownership of goods to the consumer and the consumer pays or undertakes to pay the price thereof, including any contract having as its object both goods and services;

[16]   Pursuant to Article 4(1)(d) of the Directive, 'service contract' means any contract other than a sales contract under which the trader supplies or undertakes to supply a service to the consumer and the consumer pays or undertakes to pay the price thereof;

[17]   However, cf. Recital 16, last sentence, of the Directive indicating a possibility of Member States to adopt or retain in force provisions regarding procedures of out-of-court resolution of such disputes.

[18]   The Polish ADR entities register in 2017 contained only two institutions from the banking & financial sector offering conduct of arbitral proceedings adjusted to the requirements of the Directive, i.e. Arbiter Bankowy [Bank Arbitrator] at Polish Bank Association [ZBP] (with 1,046 arbitration motions lodged with it in 2017) and the Court of Arbitration at the Polish Financial Supervision Authority (with 25 arbitration motions lodged with it in 2017; compared with: 31 in 2016, 36 on 2015, 62 in 2014, 40 in 2013, and 41 in 2012) – Cf. Information on the activity of Consumer Bank Arbitration in 2017, et. 2-3, available in Polish at: http://polubowne.gov.pl/files/152/sprawozdanie_adr_ab_2017.pdf (accessed on 25 September 2018) and The Report on Activity of the Court of Arbitration at the Polish Financial Supervision Authority in 2017, et. 3, available in Polish at: http://polubowne.gov.pl/files/155/sprawozdanie_adr_spknf_2017.pdf (accessed on 25 September 2018).

other than ADR entities in the meaning of the Directive (also in the frames of an ad hoc arbitration between a consumer and a trader) and in cases where arbitral proceedings were initiated by a trader against a consumer or in cases where one of the parties involved in a dispute is an entity (a trader or consumer) from outside of the territory of the European Union. This is because it seems that these types of cases have not been excluded from the scope of application of the new Polish regulation. The relevant provision may be applied to all rulings rendered in the context of consumer arbitration which can constitute a basis for recognition or enforcement of an arbitral award before a Polish State court.

III.2. Change of the Model of Court Control of Arbitral Awards in Consumer Disputes and New Verification Template

5.13. The new regulation substantially alters the model of control exercised by State courts over awards of arbitral tribunals in consumer cases. Previously, the Polish Code of Civil Procedure did not distinguish between the grounds for refusing the recognition or enforcement of an arbitral award depending on the type of case or entities participating in a dispute. In Article 1214(3)(1-2) CCP, the Code established two model grounds for the refusal of recognition or enforcement considered by a court ex officio at the verification of awards of domestic arbitral tribunals. Namely in situations when according to the statute provisions, a dispute is not arbitrable and when the recognition of a judgment of an arbitral tribunal or a settlement reached before an arbitral tribunal would be contrary to the basic principles of the legal order of the Republic of Poland (the public order clause). In turn, in Article 1215(2)(1-5) it determined additional grounds which a State court could take into consideration upon a motion of a party in the event of the verification of arbitral awards rendered abroad (resembling the grounds of a motion to set aside an arbitral award which follows from the fact that a motion to set aside a foreign arbitral award is excluded).[19]

---

[19] Article 1215(2) CCP: 'Notwithstanding the reasons listed in Article 1214, the court shall, at the request of a party, refuse to recognise or enforce a judgment of an arbitration court issued abroad or a settlement reached before an arbitration court abroad if the party proves that:
»   1) there was no arbitration clause, an arbitration clause is void, invalid or has expired according to relevant law,
»   2) the party was not duly notified of the appointment of an arbitrator or proceedings before an arbitration court, or was otherwise deprived of the possibility to defend his rights before an arbitration court,
»   3) a judgment of an arbitration court concerns a dispute which is not covered by an arbitration clause or falls beyond the subject-matter and scope of that clause, however, if adjudication in matters covered by

Therefore, the Polish legislator introduced a standard verification model with the source in Article 36 UNICITRAL Model Law[20] and Article V of the New York Convention on the Recognition and Enforcement of Foreign Arbitral Awards.[21]

5.14. Consequently, from the point of view of substantive law, an arbitral award could be evaluated exclusively through the prism of the public order clause. In adhering to the established case law,[22] State courts did not exercise the instance (appeal) control over arbitral awards, but merely verified their compliance with constitutional norms and primary rules governing individual areas of the law. In proceedings before a State court, a content-related control of an arbitral award was inadmissible. Therefore, State courts did not examine the correctness of evidentiary material evaluation carried out by an arbitral tribunal, the correctness of factual findings constituting the grounds of an award, construction or application of substantive law, or the legitimacy of a specific manner of settlement of a disputed legal relationship.

5.15. Whereas currently, by virtue of Article 1214(3)(3) CCP, State courts have been granted a title and at the same time an obligation to perform a content-related verification of arbitral awards rendered in cases with participation of consumers during post-arbitral proceedings. This constitutes a significant novelty in Polish civil procedure. The correct application of the regulation discussed herein will require a change in the State court's approach to the control they perform and it may not be ruled out that it will also necessitate a critical analysis of an arbitral award to a degree which had previously been excluded from the scope of competence of the State courts. This is because the question arises, whether the new ground for

---

an arbitration clause may be separated from adjudication in matters not covered by that clause or falling beyond the subject-matter and scope of that clause, a refusal to recognise or enforce of a judgment of an arbitration court may only concerns those matters which are not covered by the arbitration clause or fall beyond the subject-matter and scope of that clause,

» 4) the composition of an arbitration court or proceedings before an arbitration court were not in accordance with an agreement between the parties or, if there was no such agreement, with the law of the state where proceedings before an arbitration court were conducted,

» 5) a judgment of an arbitration court is not yet binding on the parties or has been set aside, or its enforcement has been postponed by a court of the state in which or according to whose laws the judgment was issued."

[20] United Nations Commission on International Trade Law, UNICITRAL Model Law on International Commercial Arbitration 1985: with amendments as adopted in 2006 (Vienna: United Nations, 2008).

[21] The New York Convention on the Recognition and Enforcement of Foreign Arbitral Awards, New York, 10 June 1958; ratified by Poland, Journal of Laws of 1962 No. 9, item 41.

[22] Compare among others, the judgment of the Supreme Court of 3 September 2009, I CSK 53/09, Lex no. 527154; decision of the Court of Appeals in Katowice of 26 April 2018, V AGo 11/18, Lex no. 2490086; decision of the Court of Appeals in Katowice of 19 March 2018, V Ago 13/18, Legalis no. 1775551. This stance was also accepted by the literature – cf. MARCIN ULIASZ, *Article 1214* in KODEKS POSTĘPOWANIA CYWILNEGO. TOM IV. KOMENTARZ., 1ST EDITION, Warszawa: C.H. Beck 15 (Adam Marciniak ed., 2017).

the refusal of recognition or enforcement of an arbitral award, grants State courts the competence of making their own factual findings in the case, e.g. in the context required to verify which protective norm should be applied in the case and whether its non-application deprived the consumer of the protection they are entitled to.

5.16. A template for the State court control is to be supplied by mandatory provisions of the State of habitual residence which grant protection to the consumer. The legislator did not explain which provisions are included within the scope of the notion above. However, one should agree with the stance expressed in the literature that these may not only be provisions of an imperative nature (iuris cogentis) which always apply regardless of parties' will, but also semi-imperative provisions, departures from which are possible only to the advantage of the weaker party (in this case: the consumer). Moreover, not only will these be provisions oriented specifically to protect the consumer, but rather all mandatory provisions of law that are protective in their nature.[23] It seems that domestic courts will primarily have to seek these provisions in the legislation implementing EU consumer protection rules. It may not be ruled out, however, that also specific separate regulations included in the public orders of the individual Member States will grant such protection to consumers.

5.17. The circumstances given above may undoubtedly have the impact of increasing the complexity of proceedings for the recognition or enforcement of arbitral awards in consumer cases. The application of the new control template may result in substantial problems for State courts, specifically due to the potential necessity of resorting to legal norms stemming from other public orders which so far do not constitute a significant point of reference for the verification of arbitral awards.

III.3. Change of the Arbitral Proceedings Model in Consumer Cases

5.18. The new regulation should also significantly influence the arbitral judiciary's approach to disputes where a consumer is a party. To guarantee the effectiveness of an arbitral award rendered in a consumer dispute (lack of possibility to effectively contest it in post-arbitral proceedings), arbitral tribunals currently have to take into consideration a new control template

---

[23] Compare BEATA WIĘZOWSKA-CZEPIEL, KODEKS POSTĘPOWANIA CYWILNEGO. KOMENTARZ DO ZMIAN WPROWADZONYCH USTAWĄ Z 23 WRZEŚNIA 2016 O POZASĄDOWYM ROZWIĄZYWANIU SPORÓW KONSUMENCKICH, Komentarz do Art. 1214, nb. 4, Lex/el. (2017).

established in Article 1214(3)(3) CCP and applied by State courts. This assumption interferes with one of the fundamental characteristics and advantages of arbitration – the flexibility of proceedings and, moreover, in a way limits the autonomy of parties' will. Not only in selecting the applicable law, but also in selecting the grounds of the ruling. The most explicit example of that is a circumstance that the above-given requirement for respecting the protection stemming from the mandatory provisions of law applies, on the grounds of the new Article 1194(3) CCP, also in arbitral proceedings in which the case is to be settled on the grounds of general rules of law or rules of equity.

5.19. The regulation at issue directs the arbitral tribunal to a friendly disposition towards the consumer. The obligation of taking an adequate degree of consumer protection into account in a relationship with a trader arises regardless of whether the consumer is indeed the 'weaker' party of the legal relationship. Meanwhile, oftentimes the trader has no advantage over the consumer and in this situation favouring one of the parties of the dispute may lead to violating a fundamental principle of arbitral proceedings, i.e. the principle of the equal rights of parties, in Polish law established by Article 1183 CCP.

5.20. Arbitral tribunals settling consumer disputes should display knowledge of not only mandatory provisions in the scope of consumer relations, but also the other provisions from which the protection granted to the consumer may result from. What is of relevance now, detailed criteria pertaining to the application of a specific provision are frequently ambiguous while they are given the final shape only by the case law. Despite the obligation to take into consideration the absolutely mandatory provisions protecting the consumer, in light of the Polish law, arbitral tribunals have not been granted the right to address State courts with queries regarding substantial issues related to the application of a given provision, neither do they receive any guidelines, recommendations, or indications regarding application of substantive law from State courts. In light of the arbitral tribunal's obligation, formulated in Article 1214(3)(3) CCP, to take into consideration the absolutely mandatory provisions of the law applicable to the contract a consumer is a party to (with the view of recognition or enforcement of an arbitral award), the described circumstance may breed practical problems. This is because an arbitral tribunal may not be familiar with the consumer law regulations of a foreign public order and

Czech (& Central European) Yearbook of Arbitration®

it is not authorised to address a State court in this jurisdiction with a request for an interpretation of relevant provisions of law.

5.21. Moreover, in the case of a conflict of laws, prior to rendering an award, arbitral tribunals are obligated to examine if there are grounds for the application of a corrective mechanism with the view of guaranteeing the consumer an adequate level of protection. Conducting reasoning like that may prove complicated. Consumer protection standards adopted in individual Member States may be highly diversified, since no single homogenous EU consumer law exists. As the literature correctly indicates, the consumer protection areas are to a large degree regulated in the context of harmonisation ordered by EU directives. The scope of implementation of these directives into national orders may, however, be different, ranging from a minimal standard up to a degree reaching significantly beyond the requirements of the directives. Additionally, the provisions of the State of consumer's residency will not grant the consumer more protection in each case. It may so happen that this protection will be identical or even smaller as the protection granted by the applicable law selected by the parties governing the contractual relationship.[24]

IV.   Recapitulation

5.22. The solutions contained in the new Article 1214(3)(3) CCP substantially interfere with the institution of consumer arbitration and the previously established mechanism of the verification of arbitral awards in the context of post-arbitral proceedings. According to its assumptions, its goal, similarly as the goal of the new Article 1206(2)(3) CCP and Article 1194(3) CCP, is to guarantee that the legality principle stemming from Article 11 of the Directive is realised and to guarantee an increase of parties opting for consumer arbitration in the future.

5.23. The domestic case law has not yet provided the insight that is necessary to carry out an analysis of the application of Article 1214(3)(3) CCP to arbitral awards. Neither do the published reports for the year 2017 regarding the activity of ADR entities offering consumer arbitration in Poland provide a foundation enabling one to draw any detailed conclusions on this issue.

5.24. The new regulation forces arbitral tribunals to use provisions which grant the consumer a certain minimal protection standard and introduces strong connections between arbitration and EU law which to a large degree regulates the framework of

---

[24]   ALEXANDER J. BĚLOHLÁVEK, ROZPORZĄDZENIE RZYM I I KONWENCJA RZYMSKA, KOMENTARZ, T. 1, Warszawa: C.H. Beck 1076 (2010).

national regulations oriented towards consumer protection. Adapting to the introduced solutions will oftentimes require arbitral tribunals to possess specialist knowledge in the scope of consumer law, including the knowledge facilitating a comparison of its application in different Member States. It is necessary for an arbitral award to be recognised or enforced, which, after all, is a key issue for the parties of a dispute (for a claimant consumer at least). Compliance with this condition should be, at least by assumption, feasible where disputes are settled by ADR entities listed in national registers in accordance with the provisions of the Directive. This is because these entities frequently specialise in specific sectors, and due to their function as an ADR entity, the area of their specialisation should, in particular, include regulations from the scope of consumer protection law. The practice will show if such qualifications prove sufficient and if the above-mentioned assumption is realised.

| | |

Summaries

DEU   [*Ein neuer Grund für die Verweigerung der Anerkennung bzw. der Vollstreckung von Schiedssprüchen in Verbraucher-streitigkeiten*]
Gegenstand dieses Beitrags ist eine Abhandlung zu dem in Artikel 1214 Abs. 3 (3) der polnischen Zivilprozessordnung verankerten neuen Grund für die Verweigerung der Anerkennung bzw. der Vollstreckung von Schiedssprüchen in Verbrauchersachen. Die Neuregelung datiert vom 10. Januar 2017 und hat ihren Ursprung in der Umsetzung des Artikels 11 der EU-Richtlinie über die alternative Streitbeilegung in Verbraucherangelegenheiten. Ziel des Artikels ist es, dem Leser die Bedeutung der Neuregelung nahezubringen, sowie deren Einfluss auf das Schiedsverfahren und auf das System der Kontrolle über Schiedssprüche, welche die allgemeinen Gerichte in dem an das abgeschlossene Schiedsverfahren anschließenden innerstaatlichen Verfahren ausüben. Die Autoren analysieren die Art und Weise, in der die Bestimmungen der besagten Richtlinie im polnischen Recht umgesetzt wurden. Dabei haben sie sich insbesondere auf die Beurteilung des inhaltlichen Geltungsbereichs der Bestimmungen der Richtlinie sowie der neuen Bestimmungen der polnischen Zivilprozessordnung konzentriert. Der hier abgehandelte Grund für die Verweigerung der Anerkennung bzw. der Vollstreckung von

Schiedssprüchen, die in Streitigkeiten mit Verbraucherbeteiligung ergangen sind, ist in Polen bisher nicht Gegenstand eingehenderer Diskussionen gewesen, und zwar weder in der gerichtlichen Praxis noch in der Lehre – und dies obwohl die Regelung dazu angetan ist, das System der Streitbeilegung zwischen Verbrauchern und Unternehmen im Rahmen von Verbraucherschiedsverfahren sowie die Anerkennung und Vollstreckung von in solchen Verfahren ergangenen Schiedssprüchen in erheblicher Weise umzuformen.

CZE [***Nový důvod pro odmítnutí uznání nebo výkonu rozhodčího nálezu ve spotřebitelských věcech***]

Předmětem tohoto příspěvku je pojednání o novém důvodu pro odmítnutí uznání nebo výkonu rozhodčích nálezů ve spotřebitelských věcech zakotveném v článku 1214 odst. 3 bod 3 polského občanského soudního řádu. Tato úprava byla zavedena dne 10. ledna 2017 v důsledku implementace článku 11 směrnice EU o alternativním řešení spotřebitelských sporů. Účelem tohoto článku je vysvětlit význam této nové úpravy a její vliv na rozhodčí řízení a na systém kontroly vykonávané nad rozhodčím nálezem obecnými soudy ve vnitrostátním řízení probíhajícím po skončení řízení rozhodčího. Autoři analyzují způsob, jakým byla ustanovení směrnice implementována do polského práva. Autoři se zejména zaměřili na posuzování věcné působnosti ustanovení směrnice i nových ustanovení polského občanského soudního řádu. Pojednávaný důvod pro odmítnutí uznání nebo výkonu rozhodčích nálezů vydaných ve sporech s účastí spotřebitele dosud nebyl předmětem podrobnější diskuse v polské soudní praxi ani teorii. Tato úprava však může významně přetvořit systém řešení sporů mezi spotřebiteli a podnikateli rozhodovaných ve spotřebitelském rozhodčím řízení a uznávání či výkon rozhodčích nálezů vydaných v těchto typech případů.

| | |

POL [***Nowa podstawa odmowy uznania albo stwierdzenia wykonalności wyroku sądu polubownego w sprawach z udziałem konsumentów***]

Artykuł omawia nową podstawę odmowy uznania albo stwierdzenia wykonalności wyroku sądu polubownego w sprawach z udziałem konsumentów ustanowioną w art. 1214 § 3 pkt 3 polskiego Kodeksu postępowania cywilnego. Regulacja weszła w życie 10 stycznia 2017 roku jako rezultat implementacji

Artykułu 11 unijnej dyrektywy w sprawie ADR w sporach konsumenckich (2013/11/UE z dnia 21 maja 2013 r.).

FRA [*Un nouveau motif de refus de la reconnaissance ou de l'exécution des sentences arbitrales en matière du droit de la consommation*]

Le présent texte a pour objectif d'examiner un nouveau motif de refus de la reconnaissance ou de l'exécution des sentences arbitrales en matière du droit de la consommation, prévu par l'article 1214, paragraphe 3, point 3, du Code de procédure civile polonais. Cette disposition a été adoptée le 10 janvier 2017 en transposition de l'article 11 de la directive européenne relative au règlement extrajudiciaire des litiges de consommation (directive 2013/11/UE du 21 mai 2013).

RUS [*Новая причина для отказа в признании или приведении в исполнение арбитражного решения в потребительских спорах*]

В данной статье рассматривается новая причина для отказа в признании или приведении в исполнение арбитражных решений в потребительских спорах, установленная статьей 1214 п. 3 абзац 3 польского Гражданского процессуального кодекса. Это регулирование было внедрено 10 января 2017 года как результат имплементации статьи 11 Директивы ЕС «Об альтернативном рассмотрении потребительских споров» (Директива 2013/11/ЕС от 21 мая 2013 года).

ESP [*Nuevo motivo para la negación del reconocimiento o de la ejecución del laudo arbitral en materia de consumo*]

El presente texto trata de un nuevo motivo para no reconocer o no ejecutar el laudo arbitral en materia de consumo anclado en el artículo 1214, párrafo 3, punto 3, del Código de procedimiento civil de Polonia. Dicha legislación fue introducida el día 10 de enero del 2017 a consecuencia de la implementación del artículo 11 de la Directiva de la UE relativa a la resolución alternativa de litigios en materia de consumo (Directiva 2013/11/UE del 21 de mayo del 2013).

I I I

Bibliography

MARCIN ULIASZ, *Article 1214*, in KODEKS POSTĘPOWANIA CYWILNEGO. TOM IV. KOMENTARZ., 1ST EDITION, Warszawa: C.H. Beck 15 (Adam Marciniak ed., 2017).

BEATA WIĘZOWSKA-CZEPIEL, KODEKS POSTĘPOWANIA CYWILNEGO. KOMENTARZ DO ZMIAN WPROWADZONYCH USTAWĄ Z 23 WRZEŚNIA 2016 O POZASĄDOWYM ROZWIĄZYWANIU SPORÓW KONSUMENCKICH, Komentarz do Art. 1214, nb. 4, Lex/el. (2017).

ALEXANDER J. BĚLOHLÁVEK, ROZPORZĄDZENIE RZYM I I KONWENCJA RZYMSKA, KOMENTARZ, T. 1, Warszawa: C.H. Beck 1076 (2010).

Amanda Lee | Harald Sippel

Boldness Be My Friend: Four Suggestions to Facilitate Interpretive Uniformity in the Enforcement of Arbitral Awards Set Aside at the Seat

Key words:
arbitration | enforcement
| setting aside | New
York Convention |
arbitral awards | seat |
Internationalist Approach |
Territorial Approach

Czech (& Central European) Yearbook of Arbitration®

Abstract | *The absence of a global consensus in respect of the approach to be adopted by domestic courts to the enforcement of arbitral awards set aside at the seat undermines the uniformity promised by the New York Convention. This article proposes four potential solutions to the difficulties presented by the existing recognition and enforcement dichotomy, namely: (i) amendment of the New York Convention; (ii) the establishment of a Global Enforcement and Recognition Panel; (iii) a soft law solution; and (iv) the development of a joint interpretive instrument. The authors address the advantages and disadvantages of each proposal and identify some of the practical challenges that will need to be overcome if any of the proposed solutions are to succeed. The purpose of this article is to start a wider dialogue in respect of this controversial topic in international arbitration, with a view to identifying a practical solution that will enable the promise of ease of enforcement made by arbitration to users of the arbitral process to be truly fulfilled.*

Amanda Lee, FCIArb
is a Consultant at
Seymours, London and
acts as an arbitrator.
Her practice focuses on
international arbitration
and commercial litigation.
She is dual-qualified as an
English Solicitor-Advocate
(Civil) and a New York
Attorney.
E-mail: Amanda.lee@
seymourslaw.com

**Dr. Harald Sippel, MBA
FCIArb** acts as the Head
of Legal Services at the
Asian International
Arbitration Centre
(AIAC). Heading a team
of 15 lawyers, he oversees
around 1,000 disputes in
the fields of arbitration,
adjudication, mediation
and domain names.
E-mail: harald@sippel.legal

| | |

I. Introduction

6.01. The relative ease of enforcement of arbitral awards as opposed to decisions by State courts (or any other judicial decisions, for the sake of the argument), is often cited as one of the key advantages arbitration has over other forms of dispute resolution. This must be attributed to the New York Convention on the Recognition and Enforcement of Foreign Arbitral Awards (the 'New York Convention'), which is considered by many to be perhaps 'the most successful treaty in private international law.'[1] Others have referred to it as 'one of the most important and successful United Nations treaties in the area of international trade law.'[2]

6.02. With 159 States worldwide having ratified the New York Convention as of October 2018[3] and the treaty receiving such words of praise, one would tend to believe that the New York Convention is perfect. As successful as it may be, all things considered, there are numerous problems related to the enforcement of foreign arbitral awards and arguably, the promise that arbitration makes to its users, namely the relative ease of enforcement, is oftentimes not a reality.[4] Indeed, as recently as 2013 and thus 55 years (!) after the entry into force of the New York Convention, the Secretary of UNCITRAL was only 'hopeful that with the knowledge of and access to case-law and best practices from around the world, convergence toward universal adherence to the New York Convention, together with its uniform interpretation and effective implementation, can be achieved.'

6.03. Five years later and now in the 60th year of the New York Convention, hardly any progress has been made to achieve true uniformity in the enforcement arena. Above all, there are still two main approaches when it comes to the interpretation of the New York Convention insofar as the enforcement of arbitral awards set aside at their seat is concerned, in particular, the "Territorial

---

[1]   *See* Albert Jan van den Berg, *Convention on the Recognition and Enforcement of Foreign Arbitral Awards*, UNITED NATIONS AUDIOVISUAL LIBRARY OF INTERNATIONAL LAW (2008), available at: http://legal.un.org/avl/ha/crefaa/crefaa.html (accessed on 28 December 2018); Ronald A. Brand, *Transaction Planning Using Rules on Jurisdiction and the Recognition and Enforcement of Judgments*, 358 COLLECTED COURSES OF THE HAGUE ACADEMY OF INTERNATIONAL LAW, THE HAGUE ACADEMY OF INTERNATIONAL LAW 167 (2014)., available at: http://dx.doi.org/10.1163/1875-8096_pplrdc_ej.9789004227323.009_262 (accessed on 31 December 2018).

[2]   The New York Convention Guide, *Message from the Secretary of UNCITRAL* (2013), available at: http://newyorkconvention1958.org/index.php?lvl=cmspage&pageid=10&menu=729&opac_view=-1 (accessed on 31 December 2018).

[3]   For the current status, *see* UNCITRAL, Status, available at: http://www.uncitral.org/uncitral/en/uncitral_texts/arbitration/NYConvention_status.html (last accessed on 31 December 2018).

[4]   For a discussion on difficulties, *see*, for instance, Adebayo G. Adaralegbe, *Challenges in Enforcement of Arbitral Awards in Capital-Importing States*, 23(5) JOURNAL OF INTERNATIONAL ARBITRATION 401, 401-426 (2006).; Flávio Spaccaquerche Barbosa *The Enforcement of International Investment Arbitral Awards: is There a Better Way?*, 6(21) REVISTA BRASILEIRA DE ARBITRAGEM 7, 7 – 34 (2009).

Approach" and the "Internationalist Approach." Under the former approach, the arbitral award is a product of the seat: any award set aside becomes a legal *nullum* and hence cannot be enforced anywhere else.[5] This is the approach adopted by many States.[6] Under the latter approach, as the name indicates, the arbitral award is not connected to the seat. Therefore, whether an award has been set aside plays no role whatsoever when it comes to the enforcement of the award elsewhere. The award exists in the international sphere, completely detached from the seat. This is the approach notably taken by France. Finally, there are a few States that take a mixed approach. In principle, these States follow the Territorial Approach, but they leave the door open to the Internationalist Approach in highly unusual cases.[7]

6.04. The above shows that 'the most successful treaty in private international law' is far from being interpreted and applied uniformly around the world. Against the background of the promise of the relative ease of enforcement that arbitration makes to its users, is it fair to question whether arbitral awards, in light of this inconsistency, are worth the paper they are written on?

6.05. The question would certainly have to be answered in the negative. That being said, clearly something is rotten with the New York Convention. In an attempt to improve the current status quo, this paper puts forward several proposals to overcome the current shortcomings related to inconsistent interpretation and application of the New York Convention. It is the authors' hope that these suggestions will contribute to the debate and, ultimately, lead to changes – so that the promise of the relative ease of enforcement will become more than empty words.

II. Amend the New York Convention

6.06. It may be said that demanding an amendment to the New York Convention or even suggesting that change may be required is tantamount to blasphemy. After all, why should one seek to amend 'the most successful treaty in private international law'?[8]

---

[5] For an overview on these two approaches and which countries follow what approach, *see* As to the extent to which the wording of the French text may be read as permissive, see Amanda Lee & Harald Sippel, *To enforce or not to enforce: that is the question: Arbitral Awards Set Aside at Their Seat*, 8 CZECH (& CENTRAL EUROPEAN) YEARBOOK OF ARBITRATION 135, 141 (2018).

[6] For an overview in East Asia and selected examples from around the world, *see* Sae Youn Kim & Marieke Minkkinen, *An Asian Perspective on the Enforcement of Annulled Awards*, 19 INTERNATIONAL ARBITRATION AND THE RULE OF LAW: CONTRIBUTION AND CONFORMITY, ICCA CONGRESS SERIES 382, 382 – 421 (Andrea Menaker ed., 2017).

[7] *See* Lee and Sippel, *supra* note 5.

[8] *Supra* note 1.

Indeed, we learn from professional sports that one should 'never change a winning team' or 'a winning horse.'

6.07. However, these pieces of sporting wisdom do not apply to the New York Convention for two key reasons. First, no sports team or race horse can be expected to keep winning decade after decade. Renewal is necessary and should, therefore, at least be considered when weaknesses emerge. Secondly, what 'never change a winning horse' and 'never change a winning team' ultimately amount to is – to use yet another proverb – 'if it ain't broke, don't fix it.'

6.08. Given that the Secretary of UNCITRAL himself clearly indicated that uniform interpretation of the New York Convention and its effective implementation had not been achieved by 2013, and five years later, if anything, there are more uncertainties when it comes to enforcement than before, arguably the old adage "*if it aint't broke, don't fix it*" does not apply. This holds true irrespective of whether or not the New York Convention is rightfully regarded as the most successful treaty in private international law. It is against this background that the authors – respectfully – submit that certain changes could greatly improve the effectiveness of New York Convention in this key area of enforcement and help it to achieve the goals the Secretary of UNCITRAL expressed in 2013.

6.09. It should not be forgotten that the authors are far from being the first who dared to propose an amendment of the New York Convention. Among the many proposals and discussions, Prof. van den Berg's "*Hypothetical Draft Convention on the International Enforcement of Arbitration Agreements and Awards*"[9] clearly stands out. But there are numerous others who have proposed changes.[10]

6.10. In light of the earlier proposals of change advanced by others, the authors put forward their proposal to amend the New York Convention, albeit limited solely to changes required to address the problem of the enforcement of arbitral awards set aside at their seat.

---

[9]   New York Arbitration Convention, *Preliminary Draft Convention on the International Enforcement of Arbitration Agreements and Awards: "the Miami Draft"*, available at: http://www.newyorkconvention.org/11165/web/files/document/1/6/16017.pdf (accessed on 31 December 2018).

[10]   For one of the better-known proposals, *see* V.V. Veeder, *Is There a Need to Revise the New York Convention*, in E. Gaillard (ed.), The Review of International Arbitral Awards, available at: https://www.arbitration-icca.org/media/4/65649893142747/media012773755795520veeder_is_there_a_need_to_revise_the_new_york_convention_2010.pdf (accessed on 31 December 2018).

Boldness Be My Friend: Four Suggestions to Facilitate Interpretive Uniformity in the Enforcement ...

Czech (& Central European) Yearbook of Arbitration®

II.1.   What form would such amendments take?

6.11.   Amendments to multilateral treaties can take various forms in international law. The authors propose that an additional protocol to the New York Convention – which could be named "Enforcement Protocol to the New York Convention" – would be the most practicable option. As set forth in the UN Treaty Handbook, '[t]he advantage of a protocol is that, while it is linked to the parent agreement, it can focus on a specific aspect of that agreement in greater detail.'[11] This would precisely be the case with this proposed amendment to the New York Convention. It would be linked to the parent agreement, the New York Convention, but would focus on a specific aspect, namely the enforcement of arbitral awards set aside at their seat, in greater detail. This is an aspect that the New York Convention presently does not address explicitly at all.

6.12.   In order to provide clarity, the authors propose that the approach taken by the Dutch courts in recent years may be appropriate to set as the standard for enforcement of arbitral awards set aside at their seat.[12] To recap, Dutch courts take the view that in principle, arbitral awards set aside at their seat cannot be enforced. They thus generally follow the view *ex nihilo nihil fit*, which undeniably provides for legal certainty, as even proponents of the Internationalist Approach must admit.

6.13.   However, the Dutch approach also offers a certain element of flexibility: in the most severe cases, where the Territorial Approach would lead to very unfair results – as was the case in *Yukos Capital*, where the Court of Appeal in Amsterdam held that 'it is very likely that the judgements by the Russian civil judge setting aside the arbitration decisions are the result of the dispensing of justice that must be qualified as partial and dependent'[13] – the Dutch courts adopt the Internationalist Approach and enforce despite the fact that the award has been set aside at the seat.

6.14.   For practical purposes, it is such approach that the Protocol should adopt. This would offer legal certainty, but still provide scope for the flexibility that appears necessary in extreme cases. Further, the Protocol would make clear that the party seeking to enforce an arbitral award set aside at its seat on such grounds as grave injustice would carry the burden of proof. This would

---

[11]   United Nations, Treaty Handbook, et. 62, available at: http://www.unhcr.org/en-my/protection/statelessness/4d09dbe69/united-nations-treaty-handbook.html (accessed on 31 December 2018).
[12]   For the approach taken by the Dutch courts, *see* Albert Jan van den Berg, *Enforcement of Arbitral Awards Annulled in Russia*, 27 JOURNAL OF INTERNATIONAL ARBITRATION 180 (2010).
[13]   Van den Berg, *supra* note 12.

make sure that in instances where awards are set aside at their seat, the party relying on the judgment of the courts of the place of arbitration would not need to have to defend itself against frivolous enforcement claims by having to show that the setting aside decision was not a severe case of injustice.

II.2. Advantages

6.15. The advantages of amending the New York Convention are easy to conceive. First and foremost, when there is a formal amendment to an international treaty, such amendment makes it clear precisely what the amended approach will be. The language of the amendment would put the new position beyond doubt. In other words, it would bring uniformity.

6.16. Since it is generally understood that the degree of legal certainty on offer dictates the kind of global investment that is attracted,[14] having certainty in enforcement would clearly benefit the world's economy – and thus society – as a whole. Out of the four different approaches the authors discuss in this paper, an amendment to the New York Convention is without doubt the approach that would be the most attractive from this perspective.

6.17. Another advantage is the ease of implementation. As discussed above, the proposed amendment would take the form of an additional Protocol. 'All'[15] that would be necessary to bring the additional Protocol into effect is that the States wishing to subscribe to the uniform enforcement regime would ratify it. In principle this would require minimal effort and cost.

II.3. Disadvantages

6.18. As discussed in the following sub-chapter,[16] one of the major challenges to the successful development and implementation of the proposed Protocol would be the need to persuade a sufficient number of New York Convention signatory States to 'get on board'. It appears highly unlikely that all of the States that have ratified the New York Convention to date would be willing to ratify an additional Protocol. Therefore, although the Protocol may lead to uniformity in principle, as long as there are States that fail to ratify the Protocol, a lack of uniformity will remain. As such, the promise of the Protocol would remain

---

[14] For an overview on foreign direct investment and the importance of the rule of law, *see* Risk and Return Foreign Direct Investment and the Rule of Law, available at https://www.roleuk.org.uk/sites/default/files/files/FDI%26RoL.pdf (accessed on 31 December 2018).

[15] See further below for the obvious challenges and recognition that the 'all' may be quite difficult to implement in practice.

[16] *Infra*, sub-chapter II.4.

unfulfilled. In other words, and somewhat more drastically, as long as there is just one single State that has ratified the New York Convention but not the additional Protocol, uniformity would remain a hope, but not a reality.

6.19. Another disadvantage is that the implementation of the proposed Protocol – by means of ratification by States from around the world – would take a long time. As a first step, the Protocol would have to be drafted and agreed upon. When considering the time that completion of this step typically takes for international treaties, even when taking into account that the proposed amendment is only an additional protocol and not a treaty in its own right, merely agreeing on the language would realistically take several years.

6.20. Additionally, even if one assumed that several dozen States ultimately decided to ratify the Protocol, this would not happen overnight. It would in all likelihood be a very long process, possibly one that would take as long as a decade. Accordingly the effect of the amendment would be far from immediate, and should instead be regarded as a long-term project.

II.4. What Are the Challenges Presented by this Approach

6.21. Although 'only' an additional Protocol to the New York Convention would be necessary to implement the changes the authors have in mind, in reality, the development of a successful additional Protocol to the New York Convention is a very challenging undertaking. This is for various reasons.

6.22. Firstly, a sufficient number of States must be willing to join forces and agree on a Protocol. A critical mass would have to be reached; absent a critical mass it is highly unlikely that efforts would be sufficient to encourage other States to sign the Protocol.

6.23. However, finding this critical mass of States, which in the opinion of the authors would have to be at least fifteen different States, including at least one or two States that have in the past been shown to be an "opinion leader" and have influenced others, will be a challenge. The challenges are threefold. Firstly, it would be necessary to find a sufficient number of States that are willing to ratify an additional Protocol to the New York Convention.

6.24. Secondly, an additional Protocol to the New York Convention would require that the States seeking to implement the additional Protocol share the same view. Although the enforcement of arbitral awards set aside at their seat has been the topic of significant discussion among the arbitration community, many of the 159 contracting States have yet to deal with the question of whether their courts will follow the Territorial Approach or apply the Internationalist approach – or take a new approach altogether. Addressing the second challenge would therefore mean finding a sufficient number of States that are clear about the approach to be taken in the Protocol.

6.25. This leads to the third challenge: given the second challenge, it appears highly unlikely that a consensus can be reached right away. As discussed above,[17] even if one divides the question of enforcement of arbitral awards into two worlds only, the Territorial World and the Internationalist World, several – subtle and major – differences exist as to how such world views are implemented in practice. Therefore, before drafting a Protocol it would be necessary for the proposed signatory States to reach a consensus as to what the new enforcement regime should look like.

6.26. Even if the three challenges: (i) having a critical mass of States that; (ii) are willing to work together on an amendment to the New York Convention; (iii) having agreed on the form and substance of the Protocol, can be overcome, it will not happen overnight. There is a whole mountain to climb in order to reach the goal of ratification.

II.5. Conclusion

6.27. As is clear from the above, Herculean efforts would be required to overcome the many challenges surrounding the ratification of a Protocol. The long process required to reach consensus on international treaties and the difficulty of finding a sufficient number of States that are willing to support the initiative present clear challenges. Unless a critical mass can be reached, the alliance of Protocol signatory States will remain lone wolves in their attempt to achieve uniformity.

6.28. That being said, even the mighty New York Convention grew from humble beginnings. Many of its initial signatories would not have been described as global thought leaders. Only one State ratified the New York Convention in 1958, El Salvador. In 1959, when the New York Convention entered into force, it was ratified by only five additional States: France, Israel, Morocco, Syria and Thailand.

6.29. It is important not to forget that 1958 was quite different from 2018. The Treaty of Rome, which brought about the creation of the European Economic Community (EEC), one of the

^17   *See* Lee and Sippel, *supra* note 5.

European Communities and, predecessor of the European Union, entered into force in 1958, having been signed just a year earlier. The only signatories were Belgium, France, Italy, Luxembourg, the Netherlands and West Germany. In 1958, a series of States in Africa, including Algeria, Cameroon, Ivory Coast, Nigeria, Uganda and Zimbabwe, and in other parts of the world (e.g. Jamaica, Malaysia, U.A.E. and Brunei) had yet to gain independence. Decolonisation had begun only a few years earlier.

6.30. Back in the late 1950s, finding a sufficient number of States willing to support an initiative like the New York Convention posed a far greater difficulty than it would pose today. Whether it would be a private initiative or an UNCITRAL initiative, the sheer number of States in existence today means that there is ample opportunity to find supporters. The challenge is perhaps better characterised as an opportunity.

6.31. The international legal community has shown itself to be capable of developing innovative solutions to worldwide enforcement difficulties. For example, a new initiative with respect to enforcement will soon enter into force: the *Convention* on the Enforcement of International Settlement Agreements Resulting from *Mediation, to be known as the* 'Singapore Mediation Convention'. It is unclear at this stage which States will ratify it; however, the Singapore Mediation Convention serves as a reminder that the challenges presented by treaties with significant numbers of potential signatories can be overcome with sufficient determination.

6.32. Despite the Herculean efforts required, one should not, therefore, disregard the possibility of successfully negotiating and implementing an amendment to the New York Convention without further consideration. Rather, the international legal community should think in terms of seizing opportunities rather than in terms of not being able to overcome challenges.

III. Global Enforcement and Recognition Panel

6.33. Although today's world often seems more divided than ever, there are several encouraging examples of collaboration on a global scale that have been implemented in recent years. The International Criminal Court (the "ICCt") in The Hague is one such collaboration. Established by the Rome Statute, to which 123 different States are party, the ICCt 'is a permanent institution and shall have the power to exercise its jurisdiction over persons for the most serious crimes of international concern, as referred to in this Statute, and shall be complementary to national criminal jurisdictions.'[18]

6.34. In the same vein and in order to facilitate foreign investment and international trade, a Global Enforcement and Recognition Panel (the "Global Panel"), complementary to the enforcement and recognition jurisdictions of national courts, could be established.

III.1. What Form would a Global Enforcement and Recognition Panel Take?

6.35. The proposed Global Panel would be established by an international treaty and under the treaty, the parties would grant jurisdiction to the Global Panel in respect of matters of enforcement only when an award has been set aside at its seat. As is the case with the ICCt, several pre-conditions would have to be met for the Global Panel to exercise its jurisdiction.

6.36. It is the authors' view that such a panel should only exercise its jurisdiction in respect of cases where: (i) arbitral awards have been set aside at their seat; and (ii) there are compelling grounds to disregard the setting aside judgement. Above all – and to impose appropriate limits and avoid overburdening the Global Panel with submissions in respect of all and any awards set aside at their seat – the applicant seeking to enforce the set aside award would have to establish *prima facie* why the Global Panel should review the judgment setting aside the award.

6.37. Like the ICCt and other international institutions, the Global Panel would–– have several judges reviewing the setting aside judgements referred to it. Having analysed a setting aside judgement, the Global Panel would render a recommendation, which the member States would in turn have to respect. There would be two potential outcomes: either enforcement despite the setting aside decision; or no enforcement. The international treaty establishing the Global Panel would thus make it clear that the Territorial Approach applies unless the Global Panel decides that an award should be enforced despite having been set aside by the court at the seat.

III.2. Advantages

6.38. The establishment of the Global Panel would offer legal certainty as its biggest advantage. Every matter of enforcement involving an award that had been set aside would have to be referred to the Global Panel if a party wished to seek enforcement despite

[18] Rome Statute, Article 1.

Boldness Be My Friend: Four Suggestions to Facilitate Interpretive Uniformity in the Enforcement ...

Czech (& Central European) Yearbook of Arbitration®

the award having been set aside. Unilateralism in enforcement would cease to exist as the courts of members States would have to accept the recommendation made by the Global Panel.

6.39. The establishment of the Global Panel as an internationally recognised institution would afford its decisions more weight. The judges sitting on the Global Panel would come from member States, which would give the court great importance, as is the case in respect of the ICCt or the CJEU, to name but two courts that are broadly similar in nature.

6.40. For practical purposes, it may be sensible to attach the Global Panel to the UNCITRAL Secretariat in Vienna. The Global Panel could thus become the global guardian of recognition and enforcement in arbitral proceedings. With its expertise stemming from enforcement decisions and generally, arbitration matters, it could become a vital advisor to the UNCITRAL Secretariat and play an important role in the further development of international arbitration.

III.3. Disadvantages

6.41. As great as the potential for the Global Panel to achieve uniformity in recognition and enforcement matters in respect of arbitral awards that were set aside at the seat may be, the Global Panel would not have any jurisdiction over 'regular' matters of recognition/enforcement. This could in some instances lead to contradicting approaches to questions of enforcement.

6.42. The financial implications of developing, establishing and maintaining the Global Panel cannot be underestimated. The financial disadvantages are two-fold. Firstly, any procedure before an international organ would come at a price for the party attempting to enforce the arbitral award despite its earlier setting aside. The ability to refer a set aside award to the Global Panel would accordingly add a further layer of legal costs to enforcement. Such costs may or may not compare favourably with the costs of seeking to enforce the set aside award in another contracting State, as is the prevailing practice at present.

6.43. Secondly, the Global Panel itself would require substantial funds in order to function. Although no reasonable estimate can be given as the actual cost would depend on variables such as the structure, location and number of permanent staff, to put things into perspective, the ICCt's Programme Budget for the year 2018 alone is €147,431,500.[19] This is a substantial amount. Financing for the establishment and continuing operation of the

---

[19] International Criminal Court, *The Court Today*, Updated 21 September 2018, available at: https://www.icc-cpi.int/iccdocs/PIDS/publications/TheCourtTodayEng.pdf (accessed on 31 December 2018).

Global Panel would have to be secured. New York Convention signatory States may not be prepared to finance a supranational court with such narrow jurisdication.

III.4. What Are the Challenges Presented by this Approach?

6.44. The establishment of a Global Panel is without doubt the most challenging proposal put forward by the authors. If reaching a consensus required to implement a Protocol on the uniform approach to enforcement would require many years, the same would likely take even longer for the Global Panel. This is particularly so when one takes into account the additional financial implications of establishing a supranational judicial body.

6.45. Furthermore, the other challenges mentioned above in respect of the implementation of the proposed Protocol[20] generally apply here. Above all, in order for the Global Panel to not be toothless, it would be necessary to have a significant number of States participating in the international treaty establishing it. Even if only a few States were to start and the number of States becoming a member of the Global Panel treaty was to increase over the years, this would mean that it would take a very long time before the desired goal – uniformity in enforcement decisions – would be achieved.

6.46. Finally, while the Protocol would 'only' require States to submit to the adoption of a specific approach to the recognition and enforcement of arbitral awards, the Global Panel would go substantially further. Significant effort would be required to persuade a sufficiently large group of States to surrender jurisdiction and let a supranational organ have the final say on enforcement issues *vis-à-vis* arbitral awards set aside at the seat. There would almost certainly be concerns raised that binding enforcement recommendations could, ultimately, be disadvantageous to parties from contracting States or, to make matters worse, even disadvantage the contracting States themselves (although enforcement against States could perhaps be carved-out to address this specific concern).

III.5. Conclusion

6.47. English psychiatrist Anthony Storr famously said 'Originality implies being bold enough to go beyond accepted norms' and this proposal is definitely one of the bolder ideas that one may

[20] *Infra*, sub-chapter II.4.

Boldness Be My Friend: Four Suggestions to Facilitate Interpretive Uniformity in the Enforcement ...

Czech (& Central European) Yearbook of Arbitration®

advance. Supranational courts are infrequently established and as such only a few of them exist worldwide. Setting those bodies up took decades of work and the criticism to which they continue to be subject from some quarters is manifold.[21]

6.48. That being said, as challenging as the establishment of a Global Panel may appear to be in principle, one should not dismiss the idea without careful consideration simply because of the many challenges to be overcome. Other international organs, including the ICCt to which the authors refer earlier in this sub-chapter, were successfully established and fulfil a vital role in the international legal landscape. This is what the takeaway from this proposal should be: recognition that more can be achieved should the international legal community wish, rather than the identification of an insurmountable obstacle.

IV. A 'Soft Law' Solution

6.49. There is no shortage of reference tools intended to enlighten contracting parties about the intentions of the drafters of the New York Convention and provide information about the approaches adopted by the judiciary of contracting States to the interpretation of its wording. Two key examples are the UNCITRAL Secretariat Guide on the Recognition and Enforcement of Foreign Arbitral Awards, the most recent edition of which was published in 2016,[22] and ICCA's 2011 'Guide to the Interpretation of the 1958 New York Convention: A Handbook for Judges.'[23]

6.50. Such publications provide a useful source of information and commentary on the approaches adopted by the courts of different contracting States. The UNCITRAL Secretariat Guide was prepared in recognition of UNCITRAL's mandate to prepare 'tools necessary for a thorough understanding of the instruments it develops and for their uniform interpretation.'[24] Yet such sources are by their very nature non-binding and accordingly of limited assistance when dealing with the divergent Internationalist and Territorial Approaches. Indeed, the UNCITRAL Secretariat Guide is expressly acknowledged

---

[21] For instance, in 2016, the BBC asked *"Is this the end for the International Criminal Court?"* See BBC, *Is this the end for the International Criminal Court?*, 24 October 2016, available at: https://www.bbc.com/news/world-africa-37750978 (last accessed on 12 October 2018).

[22] UNITED NATIONS COMMISSION ON INTERNATIONAL TRADE LAW, UNCITRAL SECRETARIAT GUIDE ON THE RECOGNITION AND ENFORCEMENT OF FOREIGN ARBITRAL AWARDS (NEW YORK, 1958), Vienna: United Nations (ed., 2016).

[23] INTERNATIONAL COUNCIL FOR COMMERCIAL ARBITRATION, ICCA'S GUIDE TO THE INTERPRETATION OF THE 1958 NEW YORK CONVENTION: A HANDBOOK FOR JUDGES, The Hague: International Council for Commercial Arbitration (2011).

[24] United Nations Commission on International Trade Law, *supra* note 1, at x paragraph 4.

not to be 'an independent authority' but instead characterized as 'a reference tool'.[25]

6.51. As to the existing guides, discussion in respect of the circumstances in which an award set aside at the seat may be enforced is limited to recognition of the divergent approaches adopted by the courts of different contracting States.[26] As such, although valuable, interpretive guides provide limited scope for the facilitation of interpretive uniformity in the future. Due to their nature, neither guide has nor was intended to have legal effect. There is accordingly a role to be played by a potential new and more authoritative interpretive source – a 'soft law' solution that would be accorded the status of an independently authoritative instrument, albeit one that properly recognizes and respects the regime created by the New York Convention and the intentions of the drafters.

IV.1. What Form would such 'Soft Law' Take?

6.52. Sources of soft law in respect of treaty interpretation are broad and complex, ranging from 'treaties, but which include only soft obligations ... to non-binding or voluntary resolutions and codes of conduct ... to statements ... which purport to lay down international principles'.[27] Despite the limitations in respect of weight, there is scope for considerable creativity as to form and substance when seeking to develop authoritative and persuasive sources.

6.53. A soft law instrument to provide appropriate interpretive guidance in respect of the controversial issue of the enforcement of set aside awards must carry sufficient weight to attract the respect of contracting States and the international legal community. As such, it is important that, prior to the finalization of the wording of such an instrument, contracting States have the opportunity to share their respective views on the intended scope of the wording of Article V and related article VII if such interpretive aid is to be recognized as authoritative. As such, due to its long term involvement and status, the most appropriate

---

[25]   *Ibid*, at xi paragraph. 7.

[26]   *Ibid*, at 220-223 paragraphs 27-32, addresses the position when an award has been set aside or suspended. It is acknowledged that there is considerable divergence in the approach adopted by the courts of different contracting states, which may enforce either on the basis of the word '*may*' in Article V or the provisions of Article VII(1).

[27]   Christine M. Chinkin, *The Challenge of Soft Law: Development and Change in International Law*, 38 INTERNATIONAL AND COMPARATIVE LAW QUARTERLY 850, 851 (1989).

author of an authoritative interpretive instrument is arguably UNCITRAL.

6.54. UNCITRAL has, from time to time, issued Recommendations in respect of the interpretation of specific articles of instruments such as the New York Convention.[28] Past Recommendations relating to the New York Convention have acknowledged that they are issued in recognition of the purpose of the New York Convention as a vehicle to facilitate enforcement of foreign arbitral awards to the greatest possible extent, while respecting the fact that there are five equally authentic treaty texts.[29]

6.55. Article V provides a prime example of the difficulties that may arise due to the equally authentic status of each of the five texts of the New York Convention. In particular, the English translation of the French text of Article V(1)(e) and in particular the words *'ne seront refusées'* or *'will be refused'* appears to run in direct contrast to the more permissive wording, 'can/may', adopted in the Chinese, English, Russian and Spanish versions.[30]

6.56. Accordingly, an UNCITRAL Recommendation addressing the interpretation of Article V, when read in conjunction with Article VII, may offer an appropriate soft law vehicle for the provision of welcome clarification to the judiciary of contracting States as to the intended scope of the discretion afforded by the permissive wording of Article V when dealing with the particular problem presented by parties seeking to enforce awards set aside at the seat of arbitration.

IV.2. Advantages

6.57. By granting contracting States discretion to enforce an award set aside at the seat without providing guidance as to the circumstances when enforcement will be appropriate, the drafters of the New York Convention introduced an inbuilt limitation on the scope for uniform application of its provisions.[31] The provision of the omitted guidance in respect of such circumstances via an UNCITRAL Recommendation

---

[28] See, for example, UNCITRAL Recommendation regarding the interpretation of article II, paragraph 2, and article VII, paragraph 1, of the Convention on the Recognition and Enforcement of Foreign Arbitral Awards, done in New York, 10 June 1958 (2006), available at: http://www.uncitral.org/uncitral/en/uncitral_texts/arbitration/2006recommendation.html (accessed on 31 December 2018).

[29] See Article XVI of the New York Convention, which provides that *'the Chinese, English, French, Russian and Spanish texts shall be equally authentic'.*

[30] As to the extent to which the wording of the French text may be read as permissive, *see* Lee and Sippel, *supra* note 5, 141 paragraph 7.20.

[31] Linda Silberman, *The New York Convention After Fifty Years: Some Reflections on the Role of National Law*, 30 GEORGIA JOURNAL OF INTERNATIONAL AND COMPARATIVE LAW 25, 28 (2009).

would bridge the gap and address this significant interpretive lacuna.

6.58. In terms of practicality, the adoption by the General Assembly of a Resolution recommending the use of a Recommendation would be far easier and cheaper to achieve than the development of a Protocol to amend the New York Convention. Further, as interpretive guidance is sought in respect of a limited albeit important part of the treaty, a Recommendation would enable UNCITRAL to offer guidance without the need to take into account potential amendments to the New York Convention as a whole. The limited scope of the proposed Recommendation makes it a more practical and attractive solution to the need for guidance in respect of this discrete topic.

6.59. Despite their non-binding status, soft law sources have an important role to play in the development of customary international law. By establishing the 'norms that affect the behaviour of agents' in relations between States, such instruments have the potential to have significant and lasting effect on the international legal landscape.[32] A Recommendation provides the opportunity for this potential to be fulfilled and a degree of uniformity and predictability to be restored to the enforcement of awards set aside at the seat.

IV.3. Disadvantages

6.60. Soft law is defined by its non-binding legal nature. Accordingly its value is limited and it is therefore debatable whether a Recommendation would prove to be of greater practical value that the UNCITRAL Secretariat Guide or ICCA Guide. Signatory States are not obliged to make a formal commitment to soft law solutions. As such, there is no legal sanction available in the event that States continue to adopt divergent interpretive approaches that further blur the lines in the area of enforcement.

6.61. Further, a Recommendation would have no direct effect on the law of a contracting State and would not necessitate the enactment of domestic legislation. As such, a soft law solution would in this case fail to solve the problem presented by 'incomplete contracting' by failing to introduce binding interpretive guidelines that would promote uniformity.[33] An instrument of only persuasive authority is insufficient to address

---

[32] Eric Posner & Jacob Gerson, *Soft Law*, 213 UNIVERSITY OF CHICAGO PUBLIC LAW & LEGAL THEORY WORKING PAPER 3 (2008).

[33] Gregory C. Shaffer & Mark A. Pollack, *Hard vs. Soft Law: Alternatives, Complements and Antagonists in International Governance*, 94 MINNESOTA LAW REVIEW 706, 718 (2010).

the divergences between the contracting states adopting the Internationalist and Territorial Approaches respectively.

IV.4. What Are the Challenges Presented by this Approach?

6.62. The development and ultimate drafting of an effective Recommendation is reliant, to a significant extent, on the identification of a clear way forward in respect of the interpretation of Articles V and VII and how they should be applied to the enforcement of set aside awards. Proponents of the Internationalist and Territorial Approaches have strongly held views on the appropriateness of their interpretive stances. As such, drafting a Recommendation containing guidelines that would be of greater utility than the existing guides and case law presents a significant challenge.

6.63. Further, although UNCITRAL is likely to be able to finalize a soft law instrument in a shorter period of time than it would take to debate, draft and approve an acceptable Protocol or other form of amendment to the New York Convention, it is likely that the number of stakeholders wishing to play a role will unavoidably result in a protracted discussion and drafting process. During this period of deliberation, inconsistent approaches to the enforcement of awards set aside at the seat will continue to be adopted.

IV.5. Conclusion

6.64. Soft law is, by its very nature, devoid of legally binding effect and the merits of any proposed solution must be considered with the status of any instrument that will result from it in mind. The purpose of UNCITRAL Recommendations is to 'advance the objective of harmonization' by 'provid[ing] a set of possible legislative solutions to certain issues, but not necessarily a single set of model solutions for those issues.'[34] Although Recommendations are essentially no more than guidelines for consideration by the Governments of contracting States, they provide an opportunity for the international legal community to express and for UNCITRAL to articulate a proposed interpretive approach of persuasive value. A Recommendation may accordingly carry significant weight despite the limitations inherent in its status. In the absence of a practical and

---

[34]   UNITED NATIONS COMMISSION ON INTERNATIONAL TRADE LAW, A GUIDE TO UNCITRAL BASIC FACTS ABOUT THE UNITED NATIONS COMMISSION ON INTERNATIONAL TRADE LAW, Vienna: United Nations (2013), 16 at paragraph 44.

legally binding solution, a Recommendation may provide an opportunity for States to course correct and ultimately return to the path of uniformity.

V.   Joint Interpretive Instruments

6.65.   Public international law affords contracting States the opportunity to clarify their interpretive intentions, whether retrospectively or contemporaneously with entry into a treaty.[35] As recognised by the Permanent Court of International Justice: 'it is an established principle that the right of giving an authoritative interpretation of a legal rule belongs solely to the person or body who has power to modify or suppress it.'[36]

6.66.   Article 31 of the Vienna Convention[37] expressly acknowledges that parties may choose to reach an agreement in respect of the interpretation to be applied to specific treaty provisions subsequent to entering into the relevant treaty. In this regard, Article 31(3)(a) recognises that, together with a consideration of the terms in their context, '[t]here shall be taken into account … (a) Any subsequent agreement between the parties regarding the interpretation of the treaty or the application of its provisions' (emphasis added).[38] This general rule of interpretation is expressed in mandatory language: if parties reach a subsequent agreement about the way in which a particular term is to be interpreted, this agreement cannot be disregarded.

6.67.   Joint interpretive instruments or statements are an increasingly common feature of the bilateral investment treaty landscape.[39] Such agreements do not change the text of the underlying treaty. Instead, such agreements are intended to provide a 'clear and unambiguous statement' of what was agreed in respect of provisions that may be open to divergent interpretations.[40] It accordingly remains open to all or a subset of the New York Convention signatory States to clarify their interpretive intentions subsequent to signature of the treaty.

---

[35]   UNCTAD IIA Issues Note, *Interpretation of IIAs: What States Can Do*, No. 3 at 3 (December 2011) available at: https://unctad.org/en/Docs/webdiaeia2011d10_en.pdf (accessed on 31 December 2018).

[36]   Permanent Court of International Justice, *Question of Jaworzina (Polish-Czechoslovakian Frontier)*, PCIJ Series B, No. 8 (1923) at 37.

[37]   Vienna Convention on the Law of Treaties, Vienna, 1969.

[38]   *Ibid*, Article 31.

[39]   See, for example, the Joint Interpretative Instrument on the Comprehensive Economic and Trade Agreement (CETA) between Canada and the European Union and its Member States, Brussels, 27 October 2016, 13541/16 at 3, Cl. 1(e); Joint Interpretive Notes on the Agreement between the Government of the Republic of India and the Government of the People's Republic of Bangladesh for Promotion and Protection of Investments, Dhaka, 4 October 2017 available at: https://dea.gov.in/sites/default/files/Signed%20 Copy%20of%20JIN.pdf (accessed on 31 December 2018).

[40]   Joint Interpretive Instrument on the Comprehensive Economic and Trade Agreement (CETA) between Canada and the European Union and its Member States, Brussels, 27 October 2016, 13541/16 at 3, Cl. 1(e).

Boldness Be My Friend: Four Suggestions to Facilitate Interpretive Uniformity in the Enforcement ...

Czech (& Central European) Yearbook of Arbitration®

V.1. What Form would such a Joint Interpretive Instrument Take?

6.68. There are two potential approaches that may be taken in order to develop a joint interpretive instrument relating to the New York Convention. First, a written proposal for a joint interpretive instrument may be prepared, accompanied by draft text, for circulation amongst signatory States. The draft text would be subject to discussion and agreement, with a view to the resulting joint interpretive instrument being entered into between the proposing State and such States as may choose to agree with its interpretation. Second, discussions may be initiated between signatory States, with a view to collaborating on the development of an agreed text for discussion, amendments and ultimately agreement over a period of time.

6.69. The first approach was adopted by India in conjunction with its review and termination of a number of bilateral investment treaties to which it was party. India recognized the desirability of eliminating the scope for broad interpretation of treaty provisions by tribunals in investor-State dispute settlement proceedings. The proposed mechanism to achieve this goal was the agreement of joint interpretive statements. The Government of India provided its treaty counterparties with proposed text for joint interpretive statements, with a view to signing joint interpretive statements with twenty five of its BIT counterparties thereafter.[41]

V.2. Advantages

6.70. Joint interpretive instruments provide considerable scope for New York Convention signatory States to reach agreement on the meaning to be ascribed to controversial articles of the treaty without the need for formal amendments to the wording to be made. As such, reaching agreement about what was meant with the benefit of hindsight is likely to take less time that seeking to amend what was originally agreed and achieve the agreement of a critical mass of signatory States.

6.71. Unlike Recommendations or other soft law provisions, joint interpretive instruments are afforded legally binding status by

---

[41] *See*, for example, the views of the Government of India in Office Memorandum of Harsh K Gauram, *Issuing Joint Interpretive Statements for Indian Bilateral Investment Treaties*, 8 February 2016 available at: http://indiainbusiness.nic.in/newdesign/upload/Consolidated_Interpretive-Statement.pdf (accessed on 31 December 2018).

Czech (& Central European) Yearbook of Arbitration®

the operation of Article 31(2)(b) of the Vienna Convention.[42] This was expressly recognised by the Council Legal Service of the Council of the European Union, which noted in respect of the Joint Interpretive Instrument adopted in conjunction with CETA that *'it has legal force and a binding character.'*[43]

6.72.   At present, the lack of uniform interpretation of Article V provides for considerable uncertainty for parties seeking to enforce an award that was set aside at the seat. Although national jurisprudence to date has provided an indication of the approach likely to be adopted by a number of signatory States, the lack of harmonization in this crucial area is unwelcome.

6.73.   From a practical perspective, it should be noted that the attractiveness of any given arbitral seat may increase if the interpretive stance of the contracting State in which it is based is publicly available. Further, parties seeking to enforce a set aside award in another jurisdiction would benefit from greater knowledge of the likely approach of its courts.

V.3.   Disadvantages

6.74.   The Territorial and Internationalist Approaches (not to mention hybrid approaches) are testament to the considerable divergence of opinion between the courts of signatory States on the circumstances in which it is appropriate to enforce an arbitral award set aside at the seat. It follows that signatory States whose courts have adopted one approach over the other may be unwilling to agree to an instrument by which they adopt an interpretation that would limit the capacity of their courts to rule in accordance with established jurisprudence.

6.75.   The inevitable consequence of such disagreement would be the creation of a two-tiered system: (i) States that subscribe to the joint interpretive agreement and its promise of greater certainty and predictability; and (ii) States that choose to proceed on the basis of the existing wording. If true uniformity of approach cannot be achieved then it may be difficult for States to countenance the possibility of a joint interpretive instrument, on the basis that the benefits are potentially outweighed by the cost, time and difficulty involved in developing an agreed text for those States that see fit to engage with the proposal.

---

[42]   In respect of the Joint Interpretive Agreement to be adopted by the parties on the occasion of the signature of CETA, the Council Legal Service expressly confirmed that this document *'... constitutes a document of reference that will have to be made use of if any issue arises in the implementation of CETA regarding the interpretation of its terms.'*

[43]   Statements to the Council Minutes, Brussels, 27 October 2016, 13463/1/16 REV 1 at 30, paragraph 38.

V.4. What Are the Challenges Presented by this Approach?

6.76. Although more pragmatic, the first approach identified above relies on the prospect of a signatory State to take the initiative and propose change. Such an overture may be made independently, in conjunction with other contracting States or perhaps in conjunction with UNCITRAL or a similar organization. Depending on the extent of the work involved, the time and cost involved in preparing a first draft may be significant. The implications of the divergent interpretive approaches will need to be thoroughly researched and the desired approach identified and explained.

6.77. The 'preferred' interpretive approach is unlikely to be capable of objective determination. It will unavoidably be influenced by the approach adopted by the courts of particular arbitral seats. Jurisdictions following the Territorial Approach and Internationalist Approach jurisdictions would almost certainly produce wildly different draft wording. It is not difficult to foresee that a draft instrument based on the Territorial Approach would be met with an alternative draft consistent with the Internationalist Approach.

6.78. The temptation to address wider issues in a joint interpretive agreement is likely to be irresistible. The New York Convention contains a number of phrases that have led to uncertainty over the years. By way of example, the Article I(1) reference to awards 'not considered as domestic awards' and the ambiguous references to 'terms of the submission' and 'scope of submission' in Article V(1)(c) present difficulties that would merit interpretive agreement. Attempts to draft an exhaustive interpretive instrument rather than a narrow and focused document risk failure due to an excess of ambition.

V.5. Conclusion

6.79. Successful joint interpretive instruments are the product of constructive dialogue and the achievement of consensus. On the basis that a State can be persuaded to take the first step, a joint interpretive instrument provides a practical means by which ambiguities can be clarified without the need to rip up the New York Convention or address the significant challenges involved in a formal amendment. When dealing with a multiparty treaty such as the New York Convention, the achievement of a level of consensus between the parties that would be sufficient to make a real difference poses inevitable challenges. In the investment treaty arena, counterparties normally have a common interest in limiting the potential for sizeable claims to be brought against them by investors. The development of an interpretive aid with binding effect is mutually beneficial, serving to curtail creative interpretation of clauses by unpredictable tribunals. The incentive for contracting States to contribute to the development of a uniform interpretive paradigm in this awkward but fairly narrow area of treaty application may be limited.

VI. Conclusion

6.80. The New York Convention, the 'most successful, multilateral instrument in the field of international trade law', is, to some extent, a victim of its own success.[44] Divergent interpretations of Article V introduce an unwelcome lack of uniformity into a supposedly harmonious international legal regime. As Professor Bermann observed:

> ... disparities matter all the more, given the independence among legal systems that international commercial arbitration entails and the very high expectations that the New York Convention itself has created.[45]

Any attempt to impose transnational uniformity upon the interpretation of Article V by domestic courts must clear a number of hurdles.

6.81. To propose amendment of the 'sacred text' is to court controversy.[46] As acknowledged above, much has been said about the difficulties inherent in seeking to amend the New York Convention, with particular reference to the challenges inherent in securing the agreement of a critical mass of the 159 signatory States and the decade of negotiations that are likely to precede change.[47] Perhaps, however, the critics underestimate the ability of member States to achieve results in a realistic timeframe. UNCITRAL approved the final drafts of the treaty that will be known as the 'Singapore Mediation Convention' on 25 June 2018.[48] This step was the culmination of a mere (!) three years of

---

[44] Pieter Sanders, *Foreword*, INTERNATIONAL COUNCIL FOR COMMERCIAL ARBITRATION, ICCA'S GUIDE TO THE INTERPRETATION OF THE 1958 NEW YORK CONVENTION: A HANDBOOK FOR JUDGES, The Hague: International Council for Commercial Arbitration 7 (2011).

[45] George A. Bermann, *'Domesticating' the New York Convention: the Impact of the Federal Arbitration Act*, 2(2) JOURNAL OF INTERNATIONAL DISPUTE SETTLEMENT 317, 332 (2011).

[46] V.V. Veeder, *supra* note 10. Veeder describes the New York Convention et. 186 as '... a secular, sacred text of the greatest practical significance to every inhabitant of the 21st Century's global village.'

[47] *Infra*, sub-chapter II.3.

[48] United Nations, General Assembly, *Report of the United Nations Commission on International Trade Law Fifty-first session*, A/73/17 (2018).

negotiations involving 85 member States and 35 other entities.[49] Debate was not stymied by the number of participants, nor was the timeframe excessive for the development of an international treaty. Is it really too much to expect that the contracting States of the New York Convention may be able to achieve a similar level of efficiency and pragmatism?

6.82. Further, although the establishment of a multilateral enforcement panel is fraught with difficulties, there is clear precedent for the development of such bodies. As recently as 2018, the European Union committed to negotiate a convention establishing a permanent court to resolve investment disputes.[50] The cost of developing an enforcement court and attracting suitably qualified judges is likely to be significant – these practical issues merit careful consideration. Whether the ambiguity relating to the enforcement of set aside awards is sufficient to justify the establishment of an entirely new juridical body is a separate matter.

6.83. There is no shortage of detailed guidance available to judges tasked with interpreting and putting into effect the intentions of the drafters of the New York Convention. Despite the availability of such documents, the jurisprudence in this area is testament to the arguably unintended consequences of ambiguity in treaty wording. A specific Recommendation drafted to serve the cause of harmonization is likely to be of significant persuasive value as an interpretive aid. However, like all soft law Recommendations, are constrained by their non-binding status. Would it be responsible for contracting States to put time and hope into an interpretive aid that lacks teeth?

6.84. The negotiation of a joint interpretive instrument affords contracting States the opportunity to debate the most appropriate interpretation of Article V and adopt a solution that addresses concerns from different stakeholders: parties, courts and contracting States. The attractiveness of certain arbitral seats may be enhanced by the development of a clear interpretive paradigm. However, should sufficient consensus not be obtained, the result may be a veritable smorgasbord of different interpretive agreements entered into between different contracting States: chaos becoming an unintended consequence of the quest for clarification. There is a clear danger that the

---

[49] Global Pound Conference, *The Singapore Mediation Convention: An Overview*, (12 July 2018) available at: https://www.globalpound.org/2018/07/12/the-singapore-mediation-convention-an-overview/ (accessed on 31 December 2018).

[50] Council of the European Union, *Multilateral investment court: Council gives mandate to the Commission to open negotiations*, (20 March 2018) available at: https://www.consilium.europa.eu/en/press/press-releases/2018/03/20/multilateral-investment-court-council-gives-mandate-to-the-commission-to-open-negotiations/pdf (accessed on 31 December 2018).

result may be greater uncertainty and a kaleidoscopic range of enforcement regimes.

6.85. Despite the reservations discussed above, it is important to recognize that the above proposals represent mere ideas at this stage – the first step in what the authors hope will become a more detailed dialogue that will lead to the identification of the most suitable way forward. Only by engaging in such a dialogue can the promise of the New York Convention truly be fulfilled.

| | |

Summaries

DEU [*Kühnheit, sei mein Freund: Vier Vorschläge zur Erleichterung einer einheitlichen Interpretation im Rahmen der Vollstreckung von am Schiedsort aufgehobenen Schiedssprüchen*]

Wenngleich das New Yorker Übereinkommen über die Anerkennung und Vollstreckung ausländischer Schiedssprüche als das erfolgreichste multilaterale Abkommen im Bereich des internationalen Privatrechts gilt, so haftet ihm dennoch ein großer Makel an: die Praxis der Anerkennung und Vollstreckung ist nicht vereinheitlicht. Dies gilt insbesondere für Schiedssprüche, die am Schiedsort aufgehoben worden sind.

Dieser Aufsatz erwägt vier Ansätze, diesen Makel zu beseitigen, (i) eine Änderung des New Yorker Übereinkommens; (ii) die Errichtung eines globalen Anerkennungs- und Vollstreckungsgremiums; (iii) die Vereinheitlichung mittels soft law; und (iv) die Entwicklung eines einheitlichen Interpretationsmechanismus. Die Autoren besprechen die Vor- und Nachteile jedes Vorschlags und analysieren dabei auch die Hürden in der Praxis.

Das Ziel dieses Aufsatzes ist es, erste Ansätze zu einem weiterführenden Dialog zu starten, sodass eines der wichtigsten Versprechens der Schiedsgerichtsbarkeit, die einfache Vollstreckung (praktisch) weltweit, tatsächlich erfüllt werden kann und nicht bloß eine Utopie ist.

CZE [*Smělost nechť je mým přítelem: čtyři návrhy na snazší dosažení výkladové jednoty při výkonu rozhodčích nálezů zrušených v sídle rozhodčího řízení*]

Absence globálního konsensu co do přístupu, který by měly zaujmout vnitrostátní soudy k výkonu rozhodčích nálezů zrušených v sídle rozhodčího řízení, oslabuje jednotnost slibovanou Newyorskou úmluvou. Tento článek navrhuje čtyři možná řešení problémů vznikajících ze stávající dichotomie uznání a výkonu, a to: (i) změnu Newyorské úmluvy; (ii) vytvoření Globálního instrumentu pro výkon a uznání; (iii) řešení na úrovni „soft law"; a (iv) vytvoření společného výkladového nástroje. Autoři se věnují výhodám a nevýhodám každého návrhu a poukazují na některé praktické problémy, které bude potřeba vyřešit, mají-li některá z navržených řešení uspět. Smyslem tohoto článku je zahájit širší dialog ohledně tohoto kontroverzního tématu v mezinárodním rozhodčím řízení, s cílem najít praktické řešení, které umožní, aby byl onen slib jednoduchého výkonu rozhodčích nálezů poskytovaný rozhodčím řízením jeho uživatelům skutečně naplněn.

| | |

POL   [*Odwagi! Cztery propozycje, jak przyczynić się do jednorodności interpretacyjnej w wykonywaniu orzeczeń arbitrażowych uchylonych w miejscu siedziby postępowania arbitrażowego*]
Brak globalnego konsensusu co do zalecanego podejścia sądów krajowych do wykonywania orzeczeń arbitrażowych uchylonych w siedzibie postępowania arbitrażowego osłabia jednorodność obiecywaną przez Konwencję nowojorską. Artykuł proponuje cztery możliwe rozwiązania problemów wynikających z aktualnej dychotomii uznania i wykonania. Autorzy skupiają się na zaletach i wadach każdej propozycji oraz zwracają uwagę na pewne praktyczne problemy, próbując zapoczątkować szerszy dialog na ten temat.

FRA   [*Que l'audace m'accompagne : Quatre propositions pour arriver à une interprétation unifiée des règles d'exécution des sentences arbitrales annulées au siège du tribunal arbitral*]
L'absence de consensus global quant à la position que devraient prendre les tribunaux nationaux vis-à-vis de l'exécution des sentences arbitrales annulées au siège du tribunal arbitral affaiblit le rôle unificateur qu'est censée jouer la Convention de New York. Le présent article apporte quatre solutions possibles aux problèmes engendrés par la dichotomie actuelle opposant la reconnaissance à l'exécution. Les auteurs étudient les avantages et les inconvénients de chacune de ces propositions, tout en indiquant certains problèmes pratiques, afin de stimuler un dialogue autour de ce sujet.

Czech (& Central European) Yearbook of Arbitration®

RUS [*Пусть смелость будет моим другом: четыре предложения по упрощению единства толкования при приведении в исполнение арбитражных решений, отмененных в месте проведения арбитража*]
Единство, обещанное Нью-Йоркской конвенцией, ослабляет отсутствие глобального консенсуса в подходе, который национальные суды должны применять к исполнению арбитражных решений, отмененных в месте проведения арбитража. В этой статье предложено четыре возможных решения проблем, возникающих из-за существующей дихотомии признания и приведения в исполнение. Авторы уделяют внимание преимуществам и недостаткам каждого предложения и указывают на некоторые практические проблемы для того, чтобы начать более широкое обсуждение данного вопроса.

ESP [*¡Qué la audacia sea mi compañera! Cuatro propuestas para lograr más fácilmente la unanimidad interpretativa en la ejecución de laudos arbitrales anulados en la sede del procedimiento arbitral*]
La ausencia del consenso global en lo referente a la actitud de los tribunales nacionales hacia la ejecución de los laudos arbitrales anulados en la sede del procedimiento arbitral debilita la unidad prometida por la Convención de Nueva York. El texto propone cuatro posibles soluciones de problemas que surgen a raíz de la actual dicotomía del reconocimiento y la ejecución. Los autores detallan las ventajas y las desventajas de cada propuesta y señalan varios problemas prácticos con el fin de iniciar un amplio diálogo relativo al presente tema.

| | |

Bibliography

Adebayo G. Adaralegbe, *Challenges in Enforcement of Arbitral Awards in Capital-Importing States*, 23(5) JOURNAL OF INTERNATIONAL ARBITRATION 401 (2006).

Flávio Spaccaquerche Barbosa, *The Enforcement of International Investment Arbitral Awards: is There a Better Way?*, 6(21) REVISTA BRASILEIRA DE ARBITRAGEM 7 (2009).

Albert Jan van den Berg, *Convention on the Recognition and Enforcement of Foreign Arbitral Awards*, UNITED NATIONS AUDIOVISUAL LIBRARY OF INTERNATIONAL LAW (2008).

Boldness Be My Friend: Four Suggestions to Facilitate Interpretive Uniformity in the Enforcement ...

Czech (& Central European) Yearbook of Arbitration®

Albert Jan van den Berg, *Enforcement of Arbitral Awards Annulled in Russia*, 27 JOURNAL OF INTERNATIONAL ARBITRATION 180 (2010).

George A. Bermann, *'Domesticating' the New York Convention: the Impact of the Federal Arbitration Act*, 2(2) JOURNAL OF INTERNATIONAL DISPUTE SETTLEMENT 317 (2011).

Ronald A. Brand, *Transaction Planning Using Rules on Jurisdiction and the Recognition and Enforcement of Judgments*, 358 COLLECTED COURSES OF THE HAGUE ACADEMY OF INTERNATIONAL LAW, THE HAGUE ACADEMY OF INTERNATIONAL LAW 167 (2014).

Christine M. Chinkin, *The Challenge of Soft Law: Development and Change in International Law*, 38 INTERNATIONAL AND COMPARATIVE LAW QUARTERLY 850 (1989).

Sae Youn Kim & Marieke Minkkinen, *An Asian Perspective on the Enforcement of Annulled Awards*, 19 INTERNATIONAL ARBITRATION AND THE RULE OF LAW: CONTRIBUTION AND CONFORMITY, ICCA CONGRESS SERIES 382 (Andrea Menaker ed., 2017).

Amanda Lee & Harald Sippel, *To enforce or not to enforce: that is the question: Arbitral Awards Set Aside at Their Seat*, 8 CZECH (& CENTRAL EUROPEAN) YEARBOOK OF ARBITRATION 135 (2018).

UNITED NATIONS COMMISSION ON INTERNATIONAL TRADE LAW, UNCITRAL SECRETARIAT GUIDE ON THE RECOGNITION AND ENFORCEMENT OF FOREIGN ARBITRAL AWARDS (NEW YORK, 1958), Vienna: United Nations (ed., 2016).

INTERNATIONAL COUNCIL FOR COMMERCIAL ARBITRATION, ICCA'S GUIDE TO THE INTERPRETATION OF THE 1958 NEW YORK CONVENTION: A HANDBOOK FOR JUDGES, The Hague: International Council for Commercial Arbitration (2011).

Eric Posner & Jacob Gerson, *Soft Law*, 213 UNIVERSITY OF CHICAGO PUBLIC LAW & LEGAL THEORY WORKING PAPER 3 (2008).

Gregory C. Shaffer & Mark A. Pollack, *Hard vs. Soft Law: Alternatives, Complements and Antagonists in International Governance*, 94 MINNESOTA LAW REVIEW 706 (2010).

Pieter Sanders, *Foreword*, INTERNATIONAL COUNCIL FOR COMMERCIAL ARBITRATION, ICCA'S GUIDE TO THE INTERPRETATION OF THE 1958 NEW YORK CONVENTION: A HANDBOOK FOR JUDGES, The Hague: International Council for Commercial Arbitration 7 (2011).

Linda Silberman, *The New York Convention After Fifty Years: Some Reflections on the Role of National Law*, 30 GEORGIA JOURNAL OF INTERNATIONAL AND COMPARATIVE LAW 25 (2009).

Roman Prekop | Peter Petho

Arbitral Interim Measures – Enforcement Pitfalls

Key words:
interim measure |
provisional relief |
enforcement | execution

Abstract | This article addresses the enforcement of arbitral interim measures in international arbitration. The authors find that although the enforceability of arbitral interim measures is critical for the efficacy of arbitration, there does not appear to be any worldwide recognized binding instrument requiring national courts to enforce such measures. In particular, the New York Convention does not explicitly address arbitral interim measures, which thus results in different views. Also, although the UNCITRAL Model Law explicitly provides for the recognition and enforcement of arbitral interim measures, it is merely a non-binding guideline. Consequently, the enforceability of arbitral interim measures appears to be left to the tender mercies of the national legal orders and courts. This necessarily leads to significant uncertainty for arbitration practitioners and users. The authors believe that such a state of affairs is undesirable, but they do not foresee any indication that a significant improvement could be brought about within a few years. On this basis, the authors conclude that the requesting party, usually, must seriously consider filing a request for interim measure directly with a national court.

| | |

Roman Prekop is a founding partner at Barger Prekop Attorneys admitted to practice in the Slovak Republic and in New York. He is a member of the Slovak Bar Association, New York State Bar Association, Chartered Institute of Arbitrators, UK (FCIArb), International Bar Association, American Bar Association and Austrian Arbitration Association, and is a co-chair of the Slovak chapter of New York State Bar Association's International Section. Roman Prekop focuses his practice on litigation and international arbitration, energy sector regulation, competition and projects, M&A, and on corporate and banking matters. E-mail: rprekop@ bargerprekop.com

Peter Petho is a senior associate at Barger Prekop Attorneys admitted to practice in the Slovak Republic. He is a member of the Slovak Bar Association, Chartered Institute of Arbitrators, UK (FCIArb), International Bar Association, and 'below 40' platforms of the ICC, LCIA, ICCA, Austrian Arbitration Association and Swiss Arbitration Association. Peter Petho focuses his practice on litigation and international arbitration, construction law, real estate transactions, EU law, and on general commercial matters. E-mail: ppetho@ bargerprekop.com

I.   Introduction

7.01.   Has the enforcement of your final award proved futile, simply because the debtor had too much manoeuvring space during arbitration? When inserting an arbitration clause into a cross-border contract, did you have to warn the client that the arbitrators' powers are inferior to those of court judges? Or, have you had the feeling that when it comes to international arbitration, there is an elephant in the room? If so, there may be a subtle, but common reason. Unlike foreign final awards, foreign arbitral interim measures may be simply too weak.

7.02.   As you will read below, there is likely no single regime for the enforcement of foreign arbitral interim measures, but rather a myriad of inconsistent state regimes. First, the New York Convention does not explicitly address arbitral interim measures, which necessarily results in different views and uncertainty as to its applicability. Second, the UNCITRAL Model Law,[1] although explicitly providing for the recognition and enforcement of arbitral interim measures, is only a non-binding instrument and thereby enables many different ways of its implementation. Third, a closer look at national arbitration laws reveals that even typical arbitration fora (such as England, Switzerland, or Sweden) do not enforce foreign arbitral interim measures.

7.03.   Importantly, it very often only makes sense to enforce a final award if you can preserve the status quo during arbitration. Hence, it begs the question: if you can preserve the status quo only by resorting to state courts, why agree on arbitration instead of court litigation and thus multiply the needed dispute fora? This question is even more pressing in the EU member states, where the Brussels I Regulation renders the court's interim measures enforceable in other member states.

7.04.   Some may speculate that states will gradually push arbitration to the limits of its very existence. We would say that this will not be the case if the arbitration practitioners and users unite the masters of the world and agree on an aligned arbitration trump similar to the 1958 New York Convention. It's about time.

II.   Interim Measures

7.05.   **Definition.** Interim measures can be defined as measures of provisional nature aimed at protecting a party's rights before the tribunal renders the final award or even before arbitration

---

[1]   The UNCITRAL Model Law on International Commercial Arbitration adopted in 1985, as amended in 2006.

begins.[2] Such measures can be divided into three categories.[3] First, measures aimed at facilitating arbitration, such as orders requiring a party to allow evidence to be taken.[4] Second, measures aimed at avoiding loss and preserving a certain state of affairs until the dispute has been resolved, such as orders requiring a party to continue in certain actions or to refrain from taking certain actions.[5] Third, measures aimed at facilitating the future enforcement of an award, such as orders attaching the respondent's assets either in or outside the jurisdiction in which the arbitration takes place.[6]

7.06.   **Options for interim measures.** In practice, it is not unusual that a party to arbitration may need one or more such measures. Usually, such party has two options. First, it may consider requesting such measure from the tribunal. Choosing this option would normally be logical because this option follows the presumption that the parties to an arbitration agreement wish to have their entire dispute decided in arbitration. In fact, many national arbitration laws and rules support such logic by permitting tribunals to render interim measures, some of them even as *ex parte* measures.

7.07.   Second, the party wishing to obtain an interim measure may consider requesting such measure from the respective national court. In fact, modern arbitration laws usually empower national courts to render interim measures in support of arbitration, at least before the tribunal has been constituted. Such interim measures are also often without prejudice to the parties' right to have the dispute on the merits resolved in arbitration.

7.08.   **Choosing the right forum.** From a practical point of view, choosing the right option is often critical for a party wishing to obtain an interim measure. Before making a choice, such party needs to consider a number of issues. One of such issues is what kind of redress the requesting party has against a recalcitrant party. For instance, if a party wishes to obtain an order preventing the other party from disposing of its assets, it needs to ensure that the order will be effective even if the other party refuses to comply. However, unlike national courts, arbitral tribunals do not have coercive powers. Therefore, from this perspective,

---

[2]   Decision of the Swiss Federal Supreme Court dated 13 April 2010, 4A 582/2009, paragraph 2.3.2. An English translation of this decision is available at: http://www.swissarbitrationdecisions.com (accessed on 25 February 2019).

[3]   Report of the Secretary General of the United Nations Commission on International Trade Law, Working Group on Arbitration, A/CN.9/WG.II/WP.108, 14 January 2000, paragraph 63, available at: https://undocs.org/en/A/CN.9/WG.II/WP.108 (accessed on 25 February 2019).

[4]   *Ibid.*

[5]   *Ibid.*

[6]   *Ibid.*

the applying party may be more inclined to request an interim measure from the respective national court. But, in some states, the applicable procedural law (or arbitration rules) prevents the party from doing so. Also, choosing this option may not be in the best interest of the applying party, particularly in situations where the applying party wants to avoid detailed involvement of national courts in the dispute.

7.09. **Balanced solution.** In the majority of cases, the most balanced solution is to request an interim measure from the tribunal and have such measure enforced before the respective national court. This solution ensures that all relevant issues in dispute are decided by the tribunal and minimizes the intervention of national courts to the extent of that necessary to maintain the efficacy of arbitration and future enforcement of a final award.

III. Enforcement of Interim Measures under the New York Convention

7.10. **New York Convention.** One of the main advantages of international arbitration is the world-wide reaching enforceability of foreign final awards under the New York Convention. The New York Convention sets out uniform rules for the recognition and enforcement of foreign awards, which now apply in 159 jurisdictions. There is no comparable international instrument in respect of foreign court judgments.

7.11. **Prevailing view.** However, the prevailing view seems to be that the New York Convention does not apply to arbitral interim measures, not even those issued in the form of an award.

7.12. The proponents of such view usually argue that arbitral interim measures do not satisfy the finality requirement, which they see implied in Article V(i)(e) of the New York Convention.[7] For instance, Bermann points out that "[t]he difficulty lies in considering such measures to be not only 'binding' (which they almost certainly are), but also 'final' (which is questionable)."[8]

---

[7]   NIGEL BLACKABY, CONSTANTINE PARTASIDES, ALAN REDFERN, MARTIN HUNTER, REDFERN AND HUNTER ON INTERNATIONAL ARBITRATION, Oxford: Oxford University Press paragraph 7.19 (6th ed., 2015)., Mika Savola, Interim Measures and Emergency Arbitrator Proceedings (Presentation for the 23rd Croatian Arbitration Days in Zagreb, 3-4 December 2015), page 14, available at: https://arbitration.fi/wp-content/uploads/sites/22/2016/04/23-cad-savola-interim-measures-and-emer gency-arbitrator-proceedings.pdf (accessed on 25 February 2019), and Luke Nottage & Chester Brown, Recognition and Enforcement of Foreign Arbitral Awards: The Application of the New York Convention by National Courts, National Report for Australia, page 5, available at: https://papers.ssrn.com/sol3/papers. cfm?abstract_id=2340806 (accessed on 25 February 2019).

[8]   George A. Bermann, Recognition and Enforcement Of Foreign Arbitral Awards: The Application Of The New York Convention By National Courts (July 2, 2014 draft), page 17, available at: https://www. iacl2014congress.com/fileadmin/user_upload/k_iacl2014congress/General_reports/Bermann_-_General_ Report_Recognition__Enforcement_of_Foreign_Awards_July_2_2014__2_.pdf (accessed on 25 February 2019).

Also, Poudret and Besson argue that '[w]hatever interpretation is given to [Article V(1)(e) of the New York Convention], the authors did not envisage that a decision of an arbitrator could be questioned by a subsequent decision, and this is precisely an essential characteristic of provisional measures.'[9] The proponents of this view also often refer to the Queensland (Australia) Supreme Court's decision holding that "the reference to 'arbitral award' in the Convention does not include an interlocutory order made by an arbitrator but only an award which finally determines the rights of the parties [...]."[10]

7.13. **Minority view.** On the other hand, although this is a minority view, there are certain plausible arguments for concluding that arbitral interim measures are enforceable under the New York Convention.

7.14. In particular, it appears rather questionable whether an award capable of being enforced under the New York Convention must be 'final' in any sense. The requirement that an award be final was explicitly set out in Article 1(d) of the Geneva Convention on the Execution of Foreign Arbitral Awards (the 'Geneva Convention'),[11] the predecessor of the New York Convention. However, no such requirement was transposed into the language of the New York Convention. Rather, the 'finality' requirement under the Geneva Convention was replaced with the requirement that an award be 'binding' under Article V(i)(e) of the New York Convention. As arbitral interim measures are usually considered to be 'binding', they satisfy the 'binding' requirement under Article V(i)(e) of the New York Convention.

7.15. In addition, the requirement that an award be 'binding' under Article V(i)(e) of the New York Convention does not mean that awards not satisfying this requirement fall outside the scope

---

[9] JEAN F. POUDRET, SÉBASTIEN BESSON, COMPARATIVE LAW OF INTERNATIONAL ARBITRATION, London: Sweet & Maxwell Ltd 546 (2nd ed., 2007).

[10] The Supreme Court of Queensland, *Resort Condominiums International Inc. v. Ray Bolwell* (1993) 118 ALR 655.

[11] Under Article 1(d) of the Geneva Convention, "[i]n the territories of any High Contracting Party to which the present Convention applies, an arbitral award made in pursuance of an agreement whether relating to existing or future differences (hereinafter called 'a submission to arbitration') covered by the Protocol on Arbitration Clauses, opened at Geneva on September 24, 1923 shall be recognised as binding and shall be enforced in accordance with the rules of the procedure of the territory where the award is relied upon, provided that the said award has been made in a territory of one of the High Contracting Parties to which the present Convention applies and between persons who are subject to the jurisdiction of one of the High Contracting Parties.

To obtain such recognition or enforcement, it shall, further, be necessary: [...] (d) That the award has become final in the country in which it has been made, in the sense that it will not be considered as such if it is open to opposition, appel or pourvoi en cassation (in the countries where such forms of procedure exist) or if it is proved that any proceedings for the purpose of contesting the validity of the award are pending [...]."

of the New York Convention.[12] Article V(i)(e) of the New York Convention merely provides that the enforcing court may refuse to recognize and enforce a foreign arbitral award that has not yet become binding on the parties. In other words, even non-binding awards are awards falling within the scope of the New York Convention, but enforcing courts have discretion in deciding whether to enforce such awards or not.

7.16.   Also, even if an award capable of being enforced under the New York Convention had to be 'final', Born suggests that interim measures satisfy such requirement because they "are 'final' in the sense that they dispose of a request for relief pending the conclusion of the arbitration."[13] Similarly, according to Kojovic, "[a]n interim award on provisional relief resolves whether the request for provisional measure should be granted or not. It represents a final determination of the issue thus defined."[14] This view also seems to have support in certain decisions of US and French courts,[15] and among US commentators.[16]

7.17.   Finally, from a policy perspective, the possibility to enforce such measures is critical for the efficacy of arbitration and future enforcement of a final award. For instance, Veeder points out that '[i]n the absence of an enforceable interim measure, it is sometimes possible for a recalcitrant party to thwart the arbitration procedure—completely and finally.'[17] Born concurs that if arbitral interim awards were not enforceable under the New York Convention, 'the parties will be able to and significantly more willing to refuse to comply with provisional

---

[12]   The New York Convention does not define awards through any formal or material requirements. The definition of 'arbitral awards' is set out in Article I(2) of the New York Convention, according to which "[t]he term 'arbitral awards' shall include not only awards made by arbitrators appointed for each case but also those made by permanent arbitral bodies to which the parties have submitted."

[13]   3 GARY B. BORN, INTERNATIONAL COMMERCIAL ARBITRATION, THE NETHERLANDS: KLUWER LAW INTERNATIONAL 2515 (2nd ed., 2014).

[14]   Tijana Kojovic, *Court Enforcement of Arbitral Decisions – How Final is Provisional?* 18(5) JOURNAL OF INTERNATIONAL ARBITRATION, 511, 523-524 (2001).

[15]   For instance, in *Publicis Communication and Publicis S.A.* v. *True North Communications*, the Court of Appeals for the Seventh Circuit held that the arbitral interim measure at hand was final in respect of the matters it resolved and, as such, capable of being enforced (Court of Appeals for the Seventh Circuit, *Publicis Communication and Publicis S.A.* v. *True North Communications Inc.*, 206 F.3d 725 (7th Cir. 2000)). Born also refers to the Judgment of the Paris Court of Appeal of 7 October 2004 (2005 Rev. arb. 737), according to which arbitrators' provisional measures were held to be final: 'The arbitral tribunal has definitely ruled on the request for conservatory measures ... [and has] expressed in an award their power to on an emergency request that participates in the resolution of the dispute.' (3 GARY B. BORN, *supra* note 15, at 2514).

[16]   3 GARY B. BORN, *supra* note 15, at 2514.

[17]   Van Vechten Veeder, *Provisional and conservatory measures, in* ENFORCING ARBITRATION AWARDS UNDER THE NEW YORK CONVENTION: EXPERIENCE AND PROSPECTS, Austria: United Nations Publication 21 (1999).

relief, resulting in precisely the serious harm that provisional measures were meant to foreclose.'[18]

7.18. **Conclusion.** It follows that there seems to be a significant uncertainty as to whether arbitral interim measures are enforceable under the New York Convention. In fact, the UNCITRAL Secretariat stressed this uncertainty in its 1999 Note on the Possible Future Work in the Area of International Commercial Arbitration,[19] which subsequently led to the 2006 amendment to the UNCITRAL Model Law.

IV. Enforcement of Interim Measures under the UNCITRAL Model Law

7.19. **UNCITRAL Model Law.** The UNCITRAL Model Law serves as a guideline for national legislatures wishing to have arbitration laws in accordance with modern international commercial arbitration standards. It is therefore not surprising that the 2006 amendment to the UNCITRAL Model Law introduced a comprehensive set of rules governing the recognition and enforcement of both domestic and foreign arbitral interim measures.

7.20. **Discussions in the 1980s.** According to *travaux préparatoires* (preparatory notes), the enforceability of arbitral interim measures was already discussed in the 1980s. More specifically, one of the drafts of Article 17 provided that 'if enforcement of any such interim measure becomes necessary, the arbitral tribunal may request [a competent court] [the Court specified in article V] to render executory assistance.'[20] However, the Working Group eventually decided to delete this provision because it viewed such provision as incomplete and unlikely to be accepted by many states.[21]

7.21. **UNCITRAL revisiting the topic.** In 1999, the UNCITRAL Secretariat revisited this discussion in its Note on the Possible Future Work in the Area of International Commercial Arbitration.[22] It suggested, among other things, that a further study be made and, based on such study, tentative solutions

---

[18]   3 GARY B. BORN, *supra* note 15, at 2515.
[19]   Note of the Secretary General of the United Nations Commission on International Trade Law, A/CN.9/460, 6 April 1999, paragraph 122, available at: https://undocs.org/EN/A/CN.9/460 (accessed on 14 December 2018).
[20]   Report of the Working Group on International Contract Practices on the work of its sixth session, A/CN.9/245, 22 September 1983, paragraph 70, available at: https://documents-dds-ny.un.org/doc/UNDOC/GEN/V83/619/69/PDF/V8361969.pdf?OpenElement (accessed on 14 December 2018).
[21]   *Ibid*, at paragraph 72.
[22]   Note of the Secretary General of the United Nations Commission on International Trade Law, A/CN.9/460, 6 April 1999, paragraphs 115-127, available at: https://undocs.org/EN/A/CN.9/460 (accessed on 14 December 2018).

be first presented. In March 2000, the UNCITRAL General Assembly accorded this matter high priority[23] and the UNCITRAL Secretariat then prepared a first draft of provisions governing the enforcement of both domestic and foreign arbitral interim measures.[24]

7.22.   **Two variants.** The draft included two variants. The first required a national court to enforce an arbitral interim measure (subject to certain exceptions).[25] The second entitled (but did not require) a national court to enforce such measure.[26] The UNCITRAL Secretariat also suggested that the Working Group consider additional provisions, such as those imposing a duty to inform the court of any changes regarding the interim measure, provisions making the enforcement subject to leave of the tribunal, provisions entitling the court to make the enforcement subject to the requesting party providing security, or provisions entitling the court to reformulate the arbitral interim measure.[27]

7.23.   Eventually, the Working Group adopted the first variant, arguing that 'setting forth an obligation for courts to enforce interim measures might ultimately enhance their effectiveness.'[28] The discussions about the specific language of this variant (and additional provisions outlined above) continued until July 2006, when the Working Group adopted a final text of a new Chapter IV.A dealing with interim measures and preliminary orders.[29] The recognition and enforcement of arbitral interim measures was addressed in Section 4 titled 'Recognition and enforcement of interim measures' containing two newly adopted Articles 17H and 17I.

7.24.   **Obligation to recognize and enforce.** Under Article 17H, a national court is required to recognize and enforce an arbitral

---

[23]   Report of the United Nations Commission on International Trade Law on the work of its thirty-second session, A/54/17, 1999, paragraph 373, available at: https://documents-dds-ny.un.org/doc/UNDOC/GEN/V99/854/30/PDF/V9985430.pdf?OpenElement (accessed on 14 December 2018).

[24]   Report of the Secretary General of the United Nations Commission on International Trade Law, Working Group on Arbitration, A/CN.9/WG.II/WP.110, 22 September 2000, Section II(B), available at: https://undocs.org/en/A/CN.9/WG.II/WP.110 (accessed on 25 February 2019).

[25]   Variant 1 provided that 'An interim measure of protection referred to in article 17, irrespective of the country in which it was made, shall be enforced, upon application by the interested party to the competent court of this State, unless […].' (emphasis added)

[26]   Variant 2 provided that 'The court may, upon application by the interested party, order enforcement of an interim measure of protection referred to in article 17, irrespective of the country in which it was made.' (emphasis added)

[27]   Report of the Secretary General of the United Nations Commission on International Trade Law, Working Group on Arbitration, A/CN.9/WG.II/WP.110, 22 September 2000, Section II(C), available at: https://undocs.org/en/A/CN.9/WG.II/WP.110 (accessed on 25 February 2019).

[28]   Report of the Working Group on Arbitration of the United Nations Commission on International Trade Law on the work of its thirty-third session, A/CN.9/485, 20 December 2000, paragraph 81, available at: https://undocs.org/en/A/CN.9/485 (accessed on 25 February 2019).

[29]   Report of the United Nations Commission on International Trade Law on the work of its thirty-ninth session, A/61/17, 2006, Section IV(B), available at: https://documents-dds-ny.un.org/doc/UNDOC/GEN/V06/558/15/PDF/V0655815.pdf?OpenElement (accessed on 14 December 2018).

interim measure irrespective of the country in which it was issued (subject to the provisions of Article 17I discussed below).[30] A national court may, if it considers appropriate, order the requesting party to provide appropriate security unless the arbitral tribunal has already made a determination regarding security or where such decision is necessary to protect the rights of third parties.[31] A requesting party is also required to inform the national court of any termination, suspension, or modification of the respective interim measure.[32]

7.25.   **Grounds for refusal to recognize and enforce.** Article 17I sets out the grounds for refusing the recognition and enforcement of arbitral interim measures. In particular, these grounds follow the grounds for refusing the recognition and enforcement of foreign awards set out in Article 36 of the UNCITRAL Model Law (and Article V of the New York Convention).[33] In addition, upon the responding party's objection, a national court may refuse to recognize and enforce an interim measure if (i) the requesting party failed to comply with the tribunal's determination regarding security, or (ii) the interim measure was terminated or suspended by the tribunal or, where so empowered, by the court of the state in which the arbitration takes place or under the law of which that interim measure was granted.[34] Finally, a national court may refuse to recognize and enforce an interim measure (even *ex officio*) if the interim measure is incompatible with the powers conferred upon the national court unless the court decides to reformulate the interim measure to the extent necessary to adapt it to its own powers and procedures for the purposes of enforcing that interim measure and without modifying its substance.[35] In any event, under Article 17I(2), any determination by the court is only effective for the purposes of the application to recognize and enforce the interim measure and the court must not, in making that determination, undertake a review of the substance of the interim measure.

7.26.   **Worldwide implementation.** The UNCITRAL Secretariat does not maintain a specific list of countries that have adopted Articles 17H and 17I of the UNCITRAL Model Law into their national arbitration laws. Its official website only designates 23 jurisdictions that have implemented the 2006 amendments

---

[30]   Article 17H(1) of the UNCITRAL Model Law.
[31]   Article 17H(2) of the UNCITRAL Model Law.
[32]   Article 17H(3) of the UNCITRAL Model Law.
[33]   Article 17I(1)(a)(i) and Article 17I(1)(a)(ii) of the UNCITRAL Model Law.
[34]   Article 17I(1)(a)(ii) and (iii) of the UNCITRAL Model Law.
[35]   Article 17I(1)(a)(i) of the UNCITRAL Model Law.

Czech (& Central European) Yearbook of Arbitration®

into their national laws.[36] However, this number does not seem to correspond to the number of jurisdictions that specifically adopted Articles 17H and 17I. For instance, Slovakia is listed as a country that has not implemented the 2006 amendments, but the Slovak Arbitration Act, arguably, includes rules governing the recognition and enforcement of both domestic and foreign arbitral interim measures, which are based on Articles 17H and 17I.

V.   Enforcement of Interim Measures under National Laws

7.27.   Depending on whether they enforce arbitral interim measures, national laws can be divided into three categories: (1) national laws enforcing both domestic and foreign arbitral interim measures, (2) national laws only enforcing domestic arbitral interim measures, and (3) national laws not enforcing any arbitral interim measures. We discuss these categories (together with examples of countries falling within each) in more detail below.

V.1.   National Laws Enforcing Both Domestic and Foreign Arbitral Interim Measures

7.28.   **Germany.** Arbitration in Germany is governed by Book 10 (Sections 1025 through 1066) of the German Code of Civil Procedure.[37] Under Section 1041(2), a court may permit the enforcement of an arbitral interim measure unless a corresponding measure of temporary relief has already been petitioned with a court. The court may also issue a differently worded order if this is required for the enforcement of the measure. These rules also apply to arbitrations having their seat outside of Germany.[38]

7.29.   At first sight, it may appear that German enforcement courts enjoy wide discretion in deciding whether to enforce arbitral interim measures. The threshold for obtaining an enforcement order does not seem to be high. According to Jan K. Schaefer, German courts only consider 'whether there is a valid arbitration agreement and whether the order granted is not wholly

---

[36]   Status: UNCITRAL Model Law on International Commercial Arbitration (1985), with amendments as adopted in 2006, available at: http://www.uncitral.org/uncitral/en/uncitral_texts/arbitration/1985Model_arbitration_status.html (accessed on 25 February 2019).
[37]   Code of Civil Procedure as promulgated on 5 December 2005 (Bundesgesetzblatt (BGBl., Federal Law Gazette) I page 3202, 2006 I page 431; 2007 I page 1781), as amended (the 'German Code of Civil Procedure').
[38]   Section 1062(2) of the German Code of Civil Procedure.

misbalanced.'[39] A pro-arbitration approach of the German Code of Civil Procedure also seems to follow from the court's competence to reformulate an arbitral interim measure. As Jan K. Schaefer points out, this competence aims at preventing the courts from refusing to enforce a measure that does not fit into the German legal system, although reformulating an interim measure may not be an easy task, as demonstrated by German case law.[40]

7.30.   **Austria.** Austrian arbitration is governed by the Austrian Code of Civil Procedure,[41] specifically by Sections 577 through 618. Under Section 593(3), Austrian courts are required to enforce both domestic and foreign arbitral interim measures.[42] Austrian courts may also reformulate an arbitral interim measure if such measure provides for a means of protection unknown to Austrian law. Section 593(4) further provides certain grounds for refusing to enforce an arbitral interim measure. In particular, a domestic measure cannot be enforced if the measure suffers from a defect constituting a ground for setting aside a domestic award. A foreign measure cannot be enforced if the measure suffers from a defect constituting a ground for refusal to recognize and enforce a foreign arbitral award. Irrespective of the country of its origin, an arbitral interim measure also cannot be enforced if (i) the enforcement would contradict an Austrian court measure requested or issued earlier or an earlier foreign court measure, or (ii) the measure provides for a means of protection unknown to Austrian law and no appropriate means of protection provided under Austrian law has been requested.

7.31.   **East-Asian Arbitration Meccas.** The most renowned pro-arbitration jurisdictions in East Asia are Hong Kong and Singapore. Arbitration laws governing international arbitration in both countries provide that arbitral interim measures are, with the leave of the respective court, enforceable as if they were court interim measures.[43] Under Section 61(2) of the Hong Kong Arbitration Ordinance, the court will not grant leave to enforce an arbitral interim measure unless the requesting party shows that the measure is a type of measure that may be made

---

[39]   Jan K. Schaefer, *New Solutions for Interim Measures of Protection in International Commercial Arbitration: English, German and Hong Kong Law Compared*, 2.2 ELECTRONIC JOURNAL OF COMPARATIVE LAW, Section 4.2.2.3 (1998).

[40]   *Ibid.*

[41]   Law of 1 August 1895 Austrian Code of Civil Procedure, RGBl. Nr. 113/1895, as amended (the 'Austrian Code of Civil Procedure').

[42]   GEROLD ZEILER, AUSTRIAN ARBITRATION ACT, Vienna: Neuer Wissenschaftlicher Verlag 105 (2016).

[43]   Section 61 of the 2011 Hong Kong Arbitration Ordinance Cap 609, as amended (the 'Hong Kong Arbitration Ordinance') and Section 12(6) of the Singapore International Arbitration Act, Chapter 143A, as amended (the 'Singapore International Arbitration Act').

by a tribunal seated in Hong Kong. The Singapore International Arbitration Act does not provide such limitation.

7.32. **Post-Communist Countries.** In the past couple of years, several post-communist countries adopted rules aimed at enforcing both domestic and foreign arbitral interim measures.

7.33. **Poland.** For instance, in 2005, Poland introduced Article 1181(3) of the Polish Code of Civil Procedure,[44] according to which an arbitral interim measure is enforceable 'after attachment of an enforceability clause.'[45] Polish courts declare domestic arbitral interim measures enforceable without ordering an oral hearing.[46] The grounds for refusing to enforce a domestic measure are set out in Article 1214(3), which comprise the lack of arbitrability under Polish law and contradiction with Polish public policy. Under Article 1215(1), foreign arbitral interim measures are declared enforceable after an oral hearing. The grounds for refusing to recognize and enforce a foreign measure are set out in Article 1215(2), which correspond to the grounds set out in Article V of the New York Convention.

7.34. **Slovenia.** In 2008, the Slovenian legislature adopted a new Law on Arbitration (the "Slovenian Arbitration Law"), which, among other things, established 'a unified legislative regime for the enforcement of both domestic and foreign arbitral interim measures.'[47] In particular, under Article 43(1) of the Slovenian Arbitration Law, '[t]he recognition of an interim measure issued by a domestic or foreign arbitration shall be decided by the court having jurisdiction pursuant to the rules governing the enforcement and securing of claims.' Under Article 43(2), the grounds for refusing to enforce a domestic measure correspond to the grounds for setting aside a domestic award, which are virtually identical to those set out in the UNCITRAL Model Law. The grounds for refusing to enforce a foreign measure explicitly refer to the grounds set out in Article V of the New York Convention.

7.35. **Slovakia.** Finally, in 2014, the Slovak legislature amended the Slovak Arbitration Act,[48] including the provisions addressing interim measures. According to newly introduced Section 22c, interim measures, except for *ex parte* measures, are execution

---

[44] Polish Act of 17 November 1964 - Code of Civil Procedure, as amended (the 'Polish Code of Civil Procedure').

[45] Łucja Nowak, unofficial translation into English of an excerpt from Polish Act of 17 November 1964 - Code of Civil Procedure (Dz. U. of 1964, no. 43, item 296), available at: https://www.sakig.pl/uploads/upfiles/pdf/kpc-ang.pdf (accessed on 14 December 2018).

[46] Marcin Aslanovicz, Sylvia Piotrowska, *Poland*, *in* THE BAKER & MCKENZIE INTERNATIONAL ARBITRATION YEARBOOK, Huntington: Jurisnet 361 (2013).

[47] Matija Damjan, *Arbitral Interim Measures and the Right to Be Heard*, CZECH (& CENTRAL EUROPEAN) YEARBOOK OF ARBITRATION, HUNTINGTON: JURISNET 72, 84 (2011).

[48] Act No. 244/2002 Coll. on Arbitration, as amended (the 'Slovak Arbitration Act').

titles. An enforcement court is required to refuse to enforce an arbitral interim measure if (i) the conditions for ordering an interim measure under the Act or under the parties' agreement have not been met, (ii) the requesting party has not provided the security ordered by the tribunal, (iii) the interim measure has been terminated or modified, or (iv) the interim measure contradicts Slovak public policy. Arguably, pursuant to Section 22e, these provisions also apply to foreign interim measures.[49]

V.2. National Laws Only Enforcing Domestic Arbitral Interim Measures

7.36. **England & Wales.** The English Arbitration Act,[50] albeit being generally recognized as a pro-arbitration arbitration law, only provides for the enforcement of domestic arbitral interim measures.[51] The enforcement process comprises three steps. First, a tribunal must first issue an interim measure referred to in Sections 38 or 39. Second, under Section 41(5), if a party fails to comply with such measure, the tribunal may issue a so-called 'peremptory order', i.e. an order to the same effect prescribing such time for compliance with it as the tribunal considers appropriate. Third, if a party fails to comply with the peremptory order, the requesting party or the tribunal may ask the court to enforce such order in accordance with Section 42. At the same time, the tribunal is entitled to (i) order that the defaulting party will not be entitled to rely upon any allegation or material which was the subject matter of the peremptory order, (ii) draw adverse inferences, (iii) proceed to an award on the basis of such materials as have been properly provided to it, or (iv) make such order as it thinks fit as to the payment of costs of the arbitration incurred in consequence of the non-compliance.

7.37. **Switzerland.** Just like the English Arbitration Act, a very flexible Swiss arbitration law governing international arbitration

---

[49] Under Section 22e of the Slovak Arbitration Act, '[t]he provisions of Sections 22a, 22b and 22d only apply to interim measures ordered in arbitration that is pending in the territory of the Slovak Republic.' This suggests that Section 22c (dealing with the enforcement of arbitral interim measures) also apply to foreign arbitral measures. However, under Section 2(3), only provisions of Sections 2(2) and 27 apply to arbitrations having their place outside of Slovakia. Therefore, an argument can be made that Section 22e, which aims at extending the applicability of Section 22c to foreign arbitral measures, cannot be applied in case of foreign arbitrations. Hence, the solution adopted by the Slovak legislature created unnecessary ambiguity and one may have difficulty understanding why the Slovak legislature did not amend Section 2(3) by adding a reference to Section 22c (compare with Article 1(2) of the UNCITRAL Model Law, which enumerates the provisions addressing the recognition and enforcement of arbitral interim measures (Articles 17H and 17I) in the list of provisions applicable to both domestic and foreign arbitrations).
[50] English Arbitration Act 1996, as amended (the 'English Arbitration Act').
[51] Jan K. Schaefer, *supra* note 41, at Section 4.1.2.3, the International Comparative Legal Guide to International Arbitration 2018, England & Wales, 15th Edition, Question 7.6, available at https://iclg.com/practice-areas/international-arbitration-laws-and-regulations/england-and-wales (accessed on 25 February 2019).

(Chapter 12 of the 1987 Federal Private International Law Act) (the 'Swiss PILA') also only provides for the enforcement of domestic interim measures. Under Article 183(2) of the Swiss PILA, if a party does not comply with an arbitral interim measure, the tribunal (not a party) may ask the court for assistance. The court will only enforce an arbitral interim measure if the measure is recognized by Swiss procedural law.[52] However, under Article 176 of the Swiss PILA, Article 183 only applies to arbitrations seated in Switzerland. Further, according to Swiss commentators, it is also unlikely that Swiss courts would enforce a foreign arbitral interim measure as a foreign award because the Swiss Supreme Court has held that arbitral interim measures are not 'awards'.[53]

7.38. **Hungary.** In 2017, Hungary introduced a new, modern arbitration act (Act LX of 2017 on arbitration) (the "Hungarian Arbitration Act"). The Hungarian Arbitration Act, among other things, introduced a comprehensive set of rules governing the enforcement of arbitral interim measures in Sections 26 and 27. These Sections are largely based on Articles 17H and 17I of the UNCITRAL Model Law. However, Sections 26 and 27 of the Hungarian Arbitration Act are not referred to in the list of provisions that apply also to arbitrations having their place outside of Hungary (Section 1(2) of the Hungarian Arbitration Act). Therefore, it appears rather unlikely that foreign arbitral interim measures would be enforceable in Hungary under Sections 26 and 27 of the Hungarian Arbitration Act.

V.3. National Laws Not Enforcing Any Arbitral Interim Measures

7.39. National arbitration laws that do not provide for the enforcement of domestic or foreign interim measures are, for instance, found

---

[52] The International Comparative Legal Guide to International Arbitration 2018, Switzerland, 15th Edition, Question 7.6, available at https://iclg.com/practice-areas/international-arbitration-laws-and-regulations/Switzerland (accessed on 25 February 2019).

[53] Georg von Segesser, Christopher Boog, *Interim Measures, in* INTERNATIONAL ARBITRATION IN SWITZERLAND, A HANDBOOK FOR PRACTITIONERS, The Netherlands: Kluwer Law International 123 (2013), Lukas Wyss, *Switzerland*, INTERIM MEASURES IN INTERNATIONAL ARBITRATION, HUNTINGTON: JURISNET 747 (2014), and the International Comparative Legal Guide to International Arbitration 2018, Switzerland, 15th Edition, Question 7.6, available at https://iclg.com/practice-areas/international-arbitration-laws-and-regulations/Switzerland (accessed on 25 February 2019).

in China,[54] the Czech Republic,[55] Italy,[56] and, surprisingly, even in Sweden.[57] Except for Sweden, the common feature of these arbitration laws is that they do not empower domestic arbitral tribunals to issue interim measures. Therefore, it is not surprising that these arbitration laws do not enforce also foreign interim measures. Sweden seems to be an interesting exception in the list of countries not providing for the enforcement of any interim measures. This is mainly because arbitral tribunals seated in Sweden are entitled to issue interim measures,[58] and Sweden is generally recognized as an arbitration-friendly country.

VI. Conclusion

7.40.   The enforceability of arbitral interim measures is critical for the efficacy of arbitration. However, there does not appear to be a worldwide recognized binding instrument requiring national courts to enforce such measures. In particular, it is very questionable whether arbitral measures are enforceable under the New York Convention. Given this ambiguity, it always rests with national courts to decide whether arbitral interim measures qualify as 'awards' capable of being enforced under the New York Convention. This naturally leads to different outcomes, which is clearly undesirable.

7.41.   The 2006 amendment to the UNCITRAL Model Law aimed to fix this ambiguity by introducing a comprehensive set of rules governing the enforcement of both domestic and foreign arbitral interim measures. Yet, it appears that this amendment has not been implemented into a significant number of national legal orders. Therefore, one may have serious doubts as to whether this amendment reached its goal.

7.42.   Thus, it appears that a party intending to request an arbitral interim measure always needs to review the national laws of the state where the other party's assets are located. For instance,

---

[54]   The International Comparative Legal Guide to International Arbitration 2018, China, 15th Edition, Question 7.6, available at: https://iclg.com/practice-areas/international-arbitration-laws-and-regulations/china (accessed on 25 February 2019).

[55]   The International Comparative Legal Guide to International Arbitration 2018, Czech Republic, 15th Edition, Question 7.6, available at: https://iclg.com/practice-areas/international-arbitration-laws-and-regulations/czech-republic (accessed on 25 February 2019).

[56]   The International Comparative Legal Guide to International Arbitration 2018, Italy, 15th Edition, Question 7.6, available at: https://iclg.com/practice-areas/international-arbitration-laws-and-regulations/italy (accessed on 25 February 2019).

[57]   The International Comparative Legal Guide to International Arbitration 2018, Sweden, 15th Edition, Question 7.6, available at: https://iclg.com/practice-areas/international-arbitration-laws-and-regulations/sweden (accessed on 25 February 2019).

[58]   IBA Arbitration Guide: Sweden (Updated January 2018), available at: https://www.ibanet.org/LPD/Dispute_Resolution_Section/Arbitration/Arbcountryguides.aspx (accessed on 25 February 2019).

an English claimant wishing to request a freezing order from a tribunal seated in Switzerland against a respondent having its assets in Germany needs to know whether the German legal order would enforce a Swiss arbitral freezing order.

7.43.   Depending on whether national laws enforce arbitral interim measures, they can be divided into three categories. The first category includes national laws enforcing both domestic and foreign arbitral interim measures. Such national laws are, for example, in Germany, Austria, Hong Kong, Singapore, Poland, Slovenia, and Slovakia. The second category includes national laws only enforcing domestic arbitral interim measures. A bit surprisingly, even some of the most pro-arbitration laws fall within this category, such as the English Arbitration Act and Swiss PILA. Finally, the third category includes national laws not providing for the enforcement of any arbitral interim measures. Here, we can find arbitration laws that do not empower arbitral tribunals to issue interim measures (e.g. China, the Czech Republic, and Italy), but also national laws which empower arbitral tribunals to do so (e.g. Sweden).

7.44.   This state of affairs is far from desirable when looking at it from a pro-arbitration perspective. However, it is difficult to imagine that a significant improvement will come about within a few years. Therefore, at this point of time, it appears that in the majority of cases involving a potentially recalcitrant adverse party, the party wishing to request an interim measure should seriously consider filing such request directly with a national court rather than with the tribunal lacking any coercive powers.

| | |

Summaries

DEU   [*Im Schiedsverfahren ergangene vorläufige und einstweilige Maßnahmen - Fallstricke für die Vollstreckung*]
Der Artikel befasst sich mit der Vollstreckung einstweiliger Verfügungen im internationalen Schiedsverfahren. Die Autoren vertreten die Auffassung, dass – ungeachtet der grundlegenden Bedeutung der Vollstreckbarkeit solcher einstweiligen Verfügungen im Schiedsverfahren für die Effizienz solcher Verfahren – wohl keine global anerkannte, verbindliche Rechtsquelle existiert, welche die Anerkennung solcher Verfügungen durch die Gerichte zwingend voraussetzen würde. Vor allem haben wir hier das New Yorker Übereinkommen,

welches die im Schiedsverfahren ergangenen einstweiligen Verfügungen nicht ausdrücklich erwähnt. Das hat verschiedenste Meinungen ausgelöst. Andererseits ist zu konzedieren, dass das UNCITRAL-Mustergesetz, welches die Anerkennung und die Vollstreckung von im Schiedsverfahren ergangenen einstweiligen Verfügungen ausdrücklich regelt, nur eine unverbindliche Empfehlung darstellt. Vor diesem Hintergrund sieht es so aus, als ob die Vollstreckbarkeit einstweiliger Verfügungen, welche von Schiedsrichtern erlassen wurden, dem Wohlwollen nationaler Rechtsordnungen und der innerstaatlichen Gerichte anheimgestellt ist. Dies führt unausweichlich zu erheblicher Rechtsunsicherheit. Den Autoren zufolge ist der Stand der Dinge zwar wenig wünschenswert; zugleich bestehen aber keine Anzeichen dafür, dass es in den kommenden Jahren zu einer grundsätzlichen Besserung kommen könnte. Im Hinblick darauf schließen die Autoren, dass Streitparteien, die den Erlass einer einstweiligen Verfügung anstrengen, im Regelfall nur bleibt, die Beantragung direkt bei einem innerstaatlichen (nationalen) Gericht zu erwägen.

CZE   *[**Předběžná a prozatímní opatření vydávaná v rozhodčím řízení - nástrahy pro výkon**]*
Tento článek se zabývá výkonem předběžných opatření v mezinárodním rozhodčím řízení. Autoři zastávají názor, že ačkoli je vykonatelnost předběžných opatření v rozhodčím řízení zásadní pro efektivitu rozhodčího řízení, zdá se, že neexistuje globálně uznávaný závazný pramen práva, který by vyžadoval, aby soudy taková opatření uznaly. Především je to Newyorská úmluva, která výslovně neuvádí předběžná opatření vydávaná v rozhodčím řízení, což evokuje různé názory. Současně je nutno uvést, že ačkoli Vzorový zákon UNCITRAL výslovně upravuje uznávání a výkon předběžných opatření vydávaných v rozhodčím řízení, jde pouze o nezávazné doporučení. Vzhledem k tomu se zdá, že vykonatelnost předběžných opatření vydávaných rozhodci je ponechána na milost národním právním řádům a vnitrostátním soudům. To nevyhnutelně vede ke značné nejistotě. Autoři mají za to, že tento stav je nežádoucí, ale nevidí náznaky toho, že by mohlo dojít k zásadnímu zlepšení v průběhu několika let. S ohledem na to autoři uzavírají, že strana požadující vydání předběžného opatření musí obvykle zvážit podání žádosti o předběžné opatření přímo u vnitrostátního (národního) soudu.

| | |

POL [*Środki tymczasowe i postanowienia przedwstępne orzekane w postępowaniu arbitrażowym – pułapki związane z wykonywaniem*]

W opinii autorów, chociaż wykonalność środków tymczasowych wydawanych w postępowaniu arbitrażowym ma zasadnicze znaczenie dla efektywności postępowania arbitrażowego, jednak wydaje się, że nie istnieje globalnie uznawane wiążące źródło prawa, które nakładałoby na sądy obowiązek uznawania tego typu środków. W związku z tym wydaje się, że wykonalność środków tymczasowych wydawanych w postępowaniu arbitrażowych jest zdane na łaskę krajowych porządków prawnych i sądów krajowych. Autorzy są zdania, że jest to sytuacja niepożądana, jednak nie dostrzegają żadnych sygnałów, które zwiastowałyby zasadniczą poprawę sytuacji w ciągu najbliższych lat. Autorzy konstatują, że strona występująca o wydanie środka tymczasowego musi zazwyczaj zastanowić się nad złożeniem stosownego wniosku o wydanie środka tymczasowego bezpośrednio do sądu krajowego.

FRA [*Les mesures provisoires dans la procédure d'arbitrage - les écueils de leur exécution*]

Quoique la force exécutoire des mesures provisoires prises dans le cadre d'une procédure d'arbitrage soit essentielle pour l'efficacité de cette procédure, il semble qu'il n'existe pas de source de droit contraignante et mondialement reconnue qui stipule l'obligation des juges à reconnaître de telles mesures. Partant, l'exécution des mesures provisoires prises dans le cadre d'une procédure d'arbitrage serait laissée à l'appréciation des juges nationaux appliquant les règles de droit nationales. Les auteurs sont d'avis que cet état est loin d'être souhaitable, mais estiment qu'une amélioration fondamentale est peu probable dans un proche avenir. Dans ce contexte, la partie demandant la prise d'une mesure provisoire, doit en principe considérer la possibilité de s'adresser directement à une juridiction nationale.

RUS [*Предварительные и временные меры, принятые в арбитраже - ловушки для исполнения*]

Авторы придерживаются мнения, что, хотя исполнимость предварительных мер, принимаемых арбитражем, и имеет решающее значение для эффективности арбитража, очевидно отсутствие признанного в мировом масштабе обязательного источника права, требующего, чтобы суды признавали такие меры. С учетом этого кажется, что исполнимость предварительных мер, принятых арбитражем, остается во власти национальных законодательств и национальных судов. Авторы считают, что такое состояние нежелательно, и не видят признаков серьезных улучшений в течение нескольких лет. Учитывая это, авторы пришли к выводу, что сторона, требующая принятия предварительных мер, обычно должна рассмотреть возможность подачи ходатайства о принятии предварительных мер непосредственно в национальный (внутригосударственный) суд.

ESP [*Medidas provisionales y preliminares en el procedimiento arbitral - riesgos de la ejecución*]

Los autores sostienen que, a pesar de ser la ejecutoriedad de las medidas preliminares dictadas en el procedimiento arbitral, del todo fundamental para la eficacia del procedimiento arbitral, aparentemente no existe una fuente con carácter vinculante y reconocida a nivel global que exija que tales medidas sean reconocidas por los tribunales. Es por ello, al parecer, que la ejecutoriedad de las medidas preliminares dictadas en el procedimiento arbitral está a la merced de los ordenamientos jurídicos y los tribunales nacionales. Los autores consideran esta situación indeseable, sin embargo, no prevén una mejora fundamental en los próximos años. En este sentido, los autores concluyen que aquella parte que solicita el dictamen de una medida preliminar habitualmente considera la posibilidad de que se presente la solicitud del dictamen de la medida preliminar directamente en el tribunal nacional.

Bibliography

Marcin Aslanovicz, Sylvia Piotrowska, *Poland, in* THE BAKER & MCKENZIE INTERNATIONAL ARBITRATION YEARBOOK, Huntington: Jurisnet (2013).

NIGEL BLACKABY, CONSTANTINE PARTASIDES, ALAN REDFERN, MARTIN HUNTER, REDFERN AND HUNTER ON INTERNATIONAL ARBITRATION, Oxford: Oxford University (6th ed., 2015).

Gary B. Born, *International Commercial Arbitration, in* THE NETHERLANDS: KLUWER LAW INTERNATIONAL (2nd ed., 2014).

Matija Damjan, *Arbitral Interim Measures and the Right to Be Heard, in* CZECH (& CENTRAL EUROPEAN) YEARBOOK OF ARBITRATION, Huntington: Jurisnet (2011).

Tijana Kojovic, *Court Enforcement of Arbitral Decisions – How Final is Provisional?* 18(5) JOURNAL OF INTERNATIONAL ARBITRATION 511 (2001).

JEAN F. POUDRET, SÉBASTIEN BESSON, COMPARATIVE LAW OF INTERNATIONAL ARBITRATION, London: Sweet & Maxwell Ltd (2nd ed., 2007).

Georg von Segesser, Christopher Boog, *Interim Measures, in* INTERNATIONAL ARBITRATION IN SWITZERLAND, A HANDBOOK FOR PRACTITIONERS, The Netherlands: Kluwer Law International (2013).

Jan K. Schaefer, *New Solutions for Interim Measures of Protection in International Commercial Arbitration: English, German and Hong Kong Law Compared*, 2.2 ELECTRONIC JOURNAL OF COMPARATIVE LAW (1998).

Van Vechten Veeder, *Provisional and conservatory measures*, ENFORCING ARBITRATION AWARDS UNDER THE NEW YORK CONVENTION: EXPERIENCE AND PROSPECTS, Austria: United Nations Publication (1999).

Lukas Wyss, *Switzerland*, INTERIM MEASURES IN INTERNATIONAL ARBITRATION, Huntington: Jurisnet (2014).

GEROLD ZEILER, AUSTRIAN ARBITRATION ACT, Vienna: Neuer Wissenschaftlicher Verlag (2016).

Czech (& Central European) Yearbook of Arbitration®

Lukáš Ryšavý

Recognition and Enforcement of Foreign Arbitral Awards with Respect to the Independence and Impartiality of the Arbitrator

Key words:
Arbitration | Foreign Arbitral Award | Recognition and Enforcement of Arbitral Award | Independence | Impartiality | Bias | Neutrality | Annulment of the Arbitral Award | Exclusion of the Arbitrator | Enforceability of the Arbitral Award

Abstract | Arbitration is a form of out-of-court dispute resolution and the arbitral award is a final and enforceable decision based on the merits of the case. It is therefore an enforceable title. If there is no voluntary fulfilment of the obligation imposed by the arbitral award, then there is a need to assert the obligation even against the will of the obliged party. In the case of a foreign arbitral award, it is essential that this arbitral award must be recognized before it is enforced. This article discusses the extent to which the independence and impartiality of the arbitrator can play a role in the recognition and enforcement of a foreign arbitral award; whether the independence and impartiality of an arbitrator can be found as a reason for refusing to recognize and enforce a foreign arbitral award. In this context, the article defines the concepts of independence and impartiality (but also bias and neutrality). These are the basic conditions of arbitration, from the constitution of the arbitral tribunal to the enforcement of the arbitral award. At the same time, this article introduces other possibilities guaranteeing impartial, independent and fair decision-making (including the exclusion of the arbitrator, and the annulment of the arbitral award), which are very closely related to the topic of this article. The author concludes that although the independence and impartiality of an arbitrator may appear as a reason for refusal to recognize and enforce an arbitral award, its practical application may be considered only in exceptional cases. These include where the reasons could not be applied in

Lukáš Ryšavý is a senior lecturer in the Department of International and European Law at Palacky University Olomouc, Faculty of Law. He is also a guest lecturer at the University of Salzburg, in the Salzburg Centre of European Union Studies (SCEUS). In his research he focuses on the fields of International Private Law, European Union Law, Arbitration and Mediation. E-mail: lukas.rysavy@upol.cz, l.rysavy@seznam.cz

the country of origin of the arbitral award, or respectively the application of these reasons was unsuccessful and recognition or the enforcement of an arbitral award would be incompatible with public policy.

| | |

I. Introduction

8.01.   One of many relevant reasons[1] why arbitration has become the most popular way to resolve disputes, especially in the context of international business relations, is the easier execution of foreign arbitral awards. This free movement of foreign arbitral awards, if we use the terminology of EU law, is made possible primarily by the worldwide acceptance of the New York Convention on the Recognition and Enforcement of Foreign Arbitral Awards[2] (1958). With this convention, the UN created the most important legal basis for arbitration and one of the most successful international treaties in history.[3]

8.02.   One of the basic conditions pervading arbitration, from the constitution of the arbitral tribunal to the enforcement of the arbitral award, or the recognition and enforcement of a foreign arbitral award, is that the principles of a fair trial are observed. This is so that, among other things, an independent and impartial arbitrator makes the decision.

8.03.   In the light of these facts, this article deals with the issue of the recognition and enforcement of foreign arbitral awards in terms of the independence and impartiality of the arbitrator, or the question of the role of independence and impartiality in the recognition and enforcement of foreign arbitral awards. However, the answer to this question is not possible without approaching the other institutions which guarantee impartial, independent and fair decision-making. In this respect, the main focus will not be recognition and enforcement at its general level, but only in the sense in which the independence and impartiality of the arbitrator may appear as grounds for refusal to recognize and execute a foreign arbitral award. In view of

---

[1]   For other reasons see for e.g. NIGEL BLACKABY, CONSTANTINE PARTASIDES et al., REDFERN AND HUNTER ON INTERNATIONAL ARBITRATION, New York: Oxford University Press 31 (5th ed. 2009).

[2]   Decree No. 74/1959 Coll.

[3]   The New York Convention replaced the Geneva Protocol on Arbitration Clauses of 1923 between Contracting States and the Geneva Convention on the Execution of Foreign Arbitral Awards of 1927 and currently nearly 160 States have joined this Convention, see Status of Convention on the Recognition and Enforcement of Foreign Arbitral Awards (New York, 1958), available at: http://<www.uncitral.org/uncitral/ en/uncitral_texts/arbitration/NYConvention_status.html (accessed on 15 April 2018).

this objective, it will also be necessary to define these central concepts.

II. Independence and Impartiality as a Criterion when Selecting an Arbitrator

8.04. A whole range of criteria can be given for choosing the 'right' arbitrator. Parties, or the third party, may consider, for example, the nationality of the parties, the nationality of the arbitrator, the experience of the arbitrator with the issue in dispute, the language skills of the arbitrator with respect to the parties to the dispute, the language in which the proceedings will be conducted, the scheduling possibilities of the arbitrator, the willingness to travel if it appears desirable or necessary, and the independence and impartiality of the arbitrator.[4] Parties to the dispute may also rely on references from close or familiar persons, from the arbitrator's jurisdiction to any organization, political party, or association; from the behaviour of the person, from a certain personal experience etc.[5]

8.05. In addition, the parties may deliberately appoint an arbitrator to be such a person whom they do not consider to be impartial at all. They hope they will act in their favour, or at least they are convinced that they share their legal opinion on the matter.[6] All these circumstances may, to a greater or lesser degree, increase confidence or distrust in the person or even in arbitration as such. It is the trust in a particular arbitrator on the basis of a variety of criteria, that is to say, the relationship between the party and the arbitrator, which may lead to a certain strain on the arbitrator in the light of the expectations of the parties and by the law and arbitration rules laid down by the principle of impartiality and independence.

8.06. Independence and impartiality, as legally stipulated terms, have a fundamental legal significance and influence over the whole arbitration procedure, or may affect the legality and enforceability of the arbitral award.[7]

---

[4] See e.g. MAURO RUBINO-SAMMARTANO, INTERNATIONAL ARBITRATION, LAW AND PRACTICE, Huntington, New York: Juris Publishing 460 (3rd ed. 2014); WOLFGANG KRÜGER, THOMAS RAUSCHER (eds.), MÜNCHENER KOMMENTAR ZUR ZIVILPROZESSORDNUNG. BAND 3, Sections 1025 – 1109, München: C. H. Beck 34 (4th ed. 2013).

[5] Burkhard Lotz, *Die Unparteilichkeit und Unabhängigkeit des parteiernannten Schiedsrichter,* 52(4) ANWALTSBLATT 202, 202 (2002).

[6] See HANS SMIT, THE PERNICIOUS INSTITUTION OF THE PARTY-APPOINTED ARBITRATOR, Columbia University Academic Commons 1 (2010), available at: http://hdl.handle.net/10022/AC:P:10569 (accessed on 15 April 2018).

[7] Similarly see e.g. FOUCHARD, GAILLARD, GOLDMAN ON INTERNATIONAL COMMERCIAL ARBITRATION, The Hague, Boston, London: Kluwer Law International 561 (Emmanuel Gaillard, John Savage eds., 1999); see also Judgment of the German Federal Court of Justice (Bundesgerichtshof) of 3 July 1975, Ref. No. III ZR 78/73, point 17.

II.1. The Concepts of Independence, Impartiality and Bias

8.07. Almost all legal regulations or orders of arbitration courts contain the concepts of independence and impartiality (or at least one of them),[8] but generally do not define these terms. The theoretical and practical approaches are not entirely unified, and the concepts of independence and impartiality are often confused without being attributed to different content. Additionally, the distinction of independence and impartiality is considered to be unnecessary or the boundary between the two concepts is not clear enough.[9]

8.08. Frequently used examples for distinguishing independence and impartiality are the Ethical Rules for International Arbitrators issued in 1987 by the International Bar Association (IBA Rules of Ethics for International Arbitrators),[10] which state in point 3.1:

> The criteria for the assessing questions relating to bias are impartiality and independence. Partiality arises when an arbitrator favours one of the parties, or where he is prejudiced in relation to the subject-matter of the dispute. Dependence arises from the relationship between an arbitrator and one of the parties, or with someone closely connected with one of the parties.

8.09. At the moment, there are also IBA Guidelines on Conflicts of Interest in International Arbitration from 2014,[11] which replace the Ethical Rules on certain issues, but do not change the content of the above-mentioned IBA Ethical Rules.

8.10. Similar definitions of the concepts of independence and impartiality are given by Redfern and Hunter when they state that 'an impartial arbitrator, by definition, is one who is not biased in favour of or prejudiced against, a particular party or its case, while an independent arbitrator is one who has no close relationship - financial, professional, or personal - with a party

---

[8] See Article 14 paragraph 1 Convention On The Settlement Of Investment Disputes Between States And Nationals Of Other States Done at Washington, 18 March 1965 (entered into force on 14 October 1966); Article 24 paragraph 1(a) Arbitration Act 1996.

[9] For more details see SAM LUTTRELL, BIAS CHALLENGES IN INTERNATIONAL COMMERCIAL ARBITRATION: THE NEED FOR A 'REAL DANGER' TEST, Alphen aan den Rijn: Kluwer Law International 19 (2009); similarly Scott M. Donahey, *The Independence and Neutrality of Arbitrators*, 9(4) JOURNAL OF INTERNATIONAL ARBITRATION 31, 31 (1992).

[10] IBA Rules of Ethics for International Arbitrators, available at: https://www.trans-lex.org/701100 (acessed on 10 April 2018).

[11] Available also in Czech, Pokyny pro střet zájmů v mezinárodní arbitráži, available at: http://<www. forarb.com/wp-content/uploads/2012/02/IBA-Pokyny-pro-st%C5%99et-z%C3%A1jm%C5%AF-v-mezin%C3%A1rodn%C3%AD-arbitr%C3%A1%C5%BEi.pdf (acessed on 10 April 2018).

or its counsel.'[12] However, as they later point out, the notions of independence and impartiality have also changed over time, and the two concepts are characterized as 'the opposite side of the same coin.'[13]

II.1.1. Independence

8.11. On the basis of the above, it is therefore possible to define the notion of independence, respectively lack of independence as an objective fact of the arbitrator's personal, social, professional or financial ties to the parties or close persons.[14] Some scholars also discuss the arbitrator's independence in relation to the arbitration institution.[15] Dependence can be seen, for example, in situations where an arbitrator acts or has acted as a consultant or employee of one party to the dispute. Additionally, it can be a situation where the arbitrator engages in a business transaction with one party to the dispute, for example, by investing in real estate or securities. It can also be seen where a relationship of affinity to the parties to the dispute or to legal representatives exists, or where long-term friendship exists. In most cases, independence will primarily depend on the depth and intensity of such a relationship.

II.1.2. Impartiality

8.12. Impartiality, respectively lack of impartiality is rather a subjective advantage of one party to the dispute or a manifestation of prejudice. Advantage in this sense is then to be understood as favouring one party before the other for reasons unconnected with a link to any of the parties to the dispute or the subject matter of the dispute.[16] Donahey, for example, speaks in the same sense about impartiality: 'Impartiality is the absence of impermissible bias in the mind of the arbitrator toward a party

---

[12]   ALAN REDFERN, MARTIN HUNTER, LAW AND PRACTICE OF INTERNATIONAL COMMERCIAL ARBITRATION, London: Sweet & Maxwell 220 (3rd ed. 1999).
[13]   ALAN REDFERN, MARTIN HUNTER, NIGEL BLACKABY, CONSTANTINE PARTASIDES, LAW AND PRACTICE OF INTERNATIONAL COMMERCIAL ARBITRATION, London: Sweet & Maxwell 201 (4th ed. 2004).
[14]   Similarly PŘEMYSL RABAN, ALTERNATIVNÍ ŘEŠENÍ SPORŮ, ARBITRÁŽ A ROZHODCI V ČESKÉ A SLOVENSKÉ REPUBLICE A ZAHRANIČÍ, Praha: C. H. Beck 112 (2004); EMMANUEL GAILLARD, JOHN SAVAGE (eds.), *supra* note 7, at 557.
[15]   See PETER SCHLOSSER, DAS RECHT DER INTERNATIONALEN PRIVATEN SCHIEDSGERICHTSBARKEIT, Tübingen: Mohr Siebeck 402 (2nd ed. 1989).
[16]   See Antonín Mokrý, *Nezávislost a nestrannost soudce - vzájemná souvislost* a *podmíněnost pojmů,* 41 (8) PRÁVNÍ PRAXE 459, 460 (1993); decision of the Czech Constitutional Court (Ústavní soud) of 19 July 2016, Ref. No. III. ÚS 1872/16.

or toward the subject matter in dispute."[17] This definition could also serve to define the concept of bias, which will be explained below.

II.1.3. Bias

8.13. In addition to the notion of independence and impartiality, there is also the term *bias*, which is used only in relation to the exclusion of the arbitrator. Its importance lies above all in preventing the arbitrator in question from hearing and adjudicating the dispute. The proximity of the concepts of impartiality, independence and bias is evidenced, for example, by Section 42 paragraph 2 ZPO[18] governing the possibility of rejecting a judge because of a suspicion of bias if there is reason to doubt their impartiality. Similarly, the Czech Constitutional Court's case law uses the notion of impartiality and bias in close proximity, when it examines the issue of a biased judge from the aspect of impartiality. In a recent decision, it associated the right to a fair trial with the condition that an 'independent and impartial' judge adjudicates a dispute, while the 'impartiality' of the judge is one of the main prerequisites for fair decision-making.[19]

II.1.4. Neutrality

8.14. In addition to the notion of independence, impartiality, and bias, the term 'neutrality' commonly found in literature and practice can be understood in various ways. On the one hand, it can be used as a superior term in relation to the concepts of independence and impartiality,[20] or it may also be understood as a criterion for a different, neutral nationality, habitual residence

[17] Scott M. Donahey, *The Uniform Domain Name Dispute Resolution Process and the appearance of partiality. Panelists impaled on the horns of a dilemma*, 19(1) JOURNAL OF INTERNATIONAL ARBITRATION 33, 35 (2002).

[18] The German Code of Civil Procedure - Zivilprozessordnung in der Fassung der Bekanntmachung vom 5. Dezember 2005 (BGBl. I P. 3202, ber. 2006 P. 431, 2007 P. 1781) zuletzt geändert durch Gesetz vom 21.11.2016 (BGBl. I P. 2591), hereinafter referred to as ZPO.

[19] Decision of the Czech Constitutional Court (Ústavní soud) of 27 May 2015, Ref. No. I. ÚS 1811/14; see also f.e. ALEXANDER J. BĚLOHLÁVEK, ZÁKON O ROZHODČÍM ŘÍZENÍ A VÝKONU ROZHODČÍCH NÁLEZŮ: KOMENTÁŘ, Praha: C. H. Beck 408 (2nd ed. 2012); decision of the Czech Constitutional Court (Ústavní soud) of 19 July 2016, Ref. No. III. ÚS 1872/16; decision of the Czech Constitutional Court (Ústavní soud) of 27 November 1996, Ref. No. I. ÚS 167/94.

[20] Pierre Lalive, *On the neutrality of the arbitrator and of the place of arbitration*, in RECUEIL DE TRAVAUX SUISSES SUR L'ARBITRAGE INTERNATIONAL, Zürich: Schulthess 23, 24 (Claude Reymond, Eugen Bucher eds., 1984); Marie Öhrström, *Chapter XII - SCC Rules*, in INSTITUTIONAL ARBITRATION. ARTICLE-BY-ARTICLE COMMENTARY, München: C. H. Beck, 2013, 829 (Rolf A. Schütze ed., 2013). Similarly see the Judgment of the German Federal Court of Justice (Bundesgerichtshof) of 15 May 1986, Ref. No. III ZR 192/84. In addition, Donahey refers to the use of the concept of neutrality in the same sense as impartiality, see SCOTT M. DONAHEY, *supra* note 9, at 32.

or domicile than that of the parties to the dispute.[21] In this sense, the concept of 'neutral' is also used in relation to the place of arbitration, where it may be desirable and appropriate to designate the place of the arbitration in a third, neutral, country than what could be considered a 'domestic' relationship with one of the parties.[22] Neutrality may also include legal, cultural, sociological, religious, economic, or ideological issues.

III.   Applying Reasons for Bias

III.1.   Exclusion of the Arbitrator

8.15.   The right to the exclusion of an arbitrator (Section 11 and 12 of the Czech Arbitration Act)[23,24] is an important means of protecting parties against bias during decision making in arbitration. In general, it must be assumed that it is up to the parties to evaluate the circumstances that are known to them and that could adversely affect the independence and impartiality of the arbitrator, and possibly raise the arbitrator´s bias within the prescribed period. If the reason to exclude an arbitrator is not applied in time, there is a lapse of claim and this reason cannot be relied upon, either as grounds for the setting aside the arbitral award, or as grounds for the refusal of its recognition.[25]

8.16.   The question of a time limit in which the grounds for bias may be objected deserves a short note. While according to German legislation, this right is bound for a period of two weeks from the moment the party has learned of the composition of the arbitral tribunal or the reason for the refusal of the arbitrator (Section 1037 paragraph 2, ZPO), Czech legislation is fundamentally lagging behind in this respect. The Czech Arbitration Act does not provide for any specific time limit for the application of grounds of bias in the course of the arbitration procedure and the only time limit is the general time limit in Section 33 of the Czech Arbitration Act, which only applies to the situation when the arbitral award is annulled. This inconsistency of the legislature is very problematic in practice and should be

---

[21]   For more information see Ilhyung Lee, *Practice and Predicament: The Nationality of the International Arbitrator (With Survey Results)*, 31(3) FORDHAM INTERNATIONAL L. J. 603 - 633 (2007).

[22]   See Pierre Lalive, *On the Transfer of Seat in International Arbitration*, in LAW AND JUSTICE IN A MULTISTATE WORLD. ESSAYS IN HONOR OF ARTHUR T. VON MEHREN, New York: Transnational Publishers, 515-526 (James Nafziger, Symeon Symeonides eds., 2002).

[23]   Act No 216/1994 Coll. On Arbitration and Enforcement of Arbitral Awards.

[24]   The German ZPO in this context speaks of the arbitrator's refusal (Section 1036 and 1037 German ZPO).

[25]   For more information about the preclusive period in the arbitration and before the regular court see Joachim Münch, in MÜNCHENER KOMMENTAR ZUR ZIVILPROZESSORDNUNG. BAND 3. Sections 1025 – 1109, München: C. H. Beck 237 (Wolfgang Krüger, Thomas Rauscher eds., 2013).

removed for the sake of legal certainty of both the arbitrators and the parties by setting a deadline for the application of the known circumstances (generally stipulated in Section 33 of the Czech Arbitration Act), as well as for circumstances known to the party later in the course of the arbitration proceedings.

III.2. Annulment of the Arbitral award Due to the Bias of the Arbitrator

8.17.   In general, it must be stated that the arbitral award has, according to the provisions of section 28(2) of the Czech Arbitration Act or Section 1055 ZPO, effects of a final judicial decision and is therefore enforceable.[26] It is not possible to initiate the proceedings on the exclusion of an arbitrator after the end of the arbitration procedure, and the only option is to seek the annulment of the arbitral award in the proceedings before the General Courts, while the annulment of the arbitral award is permissible only for a domestic arbitral award.

8.18.   However, if the grounds of bias without limitation would apply not only in the arbitration procedure but also in the civil proceedings for the annulment of the arbitral award, it would be regarded as an unwanted phenomenon and would also be contrary to the proceedings to exclude an arbitrator, specifically the refusal of the arbitrator (Section 11 and 12 of the Czech Arbitration Act, Section 1036 and 1037 ZPO).[27] In this respect, section 33 of the Czech Arbitration Act states that the application for annulment of the arbitral award should be dismissed if the reason relates to the person of the arbitrator and the party did not apply these grounds in the arbitration proceedings, although it could have.[28]

8.19.   In a case where reasons arose after the arbitral award was made, the view on this issue is unambiguous.[29] There is a certain conflict between the right of exclusion of the arbitrator and the

---

[26]   For differences in enforceability, see below.

[27]   See ALEXANDER J. BĚLOHLÁVEK, *supra* note 19, at 439.

[28]   Similarly Judgment of the German Federal Court of Justice (Bundesgerichtshof) of 4 March 1999, Ref. No. III ZR 72/98, Nr. 13 and 14. See f.e. JOHN-PATRICK BISCHOFF, UNABHÄNGIGKEIT UND UNPARTEILICHKEIT VON SCHIEDSRICHTERN NACH DEUTSCHEM UND ENGLISCHEM RECHT. UNTER BERÜCKSICHTIGUNG DER IBA-GUIDELINES ON CONFLICTS OF INTEREST IN INTERNATIONAL ARBITRATION, Frankfurt am Main: Peter Lang 93 et seq. (2013).

[29]   Compare Wolfgang Voit, in KOMMENTAR ZUR ZIVILPROZESSORDNUNG MIT GERICHTSVERFASSUNGSGESETZ, München: Verlag Franz Vahlen 2466 (Hans-Joachim Musielak, 2012) - rather he does not allow; JOACHIM MÜNCH, *supra* note 25, at 237 et seq. (depending on different circumstances, admits or does not allow); ADOLF BAUMBACH, WOLFGANG LAUTERBACH, JAN ALBERS, PETER HARTMANN, ZIVILPROZESSORDNUNG MIT FAMFG, GVG UND ANDEREN NEBENGESETZEN, München: C. H. Beck 2701 (73rd ed. 2015) – admits; KARL HEINZ SCHWAB, BERNARD WALTER, SCHIEDSGERICHTSBARKEIT. KOMMENTAR, München: C. H. Beck a Helbing & Lichtenhahn 116 (7th ed. 2005) - admits exceptionally.

Czech (& Central European) Yearbook of Arbitration®

legal certainty created by the arbitral award with the effects of a final judicial decision. It is therefore necessary to measure the principle of impartial decision-making which is central to the decision-making process and thus also to the *ordre public*[30] (see below) with the legal certainty created by the arbitral award and its possible setting aside.[31]

8.20. The setting aside of the arbitral award is possible only on a reasoned application filed within a specified period of three months from the delivery of the arbitral award (Section 32 paragraph 1 Czech Arbitration Act, Section 1059 paragraph 3 ZPO)[32] at the relevant court (Section 41 of the Czech Arbitration Act in connection with Section 43 of the Czech Arbitration Act, Section 1062 paragraph 1, point 4 and paragraph 5 ZPO). At the expiration of this deadline, all reasons relating to independence and impartiality are overcome,[33] but in general and for all other reasons an application for the annulment of an arbitral award is not admissible if the arbitral award has already been declared enforceable.[34]

III.2.1. The Consequences of the Annulment of the Arbitral award Due to Bias

8.21. If the arbitral award is annulled due to bias, it is possible in accordance with Section 34 paragraph 2 of the Czech Arbitration Act to continue at the request of one of the parties in the arbitration proceedings on the basis of the original arbitration agreement. Similarly, the German ZPO also sets as a result of the annulment of the arbitral award a 'restoration' ('Wiederaufleben') of the arbitration agreement (Section 1059 paragraph 5 ZPO) to create a legal certainty between the parties.[35]

---

[30] 'Public policy', see Article V paragraph 2(b) of the New York Convention.

[31] See also Judgment of the German Federal Court of Justice (Bundesgerichtshof) of 4 March 1999, Ref. No. III ZR 72/98, Nr. 14. Similarly ALEXANDER J. BĚLOHLÁVEK, *supra* note 19, at 1178.

[32] To a certain extension of this period see Section 1058 paragraph 2 ZPO; JOACHIM MÜNCH, *supra* note 25, at 478.

[33] For more information see decision of the Czech Constitutional Court (Ústavní soud) of 30 June 2010, Ref. No. III. ÚS 1208/10. For the possibility of submitting multiple proposals for the annulment of the arbitral award within a time period for a variety of reasons see JOACHIM MÜNCH, *supra* note 25, at 479 (does not allow); WOLFGANG VOIT, *supra* note 29, at 2544 (admits). The author is inclined to the second approach, since the wording of Section 1060(2) of the ZPO does not contradict this and, moreover, the reasons listed include a whole range of different reasons and the decision on one does not have to exclude another.

[34] See Section 1059(3) ZPO.

[35] In contrast to the old version of Section 1041 ZPO, from which it was generally assumed that the original arbitration agreement no longer existed, see ROLF SCHÜTZE, SCHIEDSGERICHT UND SCHIEDSVERFAHREN, München: C. H. Beck 191 (5th ed. 2012).

III.3. Recognition and Execution of Foreign Arbitral Awards with Respect to Independence and Impartiality

8.22. If the question was raised at the beginning of the role of independence and impartiality in the recognition and enforcement of foreign arbitral awards, it must be stated that the last possibility of examining compliance with the conditions of independence and impartiality is permissible only in the context of the recognition or enforcement of foreign arbitral awards.

8.23. In this context, it is necessary to briefly define the term of a foreign arbitral award, which is thus put in opposition to the concept of a domestic (national) arbitral award, and the rules are not entirely uniform in this regard. According to Section 1025 of the ZPO, for example, the decisive factor for the classification of an arbitral award as a foreign arbitral award is the real place of the arbitration. According to Section 120 of the Czech Act on International Private Law is it the place where the arbitral award was made.[36] The New York Convention contains a sort of compromise point of view, when Article 1(1) states that it applies to the recognition and enforcement of arbitral awards resulting from disputes between natural or legal persons and issued in the territory of a State other than that in which recognition and enforcement are sought. However, the principle of territoriality in Article 1, paragraph 1, the second sentence, is also extended to arbitration findings that are not considered to be local (national) findings in the State in which recognition and enforcement are sought.

III.3.1. Recognition and Enforcement of Foreign Arbitration Awards in Accordance with the National Rules

8.24. Although the issue of independence and impartiality has been regulated in the Czech Arbitration Act, in the context of the extensive recodification of Czech private law, since 1 January 2014, some international arbitration issues have been moved to Act on International Private Law. This includes the arbitration agreement, the alien's ability to be an arbitrator, the determination of the applicable law, and the recognition and enforcement of foreign arbitration findings (Section 117 - 122 of

---

[36] Czech Act No. 91/2012 Coll. On International Private Law.

the Czech Act on International Private Law). With regard to the topic of the article, the two laws are therefore complementary.

8.25. Recognition and Enforcement of Foreign Arbitral Awards is specifically regulated in Section 120 - 122 of the Czech Act on International Private Law. The issue of independence and impartiality, if mutual recognition and enforcement is ensured (Section 120 of the Czech Act on International Private Law), is covered by the provisions of Section 121 c) and d) of the Czech Act on International Private Law. Under the first provision, recognition or enforcement of a foreign arbitral award shall be refused if the foreign arbitration award is vitiated, which is the reason for the annulment of the Czech arbitration award by the court.[37] Under the second provision, recognition or enforcement will be denied if the foreign is contrary to (meaning the Czech public policy). However, as the New York Convention is binding for the Czech Republic, the provisions of the Czech Act on International Private Law on the Recognition and Enforcement of Foreign arbitration award will not be practically applicable.[38]

8.26. The German ZPO does not contain any grounds for refusing to recognize and enforce foreign arbitral awards, since it refers specifically to the application of the New York Convention in its Section 1061 paragraph 1. However, even if this explicit regulation was not included in the ZPO, the New York Convention would be preferentially applied on the basis of Article 25 of Grundgesetz (German constitution). The reasons and conclusions regarding the annulment of the domestic arbitration award under the ZPO are, with respect to the almost identical list of grounds, also applicable to the recognition and enforcement of a foreign arbitration award under the New York Convention.[39]

8.27. Although, the recognition and performance of foreign arbitral awards, it will be proceed primarily under the provisions of the New York Convention, it is appropriate to point out some differences between the regulations of to the Czech Act on International Private Law and of the New York Convention. There is no fundamental difference between the ZPO and the New York Convention with regard to their consistency.

8.28. The basic distinction lies above all in the fact that the Czech Act on International Private Law does not distinguish between the grounds which are examined only at the initiative of the

---

[37] Section 31 of the Czech Arbitration Act.
[38] See Article 10 of the Act No. 1/1993 Coll. The Constitution of the Czech Republic and Article VII(1) of the New York Convention.
[39] See the Judgment of the German Federal Court of Justice (Bundesgerichtshof) of 1 February 2001, Ref. No. III ZR 332/99.

party and those examined *ex offo* (of course, in the presence of a specific proposal for recognition and enforcement, respectively for refusal to recognize and enforce a foreign arbitral award). In that regard, the Czech Act on International Private Law contains only an exhaustive list of grounds which the court examines *ex offo* without being bound by the specific ground put forward by the party. The second difference is that while the existence of any of these grounds would lead to the denial of recognition or enforcement under the Czech Act on International Private Law without exception, the New York Convention gives (at least at first glance) a discretion as to whether or not the court refuses to recognize and enforce a foreign arbitration award (see below).

8.29. The New York Convention seeks to simplify the recognition and enforcement of foreign arbitration awards and therefore the recognition and enforcement should be refused only for important and grave grounds.[40] The process of recognition and performance itself is not regulated in the New York Convention and is left to national legislation.[41]

III.3.2. Some other International Treaties Governing the Recognition and Enforcement of Foreign Arbitral Awards

8.30. In addition to the New York Convention, other legal regulations apply to the issue of the recognition and enforcement of foreign arbitration awards. European Convention on International Commercial Arbitration of 1961 deals solely with the issue of the recognition and enforcement of arbitral awards indirectly by setting out exhaustive grounds for refusal of recognition or enforcement where, for one of those grounds, the arbitration award has been annulled in the State in which or under the law of which, the award has been made.[42] An annulment of an

---

[40] Similarly ALAN REDFERN, MARTIN HUNTER, NIGEL BLACKABY, CONSTANTINE PARTASIDES, *supra* note 13, at 445; WOLFGANG BOSCH, RECHTSKRAFT UND RECHTSHÄNGIGKEIT IM SCHIEDSVERFAHREN, Tübingen: J. C. B. Mohr (Paul Siebeck) 162 (1991); Jens Adolphsen, in MÜNCHENER KOMMENTAR ZUR ZIVILPROZESSORDNUNG, BAND 3. Sections 1025 – 1109, München: C. H. Beck 563 (Wolfgang Krüger, Thomas Rauscher eds., 2013).

[41] See e.g. RECOGNITION AND ENFORCEMENT OF FOREIGN ARBITRAL AWARDS: A GLOBAL COMMENTARY ON THE NEW YORK CONVENTION, Alphen aan den Rijn: Kluwer Law International 116 et seq. (Herbert Kronke, Patricia Nacimiento, Dirk Otto, Nicola Christine Port eds., 2010); GARY B. BORN, INTERNATIONAL COMMERCIAL ARBITRATION, (2 Volume Set), Alphen aan den Rijn: Kluwer Law International 2717 (2009).

[42] The reasons given in European Convention on International Commercial Arbitration correspond to the reasons in the New York Convention. For their mutual relationship, see Article IX paragraph 2, in conjunction with paragraph 1 of the European Convention on International Commercial Arbitration.

arbitration award for other reasons is not a reason for refusal of recognition or enforcement.[43]

8.31. Other conventions governing the recognition and performance of foreign arbitral awards are, for example, Convention on the Settlement of Investment Disputes between States and Nationals of Other States,[44] Inter-American Convention on International Commercial Arbitration signed on 30 January 1975 in Panama[45] or Arab Convention on Commercial Arbitration made on 14 April 1987 in Amman.[46] In addition to these more or less well-known and recognized multilateral treaties, there are also a number of bilateral agreements between states that also play a very important role in the recognition and enforcement of foreign arbitration awards.[47] In view of the limited number of contracting parties or the specifically defined scope of these other legal sources, and in view of the universality of the New York Convention, no further attention will be paid to these other legislation.

III.3.3. The New York Convention

Article V paragraph 1(d) of the New York Convention

8.32. However, as already indicated above, the recognition and enforcement of foreign arbitral awards will be primarily pursued under the provisions of the New York Convention.[48] Under the New York Convention, the issue of the independence and impartiality of the arbitrator is not explicitly mentioned anywhere, but it is nevertheless possible to subordinate it to a number of provisions with different approaches and impacts. Issues of independence and impartiality fall under Article V paragraph 1(d) of the New York Convention, which provides that

> Recognition and enforcement of the award may be refused, at the request of the party against whom it is invoked, only if that party furnishes to the competent authority where the recognition and enforcement is sought, proof that the composition of the arbitral

---

[43] See Article IX paragraph 1 of the European Convention on International Commercial Arbitration.
[44] See Article 53 – 55. The treaty has been ratified by 153 states and is binding on both the Czech Republic and Germany, see https://icsid.worldbank.org/en/Pages/icsiddocs/ICSID-Convention.aspx.
[45] See Article V. The so-called Panama Convention was ratified by 19 states, including the United States.
[46] See Article 35. The Convention has been ratified by 14 states.
[47] See EMMANUEL GAILLARD, JOHN SAVAGE (eds.), supra note 7, at 965.
[48] See Article 10 of the Act No. 1/1993 Coll. The Constitution of the Czech Republic and Article VII(1) of the New York Convention. See also European Convention on International Commercial Arbitration of 1961. In the Czech Act on International Private Law the Issue of Recognition and Enforcement of Foreign Arbitral Awards is regulated in Section 120 - 122. See also Section 1061(1) ZPO.

authority or the arbitral procedure was not in accordance with the agreement of the parties, or, failing such agreement, was not in accordance with the law of the country where the arbitration took place.

8.33. Although this provision gives a fundamental priority to the party autonomy, the composition of the arbitral tribunal must respect the equality of the parties to the dispute and must guarantee independent and impartial decision-making. If there is no such agreement of the parties, this statement with regard to text " *in accordance with the law of the country where the arbitration took place*" is quite unambiguous for both the Czech Republic and Germany. In the case of agreement of the parties, which would be contrary to the independence and the impartiality of the arbitrator and to the neutrality of decision making, the above conclusion within the scope of the New York Convention is not without any doubt.[49] The reasons that may lead to an incorrect composition of the arbitral tribunal include, for example, the question of the appointment of arbitrators by the third impartial person, the inequality of the parties by the constitution of the arbitral tribunal,[50] relationship of the arbitrator to the parties to the dispute or failure to notify the relationship between the arbitrator and one of the parties to the dispute.[51] These and similar reasons could directly or indirectly affect the necessary independence and impartiality of the arbitrator. Here, however, the party can only object to this reason if it has not been overcome, even if the New York Convention does not regulate periods, unlike for example European Convention on International Commercial Arbitration of 1961.[52] This is logical, because if it is possible to rely only on such unforeseen reasons in the annulment of an arbitral award, the conditions may be less restrictive in the recognition and execution of a foreign arbitral award. With regard to efforts to simplify the recognition and enforcement of foreign arbitral awards that must be quite

---

[49]   HERBERT KRONKE, PATRICIA NACIMIENTO, DIRK OTTO, NICOLA CHRISTINE PORT (eds.), *supra* note 41, at 286.

[50]   Compare Judgment of the German Federal Court of Justice (Bundesgerichtshof) of 15 May 1986, Ref. No. III ZR 192/84.

[51]   HERBERT KRONKE, PATRICIA NACIMIENTO, DIRK OTTO, NICOLA CHRISTINE PORT (eds.), *supra* note 41, at 290 et seq.; WOLFGANG VOIT, *supra* note 29, at 2446; decision of the Higher Regional Court (Oberlandesgericht) in Dresden of 6 August 2008, Ref. No. 11 Sch 02/08.

[52]   See decision of the Higher Regional Court (Oberlandesgericht) in Stuttgart of 14 October 2003, Ref. No. 1 Sch 16/02, 1 Sch 6/03. Compare also KARL HEINZ SCHWAB, BERNARD WALTER, *supra* note 29, at 463. Similarly HERBERT KRONKE, PATRICIA NACIMIENTO, DIRK OTTO, NICOLA CHRISTINE PORT (eds.), *supra* note 41, at 290; JENS ADOLPHSEN, *supra* note 40, at 542 et seq. See also KARL HEINZ SCHWAB, BERNARD WALTER, *supra* note 29, at 463.

the opposite and the reasons for refusing recognition and enforcement should be interpreted rather restrictively.[53]

8.34. The above-mentioned provision of Article V paragraph 1(d) of the New York Convention may, to a certain extent, overlap with Article V paragraph 1(b) and Article V paragraph 2(b) of the New York Convention.[54] Absence of proper notice of the appointment of the arbitrator or of the arbitration proceedings or the impossibility to present his case or requirements [Article V, paragraph 1(b)] may in certain circumstances also be a manifestation of lack of impartiality and independence.[55]

Article V paragraph 2(b) of the New York Convention

8.35. In addition to the above-mentioned provision of the New York Convention, the recognition and enforcement of an arbitral award contrary to a fair and impartial decision could be refused if the court *ex offo* found that the recognition and enforcement of the arbitral award would be contrary to public policy.[56] According to Article V paragraph 2(b) of the New York Convention recognition and enforcement of an arbitral award may also be refused 'if the competent authority in the country where recognition and enforcement is sought finds that the recognition or enforcement of the award would be contrary to the public policy of that country'.[57] The issue of the independence and impartiality of an arbitrator may be investigated (even under different conditions) in the context of the recognition and enforcement of foreign arbitral awards, both at the request of the party and on its own initiative.

8.36. However, in the case of foreign arbitral awards, the bias will play a rather limited role, and the ground for non-recognition of the arbitral award will be bias according to Article V, paragraph 2(b) of The New York Convention if the reasons could not be applied in the country of origin within the institute of exclusion of Arbitrator. This is also true if in the annulment of the arbitral award the reasons were unsuccessful and the recognition of the arbitral award would lead to a result incompatible with the

---

[53] See Judgment of the Bavarian Supreme Court in Munich (Bayerisches Oberstes Landesgericht) of 23 September 2004, Ref. No. 4Z Sch 05/04. Similarly GARY B. BORN, INTERNATIONAL COMMERCIAL ARBITRATION. (3 Volume Set), Alphen aan den Rijn: Kluwer Law International 3411 et seq. (2014).
[54] See HERBERT KRONKE, PATRICIA NACIMIENTO, DIRK OTTO, NICOLA CHRISTINE PORT (eds.), *supra* note 41, at 282; ARBITRATION IN GERMANY: THE MODEL LAW IN PRACTICE, Alphen aan den Rijn: Kluwer Law International 481 et seq. (Karl Heinz Böckstiegel, Stefan Michael Kröll, Patricia Nacimiento eds., 2nd ed. 2015); GARY B. BORN, *supra* note 53, at 3585, 3590.
[55] Similarly GARY B. BORN, *supra* note 53, at 3525.
[56] ROLF SCHÜTZE, *supra* note 35, at 155.
[57] To interconnection of Article V paragraph 1(d) and Article V paragraph 2(b) of the New York Convention see WOLFGANG VOIT, *supra* note 29, at 2562.

ordre public.[58] Public policy is an institute that is inherent in all modern legal regulations. Even the Czech legal order regulates public order in Section 121(d) of the Czech Act on International Private Law, without defining it any further.[59]

8.37. In the case of the recognition and enforcement of foreign arbitral awards, a distinction is made between public policy national and international (*ordre public interne* and *ordre public international*).[60] This distinction and associated liberal assessment of foreign arbitral awards on the issue of recognition and enforcement in the context of the *ordre public international* is not accepted unreservedly, respectively is sometimes considered to be unnecessary in view of the strict conditions for the applicability of the „general" public policy.[61]

8.38. However, such a discrepancy with public policy will be the case if the effects of an arbitral award are manifestly incompatible with the essential principles of the law of the executing State. In other words, if it is found that the arbitral award is contrary to the provision governing the foundations of the State and economic establishment or to an intolerable contradiction with the concepts of justice, generally with the elementary foundations of the legal order.[62] However, it also follows that not every contradiction with the mandatory norm is at the same time a contradiction with the *ordre public*.

8.39. Among the procedural principles of public order, we can unequivocally also include an impartial judiciary and thus also the issue of independence and impartiality of an arbitrator.[63] Typically, the controversy with the *ordre public* will be unambiguously given, for example, if one of the parties itself has been appointed as an arbitrator and thus conflicts with the principle of *'nemo iudex in causa sua'.* The principle that no one can be a judge in their own case is one of the fundamental procedural characteristics of the rule of law and, as an integral part of any judicial system, applies irrespective of whether or

---

[58] JENS ADOLPHSEN, *supra* note 40, at 560.

[59] The previous regulation of private international law in Act No. 97/1963 Coll., On Private and Procedural International Law, defined public order in Section 36 as the principles of the social and state establishment of the Czech Republic and its legal order, which must be maintained without reservation. See Resolution of the Municipal Court in Prague (Městský soud v Praze) of 14 August 2006, Ref. No. 18 Co 586/2005-534 in connection with the decision of the Czech Supreme Court (Nejvyšší soud) of 18 June 2008, Ref. No. 20 Cdo 942/2007.

[60] See Decision of the German Federal Court of Justice (Bundesgerichtshof) of 29 January 2009, Ref. No. III ZB 88/07, Decision of the German Provincial Court of Appeal in Celle (OLG Celle) of 31 May 2007, Ref. No. 8 Sch 6/06. Compare Chapter V subchapter 1 Section 1.4.

[61] See f. e. Decision of the Austrian Supreme Court (Oberster Gerichtshof) of 11 May 1983, Ref. No. 3 Ob 30/83; KARL HEINZ SCHWAB, BERNARD WALTER, *supra* note 29, at 471.

[62] See Decision of the German Federal Court of Justice (Bundesgerichtshof) of 10 March 2016, Ref. No. I ZB 99/14.

[63] See WOLFGANG VOIT, *supra* note 29, at 2538.

not this principle is explicitly regulated in the Czech Arbitration Act or in the Czech Act on International Private Law.

8.40. The contradiction of the arbitral award, and specifically its effects, with public order usually does not occur.[64] If the courts of a foreign State approach issues of bias under similar principles, as in the case with domestic courts, the application of Article V paragraph 2(b) of the New York Convention is rather theoretical. In addition, it would have to be shown that the bias of the arbitration proceedings had in a substantive manner actually taken place and that the arbitrators had to influence it in the decision-making.[65] The application of the reason for independence and impartiality will therefore be in the context of recognition and enforcement of foreign arbitral award subject to stringent criteria. This provision is a kind of 'emergency brake'. However, this does not change the fact that independence and impartiality are part of the public policy and, in the event of their breach, Article V paragraph 2(b) of the New York Convention would be applied by the court. The decision on recognition and enforcement, respectively on the refusal to recognize and enforce a foreign arbitral award is, however, limited by its effects only to the State whose courts have given that decision.

8.41. Although it follows from the wording of the above-mentioned Article V of the New York Convention that the recognition and enforcement on the basis of these reasons may be refused (mohou být odepřeny, darf versagt werden), it means more a duty to refuse recognition and enforcement of foreign arbitral award and the court does not have any room for its discretion.[66] With regard to reasons such as the non-arbitrability of the dispute or the conflict with public policy, this approach appears to be correct. If the court finds a relevant ground for refusal of recognition and enforcement, it will confine itself to declaring that the proposal for recognition and enforcement of a foreign arbitral award is denied. However, setting aside of such a foreign arbitral award is not permissible.[67] Where the national legislation

---

[64] Compare KARL HEINZ SCHWAB, BERNARD WALTER, *supra* note 29, at 472.

[65] See Judgment of the German Federal Court of Justice (Bundesgerichtshof) of 1 February 2001, Ref. No. III ZR 332/99, which at the same time applied to Article V(2)(b) of the New York Convention. The grounds for the annulment of the arbitral award contained in the ZPO are identical to those in the New York Convention and that is why that approach is entirely justified. In a similarly sense see decision of the Court of Appeals for the Second Circuit (USA) of 23 December 1974, *Parsons & Whittemore Overseas Co. Inc.* v. *Société Générale de lIndustrie du Papier* (RAKTA).

[66] See KARL HEINZ SCHWAB, BERNARD WALTER, *supra* note 29, at 456; WOLFGANG VOIT, *supra* note 29, at 2566; JENS ADOLPHSEN, *supra* note 40, at 541; JENS PETER LACHMANN, HANDBUCH FÜR DIE SCHIEDSGERICHTSPRAXIS, Köln: Verlag Dr. Otto Schmidt 627 et seq. (3rd ed. 2008).

[67] The German ZPO still accepts that the declaration of enforceability be annulled if the arbitral award has been set aside afterwards abroad, see Section 1061(3) ZPO.

requires a declaration of enforceability[68] (just like the German legislation), this condition applies to foreign arbitral awards.[69]

III.3.4. Adjournment of the decision on the enforcement of the award

8.42. In the absence of a reason for refusal of the recognition and the enforcement of a foreign arbitral award, no 'corrective' means for the sake of independence and impartiality is permissible and such a finding will be executed in accordance with the law applicable at the place of enforcement of the arbitral award.[70] In the case of the Czech Republic, a foreign arbitral award will be enforced in accordance with the Czech Code of Civil Procedure[71] or by the Czech Executory Procedure Code[72] without the court having jurisdiction to execute the decision to review the substantive accuracy of the decision being taken.[73] The only exception is the possibility provided in Article VI of the New York Convention. Under that provision, the court of the State where the arbitral award is applied may adjourn the decision on the enforcement of the award, if an application for the setting aside or suspension of the award has been made to a competent authority referred to in Article V, paragraph 1(e) of the New York Convention.[74] In such a case, the court of the State of enforcement will consider whether the suspension of the decision on the enforcement of the award is appropriate. At the request of the party claiming enforcement

---

[68] The declaration of enforceability of an arbitral award is necessary for the Enforcement of an arbitral award (Section 1060 paragraph 1 ZPO). The arbitral award has the effects of a final judgment (Section 1055 ZPO) but is not in itself an enforceable title in the sense of Section 794(1) Nr. 4a ZPO. In the proceedings for a declaration of enforceability, the reasons given in Section 1059(2) ZPO (and, for example, a contradiction with the *ordre public*) shall be examined, the court no longer deals with the reasons which have already been legally adjudicated in the proceedings for annulment of the arbitral award or is bound by a decision on these grounds. Likewise, the court does not deal with the reasons for which the preclusive period has passed. (Section 1060 paragraph 2 ZPO in connection with Section 1059 paragraph 3 ZPO). In the event that the reason for annulment is given, the proposal for declaration of enforceability of the arbitral award shall be rejected and the national arbitral award, but not the foreign award, shall be set aside *ex offo* (Section 1060 paragraph 2 ZPO). This approach is not possible under the Czech Arbitration Act, because the arbitral award itself is an enforcement title, which takes effect on the day of the delivery of a final judicial decision and is enforceable. See Section 28(2) of the Czech Arbitration Act.

[69] For compliance of the declaration of enforceability with the New York Convention see f.e. Troy L. Harris, *The Public Policy Exception to Enforcement of International Arbitration Awards Under the New York Convention*, 24(1) JOURNAL OF INTERNATIONAL ARBITRATION 9, 9 (2007); NADĚŽDA ROZEHNALOVÁ, ROZHODČÍ ŘÍZENÍ V MEZINÁRODNÍM A VNITROSTÁTNÍM OBCHODNÍM STYKU, Praha: Wolters Kluwer 370 (3rd ed. 2013).

[70] See Article III of the New York Convention.

[71] See Section 251 of the Czech Code of Civil Procedure, Act No. 99/1963 Coll. Civil Procedure Code.

[72] Act No. 120/2001 Coll. On Judicial Executors and Executory Activities.

[73] Compare decision of the Czech Supreme Court (Nejvyšší soud) of 21 July 2008, Ref. No. 20 Cdo 2273/2008, of 5 August 2008, Ref. No. 20 Cdo 4548/2007.

[74] Whereas, under Article V paragraph 1(e) the New York Convention has already happened that the award has not yet become binding or has been annulled or that its enforcement has been suspended, Article VI of the New York Convention shall apply to a situation where a proposal for annulment or suspension of the arbitration award has been made.

of the award, the court may also order the other party to give suitable security. The court of the State of enforcement will base its considerations primarily on whether an application for the annulment of an arbitration award is indeed a hope of success.[75] The purpose of this suspension of enforcement is to prevent conflicting decisions of the courts of the issuing State in which the setting aside or suspension of the enforcement of the award is sought and of the State of enforcement in which recognition and enforcement of the award are sought.

IV. Conclusion

8.43. Arbitration is a special process in which judicial principles are combined with the interests of the parties. Thus for example, confidentiality is combined with transparency, and autonomy of the parties is combined with impartiality. Independence and impartiality are some of the central conditions for the implementation of fair justice and hence the arbitration procedure. These pervade the arbitration procedure from the constitution of the arbitral tribunal to the question of annulment, recognition and enforcement of the arbitral award. They are part of the procedural principles of public order.

8.44. The maximum limit for the applicability of the grounds of bias shall be three months from the delivery of the arbitral award (Section 1059 paragraph 3 ZPO, Section 32 paragraph 1 of the Czech Arbitration Act), which is the time limit for filing an application for the annulment of the arbitral award. By the expiration of this period, all grounds of bias are overcome, and the principle of legal certainty which has been established between the parties by the arbitral award and the effects of a final judgment is given priority.

8.45. However, in the case of foreign arbitral awards, the question of independence and impartiality is still examined within the recognition and enforcement of a foreign arbitral award in accordance with Article V paragraph 1(d), resp. paragraph 1(b) and paragraph 2(b) of the New York Convention. In the case of foreign arbitral awards the bias plays a rather limited role. Bias will be a reason for non-recognition of the arbitral award if the reasons could not be applied in the country of origin, the application of the reasons was unsuccessful, or recognition of

---

[75] See JEAN-FRANÇOIS POUDRET, SÉBASTIEN BESSON, COMPARATIVE LAW OF INTERNATIONAL ARBITRATION, London: Sweet & Maxwell 873 (2nd ed. 2007); JENS ADOLPHSEN, *supra* note 40, at 563.

the arbitral award would result in a result incompatible with the *ordre public*.

| | |

Summaries

DEU   [*Anerkennung und Vollstreckung ausländischer Schiedssprüche im Hinblick auf die Unabhängigkeit und Unparteilichkeit des Schiedsrichters*]

Das Schiedsverfahren stellt eine Form der außergerichtlichen Streitbeilegung dar, und Schiedssprüche sind eine rechtskräftige und vollstreckbare Entscheidung in der Sache und damit ein Vollstreckungstitel. Werden die im jeweiligen Schiedsspruch auferlegten Pflichten nicht freiwillig erfüllt, bleibt nur deren Durchsetzung gegen den Willen des Verpflichteten. Im Falle eines ausländischen Schiedsspruchs setzt dies zwingend voraus, dass dieser vor der Vollstreckung zunächst einmal anerkannt wird. Der vorliegende Beitrag befasst sich mit der Frage, inwieweit die Problematik der Unabhängigkeit und Unparteilichkeit des Schiedsrichters bei der Anerkennung und Vollstreckung ausländischer Schiedssprüche eine Rolle spielt, m.a.W., ob die Unabhängigkeit und Unparteilichkeit eines Schiedsrichters Grund dafür sein kann, die Anerkennung und Vollstreckung eines ausländischen Schiedsspruchs zu verweigern. In diesem Zusammenhang definiert der Beitrag die Begriffe Unabhängigkeit, Unparteilichkeit, Voreingenommenheit und Neutralität – grundlegende Voraussetzungen für das Schiedsverfahren, von der Bestellung des Schiedsgerichts bis zur Vollstreckung des Schiedsspruchs. Außerdem bringt der Beitrag dem Leser weitere Rechtsinstitute nahe, welche einen unparteiischen, unabhängigen und gerechten Entscheidungsfindungsprozess garantieren (Ausschluss von Schiedsrichtern, Aufhebung von Schiedssprüchen), und welche mit der im Beitrag aufgeworfenen Frage sehr eng zusammenhängen. Der Autor gelangt zu dem Schluss, dass das Institut der Unabhängigkeit und Unparteilichkeit des Schiedsrichters als Grund für die Verweigerung der Anerkennung und Vollstreckung von Schiedssprüchen zwar vorkommen kann, in der Praxis aber wohl eher in Ausnahmefällen zur Anwendung kommen dürfte, nämlich dort, wo die Gründe im Ursprungsland des Schiedsspruchs nicht bzw. nicht erfolgreich geltend gemacht werden konnten und eine Vollstreckung des Schiedsspruchs im Ergebnis mit der öffentlichen Ordnung unvereinbar wäre.

CZE [*Uznání a výkon cizích rozhodčích nálezů s ohledem na nezávislost a nestrannost rozhodce*]
Rozhodčí řízení představuje mimosoudní způsob řešení sporů a rozhodčí nález je pravomocným a vykonatelným rozhodnutím v meritu věci a je tedy exekučním titulem. V případě, že nedojde k dobrovolnému splnění povinnosti uložené určitým rozhodčím nálezem, pak nezbývá než prosadit danou povinnost i proti vůli povinného. V případě cizího rozhodčího nálezu je nezbytné, aby byl tento rozhodčí nález před jeho výkonem uznán. Tento článek se zabývá otázkou, do jaké míry může hrát problematika nezávislosti a nestrannosti rozhodce roli při uznávání a výkonu cizího rozhodčího nálezu; zda tedy může nezávislost a nestrannost rozhodce představovat důvod pro odepření uznání a výkonu cizího rozhodčího nálezu. V této souvislosti článek vymezuje pojmy nezávislost a nestrannost, jakož i podjatost a neutralita, které představují jednu ze základních podmínek rozhodčí řízení od konstituování rozhodčího soudu až po výkon rozhodčího nálezu. Současně přibližuje ostatní instituty zaručující nestranné, nezávislé a spravedlivé rozhodování (vyloučení rozhodce, zrušení rozhodčího nálezu), které ovšem s vymezenou otázkou velmi úzce souvisí. Autor v článku dospívá k závěru, že se sice institut nezávislosti a nestrannosti rozhodce jako důvod pro odepření uznání a výkonu rozhodčího nálezu objevit může, jeho praktické uplatnění však přichází v úvahu spíše ve výjimečných případech, kdy nebylo možno uplatnit důvody v zemi původu rozhodčího nálezu, resp. uplatnění těchto důvodů nebylo úspěšné a uznání, resp. výkon rozhodčího nálezu by vedl k výsledku neslučitelnému s veřejným pořádkem.

| | |

POL [*Uznawanie i wykonywanie zagranicznych orzeczeń arbitrażowych a niezawisłość i bezstronność arbitra*]
Artykuł pochyla się nad kwestią, na ile problematyka niezawisłości i bezstronności arbitra odgrywa rolę w uznawaniu i wykonywaniu zagranicznych orzeczeń arbitrażowych, to znaczy czy niezawisłość i bezstronność arbitra może stanowić przesłankę odmowy uznania i wykonania zagranicznego orzeczenia arbitrażowego. W artykule zdefiniowano niezawisłość, bezstronność, stronniczość, neutralność, a także omówiono bliżej inne instrumenty gwarantujące bezstronność, niezależność i sprawiedliwość rozstrzygania w sprawach, a także podsunięto wniosek, że stronniczość w odniesieniu do kwestii uznawania

*i wykonywania zagranicznych orzeczeń arbitrażowych stanowi
zagadnienie natury teoretycznej.*

FRA [*La reconnaissance et l'exécution des sentences arbitrales
étrangères au vu de l'indépendance et de l'impartialité de
l'arbitre*]

*L'article se consacre aux liens qui peuvent exister entre
l'indépendance et l'impartialité de l'arbitre et la reconnaissance
et l'exécution d'une sentence arbitrale étrangère. L'auteur se
pose la question de savoir si un manque d'indépendance ou
d'impartialité de l'arbitre peut constituer un motif de refus de
la reconnaissance et de l'exécution d'une sentence arbitrale
étrangère. L'article cherche à définir les notions d'indépendance,
d'impartialité, de partialité et de neutralité, tout en réfléchissant
aux autres concepts juridiques garantissant une procédure
impartiale, indépendante et équitable. En ce qui concerne la
reconnaissance et l'exécution des sentences arbitrales étrangères,
il semble que l'argument de la partialité n'est que théorique.*

RUS [*Признание и приведение в исполнение иностранных
арбитражных решений с учетом независимости и
беспристрастности арбитра*]

*В статье рассматривается вопрос, в какой степени
проблематика независимости и беспристрастности
арбитра может влиять на признание и приведение в
исполнение иностранного арбитражного решения, т. е.
могут ли независимость и беспристрастность арбитра
послужить причиной для отказа в признании и приведении
в исполнение иностранного арбитражного решения. В
статье определены такие понятия, как независимость,
беспристрастность, предвзятость и нейтралитет;
объясняются остальные институты, гарантирующие
беспристрастное, независимое и справедливое принятие
решений, а также делается вывод о том, что применение
причин предвзятости в вопросе признания и приведения
в исполнение иностранного арбитражного решения
является скорее теоретическим размышлением.*

ESP [*Reconocimiento y ejercicio de laudos arbitrales extranjeros
en relación con la independencia y la imparcialidad del
árbitro*]

*El texto plantea la cuestión de la medida en la que la
independencia y la imparcialidad del árbitro juegan un rol en
el reconocimiento y la ejecución del laudo arbitral extranjero, es
decir, si la independencia y la imparcialidad del árbitro pueden
constituir un motivo para el no reconocimiento y la no ejecución*

del laudo arbitral extranjero. El artículo define los términos de independencia, imparcialidad, parcialidad, neutralidad y clarifica los demás institutos que garantizan una decisión imparcial, independiente y justa para concluir que utilizar el motivo de la parcialidad en el reconocimiento y ejecución del laudo arbitral extranjero constituye más bien una reflexión teórica.

| | |

Bibliography

Jens Adolphsen, *in* MÜNCHENER KOMMENTAR ZUR ZIVILPROZESSORDNUNG, BAND 3, München: C. H. Beck (Wolfgang Krüger, Thomas Rauscher eds., 2013).

ADOLF BAUMBACH, WOLFGANG LAUTERBACH, JAN ALBERS, PETER HARTMANN, ZIVILPROZESSORDNUNG MIT FAMFG, GVG UND ANDEREN NEBENGESETZEN, München: C. H. Beck (73rd ed. 2015).

ALEXANDER J. BĚLOHLÁVEK, ZÁKON O ROZHODČÍM ŘÍZENÍ A VÝKONU ROZHODČÍCH NÁLEZŮ: KOMENTÁŘ, Praha: C. H. Beck (2nd ed. 2012).

ARBITRATION IN GERMANY: THE MODEL LAW IN PRACTICE, Alphen aan den Rijn: Kluwer Law International 481 et seq. (Karl Heinz Böckstiegel, Stefan Michael Kröll, Patricia Nacimiento eds., 2nd ed. 2015).

JOHN-PATRICK BISCHOFF, UNABHÄNGIGKEIT UND UNPARTEILICHKEIT VON SCHIEDSRICHTERN NACH DEUTSCHEM UND ENGLISCHEM RECHT. UNTER BERÜCKSICHTIGUNG DER IBA-GUIDELINES ON CONFLICTS OF INTEREST IN INTERNATIONAL ARBITRATION, Frankfurt am Main: Peter Lang (2013).

NIGEL BLACKABY, CONSTANTINE PARTASIDES et al., REDFERN AND HUNTER ON INTERNATIONAL ARBITRATION, New York: Oxford University Press 31 (5th ed. 2009).

GARY B. BORN, INTERNATIONAL COMMERCIAL ARBITRATION, (2 Volume Set), Alphen aan den Rijn: Kluwer Law International (2009).

GARY B. BORN, INTERNATIONAL COMMERCIAL ARBITRATION, (3 Volume Set), Alphen aan den Rijn: Kluwer Law International (2014).

WOLFGANG BOSCH, RECHTSKRAFT UND RECHTSHÄNGIGKEIT IM SCHIEDSVERFAHREN, Tübingen: J. C. B. Mohr (Paul Siebeck) (1991).

Scott M. Donahey, *The Independence and Neutrality of Arbitrators*, 9(4) JOURNAL OF INTERNATIONAL ARBITRATION (1992).

Scott M. Donahey, *The Uniform Domain Name Dispute Resolution Process and the appearance of partiality. Panelists impaled on the horns of a dilemma*, 19(1) JOURNAL OF INTERNATIONAL ARBITRATION (2002).

FOUCHARD, GAILLARD, GOLDMAN ON INTERNATIONAL COMMERCIAL ARBITRATION, The Hague, Boston, London: Kluwer Law International (Emmanuel Gaillard, John Savage eds., 1999).

Troy L. Harris, *The Public Policy Exception to Enforcement of International Arbitration Awards Under the New York Convention*, 24(1) JOURNAL OF INTERNATIONAL ARBITRATION (2007).

RECOGNITION AND ENFORCEMENT OF FOREIGN ARBITRAL AWARDS: A GLOBAL COMMENTARY ON THE NEW YORK CONVENTION, Alphen aan den Rijn: Kluwer Law International (Herbert Kronke, Patricia Nacimiento, Dirk Otto, Nicola Christine Port eds., 2010).

WOLFGANG KRÜGER, THOMAS RAUSCHER (eds.), MÜNCHENER KOMMENTAR ZUR ZIVILPROZESSORDNUNG. BAND 3, Sections 1025 – 1109, München: C. H. Beck 34 (4th ed. 2013).

JENS PETER LACHMANN, HANDBUCH FÜR DIE SCHIEDSGERICHTSPRAXIS, Köln: Verlag Dr. Otto Schmidt (3rd ed. 2008).

Pierre Lalive, *On the neutrality of the arbitrator and of the place of arbitration, in* RECUEIL DE TRAVAUX SUISSES SUR L'ARBITRAGE INTERNATIONAL, Zürich: Schulthess (Claude Reymond, Eugen Bucher eds., 1984).

Pierre Lalive, *On the Transfer of Seat in International Arbitration, in* LAW AND JUSTICE IN A MULTISTATE WORLD. ESSAYS IN HONOR OF ARTHUR T. VON MEHREN, New York: Transnational Publishers (James Nafziger, Symeon Symeonides eds., 2002).

Ilhyung Lee, *Practice and Predicament: The Nationality of the International Arbitrator (With Survey Results)*, 31(3) FORDHAM INTERNATIONAL L. J. (2007).

Burkhard Lotz, *Die Unparteilichkeit und Unabhängigkeit des parteiernannten Schiedsrichter*, 52(4) ANWALTSBLATT (2002).

SAM LUTTRELL, BIAS CHALLENGES IN INTERNATIONAL COMMERCIAL ARBITRATION: THE NEED FOR A 'REAL DANGER' TEST, Alphen aan den Rijn: Kluwer Law International (2009).

Antonín Mokrý, *Nezávislost a nestrannost soudce - vzájemná souvislost a podmíněnost pojmů*, 41 (8) PRÁVNÍ PRAXE 459 (1993).

Joachim Münch, *in* MÜNCHENER KOMMENTAR ZUR ZIVILPROZESSORDNUNG, BAND 3, München: C. H. Beck 237 (Wolfgang Krüger, Thomas Rauscher eds., 2013).

Marie Öhrström, *Chapter XII - SCC Rules, in* INSTITUTIONAL ARBITRATION. ARTICLE-BY-ARTICLE COMMENTARY, München: C. H. Beck (Rolf A. Schütze ed., 2013).

JEAN-FRANÇOIS POUDRET, SÉBASTIEN BESSON, COMPARATIVE LAW OF INTERNATIONAL ARBITRATION, London: Sweet & Maxwell (2nd ed. 2007).

PŘEMYSL RABAN, ALTERNATIVNÍ ŘEŠENÍ SPORŮ, ARBITRÁŽ A ROZHODCI V ČESKÉ A SLOVENSKÉ REPUBLICE A ZAHRANIČÍ, Praha: C. H. Beck (2004).

ALAN REDFERN, MARTIN HUNTER, LAW AND PRACTICE OF INTERNATIONAL COMMERCIAL ARBITRATION, London: Sweet & Maxwell (3rd ed. 1999).

ALAN REDFERN, MARTIN HUNTER, NIGEL BLACKABY, CONSTANTINE PARTASIDES, LAW AND PRACTICE OF INTERNATIONAL COMMERCIAL ARBITRATION, London: Sweet & Maxwell (4th ed. 2004).

NADĚŽDA ROZEHNALOVÁ, ROZHODČÍ ŘÍZENÍ V MEZINÁRODNÍM A VNITROSTÁTNÍM OBCHODNÍM STYKU, Praha: Wolters Kluwer (3rd ed. 2013).

MAURO RUBINO-SAMMARTANO, INTERNATIONAL ARBITRATION, LAW AND PRACTICE, Huntington, New York: Juris Publishing (3rd ed. 2014).

PETER SCHLOSSER, DAS RECHT DER INTERNATIONALEN PRIVATEN SCHIEDSGERICHTSBARKEIT, Tübingen: Mohr Siebeck (2nd ed. 1989).

ROLF SCHÜTZE, SCHIEDSGERICHT UND SCHIEDSVERFAHREN, München: C. H. Beck 191 (5th ed. 2012).

KARL HEINZ SCHWAB, BERNARD WALTER, SCHIEDSGERICHTSBARKEIT, KOMMENTAR, München: C. H. Beck a Helbing & Lichtenhahn (7th ed. 2005).

HANS SMIT, THE PERNICIOUS INSTITUTION OF THE PARTY-APPOINTED ARBITRATOR, Columbia University Academic Commons (2010).

Wolfgang Voit, *in* KOMMENTAR ZUR ZIVILPROZESSORDNUNG MIT GERICHTSVERFASSUNGSGESETZ, München: Verlag Franz Vahlen (Hans-Joachim Musielak, 2012).

Alexander Sergeev |
Tatiana Tereshchenko

Key words:
*arbitral awards | New
York Convention | full
effect of recognition and
enforceability | equal
treatment | inherent legal
force | 'issue estoppel' effect |
res judicata*

'Issue Estoppel' Effect of Arbitral Awards

Abstract | *It's hard to deny the growing importance of international arbitration as one of the jurisdictional forms for commercial dispute resolution. In view of this foreign, non-domestic and domestic arbitral awards (arbitral awards) should be given the full effect of recognition and enforceability. In addition as a matter of common legislative standards, these arbitral awards should not discriminate against awards issued by national state courts, in any kind of jurisdiction[1]. Interpretation and application of provisions of the United Nations Convention on the Recognition and Enforcement of Foreign Arbitral Awards (New York, 1958)[2] (New York Convention), supported by the European Court of Human Rights' (ECHR) case precedents, are aimed to consider the inherent legal force of the arbitral awards and the consequences. However, despite the recognition of the role of arbitration, a number of questions still do not have an unambiguous assessment. Among stumbling blocks is a dispute about the 'issue estoppels' effect of arbitral awards.*

Before we proceed with further analyses, it worth to mention that in Russian legislation and court practice the terms 'prejudicial effect', 'prejuducialness' or 'prejudice' are used (on Russian – 'преюдициальность'). Generally they considered to be closely connected with the

Alexander P. Sergeev,
Doctor of Law, is a
professor in the Civil
Law and Procedure
Department at the Law
Faculty of National
Research University
'Higher School of
Economics' (St.
Petersburg). He is also
counsel with DLA Piper
Global Law Firm, a
Russian Government
Prize laureate, President
of the Arbitration Court
'IUS', and an arbitrator
in the Arbitration Court
of St. Petersburg CIC, an
arbitrator in the Russian
Arbitration Center at
the Russian Institute
of Modern Arbitration
(RIMA). He is an expert in
international disputes on
Civil, Corporate, Contract,
and Intellectual Property
Law, as well as an author
and co-editor of more than
182 articles.
E-mail: apsergeev2004@
mail.ru

Tatiana A. Tereshchenko,
Ph.D. in Law, is a professor
in the Civil Law and
Procedure Department
at the Law Faculty of
National Research
University 'Higher
School of Economics' (St.
Petersburg). She is head of
the Research Department
for the Law Firm 'Prime
Advice Saint-Petersburg',
an advocate, FCIArb
(London), an arbitrator in
the Arbitration Court 'IUS',

---

[1]   In Russia there is some semantic issue with using the word 'arbitral', which applies both for the arbitration court itself and state commercial courts. Thus, to avoid any confusion due to such different terminology traditions in this article, the terms 'arbitral' and their derivatives are used as synonyms for arbitration, while state commercial courts are addressed like 'state arbitrazhny' and the similar.

[2]   Available at: http://www.uncitral.org/pdf/english/texts/arbitration/NY-conv/New-York-Convention-E.pdf (accessed on 25 January 2019).

Czech (& Central European) Yearbook of Arbitration®

an arbitrator in the Russian Arbitration Association (RAA), an arbitrator in the Russian Arbitration Center at the Russian Institute of Modern Arbitration (RIMA). She is an expert in international disputes on Civil, Corporate, Contract, and Intellectual Property Law, and author of more than 70 articles.
E-mail: t.tereshchenko@hlbprime.com, t_t.06@mail.ru

principle 'res judicata'[3], which from Latin means literally already 'a matter judged'. As a concept 'res judicata' principle has few meanings in doctrine. Among them could be found the so called 'issue estoppels'. The later bars the re-litigation of issues of law or fact that have already been determined by a judge as part of an earlier case. In particular,
'An estoppel which has come to be known as 'issue estoppel' may arise where a plea of res judicata could not be established because the causes of action are not the same. A party is precluded from contending the contrary of any precise point which, having once been distinctively put in issue, has been solemnly and with certainty determined against him. Even if the objects of the first and second actions are different, the finding on a matter which came directly (not collaterally or incidentally) in issue in the first action, provided it is embodied in a judicial decision that is final, is conclusive in a second action between the same parties and their privies. This principle applies whether the point involved in the earlier decision, and as to which the parties are estopped, is one of fact or one of law, or one of mixed fact and law'.[4]

Taking into account said above, we consider it appropriate to use term 'issue estoppel' effect along with 'prejudicialness' like synonyms for the purpose of this article to avoid any linguistic confusion.

Practically all possible reasons to dispute the 'issue estoppel' effect ('prejudicialness') of arbitral awards, could be summed up in two main aspects. Firstly, there is a concern about the private nature of arbitration, arising from the arbitration agreement between certain parties, the confidentiality of the proceedings in general and specifically of enforcement, when the loosing party refuses to perform the arbitral award voluntary. Secondly, there is the problem with the formal approach of national enforcement bodies to national procedural legislation and its interpretation, based on tradition when they attempt to identify the award with the statehood jurisdiction.

However, are these reasons really so important as to consider them necessary and sufficient to deny the 'issue estoppel' effect ('prejudicialness') of the arbitral awards and the universal approach to it?

---

3   See more: Irina N. Lukyanova, *Problems of the institute of prejudice as a tool of legal certainty in modern civil legal proceedings*, 12 LAWS OF RUSSIA: EXPERIENCE, ANALYSIS, PRACTICE 28, 28-32 (2015).
4   See Halsbury's Laws of England, 4th ed., vol. 16, p. 1030, 1530, available at: http://www.duhaime.org/LegalDictionary/I/IssueEstoppel.aspx (accessed on 25 January 2019).

I. The Meaning and Goal of the 'Issue Estoppel' Effect ('Prejudicialness') in Jurisdiction Practice

9.01. It is considered that the decision of the state court, which entered into legal force, acquires a number of essential properties. These include, in particular, compulsion, feasibility, exclusivity, incontrovertibility and 'issue estoppel' effect ('prejudicialness').[5]

9.02. It is an established legal principle, that the facts adjudicated are not subject to the judicial re-establishment and retain their value until the termination of the judicial act in the manner prescribed by law. Thus, the 'issue estoppel' effect ('prejudicialness') does not only indicate that there is no need to prove again the facts reflected in the judicial act, but also imposes a ban on their refutation[6].

9.03. The doctrinal understanding of the 'issue estoppel' effect ('prejudicialness') concept by itself is fully consistent with its common understanding in practice.[7] The prejudicialness is the 'attribute of the enforceable court decision, according to which the facts, established by the judicial act, are mandatory, when considering other cases involving the same parties';[8] 'prejudicialness of the judicial act, which has entered into legal force, is nothing but a manifestation of its legal validity.'[9]

9.04. To conclude, the 'issue estoppel' effect ('prejudicialness') is a property of a judicial act that entered into legal force, in accordance with which the facts established by a judicial act are mandatory in the consideration of other cases involving these parties. Generally, the 'issue estoppel' effect ('prejudicialness') means not only the lack of the need to repeatedly prove the established facts, but also the prohibition of their refutation. 'It serves for maintaining the consistency of judicial decisions. And helps to give full effect to the legal certainty principle, forming stability of any legal relationship. It covers not only the 'recital'

---

[5] See, for example: Elena A. Vinogradova, ARBITRATION PROCESS: TEXTBOOK, M., 723, 723 – 725 (Vladimir V. Yarkov ed., 2010); VLADIMIR V. YARKOV, LEGAL FACTS IN THE CIVIL PROCESS, M. 480 (2012).

[6] See also: Ludmila A. Novoselova, Marina A. Rozhkova, *About the question of the power of judicial acts of the arbitral tribunal*, 5 BULLETIN OF THE SUPREME ARBITRATION COURT OF THE RUSSIAN FEDERATION (2003).

[7] See also: Ruling of the Constitutional Court as of 21 December 2011 No. 30-P 'On the case of the constitutionality of the provisions of Article 90 of the Criminal Procedure Code of the Russian Federation in connection with the complaint of citizens V.D. Vlasenko and E. A. Vlasenko', available at: http://doc.ksrf.ru/decision/KSRFDecision83184.pdf (accessed on 25 January 2019).

[8] Alexander A. Kostin, *The problem of prejudicial nature of the decisions of international commercial arbitration in the legislation of the Russian Federation*, 3 ACTUAL PROBLEMS OF RUSSIAN LAW 493, 493 – 498 (2014).

[9] Anatoly E. Bereziy, Valeriy A. Musin, *About prejudice of judicial acts*, 6 BULLETIN OF THE SUPREME ARBITRATION COURT OF THE RUSSIAN FEDERATION (2001).

part of the court decision, but also the legal assessment of the circumstances set out by the court, which are established by the decision.[10]

9.05.   At the same time the 'issue estoppel' effect ('prejudicialness') requires striking a balance between the constitutionally protected values, such as universal validity and consistency of decisions, on the one hand, and the independence of the court and adversarial proceedings - on the other. This balance is ensured by establishing limits for the 'issue estoppel' effect ('prejudicialness'), as well as the order of its rebuttal. In particular, the scope of the prejudicial decision is objectively determined by understanding, that the relevant facts, established by the court as part of its subject matter, can have a different meaning as part of the subject of evidence in another case. The items of evidence in different types of proceedings are not the same. The courts in their study are limited by their competence in a specific type of proceedings. For example, there is no need to establish the guilt in a civil proceeding, and that is opposite to a criminal proceeding, when the guilt should be proven.

9.06.   Thus, facts and circumstances, established by judicial act and not subject to re-proof and even excluded from the subject of proof, in another proceeding between the same parties, are considered to be prejudicial in another case. Therefore, the prejudicial effect allows courts to exclude any different legal assessment and qualification of the same factual circumstances involving the same interested persons.

9.07.   The development of economic relations between entities from different countries requires, at the very least, a cross-border recognition of the legal consequences of juridical facts, established in certain cases. Therefore, the question of 'issue estoppel' effect ('prejudicialness') is an intra-national matter in legal relations.[11]

9.08.   The 'issue estoppel' effect ('prejudicialness') is inextricably linked with and follows up on such characteristics of the legitimate force, such as the mandatory nature of judicial acts. The legitimate power of judicial acts means irrefutability, exclusivity and commitment,[12] maintaining the consistency of judicial decisions and legal certainty, which, in turn, corresponds to the

---

[10]   For the purpose of the present article we put aside discussion about whether 'issue estoppel' effect (in Russian terminology – prejudicialness) covers only facts established in an award or legal assessment of the circumstances as well.

[11]   Natalia Y. Erpyleva, *International commercial arbitration: an institutionally-normative mechanism of legal regulation*, 1 THE LEGISLATION AND ECONOMY 38, 38 - 58 (2011).

[12]   For more information about these features, see, for example: Nadezhda A. Chechina, *The rule of law and the decision*, 2 RUSSIAN YEARBOOK OF CIVIL AND ARBITRATION PROCESS (Vladimir V. Yarkov ed., 2004).

public policy of the state. Hence, finally practical realization of the legal force of the judicial act is carried out by accounting the 'issue estoppel' effect ('prejudicialness') of the respective decision or award.

II. Negative Approach to the 'Issue Estoppel' Effect ('Prejudicialness') of Arbitral Awards in Russian Enforcement Practice

9.09. As to whether the arbitration award has the same legal force as the decision of the state court, there is no unity of opinion. In Russian doctrine one can find both positive [13] and negative [14] positions.

9.10. Up to date the dominant trend in the development of Russian national case law is the non-recognition of the 'issue estoppel' effect ('prejudicialness') for arbitral awards. It still exists notwithstanding the international obligations such as joining the New York Convention. This action brought the obligation to comply with the principles of fair trial, enshrined in Article 6(1) of the Convention for the Protection of Human Rights and Fundamental Freedoms, 1950.[15] The recent Russian Arbitration Reform, resulted in legislative changes, based on The Federal Law 'On Arbitration in the Russian Federation' N 382-FL dated 29 December 2015[16] and The Federal Law 'On Changes to Certain Laws of the Russian Federation' N 409-FL dated 29 December 2015[17] (both came into force on 1 September 2016) (New Russian arbitration legislation).[18]

9.11. Unfortunately, this negative practice is based on very formal grounds and very narrow understanding of justice itself.

9.12. For example, as formulated in the Resolution of the Federal Arbitrazhny Court of the North-Western Region as of 15 May

---

[13]   For example: Maria. A. DUBROVINA, INTERNATIONAL COMMERCIAL ARBITRATION IN SWITZERLAND, M. 23; Nataliya S. ZVEREVA, INTERACTION OF ALTERNATIVE METHODS OF DISPUTE SETTLEMENT AND CIVIL PROCEEDINGS IN THE LAW OF RUSSIA AND FRANCE 384 (Vladimir V. Yarkov ed., 2017).

[14]   For example: YU O. SKVORTSOV, PREJUDICIAL EFFECT OF THE DECISION OF THE ARBITRATION COURT IN THE CASE OF INSOLVENCY, Kodeks-info 13 – 17 (2003); Anatoly M. BEZRUKOV, PREJUDICIAL CONNECTION OF JUDICIAL ACTS 144 (2007); Stanislav V. Nikolyukin, *Specificity and procedural features of the arbitration award*, Taxes 10 INFO-LEGAL SYSTEM CONSULTANTPLUS+ 18, 18 – 24 (2011).

[15]   Available at: https://ec.europa.eu/digital-agenda/sites/digital-agenda/files/Convention_ENG.pdf (accessed on 25 January 2019).

[16]   Available at: http://pravo.gov.ru/proxy/ips/?docbody=&firstDoc=1&lastDoc=1&nd=102386393 in Russian language (accessed on 25 January 2019).

[17]   Available at: http://kremlin.ru/acts/bank/40461 in Russian language (accessed on 25 January 2019).

[18]   See more about Russian Arbitration reform, for example: http://arbitrations.ru/en/press-centr/news/a-commentary-to-the-russian-arbitration-laws/?sphrase_id=33130, http://internationalarbitrationlaw.com/blog/the-uncertain-impact-of-the-russian-arbitration-reform-on-foreign-arbitral-institutions-and-international-arbitration/ (accessed on 25 January 2019).

2002 No. A56-1393 / 02,[19] arbitral awards don't have the 'issue estoppel' effect ('prejudicialness') exactly because provisions of the certain article of the national procedural legislation, 'which establishes circumstances of prejudicial significance, does not include among the grounds for exemption from proof in the [state]arbitrazhny proceedings the decision of the arbitral tribunal, as well as the circumstances that it establishes',

9.13. The situation becomes even more complicated if the issue of the arbitral award' effect arises in the bankruptcy procedure. Moreover, Bankruptcy practices in Russia, considering rules of the bankruptcy legislation as a top priority, has formed an extremely negative attitude to the importance of the arbitral decisions. In one case, regarding bankruptcy proceedings, the Supreme Court of the Russian Federation at the Definition as of 5 December 2016 No. 305-ES16-10852 in the case N A41-21198 / 2015,[20] pointed out the following:

> At the same time, the arbitration court in substantiation of the debt for the main (secured) obligation referred to another decision of the arbitration court in the case of recovery of the debt from the drawer (the main debtor), by which the [state] arbitrazhny court issued the writ of execution, as well as the inclusion of the bill of exchange in the register of creditors' claims regarding commercial and industrial group [legal entity] in the case of its bankruptcy. Thus, the [arbitration] court in case No. TC-78-0206 / 2013 did not independently verify the existence of a real unperformed promissory note, which is the main, in fact, recognizing the relevant circumstances as prejudicial and not requiring proof. There was the appearance of the absence of doubt on the main obligation and its indisputability, in connection with which the arbitration court considered only simple differences on the security transaction. *However, in none of the disputes concerning the issue of the existence of a promissory note (principal) debt, the creditors of the plant [legal entity] did not participate (they were not participants in the arbitration with the main debtor, cases on the application for the issuance of the writ of execution against the commercial and industrial group [legal entity], bankruptcy case of it). Not being creditors of*

---

[19] Info-legal System Consultant +.
[20] Info-legal System Consultant +.

> *the commercial and industrial group [legal entity],*
> *the creditors of the plant had no real opportunity*
> *as to challenge the decision of the arbitral tribunal*
> *in the dispute on collecting the bill of exchange from*
> *the commercial and industrial group [legal entity],*
> *[as well as] to appeal the judicial acts adopted in the*
> *procedure for obtaining the writ of execution for the*
> *enforcement of this decision, and [as well as] judicial*
> *acts issued in the framework of the bankruptcy case*
> *of the commercial and industrial group[legal entity]*

9.14. Recently, in spite of the accumulated experience of recognition and enforcement of arbitral awards, the Constitutional Court of the Russian Federation (Constitutional Court RF), whose positions are mandatory for national state courts in Russia, in the Order 'The refusal to accept for consideration the complaint of the citizen Sanaeva Tatyana Vladimirovna about violation of her constitutional rights by Article 61 of the Civil Procedure Code of the Russian Federation' as of 25 September 2014 No. 2136-O,[21] factually confirmed the negative approach and gave the following interpretation:

> In accordance with the second part of Article 61 of the Civil Procedure Code of the Russian Federation circumstances, established by a legally effective decision, rendered in the case previously considered, are mandatory for the court; these circumstances are not proved again and could not be contested with another case, involving the same persons. This statutory provision in relation to the first part of Article 1, the first part of Article 3, Article 5, paragraph 1 of Article 13 of the Civil Procedure Code of the Russian Federation means that circumstances are recognized prejudicial, if they established by judicial decisions of [state] courts of general jurisdiction, but not by the awards of the arbitration courts, which corresponds to the status of the arbitration courts as an alternative form of resolution of civil disputes, by which, as pointed out by the Constitutional Court of the Russian Federation in its Decision as of 26 May 2011 No. 10-P, justice is not carried out. The persons, involved in the case, are not deprived of the opportunity to refer to the arbitral award, taken in

---

[21] Available at: http://doc.ksrf.ru/decision/KSRFDecision177231.pdf (accessed on 25 January 2019).

respect of them, as written evidence to support their position.

9.15. The nuance of the position of the Constitutional Court RF, to which reference is made above, [22] is that it was expressed in passing by manner, just in the context of a named inquiry regarding another main topic - arbitrability of the real estate issues. In particular:

> Allowing the implementation of state registration of rights to real estate, as well as the foreclosure of the mortgaged real estate on the basis of the decision of both the state [courts] and the arbitral tribunals, ... the concept of 'court' and 'arbitration court' are not identified in the context of the administration function of justice, inherent exclusively to state court, but only equate - for state registration purposes or repossession of real estate - the consequences of a decision by a state court and through the arbitration, what is consistent with both the constitutional requirement of the administration of justice only by the [state] courts, as well as with the arbitration by nature as a recognized alternative forms of protection of civilians rights.

9.16. At first glance, it may even seems that the position of the Constitutional Court of the RF, is quite in line with the provisions of the national procedural law. For example, Article 69(2-4) of the Arbitrazhny Procedure Code of the Russian Federation[23] (Arbitrazhny Code RF) stipulates as follows:

> Circumstances established by a judicial act of the [state] arbitrazny court, that entered into legal force, in the previously reviewed case, should not be proved again, when the [state] arbitrazny court considers another case in which the same persons participate. A legally enforceable judgment of a court of general jurisdiction on a previously considered civil case is mandatory for the [state] arbitrazhny court, considering the case, on the circumstances, established by the decision of the court of general jurisdiction and relating to the persons participating

---

[22] For example paragraph 3 clause 7 of Decision 'At the case on the constitutionality of the provisions of the Article 11(1) of the Civil Code of the Russian Federation, Article 1(2) of the Federal Law 'On arbitration courts in the Russian Federation', ... in connection with the request of the Supreme Arbitration Court of the Russian Federation' as of 26 May 2011 No. 10-P // http://doc.ksrf.ru/decision/KSRFDecision63784.pdf (accessed on 25 January 2019).

[23] See also Article 22.1(2) of the Civil Procedure Code of the Russian Federation.

in the case. A verdict of a court in a criminal case, that has entered into legal force, is mandatory for the [state] arbitrazhny court on whether certain actions were taken and whether they were committed by a certain person.

9.17. However, there is no wonder the arbitral awards are not mentioned in provisions above. Arbitrazhny Code RF is adopted for state proceedings and therefore, primarily devoted to jurisdiction of state courts. Thus, it is doubtful, that mere literal text of provisions is sufficient enough to infer the presence or absence of prejudicial effect for the arbitral awards. A too formal approach creates risk such an interpretation, which seems to be contradictive to the essence of the right for protection of violated rights on the trans-border level. In fact, it seems to be opposite to the nature of arbitration[24], understanding of which has developed as a result of accepting the idea that privilege to exercise justice has its basis not with the public source of statehood, but rather emanates from the law itself.

9.18. The existence of some acts, interpreting the legislation in very narrow sense and creating the formal preconditions for denial of prejudicial effect for the arbitral awards, altogether with the extreme formalism are not the reasons to detract the validity of the prevailing approach to understanding of the prejudicial effect' essentials and to disrupt the uniformity in the interpretation of the law rules. Law enforcement errors could be quite common, when legal techniques are not perfect, and when the subject of regulation and application has complex, interdisciplinary and supra-national character.

9.19. Worth to mention that the position of the Constitutional Court RF, regarding arbitrability of the real estates disputes, not actual anymore. Now New Russian arbitration legislation does not set limits for the arbitrability of any disputes over rights to real estate (immovable property). The fact that entry in the public register of real estate rights cannot be made in the absence of a writ of execution, issued on the basis of a judicial act of the state court, doesn't change such approach. It is based on idea that starting 1 September 2016 disputes that cannot be submitted to arbitration are listed specifically, for example, at Article 33(2) of the Arbitrazhny Code RF. Additional restrictions may still be imposed by federal laws, since the list is not closed. But certain

---

[24] For the history of arbitration see: Derek Roebuck, *Sources for the History of Arbitration*, 14(3) ARBITRATION INTERNATIONAL 237-343 (1998).

provision should be explicit to exclude the presumption of arbitrability of any private dispute.

9.20. The practice of accepting arbitral awards like additional written evidences does not solve the problem, since evidences could be assessed in different ways. But this does not correspond to the principle of legal certainty and stability. In addition, such a fit is contrary to the nature of arbitration.

9.21. Accordingly, understanding the place of arbitration in the system of administration of justice, and an analysis of doctrine and modern trends in international practice helps to assert that there are grounds to acknowledge that the state court decisions and the arbitral awards as well should be characterized by the equal legal force with all the related consequences of it. Therefore the prejudicial effect, being among such consequences, should be taking into account regarding any form of jurisdiction.[25]

III. The Legal Force of the Judicial Act as a Source of the 'Issue Estoppel' Effect ('Prejudicialness')

9.22. Different types of normative acts contain provisions on the binding force for both state court decisions and the arbitral awards as well. For example, according to Article 16 of the Arbitrazhny Code RF effective judicial acts of [state] arbitrazhny courts are mandatory for public authorities, local government bodies, other bodies, organizations, state officials and individuals, and are subject to execution on the whole territory of the Russian Federation.

9.23. The similar provision could be found in the Article III of the New York Convention:

> ,...each Contracting State shall recognize arbitral awards as binding and enforce them in accordance with the rules of procedure of the territory where the award is relied upon, under the conditions laid down in the following articles. There shall not be imposed substantially more onerous conditions or higher fees or charges on the recognition or enforcement of arbitral awards to which this Convention applies

---

[25] For the purposes of this paper we will leave aside the nuances of the discussion about the interrelatedness of legal force of the judicial act and prejudicial effect. We believe it is possible to construct arguments based on assumptions made above.

than are imposed on the recognition or enforcement of domestic arbitral awards.

9.24. The fact that to execute the arbitral awards compulsorily on this or that jurisdiction' territory, it is necessary to pass the special procedure of recognition and enforcement of them through the state court system. This does not mean that prior to such procedure arbitral awards do not possess legal mandatory power.

9.25. On the contrary, the wordings of the law articles above leave no doubt that the arbitral awards shall be recognized and enforced precisely because they are binding and mandatory. This is especially so, when one considers, that according to the Article 15(4) of the Constitution of the Russian Federation as of 12 December 1993[26] (Constitution RF) 'the universally recognized norms of international law and international treaties and agreements of the Russian Federation shall be a component part of its legal system, and if an international treaty or agreement of the Russian Federation fixes other rules than those envisaged by law, the rules of the international agreement shall be applied'.

9.26. This means that the provisions of national procedure law must be interpreted and applied solely in the context of assumed international obligations of the Russian Federation, arising, in particular, from the Convention on Human Rights and the New York Convention.

9.27. It is not by chance, that in legal literature the shared opinion is that the procedure of recognition and enforcement of international arbitral awards only confirms, but not initially gives to them their legal force, equal to the binding effect of the national court decisions.[27]

9.28. It should be noted that the granting to arbitral awards the legal force equal to the state court' decisions legal force is not situational whim of the legislator or the scholars, but a reflection of appreciation of the nature of the jurisdictional activity of international arbitration, administering justice as well.

---

[26] Available at: http://www.constitution.ru/en/10003000-02.htm (accessed on 25 January 2019).
[27] See for details: Yulia G. BOGATINA, THE RESERVATION OF THE PUBLIC POLICY IN PRIVATE INTERNATIONAL LAW: THEORETICAL ISSUES AND CURRENT PRACTICE, M. 408 (2010); Tatyana N. Neshataeva, *On the recognition and enforcement of decisions on economic disputes of the the courts of the CIS states-participants of the Russian Federation*, 2(16) JOURNAL OF INTERNATIONAL PRIVATE LAW 5 (1997).

IV. Place of Arbitration in the Justice System as a Reason for the Legal Force and 'Issue Estoppel' effect ('Prejudicialness') of the Arbitral Awards

9.29. Jurisdiction as a normative set of competences should be understood broadly in its content. It may be not only of a state nature (the state court system), but also of a non-governmental character (arbitration), provided that the execution of justice is carried out in full compliance with the guarantees of a fair trial on an equal base, including public hearing within a reasonable time by an independent and impartial body.[28]

9.30. Such approach is based on the interpretation of the Article 6(1) of the Convention on Human Rights by the ECHR.i.e. 'The term 'court' should not to be understood as the jurisdiction of the classical type only, integrated into the overall judicial system of the certain state.'[29]

9.31. This conclusion corresponds to the special provision of Article 46(3) of the Constitution RF, that 'everyone has the right to apply to international bodies for the protection of human rights and freedoms, including the supranational courts outside the judicial system of a particular State'. This testifies to the link between the national statehood and the execution of justice itself. The idea of *justice* as an institution of the state' origin only and as a branch of the government, has neither historical nor actual confirmation and is internally inconsistent.

9.32. Thus, the common phrase that 'justice is carried out only by the court' (for example, in Article 118 of the Constitution RF or at similar rulings of any other national legislations) does not deny the jurisdiction of social institutions, including arbitration. To give justice the sense, that it is performed by the state exclusively, would be absolutely inconsistent with the international common principles of the rule of law.

9.33. Besides, the mere fact of the existence of supranational courts, which are not included into the judicial system of certain states (the ECHR,[30] in particular), confirms the thesis that the protection of rights and freedoms could be done by any means, including possibility to apply to international bodies.[31] It would

---

[28] For more details see: *Campbell & Fell* v. *United Kingdom*, No. 7819/77, 7878/77, 28 June 1984; Lithgov et al. v. United Kingdom, No. 9006/80, 9262/81, 9263/81, 9265/81, 9266/81, 9313/81, 9405/81, 8 June 1986; *Transado-Transportes Fluviais Do Sado, S.A.* v. *Portugal*, No. 35943/02, 16 December 2003; *Regent Company* v. *Ukraine*, No. 773/03, 3 April 2008, available at: http://www.echr.coe.int/Pages/home.aspx?p=caselaw&c= (accessed on 25 January 2019).

[29] *Ibid.*

[30] For details see: http://www.echr.coe.int (accessed on 25 January 2019).

[31] For more details see: http://www.echr.coe.int/Documents/Court_in_brief_ENG.pdf (accessed on 25 January 2019).

be necessary to take into account the dispositive (discretionary) basis of civil substantial and procedural relations, arising from the contractual freedom along with the autonomy of the will of the participants.

9.34. When the parties choose to submit the dispute to arbitration court, provided that it is performed without coercion,[32] the arbitral court receives the exceptional competence, equal in force to state courts powers, and can be annulled only with the termination of the arbitration agreement or with its invalidity. Arbitration proceedings are generally recognized as an alternative jurisdictional form of dispute resolution. The establishment of the facts and circumstances of the dispute in the international arbitration court is also based on the principles of impartiality and independence of arbitrators, the competition and the direct examination of evidence.

9.35. Therefore, arbitral awards have legal force and binding features. This shows that in fact arbitral awards involve a number of publicly significant effects, including basis for termination of litigation proceedings between the same parties on the same subject and on the same grounds. The voluntary execution of the arbitral award is the proper execution of the corresponding civil contract, by virtue of which the parties have recognized the competence of the arbitral tribunal chosen by them and the finality of its dispute resolution by social judicial institution with public features, predetermined by its value and functions.[33]

9.36. Such an attitude to the nature of arbitration explains the existence the positive practice regarding the prejudicial effect of the arbitral awards.

9.37. In the judgment of the Federal Arbitrazhny Court of the Moscow District of 22 August 2000, in case No. KG-A41 / 3640-00,[34] the decision of the arbitration court on the recognition of the arbitration agreement as invalid or unconcluded was

[32] For more details see: ECHR, *Deweer* v. *Belgium*, European Court of Human Rights, No. 6903/75, 27 February 1980, available at: http://www.echr.coe.int/Pages/home.aspx?p=caselaw&c= (accessed on 25 January 2019).
[33] All the features of arbitration described above could be found in a general sense in UNCITRAL Model Law on International Commercial Arbitration, 1985 (with amendments), available at: (http://www.uncitral.org/pdf/english/texts/arbitration/ml-arb/07-86998_Ebook.pdf (accessed on 25 January 2019)), as well as in the many rules of arbitration centers known worldwide, such as the London Court of International Arbitration (http://www.lcia.org/Dispute_Resolution_Services/lcia-arbitration-rules-2014.aspx (accessed on 25 January 2019)), ICC International Court of arbitration (http://www.iccwbo.org/products-and-services/arbitration-and-adr/arbitration/icc-rules-of-arbitration/ (accessed on 25 January 2019)) and the like.
[34] Info-Legal System Consultant +.

recognized as having prejudicial nature, since the word 'court' in national law is widely understood.

9.38. In accordance with clause 1 of Article 11 of the Civil Code of the Russian Federation, protection of violated or disputed civil rights is exercised in accordance with the jurisdiction of cases established by procedural law, the court, arbitrazhny court or arbitration court (hereinafter referred to as the court). It follows that the court at the Civil Code of the Russian Federation also implies an arbitration court.

9.39. As pointed out in the Decision of the Federal arbitrazhny court of Ural District as of 12 October 2005 No. F09-2110 / 05-C6.[35]

9.40. The existence at the territory of the Russian Federation of judicial acts of equal legal force, containing mutually exclusive conclusions ... would come into contradiction with the principle of the mandatory force of the judicial acts of the Russian court, which [the principle] is an integral part of the public policy of the Russian Federation.

9.41. A similar position was approved by the Supreme Arbitrazhny Court of Russian Federation at Order as of 27 August 2012 No. VAS-17458/11:[36] 'The decision is based on conclusion, made in the process of the implementation of the New York Convention, that state court decisions and arbitral awards has equal legal force'.

9.42. Worldwide support of the position about the equality of legal force of state court decisions and arbitral awards could be found in international practice. As pointed out by the Court of the Southern District of New York in the Decision '*Oinoussian Steamship Corporation of Panama* v. *Sabre Shipping Corporation*' (224 F. Supp. 807 (SDNY 1963)), 'The arbitral award, rendered within the volume of the arbitration clause, has prejudicial force and effect of res judicata'.[37]

9.43. ECHR at paragraph 39, 42, 46-48 of the Decision on Case of *Ates Mimarlik Muhendislik A.S.* v. *Turkey* (Application no. 33275/05)[38] emphasized that

> The national courts must, in applying the rules of procedure, avoid ... excessive formalism which would affect the fairness of the procedure'; in view of this the development and harmonization of common

---

[35] Info-Legal System Consultant +.

[36] Info-Legal System Consultant +.

[37] Quoted by: Alexander A. Kostin *Ibid.*

[38] Available at: https://www.google.ch/url?sa=t&rct=j&q=&esrc=s&source=web&cd=1&ved=2ahUKEw-jilsCO45rgAhXLQY8KHWTPC5cQFjAAegQIBBAC&url=http%3A%2F%2Fhudoc.echr.coe.int%2Fap-p%2Fconversion%2Fpdf%2F%3Flibrary%3DECHR%26id%3D001-113441%26filename%3D001-113441.pd-f%26TID%3Dihgdqbxnfi&usg=AOvVaw3uIj6SEqgPn1LWJrlLQB4N (accessed on 4 February 2018).

judicial standards led to establishment of 'rules on the recognition and enforceability of a foreign judgment in ...domestic systems with a view to ensuring legal certainty in international relations between private parties and to fostering predictability and coherence in rules and procedures.

9.44. Disregarding the probative value of the foreign decision without due reasoning led to 'interpretation and application of domestic legislation resulted in an impediment to the applicant to have the merits of its case examined by a judicial authority in such a way or to such an extent that the very essence of its right of access to a court is impaired', regarding what constitutes a violation of Article 6(1) of the Convention on Human Rights.

9.45. Despite the fact that in the case mentioned above the ECHR considered the question of the binding effect of the facts established by the foreign court decision, the findings, set out in it, are subject to the prejudicial effect of judicial acts in general and therefore, applicable to arbitral awards. This is due to the same legal force and in view of the broad understanding of the binding nature of the judicial act.

V. Conclusion

9.46. Summing up, the formal approach can hardly serve as a good reason for the revision of the role of arbitration in the whole justice system. This happens when the 'issue estoppel' effect ('prejudicialness') as the consequence of the legal force of the arbitral award is denied.

9.47. In this regard, perhaps, it is worth to discuss the need to adapt the notion of the concept of the legal force of a judicial decision in general for the purpose of accounting possible differences in the grounds of exercising the state and private (arbitration) jurisdiction. The legal force of any judicial act could be viewed not as a manifestation of the strength of the rule of law applied by the state court in the examination of the case, but as a special legal feature that incorporates all the properties of the jurisdictional decision as a procedural document and an act of justice. In fact, the legal force of a jurisdictional act demonstrates such a legal state of a decision when it becomes as inviolable and final as possible as a result of the manifestation of all its properties. It is the inviolability and finality of the judicial decision that form

Czech (& Central European) Yearbook of Arbitration®

the validity of the legal force. The same characteristics are fully applicable to acts of arbitration.

9.48. Therefore, at present there is every reason to recognize the 'issue estoppel' effect ('prejudicialness') of the arbitral awards. Another approach would violate the universally recognized norms and principles of international law.

9.49. Legal implementation practice, based on the provisions of the New York Convention and Convention on Human rights as well, demonstrates that the only way to respect the principles of legal certainty and consistency of judicial decisions is to recognize the 'issue estoppel' effect ('prejudicialness') of the arbitral awards, keeping in mind the essence of such effect, aimed to exclude the existence of parallel equal judicial acts with different assessment of law or facts.

| | |

Summaries

FRA [*« Issue Estoppel » : la force de chose jugée et les effets des sentences arbitrales*]

Le fait que la procédure d'arbitrage soit mondialement reconnue comme une procédure à part entière, menée par un organe revêtu de pouvoirs et de compétence pour rendre justice au même titre que les tribunaux de droit commun, ne permet toutefois pas d'apporter une réponse à toutes les questions litigieuses au niveau de l'application du droit. Une de ces questions concerne la force de chose jugée des sentences arbitrales. La notion de « force de chose jugée » (res judicata) renvoie aux effets d'un acte juridictionnel entré en force. La force de chose jugée, une des garanties de l'uniformité des décisions de justice, est au service du principe de sécurité juridique. Les sentences arbitrales sont destinées à passer en force de chose jugée et à devenir contraignantes. Ceci implique un grand nombre d'effets de portée publique. Par exemple, une sentence arbitrale constitue un motif pour la clôture d'une éventuelle procédure judiciaire entre les mêmes parties ayant le même objet et les mêmes motifs. Une exécution volontaire d'une sentence arbitrale traduit le respect d'un contrat civil par lequel les parties ont reconnu la compétence du tribunal arbitral choisi et le caractère contraignant (force de chose jugée) de ce mode de règlement des litiges, assuré par des tribunaux revêtant certaines caractéristiques du droit public. Le présent article se propose d'analyser les principaux arguments soulevés en la matière, y compris ceux qui procèdent de la jurisprudence nationale. En conclusion, les auteurs plaident en faveur d'une approche équilibrée de la notion de « force de chose jugée », quel que soit l'acte juridictionnel concerné. En l'espèce, toutes les conditions sont réunies pour étendre les effets de la « chose jugée » (res judicata) aux sentences arbitrales.

CZE [„*Issue Estoppel"– překážka věci rozhodnuté a účinek rozhodčích nálezů*]
Celosvětové uznávání rozhodčího řízení jako plnohodnotného řízení vedeného orgánem nadaným pravomocí a příslušností, který vykonává spravedlnost rovnocenně s obecnými soudy, neumožňuje řešení všech sporných otázek na úrovni vymáhání práva. Jednou z nich je diskuse týkající se povahy rozhodčích nálezů jako rei judicatae. Účinek „věci pravomocně rozhodnuté" („účinek rei judicatae") je běžně označován jako vlastnost aktu obecného soudu, který nabyl právní moci. Účinek „věci pravomocně rozhodnuté" („účinek rei judicatae") obecně slouží zájmu zachování jednotnosti soudních rozhodnutí. Pomáhá plné realizaci zásady právní jistoty. Rozhodčí nálezy nabývají právní moci a jsou nadány prvkem závaznosti. Tato skutečnost dokazuje, že rozhodčí nálezy mají ve skutečnosti řadu veřejně významných účinků, včetně toho, že tvoří základ pro ukončení sporného řízení soudního mezi týmiž stranami ohledně téhož předmětu a z týchž důvodů. Dobrovolný výkon rozhodčího nálezu je řádným výkonem tomu odpovídající civilněprávní smlouvy, na základě které strany uznaly pravomoc jimi zvoleného rozhodčího soudu a závaznost (právní moc) tohoto způsobu řešení sporu prostřednictvím společenských soudních institucí s veřejnoprávními vlastnostmi, předurčeným jeho hodnotou a funkcemi. Tento článek analyzuje hlavní argumenty, včetně těch, které jsou založeny na precedentech vnitrostátní praxe. Autoři dospívají k závěru, že je nezbytný vyvážený přístup k pojmu „právní moc" kteréhokoli jurisdikčního aktu. V tomto případě jsou dány všechny důvody pro přiznání účinku „věci pravomocně rozhodnuté" („účinku rei judicatae") rozhodčím nálezům.

| | |

POL [„*Issue Estoppel" – powaga rzeczy osądzonej a skutek orzeczeń arbitrażowych*]
W skali globalnej przyjęto, że orzeczenie arbitrażowe stanowi pełnowartościową alternatywę dla rozstrzygania w sporach

przez organy sądowe, tzn. że chodzi o wykonywanie kompetencji równoważnych mocy sądowej, czyli porównywalnych z wykonywaniem kompetencji przez sądy powszechne, nawet jeżeli rozjemcy nie mogą rozstrzygać we wszystkich sporach powstających na gruncie obowiązującego prawa. Jeden z problemów stanowi charakter prejudycjalny orzeczeń arbitrażowych. W artykule omówiono podstawowe argumenty „za" i „przeciw" (konkretnie na przykładzie praktyki krajowej). Autorzy dochodzą do wniosku, że konieczne jest ograniczenie pojęciowe terminu „mocy prawa" w odniesieniu do dowolnego aktu jurysdykcyjnego. Mogłoby to bowiem doprowadzić do tego, że wszystkie orzeczenia arbitrażowe będą miały skutek prejudycjalny.

DEU [*„Issue Estoppel" – das Hindernis der Res judicata und die Wirkung von Schiedssprüchen*]
Im globalen Maßstab ist unumstritten, dass das Schiedsverfahren eine vollwertige Alternative zur Entscheidung von Streitigkeiten durch Stellen der Justiz darstellt – soll heißen, dass hier Kompetenzen wahrgenommen werden, die denen der richterlichen Gewalt entsprechen bzw. mit der Ausübung der Gewalt staatlicher Gerichte vergleichbar sind, und zwar ungeachtet dessen, dass Schiedsrichter nicht alle Streitigkeiten zu entscheiden berechtigt sind, die sich im Zusammenhang mit geltendem Recht ergeben. Der präjudiziale Charakter von Schiedssprüchen stellt ein Problem dar. Der Beitrag seziert die wichtigsten Argumente «dafür und dagegen» (auf der Basis konkreter Beispiele aus der nationalen Praxis). Die Autoren kommen zum Schluss, dass dem Verständnis, wonach jedem Akt der Rechtsprechung «Gesetzeskraft» zukommt, notwendigerweise mit Vorbehalten zu begegnen ist. Im vorliegenden Fall läuft alles darauf hinaus, dass sämtliche Schiedssprüche präjudiziale Wirkung haben.

RUS [*„Issue Estoppel" эффект арбитражных решений*]
Мировое признание арбитража полноценным юрисдикционным органом, осуществляющим правосудие наравне с государственными судами, не позволяет разрешить все спорные вопросы на уровне правоприменения. Один из них – дискуссия о преюдициальном свойстве арбитражных решений. В настоящей статье анализируются основные аргументы «за» и «против» (в том числе на примере национальной практики). Авторы делают вывод о том, что необходим взвешенный подход к понятию «законной силы» любого юрисдикционного

Czech (& Central European) Yearbook of Arbitration®

акта. В таком случае есть все основания для придания арбитражным решениям преюдициального эффекта.

ESP   [*"Issue Estoppel"– impedimento de cosa juzgada y efecto de laudos arbitrales*]
El procedimiento arbitral es reconocido, a nivel global, como una alternativa plenamente válida a la resolución judicial de litigios, es decir, se trata de la ejecución de potestades correspondientes al poder judicial y, por ello, comparable con la ejecución del poder por parte de los tribunales del Estado, a pesar de que los árbitros no pueden resolver todos los litigios conforme estos surgen respecto a la legislación vigente. Constituye uno de los problemas el carácter prejudicial de los laudos arbitrales. El artículo analiza los principales argumentos "a favor" y "en contra" (concretamente en el ejemplo de la práctica nacional). Los autores llegan a la conclusión de que el enfoque restringido del concepto de la "fuerza legal" de cualquier acto jurídico resulta imprescindible. En tal caso, todo parece indicar que todos los laudos arbitrales poseen el efecto prejudicial.

| | |

Bibliography

Anatoly E. Bereziy, Valeriy A. Musin, *About prejudice of judicial acts*, 6 BULLETIN OF THE SUPREME ARBITRATION COURT OF THE RUSSIAN FEDERATION (2001).

Anatoly M. BEZRUKOV, PREJUDICIAL CONNECTION OF JUDICIAL ACTS (2007).

Yulia G. BOGATINA, THE RESERVATION OF THE PUBLIC POLICY IN PRIVATE INTERNATIONAL LAW: THEORETICAL ISSUES AND CURRENT PRACTICE, M. (2010).

Nadezhda A. Chechina, *The rule of law and the decision*, 2 RUSSIAN YEARBOOK OF CIVIL AND ARBITRATION PROCESS (Vladimir V. Yarkov ed., 2004).

Natalia Y. Erpyleva, *International commercial arbitration: an institutionally-normative mechanism of legal regulation*, 1 THE LEGISLATION AND ECONOMY 38 (2011).

Alexander A. Kostin, *The problem of prejudicial nature of the decisions of international commercial arbitration in the legislation of the Russian Federation*, 3 ACTUAL PROBLEMS OF RUSSIAN LAW 493 (2014).

Irina N. Lukyanova, *Problems of the institute of prejudice as a tool of legal certainty in modern civil legal proceedings*, 12 LAWS OF RUSSIA: EXPERIENCE, ANALYSIS, PRACTICE 28 (2015).

Tatyana N. Neshataeva, *On the recognition and enforcement of decisions on economic disputes of the the courts of the CIS states-participants of the Russian Federation*, 2(16) JOURNAL OF INTERNATIONAL PRIVATE LAW 5 (1997).

Stanislav V. Nikolyukin, *Specificity and procedural features of the arbitration award*, Taxes 10 INFO-LEGAL SYSTEM CONSULTANTPLUS+ 18 (2011).

Ludmila A. Novoselova, Marina A. Rozhkova, *About the question of the power of judicial acts of the arbitral tribunal*, 5 BULLETIN OF THE SUPREME ARBITRATION COURT OF THE RUSSIAN FEDERATION (2003).

Derek Roebuck, *Sources for the History of Arbitration*, 14(3) ARBITRATION INTERNATIONAL (1998).

YU O. SKVORTSOV, PREJUDICIAL EFFECT OF THE DECISION OF THE ARBITRATION COURT IN THE CASE OF INSOLVENCY, Kodeks-info (2003).

Elena A. VINOGRADOVA, ARBITRATION PROCESS: TEXTBOOK, M., 723 (Vladimir V. Yarkov ed., 2010).

VLADIMIR V. YARKOV, LEGAL FACTS IN THE CIVIL PROCESS, M. (2012).

Nataliya S. ZVEREVA, INTERACTION OF ALTERNATIVE METHODS OF DISPUTE SETTLEMENT AND CIVIL PROCEEDINGS IN THE LAW OF RUSSIA AND FRANCE (Vladimir V. Yarkov ed., 2017).

Albertas Šekštelo

A Prophecy of the Crisis of International Commercial Arbitration in Europe?

Key words:
Achmea | arbitration | BIT | commercial arbitration | ECJ | EU law | European Union | investment arbitration | ISDS

Albertas Šekštelo is a senior assocate at the law firm Motieka & Audzevičius, Lithuania. He has a Master's Degree in Law from the Faculty of Law, Vilnius University (2005) and a PGDip (with distinction) in International Arbitration from Queen Mary University of London (2011). In 2013, he became a Fellow of the Chartered Institute of Arbitrators (FCIArb). He usually acts as (co-)counsel in both domestic and international commercial arbitrations, as well as international investment arbitrations.
E-mail: albertas.sekstelo@motieka.com

Abstract | *The Court of Justice of the European Union granted a now-famous judgement in the Achmea case in 2018. The Court ruled that arbitration clauses contained in the intra-EU bilateral investment treaties contradict mandatory EU law. The judgement is in line with the general concerns raised by the European Union towards Investor-State Dispute Settlement provisions. The article analyses the background and reasoning of the Court of Justice in terms of the possible implications of the Achmea case on international commercial arbitration. Although the Court of Justice has distinguished international investment arbitration from international commercial arbitration, the line of the Court's arguments is not persuasive. The Court of Justice held that while international commercial arbitration originates in the freely expressed will of the parties, international investment arbitration derives from a treaty. However, such a dichotomy that the Court sees does not in fact exist. First of all, an arbitration clause contained in the intra-EU bilateral investment treaty must be interpreted separately from the contract under the separability doctrine widely applicable in international arbitration. The severability doctrine has another very important implication – applicable law for the validity and interpretation of the arbitration clause in question may be different from that applicable to the treaty. Therefore, it is not necessary that international public law be at stake when, e.g., interpreting the arbitration clause contained in the intra-EU bilateral investment treaty. Moreover, the treaty* *itself does not have an arbitration clause. It contains only an offer for any investor of another contracting State. If the investor commences arbitration proceedings, it accepts the State's offer and thus concludes the agreement to arbitrate. Thus, the treaty provides only an opt-in system and it is up to the investor which régime to choose. Furthermore, arbitration always eliminates relevant or overlapping State courts' jurisdiction. Finally, the arbitration rules for international investment and commercial arbitrations are mostly identical. Consequently, considering the growing appetite of the Court of Justice, it is only a matter of time when we will see another Achmea case, challenging the fundamental principles of international commercial arbitration.*

| | |

I.   Introduction

10.01. The Court of Justice of the European Union (Court of Justice or Court) rendered a ground-breaking decision in the *Achmea* case in 2018. The Court of Justice held that European Union (EU) law precludes a provision in an international agreement concluded between Member States under which an investor from one of those Member States may, in the event of a dispute concerning investments in the other Member State, bring proceedings against the latter Member State before an arbitral tribunal whose jurisdiction that State has undertaken to accept.

10.02. The decision has raised many issues in the legal world, in particular among international arbitration practitioners. It is a coincidence, but the French word *acmé*, which sounds similarly to Achmea, means crisis, or the end.

10.03. The purpose of this article is not to review all pros and cons of the *Achmea* decision. On the contrary, the author respectfully doubts the reasoning of the Court of Justice where the Court distinguishes between international investment arbitration and international commercial arbitration that allowed the Court to apply a different standard to international investment arbitration.[1] The Court's decision is also potentially dangerous to international commercial arbitration because the Court challenges the crux of the alternative dispute resolution mechanism – the courts' limited control influenced by the parties' autonomy of hearing disputes in the forum detached

---

[1]   Of course, such a distinction exists, but not because of the reasons the Court provided in the *Achmea* case. The differences between international commercial arbitration and investment arbitration are out of the scope of this publication.

from a particular jurisdiction. Such reasoning can encourage the Court of Justice, or the Member States' courts to go further and question the effectiveness of international commercial arbitration as well. Such implications, unfortunately, already exist. In light of the foregoing, the author seeks to look deeper into these implications.

10.04. The author will briefly discuss (I) the background and main Court's reasoning in the *Achmea* case. Then, (II) the EU position against the resolution of international investment disputes in arbitration will be presented. Subsequently, (III) the article will reveal how the Court of Justice expands the courts' powers in terms of international commercial arbitration. Finally, (IV) the author will analyse whether the divide exists between international commercial arbitration and investment arbitration in terms of conclusion of arbitration clauses and the course of arbitral procedures.

II.   Background and Primary Reasoning in the *Achmea* case

10.05. It is first necessary to provide a brief background of the *Achmea* decision.[2] In 2004, after its accession into the European Union, Slovakia decided to reform its health care system. The State opened its market for the investors proposing health care insurance services. One such investor was Achmea, a company incorporated in the Netherlands. Achmea established a subsidiary in Slovakia for providing health care insurance services. Achmea made investments and rendered its services within the territory of Slovakia through the subsidiary.

10.06. However, after the 2006 elections in Slovakia, the State went in the opposite direction and partially repealed the liberalization of the health care insurance market, causing financial damage to Achmea. The latter commenced arbitration proceedings against Slovakia under the relevant Bilateral Investment Treaty (BIT) concluded between the Netherlands and the former Republic of Czechoslovakia.[3]

10.07. The Arbitral Tribunal established under the BIT and the UNCITRAL Arbitration Rules granted the Final Award of 7 December 2012 and ordered Slovakia to compensate Achmea's damage amounting to EUR 22.1 million. As the arbitration place was in Germany, Slovakia challenged the Award before the German courts. The Supreme Federal Court referred to the Court of Justice for a preliminary ruling. The Grand Chamber

---

2   ECJ Judgement of 06 March 2018, C-248/16, *Achmea* [2018] EU:C:2018:158.
3   Now Slovakia is an accessory to the BIT.

of the Court of Justice considered the request and granted the well-known judgement in the *Achmea* case.

10.08. In the context of this article it is relevant to understand the logic of the Court of Justice provided in the judgement. The Court stressed that

> the Member States are obliged, by reason *inter alia* of the principle of sincere cooperation ... to ensure in their respective territories the application of and respect for European Union law, and to take for those purposes any appropriate measure.[4]

10.09. For such a purpose the EU has established a judicial system intended to ensure consistency and uniformity in the interpretation of EU law.[5] The keystone of such a system is the preliminary ruling procedure laid down in Article 267 of the Treaty on the Functioning of the European Union (TFEU).[6]

10.10. Then the Court of Justice raised three premises which have been subsequently answered negatively by the Court. First, the Court analysed whether the disputes under the BIT can be related to the interpretation or application of EU law.[7] Second, the Court assessed whether the Arbitral Tribunal constituted under the BIT can interpret or apply EU law and can be regarded as a court or tribunal of a Member State within the meaning of Article 267 TFEU and can benefit from referring to the Court of Justice for a preliminary ruling.[8] Third and foremost, the Court discussed whether there is an effective control mechanism for the Award granted under the BIT.[9] Thus, the Court of Justice decided that such a dispute resolution in arbitration that does not form part of the EU court's system has an adverse effect on the autonomy of EU law.[10]

10.11. Nevertheless, the scope of the analysis of this publication is paragraphs 54-55 of the *Achmea* judgement which is quoted in full:

> 54. It is true that, in relation to commercial arbitration, the Court has held that the requirements of efficient arbitration proceedings justify the review of arbitral awards by the courts of the Member States being limited in scope, provided that the fundamental provisions of EU law can be examined in the course

---

[4] ECJ Judgement of 6 March 2018, *supra* note 2 at paragraph 34.
[5] *Ibid.*, paragraph 35.
[6] *Ibid.*, paragraph 37.
[7] *Ibid.*, paragraphs 39-42.
[8] *Ibid.*, paragraphs 43-49.
[9] *Ibid.*, paragraph 50 *et seq.*
[10] *Ibid.*, paragraphs 58-59, 62.

of that review and, if necessary, be the subject of a reference to the Court for a preliminary ruling (see, to that effect, judgments of 1 June 1999, *Eco Swiss*, C-126/97, EU:C:1999:269, paragraphs 35, 36 and 40, and of 26 October 2006, *Mostaza Claro*, C-168/05, EU:C:2006:675, paragraphs 34 to 39).

55. However, arbitration proceedings such as those referred to in Article 8 of the BIT are different from commercial arbitration proceedings. While the latter originate in the freely expressed wishes of the parties, the former derive from a treaty by which Member States agree to remove from the jurisdiction of their own courts, and hence from the system of judicial remedies which the second subparagraph of Article 19(1) TEU requires them to establish in the fields covered by EU law (see, to that effect, judgment of 27 February 2018, *Associação Sindical dos Juízes Portugueses*, C-64/16, EU:C:2018:117, paragraph 34), disputes which may concern the application or interpretation of EU law. In those circumstances, the considerations set out in the preceding paragraph relating to commercial arbitration cannot be applied to arbitration proceedings such as those referred to in Article 8 of the BIT.

10.12. Although the Court of Justice expressed that '... the considerations ... relating to commercial arbitration cannot be applied to arbitration proceedings such as those referred to in Article 8 of the BIT', the lack of comprehensive and persuasive reasoning confirms that the Court of Justice rendered a political judgement.

III. The EU – Against the Resolution of International Investment Disputes in Arbitration

10.13. The outcome of the *Achmea* judgement should be visible in the EU attitude towards the necessity to terminate the intra-EU BITs, as well as relevant arbitration clauses therein, because the provisions of the BITs duplicate and to some extent contradict EU law.

10.14. But a closer look at this issue reveals the EU's fear to delegate the disputes arising out of the BITs to independent arbitrators. The EU's main concerns are summarised in the EU submission[11]

---

[11] Possible reform of investor-State dispute settlement (ISDS). Submission from the European Union. *The identification and consideration of concerns as regards investor to state dispute settlement.* A/CN.9/WG.III/WP.145.

to the United Nations Commission on International Trade Law (UNCITRAL) when considering a possible reform of investor-State dispute settlement (ISDS). The aim of the paper is to identify and consider concerns about the current system of ISDS.[12] By stressing that the international investment régime comes from the public international law domain,[13] the EU expressed its concerns towards such a régime. First, the *ad hoc* nature of the system affects consistency and predictability. In the opinion of the EU, the *ad hoc* constitution of arbitral tribunals potentially influences outcomes, since arbitrators are repeat players, or are seeking to be repeat players, in a system where the adjudicators need to be appointed afresh for each dispute. This does not enhance the stability and consistency of the system and hence the ability of the parties to the dispute to seek guidance on previous cases to try to determine how the rules will be applied in a particular set of circumstances.[14]

10.15. Second, the EU raises significant concerns of perception. The *ad hoc* nature of the ISDS arbitration where the arbitrators, by definition, have other activities, creates significant perception problems. The perception problems derive from the fact that the professional and/or personal interests of the persons involved in the system might be perceived to influence the outcomes of the disputes.[15]

10.16. Third, the parallel with the reasoning of the Court of Justice in the *Achmea* case can be seen, in that another concern of the EU regarding the existing ISDS is a limited possibility of a systemic check for correctness and consistency of awards. According to the EU, under the ICSID system, annulment is only available to correct a very limited set of errors. Article 52 of the Convention on the Settlement of Investment Disputes between States and Nationals of Other States (ICSID Convention) only provides for annulment in limited circumstances.[16] These do not touch upon

---

[12]   *Ibid.*, paragraph 1.

[13]   *Ibid.*, paragraphs 3-5.

[14]   *Ibid.*, paragraph 21. The EU argument that the *ad hoc* constitution of the arbitral tribunals helps to determine how the rules will be applied in a dispute, is not consistent with the EU idea to establish a permanent body to hear international investment cases, because the case-law of any such body also tends to be predictable.

[15]   *Ibid.*, paragraph 27. Such EU argument seems to be superficial. Each arbitration law and rule requires impartiality and independence from every arbitrator and provides for a possibility of challenging the appointed arbitrators if the arbitrators do not follow such obligations (see, for instance, Article 12 UNCITRAL Arbitration Rules; Article 14 ICC Arbitration Rules; Article 19 SCC Arbitration Rules). Therefore, each arbitrator is bound by the obligation to be impartial and independent and a party to the particular international investment arbitration has a full set of rules to challenge any bias arbitrator.

[16]   Article 52(1) of the ICSID Convention provides as far as follows:

[e]ither party may request annulment of the award by an application in writing addressed to the Secretary-General on one or more of the following grounds: (a) that the Tribunal was not properly constituted; (b) that the Tribunal has manifestly exceeded its powers; (c) that there was corruption on the part of a member of the Tribunal; (d) that there has been a serious departure

the substantive correctness of the award.[17] Similarly, domestic arbitration laws or the New York Convention limit the grounds on which recognition and enforcement of an award can be refused.[18] This means that awards can be legally incorrect, but the system does not allow for them to be corrected.[19]

10.17. Fourth, the EU raises concerns regarding the nature of appointment of adjudicators. In view of the EU, when States appoint adjudicators *ex ante* (before particular disputes arise), they act in their capacity as treaty parties and have an incentive to balance their interests, ensuring the selection of fair and balanced adjudicators that they would be happy to live with whether a future case is brought by their investors or against them as respondents.[20] In arbitration, however, the choice of arbitrator is made not in advance but *ex post* (i.e. at the time a dispute has arisen), which means that investors and State respondents make decisions about arbitrators with a view to best serving their interests in that particular case. This leads them to focus on arbitrators who are already known in the system and who are considered as having a predisposition towards one or other side (e.g. being perceived as investor or state-friendly).[21]

10.18. The EU noted that in addition to encouraging the appointment of predisposed arbitrators and a small number of repeat players,

---

from a fundamental rule of procedure; or (e) that the award has failed to state the reasons on which it is based.

[17] A/CN.9/WG.III/WP.145, *supra* note 11 at paragraph 28.

[18] *Ibid.*, paragraph 28.

[19] *Ibid.*, paragraph 29. Such an argument from the EU is surprising. It is true that the main feature of the grounds for refusal to recognize the final arbitral award is that 'no review of the merits of the arbitral award is allowed'; see ALBERT JAN VAN DEN BERG, THE NEW YORK ARBITRATION CONVENTION OF 1958: TOWARDS A UNIFORM JUDICIAL INTERPRETATION, Netherlands: Kluwer Law Taxation Publishers, 265 (1981). The same prohibition to review the merits of the award applies when the award is challenged.

> It is fundamental under virtually all national legal systems that an action for the annulment of an international arbitral award is not comparable to an appeal from a lower court judgement ... Most national arbitration legislation permits actions to annul an award only on grounds analogous to those set out in Articles V(1) and V(2) of the New York Convention and Articles 34 and 36 of the Model law ...

see 3 GARRY B. BORN, INTERNATIONAL COMMERCIAL ARBITRATION, New York: Wolters Kluwer 3186 (2014). Hence, the absence of appeal on the merits forms a distinctive and important feature of international arbitration. As rightly pointed out by learned experts of international investment law, Profs. Rudolf Dolcer and Christoph Schreuer,

> [a]n appeal facility is not necessarily the best mechanism to achieve coherence and consistency in the interpretation of investment treaties. Appeal presupposes a decision that will be attacked for some alleged flaw in order to be repaired. Rather than trying to fix the damage after the fact through an appeal, it is more economical and effective to address it preventively before it occurs.

see RUDOLF DOLCER AND CHRISTOPH SCHREUER, PRINCIPLES OF INTERNATIONAL INVESTMENT LAW, Oxford: Oxford University Press 38 (2008).

[20] A/CN.9/WG.III/WP.145, *supra* note 11 at paragraph 31.

[21] *Ibid.*, paragraph 31. However, such reasoning by the EU is not persuasive. The vast majority of arbitration rules, including the ICSID Convention and BITs, provide balanced provisions in terms of the constitution of an arbitral tribunal. For instance, the BIT analysed by the Court of Justice in the *Achmea* judgement provides in Article 8(3) that

> [t]he arbitral tribunal referred to in paragraph 2 of this Article will be constituted for each individual case in the following way: each party to the dispute appoints one member of the

one of the problems with this approach is that it leads to a continued high concentration of persons who have gained their experience as arbitrators primarily in the field of commercial arbitration involving disputes of 'private law' rather than public international law disputes. Such persons are often professionally less familiar with public international law and public law.[22]

10.19. Fifth, the EU expressed concerns regarding significant arbitration costs. In particular, the EU noted that high arbitration costs come from the lack of consistency and predictability inherent in the system where diligent counsel will run with arguments which might have been dismissed in another case because it is always possible that another tribunal will accept them. Costs are also generated by the need to identify and then appoint arbitrators.[23]

10.20. Finally, in view of the EU, the existing international investment arbitration dispute resolution system lacks transparency.[24] The EU explained that the existing system, being largely based on or derived from commercial arbitration has historically not regarded transparency as being a necessary component of dispute settlement. This is because information on investment disputes is not always provided to the public.[25]

10.21. Hence, the EU's arguments show that the EU no longer trusts the existing mechanism of international investment arbitration

---

tribunal and the two members thus appointed shall select a national of a third State as Chairman of the tribunal. Each party to the dispute shall appoint its member of the tribunal within two months, and the Chairman shall be appointed within three months from the date on which the investor has notified the other Contracting Party of his decision to submit the dispute to the arbitral tribunal.

see ECJ Judgement of 6 March 2018, *supra* note 2 at paragraph 4. A very similar provision is contained in Article 37(2)(b) of the ICSID Convention ('Where the parties do not agree upon the number of arbitrators and the method of their appointment, the Tribunal shall consist of three arbitrators, one arbitrator appointed by each party and the third, who shall be the president of the Tribunal, appointed by agreement of the parties'; in addition, see also Rule 3 of the ICSID Arbitration Rules). Thus, even if the perception about investor-and-state-friendly arbitrators existed, as the final award is usually rendered by three arbitrators, it must reflect a balanced view of the arbitral tribunal on the issues in question.

[22] A/CN.9/WG.III/WP.145, *supra* note 11 at paragraph 32. However, such an argument of the EU is predisposed disregarding the fact that usually prominent and highly-skilled persons with remarkable records are appointed as arbitrators in international investment arbitrations.

[23] *Ibid.*, paragraph 33. As rightly pointed out, 'it should not be forgotten that arbitration is a form of "one-stop-shopping", so that although its cost may not be less than that of proceedings in court (and may indeed be more) the award of the arbitrators is unlikely to be followed by a series of costly appeals to superior courts'; LAW AND PRACTICE OF INTERNATIONAL COMMERCIAL ARBITRATION, London: Sweet & Maxwell 24 (Alan Redfern *et al.* eds., 4th ed., 2004).

[24] A/CN.9/WG.III/WP.145, *supra* note 11 at paragraph 35.

[25] However, as noted by the EU itself, significant steps have been taken to improve this situation through the amendments of the ICSID Arbitration Rules to provide for certain levels of transparency, as well as the adoption of the UNCITRAL Rules on Transparency in Treaty-based Investor-State Arbitration and the United Nations Convention on Transparency in Treaty-based Investor-State Arbitration. In fact, '... this "legitimacy crisis" of investment arbitration, of which the transparency debate forms an important part, can be explained, in part, by the hybrid nature of investment arbitration...'; where from one point of view, the outcome of the investment dispute may impact large numbers of individuals and even for the host State's economy and from a different perspective, investment arbitration remains a private dispute resolution mechanism that should remain confidential; see TRANSPARENCY IN INTERNATIONAL INVESTMENT

dispute resolution. In the light of the foregoing, the Court of Justice's *Achmea* judgement is the logical consequence of such a general policy of the EU.

10.22. Such an attitude by the EU towards intra-EU BITs is evident from the EU Commission's further guidance on the protection of cross-border EU investments. On 19 July 2018, the EU Commission published a communication to the European Parliament and the Council on protection of intra-EU investment.[26] The Commission also commented on the question '[w]hat has been the Commission position on intra-EU BITs'.[27] The Commission commented that it has consistently taken the view that intra-EU BITs are incompatible with EU law and that the Energy Charter Treaty does not apply between EU Member States. This is because intra-EU BITs constitute a parallel system overlapping with single market rules. In addition, intra-EU BITs conflict with the principle of non-discrimination among EU investors within the single market by conferring rights on a bilateral basis to investors from some Member States only. Furthermore, intra-EU BITs may constitute the basis for the award of unlawful State aid in violation of the level playing field in the single market. Finally, intra-EU BITs entrust disputes dealing with EU law to non-permanent and private arbitral tribunals who are not State organs. They are thus outside the mechanism of dispute resolution which is laid down in the Treaty. They are unable to ensure the correct and uniform application of EU law, in the absence of the judicial dialogue with the ECJ.[28] Thus, the EU Commission expanded its arguments against intra-EU BITs and used them, as well as the *Achmea* judgement, as a political tool to press the Member States to terminate such BITs.[29]

10.23. However, if the EU's attitude towards international investment arbitration is due to political and economical reasons (e.g. high arbitration costs), will such a tendency of narrowing the scope of international arbitration be expanded to international commercial arbitration, for instance, related to concession or

---

ARBITRATION. A GUIDE TO THE UNCITRAL RULES ON TRANSPARENCY IN TREATY-BASED INVESTOR-STATE ARBITRATION, Cambridge: Cambridge University Press 2-3 (D. Euler, M. Gehring and M. Scherer, eds, 2015).

[26] European Commission, Communication from the Commission to the European Parliament and the Council COM(2018) 547/2 Protection of intra-EU investment, available at http://ec.europa.eu/finance/docs/policy/180719-communication-protection-of-investments_en.pdf (accessed on 24 July 2018).

[27] Commission provides guidance on protection of cross-border EU investments – Questions and Answers, available at http://europa.eu/rapid/press-release_MEMO-18-4529_en.htm (accessed on 25 January 2019).

[28] *Ibid.*, (accessed on 25 January 2019).

[29] The Commission has launched infringement procedures against five Member States for failure to terminate intra-EU BITs. Following the *Achmea* judgement, the Commission has intensified its work with the Member States concerned in order to ensure that the judgement is fully implemented, *Ibid.*, (accessed on 25 January 2019).

PPP contracts? In addition to this, the expanding interpretation of the notion of 'public order' by the Court of Justice in terms of international commercial arbitration is also worrying.

IV. The Court of Justice Expands the Courts' Powers in International Commercial Arbitration

10.24. The Court of Justice acknowledges that

> in relation to commercial arbitration, the Court has held that the requirements of efficient arbitration proceedings justify the review of arbitral awards by the courts of the Member States being limited in scope, provided that the fundamental provisions of EU law can be examined in the course of that review and, if necessary, be the subject of a reference to the Court for a preliminary ruling.[30]

10.25. However, the Court's case law steadily expands the powers of the national courts of the Member States to review arbitral awards on the merits through the 'public order' requirement stipulated in Article V(2)(b) of the New York Convention.

10.26. Even in the *Achmea* case the Court referred firstly to the *Eco Swiss* case.[31] In *Eco Swiss*, the Court recalled that the arbitral tribunal cannot refer to the Court of Justice for a preliminary ruling.[32] The Court ordered that where its domestic rules of procedure require a national court to grant an application for annulment of an arbitration award where such application is founded on the failure to observe national rules of public policy, it must also grant such an application where it is founded on a failure to comply with the prohibition for unfair competition.[33] Consequently, the Court held that such provisions prohibiting unfair competition may be regarded as a matter of public policy

---

[30] ECJ Judgement of 6 March 2018, *supra* note 2, paragraph 54. By saying this the Court referred to its previous ECJ judgements in the following cases: *Eco Swiss*, C-126/97, EU:C:1999:269, paragraphs 35, 36 and 40 and *Mostaza Claro*, C-168/05, EU:C:2006:675, paragraphs 34-39.

[31] ECJ Judgement of 1 June 1999, C-126/97, *Eco Swiss* [1999] EU:C:1999:269, paragraphs 35, 36 and 40. The background of this case was as follows: In 1986, Benetton concluded a licensing agreement for a period of eight years with Eco Swiss and Bulova Watch Company. Under the agreement, Benetton granted Eco Swiss the right to manufacture watches and clocks bearing the words 'Benetton by Bulova', which could then be sold by Eco Swiss or Bulova. The licencing agreement contained an arbitration clause. In 1991, three years before the end of the period originally provided for, Benetton terminated the agreement. Consequently, Eco Swiss and Bulova commenced arbitration proceedings in connection with the termination. In the final award made in 1995, the arbitral tribunal ordered Benetton to compensate for damages to both Eco Swiss and Bulova. Benetton applied to the court for setting aside the award. The court applied to the Court of Justice for a preliminary ruling.

[32] Under the Court's case law, an arbitration tribunal is not a 'court or tribunal of a Member State' within the meaning of TFEU; see also ECJ Judgement of 23 March 1982, C-102/81, *Nordsee* [1982] EU:C:1982:107; ECJ Judgement of 27 January 2005, C-125/04, *Transorient* [2005] EU:C:2005:69.

[33] ECJ Judgement of 1 June 1999, *supra* note 31 at paragraph 37.

within the meaning of the New York Convention.[34] Hence, the law requires that questions concerning the interpretation of the prohibitions of mandatory EU law which, in view of the Court, form part of the public policy should be open to examination by national courts when asked to determine the validity of an arbitration award and that it should be possible for those questions to be referred, if necessary, to the Court of Justice for a preliminary ruling.[35] The Court then ruled that a national court to which an application is made for annulment of an arbitration award must grant that application if the court considers that the award in question is in fact contrary to EU law provisions related to unfair competition, where the court's domestic rules of procedure require it to grant an application for annulment founded on a failure to observe a national rule of public policy.[36] This ruling of the Court was heavily criticised not only by scholars, but also by the Member States. For instance, in the *travaux préparatoires* to the Swedish Arbitration Act of 1999, which was written prior to the *Eco Swiss* ruling, the Swedish Government examined in detail whether an arbitral tribunal should consider EC competition law aspects.[37] The Swedish Government concluded that tribunals are bound by, and may not go beyond, the submission of the parties and that tribunals should not consider these aspects *ex officio*. The Government also stated that should the then pending *Eco Swiss* case have an impact on the principle concerned, the Government would reconsider its position. This has, however, not yet been done.[38] Thus, the general opinion in Sweden seems to be that an international arbitrator is under no obligation to respect the public policy of any national law except *lex contractus*, i.e. the law on the merits chosen by the parties or the arbitrators. Awards which infringe on competition law outside the EU, e.g.

---

[34]   *Ibid.*, paragraph 39. The Court reasoned that the New York Convention, which has been ratified by all the Member States, provides that recognition and enforcement of an arbitration award may be refused only on certain specific grounds, namely where the award does not fall within the terms of submission to arbitration or goes beyond its scope, where the award is not binding on the parties or where the recognition or enforcement of the award would be contrary to the public policy of the country where such recognition and enforcement are sought (Articles V(1)(c) and (e) and II(b) of the New York Convention; see ECJ Judgement of 1 June 1999, *supra* note 31 at paragraph 38.

[35]   *Ibid.*, paragraph 40.

[36]   *Ibid*, paragraph 41.

[37]   Government Bill, prop. 1998/99:35, et 58 in The Swedish Arbitration Act of 1999, FIVE YEARS ON: A CRITICAL REVIEW OF STRENGTHS AND WEAKNESSES, New York: JurisNet, LLC 114, fn. 48 (Lars Heuman and Sigvard Jarvin eds., 2006).

[38]   *Ibid.*, at 114.

U.S. antitrust laws, are not considered to fall within the scope of the public policy concept in Swedish law.[39]

10.27. Moving back to the Court of Justice's reasoning in the *Achmea* case, when building up the reasoning the Court referred to the *Mostaza Claro* case.[40] In *Mostaza Claro*, the Court ruled that the nature and importance of the public interest underlying the protection which Council Directive 93/13/EEC of 5 April 1993 on unfair terms in consumer contracts confers on consumers justify, moreover, the national court being required to assess of its own motion whether a contractual term is unfair. In this way, it compensates for the imbalance which exists between the consumer and the seller or supplier.[41]

10.28. It follows that the EU mandatory law rule equivalent to the public order within the meaning of the New York Convention can be embodied not only in the primary sources of EU law but also in secondary legislation. The Court thus expands the legislative area of such a public order allowing, in fact, the Member State courts to review arbitral awards on merits.

10.29. Further, the Court of Justice not only expands the scope of the notion 'public order' embodied in the New York Convention but interferes in other important fields of international commercial arbitration – arbitrability and interpretation of the arbitration clauses. Here the *Achmea* case is not a pioneer.

10.30. In the *Cartel Damage Claims (CDC)* case,[42] a CDC company was established for pursuing claims for damages of undertakings affected by a cartel. In that regard, *CDC* invoked agreements concerning the transfer of claims for damages entered into with 32 undertakings domiciled in 13 different Member States of the EU or of the European Economic Area (EEA). CDC brought an action for damages before a Member State court against six chemical undertakings after the European Commission found that those companies and other undertakings had participated in a single and continuous infringement of the prohibition of cartel agreements banned by EU law. The defendants, as well as other companies purchased substantial quantities of hydrogen peroxide in various EU and EEA Member States, some undertakings having supplied hydrogen peroxide to plants in several EU Member States. The defendants in the case concerned stated that some of the contracts of sale had

---

[39] *Ibid.*, at 115; see also International Arbitration in Sweden: A Practitioner's Guide: Kluwer Law International 144 (Ulf Franke, Annette Magnusson, et al. eds., 2013); Kaj Hobér, International Commercial Arbitration in Sweden: Lindskog, Skiljeförfarande, 241 (2001).
[40] ECJ Judgement of 06 March 2018, *supra* note 2, paragraph 54; ECJ Judgement of 26 October 2006, C-168/05, *Mostaza Claro* [2006] EU:C:2006:675.
[41] ECJ Judgement of 26 October 2006, *supra* note 40 at paragraph 38.
[42] ECJ Judgement of 21 May 2015, C-352/13, *Cartel Damage Claims* [2015] EU:C:2015:335.

A Prophecy of the Crisis of International Commercial Arbitration in Europe?

Czech (& Central European) Yearbook of Arbitration®

included agreements on arbitration. Consequently, the court that heard the case referred to the Court of Justice, *inter alia*, with the following question: whether, in the case of actions for damages for antitrust infringements, the requirement of effective enforcement of the prohibition of such infringements allows account to be taken of arbitration and jurisdiction clauses contained in contracts for the supply of goods, where this has the effect on excluding the jurisdiction of a court with international jurisdiction under the Brussels I Regulation in relation to the defendants and some of the claims brought.[43]

10.31. In the *CDC* case, the Court of Justice held that' ... the referring court must, in particular, regard a clause which abstractly refers to all disputes arising from contractual relationships as not extending to a dispute relating to the tortious liability that one party allegedly incurred as a result of its participation in an unlawful cartel'.[44] The Court pointed out only one reason why it had decided in such a manner. 'Given that the undertaking which suffered the loss could not reasonably foresee such litigation at the time that it agreed to the jurisdiction clause and that that undertaking had no knowledge of the unlawful cartel at that time, such litigation cannot be regarded as stemming from a contractual relationship'.[45] However, the Court's reasoning is not persuasive because of the following main reasons.

10.32. Firstly, it is evident that the Court of Justice did not have sufficient information either about the arbitration clauses contained in the supply contracts or about the supply contracts themselves.[46] The only example of the arbitration clause was provided in the Opinion of the Advocate General. Mr. Niil Jääskinen, by way of illustration, quoted the following arbitration clause contained in one of the supply contracts:

> [a]ll disputes or allegations resulting from or in connection with this contract or any infringement thereof, or concerning its termination or validity, shall be referred to an arbitration tribunal according to the rules of the Helsinki Chamber of Commerce. Arbitration shall take place in Helsinki, Finland.[47]

10.33. The *CDC* judgement, however, lacks any analysis or even examples of the arbitration clause(s) in question. The situation

---

[43]   *Ibid.*, paragraph 14.3.

[44]   *Ibid.*, paragraph 69.

[45]   *Ibid.*, paragraph 70.

[46]   Although the Court of Justice deals only with the interpretation of EU law, in practice the Court thoroughly considers the background of the case in question.

[47]   Opinion of Advocate General Jääskinen delivered on 11 December 2014 in the *Cartel Damage Claims*, C-352/13, EU:C:2014:2443, fn. 107.

with the supply contracts is similar. Thus, the Court of Justice did not pay attention to such important issues as wordings of the arbitration clauses and the supply contracts in question.

10.34. The Court explained that

> [b]efore assessing that question [about jurisdiction clauses], it must be made clear that, with regard to certain terms derogating from otherwise applicable rules allegedly contained in the contracts at issue but which do not fall within the scope of application of Regulation No 44/2001, *the Court does not have sufficient information at its disposal in order to provide a useful answer to the referring court* [Emphasis added].[48]

10.35. Hence, it is evident that the Court of Justice did not have sufficient information about the background of the issue, but nevertheless ruled on the interpretation of the jurisdictional (and arbitration) clauses.

10.36. Secondly, the Court could not interpret the arbitration clauses considering the *CDC* case. Article 1(2)(d) of the Brussels I (recast) Regulation[49] prescribes that this Regulation shall not apply to arbitration.[50] Consequently, the Court of Justice should refrain from interpreting the scope of arbitration clauses when considering EU law on courts' jurisdiction. Despite this, the Court interpreted the arbitration clauses in the *CDC* case.

10.37. Thirdly, the arbitration clause quoted by the Advocate General in the *CDC* case covered not only existing but also prospective disputes, contrary to the Court's implications, referring to '[a] ll disputes or allegations resulting from or in connection with this contract or any infringement thereof or concerning its termination or validity...'[51] Thus, such a wording shows that the parties had agreed to refer to arbitration not only the existing disputes but also any or all of them resulting from or in connection with the relevant supply contract.

10.38. There are two basic types of arbitration agreements: arbitration clauses and submission agreements.[52] An arbitration clause looks

---

[48] ECJ Judgement of 21 May 2015, *supra* note 41 at paragraph 58.

[49] Regulation (EU) No. 1215/2012 of 12 December 2012 on jurisdiction and the recognition and enforcement of judgements in civil and commercial matters (recast) [2012] OJ L351/1.

[50] The same provision was embodied in Article 1(2)(d) of Council Regulation (EC) No 44/2001 of 22 December 2000 on jurisdiction and the recognition and enforcement of judgements in civil and commercial matters [2001] OJ L12/1, relevant when the *CDC* case was pending before the Court of Justice. Moreover, Recital (12) of Regulation No. 1215/2012 provides that 'a ruling given by a court of a Member State as to whether or not an arbitration agreement is null and void, inoperative or incapable of being performed should not be subject to the rules of recognition and enforcement laid down in this Regulation, regardless of whether the court decided on this as a principal issue or as an incidental question'.

[51] Opinion of Advocate General Jääskinen *supra* note 47 at fn. 107.

[52] ALAN REDFERN *ET AL.* EDS, *supra* note 23 at 131.

to the future, whereas a submission agreement looks to the past. The first one, which is most common, is usually contained in the principal agreement between the parties and is an agreement to submit *future* disputes to arbitration. The second one is an agreement to submit *existing* disputes to arbitration.[53] In the reasoning of the Court of Justice, it noted that

> [g]iven that the undertaking which suffered the loss could not reasonably foresee such litigation [or arbitration] at the time that it agreed to the jurisdiction clause and that that undertaking had no knowledge of the unlawful cartel at that time, such litigation [or arbitration] cannot be regarded as stemming from a contractual relationship.

10.39. This shows that the Court unreasonably narrowed the scope of the arbitration clause to that of the submission agreement. Following the Court's logic, in similar cases the arbitration clause should cover only existing disputes, because the 'knowledge of the unlawful cartel' implies that such a cartel already exists and, moreover, its unlawfulness has been established.

10.40. Fourthly, the Court of Justice unreasonably held that arbitration clauses do not cover tort liability disputes related to supply contracts. In fact, in a substantial majority of all jurisdictions, national law provides that international arbitration agreements should be interpreted in the light of a 'pro-arbitration' presumption.[54] This type of presumption provides that a valid arbitration clause should generally be interpreted expansively and, in cases of doubt, extended to encompass dispute claims.[55] The Court of Justice has not followed this presumption.

10.41. Article II(1) of the New York Convention prescribes that each Contracting State must recognise an agreement in writing under which the parties undertake to submit to arbitration all or any differences which have arisen or which may arise between them with respect to a defined legal relationship, <u>whether contractual or not</u>, concerning a subject-matter capable of settlement by arbitration. The Advocate General in the *CDC* case also concluded that

> ... in certain national legal systems, the classification of the subject-matter of a dispute as a matter relating to tort, delict or quasi-delict does not itself preclude the applicability of jurisdiction or arbitration clauses,

---

[53]   *Ibid.*, at 131.
[54]   1 GARRY B. BORN, *supra* note 19, at 1326.
[55]   *Ibid.*, at 1326.

which obviously depends, in each specific case, on the wording of the clause concerned.[56]

10.42. Here, the Advocate General even provided a case-law example of the *lex arbitri*:

> ... according to the case-law of the Korkein oikeus (Supreme Court, Finland), an arbitration clause contained in a contract is applicable to a dispute concerning extra-contractual liability where failure to comply with the contract invoked constitutes fraud within the meaning of criminal law (see Korkein oikeus, judgment of 27 November 2008, KKO, 2008:102...).[57]

10.43. Even a linguistic analysis of the only arbitration clause provided by the Advocate General confirms that the clause covers damage claims related to the cartel. To recall, the relevant part of the arbitration clause provided in the *CMC* case reads as follows: '[a]ll disputes or allegations resulting from or *in connection with* this contract or any infringement thereof, or concerning its termination or validity, shall be referred to an arbitration tribunal...' [Emphasis added].[58] The linking words 'in connection with' give the broadest content to the scope of the arbitration clause, thus covering the tort damage claims connected to the supply contracts.[59] And in general, the three categories of claims are potentially within the scope of an arbitration clause: contractual claims (including claims incidental to the contract such as a *quantum meruit*), claims in tort and statutory claims.[60] The first two are self-explanatory. The third one relates to those claims that arise out of legislation which might bind the parties, such as antitrust legislation.[61]

10.44. Despite this clear legislation and case-law, the Court of Justice relied only on a subjective interpretation of the arbitration clause. The Court held that when concluding the arbitration clause, the parties did not know about the cartel. Thus, the relevant damage that had arisen out of the cartel was not related to the relevant supply agreements. In other words, the Court mentioned only an alleged intent of the parties when entering the arbitration

---

[56] Opinion of Advocate General Jääskinen *supra* note 47 at paragraph 131.
[57] *Ibid.*, fn. 148.
[58] *Ibid.*, fn. 107.
[59] 1 GARRY B. BORN, *supra* note 19, at 1350-1351.
[60] ALAN REDFERN *ET AL.* EDS, *supra* note 23, at 155.
[61] *Ibid.*, at 155.

clause. However, the Court of Justice neither analysed such an intent nor considered the content of the arbitration clause.

10.45. Finally, EU legislation confirms that the Court's reasoning in the *CDC* case was flawed. The Directive on damages for infringements of competition law[62] provides that

> ... infringers and injured parties should be encouraged to agree on compensating for the harm caused by a competition law infringement through consensual dispute resolution mechanisms, such as ... arbitration ... Such consensual dispute resolution should cover as many injured parties and infringers as legally possible. The provisions in this Directive on consensual dispute resolution are therefore meant to facilitate the use of such mechanisms and increase their effectiveness.[63]

10.46. Thus, EU legislation encourages the use of arbitration in the antitrust cases.[64]

10.47. Hence, the *CDC* case, as well as other cases mentioned in the Court's jurisprudence show that there is a general tendency of the Court of Justice to exclude statutory claims from the scope of arbitration clauses. Another tendency is to increase the powers of the national courts of the Member States when reviewing arbitral awards in challenge or recognition procedures. Then, naturally, the question arises whether there is a clear distinction between international commercial arbitration and international investment arbitration in terms of the scope of relevant arbitration clauses and arbitral procedures.

V. Does the divide, that relites to conclusion of arbitration clauses and the course of arbitral procedures, exist between international commercial arbitration and investment arbitration?

10.48. Article 8 of the Netherlands-Slovakia BIT referred to in the *Achmea* case provides a standard investor-State dispute resolution clause and though lengthy, is worth quoting in full:

> 1. All disputes between one Contracting Party and an investor of the other Contracting Party concerning

---

[62] Directive 2014/104/EU of 26 November 2014 on certain rules governing actions for damages under national law for infringements of the competition law provisions of the Member States and of the European Union [2014] OJ L349/1.
[63] *Ibid.*, Recital (48).
[64] See also Miriam Driessen-Reilly, *Private Damages in EU Competition Law and Arbitration: A Changing Landscape*, 31(4) Arb. Int'l, 567, 572.

an investment of the latter shall, if possible, be settled amicably.

2. Each Contracting Party hereby consents to submit a dispute referred to in paragraph 1 of this Article to an arbitral tribunal, if the dispute has not been settled amicably within a period of six months from the date on which either party to the dispute requested amicable settlement.

3. The arbitral tribunal referred to in paragraph 2 of this Article will be constituted for each individual case in the following way: each party to the dispute appoints one member of the tribunal and the two members thus appointed shall select a national of a third State as Chairman of the tribunal. Each party to the dispute shall appoint its member of the tribunal within two months, and the Chairman shall be appointed within three months from the date on which the investor has notified the other Contracting Party of his decision to submit the dispute to the arbitral tribunal.

4. If the appointments have not been made in the abovementioned periods, either party to the dispute may invite the President of the Arbitration Institute of the Chamber of Commerce of Stockholm to make the necessary appointments. If the President is a national of either Contracting Party or if he is otherwise prevented from discharging the said function, the Vice-President shall be invited to make the necessary appointments. If the Vice-President is a national of either Contracting Party or if he too is prevented from discharging the said function, the most senior member of the Arbitration Institute who is not a national of either Contracting Party shall be invited to make the necessary appointments.

5. The arbitration tribunal shall determine its own procedure applying the United Nations Commission on International Trade Law (UNCITRAL) arbitration rules.

6. The arbitral tribunal shall decide on the basis of the law, taking into account in particular though not exclusively:
   – the law in force of the Contracting Party concerned;
   – the provisions of this Agreement, and other relevant agreements between the Contracting Parties;
   – the provisions of special agreements relating to the investment;
   – the general principles of international law.

7. The tribunal takes its decision by majority of votes; such decision shall be final and binding upon the parties to the dispute.[65]

10.49. The Court of Justice held in the *Achmea* case that

[h]owever, arbitration proceedings such as those referred to in Article 8 of the BIT are different from commercial arbitration proceedings. While the latter originate in the freely expressed wishes of the parties, the former derive from a treaty by which Member States agree to remove from the jurisdiction of their own courts, and hence from the system of judicial remedies... TEU requires them to establish in the fields covered by EU law.[66]

10.50. The only reason employed by the Court of Justice, at least in the *Achmea* case, distinguishing international investment arbitration from international commercial arbitration, is very formal – the nature of the document that contains the arbitration clause. If such an underlying document is a contract, the Court of Justice sees no problems. But if it is a BIT, then there is a problem. Such a position by the Court does not withstand scrutiny.

10.51. First of all, it is not the document that contains the arbitration clause but the clause itself that determines the validity of the agreement to arbitrate. The separability presumption is one of the conceptual and practical cornerstones of international arbitration.[67] The doctrine of separability recognises the arbitration clause in a main contract as a separate contract, independent and distinct from the main contract. The essence of the doctrine is that the validity of an arbitration clause is not bound to that of the main contract and vice versa.[68] As this is a separate contract, it can be concluded on the offer-acceptance basis.

10.52. The vast majority of BITs contain clauses referring to investment arbitration. The basic mechanism is as follows: the State parties to the BIT offer consent to arbitration to investors who are nationals of the other contracting party. The arbitration agreement is perfected through the acceptance of that offer by an eligible investor.[69] Thus, technically, the agreement to arbitrate may be concluded not between two contracting States,

---

[65] ECJ Judgement of 6 March 2018, *supra* note 2, paragraph 4.
[66] *Ibid.*, paragraph 55.
[67] 1 GARRY B. BORN, *supra* note 19, at 350.
[68] *Ibid.*, at 350-351, see also JULIAN D M LEW, LOUKAS A MISTELIS, STEFAN M KRÖLL, COMPARATIVE INTERNATIONAL COMMERCIAL ARBITRATION, The Hague: Kluwer Law International 102 (2003).
[69] Christoph Schreuer, Consent to Arbitration available at http://www.univie.ac.at/intlaw/con_arbitr_89.pdf at 6, (accessed on 25 January 2019).

but between such a State and the investor of another contracting State. In this regard, there is no fundamental difference between arbitration clauses contained in a BIT and in a commercial contract; for instance, when the State concludes a PPP contract.

10.53. The arbitral clause is doubly autonomous or separable, both in relation to the arbitral agreement and in relation to the law of the contract.[70] Thus, one of the practical implications of the separability doctrine is the possible application of a different national law, or a different set of substantive legal rules, to the arbitration agreement than to the underlying contract.[71] Therefore, it is not necessary that sources of public international law such as the Vienna Convention on the Law of Treaties would be applicable to the interpretation and validity of arbitration clauses contained in BITs. Rather, the conflict of law rules of *lex arbitri* will determine the law governing the relevant arbitration clause of the BIT.

10.54. Moreover, in practice, a breach of the particular commercial contract between the investor and the State implies a breach of the BIT as well. Therefore, provisions of the BIT concerned in the *Achmea* case prescribe that the arbitral tribunal should decide, *inter alia*, on the basis of the law, taking into account the law in force of the Contracting Party concerned and the provisions of special agreements relating to the investment.[72]

10.55. Consequently, the rules applicable to the validity and interpretation of the arbitration clause contained in the BIT do not materially differ from those applicable to arbitration clauses in regular international commercial contracts. Therefore, the nature of the underlying contract does not have any decisive impact on the rules of law applicable to the validity and interpretation of the arbitration clause in question.

10.56. Secondly, the States provide several options in their BITs for how to resolve investor-State disputes – in *ad hoc* arbitration, or in investment arbitration such as the ICSID Convention or the State's courts. In this situation, the Court of Justice has discriminated arbitration in the *Achmea* case as a dispute resolution method. If the investor opts for the court of the

---

[70] 1 GARRY B. BORN, *supra* note 19, at 352.
[71] *Ibid.*, at 351, 473, 475.
[72] ECJ Judgement of 06 March 2018, *supra* note 2, paragraph 4.

Member State that has allegedly breached the BIT,[73] such a dispute resolution mechanism will be in line with EU law.

10.57. One of the cornerstone reasons employed by the Court of Justice, as well as by the EU authorities, is the lack of effective control of arbitral awards by Member State courts. Such a line of arguments is a decades-old throwback. One of the fundamental characteristics and advantages of both international commercial and investment arbitrations is no review of arbitral awards on merits.[74] In this regard, the Court of Justice held in the *Achmea* judgement that

> ... the requirements of efficient arbitration proceedings justify the review of arbitral awards by the courts of the Member States being limited in scope, provided that the fundamental provisions of EU law can be examined in the course of that review and, if necessary, be the subject of a reference to the Court for a preliminary ruling...[75]

10.58. However, such a line of arguments is not persuasive. In fact, in some exceptions,[76] the recognition and enforcement of an award granted in international investment arbitration falls within the scope of the New York Convention, the same Convention applicable to the recognition and enforcement of awards rendered in international commercial arbitration. The same situation would apply with set-aside proceedings. Therefore, following the wording of the Court of Justice, the courts of the Member State would usually have the same tools to review the

---

[73] Now the European Commission encourages the investors to choose Member State courts, see European Commission, *supra* note 26, available at http://ec.europa.eu/finance/docs/policy/180719-communication-protection-of-investments_en.pdf (accessed on 24 July 2018).
[74] See, *e.g.*, Article 34(2) UNCITRAL Model Law on International Commercial Arbitration 1985 with amendments as adopted in 2006; Article V of the New York Convention, that provide limited grounds for setting aside arbitral awards. Article 34 of the UNCITRAL Model Law deals with an issue that is of utmost importance in the delicate balance between the autonomy of arbitration on the one hand and judicial control on the other. This balance weighs arbitration's quest to achieve the greatest possible independence from the courts in order to fully accomplish the advantages of speed and efficiency, which are commonly lost when a municipal court becomes involved, against the confidence in arbitration. This is especially in the awards rendered by arbitral tribunals, which can only be achieved if there remains the option to set aside an award that was made under an evidently unjust procedure; PETER BINDER, INTERNATIONAL COMMERCIAL ARBITRATION AND CONCILIATION IN UNCITRAL MODEL LAW JURISDICTIONS, London: Sweet & Maxwell, Thomson Reuters 377-378 (3rd ed. 2010). A main feature of the grounds for the refusal of recognition and enforcement of the awards in the New York Convention is that no review of the merits of the arbitral award is allowed; see ALBERT JAN VAN DEN BERG, *supra* note 19, at 265.
[75] ECJ Judgement of 06 March 2018, *supra* note 2, paragraph 54.
[76] For instance, Article 52 ICSID Convention provides an autonomous annulment procedure detached from grounds for refusal prescribed in the New York Convention.

Czech (& Central European) Yearbook of Arbitration®

Czech (& Central European) Yearbook of Arbitration®

arbitral awards granted either in international commercial, or investment arbitrations.

10.59. Therefore, generally there is no procedural differences between setting aside or recognition and enforcement of international commercial and investment arbitrations.[77]

10.60. Thirdly, usually the same sets of procedural rules are applicable to both international commercial and investment arbitrations. Thus, the same UNCITRAL, ICC, SCC or other arbitral rules are applicable similarly to both commercial and investment disputes.

10.61. In light of the foregoing, the distinction between international commercial arbitration and international investment arbitration, as described by the Court of Justice, does not exist in fact. Therefore, it seems that the Court rendered a political decision. A brief analysis of the Court's case law indicates the tendency to push some statutory claims away from arbitration. Thus, considering the Court of Justice case law enhancing the powers of Member State courts to control arbitral awards, taking into account the general EU mistrust of large-scale international arbitration because of the lack of effective control, high costs and *ex post* formation of the tribunals, it is only a matter of time when international commercial arbitration, resolving, for instance, PPP disputes, will meet the same destiny on intra-EU level as *Achmea*.

| | |

Summaries

FRA   [*Faut-il s'attendre à une crise de l'arbitrage commercial international en Europe ?*]
En 2018, la Cour de justice de l'Union européenne a rendu l'arrêt dans l'affaire Achmea, désormais notoirement connu. La Cour a statué en ce sens que les clauses compromissoires contenues dans des accords bilatéraux relatifs au soutien et à la protection des investissements à l'intérieur de l'Union européenne sont contraires aux normes impératives de l'UE. Cet arrêt s'inscrit dans le prolongement des réserves que l'Union européenne a exprimées au sujet des dispositions relatives au règlement des litiges entre investisseurs et États. L'article analyse les principaux éléments de fait et la motivation de l'arrêt de la

---

[77]   As mentioned, the ICSID Convention provides for an autonomous annulment procedure and is an exception of such a general rule. However, at least recently, the ICSID Convention is not a target of either the EU or the Court of Justice in terms of the Convention's invalidity on intra-EU level.

Cour de justice au vu des éventuelles répercussions de l'affaire Achmea sur l'arbitrage commercial international. Si la Cour de justice a retenu la distinction entre arbitrage d'investissement et arbitrage commercial, son argumentation n'est pourtant pas convaincante. En effet, selon la Cour, un arbitrage commercial international procèderait de l'autonomie de la volonté des parties, alors qu'un arbitrage d'investissement international procèderait d'un accord international. Une telle dichotomie, en réalité, n'a aucun fondement réel. Premièrement, une clause compromissoire contenue dans un accord bilatéral relatif au soutien et à la protection des investissements dans le cadre de l'UE doit être interprétée, conformément au principe de divisibilité largement appliqué dans l'arbitrage international, indépendamment de l'accord. Le principe de divisibilité emporte une autre conséquence importante : la loi applicable à la validité et à l'interprétation de la clause compromissoire en cause peut être différente de la loi applicable à l'accord. Il n'est donc pas nécessaire, lors de l'interprétation d'une clause compromissoire contenue dans un accord bilatéral relatif au soutien et à la protection des investissements à l'intérieur de l'Union européenne, que le droit international public soit appliqué. De plus, l'accord international ne comporte pas de clause compromissoire, mais uniquement une proposition destinée à l'investisseur originaire d'un autre État contractant. En intentant une procédure d'arbitrage, l'investisseur accepte cette proposition et conclut ainsi un accord d'arbitrage. L'accord international prévoit donc un système « opt-in », qui laisse à l'investisseur la liberté de choisir le régime qui lui convient. En outre, la procédure d'arbitrage élimine systématiquement la compétence des juridictions de droit commun qui pourrait intervenir dans cette procédure. Enfin, les règles applicables aux arbitrages d'investissement internationaux et aux arbitrages commerciaux internationaux sont en règle générale identiques. Étant donné l'appétit grandissant de la Cour de justice, des affaires analogues pourraient se multiplier dans un proche avenir, et donner lieu à la mise en question des principes fondamentaux de l'arbitrage commercial international.

CZE [*Proroctví krize mezinárodní obchodní arbitráže v Evropě?*]
Soudní dvůr Evropské unie vydal rozsudek ve věci Achmea, nyní již velmi dobře známý, v roce 2018. Soud rozhodl tak, že rozhodčí doložky obsažené ve dvoustranných dohodách o podpoře a ochraně investic v rámci Evropské unie jsou v rozporu s kogentním právem EU. Tento rozsudek je v souladu s obecnými výhradami, které má Evropská unie vůči ustanovením o urovnávání sporů

mezi investory a státy. Článek analyzuje základní skutkové okolnosti a odůvodnění rozsudku Soudního dvora, pokud jde o možné dopady případu Achmea na mezinárodní obchodní arbitráž. Přestože Soudní dvůr rozlišoval mezi mezinárodní investiční arbitráží a mezinárodní obchodní arbitráží, není argumentační linie Soudního dvora přesvědčivá. Soudní dvůr konstatoval, že zatímco mezinárodní obchodní arbitráž vychází ze svobodně vyjádřené vůle stran, mezinárodní investiční arbitráž vychází z mezinárodní dohody. Žádná takováto dichotomie, k níž Soudní dvůr dospěl, však ve skutečnosti neexistuje. Zaprvé, rozhodčí doložka obsažená ve dvoustranné dohodě o podpoře a ochraně investic v rámci EU musí být dle doktríny oddělitelnosti, která je v mezinárodní arbitráži široce uplatňována, vykládána odděleně od dohody. Doktrína oddělitelnosti má i další významný důsledek – právo použitelné na platnost a výklad předmětné rozhodčí doložky se může lišit od práva použitelného na danou mezinárodní dohodu. Není proto nezbytné, aby například při výkladu rozhodčí doložky obsažené ve dvoustranné dohodě o podpoře a ochraně investic v rámci EU šlo o mezinárodní právo veřejné. Navíc samotná mezinárodní dohoda rozhodčí doložku neobsahuje. Obsahuje pouze nabídku určenou investorovi jiného smluvního státu. Pokud investor rozhodčí řízení zahájí, přijímá nabídku státu a uzavírá tak dohodu o rozhodčím řízení. Mezinárodní dohoda tak zakotvuje pouze tzv. systém „opt-in" a záleží na investorovi, který režim si zvolí. Rozhodčí řízení navíc vždy eliminuje relevantní nebo do rozhodčího řízení zasahující pravomoc obecných soudů. Konečně, rozhodčí pravidla pro mezinárodní investiční a obchodní arbitráže jsou většinou totožná. Proto je vzhledem k rostoucímu apetitu Soudního dvora pouze otázkou času, kdy uvidíme další případ Achmea, v němž dojde ke zpochybnění základních zásad mezinárodní obchodní arbitráže.

| | |

POL [*Proroctwo kryzysu międzynarodowego arbitrażu handlowego w Europie?*]
Artykuł przedstawia refleksje na temat politycznego charakteru argumentacji Trybunału Sprawiedliwości Unii Europejskiej w sprawie Achmea. W artykule przeanalizowano również potencjalne skutki tego orzeczenia w sferze nie tylko postępowania arbitrażowego w sporach inwestycyjnych, ale również postępowania arbitrażowego w sporach handlowych.

Czech (& Central European) Yearbook of Arbitration ®

DEU   [*Vorboten einer Krise der internationalen Handels-schiedsgerichtsbarkeit in Europa?*]
Dieser Beitrag legt Erwägungen zur politisch motivierten Argumentation des Europäischen Gerichtshofs in Sachen Achmea vor, und beurteilt zugleich die möglichen Folgen der Entscheidung nicht nur für Schiedsverfahren in Investitionsstreitigkeiten, sondern auch für Schiedsverfahren in Handelssachen.

RUS   [*Пророчество кризиса международного коммерческого арбитража в Европе?*]
В данной статье представлены размышления о политически мотивированной аргументации Европейского суда в деле Ахмеа (Achmea). В статье также рассматриваются возможные последствия этого решения не только для арбитража в области инвестиционных споров, но и для арбитража в области коммерческих споров.

ESP   [*¿Profecía sobre la crisis del arbitraje comercial internacional en Europa?*]
El presente artículo reflexiona sobre la argumentación políticamente motivada que fue empleada por el Tribunal de Justicia de la Unión Europea en el asunto Achmea. El texto también evalúa las posibles consecuencias de dicha resolución no solo en el ámbito del procedimiento arbitral de litigios relacionados con la inversión, sino también en el procedimiento arbitral de controversias comerciales.

| | |

Bibliography

ALBERT JAN VAN DEN BERG, THE NEW YORK ARBITRATION CONVENTION OF 1958: TOWARDS A UNIFORM JUDICIAL INTERPRETATION, Netherlands: Kluwer Law Taxation Publishers, 265 (1981).

PETER BINDER, INTERNATIONAL COMMERCIAL ARBITRATION AND CONCILIATION IN UNCITRAL MODEL LAW JURISDICTIONS, London: Sweet & Maxwell, Thomson Reuters 377-378 (3rd ed. 2010).

GARRY B. BORN, INTERNATIONAL COMMERCIAL ARBITRATION, New York: Wolters Kluwer 3186 (2014).

RUDOLF DOLCER, CHRISTOPH SCHREUER, PRINCIPLES OF INTERNATIONAL INVESTMENT LAW, Oxford: Oxford University Press 38 (2008).

Czech (& Central European) Yearbook of Arbitration®

Miriam Driessen-Reilly, *Private Damages in EU Competition Law and Arbitration: A Changing Landscape,* 31(4) ARB. INT'L, 567, 572.

FIVE YEARS ON: A CRITICAL REVIEW OF STRENGTHS AND WEAKNESSES, New York: JurisNet, LLC 114, fn. 48 (Lars Heuman and Sigvard Jarvin eds., 2006).

KAJ HOBÉR, INTERNATIONAL COMMERCIAL ARBITRATION IN SWEDEN: Lindskog, Skiljeförfarande, 241 (2001).

INTERNATIONAL ARBITRATION IN SWEDEN: A PRACTITIONER'S GUIDE: Kluwer Law International 144 (Ulf Franke, Annette Magnusson, et al. eds., 2013).

LAW AND PRACTICE OF INTERNATIONAL COMMERCIAL ARBITRATION, London: Sweet & Maxwell 24 (Alan Redfern *et al.* eds., 4th ed., 2004).

JULIAN D. M. LEW, LOUKAS A. MISTELIS, STEFAN M. KRÖLL, COMPARATIVE INTERNATIONAL COMMERCIAL ARBITRATION, The Hague: Kluwer Law International 102 (2003).

TRANSPARENCY IN INTERNATIONAL INVESTMENT ARBITRATION. A GUIDE TO THE UNCITRAL RULES ON TRANSPARENCY IN TREATY-BASED INVESTOR-STATE ARBITRATION, Cambridge: Cambridge University Press 2-3 (D. Euler, M. Gehring and M. Scherer, eds, 2015).

Case Law

Czech (& Central European) Yearbook of Arbitration®

Selected Case Law of Czech Courts Related to Arbitration

Alexander J. Bělohlávek

ORCID iD 0000-0001-5310-5269
https://orcid.org/0000-0001-5310-5269

Section 38 [Recognition and enforcement of foreign arbitral awards][1]

Arbitral awards made abroad shall be recognized and enforced in the Czech Republic like Czech arbitral awards, on condition of reciprocity. The requirement of reciprocity shall also be considered fulfilled if the foreign country generally declares foreign arbitral awards enforceable on condition of reciprocity. However, the decision on enforcement of a foreign arbitral award must always be reasoned.

Rules effective from 1 January 2014 (PIL):
[Recognition and enforcement of foreign arbitral awards][2]
Section 120 of the PIL[3]

Arbitral awards made abroad shall be recognized and enforced in the Czech Republic like Czech arbitral awards, on condition of reciprocity. The requirement of reciprocity shall also be considered fulfilled if the foreign country generally declares foreign arbitral awards enforceable.

Section 121 of the PIL
[Quoted in the commentary to Section 39 of the ArbAct.]

---

[1] This provision is repealed with effect from 1 January 2014 and will be materially replaced with Section 117 of the PIL. See Section 124(16) of Act No. 91/2012, on Private International Law (PIL).
[2] This heading is part of the quoted normative text.
[3] Save for certain changes in terminology, this provision is identical to the first and second sentences of Section 38 of the ArbAct; Section 120 of the PIL, in conjunction with Section 122(2) of the PIL, replaces Section 38 of the ArbAct with effect from 1 January 2014.

Section 122 of the PIL

(1) A foreign arbitral award shall be recognized without any special decision being required. A foreign arbitral award is recognized by the award being taken into consideration, subject to the requirements stipulated in Sections 120 and 121, as if it were a Czech arbitral award. **(2)** The enforcement of a foreign arbitral award shall be ordered by a reasoned decision of a Czech court.[4]

PART EIGHT – [TRANSITIONAL AND FINAL PROVISIONS]
Section 123 of the PIL [Transitional provisions]

(1) *[Quoted in the commentary to Sections 36 and 37 of the ArbAct.]*
(2) Proceedings commenced before the effective date of this Act shall continue to be governed by the provisions of the laws and regulations on the jurisdiction of Czech courts applicable until the effective date of this Act. This also applies to proceedings in matters of the recognition and enforcement of foreign decisions and foreign arbitral awards with respect to the conditions for their recognition and enforcement.

Related provisions: Sections 17, 39, 40, 47, 48
Related laws: Sections 1 and 54 of the PILP;[5] Article 35 of the UML; Article I(1), Article II(1), Article III, Article IV of the NYConv;* Article IX of the EConv; Constitutional Act No. 4/1993 Coll.; Section 55 of the ExecProcC; Section 268, Section 274(h), Section 303, Section 321, Section 322 of the CCP; Sections 13,[6] 120, 121, 122, 123, 124(16) of the PIL [*The list of the NYConv signatories is available at: http://www.uncitral.org/uncitral/en/uncitral_texts/arbitration/NYConvention_status.html][7]

---

[4]   Save for the (updated) reference to "Czech courts", this provision is identical to the previous wording of the provision.
[5]   PILP – Section 54 – *"Declaration of reciprocity exercised by a foreign state, issued by the Ministry of Justice upon agreement with the Ministry of Foreign Affairs and other relevant ministries, is binding on the courts and other state authorities."* The same rule also applies in Slovakia.
[6]   PIL – Section 13 – Determination of reciprocity – *"The Ministry of Justice shall provide to the court, on request, a declaration of reciprocity exercised by a foreign state."*
[7]   On the day the manuscript of this book was finished, the NYConv status included 146 states.

I. The term "foreign arbitral award" under the law of national origin (ArbAct) and under the New York Convention (NYConv)

I.1. Importance of the NYConv (NYConv) and the concept of arbitration / arbitral award in the state of recognition/enforcement

11.01. Most countries distinguish between national (domestic) and international (foreign) awards. Domestic arbitral awards are awards rendered in the state where the court is located, whereas foreign awards are rendered in a different state. But it is not the same difference as between domestic and international arbitration. A domestic arbitral award may be rendered both in a domestic and in an international dispute. The rules for the recognition and enforcement of domestic arbitral awards often differ from the rules for the recognition and enforcement of foreign arbitral awards.[8] But it is necessary to emphasize the importance of the rules of international origin (international treaties) which have come to assume major importance for the enforcement of foreign arbitral awards.

11.02. The court with jurisdiction over the recognition and enforcement of an arbitral award is a national (domestic) court. The jurisdiction of a particular court is determined according to national (domestic) laws.

I.1.1. Importance of the NYConv (NYConv)

11.03. Sections 38 and 39 of the ArbAct apply to *foreign arbitral awards*. The term is crucial for the applicability of these provisions despite the fact that Czech law does not set forth any definition of the term. But many other legal systems contain no explicit definition either. Nonetheless, it is still necessary to distinguish between a foreign and, conversely, a domestic arbitral award. The general consensus is that the crucial instrument for the practice of international arbitration is the New York Convention on the Recognition and Enforcement of Foreign Arbitral Awards of 1958 (NYConv). Considering the number of signatories (it has been ratified by 146 states)[9] and its more than fifty-year history of application in almost two hundred states, the NYConv is perceived as the basis for any conclusions on these

---

[8]   See JEAN-FRANCOIS POUDRET, SEBASTIEN BESSON; S. BIRTI, COMPARATIVE LAW OF INTERNATIONAL ARBITRATION, London: Sweet & Maxwell marg. 849 (2nd ed., 2007).
[9]   Available at: http://www.uncitral.org/uncitral/en/uncitral_texts/arbitration/NYConvention_status. html (accessed on 3 February 2019).

issues. Determination of the status of an arbitral award is also significantly dependent on the concept of the nature (essence) of the arbitral award in the state where recognition/enforcement are sought. The concept of an arbitral award is determined by the concept of arbitration as such – see the detailed analysis in the commentary to Section 1 of the ArbAct. Hence, the overview below is only a brief outline of the influence of the concept of arbitration on the nature of the arbitral award in two major directions. For more details and divergences from these approaches, see the detailed commentary to Section 1 of the ArbAct.

I.1.2. Contractual concept of the arbitral award

11.04. The contractual theory is based on the concept of the arbitral award as a direct effect of the arbitration agreement, i.e. a continuation and fulfillment of the agreement. The arbitral award, as a consequence of the arbitration agreement, gives rise to rights and obligations of a private-law nature. If the successful claimant has a claim for performance against the respondent (the contractual theory maintains that the claim is of a private-law nature), then the enforcement of performance requires a petition filed with a court. Consequently, the declaration of enforceability requires a court decision. There is no reason to treat domestic arbitral awards differently from foreign arbitral awards – just as the pursuit of private-law claims in court is not prevented by the fact that the respective legal relationship was established abroad.[10]

I.1.3. Jurisdictional concept of the arbitral award (arbitral award as a judgment)

11.05. The jurisdictional theory is based on the adversarial nature of arbitration – arbitrators exercise and are endowed with the decision-making power vested in them by the law which permits arbitration. According to this theory, a foreign arbitral award is not a basis for a private-law claim; it is a manifestation of the decision-making power based on foreign law (on foreign *lex arbitri* or other laws especially in the country where the arbitral award was made).[11] The author opines that the Czech *lex arbitri* is based on the jurisdictional theory rather than the

---

[10] ZDENĚK KUČERA, MEZINÁRODNÍ PRÁVO SOUKROMÉ [Title in translation: PRIVATE INTERNATIONAL LAW], Brno: Doplněk 429 et seq. (6th ed., 2004).
[11] ZDENĚK KUČERA, MEZINÁRODNÍ PRÁVO SOUKROMÉ [Title in translation: PRIVATE INTERNATIONAL LAW], Brno: Doplněk 430 (2004).

contractual theory, despite the fact that between 2002 and 2011 the ConCourt CR rendered many decisions in which the Court advocated the opposite approach.[12] However, it is necessary to refer to the landmark decision of the ConCourt CR, Judgment of 8 March 2011,[13] which significantly shifted the concept of arbitration to a different level which, in the author's opinion, is more in line with the contemporary approach to arbitration, as well as with Czech constitutional and legal doctrine. The decision approaches arbitration more from the perspective of the jurisdictional theory and classifies the arbitral tribunal as a "different authority".[14] The arbitral award is thereby attributed a jurisdictional nature (the quality of a judgment). The jurisdictional nature is also supported by the nature of the arbitral award, as articulated in Section 28 of the ArbAct.[15]

I.1.4. International treaties

11.06. Considering domestic Czech law, namely Section 47 of the ArbAct, only the provisions of the Act on recognition and enforcement of foreign arbitral awards apply, unless an international treaty binding upon the Czech Republic stipulates otherwise. The recognition and enforcement of arbitral awards are provided for in a number of bilateral treaties, namely many legal assistance treaties which the CR negotiated and concluded in the past, previously also in the Agreement on Trade and Shipping with the then Soviet Union (USSR), in agreements on the recognition and enforcement of court decisions, as well as in certain treaties regulating international legal assistance and the recognition and enforcement of decisions. Principal importance is attributed to multilateral treaties, primarily (as mentioned above) the NYConv (for more details, see the commentary to Section 47 of the ArbAct). Whereas the commentary to Section 47 of the ArbAct focuses on other sources of international origin, the scope and, especially, purpose of Section 38 (in connection with Section 39) of the ArbAct and the scope and purpose of the NYConv merit an analysis of the NYConv in the commentaries to Sections 38 and 39 of the ArbAct, i.e. in this chapter. As

---

[12]   See Judgment of the ConCourt CR, Case No. IV. ÚS 174/02 of 15 July 2002, and a number of later decisions of the ConCourt CR, the SC CR, and other courts. The decisions of the ConCourt CR are especially analyzed in great detail and cited in the commentary to Section 1 of the ArbAct, partially also in connection with other provisions.

[13]   Judgment of the ConCourt CR, Case No. I. ÚS 3227/07 of 8 March 2011.

[14]   See also Alexander Bělohlávek, Ústavní soud České republiky opustil striktní smluvní výklad koncepce rozhodčího řízení. [Title in translation: *The Constitutional Court of the Czech Republic Has Abandoned Its Strict Contractual Interpretation of the Concept of Arbitration*], 12 BULLETIN ADVOKACIE 40–43 (2011.

[15]   A duly served arbitral award is deemed to have the effects of a final and conclusive court decision, subject to the conditions stipulated in Section 28 of the ArbAct.

concerns the NYConv, it is necessary to point out that the Czech Republic formulated a reservation to the NYConv regarding the possibility of applying the NYConv to the recognition and enforcement of arbitral awards made in the territory of a state other than a contracting state. This possibility is preserved for the Czech Republic even under the NYConv regime, but only on condition of reciprocity.

11.07. Despite the fact that the ArbAct does not apply to the hearing and resolution of so-called investment disputes,[16] it is necessary to emphasize that the NYConv also specifically applies to disputes of an investment nature. After all, even the resolution of investment disputes is associated with the use of private-law mechanisms, i.e. primarily arbitration.

I.1.5. Connection between the NYConv and other international treaties and national rules

11.08. Article VII of the NYConv provides for the relationship of the Convention to other international treaties and laws of national origin. It incorporates two main rules.[17] First of all, the **most favorable treatment rule** which allows the party to request recognition and enforcement of an arbitral award pursuant to a different international treaty or national law. Second, the **compatibility clause** which stipulates that the NYConv does not affect the validity of other international treaties. Whereas the relation to national laws is only influenced by the rule (regime) of the most favorable treatment, the relationship to other international treaties must also take account of the compatibility clause.[18]

11.09. The purpose of the most favorable treatment regime is to secure enforcement of arbitral awards to the greatest possible extent. But it is unclear whether the application of national law (law of national origin) or another international treaty, as proposed by the parties, excludes the application of the NYConv. Some opinions argue that Article VII allows the parties to choose from the individual recognition and enforcement regimes but

---

[16]   See also Alexander Bělohlávek, *Pojem investice z pohledu mezinárodněprávní ochrany (podmínky ratione materiae, ratione tempori a ratione voluntatis pro využití mechanismů mezinárodní ochrany investic).* [Title in translation: *The Concept of Investment from the Perspective of International Protection (Requirements Ratione Materiae, Ratione Tempori and Ratione Voluntatis for the Application of the Mechanisms of the International Protection of Investments)*], 19(3-Part I) 19(4-Part II) OBCHODNÍ PRÁVO 2–26 et 2–18 et al. (2010).

[17]   Article VII(1) of the NYConv.

[18]   ALBERT JAN VAN DEN BERG, THE NEW YORK ARBITRATION CONVENTION OF 1958, Den Haag: T.M.C. Asser Institute 81–82 (1981).

does not allow combining them.[19] Others advocate the opposite view which allows an intentional selection and combination of the most advantageous institutions according to the applicant's choice, selected from more applicable (possible) sources,[20] i.e. their combination.[21] The most favorable treatment clause also applies to the recognition and enforcement of foreign arbitral awards. It should also be mentioned that the rule does not permit a more favorable choice of the relevant rules for the entire arbitral proceedings, only those rules which apply to recognition and enforcement.[22] This issue is also analyzed in the commentary to **Section 47 of the ArbAct**. The author agrees with the opinion that usually the choice of one specific regime by the applicant excludes the simultaneous application of other sources with an identical purpose. The specific instrument applicable to the given case applies as a whole, and, at the stage of drafting the instrument (adopting international treaties, passing national laws), it can hardly take account of all other, potentially applicable, instruments, let alone those which will be adopted in the future. Moreover, an advantage for one of the parties may simultaneously constitute a disadvantage for another party. Consequently, it is not possible to choose only those aspects which are favorable for one of the parties but disadvantage the other one. Nonetheless, each case must be approached individually, and it is not inconceivable that sometimes it will be possible to combine multiple sources, although the author considers such a situation rather exceptional. As concerns the sources of international origin, it is also necessary to take account of the international interpretation and the rules of interpretation applicable to instruments which constitute sources of international origin, although in a particular case they can directly give rise to rights accruing to private entities.

---

[19]   ALBERT JAN VAN DEN BERG, THE NEW YORK ARBITRATION CONVENTION OF 1958, Den Haag: T.M.C. Asser Institute 85–86 (1981).; NADĚŽDA ROZEHNALOVÁ, ROZHODČÍ ŘÍZENÍ V MEZINÁRODNÍM A VNITROSTÁTNÍM OBCHODNÍM STYKU. [Title in translation: ARBITRATION IN INTERNATIONAL AND NATIONAL COMMERCE], Prague: ASPI, Wolters Kluwer 96 (2008).
[20]   DOMENICO DIPIETRO; MARTIN PLATTE, ENFORCEMENT OF INTERNATIONAL ARBITRATION AWARDS – THE NEW YORK CONVENTION, London: Cameron May 171–173 (2001).
[21]   Cf. also Decision of the Debrecen District Court, Case No. Pkf.III.20.503/2005 of 2005. Source: *Complex*, Hungarian legal information database, Ref. No. BDT 2006.1356. The information available to the author suggests that the opinion has been principally accepted and has not been challenged by theory or practice, despite the fact that it was articulated by a regional court, not by the Hungarian Supreme Court. A detailed annotation also in: Alexander J. Bělohlávek, *Special Case Law of the Courts on the Relation of Arbitration and Constitutional Issues: 5. Hungary*, 1 CYArb 363–371 (Alexander J. Bělohlávek; Naděžda Rozehnalová, eds., 2011)., here pp. 366–369, marg. 23.12-23.15. For more details, see also the commentary to Section 47 of the ArbAct.
[22]   JEAN-FRANCOIS POUDRET; SEBASTIEN BESSON, COMPARATIVE LAW OF INTERNATIONAL ARBITRATION, London: Sweet & Maxwell, 821. (2nd ed., 2007).

I.2. Scope of the New York Convention in connection with Sections 38 and 39 of the ArbAct

I.2.1. Scope of the New York Convention (NYConv)

11.10. The scope of the NYConv is defined in its Article 1(1) according to which (cit.:) "*This Convention shall apply to the recognition and enforcement of arbitral awards made in the territory of a State other than the State where the recognition and enforcement of such awards are sought, and arising out of differences between persons, whether physical or legal. It shall also apply to arbitral awards not considered as domestic awards in the State where their recognition and enforcement are sought.*" The scope of the NYConv therefore suggests that there are **two types of foreign arbitral awards** to which the NYConv applies,[23] namely: **(i)** arbitral awards made in the territory of a state other than the state where the recognition and enforcement of such awards are sought and **(ii)** arbitral awards which are not considered local (national, domestic) awards in the state where their recognition is sought.

11.11. The reason for such approach (classification of arbitral awards) in terms of Article 1(1) of the NYConv consists in the differences in the interpretation of the status (domestic or foreign) of an arbitral award from the perspective of various doctrines, i.e. a different approach adopted by various states.[24]

11.12. The first case[25] covers the *traditional* interpretation of a foreign arbitral award. A foreign arbitral award is considered to be an award made in a state (in a territory) other than the one in which recognition and enforcement are sought. In other words, the important issue is where the proceedings were conducted and where the arbitral award was rendered. On the other hand, the difference between a foreign and a domestic arbitral award does not depend on the place where the award was signed.[26] However, the importance of the place where the arbitral award was made has been continuously diminishing in international practice as well as in the practice of individual states. This is because many procedural acts between members of the arbitral panel, and

---

[23]   GARY B. BORN, INTERNATIONAL COMMERCIAL ARBITRATION: COMMENTARY AND MATERIALS, Den Haag: KLI 712–729 (2nd ed., 2001).
[24]   NADĚŽDA ROZEHNALOVÁ, ROZHODČÍ ŘÍZENÍ V MEZINÁRODNÍM A VNITROSTÁTNÍM OBCHODNÍM STYKU. [Title in translation: ARBITRATION IN INTERNATIONAL AND NATIONAL COMMERCE],, Prague: ASPI / Wolters Kluwer 325. (2nd ed., 2008).
[25]   Arbitral awards issued in the territory of a state other than the state in which their recognition and enforcement are sought.
[26]   JEAN-FRANCOIS POUDRET; SEBASTIEN BESSON, COMPARATIVE LAW OF INTERNATIONAL ARBITRATION, London: Sweet & Maxwell 819 (2nd ed., 2007).

frequently also between the arbitral tribunal and the parties, are executed by means of distant communication. Telephone conferences and video conferences have been employed more and more often, awards are often *signed* by each member of the arbitral panel in a different place, etc. Consequently, the seat of arbitration agreed by the parties or determined by the arbitral tribunal, in the sense of an autonomous domiciliation of the dispute to a particular place, has become more important than in the past. It is often completely irrelevant that no oral hearing has been held and that none of the parties or none of the arbitrators have their residence (or any other kind of *domicile*) there.[27]

11.13. The second case[28] mainly concerns disputes between parties from the same country which were resolved by a local arbitral tribunal, but the applicable law chosen by the parties (especially the law chosen to apply to the arbitration agreement and / or the proceedings as such) differs from the law of the seat of arbitration.[29] Due to the different applicable law, the state where the arbitration was held could not enforce the resultant arbitral award as a domestic award, and, at the same time, the award would not meet the criterion under the first alternative.[30] This is, however, rather rare in practice.

I.2.2. Concept of "arbitral award" under the New York Convention

11.14. The New York Convention [NYConv] provides no definition of an arbitral award;[31] it is therefore left for the discretion of the national courts which will apply the NYConv. The question is whether we should apply the law of the state of the seat of arbitration (the place where the arbitral award was made) or the law of the state where recognition/enforcement is sought or whether it is necessary to apply an autonomous definition of an arbitral award in compliance with the international (as a matter of fact, global) nature and purpose of the NYConv. But it is not possible to come up with an autonomous definition which would disregard the various specifics of the national legal systems. In order to determine whether the respective arbitral

---

[27] See also the commentary to Section 17 of the ArbAct.
[28] Arbitral awards which are not considered local (national) awards in the state in which their recognition is sought.
[29] See Sections 30 and 36 of the ArbAct.
[30] Cf. NADĚŽDA ROZEHNALOVÁ, ROZHODČÍ ŘÍZENÍ V MEZINÁRODNÍM A VNITROSTÁTNÍM OBCHODNÍM STYKU. [Title in translation: ARBITRATION IN INTERNATIONAL AND NATIONAL COMMERCE], Prague: ASPI/Wolters Kluwer 325 (2nd ed., 2008).
[31] The New York Convention only stipulates in Article I(2) that the term includes the decisions of *ad hoc* arbitrators as well as the decisions of permanent arbitral institutions.

award meets the criteria of a foreign arbitral award, it is always necessary to have regard to the law of the state to which the award has a certain (non-negligible) relationship. Some authors claim that only a final decision which constitutes *res iudicata* can be enforceable.[32] Other authors, however, claim that the NYConv could also be applied to other types of decisions. Consequently, the following decisions are not considered foreign arbitral awards under the NYConv, *inter alia*:[33] **(i)** decisions dealing with procedural issues,[34] **(ii)** preliminary (provisional), non-final, decisions/injunctions (as opposed to decisions which partially resolve the parties' mutual rights with final force and effect),[35] **(iii)** decisions which depend on the agreement of the parties such as *lodo irrituale*,[36] **(iv)** court decisions on the recognition and enforcement of an arbitral award, **(v)** delocalized (denationalized)[37] arbitral awards which are not subject to judicial control in any state.[38]

11.15. According to the same sources (cited in the preceding paragraph), arbitral awards covered by the NYConv include:[39] **(i)** a *consent award*, **(ii)** an award which can no longer be challenged due to a valid waiver of the right to challenge the award in court

---

[32] STEFAN M. KRÖLL; JULIAN D. M LEW; LOUKAS A. MISTELIS, COMPARATIVE INTERNATIONAL COMMERCIAL ARBITRATION, Den Haag: KLI 699 (2003).

[33] *Besson, S. et Poudret, J.* Comparative Law of International Arbitration. 2nd ed. London: Sweet & Maxwell, 2007, pp. 811–817.

[34] It is necessary to bear in mind that the dividing line between substantive and procedural law is interpreted differently under the individual legal systems. In particular, we must not forget that *common law* specifically classifies jurisdiction as a substantive-law issue and as a component of the decision in the merits. Jurisdiction issues (jurisdictional challenges) in *common law* countries are therefore often the subject of partial arbitral awards. On the other hand, some national laws on arbitration (rules of national origin on the recognition and enforcement of arbitral awards) expressly allow the recognition and enforcement of such awards as well, for instance Austria. It is also necessary to emphasize that in a number of countries the recognition proceedings (*exequatur*) and the enforcement proceedings (execution) are separate, and it is possible to apply for recognition without simultaneously applying for enforcement of a foreign award. Such separate recognition without enforcement can be especially relevant if the party wishes to establish *lis pendens* in other countries. The practice of arbitration is highly internationalized, but it is still possible to come across major national differences even as concerns principal conceptual issues.

[35] Jean-Paul Beraudo, *Recognition and Enforcement of Interim Measures of Protection Ordered by Arbitral Tribunals*, 3 JOURNAL OF INTERNATIONAL ARBITRATION 247–252 (2005).

[36] An award based on the Italian *arbitrato irrituale*. In Italian law, this institution does not fall within the Italian legal rules on arbitration; it is based solely on the agreement between the parties. An award rendered in such proceedings (*lodo irrituale*) does not have the same legal effects as an award issued in arbitration governed by Italian law (*arbitratio rituale*).

[37] Concerning this issue, see also Naděžda Rozehnalová, *Institut zrušení rozhodčího nálezu v mezinárodním prostředí.* [Title in translation: *The Annulment of Arbitral Awards in the International Arena*.], 4 ČASOPIS PRO PRÁVNÍ VĚDU A PRAXI 352–353 (1999). The author of this commentary denies the existence of so-called delocalized arbitral awards and insists that it is a purely artificial concept. Concerning this issue, see also the commentary to Section 17 of the ArbAct.

[38] There is no uniform opinion on this issue; the opinions of the individual authors and the views held by the individual national courts which had to address it in their rulings exhibit major differences. The prevailing opinion is that these awards cannot be subject to the provisions of the NYConv.

[39] JEAN-FRANCOIS POUDRET, SEBASTIEN BESSON; S. BIRTI, COMPARATIVE LAW OF INTERNATIONAL ARBITRATION, London: Sweet & Maxwell 818–819 (2nd ed., 2007).

(according to the law of the state the award is subject to),[40] **(iii)** a final, partial, and interim arbitral award; the interim award can be only recognized, it cannot be enforced (it contains no order which could be enforced), **(iv)** a *default award*. This catalog has been adopted by many other sources, but it is heavily influenced by *common law*. The author is of the opinion that this list is by no means indisputable.

11.16. The International Law Association (ILA) tried to define ***res iudicata*** specifically in connection with arbitration and any related issues of enforceability of an arbitral award. According to the ILA, the following arbitral awards can be considered as *res iudicata*:[41] (•) an arbitral award which is final and binding in the place where it was made (the seat of arbitration), (•) it is capable of recognition in the seat of arbitration, namely (•) to the extent to which the award covers the subject of each new claim (action), (•) was rendered between the same parties, and (•) is based upon the same cause of action as the claim which was disposed of or decided on by an arbitral award.

11.17. The definition of arbitral award is crucial for the NYConv, because it is the only type of decision which can benefit from the regime of the Convention. The NYConv itself only offers an attempt at a definition *("quasi definition")* of an arbitral award.[42] The NYConv stipulates that the concept of arbitral award covers both arbitral awards made by *ad hoc* arbitrators and arbitral awards made by permanent arbitral institutions.

11.18. Consequently, if the NYConv lacks any definition of an arbitral award, then we need to ask which law should govern the determination of whether a particular decision is an arbitral award or not. There are a number of possibilities, such as (i) the law of the state of enforcement, or *lex loci arbitri* (the law of the seat of arbitration), (ii) or the term must be construed autonomously in terms of the systematics of the system and the purpose.[43] The opinions on this issue diverge. The Convention does not represent an exhaustive (comprehensive) set of arbitration rules. It only regulates the requirements concerning recognition and enforcement (together with cases of potential refusal of recognition and enforcement). Consequently, the application of terms and definitions from national legal

---

[40] Academic writings do not, however, provide any opinion on situations in which the waiver of the right to annulment of an arbitral award would be contrary to public policy. We might possibly conclude that this would be the case under the Czech rules on arbitration or Czech law in general.

[41] Denis Bensaude, *The International Law Association's Recommendations on Res Judicata and Lis Pendens in International Commercial Arbitration*, 4 Journal of International Arbitration 417 (2007).

[42] Article I(2) of the NYConv.

[43] JEAN-FRANCOIS POUDRET, SEBASTIEN BESSON; S. BIRTI, COMPARATIVE LAW OF INTERNATIONAL ARBITRATION, London: Sweet & Maxwell 811 (2nd ed., 2007).

systems is, to some extent, inevitable.[44] *Berg* inclines towards the application of the *lex loci arbitri* as the law which ought to determine whether the arbitrators' decision is an award in terms of the NYConv.[45] *Poudret and Besson* do not deny the role of the *lex loci arbitri* either.[46] *Fouchard and Born* are more inclined towards an autonomous interpretation.[47] The case law of national courts leaves the question of the law applicable to the concept of arbitral award more or less unanswered, save for certain exceptions, such as the decision of the Bavarian court – OLG, Case No. 4 Z Sch 13/02.[48] In determining whether the decision is an arbitral award for the purposes of the NYConv, this decision refers to the *lex loci arbitri*. This decision maintains that the *"[s] ubmitted* [in the given case] *arbitral award is an enforceable award within the meaning of* [*the NYConv*] *from the moment it was confirmed by a California court.* [...] *A decision which only has the effects of a contract, not the effects of a judgment, is not enforceable under the Convention. The relevant provision of the California Code of Civil Procedure stipulates that an arbitral award which was not confirmed*[49] *has the same effects as a written agreement between the parties to the arbitration. Nonetheless, the arbitral award can still be subject to enforcement, because the California Code of Civil Procedure stipulates that, after the award is confirmed, it has the same effects as a court judgment."*

11.19. Throughout the history of the NYConv, theory and practice have both presented their opinions on which decisions fall within the scope of the Convention and are considered arbitral awards for the purposes thereof. The delimitation principally does not refer to the *lex loci arbitri* or the legal system of the state of enforcement; it is based primarily on the contents and

---

[44]   Ibid, et. 811.

[45]   Albert J. van den Berg, *Why are Some Awards not Enforceable*, NEW HORIZONS IN INTERNATIONAL COMMERCIAL ARBITRATION AND BEYOND. Den Haag: KLI 317 (2005).

[46]   JEAN-FRANCOIS POUDRET, SEBASTIEN BESSON; S. BIRTI, COMPARATIVE LAW OF INTERNATIONAL ARBITRATION, London: Sweet & Maxwell 811 (2nd ed., 2007).

[47]   PHILIPPE FOUCHARD; EMMANUEL GAILLARD; BERTHOLD GOLDMAN, ON INTERNATIONAL COMMERCIAL ARBITRATION. Den Haag: KLI 745 (1999).; GARY B. BORN, INTERNATIONAL COMMERCIAL ARBITRATION. VOL. II., Austin: Wolters Kluwer 2350 (2009).

[48]   Decision of the Bavarian OLG, Case No. 4 Z Sch 13/02 of 22 November 2002. The case concerned a dispute between a film distributor and a film producer. Based on a licensing agreement entered into with the film producer in 2000, the film distributor had the right to distribute an unfinished film in the European market in consideration of a minimum fee and a loan for the purpose of finishing the film. The contract contained an arbitration clause. The arbitration was to be governed by the Rules for International Arbitration of the American Film Marketing Association. After the dispute arose, the distributor commenced arbitration in California [USA], and the arbitrator issued an arbitral award in the distributor's favor. The distributor requested confirmation of the award in a California court (in compliance with the requirements for enforceability of arbitral awards under the law of the state of California) and subsequently an enforcement of the award in Germany.

[49]   Confirmation by the court in the seat of arbitration, i.e. fulfillment of the condition for enforceability in the seat of arbitration. For instance, where there is no *exequatur* prescribed for local arbitral awards (e.g. in the Czech Republic, in Austria, and in many other countries), such procedure does not exist.

the purpose of the decisions made in arbitration. This approach has gradually shaped a more or less autonomous definition of an arbitral award for the purposes of the Convention.[50]

11.20. Poudret and Besson provide the following definition: *"An arbitral award in terms of [the NYConv] is a decision made by the arbitrators which finally resolves all or some of the claims made, or the procedural issue leading to the termination of arbitration, or which contains a settlement agreed between the parties. It is a decision rendered in arbitration which is connected with the law of a particular state, primarily the law of the state where the arbitration took place [lex loci arbitri]."*[51] The second part of the definition is a reaction to the application of the NYConv to so-called private arbitral awards. The New York Convention certainly applies to arbitral awards which finally determine the claims submitted to arbitration. According to the quoted opinion, the NYConv applies to final as well as partial arbitral awards.[52] We need to point out, though, that some countries refuse to enforce both interim and partial arbitral awards for doctrinal and conceptual reasons.[53] These awards are enforcement titles, i.e. the Convention allows their recognition and enforcement. The Convention also applies to arbitral awards containing a settlement between the parties.[54] According to the authors cited in the opening part of this paragraph (Poudret and Besson), the Convention also applies to an interim arbitral award which only determines the basis of the claim; such an award,

---

[50]   GARY B. BORN, INTERNATIONAL COMMERCIAL ARBITRATION. VOL. II., Austin: Wolters Kluwer 2350 (2009).

[51]   JEAN-FRANCOIS POUDRET; SEBASTIEN BESSON, COMPARATIVE LAW OF INTERNATIONAL ARBITRATION, London: Sweet & Maxwell 819 (2nd ed., 2007).

[52]   JEAN-FRANCOIS POUDRET; SEBASTIEN BESSON, COMPARATIVE LAW OF INTERNATIONAL ARBITRATION, London: Sweet & Maxwell 818 (2nd ed., 2007).; Albert J. van den Berg, *Why are Some Awards not Enforceable*, NEW HORIZONS IN INTERNATIONAL COMMERCIAL ARBITRATION AND BEYOND. Den Haag: KLI 317 (2005).

[53]   Cf., for instance, Resolution of the Bulgarian Supreme Court of Cassation No. 356, Commercial Case No. 24/1999 of 23 February 2009 (*A. OOD, USA v. K.A.*, Bulgaria), in which the court ruled that only a final arbitral award was binding upon the parties and could be recognized and enforced in Bulgaria. Surprisingly, the same decision regarding the recognition and enforcement of arbitral awards under the NYConv explicitly states that the procedure of recognition and enforcement is only governed by the procedural laws of the forum, i.e. the procedural rules applicable in the state in which the recognition and enforcement are proposed. Source: APIS 7 PRAVO [АПИС 7 ПРАВО Bulgarian legal information database] and case law published in the Bulletin of the Supreme Court of Cassation of the Republic of Bulgaria, 1998, Vol. 9–10. Also annotated in: Alexander J. Bělohlávek, I CYArb 247–248 (2011).

[54]   JEAN-FRANCOIS POUDRET; SEBASTIEN BESSON, COMPARATIVE LAW OF INTERNATIONAL ARBITRATION, London: Sweet & Maxwell 818 (2nd ed., 2007); PHILIPPE FOUCHARD, EMMANUEL GAILLARD, BERTHOLD GOLDMAN, ON INTERNATIONAL COMMERCIAL ARBITRATION, Den Haag: KLI 744–746 (1999).; Gino Lörcher, *Enforceability of Agreed Awards in Foreign Jurisdictions*, 17(3) Arbitration International 279 (2001).; JULIAN D. M. LEW; LOUKAS A. MISTELIS; STEFAN M. KRÖLL, COMPARATIVE INTERNATIONAL COMMERCIAL ARBITRATION. Den Haag: KLI 636 (2003).; ANDREW TWEEDDALE; KAREN TWEEDDALE, ARBITRATION OF COMMERCIAL DISPUTES: INTERNATIONAL AND ENGLISH LAW AND PRACTICE, Oxford: Oxford University Press 335 (2005).

however, can only be subject to recognition, not enforcement.[55] The approach to the enforcement of foreign awards under Czech law, according to which the application for recognition cannot be separated from the application for enforcement,[56] precludes the possibility of a separate recognition of an arbitral award. Consequently, only final arbitral awards can be subject to recognition (recognition and enforcement). In the author's opinion, recognition is also possible with respect to partial arbitral awards, if allowed by the nature of the [partial] order of the award.

11.21. The New York Convention does not apply to procedural decisions made by arbitrators.[57] But each decision must be assessed according to its contents and its purpose. This means that, even if a decision is designated as a procedural one, it can in actual fact be an arbitral award. What matters is its material contents.

11.22. Application of the NYConv to preliminary (provisional) measures made by arbitrators, where the applicable *lex arbitri* allows the arbitrators to issue preliminary measures, is a matter of dispute. The basic quality required of any award for the purposes of the Convention is its finality. Interim measures do not possess this quality. Some opinions argue that the Convention therefore does not apply to these injunctions.[58] The author of this commentary shares these opinions. But there are also opposite views. In this particular situation, *Berg* considers the original concept of the *lex loci arbitri* as the crucial factor. He maintains that, if a preliminary measure is an enforceable award in terms of the *lex loci arbitri*, it can be recognized and enforced under the Convention.[59] As mentioned above, the author does not support that opinion.

11.23. It is also unclear whether the NYConv applies to arbitral awards which only resolve the issue of jurisdiction of the arbitrators. Such decisions are rather frequent, because *common law*

---

[55]   JEAN-FRANCOIS POUDRET; SEBASTIEN BESSON, COMPARATIVE LAW OF INTERNATIONAL ARBITRATION, London: Sweet & Maxwell 818 (2nd ed., 2007).

[56]   See also Alexander J. Bělohlávek, *Zavedení tzv. exequatur do českého právního řádu.* [Title in translation: *The Introduction of So-Called Exequatur in Czech Law*], 5 PRÁVNÍ ZPRAVODAJ 16–17 (2004).

[57]   JEAN-FRANCOIS POUDRET; SEBASTIEN BESSON, COMPARATIVE LAW OF INTERNATIONAL ARBITRATION, London: Sweet & Maxwell 811 (2nd ed., 2007).; JULIAN D. M. LEW; LOUKAS A. MISTELIS; STEFAN M. KRÖLL, COMPARATIVE INTERNATIONAL COMMERCIAL ARBITRATION, Den Haag: KLI 699 (2003).

[58]   JEAN-FRANCOIS POUDRET; SEBASTIEN BESSON, COMPARATIVE LAW OF INTERNATIONAL ARBITRATION, London: Sweet & Maxwell 812 (2nd ed., 2007).; JULIAN D. M. LEW; LOUKAS A. MISTELIS; STEFAN M. KRÖLL, COMPARATIVE INTERNATIONAL COMMERCIAL ARBITRATION, Den Haag: KLI 699-700 (2003).

[59]   Albert J. van den Berg, *The Application of the New York Convention by the Court*, 9 IMPROVING THE EFFICIENCY OF ARBITRATION AGREEMENTS AND AWARDS: 40 YEARS OF APPLICATION OF THE NEW YORK CONVENTION, ICCA CONGRESS SERIES - 1998, Den Haag: KLI 28–29 (1999).

classifies jurisdiction as a substantive-law matter (i.e. as part of the decision in the merits), not a procedural requirement, which is typical for most continental *civil law* doctrines. From the *common law* perspective, such arbitral awards [regarding jurisdiction] meet the requirement of finality, because they finally determine a particular issue which is classified as a substantive-law issue under the law of the state of the seat of arbitration. On the other hand, many countries (especially those which subscribe to a doctrine based on civil law) classify such awards as procedural decisions. If the arbitrators conclude that they lack jurisdiction, then they terminate the arbitration. In such case, the definition offered by *Poudret* and *Besson* (see above) would be met. This opinion is also shared by *Born* who argues that decisions on jurisdiction are awards and fall within the scope of the Convention.[60] According to the Convention, they can only be subject to recognition. The author of this commentary believes that such approach is unacceptable, not just because Czech law does not allow "recognition without enforcement". The author of this commentary believes that, from this perspective, we must also consider the basic premises of the state of recognition/enforcement. True, recognition/ enforcement are primarily governed by the NYConv, but the NYConv contains no procedural provisions. Consequently, the *procedure* of recognition/enforcement must always be governed by the procedural laws of the state of recognition/ enforcement. The author of this commentary therefore believes that recognition of a decision on jurisdiction under the regime of the NYConv would violate the *ordre public* of the state of recognition/enforcement, despite the fact that the law of the state of recognition/enforcement classifies jurisdiction as a procedural issue (procedural requirement). We must point out, though, that even such decisions are commonly recognized in a number of other countries.

11.24. Nevertheless, an arbitral award falling within the scope of the NYConv must always be the result of proceedings of a jurisdictional nature. In other words, the Convention does not cover the *results* of proceedings, which could perhaps be designated as "arbitral proceedings" ("arbitration" etc.) but the purpose or nature of which are different.[61]

---

[60]   GARY B. BORN, INTERNATIONAL COMMERCIAL ARBITRATION. VOL. II., Austin: Wolters Kluwer 2359 (2009).

[61]   DOMENICO DIPIETRO; MARTIN PLATTE, ENFORCEMENT OF INTERNATIONAL ARBITRATION AWARDS – THE NEW YORK CONVENTION, London: Cameron May 31–57 (2001).; JULIAN D. M. LEW, LOUKAS A. MISTELIS, STEFAN M. KRÖLL, COMPARATIVE INTERNATIONAL COMMERCIAL ARBITRATION, Den Haag: KLI 699 (2003).

I.2.3. Foreign arbitral award

11.25. The NYConv employs two criteria to define a **foreign** arbitral award: (i) **a territorial criterion** and (ii) a **criterion** which is commonly referred to as **functional**.

(a) Territorial criterion

11.26. **The first and foremost criterion is the territorial aspect**, more precisely the place where the arbitral award was made (or the seat of arbitration and the place where the award was rendered). For the purposes of the NYConv, a foreign arbitral award is an award issued in the territory of a state other than the state in which the recognition and enforcement of the award are sought.[62] No other conditions are prescribed. The Convention is therefore based on the **principle of universality**, i.e. arbitral awards are treated the same whether rendered in the Contracting States or in third countries.[63]

11.27. However, the principle of universality was not a generally recognized principle when the NYConv was adopted. The Contracting States were therefore allowed to make a reservation regarding the application of this rule. Consequently, the applicability of the Convention can be limited to arbitral awards issued in the territory of another **Contracting** State. Such reservation is commonly referred to as the reciprocity exception. The Czech Republic has partly availed itself of this possibility. Application of the principle of universality was made contingent on a reciprocal approach by the respective non-contracting state. Considering the present number of the Contracting States, which guarantees that the NYConv is indeed a global instrument, the importance of this exception is minimal in practice.

11.28. The New York Convention **does not require the existence of any international dimension in the arbitration in which the arbitral award was made.**[64] In theory, the Convention is therefore applicable to an arbitral award rendered in a case which is considered a purely domestic case in the state of the proceedings (in the state where the arbitral award was made). **The applicability of the NYConv does not depend on the nationality, residence, or registered office/seat of**

---

[62] Article I(1).

[63] ALBERT J. VAN DEN BERG, THE NEW YORK ARBITRATION CONVENTION OF 1958, Den Haag: T.M.C. Asser Institute 12 (1981).

[64] JULIAN D. M. LEW; LOUKAS A. MISTELIS; STEFAN M. KRÖLL, COMPARATIVE INTERNATIONAL COMMERCIAL ARBITRATION, Den Haag: KLI 700 (2003).; ALBERT J. VAN DEN BERG, THE NEW YORK ARBITRATION CONVENTION OF 1958, Den Haag: T.M.C. Asser Institute 17 (1981).; MAURO RUBINO-SAMMARTANO, INTERNATIONAL ARBITRATION LAW AND PRACTICE, Den Haag: KLI 546 (2nd ed., 2001).

the parties.[65] **The Convention covers arbitral awards which were rendered in arbitration between parties who have the same nationality.**[66] The Convention therefore also applies to an arbitral award made in arbitration between parties of the same nationality, providing the arbitration was held in a state other than the state whose nationals the parties are.[67] Assessment of proceedings, in which the only international dimension is the place of arbitration, can be a problem.[68] An arbitral award issued in such proceedings is capable of recognition and enforcement under the NYConv. The only conceivable reason for a refusal of recognition[69] is a violation of public policy,[70] but only if the recognition is sought in a state with which the case apparently has all connections. However, the reason why the parties opted for arbitration in a different country will be important. If their aim was to evade certain important mandatory rules, then the application of public policy could be justified.[71]

11.29. The territorial criterion is the basic and always applicable criterion. If the arbitral award is rendered in a state other than the state where the recognition and enforcement are sought, then the NYConv shall apply.[72] The prevailing opinions maintain that an arbitral award is rendered in the state where the seat of arbitration[73] is located (see the commentary to Section 17 of the

---

[65] See also Decision of the Court for the Geneva Canton, Switzerland, of 14 April 1983 (*Carbomin S.A. v. Ekton Corporation*).

[66] ALBERT J. VAN DEN BERG, THE NEW YORK ARBITRATION CONVENTION OF 1958, Den Haag: T.M.C. Asser Institute 17–18 (1981).; PHILIPPE FOUCHARD, EMANUEL GAILLARD, BERTHOLD GOLDMAN, ON INTERNATIONAL COMMERCIAL ARBITRATION, Den Haag: KLI 966 (1999).; MAURO RUBINO-SAMMARTANO, INTERNATIONAL ARBITRATION LAW AND PRACTICE, Den Haag: KLI 546 (2nd ed., 2001).

[67] In several cases, the U.S. courts did not consider such awards foreign awards within the meaning of the NYConv, but domestic awards. For more details, see GARY B. BORN, INTERNATIONAL COMMERCIAL ARBITRATION. VOL. II, Austin: Wolters Kluwer 2374–2375 (2009).; for an opposite view, see also the following decisions: (•) Corte di Appello Milano, Italy, of 24 March 1998 (*Virgilio de Agostini and Loris et Enrico Germani v. Milloil SpA, Pia et Gabriela Germani et Andrea de Agostini*) or (•) High Court Queen's Bench Division, Commercial Court, Great Britain [England] of 27 April 2005 (*IPCO Nigeria Limited v. Nigerian National Petroleum Corporation*).

[68] NADĚŽDA ROZEHNALOVÁ, ROZHODČÍ ŘÍZENÍ V MEZINÁRODNÍM A VNITROSTÁTNÍM OBCHODNÍM STYKU. [Title in translation: ARBITRATION IN INTERNATIONAL AND NATIONAL COMMERCE], Prague: ASPI 47–48 (2nd ed., 2008). See also the commentary to Section 17 of the ArbAct in this book.

[69] Unless, of course, the arbitration as such or the arbitral award suffer from defects in terms of Article V of the NYConv.

[70] Article V(2)(b) of the NYConv.

[71] ALBERT J. VAN DEN BERG, THE NEW YORK ARBITRATION CONVENTION OF 1958. The Hague: Asser 18 (1981).

[72] Albert J. van den Berg, *Non-domestic Arbitral Awards under the 1958 New York Convention*, 2(3) ARB. INT. 198 (1986).; Michael Pryles, *Foreign Awards and the New York Convention*, 9(3) ARB. INT. 268 (1993).; MAURO RUBINO-SAMMARTANO, INTERNATIONAL ARBITRATION LAW AND PRACTICE, Den Haag: KLI 945 (2nd ed., 2001).; GARY B. BORN, INTERNATIONAL COMMERCIAL ARBITRATION. VOL. II, Austin: Wolters Kluwer 2367 (2009).

[73] JEAN-FRANCOIS POUDRET; SEBASTIEN BESSON, COMPARATIVE LAW OF INTERNATIONAL ARBITRATION, London: Sweet & Maxwell 819 (2nd ed., 2007).; JULIAN D. M. LEW; LOUKAS A. MISTELIS; STEFAN M. KRÖLL, COMPARATIVE INTERNATIONAL COMMERCIAL ARBITRATION,

ArbAct). If the seat of arbitration is in doubt, then the court of the state where enforcement is sought ought to decide where the award was made.[74] The application of the territorial criterion has not created any major problems in practice. Nonetheless, there are certain decisions which considered an arbitral award rendered in a different state a domestic award, and the court refused to apply the NYConv. Such decisions are, however, very rare.[75]

(b) Functional criterion

11.30. The other criterion employed by the New York Convention to determine whether a particular arbitral award is a foreign award (apart from the territorial criterion) is the so-called functional criterion. An arbitral award is a foreign award if it is not considered a domestic award in the country where its recognition and enforcement are sought. The original draft of the Convention presented by the ECOSOC only contained the territorial criterion. At a conference in New York, however, the representatives of certain countries raised the objection that this criterion was inadequate.[76] Especially the representatives of Germany and France argued that certain jurisdictions allow the parties to choose a legal system other than the law of the seat of arbitration as the law applicable to their arbitration.[77] The result was a compromise solution – the relevant provision of the Convention incorporating the territorial criterion was broadened to include another criterion, namely the *functional* criterion. The same reason was behind the additional text incorporated in Article V(1)(a) and (e).[78]

11.31. The functional criterion extends the application of the NYConv. The basic criterion is the territorial criterion. The Convention applies whenever the award is rendered in a different state. But the functional criterion allows application of the NYConv even if the arbitral award is made in the state of enforcement, providing the award is not considered a domestic award in

---

Den Haag: KLI 700 (2003).; F. A. Mann, *Where is an Award Made*, 1(1) ARBITRATION INTERNATIONAL 107–108 (1985).; GARY B. BORN, INTERNATIONAL COMMERCIAL ARBITRATION. VOL. II, Austin: Wolters Kluwer 2368–2370 (2009).; see also Section 1054 of the ZPO [DEU], Section 53 of the AA.

[74]   JULIAN D. M. LEW; LOUKAS A. MISTELIS; STEFAN M. KRÖLL, COMPARATIVE INTERNATIONAL COMMERCIAL ARBITRATION, Den Haag: KLI 700 (2003).

[75]   For more details, see Michael Pryles, *Foreign Awards and the New York Convention*, 9(3) ARB. INT. 259–274 (1993).; Justice V. S. Deshpande, *Jurisdiction Over Foreign and Domestic Awards in the New York Convention, 1958*, 7(2) ARBITRATION INTERNATIONAL 123–136 (1991).; GARY B. BORN, INTERNATIONAL COMMERCIAL ARBITRATION. VOL. II, Austin: Wolters Kluwer 2376 (2009).

[76]   For more details, see Albert J. van den Berg, *Non-domestic Arbitral Awards under the 1958 New York Convention*, 2(3) ARBITRATION INTERNATIONAL 195–197 (1986).

[77]   ALBERT J. VAN DEN BERG, THE NEW YORK ARBITRATION CONVENTION OF 1958, The Hague: Asser 23 (1981).

[78]   ALBERT J. VAN DEN BERG, THE NEW YORK ARBITRATION CONVENTION OF 1958, The Hague: Asser 23 (1981).

the said state.[79] The functional criterion can only be employed if the arbitral award is made in the territory of the state in which the enforcement thereof is sought. Application of the criterion is at the court's discretion.[80] The author believes that this approach is not applicable in the Czech Republic. It is true that the parties are endowed with broad autonomy as concerns agreements on procedure (Section 19 of the ArbAct), and, in cases with an international dimension, they can also agree on the law applicable to their arbitration agreement (Section 36 of the ArbAct). But the arbitration is always considered domestic (*a contrario* the applicability of Section 38 et seq. of the ArbAct on recognition and enforcement of foreign arbitral awards) if the Czech Republic is the seat of arbitration (Section 17 of the ArbAct). Consequently, Czech law does not attribute any special significance to the place where the arbitral award is made, because the Czech *lex arbitri* is based on the irrebuttable presumption that the arbitral award is issued in the seat of arbitration.

11.32.　The NYConv itself has no specific provision which would stipulate which arbitral award ought to be considered a foreign award in the state of enforcement. Consequently, the determination of whether an award is a foreign arbitral award is at the discretion of the state (the court of the state) in which the recognition and enforcement are sought. The traditional interpretation of the criterion is that an arbitral award is considered a foreign award if the arbitration was governed by the *lex arbitri* of another state.[81] The Convention thereby confirmed the right of the parties to choose a *lex arbitri* different from the law of the seat of arbitration. But whether such possibility is indeed open to the parties in a particular case must, in the author's opinion, be determined only according to the rules of *lex arbitri* of the state in which the arbitration itself is domiciled (cf. Section 17 of the

---

[79]　Albert J. van den Berg, *Non-domestic Arbitral Awards under the 1958 New York Convention*, 2(3) ARBITRATION INTERNATIONAL 198 (1986).; Albert J. van den Berg, *The New York Convention: Summary of Court Decisions*, THE NEW YORK CONVENTION OF 1958: A COLLECTION OF REPORTS AND MATERIALS DELIVERED AT THE ASA CONFERENCE HELD IN ZURICH ON 2 FEBRUARY 1996, Zurich: ASA 9 (1996).

[80]　ALBERT J. VAN DEN BERG, THE NEW YORK ARBITRATION CONVENTION OF 1958, The Hague: Asser 24-27 (1981).

[81]　DOMENICO DIPIETRO; MARTIN PLATTE, ENFORCEMENT OF INTERNATIONAL ARBITRATION AWARDS – THE NEW YORK CONVENTION, London: Cameron May 29 (2001).; ALBERT J. VAN DEN BERG, THE NEW YORK ARBITRATION CONVENTION OF 1958, The Hague: Asser 23 (1981).; JULIAN D. M. LEW; LOUKAS A. MISTELIS; STEFAN M. KRÖLL, COMPARATIVE INTERNATIONAL COMMERCIAL ARBITRATION, Den Haag: KLI 701 (2003).; Albert J. van den Berg, *Non-domestic Arbitral Awards under the 1958 New York Convention*, 2(3) ARBITRATION INTERNATIONAL 200-201 (1986).; Albert J. van den Berg, *The Application of the New York Convention by the Court*, 9 IMPROVING THE EFFICIENCY OF ARBITRATION AGREEMENTS AND AWARDS: 40 YEARS OF APPLICATION OF THE NEW YORK CONVENTION, ICCA CONGRESS SERIES - 1998, Den Haag: KLI, 26 (1999).

ArbAct). As mentioned above, the author believes that Czech law does not allow the parties to agree on the application of any *lex arbitri* other than the law of the state of the seat of arbitration. Application of the functional criterion in the traditional sense is rather marginal in international practice.[82]

11.33. But the U.S. courts have, conversely, come up with an even broader interpretation of the functional criterion. In this regard, the landmark decision is the ruling of the *Court of Appeals for the Second Circuit* in *Bergesen v. Müller*.[83] The case concerned an arbitral award made in the state of New York, in an arbitration conducted between parties from Norway and Switzerland, respectively.[84] The court concluded that an arbitral award which is not considered a domestic award means an award made under the legal system of a different state, i.e. made pursuant to foreign law or between parties with their residence or their principal place of business outside the state of enforcement.[85] The *Court of Appeals* based its conclusion primarily on the nationality of the parties. The nationality of the parties has no importance for the

---

[82] See also GARY B. BORN, INTERNATIONAL COMMERCIAL ARBITRATION. VOL. II, Austin: Wolters Kluwer, 2381 (2009).

[83] Decision of the *Court of Appeals for the Second Circuit*, USA, of 17 June 1983 (*Sigval Bergesen v. Joseph Müller AG*), cited according to Albert J. van den Berg, *The Application of the New York Convention by the Courts*, 9 IMPROVING THE EFFICIENCY OF ARBITRATION AGREEMENTS AND AWARDS: 40 YEARS OF APPLICATION OF THE NEW YORK CONVENTION, ICCA CONGRESS SERIES – 1998, Den Haag: KLI 27 (1999).; Albert J. van den Berg, *Non-domestic Arbitral Awards under the 1958 New York Convention*, 2(3) ARBITRATION INTERNATIONAL 191–194 (1986).; Michael Pryles, *Foreign Awards and the New York Convention*, 9(3) ARBITRATION INTERNATIONAL 269–271 (1993).; JEAN-FRANCOIS POUDRET, SEBESTIEN BESSON, COMPARATIVE LAW OF INTERNATIONAL ARBITRATION, London: Sweet & Maxwell 819 (2nd ed., 2007).; JULIAN D. M. LEW, LOUKAS A. MISTELIS, STEFAN M. KRÖLL, COMPARATIVE INTERNATIONAL COMMERCIAL ARBITRATION, Den Haag: KLI 701–702 (2003).

[84] *Bergesen*, the owner of the ship from Norway, and a Swiss corporation *Müller* entered into several shipping contracts for the transportation of cargo. Each contract contained the following arbitration clause: *"Arbitration shall be held in and pursuant to the law of the state of New York. An arbitral award made by the majority of arbitrators can be enforced by any court and shall be final and binding on the parties all over the world."* Arbitration was opened after a dispute arose between the parties regarding some of the contracts. The arbitrators rendered an arbitral award in New York in favor of *Bergesen*. *Bergesen* sought enforcement of the award in Switzerland under the NYConv. The trial court declared the award enforceable; the decision was upheld by the appellate court. *Müller* appealed to the Tribunal Fédéral (Federal Supreme Court) arguing that the award was not binding in terms of the NYConv. *Müller* relied on a provision incorporated in the law of the state of New York according to which a court must, at the request of a party, confirm an arbitral award within one year after the award is served. The confirmation is a *conditio sine qua non* for the award to become binding in terms of the NYConv. The Convention does not prescribe any such confirmation; nevertheless, to be on the safe side, *Bergesen* filed a petition for the confirmation of the award in the *District Court of New York*. The above-mentioned provision of the law of the state of New York stipulates that the petition must be filed within one year after the award is served. Conversely, the law implementing the NYConv stipulates a period of three years. In his petition, *Bergesen* therefore relied on the law implementing the Convention, because he missed the one-year deadline. The *District Court* was thus called upon to resolve the issue of whether enforcement of the award falls within the scope of the Convention and the implementing legislation. The *District Court* concluded that the award falls within the scope of the Convention. The decision was upheld by the *Court of Appeals*.

[85] Albert J. van den Berg, *The Application of the New York Convention by the Courts*, 9 IMPROVING THE EFFICIENCY OF ARBITRATION AGREEMENTS AND AWARDS: 40 YEARS OF APPLICATION OF THE NEW YORK CONVENTION, ICCA CONGRESS SERIES – 1998, Den Haag: KLI 27 (1999).

territorial criterion, but the NYConv does not explicitly prohibit the courts from taking account of the parties' nationality when they apply the functional criterion. After all, the Convention does not define when an award is not to be considered a domestic award.[86] The *Court of Appeals* reached this conclusion based on the law implementing the NYConv in the U.S., i.e. Chapter 2 of the *Federal Arbitration Act* (FAA). Section 202 of the FAA[87] stipulates that an arbitral award that arises out of a commercial relationship between two U.S. citizens does not fall under the Convention, unless the relationship involves property located abroad, envisages performance abroad, or has some other *reasonable* connection with one or more foreign states.[88] But the purpose of the provision is not to define an arbitral award which is not considered domestic; the purpose is to divide competences between Chapter 1 and Chapter 2 of the FAA.[89] *Poudret* and *Besson* argue that the decision confused the classification of arbitration into national (domestic) and international on the one hand and the classification of awards into domestic and foreign awards on the other hand.[90] The author of this commentary shares this opinion. Section 202 of the FAA apparently intended to distinguish between national and international arbitration. The functional criterion in Article I of the NYConv cannot be interpreted in an isolated manner; it is necessary to take into account the other provisions of the NYConv, too. This primarily applies to Article V(1)(e) of the NYConv, which refers to the law of the state in which the award was made or the law of the state pursuant to which it was made. Indeed, the final wording of Article V(1)(e) of the NYConv was influenced by the fact that the functional criterion was incorporated in the NYConv at the final stage of the negotiations on the Convention. Article V(1)(e) of the NYConv suggests that a foreign arbitral award means an award rendered pursuant to foreign *lex arbitri*. In the *Bergesen* case, the U.S. court applied the New York Convention to the enforcement of an award made

---

[86]   Albert J. van den Berg, *Non-domestic Arbitral Awards under the 1958 New York Convention*, 2(3) Arbitration International 202–204 (1986).
[87]   For a translation of the FAA to Czech, see ALEXANDER J. BĚLOHLÁVEK, ROZHODČÍ ŘÍZENÍ, ORDRE PUBLIC A TRESTNÍ PRÁVO: INTERAKCE MEZINÁRODNÍHO A TUZEMSKÉHO PRÁVA SOUKROMÉHO A VEŘEJNÉHO. [Title in translation: ARBITRATION, ORDRE PUBLIC AND CRIMINAL LAW: INTERACTION BETWEEN INTERNATIONAL AND DOMESTIC PRIVATE AND PUBLIC LAW], Volume II, Prague: C. H. Beck, (2008). (Annexes to the core part – U.S. arbitration laws).
[88]   JULIAN D. M. LEW; LOUKAS A. MISTELIS; STEFAN M. KRÖLL, COMPARATIVE INTERNATIONAL COMMERCIAL ARBITRATION, Den Haag: KLI 702 (2003).
[89]   Albert J. van den Berg, *Non-domestic Arbitral Awards under the 1958 New York Convention*, 2(3) ARBITRATION INTERNATIONAL 204 (1986).
[90]   JEAN-FRANCOIS POUDRET; SEBASTIEN BESSON, COMPARATIVE LAW OF INTERNATIONAL ARBITRATION, London: Sweet & Maxwell 819 (2nd ed., 2007).

in the U.S. The NYConv would be applied in the same way by a court of any other state, if petitioned to enforce the award. Consequently, from the perspective of the NYConv, the award would not in fact be deemed a domestic award in any country, which mainly contradicts Article V(1)(e) that basically requires that an arbitral award be domiciled in a particular state.[91]

I.2.4. Foreign arbitral award within the meaning of Sections 38 and 39 of the ArbAct

11.34. As concerns the definition of foreign arbitral award in connection with Sections 38–40 of the ArbAct (which regulate recognition and enforcement of foreign arbitral awards in the Czech domestic legal system), *Kučera* refers to the first sentence of Section 38 of the ArbAct and states that a *"foreign arbitral award means an arbitral award made in a foreign country"*.[92] We can therefore argue that Czech law is based on the territorial criterion inspired by the New York Convention. Moreover, considering the fact that the NYConv has been signed by so many Contracting States that it can be deemed universally applicable, the cases in which the domestic Czech law of national origin would apply (ArbAct) are indeed most exceptional (see Section 47 of the ArbAct).

11.35. The differentiation between a domestic arbitral award and a foreign arbitral award depends on the place where the award is made (the principle of territoriality of the award) or the seat of arbitration, as applicable.

II.   Recognition and enforcement

11.36. The enforcement of foreign arbitral awards is based on the nature of arbitral awards as enforceable titles issued in adversarial proceedings, but by an entity of private law. Consequently, it is possible to disregard the principle of sovereignty,[93] which is taken into consideration in the recognition and enforcement of

---

[91] Albert J. van den Berg, *Non-domestic Arbitral Awards under the 1958 New York Convention*, 2(3) ARBITRATION INTERNATIONAL 206–211 (1986). Later on, *Berg* advocated the opposite view, but his arguments in the latter case appear less persuasive. See Albert J. van den Berg, *The Application of the New York Convention by the Courts*, 9 IMPROVING THE EFFICIENCY OF ARBITRATION AGREEMENTS AND AWARDS: 40 YEARS OF APPLICATION OF THE NEW YORK CONVENTION, ICCA Congress Series – 1998, Den Haag: KLI 27 (1999).; similarly JULIAN D. M. LEW; LOUKAS A. MISTELIS; STEFAN M. KRÖLL, COMPARATIVE INTERNATIONAL COMMERCIAL ARBITRATION, Den Haag: KLI 702 (2003).

[92] ZDENĚK KUČERA, MEZINÁRODNÍ PRÁVO SOUKROMÉ [Title in translation: PRIVATE INTERNATIONAL LAW], Brno: Doplněk 430 (6th ed., 2004).

[93] Naturally, this is not to imply that sovereignty in enforcement should not be considered in those cases in which the order of the arbitral award is directed against the state or against an entity which is endowed with the same or a comparable sovereignty in enforcement as the state.

foreign court decisions, despite the fact that the foreign award could not be rendered in the foreign state if the procedure were not approved by the law of the state where the award was made. The main issue is whether the country in which the arbitral award was made recognizes and enforces arbitral awards made in the territory of the Czech Republic. This is the reason why the enforcement of foreign arbitral awards is only facing one obstacle, namely the requirement of reciprocity. It is irrelevant whether enforcement only means enforcement by the court in compliance with the Code of Civil Procedure or whether it also includes enforcement pursuant to the Executory Procedure Code. The Arbitration Act contains no provisions regarding the authority empowered to confirm reciprocity or to declare lack of reciprocity in the enforcement of foreign arbitral awards. Consequently, it is necessary to apply Section 54 of the PILP[94] which stipulates that issues of reciprocity are resolved by the Ministry of Justice of the Czech Republic. This also complies with the purpose of the Act on Private International Law and Procedure, Section 1 [of the PILP]. The enforcement of any title means enforcement with the use of state power. Relationships with an international dimension must be governed by the above-cited special law, namely the Act on Private International Law and Procedure.

11.37. The differentiation between a foreign arbitral award and a domestic arbitral award under the ArbAct is based on the place where the award was made; in proceedings governed by the ArbAct, the said place must be considered the same as the seat of arbitration. Regarding the seat of arbitration (the place where the arbitral award is made), see the commentary to Section 17 of the ArbAct. An analysis of foreign arbitration and a foreign arbitral award is also the subject matter of the commentary to Section 36 of the ArbAct.

11.38. When ordering enforcement of a foreign arbitral award, the domestic court is not entitled to review the merits of the foreign award. The court must only verify whether the award is a foreign award and whether there are any grounds which would necessitate refusal of the enforcement in terms of Section 39 of the ArbAct. As prescribed by Article IV of the NYConv, the motion to recognize and enforce a foreign arbitral award must be submitted together with the original or a certified copy of the arbitral award and the original or a certified copy

---

[94] With effect from 1 January 2014, this provision will be replaced by new law (PIL); as concerns the determination (confirmation) of reciprocity, see Section 13 [of the PIL]. Both provisions (Section 54 of the PILP and Section 13 of the PIL) are cited in a note in the opening part of this commentary to Section 38 of the ArbAct, in the list of related laws.

of the arbitration agreement establishing the jurisdiction of the arbitrators. The courts also usually require documents proving that the arbitral award was served on all parties, or especially those persons against whom the enforcement is proposed. In the case of an award issued in institutionalized arbitration, the courts of many countries, including Czech courts, only require a declaration of the permanent arbitral institution or a confirmation of legal force and effect issued by the institution. Such confirmation can be issued in compliance with the rules of the permanent arbitral institution after the arbitral award is duly served on the parties to the dispute. It is necessary to point out that many countries are unfamiliar with instruments analogous to the domestic Czech confirmation of legal force and effect and confirmation of enforceability. What is more, many legal systems do not even recognize the concept of material legal force and effect, which is the basis of Czech law. Consequently, it is also necessary to accept any document attesting to the finality of the arbitral award and its eligibility for enforcement in the country where the award was made. What matters are the last-mentioned circumstances, not the manner of proving these circumstances in the proceedings for recognition/enforcement.[95]

11.39. Identical to the enforcement of decisions rendered by foreign courts pursuant to Section 65 of the PILP, the recognition of a foreign arbitral award is not pronounced by any special order (see Section 40 of the ArbAct)[96] in any special proceedings (save for certain specific cases, such as decisions in matters of status). If the court in the enforcement proceedings (execution) concludes that the instrument is an arbitral award and that there are no grounds which would necessitate refusal of the enforcement thereof, then the court has regard to the foreign award. But the court's decision on enforcement of a foreign arbitral award must always be reasoned. These principles are, indeed, also reflected in Section 122 of the PIL (effective date 1 January 2014).[97]

11.40. Arbitration practice also requires an answer to the question whether a partial or an interim arbitral award can be subject to enforcement, too. Although Czech law contains no provisions regarding partial or interim awards, Czech arbitral practice also

---

[95]   See also Resolution of the ConCourt, Case No. IV. ÚS 189/10 of 10 May 2010, which is partially cited in the final part of this commentary to Section 38 of the ArbAct, and in greater detail in the commentary to Section 39 of the ArbAct.

[96]   This provision will be replaced with Section 122 of the PIL with effect from 1 January 2014.

[97]   With effect from 1 January 2014, the PIL repeals Part Five of the ArbAct in its entirety and replaces it with special provisions directly incorporated in the PIL. Concerning this change, see the final part of the commentary to Section 36 of the ArbAct. It is necessary to highlight that, save for several less important exceptions, there will principally be no major changes compared to the regime which is currently laid down by the ArbAct.

knows partial arbitral awards. Such an award must be perceived as a final award with respect to the subject matter of the decision, providing it was adopted in compliance with the law applicable in the country where it was made or in compliance with the provisions applicable to the given proceedings. The author believes that a partial arbitral award can also be subject to enforcement, but on the condition the decision stipulates a specific obligation the performance of which can be enforced by instruments of state power. In other words, such decision imposes an obligation the performance of which can be subject to execution.[98] Conversely, interim arbitral awards cannot be subject to enforcement in the Czech Republic (in the author's opinion). The only purpose of such awards is to clarify and determine a particular issue important for further assessment and resolution of the claim. Nonetheless, the author is of the opinion, that the issuance of an interim arbitral award may be significant for the determination of whether there are grounds justifying an interim (provisional) measure by court during the arbitral proceedings or not.

11.41. As repeatedly mentioned in this book, the assessment of enforceability and the order of enforcement of foreign arbitral awards are primarily governed by international treaties binding upon the Czech Republic. The factors relevant for the assessment of applicability of the NYConv include the place where the arbitral award was made (cf. Sections 17 and 36 of the ArbAct), not the registered office/seat or the place of residence of the parties to the proceedings. For instance, Article I(1) of the NYConv allows the enforcement of a foreign arbitral award which was made in proceedings between parties from one and the same state, i.e. even if both parties come from the state of the seat of arbitration, and the proceedings are therefore considered "domestic". Thus, the award is considered a domestic arbitral award in the place where the arbitral award was made. Conversely, these cases exclude the application of the European Convention, because the EConv applies (Article I(1) of the

---

[98] Cf. also FRANZ LASCHET. ZUR ANERKENNUNG AUSLÄNDISCHER ZWISCHENSCHIEDSSPRÜCHE, Praxis des Internationalen Privat- und Verfahrensrechtes 72 et seq. (1984)., or E. MEZGER, NOCHMALS ZUR ANERKENNUNG AUSLÄNDISCHER ZWISCHENSCHIEDSSPRÜCHE, Praxis des Internationalen Privat- und Verfahrensrechtes 194 et seq. (1984). Although the prevailing practice is that partial foreign arbitral awards can be especially subject to enforcement, there are several contrary examples (see the above-mentioned foreign authors).

EConv) if the parties to the dispute come from different states which are bound by this international treaty.

11.42. If the enforcement concerns an arbitral award rendered in disputes arising from international investments[99] and pursuant to any of the treaties on mutual assistance and protection of investments binding upon the Czech Republic, then the arbitral award must be made in one of the Member States to the NYConv.

11.43. Special provisions regarding the enforceability of foreign arbitral awards are also incorporated in other international treaties binding upon the Czech Republic, the application of which in regular practice is rather exceptional, though. For instance, Article 16(2) of the Convention concerning International Carriage by Rail of 9 May 1980[100] stipulates that the arbitration tribunal's award in relation to transport undertakings or users, issued in the proceedings pursuant to Title III et seq. of the Convention, becomes enforceable in each of the Member States on completion of the formalities required in the state where enforcement is to take place. The merits of the case shall not be subject to review. As concerns the application of sources of international origin to the enforcement of foreign arbitral awards, the author also refers to the commentary to Section 47 of the ArbAct, which especially focuses on the application of legal assistance treaties.

III. Correlation between recognition and enforcement of foreign arbitral awards and standards applicable to the proceedings

11.44. The issue of the laws and rules applicable to arbitration may also become relevant at the stage of enforcement of arbitral awards. The important difference between judicial case management and proceedings before arbitrators inheres in the broad enforceability

---

[99] See also Vladimír Kostka, *Washingtonská úmluva o řešení investičních sporů mezi státy a příslušníky z druhých států z 18. 3. 1965.* [Title in translation: *The Washington Convention on the Settlement of Investment Disputes between States and Nationals of Other States of 18 March 1965*], 1 Acta Universitatis Carolinae-Iuridica 3 et seq. (1991)., or Alexander J. Bělohlávek, *Ochrana majetkových práv zahraničních osob a rozhodčí řízení ve věcech mezinárodních investic.* [Title in translation: *The Protection of Property Rights of Foreign Persons and Arbitration in Light of International Investments*], 9(6) DAŇOVÁ A HOSPODÁŘSKÁ KARTOTÉKA B 53–B 58 (2001)., JOY CHERIAN, INVESTMENT CONTRACTS AND ARBITRATION: THE WORLD BANK CONVENTION ON THE SETTLEMENT OF INVESTMENT DISPUTES, Leyden: Sijthoff (1975)., and other writings.

[100] The Convention concerning International Carriage by Rail (COTIF) was negotiated in Bern on 9 May 1980 and signed on behalf of the then CSSR in Bern on 29 December 1980. COTIF entered into force (also for Czechoslovakia) on 1 May 1985 and was promulgated in the Annex to the Decree of the Minister of Foreign Affairs of 2 August 1984 under No. 8/1985 Coll. (as amended in the meantime by No. 61/1991 Coll., No. 251/1991 Coll., No. 274/1996 Coll., and No. 8/2004 Coll. Int. Tr.).

of awards.[101] No state is usually required to recognize and enforce decisions rendered by the courts of another state (as concerns the principles of accepting the manifestations of state power of another state in the broadest sense and from the perspective of general principles of international law). Similarly, no state is bound to recognize and enforce awards made by arbitrators in a different state (exclusively from the perspective of the principles of international law). The obligation of recognition and enforcement may be established by an international treaty. As concerns the enforcement of arbitral awards, the basic law of international origin, ratified by a significant number of member states, is the NYConv, analyzed in great detail above. The NYConv also allows posing the question of the procedural laws with which the award must comply. The New York Convention, similarly to modern *leges arbitri*, does not stipulate any specific procedural rules. It only requires that the fundamental rules of due process be honored.

11.45. The law of civil court proceedings does not usually apply to arbitration. Hence, the fact that the arbitrators do not abide by the procedural laws of the seat of arbitration does not constitute grounds under the NYConv for challenging the award or refusing enforcement of the award abroad. International opinions are basically uniform in that the NYConv does not allow refusal of enforcement of an award for failure to observe the laws of civil procedure.[102] The New York Convention does not allow refusing enforcement of an award for breach of procedural rules. Refusal can only be justified by a breach of any of the essential procedural principles. Indeed, this has also been reflected in the ILA recommendations regarding the application of the procedural *ordre public* as grounds for a refusal to recognize and enforce a foreign arbitral award rendered in foreign arbitration (2002 Recommendation). In this regard, the ILA continues by stating that when enforcing awards, the courts should apply the procedural rules applicable to court proceedings only if such rules are considered acceptable in the international community (cit.:) *"Nevertheless, in order to determine whether a principle forming part of its legal system must be considered sufficiently fundamental to justify a refusal to recognise or enforce an award, a court should take into account, on the one hand, the*

---

[101] The author intentionally disregards the special EU regime (EU law) which, conversely, guarantees the extensive enforceability of court decisions (at least in most civil and commercial matters). The author is trying to approach this issue from the global perspective.

[102] After all, the recent *fiftieth anniversary* of the NYConv was an opportunity for analyzing the Convention from many perspectives and by many different *fora*. For instance, there are a number of working and expert groups in the ICC Commission on Arbitration, as well as under the auspices of IBA, UNCITRAL, etc., which focus on the Convention, and their view of the respective issue is basically the same.

international nature of the case and its connection with the legal system of the forum, and, on the other hand, the existence or otherwise of a consensus within the international community as regards the principle under consideration."[103]

11.46. Courts in foreign countries commonly accept that the procedural regime of conducting domestic disputes in court proceedings is not tailored to arbitration, whether international or national. This postulate can be illustrated, for instance, in the rich case law of the Swiss Supreme Court. The said Court has held that
- the rules of national origin regulating civil court proceedings, for instance the rules on evidence, **do not apply to arbitration**,
- an arbitral award can be set aside for a breach of procedural rules only if the violation can be considered a breach of the procedural *ordre public*, namely violation of the right to equal treatment and the principle of due and fair hearing of the case (concerning this issue, see also the commentary to Section 30 of the ArbAct), and ● the requirements of national law regarding litigation in courts do not constitute such procedural *ordre public*. For instance, the Swiss Supreme Court, in its decision of 14 November 1991, rejected the argument that rules on the examination of evidence contained in the Swiss law of civil procedure are part of the requirements for equal treatment and a fair and equitable hearing of the case within the framework of the procedural *ordre public*. The respondent referred to such requirements in the reasons supporting his motion to annul the arbitral award. The said Court held that, although the respondent referred in his defense to Article 190(2)(d) of the IPRG [CHE], the provision has nothing in common with the principles of equal treatment and a fair and equitable hearing of the dispute. The Court held that the respondent had admitted that the arbitral tribunal allowed him to present his case in two exchanges of procedural pleadings. The Court then concluded that the limits of the timing and the form of the parties' proposals for evidence, as well as the provisions regulating this issue for the purposes of civil court proceedings, do not represent part of the procedural *ordre public*, i.e. they are not part of the requirement for equal treatment and a fair and equitable hearing of the case.[104]

---

[103] Recommendation 2b.
[104] Fernando Mantilla-Serrano, *Towards a Transnational Procedural Public Policy*, TOWARDS A UNIFORM INTERNATIONAL ARBITRATION LAW, New York: Juris Publishing 186 (Degos, L., Pinsolle, P. et Schläpfer, A.-V. eds., 2005).

IV.   Case law

11.47.   Resolution of the DC in Ústí nad Orlicí, Case No. 5 E 1245/98-18 of 30 March 1999:[105] **[recognition/enforcement of a foreign arbitral award; NYConv; enforceability; finality of AA; confirmation of enforceability] (1)** The enforceability of a foreign arbitral award is sufficiently confirmed if the competent personnel of the permanent arbitral institution confirm that the enforced arbitral award was duly *notified* to the debtor, which renders the arbitral award final and binding.[106] **(2)** If the conditions for application of the New York Convention [NYConv] are fulfilled, then the decisions on recognition/enforcement are governed by the NYConv.[107] Thus, the recognition/enforcement may only be refused for the reasons specified in Article V of the NYConv. **(3)** Hence, it is irrelevant for the recognition and enforcement of the arbitral award whether the debtor [still] conducts business activities or not or whether the debtor does not have sufficient finances in his or her accounts.

11.48.   Resolution of the RC in Hradec Králové, Case No. 19 Co 337/99-42 of 30 November 1999:[108] **[exclusion of review in the merits in** *exequatur* **/ enforcement proceedings; application of the NYConv; standing; public policy] (1)** The court conducting proceedings for ordering enforcement may only examine procedural issues. The court must not assess the

---

[105] As amended by Corrective Resolution Case No. 5 E 1245/98-27 of 23 April 1999. The decision was affirmed by the following decisions in the same case: (i) Resolution of the RC in Hradec Králové, Case No. 19 Co 337/99-42 of 30 November 1999 (annotated separately) and (ii) Resolution of the SC, Case No. 21 Cdo 1511/2000 of 29 March 2001. Information regarding the decision of the DC was adopted from the reasons for the SC resolution.

[106] In this case, a confirmation issued by the Secretary General of ICC International Court of Arbitration (International Chamber of Commerce).

For an identical conclusion, see also:

»   Resolution of the DC in Ústí nad Orlicí, Case No. 5 E 1246/98-16 of 30 March 1999, which was upheld by Resolution of the RC in Hradec Králové, Case No. 19 Co 322/99-47 of 27 January 2000 and Resolution of the SC, Case No. 21 Cdo 1876/2000 of 26 March 2001 (enforcement of AA rendered in arbitration at the ICC Court No. ICC 8.798 of 8 July 1998);

»   Resolution of the DC in Ústí nad Orlicí, Case No. 11 E 3835/98-36 of 30 March 1999, which was upheld by Resolution of the RC in Hradec Králové, Case No. 19 Co 274/99-50 of 26 October 1999 and Resolution of the SC, Case No. 21 Cdo 258/2000 of 27 March 2001 (enforcement of the same AA);

»   Resolution of the DC in Ústí nad Orlicí, Case No. 5 E 1244/98-12 of 30 March 1999, which was upheld by Resolution of the RC in Hradec Králové, Case No. 19 Co 323/99-31 of 26 October 1999 and Resolution of the SC, Case No. 21 Cdo 574/2000 of 26 March 2001; and

»   Resolution of the DC in Ústí nad Orlicí, Case No. 11 E 3836/98-7 of 30 March 1999, which was upheld by Resolution of the RC in Hradec Králové, Case No. 19 Co 271/99-25 of 30 November 1999 and Resolution of the SC, Case No. 21 Cdo 753/2000 of 26 March 2001.

[107] In this case with reference to Section 35 of the 1963 ArbAct – analogous to Section 47 of the ArbAct. As concerns recognition/enforcement of foreign arbitral awards, it is principally irrelevant if the law applied to the case is Act No. 98/1963 Coll. (1963 ArbAct; very rare in contemporary practice) or the ArbAct.

[108] The preceding decision was the Resolution of the DC in Ústí nad Orlicí, Case No. 5E 1245/98-18. The decision of the RC was affirmed by Resolution of the SC, Case No. 21 Cdo 1511/2000 of 29 March 2001. Information regarding the decision of the RC was adopted from the reasons for the SC resolution.

material correctness of the enforcement title, including the issue of the potential standing of the debtor's legal predecessor. **(2)** The issue of the respondent's standing in the merits has no connection to the public policy of the Czech Republic but to an issue of substantive law. Such issue cannot be subject to review in the proceedings for recognition/enforcement of a foreign arbitral award.[109] **(3)** The issue of the respondent's standing is subject to assessment pursuant to the substantive law applicable to the merits.[110]

11.49. **Resolution of the SC, Case No. 21 Cdo 1511/2000 of 29 March 2001:**[111] **[recognition/enforcement of a foreign award; prohibition of review in the merits; scope of application of foreign law; succession; guarantee]** **(1)** Courts in the proceedings for recognition/enforcement do not examine the substantive relationships between the creditor and the debtor. They only focus on whether the title for recognition/enforcement issued by a foreign authority can be enforced in the Czech Republic. **(2)** In the recognition and enforcement of a foreign arbitral award, the courts do not apply foreign law; they decide according to domestic Czech law or according to an applicable provision of international origin (here the NYConv). The courts address neither the issue of (in)correct application of foreign law in the merits nor the issue of (in)correct determination of

---

[109] The applicable substantive law was Austrian law, chosen by the parties in their licensing agreement. The case was resolved in arbitration conducted at the ICC International Court of Arbitration (AA, Case No. ICC 8798 of 8 July 1998).

The enforcement of the same arbitral award was also the subject matter of the following decisions:

» Resolution of the DC in Ústí nad Orlicí, Case No. 5 E 1246/98-16 of 30 March 1999, upheld by Resolution of the RC in Hradec Králové, Case No. 19 Co 322/99-47 of 27 January 2000, followed by a cassation appeal dismissed by Resolution of the SC, Case No. 21 Cdo 1876/2000 of 26 March 2001 (the conclusions were the same, these decisions are therefore not separately annotated);

» Resolution of the DC in Ústí nad Orlicí, Case No. 11 E 3835/98-36 of 30 March 1999, upheld by Resolution of the RC in Hradec Králové, Case No. 19 Co 274/99-50 of 26 October 1999, followed by a cassation appeal dismissed by Resolution of the SC, Case No. 21 Cdo 258/2000 of 27 March 2001 (the conclusions were the same, these decisions are therefore not separately annotated);

» Resolution of the DC in Ústí nad Orlicí, Case No. 5 E 1244/98-12 of 30 March 1999, upheld by Resolution of the RC in Hradec Králové, Case No. 19 Co 323/99-31 of 26 October 1999, followed by a cassation appeal dismissed by Resolution of the SC, Case No. 21 Cdo 574/2000 of 26 March 2001; as well as

» Resolution of the DC in Ústí nad Orlicí, Case No. 11 E 3836/98-7 of 30 March 1999, upheld by Resolution of the RC in Hradec Králové, Case No. 19 Co 271/99-25 of 30 November 1999, followed by a cassation appeal dismissed by Resolution of the SC, Case No. 21 Cdo 753/2000 of 26 March 2001.

[110] The applicable substantive law was Austrian law, chosen by the parties in their licensing agreement. The case was resolved in arbitration conducted at the ICC International Court of Arbitration (AA, Case No. ICC 8798 of 8 July 1998).

[111] Preceding decisions: (i) Resolution of the DC in Ústí nad Orlicí, Case No. 5E 1245/98-18 (annotated separately in this book) and (ii) Resolution of the RC in Hradec Králové, Case No. 19 Co 337/99-42 of 30 November 1999 (also annotated separately). The case concerned recognition/enforcement of an AA rendered in arbitration at the ICC International Court of Arbitration (AA, Case No. ICC 8798 of 8 July 1998). See also identical decisions rendered with respect to enforcement of the same AA:

» Resolution of the SC, Case No. 21 Cdo 1876/2000 of 27 March 2001, and

» Resolution of the SC, Case No. 21 Cdo 258/2000 of 27 March 2001.

applicable law by the arbitrators. **(3)** Section 251 of the CCP[112] applies to the enforcement of decisions rendered in civil court proceedings, as well as to the enforcement of other titles listed in Section 274 of the CCP.[113] **(4)** When enforcing a decision [i.e. including a foreign arbitral award], the court is not allowed to review the correctness of the merits of the enforced decision or another enforcement title. The court is bound by, and obliged to observe, the contents of the decision (another enforcement title), i.e. the operative part thereof, the enforcement of which is proposed. **(5)** The obligor (debtor) argues that the [foreign] arbitral award proposed for enforcement is contrary to Czech public policy. This is because the arbitrator concluded in the reasons for the arbitral award that "Austrian law shall also govern the guarantee provided by the original contracting party for commitments arising from the licensing agreement which the other contracting party breached". This was concluded despite the fact that "the debtor could not, after the takeover of the privatized property, influence in any manner the performance or non-performance of the obligations under the licensing agreement by the new contracting party" and that "the Austrian party knew about the transfer of rights and obligations to the new contracting party and negotiated with the new party with respect to the licensing agreement". (This should have constituted grounds for a refusal to enforce the decision against the debtor pursuant to Article V(2)(b) of the NYConv.) Hence, the debtor's arguments are not in fact challenging the requirements for opening the enforcement proceedings (and only these requirements can be subject to review), but the correctness of the merits of the arbitral award proposed for enforcement.

11.50. **Resolution of the SC, Case No. 20 Cdo 82/2001 of 12 September 2002:[114] [passing of arbitration agreement as a result of sale of property; privatization; recognition and enforcement; NYConv; temporal scope of the ArbAct] (1)** If the case concerns an arbitral award made in a foreign country and the main contract (in the present case, the licensing agreement) was concluded on 25 February 1991 and contains an

---

[112]   (Cit.:) *"Unless the debtor voluntarily performs the obligation imposed by the enforceable decision, the creditor may file a motion to enforce the decision by court."*

[113]   However, arbitral awards cannot be classified as titles under Section 274(h) of the CCP, but as titles under Section 274(c) of the CCP.

[114]   The preceding stages of the litigation involved the following decisions: (i) Resolution of the DC in Ústí n. Orlicí, Case No. 5 E 1357/99-23 of 20 January 2000 (as amended by Corrective Resolution of 28 January 2000) and (ii) Resolution of the RC in Hradec Králové, Case No. 19 Co 120/2000-39 of 5 October 2000.
As concerns the same arbitral award, see also the annotation of Resolution of the SC, Case No. 21 Cdo 1511/2000 of 29 March 2001 and the associated decisions cited in a footnote.

agreement stipulating that all disputes arising from the contract shall be finally resolved according to the Rules of Conciliation and Arbitration at the International Chamber of Commerce in Paris [ICC Rules], by one or more arbitrators appointed in accordance with the said Rules (arbitration agreement), then the case must be assessed pursuant to Act No. 98/1963 Coll., on Arbitration in International Commercial Transactions and Enforcement of Arbitral Awards (cf. Section 48 of the ArbAct). **(2)** The New York Convention (NYConv) has become part of the laws of the Czech Republic (cf. Article I of Constitutional Act No. 4/1993 Coll., on Measures Relating to the Dissolution of the Czech and Slovak Federal Republic). Due to the fact that the Convention applies to the recognition and enforcement of arbitral awards made in the territory of a state other than the state where the recognition and enforcement of such awards are sought, and arising out of differences between persons, whether physical or legal (first sentence of Article I(1) of the NYConv), the recognition and enforcement of the arbitral award in this case shall be governed by the NYConv, considering Section 35 of Act No. 98/1963 Coll. **(3)** The assessment of recognition and enforcement or the possibility to refuse recognition/enforcement depends on whether the debtor or, as in the present case, the legal predecessor of the debtor entered into the arbitration agreement and whether the rights and obligations arising from the concluded arbitration agreement were passed on to the debtor. Although the agreement lacks information about legal form, it is sufficient if the agreement contains information which allows an unequivocal identification of the party to the agreement. **(4)** The transfer of rights and obligations of a particular entity to a new entity pursuant to Act No. 92/1991 Coll., on Conditions of Transfer of State Property to Other Parties, also entailed the transfer of rights and obligations arising from an arbitration agreement. Pursuant to Section 15(1) of Act No. 92/2001 Coll., the (ownership) title to the privatized property is transferred to the transferee together with the other rights and obligations relating to the privatized property. In the given case, this applied to rights to intangible assets as well as arbitration clauses relating to the use of such rights (here the licensing agreement). **(5)** The transfer of tangible and intangible assets, or the transfer of rights, obligations, and claims,[115] also

---

[115]   Here pursuant to Act No. 92/1991 Coll., as subsequently amended. But this *ratio decidendi* intentionally generalizes the postulate; if it applies to this special case, there is no reason to doubt that the conclusion also applies to succession in general.

entails the transfer of rights and obligations under arbitration agreements connected with these rights and obligations.

11.51. Resolution of the SC, Case No. 20 Cdo 456/2003 of 28 January 2004:[116] **[recognition and enforcement of a foreign AA; grounds for a refusal of recognition and enforcement; NYConv] (1)** As concerns the recognition and enforcement of a foreign arbitral award, it is irrelevant whether the court proceeded pursuant to the ArbAct and not pursuant to Act No. 98/1963 Coll. (the arbitration agreement was entered into on 15 December 1994), if the law to be applied is the NYConv. The regime of application of the NYConv is the same whether the case is governed by the ArbAct or by the previous law. **(2)** The objection of an incorrect application of substantive law concerns the proceedings preceding the execution and is irrelevant with respect to recognition and enforcement of the arbitral award. **(3)** The recognition and enforcement of a decision principally only depend on fulfillment of the requirements stipulated in Article IV of the NYConv. **(4)** In the proceedings for ordering execution – in which neither the first-instance court nor the court of appeals need to summon a hearing[117] – the prerequisites which allow the motion to be granted are usually ascertained from the documents, without the court examining any evidence. This implies that when considering the possibility of enforcing the arbitral award,[118] the court examines, of its own motion, only the circumstances listed in Article V(2)(a) and (b) of the NYConv. **(5)** The existence of circumstances preventing the recognition and enforcement of a foreign arbitral award pursuant to Article V(1)(a) through (e) of the NYConv must be proven by the debtor. That is why the objections regarding such circumstances should be concentrated in the proceedings for terminating the execution.[119] The objection that the arbitral tribunal applied a different law to the dispute between the parties (Chinese law instead of Czech law) could therefore only be important in the proceedings for terminating the execution, if it were possible to classify such objection under Article V(1) of the NYConv at all.[120] *[From the factual and legal findings]:*

---

[116] The preceding stages of the litigation also involved the following decisions: (i) Resolution of the CDC for Prague 3, Case No. E-Nc 11622/2002-54 of 22 April 2002 and (ii) Resolution of the MC in Prague, Case No. 19 Co 266/2000-110. Also cited in: Ľuboš Fojtík; Lenka Macáková, *Otazníky nad uznáním a výkonem cizích rozhodčích nálezů.* [Title in translation: *Question Marks Over the Recognition and Enforcement of Foreign Arbitral Awards*], 6(5) PRÁVNÍ FÓRUM, 184–189 et al. (2009).

[117] Cf. Section 52(1) of the ExecProcC, Section 253(2), Section 214(2)(c) of the CCP.

[118] Section 40(1)(c) of the ExecProcC.

[119] Section 55(1) of the ExecProcC, Section 268(1)(h) of the CCP.

[120] The prevailing international opinion is that an error in the application of applicable law or an erroneous determination of applicable law is principally irrelevant in proceedings for recognition and enforcement of an arbitral award. Only very special circumstances would justify the possibility of annulment of the arbitral

The case concerned recognition and enforcement of an arbitral award rendered by the Chinese International Economic and Trade Arbitration Commission (CIETAC), No. 0193 of 1 June 1999. The first-instance court ordered enforcement and charged an executor with implementing the execution. The court of appeals upheld the decision. The petitioner raised objections to the proceedings, arguing that the decision was rendered without a hearing and without examining the evidence proposed by him (witness interrogation) and that the courts accepted a trade licensing certificate issued by an administrative authority of the People's Republic of China as the only evidence of existence of the claimant as a legal person under foreign law. The Supreme Court dismissed the cassation appeal.

11.52. **Resolution of the ConCourt, Case No. IV. ÚS 189/10 of 10 May 2010**: An objection that the arbitral award is not **stamped with a confirmation of legal force and effect and the confirmation of enforceability** is incongruous. The reason is that the [NYConv], which prevails over statutes, namely Section 39 [of the ArbAct], does not prescribe any such requirement (cf. Article IV [of the NYConv]). It is sufficient if the arbitral award is final and binding upon the parties and that the parties undertake to perform under the award without delay (cf. Article 32.2 of the UNCITRAL Rules).[121] *[For other rationes decidendi and a summary of the factual and legal findings, see the commentary to Section 39 of the ArbAct.]*

V. Comparison with the law of the Slovak Republic (SlovArbAct)[122]

PART EIGHT - RECOGNITION AND ENFORCEMENT OF ARBITRAL AWARD

Domestic arbitral award

11.53. Section 44

    (1) A domestic arbitral award is an award made in the territory of the Slovak Republic.

    (2) A domestic arbitral award which has become final and conclusive becomes enforceable in the Slovak Republic

---

award under the *lex arbitri* in the state of the seat of arbitration (place where the arbitral award was made) if it were proven that the arbitrators refused to address the issue of applicable law. However, the situation would also have to involve breach of the equality of the parties and failure to provide one of the parties with an opportunity to assert his or her rights in consequence of the above-mentioned circumstances.

[121] The author has applied the uniform terminology chosen for this book. The original of the ConCourt judgment refers to „Rozhodčí řád UNCITRAL" ("UNCITRAL Arbitration Rules").

[122] See also the following provisions:

»   CCP [SVK] – Sections 250w through 250y, Section 261;

»   Act No. 233/1995 Coll., on Judicial Executors and Executory Activities (Executory Procedure Code)

pursuant to special laws upon expiration of the time limit for performance.[15])

[15]) Section 274(h) of the Code of Civil Procedure. Section 41(2) of Act of the Slovak National Council No. 233/1995 Coll., on Judicial Executors and Executory Activities (Executory Procedure Code) and Amending and Supplementing Other Legislation, as subsequently amended.

11.54. Section 45

(1) The court with jurisdiction over enforcement or execution pursuant to special laws [16]) terminates the enforcement or the execution at the request of a party against whom the enforcement of the arbitral award is sought: **(a)** for grounds specified in a special law, [17]) **(b)** if the arbitral award suffers from a defect specified in Section 40(a) and (b), or **(c)** if the arbitral award orders the party to the arbitration to provide performance which is objectively impossible, unlawful or contra bonos mores.

(2) The court with jurisdiction over enforcement or execution shall terminate the enforcement of the arbitral award or the execution of its own motion (sua sponte) if the court discovers that the arbitration suffered from defects specified in subsection 1(b) or (c).

(3) The court decisions under subsections 1 and 2 can be appealed.

[16]) Section 252 of the Code of Civil Procedure. Section 45 of Act of the Slovak National Council No. 233/1995 Coll., as subsequently amended.

[17]) Section 268 of the Code of Civil Procedure. Section 57 of Act of the Slovak National Council No. 233/1995 Coll., as subsequently amended.

Foreign arbitral award

11.55. Section 46

(1) For the purposes of this Act, a foreign arbitral award means an arbitral decision in the merits which was

rendered in arbitration and which was made in the territory of a state other than the Slovak Republic.

(2) A foreign arbitral award can be recognized and enforced in the Slovak Republic subject to the conditions stipulated by this Act.

11.56. Section 47

(1) A party to the proceedings who requests recognition and enforcement of a foreign arbitral award must submit the written petition for recognition and enforcement of the foreign arbitral award together with the original of the foreign arbitral award, or a certified copy thereof, and the original of the arbitration agreement, or a certified copy thereof.

(2) If the foreign arbitral award or the arbitration agreement are not written in the official language of the Slovak Republic, the party shall arrange for their official translation into this official language.

11.57. Section 48

If a motion to annul the foreign arbitral award was filed abroad, the court in the Slovak Republic may suspend enforceability of the foreign arbitral award at the request of the party who filed the motion to annul the foreign arbitral award.

11.58. Section 49

(1) A foreign arbitral award shall be recognized without any special decision being required. A foreign arbitral award is recognized by the award being taken into consideration by the court with jurisdiction over the enforcement or execution, as if it were a domestic arbitral award.

(2) A foreign arbitral award shall be enforced in the Slovak Republic just like a domestic arbitral award.

11.59. Section 50

(1) The court may refuse recognition and enforcement of a foreign arbitral award at the request of a party to the proceedings against whom it is invoked, only if that party furnishes to the competent court where the enforcement or the execution is sought, proof that: **(a)** as a party to the arbitration agreement (Section 3(1)), the party could not exercise his or her rights, or the arbitration agreement was not concluded in compliance with the law to which the parties have subjected it or, failing any indication thereon, under the law of the country where the award was made; **(b)** the party was not given proper notice of the appointment

Czech (& Central European) Yearbook of Arbitration®

of the arbitrator or of the arbitration proceedings or was otherwise unable to attend the arbitration for serious reasons specified explicitly in the petition; **(c)** the award deals with a difference not contemplated by or not falling within the terms of the submission to arbitration, or it contains decisions on matters excluded from arbitration under the law to which the parties have subjected the arbitration agreement or, failing any indication thereon, under the law of the country where the award was made; **(d)** the composition of the arbitral authority or the arbitral procedure was not in accordance with the agreement of the parties, or, failing such agreement, was not in accordance with the law of the country where the arbitration took place; or **(e)** the award has not yet become final and binding on the parties to the arbitration, or has been set aside or suspended by a court of the country in which, or under the law of which, that award was made.

(2) The court with jurisdiction over the enforcement or execution shall refuse recognition and enforcement of the foreign arbitral award upon a motion of the party to the proceedings against whom the foreign arbitral award is invoked, or of the court's own motion if the court finds that the subject matter of the difference is not capable of settlement by arbitration under the law of the Slovak Republic, or the recognition and enforcement of the award would be contrary to the public policy.

(3) The court with jurisdiction over the enforcement or execution must always provide reasons for its decision whereby the recognition and enforcement of a foreign arbitral award are refused.

(4) The decision of the court whereby the recognition and enforcement of a foreign arbitral award are refused can be appealed.

VI. Bibliography

B. Ancel, *The Brussels I Regulation, Comment*, III YEARBOOK OF PRIVATE INTERNATIONAL LAW, Den Haag: Kluwer Law International (2001).

ENA-MARLIS BAJONS, ENFORCING ANNULLED ARBITRAL AWARDS: A COMPARATIVE VIEW, Croatian Arbitration Yearbook, Croatian Chamber of Commerce 55–69 (2000).

Patrick M. Baron; Stefan A. Liniger, *A Second Look at Arbitrability. Approaches to Arbitration in the United States, Switzerland and Germany*, 1 ARB. INT. 32 et seq. (2003).

Alexander J. Bělohlávek, *Rozhodčí řízení – spása při řešení majetkových sporů?* [Title in translation: *Arbitration – Salvation in the Resolution of Property Disputes?*] 2 PRÁVNÍ RÁDCE (1995).

Alexander J. Bělohlávek, *Rozhodčí řízení v USA* [Title in translation: *Arbitration in the USA*], 3(I-Part I) (II-Part II) DHK (1995).

Alexander J. Bělohlávek; Vladimír Jašek, *Rozhodčí řízení v SRN*. [Title in translation: *Arbitration in the Federal Republic of Germany*], 4(4-Part I) 4(5- Part II) DHK 37-44 et 45-50 (1995).

Alexander J. Bělohlávek, *Výkon rozhodnutí na Slovensku – vzor pro nás?* [Title in translation: *The Enforcement of Decisions in Slovakia – A Model for Us?*] 3 PRÁVNÍ RÁDCE 11-12 (1997).

Alexander J. Bělohlávek; Vladimír Jašek, *Rozhodčí řízení v Rakousku.* [Title in translation: *Arbitration in Austria*], 5(17-Part I) 5(18-Part II) DHK 175-181 et 185-191 (1997).

Alexander J. Bělohlávek; Vladimír Jašek, *Rozhodčí řízení na Slovensku z pohledu české právní úpravy* [Title in translation: *Arbitration in Slovakia from the Perspective of Czech Laws*], 6(16) 185-2000 DHK (1998).

ALEXANDER J. BĚLOHLÁVEK, MIŽNARODNIJ TORGOVIJ ARBIRAŽ / INTERNATIONAL COMMERCIAL ARBITRATION, Kiev: Taxon (1998).[123]

Alexander J. Bělohlávek, *Uznání a výkon rozhodnutí německých orgánů majetkové věci.* [Title in translation: *The Recognition and Enforcement of Decisions Rendered by German Authorities – Property Matters*], 2 PRÁVNÍ RÁDCE 27 et seq. (1999).

Alexander J. Bělohlávek, *Nové perspektivy pro výkon zahraničních rozhodnutí a tzv. Luganská úmluva.* [Title in translation: *New Perspectives for the Enforcement of Foreign Decisions and the Lugano Convention*], 1 PRÁVNÍ PRAXE V PODNIKÁNÍ 37–40 (1999).

Alexander J. Bělohlávek, *Zavedení tzv. exequatur do českého právního řádu.* [Title in translation: *The Introduction of So-Called Exequatur in Czech Law*], 5 PRÁVNÍ ZPRAVODAJ 16-17 (2004).

Alexander J. Bělohlávek, *Pravomoci soudců a výkon rozhodnutí v kontextu vývoje evropského civilního procesu.* [Title in translation: *Powers of Judges and the Enforcement of Decisions in the Context of Developments in the European Civil Procedure*], 12 PRÁVNÍ RÁDCE 15-19 (2004).

---

[123] Bilingual – Ukrainian and English.

ALEXANDER BĚLOHLÁVEK, ROZHODČÍ ŘÍZENÍ, ORDRE PUBLIC A TRESTNÍ PRÁVO: INTERAKCE MEZINÁRODNÍHO A TUZEMSKÉHO PRÁVA SOUKROMÉHO A VEŘEJNÉHO. [Title in translation: ARBITRATION, ORDRE PUBLIC AND CRIMINAL LAW: INTERACTION BETWEEN INTERNATIONAL AND DOMESTIC PRIVATE AND PUBLIC LAW], Volumes I and II, Prague: C. H. Beck, (2008).

Alexander J. Bělohlávek, *Czech Republic: Procedure for Recognition and Enforcement of New York Convention Awards*, 727E GUIDE TO NATIONAL RULES OF PROCEDURE FOR RECOGNITION AND ENFORCEMENT OF NEW YORK CONVENTION AWARDS, ICC Publication, Paris: International Chamber of Commerce / ICC Publishing 98-102 (2009).

Alexander J. Bělohlávek, *West Tankers as a Trojan Horse with Respect to the Autonomy of Arbitration Proceedings and the New York Convention 1958: On the contentious concept of the importance of the disputed subject matter in light of subsequent decisions on the fate of anti-suit injunctions from the vantage point of Brussels-Luxembourg officialdom*, 4 ASA BULLETIN, Basel / Den Haag: ASA / KLI 646 – 670 (2009).

ALEXANDER J. BĚLOHLÁVEK, MEZINÁRODNÍ PRÁVO SOUKROMÉ EVROPSKÝCH ZEMÍ. [Title in translation: PRIVATE INTERNATIONAL LAW OF EUROPEAN COUNTRIES], Prague: C. H. Beck (2010).

Alexander J. Bělohlávek, *Pojem investice z pohledu mezinárodněprávní ochrany (podmínky ratione materiae, ratione tempori a ratione voluntatis pro využití mechanismů mezinárodní ochrany investic).* [Title in translation: *The Concept of Investments from the Perspective of International Protection (Requirements Ratione Materiae, Ratione Tempori and Ratione Voluntatis for the Application of the Mechanisms of International Protection of Investments)*], 19(3-PartI) 19(4-Part II) OBCHODNÍ PRÁVO 2-26 et 2-18 (2010).

Alexander J. Bělohlávek, Rozhodčí řízení v tzv. smluvních vztazích spotřebitelského typu. [Title in translation: *Arbitration in So-Called Consumer Contractual Relationships*], 7(3) PRFO 89-99 (2010).

Denis Bensaude, *The International Law Association's Recommendations on Res Judicata and Lis Pendens in International Commercial Arbitration*, 4 JOURNAL OF INTERNATIONAL ARBITRATION (2007).

Jean-Paul Beraudo, *Recognition and Enforcement of Interim Measures of Protection Ordered by Arbitral Tribunals*, 3 JOURNAL OF INTERNATIONAL ARBITRATION 247–252 (2005).

Albert J. van den Berg, *Non-domestic Arbitral Awards under the 1958 New York Convention*, 2(3) ARBITRATION INTERNATIONAL (1986).

Albert J. van den Berg, *The Application of the New York Convention by the Court*, 9 IMPROVING THE EFFICIENCY OF ARBITRATION AGREEMENTS AND AWARDS: 40 YEARS OF APPLICATION OF THE NEW YORK CONVENTION, ICCA CONGRESS SERIES 1998, Den Haag: KLI 28 et seq (1999).

ALBERT J. VAN DEN BERG, THE NEW YORK ARBITRATION CONVENTION OF 1958, Den Haag: T.M.C. Asser Institute (1981).

Albert J. van den Berg, *The New York Convention: Summary of Court Decisions*, THE NEW YORK CONVENTION OF 1958: A COLLECTION OF REPORTS AND MATERIALS DELIVERED AT THE ASA CONFERENCE HELD IN ZURICH ON 2ND FEBRUARY 1996, Zurich: ASA (1996).

KLAUS P. BERGER, DIE REGELUNG DER GERICHTLICHEN ANFECHTBARKEIT INTERNATIONALER SCHIEDSSPRÜCHE IN EUROPÄISCHEN SCHIEDSGERICHTSGESETZEN, RIW 850–857 (1989).

T. R Bertheau, *Das New Yorker Abkommen vom 10. Juni 1958 über die Anerkennung und Vollstreckung ausländischer Schiedssprüche*, DISSERTATION THESIS SUCCESSFULLY DEFENDED AT THE UNIVERSITY OF ZÜRICH (1965).

R. Birne, *The Arbitrability of Intellectual Property Disputes with Particular Emphasis on the Situation in Switzerland*, 728 WIPO PUBLICATION (1994).

Marc Blessing, *Mandatory Rules of Law versus Party Autonomy in International Arbitration* 4 JIA 23 et seq (1997).

Karl-Heinz Böckstiegel, *Public Policy and Arbitrability*, 3 COMPARATIVE ARBITRATION PRACTICE AND PUBLIC POLICY IN ARBITRATION, ICCA CONGRESS SERIES 177 et seq. (Peter Sanders ed., 1987). In KARL-HEINZ BÖCKSTIEGEL, SCHIEDSGERICHTSBARKEIT IM UMFELD VON POLITIK, WIRTSCHAFT UND GERICHTSBARKEIT, Köln a. R.: Carl Heymann (1992).

Karl-Heinz Böckstiegel, *Die Bedeutung der Schiedsgerichtsbarkeit im gegenwärtigen politischen und wirtschaftlichen Umfeld*, SCHIEDSGERICHTSBARKEIT IM UMFELD VON POLITIK, WIRTSCHAFT UND GERICHTSBARKEIT, Köln a. R.: Carl Heymann 17 et seq. (Karl-Heinz Böckstiegel ed.,1992).

MICHAEL BOGDAN, THE BRUSSELS JURISDICTION AND ENFORCEMENT CONVENTION: AN EC COURT CASEBOOK, Stockholm: Kluwer Law International (1996).

GEORG BORGES, DAS DOPPELEXEQUATUR VON SCHIEDSSPRÜCHEN: DIE ANERKENNUNG AUSLÄNDISCHER SCHIEDSSPRÜCHE UND EXEQUATURENSCHEIDUNGEN (1977).

Georg Borges, *Die Anerkennung und Vollstreckung von Schiedssprüchen nach dem neuen Schiedsverfahrensrecht*, 111 ZZP 487–513 (1998).

Alexander Brunns, *Der anerkennungsrechtliche ordre public in Europa und den USA*, JZ 278–287 (1999).

Alfred Burgstaller, *Vollstreckung ausländischer Schiedssprüche in Österreich. Zeitschrift für Rechtsvergleichung*, 41(3) INTERNATIONALES PRIVATRECHT UND EUROPARECHT 83–93 (2000).

Katarína Chovancová, *Enforcement of Arbitral Awards in the New Countries of the European Union*, 16(6) EUROPEAN REVIEW OF PRIVATE LAW 995-1007 (2008).

Katarína Chovancová, *Medzinárodná obchodná arbitráž – definícia a charakteristika*. [Title in translation: *International Commercial Arbitration – Definition and Characteristics*], 9(1) OBCHODNÉ PRÁVO (2008).

Katarína Chovancová, *Res iudicata v medzinárodnej arbitrážnej praxis*, [Title in translation: *Res Judicata in International Arbitration Practice*], 14(9-Part I) 14(10-Part II) BULLETIN SLOVENSKEJ ADVOKÁCIE 29-38 et 20-28 (2008).

Anthony Cioni, *The First Pancake Always Has Lumps: Alberta Petroleum Companies, Arbitration and Arbitral Award Enforcement in the Russian Federation*, 35 Alberta Law Review 726 et seq. (1997).

Thomas Clay, *La Convention de New York vue par la doctrine française*, 26(3) ASA BULLETIN 467-478 (2008).

Gilles Cuniberti, *England - Enforcement of Arbitration Agreements: The End of the English Exception. Enforcement of Arbitration Agreements by Anti-Suit Injunctions in Europe - From Turner to West Tankers*, 9 YEARBOOK OF PRIVATE INTERNATIONAL LAW 449-458 (2007).

Josef Černohlávek, *Konkurzní řízení s mezinárodním prvkem*, [Title in translation: *Bankruptcy with an International Dimension*], 9 BULLETIN ADVOKACIE 25 et seq. (1996).

RENÉ DAVID, ARBITRATION IN INTERNATIONAL TRADE, Deventer (1985).

V. S. Deshpande, *Jurisdiction Over Foreign and Domestic Awards in the New York Convention, 1958*, 7(2) ARBITRATION INTERNATIONAL 123–136 (1991).

DOMENICO DIPIETRO; MARTIN PLATTE, ENFORCEMENT OF INTERNATIONAL ARBITRATION AWARDS - THE NEW YORK CONVENTION, London: Cameron May (2001).

Petr Dobiáš, *Uznání a výkon rozhodčích nálezů zrušených ve státě původu podle relevantní judikatury zahraničních obecných soudů*. [Title in translation: *The Recognition and Enforcement of Arbitral Awards Annulled in the State of Origin Pursuant to the Relevant Case Law of Foreign Courts*], 146(3) PRÁVNÍK 325-336 (2007).

Petr Dobiáš, *Uznání a výkon cizích rozhodčích nálezů ve Spolkové republice Německo podle judikatury německých obecných soudů*. [Title in translation: *The Recognition and Enforcement of Foreign Arbitral Awards in the Federal Republic of Germany According to the Case Law of German Courts*], 1 ACTA UNIVERSITATIS CAROLINAE – IURIDICA 37-47 (2008).

Klára Drličková, *Deletion of the Arbitration Exception in the Regulation Brussels I – The Way Towards the European Regulation of Arbitration?*, HARMONIZATION AND UNIFICATION OF LAW IN THE EUROPEAN CONTEXT, BRATISLAVA: KOMENSKÝ UNIVERSITY IN BRATISLAVA, FACULTY OF LAW 247-258 (2011).

Florian Eichel, *Inhaltskontrolle von AGB-Schiedsklauseln im internationalen Handelsverkehr*, 3 IPRAX (2010).

Josef Fiala, *Spory vznikající z podnětu výkonu rozhodnutí (exekuční spory)* [Title in translation: *Disputes Arising from Enforcement Proceedings (Execution Disputes)*], ACTA UNIVERSITATIS CAROLINAE – IURIDICA. MONOGRAPHIA XVI, PRAGUE: CHARLES UNIVERSITY (1972).

Ľuboš Fojtík; Lenka Macáková, *Otazníky nad uznáním a výkonem cizích rozhodčích nálezů*. [Title in translation: *Question Marks Over the Recognition and Enforcement of Foreign Arbitral Awards*], 6(5) PRÁVNÍ FORUM 184-189 (2009).

Emmanuel Gaillard, *Enforcement of Awards Set Aside in the Country of Origin: The French Experience*, IMPROVING THE EFFICIENCY OF ARBITRATION AGREEMENTS AND AWARDS: 40 YEARS OF APPLICATION OF THE NEW YORK CONVENTION. ICCA INTERNATIONAL ARBITRATION CONFERENCE, PARIS 507–509 (Albert J. van den Berg (ed.) 1998).

LOUIS GARB; JULIAN D. M. LEW, ENFORCEMENT OF FOREIGN JUDGMENTS, Den Haag: KLI (1994).

HAMID G. GHARAVI, INTERNATIONAL EFFECTIVENESS OF THE ANNULMENT OF AN ARBITRAL AWARD, Den Haag / New York: Kluwer Law International (2002).

Arfazadeh Hamayoon, *Arbitrability under the New York Convention: The Lex Fori Revised*, 1 ARB. INT. 85 et seq. (2001).

Bernard Hanotiau, *What Law Governs the Issue of Arbitrability*, 12 Arb. Int. 394 et seq. (1996).

Bernard Hanotiau, *The Law Applicable to Arbitrability*, 9 IMPROVING THE EFFICIENCY OF ARBITRATION AGREEMENTS AND AWARDS: 40 YEARS OF APPLICATION OF THE NEW YORK CONVENTION. IN: ICCA CONGRESS SERIES, (1998), Den Haag: KLI, (Albert J. van den Berg (ed.) 1999).

RAGNAR HARBST, DIE ROLLE DER STAATLICHEN GERICHTE IM SCHIEDSVERFAHREN: EIN RECHTSVERGLEICH ZWISCHEM DEM ENGLISCHEN ARBITRATION ACT 1996 UND DEM SCHIEDSVERFAHRENSRECHT, Heidelberg: Verlag Recht und Wirtschaft (2002).

Troy L. Harris, *The Public Policy Exception to Enforcement of International Arbitration Awards under the New York Convention*, 1 JIA 9-24 (2007).

M. K. Hentzen, *Enforcing Foreign Arbitral Awards in the Federal Republic of Germany: The Example of a United States Award*, 2 TRANSNATIONAL LAW 49 et seq. (1989).

PETR HLAVSA, EXEKUČNÍ ŘÁD S VÝKLADEM A PROVÁDĚCÍMI PŘEDPISY [Title in translation: EXECUTORY PROCEDURE CODE WITH A COMMENTARY AND IMPLEMENTING LEGISLATION], Prague: Linde 48–50 (2001).

Kaj I. Hobér, *Defenses to Recognition and Enforcement of Foreign Arbitral Awards in the United States*, 48 NORDISK TIDSSKRIFT FOR INTERNATIONAL RET 38-57 (1978).

Kaj I. Hobér, *Ogiltighet och klander i internationella skiljeförfaranden. Högsta domstolen meddelar beslut i Uganda-målet* [Title in translation: *Invalidity and Defense Against Arbitral Awards in International Arbitration. The Supreme Court Decides the Uganda case*], YEARBOOK OF THE ARBITRATION INSTITUTE OF THE STOCKHOLM CHAMBER OF COMMERCE (1989).

Kaj I. Hobér, *Arbitration and the Swedish Courts*, YEARBOOK OF THE ARBITRATION INSTITUTE OF THE STOCKHOLM CHAMBER OF COMMERCE 56 et seq. (1990).

Kaj I. Hobér, *Enforcing Foreign Arbitral Awards Against Russian Entities*, 35 ACTA JURIDICA HUNGARICA 257-304 (1993).

Kaj I. Hobér, *Enforcing Foreign Arbitral Awards Against Russian Entities*, 10(1) ARB. INT. (1994).

GÜNTHER J. HORVATH, THE DUTY OF THE TRIBUNAL TO RENDER AN ENFORCEABLE AWARD, JIA 135 et seq. (1994).

ZHENJIE HU, CHINESE PERSPECTIVES ON INTERNATIONAL JURISDICTION AND THE ENFORCEMENT OF JUDGMENTS IN CONTRACTUAL MATTERS: A COMPARATIVE STUDY OF THE RELEVANT PROVISIONS OF CHINESE, SWISS AND US

LAW, OF THE EUROPEAN CONVENTIONS AND OF OTHER INTERNATIONAL TREATIES, Zürich: Schulthess (1999).

MICHAEL HWANG; ANDREW CHAN, ENFORCEMENT AND SETTING ASIDE OF INTERNATIONAL ARBITRAL AWARDS: THE PERSPECTIVE OF COMMON LAW COUNTRIES. IN: INTERNATIONAL ARBITRATION AND NATIONAL COURTS: THE NEVER ENDING STORY 145 et seq. (2001).

IA. HCCH: *The Future Convention on Exclusive Choice of Court Agreements and Arbitration - Parallel proceedings and possible treaty conflicts, in particular with ICSID and the New York Convention on the Recognition and Enforcement of Foreign Arbitral Awards*, 3(5) TDM (2006).

Jean-Michel Jacquet, *La fonction supranationale de la règle de conflits de lois*, REC. DES COURS DE LA HAYE, T.292 151-248 (2002).

Milan Jančo, *Aktuálne otázky koncepcie absolútnej neplatnosti právnych úkonov podľa § 39 Obč. zákonníka.* [Title in translation: *Current Issues of the Concept of Invalidity of Juridical Acts Pursuant to Section 39 of the Civil Code*], 14(10-PartI) 14(11-PartII) BULLETIN SLOVENSKEJ ADVOKÁCIE, 29-38 et 32-40.

Robert M. Jarvis, *The Use of Civil Rico in International Arbitration: Some Thoughts After Shearson/American Express v. McMahon*, 1 TRANSNATIONAL LAW 1–41 (1988).

DAVID JOSEPH, JURISDICTION AND ARBITRATION AGREEMENTS AND THEIR ENFORCEMENT, London: Sweet & Maxwell (2005).

Roman Kozel, *Věcná příslušnost soudů podle § 9 odst. 3 písm. a) o. s. ř.* [Title in translation: *The Subject-Matter Jurisdiction of Courts Under Section 9(3)(a) of the CCP*], 6-7 BULLETIN ADVOKACIE 45 et seq. (1997).

HERBERT KRONKE; PATRICIA NACIMIENTO; DIRK OTTO; NICOLA CHR. PORT, RECOGNITION AND ENFORCEMENT OF FOREIGN ARBITRAL AWARDS: A GLOBAL COMMENTARY ON THE NEW YORK CONVENTION, Alphen aan den Rijn: KLI (2010).

VLADIMÍR KURKA; LJUBOMÍR DRÁPAL, VÝKON ROZHODNUTÍ V SOUDNÍM ŘÍZENÍ [Title in translation: ENFORCEMENT OF DECISIONS IN COURT PROCEEDINGS], Prague: Linde (2004).

Pierre Lalive, *Absolute Finality of Arbitral Awards?* 6 REVISTA INTERNACIONAL DE ARBITRAGEM E CONCILIAÇÃO, ASSOCIAÇÃO, PORTUGUESA DE ARBITRAGEM 109-127 (2008).

C. B. Lamm, et F. Sperenberg, *The Enforcement of Foreign Arbitral Awards under the New York Convention: Recent Developments*, 2001(2) STOCKHOLM ARBITRATION REPORT 4-9 (2001).

FRANZ LASCHET, ZUR ANERKENNUNG AUSLÄNDISCHER ZWISCHENSCHIEDSSPRÜCHE, Praxis des Internationalen Privat- und Verfahrensrechtes 72 et seq. (1984).

Pierre Lastenouse, *Why Setting Aside an Arbitral Award is Not Enough to Remove It from the International Scene*, JOURNAL OF INTERNATIONAL ARBITRATION, KLUWER LAW INTERNATIONAL (1999).

Laurent Levy; Elliott Geisiner, *Lis Alibi Pendens in International Commercial Arbitration*, ICC BULLETIN, SPECIAL SUPPLEMENT, COMPLEX ARBITRATION 55-73 (2003).

Josef Macur, *Kurs občanského práva procesního – Exekuční právo.* [Title in translation: *Course in the Law of Civil Procedure – The Law of Enforcement (Execution)*], Prague: C. H. Beck.

ULRICH MAGNUS; PETER MANKOWSKI; ALFONSO-LUIS C. CARAVACA; JOHN BLAKELEY, BRUSSELS I REGULATION, München: Sellier European Law Publishers (2007).

Fernando Mantilla-Serrano, *Towards a Transnational Procedural Public Policy*, 20(4) ARB. INT. 334 et seq.

Vilém Másílko, *Výkon rozhodnutí s cizím prvkem, vydaného řádným či rozhodčím soudem.* [Title in translation: *The Enforcement of Decisions with a Foreign Dimension, Made by Courts or Arbitral Tribunals*], PRÁVNÍ ZPRAVODAJ ČESKOSLOVENSKÉHO ZAHRANIČNÍHO OBCHODU. PRAGUE: CZECHOSLOVAK CHAMBER OF COMMERCE AND INDUSTRY (1980).

ANTON G. MAURER, THE PUBLIC POLICY EXCEPTION UNDER THE NEW YORK CONVENTION: HISTORY, INTERPRETATION AND APPLICATION. HUNTINGTON, New York: Juris Net (2012).

Pierre Mayer; Audley Sheppard, *Final ILA Report on Public Policy as a Bar to Enforcement of International Arbitral Awards*, 19(2) ARB. INT. 249-263.

Richard B. von Mehren, *The Eco-Swiss Case and International Arbitration*, 4 ARB. INT. 468 et seq. (2003).

Mezger, *Nochmals zur Anerkennung ausländischer Zwischenschiedssprüche*, PRAXIS DES INTERNATIONALEN PRIVAT- UND VERFAHRENSRECHTES 194 et seq. (1984).

LOUKAS A. MISTELIS, ARBITRABILITY – INTERNATIONAL AND COMPARATIVE PERSPECTIVES, Arbitrability: International & Comparative Perspective, Alphen aan den Rijn: KLI 49 et seq. (Loukas A. Mistelis et Stavros L. Brekoulakis ed., 2009)

Peter Molnár, *Uznávanie vykonateľnosti cudzích exekučných titulov v Slovenskej republike.* [Title in translation: *Recognition of Enforceability of*

Czech (& Central European) Yearbook of Arbitration®

Foreign Enforcement Titles in the Slovak Republic], 14(1-2) BULLETIN SLOVENSKEJ ADVOKÁCIE 8-12 (2008).

Aleksandr I. Muranov, *Nekotoryje probljemy priznanija i privedenija v ispolnenie rešenij morskoj arbitražnoj komissiji pri torgovo promyšljennoj palate Rossijskoj federaciji* [Title in translation: *Selected Issues of the Recognition and Enforcement of Decisions Made by the Maritime Arbitral Commission at the Chamber of Commerce and Industry of the Russian Federation*], MOSKOVSKIJ ŽURNAL MEŽDUNARODNOGO PRAVA 35 et seq. (2001).

ALEKSANDR I. MURANOV, USPOLNENIJE INOSTRANNYCH SUDEBNYCH I ARBITRAŽNYCH REŠENIJ. KOMPETENCIJA ROSSIJSKUCH SUDOV, Moscow: Justicinform (2002).

Tamara N. Nešataeva, *Obščije zamječanija po voprosu o priznaniji i ispolneniji rešenij sudov i arbitražej po ekonomičeskim sporam*, 3 SPECIJALNOJE PRILOŽENIJE K VJESTNIKU VAS RF (1999).

Tamara N. Nešataeva, *O sudebnom kontrole za alternativnymi sposobami razrešenija predprinimatelskuch konfliktov*, 4 VOPROSY PRAVOPRIMENENIJA 23 (2001).

Ioannis M. Papagiannis, *Die Vollstreckung ausländischer Schiedssprüche nach ihrer Annullierung im Herkunftsstaat*, 98(2) ZVGLRWISS 139-174 (1999).

Jan Paulson, *Enforcing Arbitral Awards Notwithstanding a Local Standard Annulment (LSA)*, 9(1) ICC BULLETIN (1998).

Jan Paulson, *May or Must Under the New York Convention: An Exercise in Syntax and Linguistics*, 14(2) ARB. INT. 227 et seq. (1998).

Nina V. Pavlova, *Nekotoryje osnovanija otkaza i priznanii i privjedenii v ispolnenije arbitražnych rešenij*, 3 SPECIJALNOJE PRILOŽENIJE K VESTNIKU VYSŠEGO ARBITRAŽNOGO SUDA ROSSIJSKOJ FEDERACII, MOSCOW, 17–23 (1999).

Jill A. Pietrowski, *Enforcing International Commercial Arbitration Agreements: Post-Mitsubishi Motors Corp. v. Soler Chrysler-Plymouth*, 36 INC. AMERICAN UNIVERSITY LAW REVIEW 57 et seq. (1986).

John Prebble, *Choice of Law to Determine the Validity and Effect of Contracts: A Comparison of English and American Approaches to the Conflict of Laws*, 58 COLUMBIA LAW REVIEW 433 et seq. (1973).

Michael Pryles, *Foreign Awards and the New York Convention*, 9(3) ARBITRATION INTERNATIONAL (1993).

L. G. RADICATI DI BROZOLO, MONDIALISATION, JURIDICTION, ARBITRAGE: VERS DES REGLES D'APPLICATION SEMI-NECESSAIRES ? Rev. crit. DIP 1 et seq. (2003).

Czech (& Central European) Yearbook of Arbitration®

Pippa Reed, *Delocalization of International Commercial Arbitration: Its Relevance in the New Millennium*, 10 THE AMERICAN REVIEW OF INTERNATIONAL ARBITRATION 179–180 (1999).

David W. Rivkin, *Enforceability of Arbitral Awards based on Lex Mercatoria*, 9 ARB. INT. 67 et seq. (1993).

Andrew Rogers, *Arbitrability*, 3 ARB. INT. 263 et seq. (1994).

Kristin T. Roy, *The New York Convention and Saudi Arabia: Can a Country Use the Public Policy Defense to Refuse Enforcement of Non-Domestic Arbitral Awards?* 18 FORDHAM INTERNATIONAL LAW JOURNAL 920 et seq. (1995).

Naděžda Rozehnalová, *Rozhodčí řízení v mezinárodním a vnitrostátním obchodním styku*. [Title in translation: *Arbitration in International and National Commerce*], ASPI WOLTERS KLUWER (2008).

Květoslav Růžička, *Uznání a výkon cizích rozhodčích nálezů*. [Title in translation: *The Recognition and Enforcement of Foreign Arbitral Awards*], 8 PRÁVO A PODNIKÁNÍ 10 et seq. (1993).

Květoslav Růžička, *Rozhodčí řízení před Rozhodčím soudem při Hospodářské komoře České republiky a Agrární komoře České republiky* [Title in translation: *Arbitration in the Arbitration Court at the Economic Chamber of the Czech Republic and Agricultural Chamber of the Czech Republic*], DOBRÁ VODA U PELHŘIMOVA: ALEŠ ČENĚK 179–184 (2003).

Peter Sanders, *Comparative Arbitration Practice and Public Policy in Arbitration*, 3 ICCA CONGRESS SERIES (Peter Sanders ed., 1987).

FRANZ SATMER, VERWEIGERUNG DER ANERKENNUNG AUSLÄNDISCHER SCHIEDSSPRÜCHE WEGEN VERFAHRENSMÄNGELN, Zürich: Schulthess (1994).

Haimo Schack, *Höchstrichterliche Rechtsprechung zum Internationalen Privat- und Verfahrensrecht*, C.H.BECK´SCHE VERLAGSBUCHHANDLUNG, (2nd ed., 2000).

Peter Schlosser, *„Brüssel I" und Schiedsgerichtsbarkeit*, SCHIEDSVZ 129-139 (2009).

Karel Střelec, *K možnosti uznání a výkonu zrušeného cizího rozhodčího nálezu* [Title in translation: *Regarding the Possibility of Recognition and Enforcement of an Annulled Foreign Arbitral Award*], 3 BULLETIN ADVOKACIE 34–44 (2004).

Louise E. Teitz, *Both Sides of the Coin: A Decade of Parallel Proceedings and Enforcement of Foreign Judgments in Transnational Litigation*, 3(5) TDM (2006)

Johannes Trappe, *„Révision au fond" bei der Vollstreckung eines Schiedsspruchs – eine Anmerkung,* 2 RECHT UND PRAXIS DER SCHIEDSGERICHTSBARKEIT 7 et seq. (2000).

Antonín Tripes, *Exekuce v soudní praxi* [Title in translation: *Enforcement Proceedings (Execution) in the Practice of Courts*], Prague: C. H. Beck (2nd ed., 2001).

JAN VESELÝ; ADAM RAKOVSKÝ; PETR MIKŠOVSKÝ; RADKA ŠIMKOVÁ, ZÁKON O VEŘEJNÝCH DRAŽBÁCH, KOMENTÁŘ [Title in translation: THE PUBLIC AUCTIONS ACT, A COMMENTARY], Prague: C. H. Beck (2001).

J. VOSKA, KOMENTÁŘ KE KONKURSNÍMU ŘÁDU (64/1931 SB.) [Title in translation: A COMMENTARY ON THE BANKRUPTCY CODE (64/1931 COLL.)], Prague (1931).

Peter Wahl, *Enforcement of Foreign Arbitral Awards Set Aside in Their Country of Origin. The Chromalloy Case Revisited,* 16(4) JOURNAL OF INTERNATIONAL ARBITRATION, KLUWER LAW INTERNATIONAL 131–140 (1999).

F. Weinacht, *Enforcement of Annulled Foreign Arbitral Awards in Germany. Journal of International Arbitration,* 19(4) KLUWER LAW INTERNATIONAL 330 et seq. (2002).

JAROSLAV ZELENKA, INSOLVENČNÍ ZÁKON (ZÁKON Č. 182/2006 SB.: POZNÁMKOVÉ VYDÁNÍ S DŮVODOVOU ZPRÁVOU A NAŘÍZENÍM RADY ES 1346/2000). [Title in translation: THE INSOLVENCY ACT (ACT NO. 182/2006 COLL.: ANNOTATED EDITION WITH EXPLANATORY MEMORANDUM AND COUNCIL REGULATION (EC) 1346/2000)], Prague: Linde (2007).

Michal Žižlavský, *Prodej nemovitosti správcem konkurzní podstaty,* [Title in translation: *The Sale of Real Property by a Bankruptcy Trustee*], 9 BULLETIN ADVOKACIE 38 et seq. (1996).

Section 39 [Refusal to enforce a foreign award][124]

Recognition or enforcement of a foreign arbitral award shall be refused if:

(a) The arbitral award is not final and conclusive or enforceable according to the law of the state where it was made,

(b) The arbitral award suffers from any of the defects listed in Section 31,

(c) The arbitral award is contrary to public policy.

Rules effective from 1 January 2014 (PIL):

[Recognition and enforcement of foreign arbitral awards][125]

Section 120 of the PIL

[Quoted in the commentary to Section 38 of the ArbAct.]

Section 121 of the PIL

Recognition or enforcement of a foreign arbitral award shall be refused if the foreign arbitral award:

a) Is not final and conclusive or enforceable according to the law of the state where it was made,

b) Was annulled in the state where it was made or according to the law of which it was made,

c) Suffers from a defect which constitutes grounds for annulment of a Czech arbitral award by the court, or

d) Is contrary to public policy.

Section 122 of the PIL

[Quoted in the commentary to Section 38 of the ArbAct.]

PART EIGHT – [TRANSITIONAL AND FINAL PROVISIONS]

Section 123 of the PIL [Transitional provisions]

(1) *[Quoted in the commentary to Sections 36 and 37 of the ArbAct.]*

(2) Proceedings commenced before the effective date of this Act shall continue to be governed by the provisions of the laws and regulations on the jurisdiction of Czech courts applicable until the effective date of this Act. This also applies to proceedings in matters of the recognition and enforcement of foreign decisions and foreign arbitral awards with respect to the conditions for their recognition and enforcement.

Related provisions: Sections 36, 38, 40, 47

Related laws: Article 38 of the UML; Articles V and VII of the NY-Conv;* Article IX of the EConv; PILP; Sections 120, 121, 122, 123, 124(16) of the PIL

[*The list of the NYConv signatories is available at: http://www.uncitral.org/uncitral/en/uncitral_texts/arbitration/NYConvention_status.html.][126]

---

124   This provision is repealed with effect from 1 January 2014 and will be materially replaced with Section 117 of the PIL. See Section 124(16) of Act No. 91/2012, on Private International Law (PIL).
125   This heading is part of the quoted normative text.
126   On the day the manuscript of this book was finished, the NYConv status included 146 states.

I. Priority application of the rules of international origin

11.60. Giving priority application to the rules of international origin is very frequent in international practice, especially in connection with the enforcement of foreign arbitral awards. The oldest and most successful treaty relating to arbitration is the New York Convention (NYConv),[127] ratified by 146 states,[128] which regulates the recognition of foreign arbitral awards in states which are bound by the Convention. Article V of the NYConv contains an exhaustive list of alternative grounds justifying the refusal of recognition of an arbitral award. The grounds listed in Article V(1) of the NYConv may only be applied if invoked by the party against whom the enforcement is sought. They include invalidity of the arbitration agreement (subparagraph (a)), breach of the right to present one's case (subparagraph (b)), decision *ultra petita* (subparagraph (c)), incorrect constitution of the arbitral panel (subparagraph (d)), and a situation where the arbitral award has not yet become binding (subparagraph (e)). The grounds specified in Article V(2) of the NYConv may be applied by the national court of its own motion (*sua sponte*). Such grounds include lack of arbitrability of the dispute (subparagraph (a)) and violation of public policy (subparagraph (b)).

11.61. In the countries which have adopted the NYConv and whose lex arbitri is based on the UNCITRAL Model Law (UML),[129] the NYConv principally prevails, in compliance with the principle of precedence (preferential application) of the law of international origin (an international treaty). This also applies in the Czech Republic in terms of Section 47 of the ArbAct,[130] in conjunction with Article 10 of the Constitution. However, the structure of Article 36(1) of the UML is identical to the structure of Article V of the NYConv and lists the same grounds for which a national court may refuse recognition and enforcement of a foreign arbitral award.

11.62. Another important treaty is the European Convention on International Commercial Arbitration of 1961 ("EConv").[131] The EConv, however, does not primarily focus on the enforcement of arbitral awards; the provisions of the EConv regulating these

---

[127] Available at: http://www.uncitral.org/pdf/english/texts/arbitration/NY-conv/XXII_1_e.pdf (accessed on 15 February 2019)

[128] Available at: http://www.uncitral.org/uncitral/en/uncitral_texts/arbitration/NYConvention_status.html (accessed on 15 February 2019)

[129] Naturally, not only in these countries. It is a broadly applied principle.

[130] With effect from 1 January 2014, see also Section 2 of the PIL.

[131] European Convention on International Commercial Arbitration, done in Geneva on 21 April 1961.

matters are based on the NYConv.[132] Nevertheless, it does not limit the grounds for the refusal to enforce an award by limiting the consequences of the annulment of the award in the country where it was made. This Convention has been signed by 32 states.

II. Rules of national origin applicable where rules of international origin cannot be applied (Section 39 of the ArbAct / 121 of the PIL)

11.63. The annulment of an arbitral award by a court is a procedure conducted in the state where the arbitral award was made. By contrast, the proceedings for recognition or enforcement of a foreign arbitral award are conducted in a country different from the country in which the arbitral award was made. (This is naturally subject to the condition that the law of the state where the proceedings are conducted is familiar with the proceedings for annulment of an arbitral award.) Hence, it becomes necessary to answer the crucial issue[133] of exterritoriality (existence or non-existence) of the effects of the decision on annulment of the award in the country of enforcement. The answer to this question is all the more important with regard to the fact that, as opposed to the arbitral award itself, the decision on annulment of the award is not a decision of an entity of private law. Such decision is that of an authority exercising the jurisdictional sovereignty of another state.

11.64. If the court determines that the grounds for a refusal of enforcement only affect part of the arbitral award, which is separable from other parts of the order of the arbitral award, then the other parts are enforceable.[134] It is necessary to emphasize, though, that partial recognition and enforcement is not permitted in certain states. The author believes, though, that Czech law does not prohibit such procedure.

11.65. As concerns the application of sources of international origin to the enforcement of foreign arbitral awards, the author also refers to the commentary to Section 47 of the ArbAct. Application of the NYConv and other rules of international

---

[132] See Fouchard, Gaillard, Goldman on International Commercial Arbitration, 1999, marg. 1714–1715.

[133] Naděžda Rozehnalová, *Mezinárodní právo obchodní. II. díl – Řešení sporů.* [Title in translation: *International Commercial Law. Part II – Resolution of Disputes*], 214 TEXTBOOKS OF THE FACULTY OF LAW, MU, Brno: Faculty of Law, MU 145 (1999).

[134] Also in compliance with applicable practice, see also KARL-HEINZ SCHWAB; GERHARD WALTER; ADOLF BAUMBACH, SCHIEDSGERICHTSBARKEIT: SYSTEMATISCHER KOMMENTAR ZU DEN VORSCHRIFTEN DER ZIVIL PROZESSORDNUNG, DES ARBEITSGESETZES, DER STAATSVERTRÄGE UND DER KOSTENGESETZE ÜBER DAS PRIVATRECHTLICHE SCHIGERICHTSVERFAHREN, München: C. H. Beck Verlag, Chapter 57, paragraph 6 (6th ed., 2000).

origin to the recognition and enforcement of foreign arbitral awards (including the grounds for a refusal of recognition and enforcement pursuant to the NYConv and the EConv) was analyzed in the commentary to Section 38 of the ArbAct.

III.   Section 39(a) of the ArbAct / Section 121(a) and (b) of the PIL

11.66.   Czech law has adopted a relatively strict approach to this issue. An arbitral award cannot be enforced in the Czech Republic unless it has become final, conclusive, and enforceable in the country in which it was made. In other words, an arbitral award cannot be enforced in the Czech Republic if, for instance, it was set aside in the country where it was made, in proceedings governed by the procedural laws of that country. However, this postulate, enshrined in Section 39(a) of the ArbAct, need not always apply without exceptions; as a matter of fact, it is contrary to currently prevailing international practice. It is necessary to emphasize, though, that from 1 January 2014, Section 39 of the ArbAct will be replaced with Section 121 of the PIL which is principally identical to Section 39 of the ArbAct. Section 121(a) of the PIL copies Section 39(a) of the ArbAct. Section 121(b) of the PIL introduces new grounds for a refusal to recognise and enforce an arbitral award in those cases in which the arbitral award was annulled in the country where it was made. Until now, Czech law has not been familiar with these grounds.

11.67.   But it is necessary to point out that, if the NYConv applies, the courts are not *obliged to* refuse the recognition and enforcement of the foreign arbitral award; they only have the possibility to do so. This also applies in the Czech Republic if the foreign arbitral award is proposed for recognition and enforcement under the regime of the NYConv or the EConv. Pursuant to Section 47 of the ArbAct (or also Article 10 of the Constitution and, in the future, Section 2 of the PIL), it is necessary to again highlight that the application of both conventions takes precedence over the laws of national origin, i.e. including the application of Section 39 of the ArbAct (Section 121 of the PIL with effect from 1 January 2014). Firstly, Article V(2) of the NYConv does not incorporate an obligation to refuse enforcement of the arbitral award but only a *possibility* (not an obligation) to refuse such enforcement.[135] International practice confirms that there are

---

[135]   For a linguistic interpretation of the NYConv and examples from international practice, see a detailed analysis in Karel Střelec, *K možnosti uznání a výkonu zrušeného cizího rozhodčího nálezu.* [Title in translation: *Regarding the Possibility of the Recognition and Enforcement of an Annulled Foreign Arbitral Award*], 3 BULLETIN ADVOKACIE 34–44 (2004).

many examples in international arbitration which corroborate the fact that enforcement (or recognition and enforcement) of arbitral awards is sometimes permitted, despite the fact that the award was annulled in the country where it was made or has not become enforceable for any other reason according to the law applicable in that country. Another major argument supporting the conclusion that enforcement of an arbitral award annulled in the country where it was made need not be refused in the Czech Republic, despite Section 39 of the ArbAct (cf. Section 121(b) of the PIL), is Article IX of the EConv. The grounds for a refusal of enforcement of an arbitral award in the Czech Republic are broader than the grounds under this convention. Besides, it is necessary to point out that some bilateral treaties binding upon the Czech Republic (usually legal assistance treaties) also demand that the contracting parties recognize and enforce foreign arbitral awards. According to Article VII(1) of the NYConv, the application of bilateral treaties prevails over the application of the NYConv. Consequently, the preferred rule is to follow the principle of advantageousness, i.e. apply the instrument which provides the petitioner with a higher standard of rights and guarantees. For a detailed commentary on this issue, see especially the commentary to Section 47 of the ArbAct and partially also the commentary to Section 38 of the ArbAct.

11.68. Consequently, Section 39 of the ArbAct (Section 121 of the PIL) fully applies only vis-à-vis those countries with respect to which no other international commitment of the Czech Republic can be applied. It is therefore necessary to presume that even an arbitral award, which was, for instance, set aside in the country where it was made, can be enforced in the Czech Republic under one of the above-mentioned international treaties. Considering the number of countries which are bound by the NYConv, the unconditional application of Section 39(a) of the ArbAct (Section 121(a) or (b) of the PIL, as applicable) will be rather exceptional. Paradoxically, the reason for such procedure inheres, *inter alia*, in the wording of Section 39 of the ArbAct itself (Section 121 of the PIL), namely Section 39(c) of the ArbAct (Section 121(d) of the PIL). The reason is that the foreign arbitral award could have been set aside in the country where it was made for violation of a principle which is contrary to the fundaments of the Czech legal and social order. For instance, the arbitral award might have been set aside in the country where it was made only because the arbitrator, or one of the arbitrators, was a woman.

11.69. However, the grounds under Section 39(a) of the ArbAct (Section 121(a) of the PIL) cannot cover those cases in which the arbitral award became final and conclusive in the country where it was made, but its enforceability has not been permitted. (This is providing such a decision on enforceability is required in case enforcement is sought in the country where the arbitral award was made). The reason is that it is not necessary to apply for enforcement of an arbitral award in the country where it was made at all. Such procedure would not make sense and would only result in a double *exequatur*.[136] The only requirement is that the decision is an arbitral award which became final and conclusive in the place where it was made and the time limit for voluntary performance of the obligations imposed by the award has expired.[137] Alternatively, the award meets other requirements which domestic Czech terminology would designate as so-called material enforceability or the requirements of material enforceability.

IV. Section 39(b) of the ArbAct / Section 121(c) of the PIL

11.70. Section 39(b) of the ArbAct (Section 121(c) of the PIL) stipulates that the recognition and enforcement of a foreign arbitral award shall also be refused if the arbitral award, or the proceedings in which the award was made, suffer(s) from any of the defects under Section 31 of the ArbAct, i.e. defects which justify a motion to annul a domestic arbitral award. However, a foreign arbitral award cannot be set aside (see the commentary to Section 31 of the ArbAct). The existence of such reasons only justifies refusal of enforcement of the award (or recognition and enforcement) in the territory of the Czech Republic. Naturally, this does not mean that the arbitral award can not be recognized and enforced in another country. Hence, the refusal of recognition and enforcement of a foreign arbitral award does not prejudice its "international" validity. International practice focuses specifically on the issue of refusal of recognition or enforcement of a foreign arbitral award where the party was not provided with the opportunity to plead his or her case before

---

[136] Alexander J. Bělohlávek, *Zavedení tzv. exequatur do českého právního řádu.* [Title in translation: *Introduction of So-Called Exequatur in Czech Law*], 5 PRÁVNÍ ZPRAVODAJ 16–17 (2004).

[137] Cf. FRIEDRICH STEIN, MARTIN JONAS, PETER SCHLOSSER ZIVILPROZESSORDNUNG. KOMMENTAR, München, commentary to Section 1044 of the ZPOG, paragraph 73 et seq. (21st ed., 1994).; or ALBERT J. VAN DEN BERG, THE NEW YORK ARBITRATION CONVENTION OF 1958, Deventer/ Den Haag: Kluwer Law International 337 et seq. (1980).

the arbitrators. Such situation constitutes grounds for a refusal of enforcement in connection with Section 31(e) of the ArbAct, which copies the reason under Article V(1)(b) of the NYConv, or grounds for annulment of arbitral award rendering the award unenforceable under Article IX(1)(b) of the EConv.

11.71. The court shall refuse enforcement of the arbitral award of its own motion unless the requirements for its recognition and enforcement are met.

11.72. The court is not entitled to review the merits of the arbitral award, i.e. the *"révision au fond"* is prohibited (see also the commentary to Section 38 of the ArbAct). This procedure also complies with prevailing international practice.[138] There is one exception in this respect, namely assessment of the arbitral award in terms of Section 39(b) of the ArbAct (Section 121(c) of the PIL) in connection with the grounds under Section 31(i) of the ArbAct.[139]

11.73. The reference to Section 31(f) of the ArbAct, i.e. the case where arbitrators made a decision *ultra petita*, partly copies (according to the interpretation of the New York Convention) the grounds for refusal of enforcement pursuant to Article V(1)(c) of the NYConv. However, no one has focused on the issue of a decision *infra petita*, i.e. some of the claims made by the parties were left unsolved. Prevailing international practice holds that *infra petita* does not influence the (un)enforceability of the arbitral award abroad.[140] This problem will have to be solved in the country exclusively according to the arbitration laws valid in that country where the arbitral award was made. Indeed, the same conclusion could be inferred from domestic practice, i.e. the practice of enforcement of domestic Czech arbitral awards. But the issue of *infra petitum* becomes relevant only exceptionally – it usually concerns a case where the arbitrator(s) entirely omitted part of the claim. Just like in domestic Czech arbitration practice, this problem is solved by a supplemental arbitral award (see the commentary to Section 23 of the ArbAct).

11.74. The international standard in the application of the NYConv requires that the party objecting the recognition and enforcement of a foreign arbitral award in a particular country must also prove that the party had already raised such objections in the course of the proceedings themselves. (Naturally, this applies in

---

[138] GUNTER HENN, SCHIEDSVERFAHRENSRECHT, paragraph 494, (3rd ed., 2000). or ROLF A. SCHÜTZE, SCHIEDSGERICHT UND SCHIEDSVERFAHREN. München: C. H. Beck'sche Verlagsbuchhandlung, paragraph 252. (1998).
[139] Before the Amendment to the ArbAct, these grounds were classified under Section 38(i) of the ArbAct.
[140] ALBERT J. VAN DEN BERG, THE NEW YORK ARBITRATION CONVENTION OF 1958, Deventer/ Den Haag: KLI 320 et seq. (1980).

those cases where objections could have been made, providing the party had the opportunity to do so).[141] This concept is also incorporated in Section 33 of the ArbAct. However, the international scope of this approach is substantially broader and requires that the parties, wherever possible, raise any objection during the course of the arbitral proceedings. Most objections which are not made during the arbitral proceedings disqualify the possibility of successfully pleading the objection later, whether in the proceedings for annulment or in the *exequatur* or execution proceedings.

V.   Section 39(c) of the ArbAct / Section 121(d) of the PIL

11.75.   Only the grounds under Section 39(c) of the ArbAct can be applied without reservations. The purpose of the provision is to prevent the legal effects of an arbitral award as an enforceable title which would have undesirable effects, contrary to the overriding mandatory principles of the social and political order. A similar approach is also adopted in the case of a refusal to enforce foreign decisions (meaning court decisions) in terms of Section 64(d) of the PILP,[142] as the term is defined in Section 36 of the PILP.[143] But it is necessary to highlight that the grounds for a refusal to recognize a foreign arbitral award under Section 39(c) of the ArbAct (Section 121(d) of the PIL) are targeted at procedural public policy.

11.76.   It is not possible to differentiate between a special public policy for domestic arbitral awards and a special public policy applicable to awards made abroad, although it is sometimes argued that the public policy exception applied to foreign decisions must be subjected to a less rigorous assessment than the public policy

---

[141]   Regarding foreign practice with respect to this issue, in connection with the application of the NYConv, see also Decision of the U.S. Court of Appeal, Second Circuit, Case No. 1147 / Docket 83-9078 of 11 May 1984 (*La Societe Nationale Pour La Recherche, La Production, Le Transport, La Transformation et La Commercialisation des Hydrocarburest* v. *Shaheen Natural Resources Company, Inc.*). The U.S. court adjudicated as follows: "*The party who opposes the motion to enforce an arbitral award should have filed their motions with the arbitral panel during the arbitration. Raising at this stage, i.e. at the stage of recognition and enforcement of the arbitral award, an objection consisting in circumstances which the party knew about already during the arbitral proceedings, would be contrary to the goal and the purpose of the NYConv, that is, the summary procedure to expedite the recognition and enforcement of arbitration awards.*"; published in (*neutral citation*): 585 F. Supp. 57, 62, 65 (S.D.N.Y. 1983), *aff'd*, 733 F.2d 260 (2d Cir.), *cert. denied*, 469 U.S. 883 (1984). The decision was affirmed both by the Court of Appeals and by the Supreme Court. Cf. also ALEXANDER J. BĚLOHLÁVEK, ROZHODČÍ ŘÍZENÍ, ORDRE PUBLIC A TRESTNÍ PRÁVO. [Title in translation: ARBITRATION, ORDRE PUBLIC AND CRIMINAL LAW], Prague: C. H. Beck, marg. 774 (2008).; Georges R. Delaume, *Recognition and Enforcement of State Contract Awards in the United States: A Restatement*, 91(3) THE AMERICAN JOURNAL OF INTERNATIONAL LA 476–489 (1997)., or Howard Latin, *Legal and Economic Considerations in the Decisions of Judge Breyer*, 50(4) LAW AND CONTEMPORARY PROBLEMS, ECONOMISTS ON THE BENCH 57–86, (1987). and other writings.

[142]   Cf. Section 15(e) of the PIL with effect from 1 January 2014.

[143]   Cf. Section 4 of the PIL with effect from 1 January 2014.

exception applied to domestic decisions (or juridical acts as such).[144] A decision is principally considered contrary to public policy if the effects thereof would conflict with the overriding mandatory principles of law or with the fundamental principles of the social order. In any case, prevailing international practice maintains that foreign awards (or decisions as such) are contrary to *ordre public* if they impose obligations the performance of which is contrary to the mandatory law of the place in which recognition/enforcement of the foreign arbitral award is sought and/or obligations the performance of which would be punished by a public-law penalty or entail similar consequences.[145] But it is by no means possible to claim that *ordre public* is the same thing as mandatory rules. Nevertheless, it is usually possible to classify under *ordre public* some of the special issues provided for in the mandatory provisions.

VI. Enforcement of foreign arbitral awards rendered in consumer disputes

VI.1. Grounds for refusal of recognition and enforcement

11.77. The enforcement of foreign arbitral awards may also entail certain consumer protection issues, primarily if any of the parties invokes the (un)enforceability of an arbitral award due to a breach of consumer protection laws. This is especially so when the court must determine whether to refuse the recognition and enforcement of an award, the making of which might have violated consumer protection laws.

11.78. The recognition and enforcement of foreign arbitral awards are principally governed by the courts' own procedural laws (*lex fori*). But it is necessary to point out that the recognition and enforcement of foreign arbitral awards made in consumer matters requires the priority application of international treaties, if the given state is bound by such instruments. The recognition and enforcement of foreign arbitral awards is also governed by

---

[144] Cf. REINHOLD GEIMER; E. GEIMER, ET G. GEIMER, INTERNATIONALES ZIVILPROZESSRECHT 4TH ED., REVISED AND EXPANDED EDITION. Köln/R.: Dr. Otto Schmidt, paragraph 3773, p. 1082 (2001).; or ULRICH HAAS, ANERKENNUNG UND VOLLSTRECKUNG AUSLÄNDISCHER UND INTERNATIONALER SCHIEDSSPRÜCHE. Berlin: Duncker & Humblot 221 (1991).; or CHRISTIAN VÖLKER, ZUR DOGMATIK DES ORDRE PUBLIC – DIE VORBEHALTSKLAUSELN BEI DER ANERKENNUNG FREMDER GERICHTLICHER ENTSCHEIDUNGEN UND IHR VERHÄLTNIS ZUM ORDRE PUBLIC DES KOLLISIONSRECHTS. Berlin: Duncker & Humblot 257 et seq. (1998).
[145] Cf. REINHOLD GEIMER, E. GEIMER, ET G. GEIMER, INTERNATIONALES ZIVILPROZESSRECHT. 4TH ED. Köln/R.: Dr. Otto Schmidt 1084 (2001).

the NYConv. Conversely, the possibility of applying the EConv in consumer matters is rather limited, or even excluded.

11.79. Subject to the specific conditions of consumer arbitration, the enforcement of arbitral awards may be refused on various grounds, including lack of arbitrability or invalidity of the arbitration agreement. Violation of public policy is another possible reason.[146]

11.80. As concerns the absence of arbitrability, the question is whether this reason could constitute grounds for a refusal to recognize and enforce an arbitral award which was rendered pursuant to a regime (laws) which provide(s) very extensive protection to the consumer, such as the laws of several European countries. This could apply to a limited number of situations and legal systems. For instance, disputes not exceeding 5,000 GBP cannot be submitted to arbitration in the United Kingdom. However, it has been argued that these rules should also be considered contrary to the NYConv and therefore inapplicable in cases falling within the scope of the NYConv.[147] In any case, consumer disputes under EU law (under the regime of the Directive) are principally arbitrable,[148] just as they are principally arbitrable subject to the requirements stipulated by special laws in certain EU Member States (the Czech Republic, Germany, and others) and certain non-Member States, e.g. Switzerland.[149] It is indeed very exceptional that the arbitrability of consumer disputes would be principally precluded. National laws usually only set forth certain special and limiting rules for the purpose of protecting the consumer in the conclusion of arbitration agreements and, to a lesser extent, during the arbitration itself. Consequently, the absence of arbitrability of a consumer dispute in the country of recognition/enforcement does not usually constitute grounds for a refusal to enforce the arbitral award. This is providing that the dispute is arbitrable according to the law applicable to the arbitration agreement and, subsidiarily, according to the law of the seat of arbitration. Similarly, it is not possible to refuse recognition/enforcement of a foreign

---

[146] However, as developing practice in individual countries shows, the approach of states regarding the application of the public policy exception in consumer disputes is not homogenous. For instance, in its Decision Case No. 3 Ob 144/09m of 22 July 2009, the Austrian Supreme Court (OGH [AUT]) concluded that this particular reason for refusal of recognition and enforcement of the award (here an arbitral award made in Denmark [DNK]) does not apply. Conversely, the Polish Supreme Court in its Decision Case No. No IV CSK 200/06 of 22 February 2007 refused to enforce the respective arbitral award (an arbitral award made in the U.S.).

[147] Charles Jarrosson, *Note on Cour d'appel de Paris, 7 December 1994.* 2 REV. ARB. 256 (1996).

[148] For a detailed commentary on EU law, see above.

[149] See XAVIER FAVRE-BULLE, ARBITRAGE ET RÈGLEMENT ALTERNATIVE DES LITIGES (ADR): UNE AUTRE JUSTICE POUR LES CONSOMMATEURS?, Droit de la consommation, Liber Amicorum Bernd Stauder, Genève: Schulthess, 97 et seq. (L. Théovenoz, et N. Reich, eds., 2006) here et. 101–103.

arbitral award in consumer disputes, or any other disputes, on grounds of invalidity of the arbitration agreement under the law of the country of recognition/enforcement, if the arbitration agreement is valid under the law applicable to the arbitration agreement. Such a situation is easily conceivable in practice – many countries require the fulfillment of specific criteria regarding the form of the arbitration agreement in consumer disputes on pain of invalidity.[150]

11.81. As concerns the validity of the arbitration agreement, the NYConv stipulates that enforcement may be refused if any of the parties proves that the [arbitration] agreement is not valid under the law which governs the [arbitration] agreement (Article V(1)(a) of the NYConv). Consequently, if the arbitration agreement is governed by law which generally allows arbitration in consumer disputes, such as Czech, German, Spanish, U.S., and others nations' laws, then the arbitration agreement may still be found invalid on other grounds. These grounds are usually stipulated in, or at least based on, general legal principles or provisions of contract law.

11.82. **Model situation:** Take for instance a situation where a contract concluded online between a Belgian consumer and a U.S. professional contains an arbitration clause governed by California law. The New York Convention (NYConv) does not allow Belgian courts to refuse enforcement on grounds of validity of the arbitration agreement unless the agreement is invalid under California law.

11.83. The exclusion of arbitration or the submission of such disputes to the exclusive jurisdiction of courts in consumer disputes may influence the validity of the arbitration agreement or may be considered contrary to public policy in some states. In this connection, however, it is necessary to emphasize that at least Article V(2)(b) of the NYConv concerns **international public policy**, which must be principally distinguished from national public policy. These are frequently two completely different categories. When deciding on compliance of the award with the public policy, the courts do not assess the award itself; they assess its effects under their national legal system. As concerns consumers residing in the country where the recognition and enforcement of the foreign arbitral award are sought, arbitral awards rendered in consumer disputes may conflict with the rules which prescribe the exclusive jurisdiction of a particular

---

[150]   Cf. also H. MOLLER, SCHIEDSVERFAHRENSNOVELLE UND VOLSTRECKUNG AUSLÄNDISCHER SCHIEDSSPRÜCHE. NZG et. 143–146, (1999). here et. 145 and Note No. 34; demonstrated by *H. Moller* on the example of Section 1032(5) of the ZPOG in conjunction with the application of the NYConv.

authority for consumer disputes.[151] Hence, arbitral awards rendered in consumer disputes may also be viewed as decisions conflicting with public policy, due to the fact that arbitration clauses are excluded in consumer contracts. However, it needs to be emphasized that this conclusion cannot be considered generally (universally) applicable. (According to Austrian law, arbitration clauses are prohibited in consumer disputes, and such disputes may only be subject to post-dispute arbitration agreements, i.e. agreements with respect to each individual dispute.) As Austrian case law indicates, the courts may arrive at the conclusion that it is not a case of violation of public policy within the meaning of Article V(2)(b) of the NYConv. A contrario, states which principally allow the arbitrability of consumer disputes (the Czech Republic, Germany, Spain, the U.S., and many other countries) cannot arrive at the conclusion that the arbitrability of consumer disputes is contrary to international or national public policy. As concerns the Czech Republic, it is necessary to conclude that foreign arbitral awards made in consumer disputes are capable of recognition and enforcement pursuant to the NYConv and principally cannot be refused, on the grounds specified in Article V(2)(b) of the NYConv in connection with special consumer protection. However, the author believes that the given situation, i.e. special consumer protection, does not fall within the scope of Article V(2)(b) of the NYConv, and moreover – as explicitly mentioned above – it is hardly conceivable in those countries which generally consider consumer disputes arbitrable.

11.84.   In matters relating to EU law, the courts of the Member States may have regard to EU public policy in deciding on the enforceability of awards; the author intentionally leaves aside certain doubts about this concept, namely so-called EU public policy.[152] But even the ECJ (CJEU) itself has not yet ruled that consumer protection would be a component of EU public policy. The decision in *Elisa María Mostaza Claro* v. *Centro Móvil Milenium SL*[153]only refers to a special public interest in

---

[151]   For instance, Sections 21 and 22 of the Swiss Federal Act on Court Jurisdiction in Civil Matters of 24 March 2000, RS 272.

[152]   Cf. Alexander J. Bělohlávek, *Public Policy and Public Interest in International Law and EU Law*, 3 CYIL 117–148 (2012).; ALEXANDER J. BĚLOHLÁVEK, ŘÍMSKÁ ÚMLUVA / NAŘÍZENÍ ŘÍM I. KOMENTÁŘ. [Title in translation: ROME CONVENTION / ROME I REGULATION. A COMMENTARY], Prague: C. H. Beck (2009). commentary to Section 21 of the Rome I Regulation; Pavel Mates; Michal Bartoň, *Public versus Private Interest – Can the Boundaries Be Legally Defined?*, 2 CYIL 171–190 (2011)., and other writings.

[153]   ECJ Judgment, Case C-168/05 of 26 October 2006 (*Elisa María Mostaza Claro* v. *Centro Móvil Milenium SL*), published in: ECR 2006, p. I–1421. CELEX 62005CJ0168. Language of the case: Spanish. For a detailed analysis, see also ALEXANDER J. BĚLOHLÁVEK OCHRANA SPOTŘEBITELŮ V ROZHODČÍM ŘÍZENÍ. [Title in translation: CONSUMER ARBITRATION], Prague: C. H. Beck, , marg. 201 et seq. (2012). Ms. *Mostaza Claro* was the respondent in arbitration in which she failed to plead unfairness of the arbitration

consumer protection. Public interest is by no means in the same category as public policy,[154] especially not the specific public policy enshrined in Article V(2)(b) of the NYConv. The fact that public policy and public interest are two completely different categories is corroborated, for instance, by the concept of the so-called overriding mandatory provisions employed by EU conflict-of-laws (European private international law). However, overriding mandatory provisions are a category completely different from public policy. Public interest may influence the classification of a particular provision as an overriding mandatory provision which neutralizes the application of applicable (substantive) law (substantive standard) and applies to the extent of the obligation it mandates instead of the provision of applicable substantive law. Conversely, public policy, as a component of the fundamental pillars of the legal system, has negative effects. It (the substantive public policy) does not contain any specific rule, but it eliminates the effects of the application of foreign law[155] without stipulating its own substantive standard to be applied.

11.85. Apart from that, the courts of the EU Member States may also apply Commission (EC) Recommendation No. 98/257/EC. Any award which does not comply with the principles stipulated

---

clause, although, according to the Spanish court, there are no doubts that the clause was indeed unfair. Ms. *Mostaza Claro* contested the result of the arbitration in a civil court only after the arbitral proceedings were finished and pleaded unfairness only in these court proceedings for annulment of the arbitral award. Further conclusions articulated in this decision are also annotated in the commentary to Sections 31 and 33 of the ArbAct.

[154] Cf. Alexander J. Bělohlávek. *Public Policy and Public Interest in International Law and EU Law*, 3 CYIL117–148 (2012).; DANIELA DOSTÁLKOVÁ; KATEŘINA KŘIVKOVÁ, PROBLÉMY DEFINOVÁNÍ A PROSAZOVÁNÍ VEŘEJNÉHO ZÁJMU. [Title in translation: PROBLEMS WITH THE DEFINITION AND ENFORCEMENT OF PUBLIC INTEREST.], Sborník referátů z teoretického semináře pořádaného katedrou veřejné ekonomie ESF MU Brno ve spolupráci s asociací veřejné ekonomie [Collection of Papers from the Theoretical Seminar Organized by the Department of Public Economics, Faculty of Economics and Administration, Masaryk University in Brno, in Cooperation with the Public Economics Association], Brno MU 28 et seq. (Ivan Malý, ed., 1999).; ROCHDI GOULLI, PROBLÉMY DEFINOVÁNÍ A PROSAZOVÁNÍ VEŘEJNÉHO ZÁJMU. [Title in translation: PROBLEMS WITH THE DEFINITION AND ENFORCEMENT OF PUBLIC INTEREST.], op. cit., p. 10 et seq. (Ivan Malý, (ed.); DUŠAN HENDRYCH, SPRÁVNÍ PRÁVO. OBECNÁ ČÁST. [Title in translation: ADMINISTRATIVE LAW. GENERAL PART], Prague: C. H. Beck 86 (7th ed., 2009).; Vladimír Hyánek, Problémy definování a prosazování veřejného zájmu. [Title in translation: Problems with the Definition and Enforcement of Public Interest.], op. cit., p. 60 et seq. (Ivan Malý (ed.)); JAROSLAV REKTOŘÍK, PROBLÉMY DEFINOVÁNÍ A PROSAZOVÁNÍ VEŘEJNÉHO ZÁJMU. [Title in translation: PROBLEMS WITH THE DEFINITION AND ENFORCEMENT OF PUBLIC INTEREST.], , op. cit., p. 29 et seq., (Ivan Malý (ed.)).

[155] Substantive public policy must be distinguished from procedural public policy. The latter eliminates the effects of a foreign decision if a fundamental procedural standard was breached during the making of the decision. Cf. also Alexander Bělohlávek, *Výhrada veřejného pořádku hmotněprávního a procesního ve vztazích s mezinárodním prvkem*. [Title in translation: *A Substantive and Procedural Public Policy Exception in Relationships with an International Dimension*]. 145(11) PRÁVNÍK (2006).

in the *Recommendation* may be considered contrary to public policy. These principles include:

11.86. ▶ **Independence** of the decision-making body. If the arbitral institution is perceived as an institution with a too close relationship to one of the parties,[156] especially the professional, the situation may constitute grounds for a refusal to enforce the award rendered by the institution.

11.87. ▶ The observance of the **adversarial** principle is largely comparable to the grounds for refusal pursuant to Article V(1)(b) of the NYConv regarding the right to state one's case. Specifically, consumer disputes require that the arbitrators take care to provide sufficient opportunity to the consumer to exercise his or her rights. Consequently, it must be kept in mind that the consumer might not approach the proceedings so professionally as the professional.

11.88. ▶ The principle which stipulates that the arbitral award must not deprive the consumer of the protection provided to him or her by the mandatory provisions of the state in the territory of which the decision-making authority exercises its jurisdiction.

11.89. ▶ Prohibition of pre-arbitral clauses. It has to be pointed out, specifically with reference to this point, that the *Recommendation* is not binding. Not all Member States prohibit arbitration clauses (pre-arbitral clauses) in consumer disputes. Consequently, the *Recommendation* is obviously only a certain generalizing guideline which can represent neither a binding rule nor a binding interpretation of EU law.

11.90. But the above-mentioned *Recommendation* is not a binding, let alone a directly applicable, EU law. Moreover, it is a source which can only principally influence the interpretation of substantive standards compliant with EU law, not procedural standards which are the exclusive domain of national law. The application or consideration of the *Recommendation* is even less possible in those cases in which the NYConv would have to apply as a source of international law. The reason is that a source of international law prevails over EU laws if the given state is bound by the former.

11.91. It is also necessary to point out that the laws in individual countries stipulate different levels of consumer protection standards, and consequently different limits for arbitration. Moreover, individual countries also differ with respect to their approach to certain sectors of commercial transactions.

---

[156] This is probably the case of the National Arbitration Forum (NAF) in the United States. At the time of drafting this book, the NAF is being sued by San Francisco for its decisions in consumer credits, the overwhelming majority of which favored professionals. See Wall Street Journal Law Blog, 7 April 2008. Also available at: http://blogs.wsj.com/law/ (accessed on 15 February 2019).

As concerns public policy and questions connected with the enforcement of an arbitral award, public policy may have a different intensity in different sectors; the intensity attributed to consumer protection may differ as well. For example, the protection of consumers in medical care would probably enjoy a higher importance (intensity) than the sale of consumer goods.

VI.2. Enforcement of arbitral awards rendered in states with a lower degree of consumer protection

11.92. The internet has expanded consumers' possibilities and allowed them to enter into contracts away from their habitual residence. In doing so, they may (intentionally or not) enter into arbitration agreements governed by the law of third countries. As mentioned above, individual legal systems exhibit major differences in their approach to consumer arbitration.

11.93. For instance, if we look at the U.S. as one of the leading representatives of the internet economy, then it is by no means exceptional that consumers accept contractual terms containing arbitration clauses in contracts (contract terms and conditions) offered by these overseas merchants. These arbitration clauses are usually valid and enforceable in the U.S.[157] However, these arbitration clauses anticipate that the arbitration will take place in the U.S., with or even without the consumer's attendance. The arbitration clause is usually held valid in the place of arbitration and under the law applicable to the arbitration agreement. As concerns the form of these arbitration agreements and their validity, it is a valid term. It is hardly conceivable that enforcement of such an arbitral award would be refused on grounds such as failure to meet formal requirements.[158] Nonetheless, enforcement of the award could in many countries be refused, because, for instance, the arbitration clause would de facto constitute an obstacle to consumer protection in terms of an effective right to oppose the claim.[159]

---

[157] Recently, however, purchases by consumers via websites of merchants established in Asian countries have become just as common.
[158] Cf. also H. MOLLER, SCHIEDSVERFAHRENSNOVELLE UND VOLSTRECKUNG AUSLÄNDISCHER SCHIEDSSPRÜCHE. NZG 143–146, here 145 and Note No. 34 (1999).; demonstrated by H. Moller in the example of Section 1032(5) of the ZPOG in conjunction with the application of the NYConv.
[159] Cf. also the Decision of the Polish Supreme Court, Case No. No IV CSK 200/06 of 22 February 2007, whereby the enforcement of an arbitral award made in the U.S. was refused. The cited Polish decision is annotated elsewhere in this book – see this section regarding the enforcement of foreign arbitral awards.

VI.3. Decisions of courts in EU Member States in cases of enforcement of a foreign arbitral award rendered in a consumer dispute

VI.3.1. Decision of the Austrian Supreme Court (OGH), Case No. 3 Ob 144/09m of 22 July 2009:[160] Breach of consumer protection laws does not form part of international or EU public policy

11.94. The question of whether (or not) the breach of consumer protection laws in the country where the arbitral award was made constitutes grounds for refusal to recognize and enforce the arbitral award in a different country has probably been most rigorously analyzed by the Austrian Supreme Court (OGH) in Case No. 3 Ob 144/09m of 22 July 2009.[161] In this decision, the court held that consumer protection is neither part of international public policy nor part of EU public policy. The court thus confirmed the conclusions reached by the ECJ in *Asturcom*,[162] i.e. that consumer protection under EU standards does not extend into the cross-border arena with respect to the enforcement and recognition of foreign arbitral awards. This is probably the first and, as yet, only decision which deals with consumer protection issues and the limitation of arbitrability under the law of the state where recognition and enforcement are sought, as concerns foreign arbitral awards and with respect to the NYConv. Moreover, it is a decision which has addressed all the relevant issues in great detail.[163] Indeed, such approach is typical for Austrian decisions, which are well-known for their clarity and high erudition.

11.95. The Austrian Supreme Court (OGH) held that the loss of right to invoke the invalidity of an arbitration agreement cannot be

---

[160] For a detailed annotation and analysis (including a description of the factual and legal findings and references to related legislation applied in the case together with an approximate translation), see ALEXANDER J. BĚLOHLÁVEK, OCHRANA SPOTŘEBITELŮ V ROZHODČÍM ŘÍZENÍ. [Title in translation: CONSUMER ARBITRATION]. Prague: C. H. Beck, marg. 690 et seq. (2012).

[161] Decision of the OGH [AUT], Case No. 3 Ob 144/09m of 22 July 2009. Published in: (i) SZ 010/21 (Öhlberger) and in: (ii) Austrian Arbitration Association (ArbAut) Bulletin.

[162] ECJ Judgment, Case C-40/08 of 6 October 2009 (*Telecomunicaciones SL* v. *Cristina Rodríguez Nogueira* [*Asturcom*]), CELEX 62008CA0040, the judgment was published in: ECR 2009, p. I–09579. Language of the case: Spanish. For a detailed analysis, see also ALEXANDER J. BĚLOHLÁVEK, OCHRANA SPOTŘEBITELŮ V ROZHODČÍM ŘÍZENÍ. [Title in translation: CONSUMER ARBITRATION]. Prague: C. H. Beck, marg. 241 et seq. (2012). Further conclusions are also annotated in the commentary to Sections 31 and 32 of the ArbAct.

[163] This is certainly an indisputable advantage of Austrian law and case law. Conversely, it is definitely a pity that, for instance, the reasons elaborated by French courts in their decisions are very brief. Moreover, Austrian case law and Austrian laws are easily accessible online and the publicly available databases are very well-organized. From the global perspective, this perfectly structured organizational system and public accessibility are unique.

subsequently remedied in a different country (the country of enforcement) by a refusal to recognize and enforce the arbitral award for a breach of public policy. According to this decision, an arbitration clause in business-to-consumer contracts does not automatically violate Austrian public policy, despite the fact that Austrian laws do not allow arbitration clauses and only allow post-dispute arbitration agreements. This automatically implies that the breach of consumer protection laws does not violate EU public policy, let alone international public policy.

11.96. Arbitration agreements in consumer relations do not *per se* constitute a breach of (substantive) public policy (*ordre public*). Any defects of the arbitration agreement must be pleaded in the arbitral proceedings. Failure to raise the plea remedies the defect; this principle is also enshrined in some of the broadly applied international standards, such as Article V of the EConv.[164] Interestingly, the Austrian Supreme Court did not directly apply the EConv in the given case but still acknowledged the standard of this convention for the recognition and enforcement of foreign arbitral awards rendered in consumer disputes. The Danish Institute of Arbitration, which conducted the arbitration, concluded that the plea was belated under applicable procedural law (and therefore the right to make the plea was *extinguished* from the procedural perspective). The Austrian Supreme Court held that national laws (national *lex arbitri*) which limit arbitration agreements in consumer contracts cannot be applied to the recognition and enforcement of foreign arbitral awards.[165] Besides, the Austrian Supreme Court continued, even if domestic laws (*lex arbitri*) allowed the court to have regard to consumer protection laws in *exequatur* or in enforcement proceedings,[166] such laws could not be used in those cases to which the NYConv applies. Domestic (Austrian) law would conflict with the NYConv, the application of which takes precedence. Indeed, the same conclusion must be drawn under Czech law. The Austrian court explicitly stated that a domestic provision limiting consumer arbitration does not apply to foreign arbitral awards.[167] A conflict with consumer

---

[164] The OGH invokes its former case law, in particular Decision Case No. 3 Ob 221/04b, also published in: (i) SZ 2005/9 and (ii) IPrax, 2006, p. 496 et seq. Besides, the existing commentaries share this opinion.

[165] It is necessary to point out that the Austrian *lex arbitri* (ZPOA) contains explicit rules on the territorial scope of its application (Section 577 of the ZPOA). According to Section 577 of the ZPOA, provisions limiting the arbitrability of consumer disputes do not have any exterritorial effects. Such effects would neither exist in the present case (recognition and enforcement of foreign arbitral awards) in relation to persons with their place of residence/registered office in Austria until the seat of arbitration is determined (unless, for instance, the seat of arbitration is agreed in the arbitration agreement or by reference to procedural rules).

[166] As the ECJ ruled in *Asturcom*, even EU laws leave this issue entirely at the discretion of the Member States. No EU imperative can be applied in this regard.

[167] Apart from Section 617 of the ZPOA, the OGH [AUT] explicitly invokes Section 577(2) of the ZPOA.

protection laws may, in principle, breach substantive public policy.[168] In connection with Article V(2)(b)[169] of the NYConv, however, such effects must be refused. Such agreement is also allowed in business-to-consumer contracts.

VI.3.2. Decision of the Polish Supreme Court, Case No. No IV CSK 200/06 of 22 February 2007

11.97. Conversely, according to the legal opinion of the Polish Supreme Court, a breach of the fundamental principles of consumer protection[170] also constitutes grounds for a refusal to recognize and enforce a foreign arbitral award pursuant to the NYConv.[171]

11.98. In the respective case, the *[only]* party with the right to choose between a lawsuit in court and a request for arbitration was the professional. The contract also anticipated the application of foreign law which represented substantially different legal conditions for the consumer than those prescribed by the European legal framework. At the same time, the application of arbitral procedure made it substantially more difficult for the Polish consumer to attend the hearings, because the place of arbitration was in the U.S. (Moreover, the simplified procedure for the entry of Polish citizens to U.S. territory was only introduced after the finding proceedings were held, and the granting of U.S. entry visas to Polish citizens was subject to relatively major restrictions at that time.) All of these circumstances have been classified by the Polish Supreme Court as conditions discriminating against the consumer. The decision of the Polish Supreme Court must be viewed with a certain reservation. The Polish decision primarily considered the *factual* obstacles which prevented the Polish consumer from attending the hearing of the dispute and the discrimination against the

---

[168] Cf. also Article L 132-1 of the French Consumer Protection Act [FRA] implemented by Act [FRA] No. 95-96 of 1 February 1995, Article 1, published in the Annex to JOFR of 2 February 1995 and Regulation [FRA] No. 2001-741 of 23 August 2001, Article 16, published in JOFR of 25 August 2001. The legislation explicitly stipulates that the rules (unfair terms in consumer contracts) are part of public policy. In connection with arbitration, these issues are also analyzed in great detail and cited (including approximate translations) in: ALEXANDER BĚLOHLÁVEK, OCHRANA SPOTŘEBITELŮ V ROZHODČÍM ŘÍZENÍ. [Title in translation: CONSUMER ARBITRATION].

[169] The Austrian decision explicitly invokes Article V(2)(a) of the NYConv. However, that is an obvious typographical error.

[170] Regarding consumer protection in connection with arbitration, see also ALEXANDER BĚLOHLÁVEK, OCHRANA SPOTŘEBITELŮ V ROZHODČÍM ŘÍZENÍ. [Title in translation: CONSUMER ARBITRATION]. Prague: C. H. Beck, marg. 526 et seq. (2012).

[171] Decision of the Polish Supreme Court [POL], Case No. No IV CSK 200/06 of 22 February 2007. The decision is also available online at: (i) http://dokumenty.e-prawnik.pl/orzecznictwo/sad-najwyzszy/izba-celna/1ivcsk06200.html (accessed on 15 February 2019), (ii) http://static.e-prawnik.pl/pdf/orzeczenia/1_IV_CSK_06_200.pdf (accessed on 15 February 2019), and (iii) http://arbitraz.laszczuk.pl/orzecznictwo/234,postanowienie_sadu_najwyzszego_z_dnia_22_lutego_2007_r_iv_csk_200_06.html (accessed on 15 February 2019).

consumer with respect to the choice of *forum*. The applicability of this decision as a *benchmark* decision with respect to Article V(2)(b) of the NYConv is significantly limited. We can therefore conclude that the above-cited and annotated decision of the Austrian Supreme Court is undoubtedly more important. This is especially because Austrian laws principally prohibit arbitration clauses in consumer contracts and only allow post-dispute arbitration agreements, i.e. agreements relating to a particular, *[de facto]* pre-existing dispute.

11.99. However, the Polish Supreme Court also addressed the issue of form of an arbitration agreement concluded via an internet website in international transactions, in connection with the application of the NYConv. Unless the arbitral award is set aside, the interpretation of Article II(2) et seq. of the NYConv does not permit the conclusion that the arbitration agreement does not meet the requirement of proper written form or any other requirements prescribed for business-to-consumer arbitration agreements. Similarly, there is no reason to maintain that the terms of an agreement displayed on a *website* are not equivalent to the terms presented in an agreement concluded in a written form. This especially holds true for the application of the NYConv which only requires the written form and does not contain any specific rules regarding issues such as the moment of conclusion of the agreement (for instance, between parties present at the same moment) or the place and manner of accepting the *"online"* offer. Article 1162(2) of the Polish Code of Civil Procedure (K.p.c.) stipulates that the requirement of written form is fulfilled if the arbitration clause was contained in an exchange of letters and distance communication messages which allow recording the contents thereof or in a written agreement concluded in a separate document containing a clause on submitting the dispute to arbitration. Visiting a website with a draft contract addressed to an unspecified group of potential recipients and confirming online one's will to enter into the contract does not constitute a statement which would enable recording a particular expression of will with respect to a specific, individualized contractual relationship. In the given case, the Polish Supreme Court held that a computer "confirmation" of a contract – as opposed to a standard electronic signature which at least safeguards the minimum degree of credibility – did not constitute a basis for the identification or reproduction of the contents of such an expression of will. The requirement would be met if a specific expression of will were at least sent by an individual electronic mail (e-mail) which would enable identification of the sender. In this connection, it is appropriate to point out that several Czech decisions have interpreted the requirements of form even more rigorously, holding that the parties must use an electronic (verified) signature. See also the commentary to Section 3 of the ArbAct, in connection with the case law of the MC in Brno. But the interpretation advocated by the Brno court is very extensive and undoubtedly unsustainable in the international environment.

VII. Case law

11.100. **Resolution of the RC in Hradec Králové, Case No. 19 Co 337/99-42 of 30 November 1999:**[172] **[exclusion of review in the merits in exequatur/enforcement proceedings; application of the NYConv; standing; public policy]** (1) The court conducting the proceedings for ordering enforcement may only examine procedural issues. The court must not assess the material correctness of the enforcement title, including the issue of the potential standing of the debtor's legal predecessor. (2) The issue of the respondent's standing in the merits has no connection to the public policy of the Czech Republic but to an issue of substantive law. Such issue cannot be subject to review in the proceedings for recognition/enforcement of a foreign arbitral award.[173]

11.101. **Resolution of the SC, Case No. 21 Cdo 1511/2000 of 29 March 2001:**[174] **[recognition/enforcement of a foreign award; prohibition of review in the merits; scope of application of foreign law; succession; guarantee]** (4) When enforcing a decision [i.e. including a foreign arbitral award], the court is not allowed to review the correctness of the merits of the enforced decision or another enforcement title. The court is bound by, and obliged to observe, the contents of the decision (another enforcement title), i.e. the operative part thereof, the enforcement of which is proposed. (5) The obligor (debtor) argues that the [foreign] arbitral award proposed for enforcement is contrary to Czech public policy. This is because the arbitrator concluded in the reasons for the arbitral award that "Austrian law shall also govern the guarantee provided by the original

---

[172] Preceded by Resolution of the DC in Ústí nad Orlicí, Case No. 5E 1245/98-18. The decision of the RC was affirmed by Resolution of the SC, Case No. 21 Cdo 1511/2000 of 29 March 2001. Information regarding the decision of the RC was adopted from the reasons for the SC resolution.

[173] The applicable substantive law was Austrian law, chosen by the parties in their licensing agreement. The case was resolved in arbitration conducted at the ICC Court (AA, Case No. ICC 8.798 of 8 July 1998).

[174] Preceding decisions: (i) Resolution of the DC in Ústí nad Orlicí, Case No. 5E 1245/98-18 (annotated separately in this book) and (ii) Resolution of the RC in Hradec Králové, Case No. 19 Co 337/99-42 of 30 November 1999 (also annotated separately). The case concerned recognition/enforcement of an AA rendered in arbitration at the ICC International Court of Arbitration (AA, Case No. ICC 8798 of 8 July 1998).

contracting party for commitments arising from the licensing agreement which the other contracting party breached". This was concluded despite the fact that "the debtor could not, after the takeover of the privatized property, influence in any manner the performance or non-performance of the obligations under the licensing agreement by the new contracting party" and that "the Austrian party knew about the transfer of rights and obligations to the new contracting party and negotiated with the new party with respect to the licensing agreement". (This should have constituted grounds for a refusal to enforce the decision against the debtor pursuant to Article V(2)(b) of the NYConv.) Hence, the debtor's arguments are not in fact challenging the requirements for opening of the enforcement proceedings (and only these requirements can be subject to review), but the correctness of the merits of the arbitral award proposed for enforcement. *[Further conclusions reached by the court in this decision are annotated in the commentary to Section 38 of the ArbAct.]*

11.102. Resolution of the ConCourt, Case No. IV. ÚS 189/10 of 10 May 2010: (1) (a) The state of recognition is allowed to review the arbitral award from the perspective of compliance of its effects with the fundamental principles of the state's law [public policy exception pursuant to Article V(2)(b) of the NYConv]. **(1) (b)** Due to the absence of any uniform and internationally recognized definition of public policy, the term must be interpreted [in each individual case] consistently with jurisprudence and practice in the particular country of recognition and enforcement. Generally, a conflict with public policy would occur if the enforceability of the arbitral award were **contrary to the fundamental principles of the constitutional and legal order, the social order, and public policy as such, and the breach would concern an interest which must be insisted on, unequivocally and in every respect.** **(1) (c)** A conflict with public policy arises in those cases where the **fundamental rights of the party to the proceedings** were breached in the proceedings in which the respective decision of the foreign court was rendered.[175] Insistence on the protection of the individual's fundamental rights undoubtedly belongs to such essential principles of Czech law.[176] **(1) (d)** The concept of public policy ought to be **interpreted in a relatively restrictive**

---

[175] The author is of the opinion that the ConCourt adjudicated correctly, i.e. that Article V(2)(b) of the NYConv mainly covers procedural public policy, i.e. the issue of whether overriding fundamental procedural standards were observed in the proceedings.

[176] The Constitutional Court invoked the Judgment of the ConCourt, Case No. I. ÚS 709/05, published in: Sb.n.u. [Reports of Judgments and Resolutions], Vol. 41, et. 143.

manner; mere differences in the procedural laws of a foreign arbitral tribunal and the state of recognition do not establish a conflict with public policy.[177] **(2) (a)** Therefore, an argument stating that other parties to the proceedings were represented by more legal counsels, and consequently incurred higher **costs of proceedings**, focuses only on the issue of interpretation. Application of the words "reasonable" or "adequate" regarding the costs of proceedings, as such, cannot establish a conflict with constitutional law. **(2) (b)** If the applicant argues that the costs which the applicant incurred in the part of the proceedings in which the forum ruled on the disqualification of an arbitrator for being biased were unreasonable, then such objection cannot be found justified. **It is certainly in the interest of all parties to the proceedings, including the applicant, to make sure that the proceedings and the decision in the merits do not suffer from any defect which would undermine their correctness and equitableness.** It is only natural that the costs are paid by the party who did not have standing in the merits and did not succeed in the proceedings. **(3)** An objection criticizing the **delivery of an arbitral award by a messenger service**, not by the holder of a postal license or in any other manner provided for in the CCP, is formalistic and groundless. The main point is that the arbitral award entered the sphere of the applicant, or his or her legal counsel, in compliance with the [**UNCITRAL Rules**]. **(4)** An objection that the arbitral award **is not stamped with a confirmation of legal force and effect and the confirmation of enforceability** is incongruous. The reason is that the [NYConv], which prevails over statutes, namely Section 39 [of the ArbAct], does not prescribe any such requirement (cf. Article IV [of the NYConv]). It is sufficient if the arbitral award is final and binding upon the parties and the parties undertake to perform under the award without delay (cf. Article 32(2) of the UNCITRAL Rules).[178] *[From the factual and legal findings]:* The case concerned enforcement of an LCIA arbitral award. The claims under the award were subject to execution which was ordered pursuant to Section 44(2) of the ExecProcC. The court upheld the decision. The applicant

---

[177] The Constitutional Court held that, if the court of the state of origin proceeded in compliance with procedural laws, a conflict with public policy is only possible in the most exceptional cases. The ConCourt invoked: VIKTOR VAŠKE, UZNÁNÍ A VÝKON CIZÍCH ROZHODNUTÍ V ČESKÉ REPUBLICE. [Title in translation: RECOGNITION AND ENFORCEMENT OF FOREIGN DECISIONS IN THE CZECH REPUBLIC]. Prague: C. H. Beck 44 (2007).. In this connection, the ConCourt again confirmed that the public policy exception under Article V(2)(b) of the NYConv should rather be interpreted as a procedural public policy exception.

[178] The author has applied the uniform terminology chosen for this book. The original of the ConCourt judgment refers to „Rozhodčí řád UNCITRAL" ("UNCITRAL Arbitration Rules").

argued that the arbitral award was neither final nor enforceable, because it lacked reasons, was not stamped with a confirmation of legal force and effect and a confirmation of enforceability, and the delivery by a messenger service cannot be deemed proper delivery under the CCP. The applicant also argued that the award was contrary to public policy due to an excessively high amount of the costs of proceedings to be paid by the applicant and due to the fact that the award practically lacked any reasons. All of the above-said constitutes breach of the right to a fair trial, i.e. conflicts with public policy. In this regard, the applicant also considered it unacceptable that the applicant should share the costs of the proceedings for disqualification of arbitrator whom the applicant did not challenge; moreover, this stage of the proceedings did not concern the merits. The ConCourt dismissed the constitutional complaint as manifestly unsubstantiated.

VIII. Comparison with the law of the Slovak Republic (SlovArbAct)

11.103. The applicable Slovak law is cited in the commentary to Section 38 of the ArbAct.

IX. Bibliography

ACHIM VON AHRENDT, DER ZUSTÄNDIGKEITSSTREIT IM SCHIEDSVERFAHREN, Studien zum ausländischen und internationalen Privatrecht, Bd. 48, Tübingen: J. B. Mohr (1996).

FRÉDÉRIC BACHAND, CONSENSUAL ARBITRATION IN QUEBEC, McGill Law (2008).[179]

E.–M. BAJONS, ENFORCING ANNULLED ARBITRAL AWARDS – A COMPARATIVE VIEW. CROATIAN ARBITRATION YEARBOOK, Croatian Chamber of Commerce. Zagreb 55–69 (2000).

Horst Barber, Objektive Schiedsfähigkeit und ordre public in der internationalen Schiedsgerichtsbarkeit, dissertation thesis successfully defended at Frankfurt a. M. University in 1993;

Jürgen Basedow, Die Verselbständigung des europäischen *ordre public*. In: *Coester, M., Martiny, D. et Gessaphe, K. A. P. von* Privatrecht in Europa - Vielfalt, Kollision, Kooperation, Festschrift für Hans Jürgen Sonnenberger zum 70. Geburtstag, München 291 et seq. (2004).

ANDREAS BAUMERT, EUROPÄISCHER ORDRE PUBLIC UND SONDERANKNÜPFUNG ZUR DURCHSETZUNG VON EG-

---

[179] Available online at: http://www.mcgill.ca/arbitration/law (accessed on 15 February 2019).

RECHT UNTER BESONDERER BERÜCKSICHTIGUNG DER SOGENANNTEN UNMITTELBAREN HORIZONTALEN WIRKUNG VON EG-RICHTLINIENBESTIMMUNGEN, Frankfurt a. M.: Peter Lang (1994).

JACK BEATSON; DANIEL FRIEDMANN, GOOD FAITH AND FAULT IN CONTRACT LAW, Oxford: Clarendon Press (1995).

Rolf Belke, *Grundfragen des Kartellverbots*, 143 ZHR 74-94 (1979).

Alexander J. Bělohlávek, *Nové perspektivy pro výkon zahraničních rozhodnutí a tzv. Luganská úmluva* [Title in translation: *New Perspectives for the Enforcement of Foreign Decisions and the Lugano Convention*], in: 1 PRÁVNÍ PRAXE V PODNIKÁNÍ 37–40 (1999).

Alexander J. Bělohlávek, *Pravomoci soudců a výkon rozhodnutí v kontextu vývoje evropského civilního procesu.* [Title in translation: *The Jurisdiction of Judges and the Enforcement of Decisions in the Context of Developments in European Civil Procedure*], 12 PRÁVNÍ RÁDCE 15-19 (2004).

Alexander J. Bělohlávek, *Zavedení tzv. exequatur do českého právního řádu.* [Title in translation: *Introduction of So-Called Exequatur in Czech Law*], 5 PRÁVNÍ ZPRAVODAJ 16-17 (2004).

Alexander J. Bělohlávek, *Výhrada veřejného pořádku hmotněprávního a procesního ve vztazích s mezinárodním prvkem.* [Title in translation: *Substantive and Procedural Public Policy Exception in Relationships with an International Dimension*], 145(11) PRÁVNÍK 1267-1301 (2006).

Alexander J. Bělohlávek, *Rozhodčí řízení, ordre public a trestní právo: Interakce mezinárodního a tuzemského práva soukromého a veřejného.* [Title in translation: *Arbitration, Ordre Public and Criminal Law: Interaction between International and Domestic Private and Public Law*], I et II PRAGUE: C. H. BECK (2008).[180]

Alexander J. Bělohlávek, *Rozhodčí řízení a trestní právo v tuzemském a mezinárodním kontextu.* [Title in translation: *Arbitration and Criminal Law in Domestic and International Contexts*], 5(4) PRÁVNÍ FÓRUM 140-152 (2008).

Alexander J. Bělohlávek, *Czech Republic: Procedure for Recognition and Enforcement of New York Convention Awards. In: Guide to National Rules of Procedure for Recognition and Enforcement of New York Convention Awards*, 727E ICC PUBLICATION, Paris: International Chamber of Commerce / ICC Publishing 98-102 (2009).

Alexander J. Bělohlávek, *West Tankers as a Trojan Horse with Respect to the Autonomy of Arbitration Proceedings and the New York Convention 1958: On the contentious concept of the importance of the disputed*

180 The cited edition is in Czech. The book is also available in English and Russian.

subject matter in light of subsequent decisions on the fate of anti-suit injunctions from the vantage point of Brussels-Luxembourg officialdom, 4 ASA BULLETIN 646 – 670 (2009).

Alexander J. Bělohlávek, *Mezinárodní právo soukromé evropských zemí.* [Title in translation: *Private International Law of European Countries*], PRAGUE: C. H. BECK (2010).

Alexander J. Bělohlávek, *Rozhodčí řízení v tzv. smluvních vztazích spotřebitelského typu.* [Title in translation: *Arbitration in So-Called Consumer Contractual Relationships*], 7(3) PRFO 89-99 (2010).

Alexander J. Bělohlávek, Ústavní soud České republiky opustil striktní smluvní výklad koncepce rozhodčího řízení. [Title in translation: *The Constitutional Court of the Czech Republic Has Abandoned Its Strict Contractual Interpretation of the Concept of Arbitration*], 12 BULLETIN ADVOKACIE 40-43 (2011).

Alexander J. Bělohlávek, *Hmotněprávní a procesní ordre public a jeho reálná podoba v době globalizace a europeizace.* [Title in translation: *Substantive and Procedural Ordre Public and Its Real Form in the Age of Globalization and Europeanization*], 1 DIES IURIS TYRNAVIENSIS – TRNAVSKÉ PRÁVNICKÉ DNI [TRNAVA DAYS OF LAW]: PRÁVO V EURÓPSKEJ PERSPEKTÍVE / LAW IN EUROPEAN PERSPECTIVE, TRNAVA [SLOVAKIA]: TRNAVA UNIVERSITY IN TRNAVA, FACULTY OF LAW, SLOVAK REPUBLIC 36-53 (Peter Blaho, et A. Švecová, eds., 2011).

Klaus P. Berger, *Die Regelung der gerichtlichen Anfechtbarkeit internationaler Schiedssprpche in europäischen Schiedsgesetzen*, 35 RIW 850–857 (1989).

T. R. Bertheau, Das New Yorker Abkommen vom 10. Juni 1958 über die Anerkennung und Vollstreckung ausländischer Schiedssprüche, dissertation thesis successfully defended at the University of Zürich (CH), 1965;

Veronika Bílková, *Mezinárodní úmluva o potlačování financování terorismu.* [Title in translation: *The International Convention for the Suppression of the Financing of Terrorism*], 145(6) PRÁVNÍK 672-696 (2006).

Marc Blessing, *Mandatory Rules of Law versus Party Autonomy in International Arbitration*, 4 JIA 23 et seq. (1997).

Karl-Heinz Böckstiegel, *Public Policy and Arbitrability*, 3 Comparative Arbitration Practice and Public Policy in Arbitration, ICCA Congress Series 177 et seq. (Peter Sanders ed., 1987).

KARL-HEINZ BÖCKSTIEGEL, SCHIEDSGERICHTSBARKEIT IM UMFELD VON POLITIK, WIRTSCHAFT UND GERICHTSBARKEIT, Köln a. R.: Carl Heymann (1992).

Karl-Heinz Böckstiegel, *Die Bedeutung der Schiedsgerichtsbarkeit im gegenwärtigen politischen und wirtschaftlichen Umfeld*, SCHIEDSGERICHTSBARKEIT IM UMFELD VON POLITIK, WIRTSCHAFT UND GERICHTSBARKEIT, Köln a. R.: Carl Heymann 17 et seq. (Karl-Heinz Böckstiegel ed., 1992).

MICHAEL BOGDAN, THE BRUSSELS JURISDICTION AND ENFORCEMENT CONVENTION: AN EC COURT CASEBOOK, Stockholm: Kluwer Law International (1996).

GEORG BORGES, DAS DOPPELEXEQUATUR VON SCHIEDSSPRÜCHEN: DIE ANERKENNUNG AUSLÄNDISCHER SCHIEDS SPRÜCHE UND EXEQUATURENSCHEIDUNGEN, Berlin: der Gruyter, (1997).

Mark A. Buchanan, *Public Policy and International Commercial Arbitration*, 26 AMERICAN BUSINESS LAW JOURNAL 511 et seq. (1988).

William W. Burke-White; Andreas von Staden, *Private Litigation in a Public Law Sphere: The Standard of Review in Investor-State Arbitrations*, 35(2) YALE JOURNAL OF INTERNATIONAL LAW 283-346 (2010).

Erwin Chemerinsky, *Constitutional Law: Principles and Policies*, SERIES - ASPEN TREATISE SERIES, NEW YORK: ASPEN PUBLISHERS (3rd ed., 2006).

Adeline Chong, *The Public Policy and Mandatory Rules of Third Countries in International Contracts*, 2 JOURNAL OF PRIVATE INTERNATIONAL LAW 27 et seq. (2006).

Katarína Chovancová, *Lex Causae a Lex Mercatoria v medzinárodnej arbitrážnej praxi: Švajčiarsky príklad*. [Title in translation: *Lex Causae and Lex Mercatoria in the Practice of International Arbitration: The Swiss Example*], 13(12) BULLETIN SLOVENSKEJ ADVOKÁCIE 27-37 (2007).

Katarína Chovancová, *Enforcement of Arbitral Awards in the New Countries of the European Union*, 16(6) EUROPEAN REVIEW OF PRIVATE LAW 995-1007 (2008).

Katarína Chovancová, *Res iudicata v medzinárodnej arbitrážnej praxi*. [Title in translation: *Res Judicata in International Arbitration Practice*], 14(9 – Part I) 14(10 - Part II) BULLETIN SLOVENSKEJ ADVOKÁCIE 29-38 et 20-28 (2008).

Anthony Cioni, *The First Pancake Always Has Lumps: Alberta Petroleum Companies, Arbitration and Arbitral Award Enforcement in the Russian Federation*, 35 ALBERTA LAW REVIEW 726 et seq. (1997).

EMMANUELLE CLAUDEL, ENTENTES ANTICONCURRENTIELLES ET DROIT DES CONTRATS: THESE

POUR LE DOCTORAT EN DROIT PRESENTEE ET SOUTENUE PUBLIQUEMENT LE 14. DECEMBRE 1994;[181]

ROBERT CONLE, PUBLIC POLICY AND ENFORCEMENT OF INTERNATIONAL COMMERCIAL AWARDS – CURSE OR BLESSING?, Cape Town: School for Advanced Legal Studies (2007).

Marieke de Goede, *The Politics of Preemption and the War on Terror in Europe*, 14(1) EUROPEAN JOURNAL OF INTERNATIONAL RELATIONS 161-185 (2008).

CH. DELANOY, LE CONTROLE DE L'ORDRE PUBLIC AU FOND PAR LE JUGE DE L'ANNULATION: TROIS CONSTATS, TROIS PROPOSITIONS, Rev. arb., 177 et seq. (2007).

Petr Dobiáš, *Uznání a výkon rozhodčích nálezů zrušených ve státě původu podle relevantní judikatury zahraničních obecných soudů.* [Title in translation: *The Recognition and Enforcement of Arbitral Awards Annulled in the State of Origin Pursuant to the Relevant Case Law of Foreign Courts*], 146(3) PRÁVNÍK 325-336 (2007).

Petr Dobiáš, *Uznání a výkon cizích rozhodčích nálezů ve Spolkové republice Německo podle judikatury německých obecných soudů.* [Title in translation: *The Recognition and Enforcement of Foreign Arbitral Awards in the Federal Republic of Germany According to the Case Law of German Courts*], 1 ACTA UNIVERSITATIS CAROLINAE – IURIDICA 37-47 (2008).

J. Donald, *Applying the Public Policy-Exception to Labor Arbitration Awards*, DISPUTE RESOLUTION JOURNAL (2003-2004)[182]

TAMARA EGBEDI, AN ANALYSIS OF THE EFFECT OF PUBLIC POLICY ON PARTY AUTONOMY IN INTERNATIONAL ARBITRATION, Definizione e funzionamento dell'ordine pubblico nel diritto internazionale privato, Roma: Quasar (C. F. Emanuele, ed.,1996).

Nelson Enonchong, *Public Policy in the Conflict of laws: A Chinese Wall Around Little England?*, 3 ICLQ 663-661 (1996).

Ibrahim Fadlallah, *L'ordre public dans les sentences arbitrales*, V RCADI 377. et seq. (1994).

Ibrahim Fadlallah, *Arbitrage international et litiges fiscaux*, REV. ARB. 299–310 (2001).

Josef Fiala, *Spory vznikající z podnětu výkonu rozhodnutí (exekuční spory)* [Title in translation: *Disputes Arising from Enforcement Proceedings (Execution Disputes)*], ACTA UNIVERSITATIS CAROLINAE – IURIDICA, Monographia XVI, Prague: Charles University (1972).

---

[181] Available online at: http:// glose.org (accessed on 15 February 2019).
[182] Available online at: http://findarticles.com/p/articles/mi_qa3923/is_200311/ai_n9463726 (accessed on 15 February 2019).

Ľuboš Fojtík; Lenka Macáková, *Otazníky nad uznáním a výkonem cizích rozhodčích nálezů*. [Title in translation: *Question Marks Over the Recognition and Enforcement of Foreign Arbitral Awards*], 6(5) PRÁVNÍ FÓRUM 184-188 (2009).

Emmanuel Gaillard, *Enforcement of Awards Set Aside in the Country of Origin: The French Experience*, IMPROVING THE EFFICIENCY OF ARBITRATION AGREEMENTS AND AWARDS, Den Haag: KLI, (1994).

REINHOLD GEIMER, ANERKENNUNG AUSLÄNDISCHER ENTSCHEIDUNGEN IN DEUTSCHLAND, München: Beck (1995).

Aleš Gerloch, *Mezinárodní smlouvy o lidských právech jako pramen českého práva*. [Title in translation: *International Treaties on Human Rights as a Source of Czech Law*], 43(1) ACTA UNIVERSITATIS CAROLINAE - IURIDICA, Prague: Charles University 41-46 (1997).

G. Gest, J.-P. Le Gall, Philippe Martin; P. Pouliguen, et P. Saint-Amand, *L'ordre fiscal international*, 37 DROIT FISCAL 822 et seq. (13th ed., 2007);

HAMID G. GHARAVI, THE INTERNATIONAL EFFECTIVENESS OF THE ANNULMENT OF AN ARBITRAL AWARD, Den Haag / New York: Kluwer Law International (2002).

ULRICH HAAS, ANERKENNUNG UND VOLLSTRECKUNG AUSLÄNDISCHER UND INTERNATIONALER SCHIEDSSPRÜCHE, Berlin: Duncker & Humblot (1991).

WALTER J. HABSCHEID, DIE SCHIEDSGERICHTSBARKEIT UND DER ORDRE PUBLIC, Liber amicorum Max Keller, Zürich: Schulthess 575-587 (Peter Forstmoser ed., 1989).

Bernard Hanoatiau, *What Law Governs the Issue of Arbitrability?*, 12(4) Arb. Int. 373-390 (1996).

Ragnar Harbst, *Korruption und andere ordre public Verstöße als Einwände im Schiedsverfahren*, 5 SCHIEDSVZ 22-31 (2007.

Troy L. Harris, *The Public Policy Exception to Enforcement of International Arbitration Awards under the New York Convention*, 1 JIA 9-24 (2007).

Anton Heini, *Der materiellrechtliche Ordre public im neuen schweizerischen Recht der internationalen Schiedsgerichtsbarkeit*, WALTER F. LINDACHER, FESTSCHRIFT FÜR WALTHER J. HABSCHEID ZUM 65. GEBURTSTAG, BIELEFELD: GIESEKING 153–159 (1989).

EKKHARDT HEYMANN, DER ORDRE PUBLIC IN DER PRIVATEN SCHIEDSGERICHTSBARKEIT, Bielefeld: Gieseking (1969).

BURKHARD HESS, URTEILSFREIZÜGIGKEIT UND ORDRE PUBLIC-VORBEHALT BEI VERSTÖSSEN GEGEN

VERFAHRENSGRUNDRECHTE UND MARKTFREIHEITEN, Praxis des internationalen Privat- und Verfahrensrechts (2001).

PETR HLAVSA, EXEKUČNÍ ŘÁD S VÝKLADEM A PROVÁDĚCÍMI PŘEDPISY [Title in translation: THE EXECUTORY PROCEDURE CODE WITH A COMMENTARY AND IMPLEMENTING LEGISLATION], Prague: Linde 48–50 (2001.

Kaj I. Hobér, *Defenses to Recognition and Enforcement of Foreign Arbitral Awards in the United States*, 48 NORDISK TIDSSKRIFT FOR INTERNATIONAL RET 38-57 (1978.

Kaj I. Hobér, *Ogiltighet och klander i internationella skiljeförfaranden. Högsta domstolen meddelar beslut i Uganda-målet* [Title in translation: *Invalidity and Defense Against Arbitral Awards in International Arbitration. The Supreme Court Decides the Uganda Case*], YEARBOOK OF THE ARBITRATION INSTITUTE OF THE STOCKHOLM CHAMBER OF COMMERCE (1989).

Kaj I. Hobér, *Enforcing Foreign Arbitral Awards Against Russian Entities*, 35 Acta Juridica Hungarica 257-304 (1993).

Kaj I. Hobér, *Enforcing Foreign Arbitral Awards Against Russian Entities*, 10(1) ARB. INT. (1994).

PAVEL HOLLÄNDER, ÚSTAVNĚPRÁVNÍ ARGUMENTACE: OHLÉDNUTÍ PO DESETI LETECH ÚSTAVNÍHO SOUDU [Title in translation: CONSTITUTIONAL LAW ARGUMENTS: LOOKING BACK AFTER TEN YEARS OF THE CONSTITUTIONAL COURT], Prague: Linde (2003).

Libor Holý, *Zásada dobrých mravů v řízení o uznání a výkonu cizích exekučních rozhodnutí v české rozhodovací praxi / Principle of Good Manners in the Process of Recognition and Enforcing a Foreign Enforcement Order. In: The Czech Jurisdiction. Paper presented at the COFOLA 2011 Conference*, 390 COLLECTION OF ARTICLES, SPISY PRÁVNICKÉ FAKULTY MU [COLLECTION OF PAPERS, FACULTY OF LAW, MASARYK UNIVERSITY], ACADEMIC SERIES, BRNO: MASARYK UNIVERSITY 47-56 (Eva Žatecká; Lucia Kováčová; Ján Horecký; Vojtěch Vomáčka eds., 2011).[183]

GÜNTHER J. HORVATH, THE DUTY OF THE TRIBUNAL TO RENDER AN ENFORCEABLE AWARD, JIA 135 et seq. (1994).

JÁN HUSÁR, PRÁVNA REGULÁCIA INGERENCIE VEREJNEJ MOCI DO PODNIKANIA [Title in translation: LEGAL REGULATION OF THE INTERVENTION OF STATE POWER IN BUSINESS], Košice: Equilibria (2007).

---

[183] Also available online at: http://www.law.muni.cz/sborniky/cofola2011/files/mravy/Holy_Libor_6296.pdf (accessed on 15 February 2019).

Michael Hwang; Amy Lai, *Do egregious errors amount to a breach of public policy?*, 71(1) ARBITRATION 1-24 (2005).

IA, OMEZENÍ AUTONOMIE VŮLE SMLUVNÍCH STRAN [TITLE IN TRANSLATION: LIMITING THE AUTONOMY OF WILL OF THE CONTRACTING PARTIES], E-Polis;[184]

J.-M. JACQUET, LA FONCTION SUPRANATIONALE DE LA RÈGLE DE CONFLITS DE LOIS, Rec. des Cours de La Haye, t.292, 151-248 (2002).

Antone Johnson, *Illegal Contracts and Arbitration Clauses*, 2 INTERNATIONAL ARBITRATION LAW REVIEW 35 et seq. (1999).

DAVID JOSEPH, JURISDICTION AND ARBITRATION AGREEMENTS AND THEIR ENFORCEMENT, London: Sweet & Maxwell (2005).

VIEROSLAV JÚDA, PRÁVNA ÚPRAVA PROBLEMATIKY PRANIA ŠPINAVÝCH PENAZÍ V EURÓPSKEJ ÚNII. [Title in translation: THE LEGAL REGULATION OF MONEY LAUNDERING IN THE EUROPEAN UNION], Jaroslav Klátik, Integrácia a unifikácia práva Európskej únie v oblasti trestného zákonodarstva [Title in translation: Integration and Unification of European Union Law in Criminal Legislation], Collection of Papers from the International Virtual Interdisciplinary Academic Conference held on 30 December 2008 at the Faculty of Law, UMB in Banská Bystrica, Banská Bystrica: Matej Bel University, Faculty of Law, Public Law Department 52-61 (2008).

Ajay Jugran, *Meaning of "Public Policy"*, 3(5) TDM (2006).

PHILIPPE KAHN, LES PRINCIPES GENERAUX DU DROIT DEVANT LES ARBITRES DU COMMERCE INTERNATIONAL, JDI 305-327 (1989).

Zdeněk Kapitán, *Teorie veřejného pořádku a kritéria jeho použití.* [Title in translation: *The Theory of Public Policy and the Criteria of Its Application*], 3(Part I) 4(Part II) ČASOPIS PRO PRÁVNÍ VĚDU A PRAXI (2004).

Roman Kozel, *Věcná příslušnost soudů podle § 9 odst. 3 písm. a) o. s. ř.* [Title in translation: *The Subject-Matter Jurisdiction of Courts under Section 9(3)(a) of the CCP*], 6-7 BULLETIN ADVOKACIE 45 et seq. (1997).

VLADIMÍR KURKA; LJUBOMÍR DRÁPAL, VÝKON ROZHODNUTÍ V SOUDNÍM ŘÍZENÍ [Title in translation: THE ENFORCEMENT OF DECISIONS IN COURT PROCEEDINGS], Prague: Linde (2004).

---

[184] Available online at: http://www.e-polis.cz/mezinarodni-pravo/154-rimska-umluva-o-pravu-pouzitelnem-pro-zavazky-ze-smluv-4-omezeni-autonomie-vule-smluvnich-stran.html (accessed on 15 February 2019).

PIERRE LALIVE, TRANSNATIONAL (OR TRULY INTERNATIONAL) PUBLIC POLICY AND INTERNATIONAL ARBITRATION: PROCEEDINGS OF THE ICCA NEW YORK CONFERENCE (1986).

Pierre Lalive, *Transnational Public Policy and International Arbitration*, 3 ICCA CONGRESS SERIES 257-318 (1987).

Pierre Lalive, *Absolute Finality of Arbitral Awards?* 6 REVISTA INTERNACIONAL DE ARBITRAGEM E CONCILIAÇÃO, ASSOCIAÇÃO, PORTUGUESA DE ARBITRAGEM 109-127 (2008).

Pierre Lalive, *L´ordre public transnational et l´arbitre international*, LIBER FAUSTO POCAR, PART II: NOUVEAUX INSTRUMENTS DU DROIT INTERNATIONAL PRIVE. MILAN: DOTT. A. GIUFFRÈ EDITORE, S.P.A 599-611 (G. Venturini, et S. Bariatti, eds., 2009).

Pierre Lastenouse, *Why Setting Aside an Arbitral Award is Not Enough to Remove It from the International Scene*, 2 JIA 25-48 (1999).

Dieter Leipold, *Neuere Erkenntnisse des EuGH und des BGH zum anerkennungsrechtlichen ordre public*, LIBER AMICORUM HANS STOLL, TÜBINGEN: J. C. B. MOHL (PAUL SIEBECK), 625-646 (G. Hohloch, ed., 2001).

Jiři Malenovský, *Postavení mezinárodních smluv o lidských právech v českém právu po 1. červnu 2002.* [Title in translation: *The Status of International Human Rights Treaties in Czech Law After 1 June 2002*], 9 PRÁVNÍK 917 et seq. (2002).

Fernando Mantilla-Serrano, *Towards a transnational procedural public policy*, 20(4) ARB. INT. 333-353 (2004).

VILÉM MÁSÍLKO, MEZE POUŽITÍ CIZÍHO PRÁVA U ČESKOSLOVENSKÝCH SOUDŮ A NOTÁŘSTVÍ. [Title in translation: THE LIMITS OF APPLYING FOREIGN LAW IN CZECHOSLOVAK COURTS AND NOTARIES]. Socialistická zákonnost 74 et seq. (1974).

ANTON G. MAURER, THE PUBLIC POLICY EXCEPTION UNDER THE NEW YORK CONVENTION: HISTORY, INTERPRETATION AND APPLICATION. HUNTINGTON, New York: Juris Net (2012).

Pierre Mayer; Audley Sheppard, *Final ILA Report on Public Policy as a Bar to Enforcement of International Arbitral Awards*, 19(2) ARB. INT. 249-263 (2003.

PIERRE MAYER, LA SENTENCE CONTRAIRE A L'ORDRE PUBLIC AU FOND, Rev. Arb. 615 et seq. (1994).

R. B. von Mehren, *The Eco-Swiss Case and International Arbitration*, 19(4) Arb. Int. 465-476 (2003).

OLAF MEYER, THE CIVIL LAW CONSEQUENCES OF CORRUPTION, Baden-Baden: Nomos (2009).

Alex Mills, *The Dimensions of Public Policy in Private International Law*, 4(2) JPIL 201-236 (2008).

Loukas Mistelis, *Keeping the Unruly Horse in Control or Public Policy as a Bar to Enforcement of (Foreign) Arbitral Awards*, 2 International Law Forum Du Droit International 248 et seq. (2000).

J.-H. MOITRY, ARBITRAGE INTERNATIONAL ET DROIT DE LA CONCURRENCE: VERS UN ORDRE PUBLIC DE LA LEX MERCATORIA. RdA 3-36 (1989).

Peter Molnár, *Uznávanie vyknateľnosti cudzích exekučných titulov v Slovenskej republike.* [Title in translation: *The Recognition of Enforceability of Foreign Enforcement Titles in the Slovak Republic*], 14(1-2) BULLETIN SLOVENSKEJ ADVOKÁCIE 8-12 (2008).

ALEKSANDR I. MURANOV, USPOLNENIJE INOSTRANNYCH SUDEBNYCH I ARBITRAŽNYCH REŠENIJ. KOMPETENCIJA ROSSIJSKUCH SUDOV, Moscow: Justicinform (2002).

Tamara N. Nešataeva, *O sudebnom kontrole za alternativnymi sposobami razrešenija predprinimatelskuch konfliktov*, 4 Voprosy pravoprimenenija 23 (2001).

PAUL OBERHAMMER, GEMEINSCHAFTSRECHT UND SCHIEDSRECHTLICHER ORDRE PUBLIC, Österreichisches Recht der Wirtschaft 62 et seq. (1999).

P. PAJARDI, CODICE DE FALLIMENTO, Milano: Giuffre (4th ed., 1993).

Ioannis M. Papagiannis, *Die Vollstreckung ausländischer Schiedssprüche nach ihrer Annullierung im Herkunftsstaat*, 98(2) ZVGLRWISS 139-174 (1999).

S. PATTI, U. STEIN, S. BARIATTI, CHR. BECKER, L. SALAZAR, ET K. NEHM, KLAUSELRICHTLINIE - MOBILIARSICHERHEITEN - STRAFVERFOLGUNG, Heidelberg: C. H. Müller Verlag (2005).

Monika Pauknerová, *Eingriffsnormen im tschechischen Internationalen Privatrecht*, PRIVATRECHT IN EUROPA, Vielfalt, Kollision, Kooperation. Liber amicorum Sonnenberger, München: C. H. Beck 575 et seq. (M. Coestner; D. Martiny; Karl A. von Sachsen Gessaphe, eds., 2004).

Mark Pilkington, *Illegal Residence & the Acquisition of a Domicile of Choice*, 33 ICLQ 885 et seq. (1984).

JEAN-FRANCOIS POUDRET; SEBASTIEN BESSON, COMPARATIVE LAW OF INTERNATIONAL ARBITRATION, London: Thomson / Sweet & Maxwell (2nd ed., 2007).

L. G. RADICATI DI BROZOLO, MONDIALISATION, JURIDICTION, ARBITRAGE: VERS DES RÈGLES D'APPLICATION SEMI-NÉCESSAIRES?, Rev. crit. DIP 1 et seq. (2003).

L. G. Radicati di Brozolo, *Antitrust: A Paradigm of the Relations Between Mandatory Rules and Arbitration - A Fresh Look at the "Second Look"*, 7(1) INTERNATIONAL ARBITRATION LAW REVIEW 23-37 (2004.

L. G. Radicati di Brozolo, *Arbitrage commercial international et lois de police: considérations sur les conflits de juridictions dans le commerce international*, 315 RECUEIL DES COURS 265-501 (2005).

L. G. RADICATI DI BROZOLO, L'ILLICEITE QUI CREVE LES YEUX: CRITERE DE CONTROLE DES SENTENCES ARBITRALES AU REGARD DE L'ORDRE PUBLIC INTERNATIONAL, Rev. arb. 530 et seq. (2005).

PETR RADOSOVSKÝ, ROZHODNE PRAVO V ZAVAZKOVÝCH VZTAZICH Z MEZINARODNIHO OBCHODU: NUTNE POUZITELNE NORMY, VÝHRADA VEREJNEHO PORADKU [Title in translation: APPLICABLE LAW IN OBLIGATIONS ARISING FROM INTERNATIONAL TRADE: OVERRIDING MANDATORY RULES, PUBLIC POLICY EXCEPTION];[185]

HILMAR RAESCHKE-KESSLER, BINNENMARKT, SCHIEDSGERICHTSBARKEIT UND ORDRE PUBLIC, EuZW 145-150 (1990).

G. REICHELT, „EUROPÄESCHER" ORDRE PUBLIC IM AUTONOMEN KOLLSIONSRECHT, ZfRV 217 et seq. (1975).

MICHAEL W. REISMAN, SYSTEMS OF CONTROL IN INTERNATIONAL ADJUDICATION AND ARBITRATION, Durham (North Carolina / USA) (1992).

MICHAEL W. REISMAN, LAW, INTERNATIONAL PUBLIC POLICY (SO-CALLED) AND ARBITRAL CHOICE IN INTERNATIONAL COMMERCIAL ARBITRATION, ICCA Paper for delivery in Montreal (2006).

Oliver Remien, *Europäisches Kartellrecht (Artt. 81 f. EG-Vertrag) als Eingriffsnorm oder ordre public in neueren internationalen Schiedsrechtsfällen*, DIE RICHTIGE ORDNUNG: FESTSCHRIFT FÜR JAN KROPHOLLER ZUM 70. GEBURTSTAG, Tübingen: Mohr Siebeck (D. Baetge, Jan von Hein; Michael von Hinden eds., 2008).

---

[185] Available online at: epravo.cz as Document No. 22.523 and available at: http://www.epravo.cz/top/clanky/rozhodne-pravo-v-zavazkovych-vztazich-z-mezinarodniho-obchodu-nutne-pouzitelne-normy-vyhrada-verejneho-poradku-22523.html (accessed on 15 February 2019).

THILO RENNSMANN, ANATIONALE SCHIEDSSPRÜCHE – EINE UNTERSUCHUNG ZU DEN WIRKUNGEN ANATIONALER SCHIEDSSPRÜCHE IM NATIONALEN RECHT (1997).

BOHUMIL REPÍK, ĽUDSKÉ PRÁVA V SÚDNOM KONANÍ [Title in translation: HUMAN RIGHTS IN COURT PROCEEDINGS], Bratislava: MANZ (1999).

Francis Reynolds, *Illegality by the lex loci solutionis*, 107 LQR 553 et seq. (1991).

MARKUS S. RIEDER; ANDREAS SCHOENEMANN, KORRUPTIONSVERDACHT, ZIVILPROZESS UND SCHIEDSVERFAHREN, NJW 1169-1175 (2011.

Jose Rosell; Harvey Prager, *Illicit Commissions and International Arbitration: The Question of Proof*, 15 ARB. INT. 329 et seq. (1999).

Wulf-Henning Roth, *Der Einfluss der Grundfreiheiten auf das internationales Privat- und Verfahresrechtr*, SYSTEMWECHSEL IM EUROPÄISCHEN KOLLISIONSRECHT, München: C. H. Beck 47 et seq. (J. F. Baur; Peter Mansel eds., 2002).

Naděžda Rozehnalová, *K uznání a výkonu cizích rozhodčích nálezů.* [Title in translation: *Regarding the Recognition and Enforcement of Foreign Arbitral Awards*], 12(2) OBCHODNÍ PRÁVO 2-9 (2003).

NADĚŽDA ROZEHNALOVÁ, ROZHODČÍ ŘÍZENÍ V MEZINÁRODNÍM A VNITROSTÁTNÍM OBCHODNÍM STYKU. [Title in translation: ARBITRATION IN INTERNATIONAL AND NATIONAL COMMERCE], ASPI Wolters Kluwer (2008).

KVĚTOSLAV RŮŽIČKA, ROZHODČÍ ŘÍZENÍ PŘED ROZHODČÍM SOUDEM PŘI HOSPODÁŘSKÉ KOMOŘE ČESKÉ REPUBLIKY A AGRÁRNÍ KOMOŘE ČESKÉ REPUBLIKY. [Title in translation: ARBITRATION IN THE ARBITRATION COURT AT THE ECONOMIC CHAMBER OF THE CZECH REPUBLIC AND AGRICULTURAL CHAMBER OF THE CZECH REPUBLIC], Dobrá Voda u Pelhřimova: Aleš Čeněk 179–184 (2003).

Peter Sanders, *Comparative Arbitration Practice and Public Policy in Arbitration*, 3 ICCA CONGRESS SERIES (1987).

Peter Sanders, *Comparative Arbitration Practise and Public Policy*, 3 Arbitration. International Council for Commercial Arbitration Congress, Deventer (1987).

OTTO SANDROCK, ZUM ORDRE PUBLIC BEI DER ANERKENNUNG UND VOLLSTRECKUNG AUSLÄNDISCHER SCHIEDSSPRÜCHE, „LOCAL REMEDIES", UNPARTEILICHKEIT UND UNABHÄNGIGKEIT VON SCHIEDSRICHTERN (ZU BGH, URTEIL VOM 1.2.2001 – AZ. III ZR 332/99), IPax 550-557 (2001).

OTTO SANDROCK, ZUM ORDRE PUBLIC BEI DER ANERKENNUNG UND VOLLSTRECKUNG AUSLÄNDISCHER SCHIEDSSPRÜCHE, IPRax 550 et seq. (2001.

CHRISTOPHE SERAGLINI, LOIS DE POLICE ET JUSTICE ARBITRALE INTERNATIONALE, Paris: Dalloz (2001).

Christophe Seraglini, *L'affaire Thalès et le non-usage immodéré de l'exception d'ordre public (ou les dérèglements de la déréglementation)*, 3 GAZ. PAL., CAH. DE L'ARBITRAGE 87 et seq. (2006).

Christophe Seraglini, *Les parties faibles face à l'arbitrage international: à la recherche de l'équilibre*, 4 GAZ. PAL., CAH. DE L'ARBITRAGE 5 et seq. (2007).

Vesselina Shaleva, *The Public Policy Exception to the Recognition and Enforcement of Arbitral Awards in the Theory and Jurisprudence of the Central and East European States and Russia*, 19(1) ARB. INT. 67-93 (2003).

Audley Sheppard, *Interim ILA Report on Public Policy as a Bar to Enforcement of International Arbitral Awards*, 19(2) Arb. Int. 217-248 (2003).

Audley Sheppard, *Public Policy and the Enforcement of Arbitral Awards: Should There be a Global Standard?*, 1(1) Transnational Dispute Management (2004).[186]

Matthias Scherer, *Three Recent Decisions of the Swiss Federal Tribunal Regarding Assignments and Transfer of Arbitration Agreements*, 1 ASA Bulletin 109–119 (2002).

Fabian von Schlabendorff, *Geldwäsche in internationalen Schiedsverfahren, Grenzüberschreitungen*, LIBER AMICORUM P. SCHLOSSER, Tübingen: Mohr Siebeck 851 et seq. (Birgid Bachmann; Stephan Breidenbach; Dagmar Coester-Waltjen; Burkhard Hess; Andreas Nelle; Christian Wolf eds., 2005).

PETER SCHLOSSER, AUSLÄNDISCHE SCHIEDSSPRÜCHE UND ORDRE PUBLIK „INTERNATIONAL" (ZU BHG, 18. 1. 1990 – III ZR 269/88), Iprax 218-220 (1991).

P. SCHMIT, LA COMMUNAUTARISATION DE L'ORDRE PUBLIC EN DROIT INTERNATIONAL PRIVE. Ann. dr. lux. 333-418 (2005).

H. C. SCHULTHESS, DER VERFAHRENSRECHTLICHE ORDRE PUBLIC IN DER INTERNATIONALEN SCHIEDSGERICHTSBARKEIT IN DER SCHWEIZ, Zürich: ADAG Administration und Druck AG (1981).

---

[186] Available online at: http://www.transnational-dispute-management.com/samples/freearticles/tv1-1-article_67.htm. (accessed on 15 February 2019).

Stephen M. Schwebel; Susan G. Lahne, *Public Policy and Arbitral Procedure*, 3 COMPARATIVE ARBITRATION PRACTICE AND PUBLIC POLICY IN ARBITRATION. ICCA CONGRESS SERIES, Deventer: Kluwer Law and Taxation Publishers 205-226 (Peter Sanders ed., 1987).

Hrvoje Sikirič, *Arbitražni postupak i javni poredak*, 51(1) Zbornik Pravnog fakulteta u Zagrebu 57-82 (2001).

S. I. Strong, *Enforcing Class Arbitration in the International Sphere: Due Process and Public Policy Concerns*, 30 U. PA. J. INT'L L. 1 et seq. (2008-2009.

Karel Střelec, *K možnosti uznání a výkonu zrušeného cizího rozhodčího nálezu.* [Title in translation: *Regarding the Possibility of Recognition and Enforcement of an Annulled Foreign Arbitral Award*], 3 BULLETIN ADVOKACIE 34–44 (2004).

JÁN SVÁK; ĽUBOR CIBULKA, ÚSTAVNÉ PRÁVO SLOVENSKEJ REPUBLIKY. [Title in translation: CONSTITUTIONAL LAW OF THE SLOVAK REPUBLIC], Žilina: Poradca podnikateľa (2006).

Klára Svobodová-Drličková, *Arbitrabilita jako důvod pro odmítnutí uznání a výkonu cizího rozhodčího nálezu.* [Title in translation: *Arbitrability as a Reason for a Refusal to Recognize and Enforce a Foreign Arbitral Award*], 374 COFOLA 2010: COLLECTION OF PAPERS. SPISY PRÁVNICKÉ FAKULTY MU, ŘADA TEORETICKÁ [COLLECTION OF PAPERS, FACULTY OF LAW, MASARYK UNIVERSITY, ACADEMIC SERIES], Brno 919-940 (2010).[187]

Pavel Šturma, *Mezinárodní závazky v rámci kontrolních mechanismů v oblasti lidských práv.* [Title in translation: *International Obligations Within the Framework of Human Rights Control Mechanisms*], IMPLEMENTACE LIDSKÝCH PRÁV A MEZINÁRODNÍ KONTROLNÍ MECHANISMY [Title in translation: THE IMPLEMENTATION OF HUMAN RIGHTS AND INTERNATIONAL CONTROL MECHANISMS], Prague: Vodnář / Faculty of Law, Charles University Prague 11-43 (1999).

Johannes Trappe, *„Révision au fond" bei der Vollstreckung eines Schiedsspruchs – eine Anmerkung*, 2 Recht und Praxis der Schiedsgerichtsbarkeit 7 et seq. (2000).

ANTONÍN TRIPES, EXEKUCE V SOUDNÍ PRAXI [Title in translation: ENFORCEMENT PROCEEDINGS (EXECUTION) IN THE PRACTICE OF COURTS], Prague: C. H. Beck (2nd ed., 2001).

FRANCK VALENCIA, PARTIES FAIBLES ET ACCÈS À LA JUSTICE EN MATIÈRE D'ARBITRAGE, Rev. arb. 45 et seq. (2007).

---

[187] Also available online at: http://www.law.muni.cz/sborniky/cofola2010/files/sbornik/sbornik.pdf (accessed on 15 February 2019).

J. Varšo, *Postavenie ordre public v medzinárodnom súkromnom práve.* [Title in translation: *The Status of Ordre Public in Private International Law*], ZBORNÍK K AKTUÁLNYM OTÁZKÁM ROZVOJA SÚČASNÉHO MEDZINÁRODNÉHO PRÁVA [Title in translation: COLLECTION OF PAPERS REGARDING CURRENT DEVELOPMENTS IN CONTEMPORARY INTERNATIONAL LAW], Bratislava 225–237 (1984).

VIKTOR VAŠKE, UZNÁNÍ A VÝKON CIZÍCH ROZHODNUTÍ V ČESKÉ REPUBLICE. [Title in translation: THE RECOGNITION AND ENFORCEMENT OF FOREIGN DECISIONS IN THE CZECH REPUBLIC]. Prague: C. H. Beck (2007).

JAN VESELÝ; ADAM RAKOVSKÝ; PETR MIKŠOVSKÝ; RADKA ŠIMKOVÁ, ZÁKON O VEŘEJNÝCH DRAŽBÁCH, KOMENTÁŘ. [Title in translation: THE PUBLIC AUCTIONS ACT, A COMMENTARY], Prague: C. H. Beck (2001).

E. A.Vinogradova, *Rossijskij sud ne vprave otmenit rešenije tretejskogo suda, vynesennoc na territorii drugogo gosudarstva,* 6 ROSSIJSKAJA JUSTICIJA 31 et al. (2002).

CHRISTIAN VÖLKER, ZUR DOGMATIK DES ORDRE PUBLIC – DIE VORBEHALTSKLAUSELN BEI DER ANERKENNUNG FREMDER GERICHTLICHER ENTSCHEIDUNGEN UND IHR VERHÄLTNIS ZUM ORDRE PUBLIC DES KOLLISIONSRECHTS (1998).

J. VOSKA, KOMENTÁŘ KE KONKURSNÍMU ŘÁDU (64/1931 SB.). [Title in translation: A COMMENTARY ON THE BANKRUPTCY CODE (64/1931 COLL.)], Prague (1931).

Peter Wahl, *Enforcement of Foreign Arbitral Awards Set Aside in their Country of Origin. The Chromalloy Case Revisited,* 14(4) JOURNAL OF INTERNATIONAL ARBITRATION, Den Haag: Kluwer Law International 131–140 (1999).

Ramses A. Wessel, *Editorial: The UN, the EU and Jus Cogens,* 3 INTERNATIONAL ORGANIZATIONS LAW REVIEW, Leiden (NL): Koninklijke Brill NV 1-6 (2006).

Elise P. Wheeless, *Recent Development, Article V(1)(b) of the New York Convention,* 7 EMORY INTERNATIONAL LAW REVIEW 805 et seq. (1993).

ACHIM VON WINTERFELD, NOCH EINMAL: DER DEUTCHE ORDRE PUBLIC IN DER INTERNATIONALEN SCHIEDSGERICHTSBARKEIT, NJW 3059-3061 (1987).

REGINA WUNDERER, DER DEUTSCHE „ORDRE PUBLIC D' ARBITRAGE INTERNATIONAL" UND METHODEN SEINER KONKRETISIERUNG, Frankfurt a. M.: Lang (1993).

Alexander Yanos; Cassandra Marshall; Daina Bray, *Getting the Money: When Can a Sovereign's Assets be Attached Before a Judgment Has Been Obtained on a Successful Arbitral Award?*, 3(5) TDM (2006).

JAROSLAV ZELENKA, INSOLVENČNÍ ZÁKON (ZÁKON Č. 182/2006 SB.: POZNÁMKOVÉ VYDÁNÍ S DŮVODOVOU ZPRÁVOU A NAŘÍZENÍM RADY ES 1346/2000). [Title in translation: THE INSOLVENCY ACT (ACT NO. 182/2006 COLL.: ANNOTATED EDITION WITH EXPLANATORY MEMORANDUM AND COUNCIL REGULATION (EC) 1346/2000)]. Prague: Linde (2007).

Miša Zgonec-Rozei, *Kadi & Al Barakaat v. Council of the EU & EC Commission: European Court of Justice Quashes a Council of the EU Regulation Implementing UN Security Council Resolutions*, 12(22) ASIL Insights (2008).

Vladimír Zoubek, Ústavní zákon o bezpečnosti České republiky. [Title in translation: *Constitutional Act on the Security of the Czech Republic*], 34(2) MEZINÁRODNÍ VZTAHY 23-31 (1999).

Michal Žižlavský, *Prodej nemovitosti správcem konkurzní podstaty.* [Title in translation: *The Sale of Real Property by a Bankruptcy Trustee*], 9 BULLETIN ADVOKACIE 38 et seq. (1996).

Section 40 [Recognition of a foreign arbitral award]

A foreign arbitral award shall be recognized without any special decision being required. A foreign arbitral award is recognized by the award being taken into consideration, subject to the requirements stipulated in Section 39.

Rules effective from 1 January 2014 (PIL)
[Recognition and enforcement of foreign arbitral awards][188]

Section 120 of the PIL

Arbitral awards made abroad shall be recognized and enforced in the Czech Republic like Czech arbitral awards, on condition of reciprocity. The requirement of reciprocity shall also be considered fulfilled if the foreign country generally declares foreign arbitral awards enforceable.

Section 121 of the PIL

[Quoted in the commentary to Section 39 of the ArbAct.]

Section 122 of the PIL

(1) A foreign arbitral award shall be recognized without any special decision being required. A foreign arbitral award is recognized by the award being taken into consideration, subject to the requirements stipulated in Sections 120 and 121, as if it were a Czech arbitral award.

(2) The enforcement of a foreign arbitral award shall be ordered by a reasoned decision of a Czech court.

PART EIGHT – [TRANSITIONAL AND FINAL PROVISIONS]

Section 123 of the PIL [Transitional provisions]

(1) *[Quoted in the commentary to Sections 36 and 37 of the ArbAct.]*

(2) Proceedings commenced before the effective date of this Act shall continue to be governed by the provisions of the laws and regulations on the jurisdiction of Czech courts applicable until the effective date of this Act. This also applies to proceedings in matters of the recognition and enforcement of foreign decisions and foreign arbitral awards with respect

---

[188]   This heading is part of the quoted normative text.

to the conditions for their recognition and enforcement.
Related provisions: Sections 38, 39
Related laws: PILP; Sections 120, 121, 122, 123, 124(16) of the PIL, NYConv

I.   Section 40 of the ArbAct

11.104. As mentioned above in the commentary to Section 38 of the ArbAct, an arbitral award is a special decision, similar to most foreign decisions in terms of Section 65 of the PILP.[189] This also corresponds to the entire concept of the enforcement of foreign titles as such. Ever since the adoption of the Act on Private International Law and Procedure, the legislator no longer requires special (separate) *exequatur* proceedings. (The result of such proceedings is the issue of a separate order pronouncing the (un)enforceability of the foreign title.)[190] After the fulfillment of the formal requirements is ascertained, the foreign decision, as an enforceable title, is taken into consideration in the enforcement proceedings as if it were a domestic title. Hence, the court examines: (i) whether the decision is an arbitral award and (ii) whether there are any grounds for refusing enforcement pursuant to Section 39 of the ArbAct or pursuant to an international treaty binding upon the Czech Republic. In this connection, it is necessary to again emphasize that most proceedings for enforcement (recognition and enforcement) of foreign arbitral awards are governed by the NYConv due to its widespread use.

II.   Section 122 of the PIL

11.105. With effect from 1 January 2014 and in connection with the recodification of domestic civil law, Part Five of the ArbAct will be replaced in its entirety from the said date by the provisions incorporated in the PIL. These changes are analyzed in the commentaries to the preceding provisions of this Part of the ArbAct. It is necessary to point out that no material change will actually occur with respect to the subject matter of Section 40 of the ArbAct. Section 40 of the ArbAct is transposed to Section 122(1) of the PIL. Section 122(2) of the PIL adopts the

---

[189] PILP – Section 65 – *"Recognition of a foreign decision in property matters is not pronounced by any special order. The foreign decision is recognized by being taken into consideration by the Czechoslovak authority, as if it were a decision of a Czechoslovak authority."*
[190] A special (formal) *exequatur* decision has been reintroduced into Czech law in consequence of the implementation of EU law; from the perspective of Czech private international law and procedure, this must be considered a step back.

current rules, but under the regime of the PILP which concerns procedure. It supplements Section 40 of the ArbAct. The new rules incorporated in Section 122 of the PIL will especially directly follow the regime of Section 120 of the PIL. The latter provision, however, also principally adopts the current standard under the PILP.

III. Comparison with the law of the Slovak Republic (SlovArbAct)

11.106. The applicable Slovak law is quoted in the commentary to Section 38 of the ArbAct.

IV. Bibliography

J. BÁRTA, NĚKTERÉ OTÁZKY PŘÍSTUPU K MEZINÁRODNÍ ÚMLUVĚ A POTŘEBY TRANSFORMACE DO VNITROSTÁTNÍHO PRÁVA (ÚVAHA NAD VÍDEŇSKOU ÚMLUVOU O OBČANSKOPRÁVNÍ ODPOVĚDNOSTI ZA JADERNÉ ŠKODY). [TITLE IN TRANSLATION: SELECTED ISSUES OF ACCESSION TO AN INTERNATIONAL TREATY AND THE NECESSITY OF TRANSFORMATION INTO DOMESTIC LAW (ABOUT THE VIENNA CONVENTION ON CIVIL LIABILITY FOR NUCLEAR DAMAGE)], No. 9, p. 801 et seq. (1994).

Alexander Bělohlávek, *Zavedení tzv. exequatur do českého právního řádu.* [Title in translation: *Introduction of the So-Called Exequatur in Czech Law*], 5 PRÁVNÍ ZPRAVODAJ, 16–17 (2004).

Petra Bohůnová; Zdeněk Kapitán, *Systém uznání a výkonu cizích soudních rozhodnutí.* [Title in translation: *The System of Recognition and Enforcement of Foreign Court Decisions*], 6 PRÁVNÍ FÓRUM 228 et seq. (2008).

G. BORGES, DAS DOPPELEXEQUATUR VON SCHIEDSSPRÜCHEN: DIE ANERKENNUNG AUSLÄNDISCHER SCHIEDSSPRÜCHE UND EXEQUATURENSCHEIDUNGEN, Berlin: der Gruyter, (1997).

MARCIN CZEPELAK, UMOWA MIĘDZYNARODOWA JAKO ŹRÓDŁO PRAWA PRYWATNEGO MIĘDZYNARODOWEGO, Warsaw: Wolters KLI Polska (2008).

VLADISLAV DAVID; PAVEL SLADKÝ; FRANTIŠEK ZBOŘIL, MEZINÁRODNÍ PRÁVO VEŘEJNÉ S KAZUISTIKOU [TITLE IN TRANSLATION: PUBLIC INTERNATIONAL LAW WITH CASE LAW], Prague: Leges (2010).

R. Harbst, *Korruption und andre orre public-Verstöße als Einwände im Schiedsverfahren – Inwieweit sind staatliche Gerichte an*

Sachverhaltsfeststellungen es Schiedsgerichts gebunden?, 5(1) SCHIEDSVZ 22-31 (2007).

Jan Kněžínek, *Vyhlašování mezinárodních smluv v české a československé právní úpravě* [Title in translation: *The Promulgation of International Treaties into Czech and Czechoslovak Law*], 6(4) PART I. PRFO 133 et seq. (2009).

Jan Kněžínek, *Vyhlašování mezinárodních smluv v české a československé právní úpravě* [Title in translation: *The Promulgation of International Treaties into Czech and Czechoslovak Law*], 6(5) PART II. PRFO 173 et seq. (2009).

Pierre Lalive, *Absolute Finality of Arbitral Awards?*, 6 REVISTA INTERNACIONAL DE ARBITRAGEM E CONCILIAÇÃO, ASSOCIAÇÃO, PORTUGUESA DE ARBITRAGEM 109-127 (2008).

Jiří Malenovský, *Mezinárodní smlouvy podle čl. 10a Ústavy ČR.* [Title in translation: *International Treaties Pursuant to Article 10a of the Constitution of the Czech Republic*], 142(9) PRÁVNÍK 841-854 (2003).

Petr Mlsna, *K nepublikování předpisů práva ES/EU v českém jazyce v Úředním věstníku EU.* [Title in translation: *Regarding the Non-Publication of EC/EU Laws in Czech in the Official Journal of the EU*], 9 PRZP 6-9 (2004).

Petr Mlsna, *Novela zákona č. 309/1999 Sb. z pohledu práva ES/EU.* [Title in translation: *Amendment to Act No. 309/1999 Coll. from the Perspective of EC/EU Law*], 10 PRZP 7-10 (2005).

Ioannis M. Papagiannis, *Die Vollstreckung ausländischer Schiedssprüche nach ihrer Annullierung im Herkunftsstaat*, 98(2) ZVGLRWISS 139-174 (1999).

DAVID SEHNÁLEK, EXTERNAL RELATIONS OF THE EC/EU, Days of Public Law, Brno: MU 1156-1164 (2007).

Matthias Scherer, *Three Recent Decisions of the Swiss Federal Tribunal Regarding Assignments and Transfer of Arbitration Agreements*, 1 ASA BULLETIN 109–119 (2002).

Hans-Peter Schroeder; Oppermann, B., *Anerkennung und Vollstreckung von Schiedssprüchen nach lex mercatoria in Deutschland, England und Frankreich*, 99(4) ZVGTRWISS 410-443 (2000).

Rolf A. Schütze, *Aktuelle Fragen der Anerkennung und Vollstrecktbarerklarung von US-amerikanischen Schiedsspruchen und Gerichtsurteilen in Deutschland*, 104(4) ZVGLRWISS 427-443 (2005).

Naděžda Šišková, *Mezinárodní smlouvy podle čl. 10 Ústavy ČFR a otázky související.* [Title in translation: *International Treaties Pursuant to Article 10 of the Constitution of the CFR and Related Issues*], 2(8) PRÁVNÍ FÓRUM 291-297 (2005).

Aleš Šrámek; Helena Sluková; Vladimír Sládeček, *Federální zákon o Sbírce zákonů*, [Title in translation: *The Federal Act on the Collection of Laws*], 10 P 901 et seq. (1990).

Vladimír Týč, *Aplikace mezinárodních smluv ve vnitrostátním právu.* [Title in translation: *The Application of International Treaties in National Law*], 4 P 334 et seq. (1993).

Vladimír Týč, *Implementace mezinárodních závazků České republiky ve vnitrostátním právu.* [Title in translation: *The Implementation of International Commitments of the Czech Republic into National Law*], 10 O VZTAHU ÚSTAVNÍHO A MEZINÁRODNÍHO PRÁVA. [Title in translation: REGARDING THE RELATIONSHIP BETWEEN CONSTITUTIONAL AND INTERNATIONAL LAW]. AUC-I 23 et seq. (1997).

Vladimír Týč, *Pravomoci ES k uzavírání mezinárodních smluv* [Title in translation: *Jurisdiction of the EC to Conclude International Treaties*], 54(12) AUC-I 397-403 (2008).

[A further bibliography is especially cited in the commentaries to Sections 38 and 39 of the ArbAct.]

Poland

Arbitration Case Law 2018

Agnieszka Pazdan, associate, Kubas Kos Gałkowski, Agata Wojtczak, associate, Kubas Kos Gałkowski, Kamil Zawicki, attorney at law, partner, Kubas Kos Gałkowski (ed.)

Key words:
comprehensive consideration of the case | court of arbitration | public order clause | Polish arbitration law

States involved:
> [**POL**] - [Poland]

Laws Taken into Account in This Ruling:

> Kodeks postępowania cywilnego z dnia 17 listopada 1664 r. [*Code of Civil Procedure of 17 November 1964*] [k.p.c.] [POL], published in: Dziennik Ustaw [*Journal of Laws*] 1964, No. 43, item 296, as amended; Articles 233, 1184, 1197, 1206[1]

[Rationes Decidendi]:

12.01. The fact that the court of arbitration is not a court composed of professional judges cannot explain the lack of comprehensive

---

[1]   Article 233. k.p.c. [POL] (unofficial translation) § 1. The court shall assess the reliability and validity of evidence at its discretion, following extensive deliberations of the available material.
§ 2. The court shall assess the significance of a party's refusal to present evidence or a party's interference with the taking of evidence despite the court decision on the same basis.
Article 1184. k.p.c. [POL] (unofficial translation) § 1. Unless otherwise provided for by this Act, the parties may determine the terms and conditions and the procedure of proceedings before an arbitration court.
§ 2. Unless the parties have agreed otherwise, an arbitration court may, subject to the provisions of this Act, conduct proceedings in a manner which the arbitration court deems proper. The arbitration court is not bound by the provisions on proceedings before the court.
Article 1197. k.p.c. (unofficial translation) § 1. A judgment of an arbitration court should be made in writing and signed by the issuing arbitrators. If a judgment is issued by an arbitration court panel of three or more arbitrators, the signatures of the majority of arbitrators, accompanied by an explanation why the other signatures are not provided, are sufficient.
§ 2. A judgment of an arbitration court should include the *ratio decidendi*.
§ 3. A judgment of an arbitration court should contain reference to the arbitration clause on the basis of

recognition of the case. On the other hand, non-subordination to the legal provisions with regard to the examination of civil law cases, collecting evidence, its assessment and expressing opinions about its value does not mean that some obvious standards of fair and equal treatment for the parties were not applicable. The evidence provided by the parties of the proceedings shall be carried out and referred to, and therefore not only to those which are the basis supporting a final resolution but also to evidence to the contrary, its credibility, integrity, because it shall allow the court's reasoning to be followed.

[Descriptions of the Facts and Legal Issues]:

12.02. The dispute in this case concerned the effectiveness of the withdrawal by A – the Plaintiffs, on 5 October 2012 from a construction works contract within the framework of the Project "B in W." concluded on 22 December 2009 with B – the Defendant.

12.03. In the preliminary judgment on 29 September 2016, the Court of Arbitration at the Polish Chamber of Commerce established that A effectively withdrew from the abovementioned contract.

12.04. B submitted a complaint against the judgment and claimed that the decision of the Court of Arbitration violated the basic principles of the legal order of the Republic of Poland, pursuant

---

which the judgment was issued, identify the parties and the arbitrators and specify the date and place of issue. If each arbitrator signs the judgment in a different state and the parties did not determine the place of issuance of the judgment, that place is determined by the arbitration court.

§ 4. A judgment of an arbitration court is served on the parties.

Article 1206. k.p.c. [POL] (unofficial translation) § 1. A party may file a motion to set aside a judgment of an arbitration court if:

1) there was no arbitration clause, or an arbitration clause is void, invalid or has expired according to relevant law,

2) a party was not duly notified of the appointment of an arbitrator or proceedings before an arbitration court, or was otherwise deprived of the possibility to defend his rights before an arbitration court,

3) a judgment of an arbitration court concerns a dispute which is not covered by an arbitration clause or falls beyond the subject-matter and scope of that clause, however, if adjudication in matters covered by an arbitration clause may be separated from adjudication in matters not covered by that clause or falling beyond the subject-matter and scope of that clause, a judgment may only be set aside insofar as it concerns those matters which are not covered by the arbitration clause or fall beyond the subject-matter and scope of that clause; the fact that a judgment falls beyond the subject-matter and scope of an arbitration clause may not be a basis to set that judgment aside if a party who attended proceedings did not raise allegations against the hearing of claims falling beyond the subject-matter and scope of the arbitration clause,

4) requirements concerning the composition of an arbitration court or the basic principles of proceedings before that court, as provided for by this Act or determined by the parties, were not met,

5) a judgment was achieved by means of an offence or on the basis of a false or falsified document,

6) a non-appealable court judgment has been issued in the same case between the same parties.

§ 2. Moreover, a judgment of an arbitration court shall be set aside if the court determines that:

1) the dispute cannot be settled by an arbitration court according to this Act,

2) a judgment of an arbitration court is contrary to the basic principles of the legal order of the Republic of Poland (the public order clause),

3) a ruling of an arbitration court deprives a consumer of the protection afforded to them by the mandatory provisions of the law applicable to the agreement to which the consumer is a party, and where the applicable law is a law selected by the parties - the protection afforded to the consumer by the mandatory provisions of the law which would be applicable should no law have been selected.

to Article 1206 section 1 point 2 k.p.c. [POL], in particular: the principle of comprehensive consideration of the case, including all the collected evidence and its assessment, which resulted in the lack of recognition of the essence of the case in regard to the effectiveness of the withdrawal; the principle of the burden of proof expressed in Article 6 of the k.c. [POL] which caused the lack of recognition of the case in regard to the effectiveness of the withdrawal; gross violation of the substantive law, i.e. Article 476, Article 491 and Article 640 k.c. [POL]. resulting in the violation of the principle of equality of the parties to civil law proceedings and the adequacy of the rights of the parties to civil law proceedings in the event of the other party's infringement.

12.05. The complainant requested the setting aside of the contested preliminary ruling and awarding the costs of the proceedings jointly from the other party.

12.06. Having identified the complaint, in its decision of 7 February 2017, the Court of Appeal set aside the abovementioned ruling of the Court of Arbitration. In the reasoning, the Court indicated that a state court does not evaluate an arbitration court's decision in substance, the complaint to set aside that decision is not an ordinary remedy, as a result of which the court shall reconsider the case in as to the merits and its accurate recognition by the court of arbitration.

12.07. Considering that the contested decision violates the basic principles of the legal order of the Court of Appeal referred to constitutional principles and assuming that the Court of Arbitration in this case violated the basic principal in civil procedure, the case has therefore not been considered comprehensively and the collected evidence has not been assessed overall but selectively, relying on part of the documents and disregarding other documents entirely without an explanation. The Court of Appeal indicated that significantly higher freedom to carry out the proceedings, including proceedings to take evidence, by the court of arbitration in comparison with the state court shall not lead to the lack of recognition of the case because its leads to delivering an unfair decision as it has happened in this case. Furthermore, the Court of Appeal stated that the allegations included in B's complaint which concerned: the burden of proof and the violation of substantive law with regard to the principle of equality of the parties to civil law proceedings and the sustainability of the civil law relationship, especially towards the conclusion of the agreement that the procedure for its termination by way of withdrawal, are unreasonable.

12.08. Ultimately, A filled a cassation complaint to the Supreme Court in which A requested the setting aside of the contested preliminary judgment and the referring of the case back for rehearing, with the order to pay the costs of the proceedings.

[Decision of the Supreme Court]:

12.09. The Supreme Court ruled in favour of B and dismissed A's cassation complaint.

12.10. Firstly, the Supreme Court stated that the Court of Appeal rightly pointed out that its duty is not the substantive recognition of the case because it is not an appeal body for the court of arbitration's decisions. This results from the fact that by making the arbitration clause, the parties limit their constitutional right to a trial, whereas the proceedings to set aside an arbitration court's decision is an extraordinary remedy and its conditions shall be interpreted strictly.

12.11. The essence of this case comes down to the consideration of the cassation complaint's content in terms of failure to comply – or to the contrary – fulfilment by the preliminary decision of the Court of Arbitration at the Polish Chamber of Commerce, of the conditions for infringement of the basic principles of the legal order of the Republic of Poland, hence the necessity of reaching for the public order clause to set aside the decision. According to the Court of Appeal, this necessity occurred due to a violation of the basic principle in civil procedure which is the court's obligation to a comprehensive consideration of the case, including the collected evidence and its assessment, which results in the lack of recognition of the essence of the case. In this case, it was about the lack of recognition of the essence of the dispute with regard to the effectiveness of the withdrawal from the agreement - firstly by one of the parties and further by the other party.

12.12. Subsequently, the Supreme Court indicated that the public order clause applied by the Court of Appeal, due to the lack of comprehensive recognition of the case by the Court of Arbitration, concerns the basic principles of the legal order, although it is not precise, which leaves the ruling court a lot of freedom in this case. .

12.13. The phrase "the basic principles of the legal order", applied in Article 1206 section 1 point 2 k.p.c. [POL], refers to such violation of the substantive provisions which leads to a violation of the rule of law's principles (principle of legality) and the decision violates the ground rules in force in the Republic of

Poland and affects the current legal order, therefore infringing on the systemic, political and socio-economic principles in force. It is considered that it is about principle matters for the law and civil law procedure, and hence for the course of the proceedings, particularly the preservation of the equality of the parties. However, it is reiterated that when the parties decide to include an arbitration clause in the agreement, they willingly resign from the formal protection given by the different provisions of civil law procedure. As a result, they also accept procedural conditions which consist in significant autonomy of the arbitration procedure, leading to only a minor external audit of the court's decisions.

12.14. Considering the above, the Supreme Court indicated that the procedural public order might be the basis for court of arbitration's decision in two aspects: conformity assessment of the procedure leading to the establishment of the decision by the court with the basic procedural principles of the legal order and the consequences of the said decision in terms of its conformity with the procedural legal order, i.e. if the said principles can be reconciled with the procedural law. The Supreme Court agreed with such an understanding of the public order clause under the conditions specified in this case.

12.15. The Supreme Court explained that in the case of assuming that the lack of comprehensive consideration of the case leading to the lack of recognition, the essence of the case is the basic principle of the proceedings, which is one of the legal order principles in the Republic of Poland. It shall be considered that pointing out a violation of such a legal order means compliance with the condition required to implement the public order clause expressed in Article 1206 section 1 point 2 k.p.c. [POL].

12.16. The Supreme Court indicated that the fact that the court of arbitration is not a court composed of professional judges cannot explain the lack of comprehensive recognition of the case. On the other hand, the non-subordination to the legal provisions with regard to the examination of civil law cases, collecting evidence, its assessment and expressing opinions about its value does not mean that some obvious standards of fair and equal treatment for the parties were not applicable. The evidence provided by the parties of the proceedings shall be carried out and referred to, and therefore not only to those which are the basis supporting the final resolution but also to evidence to the contrary, its credibility, integrity, because it shall allow the court's reasoning to be followed.

12.17.   Further, in the case of the arbitration court's decision, the essence of the case is not only the essence of the dispute which arises between the parties, e.g. the performance or non-performance of the agreement and withdrawal from it, as in this case. However, it does not mean the necessity of reference to each and every piece of evidence, e.g. a large number of documents, but this cannot – as stated in the statement of reasons by the Court of Appeal – regard different periods other than those relevant for the date of ruling or be omitted in their entirely or even left unmentioned. Similarly, this concerns witness statements, in particular expert testimony, appointed to assist the court in specialised matters. The concealment of some evidence in the statement of reasons by the Court of Arbitration results in the fact that the decision becomes unconvincing in its grounds, especially for the party for which it is negative. This comes down to the lack of comprehensive consideration of the case. The result of failing to comply with comprehensive consideration of the case is lack of recognition of the essence of the case, which is subject to the dispute in respect of the effectiveness of the withdrawal from the agreement concluded between the parties to the case.

12.18.   As to the grounds of the Court of Arbitration's decision, allegations against it in the appealed judgment of the Court of Appeal, and subsequently, allegations included in the cassation complaint, it should be noted that within the meaning of Article 1197 section 2 k.p.c. [POL] the term "motives" does not literally mean "reasoning" within the meaning of Code of Civil Procedure and in that provision, the term "motives" is used deliberately. However, those aspects of the court's understanding which shall indicate the relevance (accuracy) of the determination in the light of overall evidence collected during the proceedings shall be included in the content of the motives. The Arbitration Rules of the Court of Arbitration at the Polish Chamber of Commerce that underlies the proceedings in the present case, uses the term "reasoning" to cover the motives that guided arbitrators while making the decision. The motives are the component of the reasoning following the determination, although the motives do not constitute a distinct part of the decision as it has in the decisions of the state court. Therefore, the motives shall include a reference to the overall evidence in order to indicate its comprehensive consideration.

12.19. Certainly, from the essence of the proceedings, the constitutional requirements of the administration of justice by an empowered authority, and therefore also by the court of arbitration, finally from the Arbitration Rules of the Court of Arbitrations, in front of which the proceedings took place, results in the fact that the comprehensive consideration of the case, and hence the overall examination of the circumstances, in particular the performance of taking the required documents, witness statements, expert evidence, hearing of the parties, depending on the subject matter, followed by the assessment of such evidence, constitutes one of the principles of the legal order of the Republic of Poland – the public order clause. The fact that the court of arbitration shall not be bound by the provisions applied before the state court and that pursuant to Article 1184 of k.p.c. [POL] shall itself establish the rules and manner of proceeding, pursuant to the arrangements with the parties, does not mean arbitrariness in respect of the principle of civil law proceedings, which is adversarial.

12.20. According to the Supreme Court, the arbitrators are obliged to assess the credibility and strength of evidence according to its discretion, which means that this discretion shall be expressed in the motives with reference to the evidence relevant to the determination of the issue in the case, and also indicate the reasons which resulted in the other evidence's strength claimed by the requested party being refused. This does not imply only formal shortcomings of the contested decision but also recognition that the case has been examined without the sufficient consideration of the position of the complainant in the proceedings to take evidence.

Key words:

Declaration of the enforceability | postponement | public order clause | Polish arbitration law

States involved:
    [POL] - [Poland]

Laws Taken into Account in This Ruling:

             Kodeks postępowania cywilnego z dnia 17 listopada 1664 r. [*Code of Civil Procedure of 17 November 1964*] [k.p.c.] [POL], published in: Dziennik Ustaw [*Journal of Laws*] 1964, No. 43, item 296, as amended; Articles 1206, 1216 § 1, 1217[2]

[Rationes Decidendi]:

12.21. In a complaint against the decision to declare the enforceability the debtor reiterated pleas made in the proceedings to set aside the arbitration court's award. In proceedings initiated on the basis of the motion to set aside the award, the court examined these issues. [...] The Debtor did not argue that the facts of the case were altered, but entered into a polemic with the Regional Court's reasoning with reference to the argumentation raised in the cassation complaint. The recognition of the cassation complaint is a matter for the Supreme Court (Decision of the

---

[2]   Article 1206. k.p.c. [POL] (unofficial translation) § 1. A party may file a motion to set aside a judgment of an arbitration court if:

1) there was no arbitration clause, or an arbitration clause is void, invalid or has expired according to relevant law,

2) a party was not duly notified of the appointment of an arbitrator or proceedings before an arbitration court, or was otherwise deprived of the possibility to defend his rights before an arbitration court,

3) a judgment of an arbitration court concerns a dispute which is not covered by an arbitration clause or falls beyond the subject-matter and scope of that clause, however, if adjudication in matters covered by an arbitration clause may be separated from adjudication in matters not covered by that clause or falling beyond the subject-matter and scope of that clause, a judgment may only be set aside insofar as it concerns those matters which are not covered by the arbitration clause or fall beyond the subject-matter and scope of that clause; the fact that a judgment falls beyond the subject-matter and scope of an arbitration clause may not be a basis to set that judgment aside if a party who attended proceedings did not raise allegations against the hearing of claims falling beyond the subject-matter and scope of the arbitration clause,

4) requirements concerning the composition of an arbitration court or the basic principles of proceedings before that court, as provided for by this Act or determined by the parties, were not met,

5) a judgment was achieved by means of an offence or on the basis of a false or falsified document,

6) a non-appealable court judgment has been issued in the same case between the same parties.

§ 2. Moreover, a judgment of an arbitration court shall be set aside if the court determines that:

1) the dispute cannot be settled by an arbitration court according to this Act,

2) a judgment of an arbitration court is contrary to the basic principles of the legal order of the Republic of Poland (the public order clause),

3) a ruling of an arbitration court deprives a consumer of the protection afforded to them by the mandatory provisions of the law applicable to the agreement to which the consumer is a party, and where the applicable law is a law selected by the parties - the protection afforded to the consumer by the mandatory provisions of the law which would be applicable should no law have been selected.

Article 1216 § 1. k.p.c. [POL] (unofficial translation) If an application to set aside an arbitration court's award pursuant to Title VII is filed, the court with which an application for recognition or enforcement of the award has been filed may postpone hearing of the case. That court may also, on application of a party seeking recognition or enforcement of the award, order the other party to provide appropriate security.

Article 1217 k.p.c. [POL] (unofficial translation) Art. 1217. In proceedings for recognition or enforcement of an arbitration court's award issued in the Republic of Poland or a settlement agreement made before an arbitration court in the Republic of Poland, the court does not examine the circumstances referred to in Article 1214 § 3 if an application to set aside the award is validly dismissed.

Regional Court in Katowice of 15 February 2018, case no. V ACa 53/16).

[Description of Facts and Legal Issues]:

12.22. In the facts of the case the Creditor (the claimant in arbitration proceedings) filed for a declaration of the enforceability of the arbitration court award's in a case, in which the defendant (the debtor) brought forth an action for the annulment of the abovementioned award and received an unfavourable final judgement.

12.23. The dispute on which the arbitration court ruled was related to the performance of the contract of 30 May. Three years later – on 29 October 2014 - the parties, aiming to enter into the initial contract, concluded an additional agreement. In the latter agreement, the parties included a provision not to use this document as evidence in arbitration proceedings.

12.24. The arbitration court ruled in favour of the Creditor. Following the award, the debtor undertook steps to eliminate the said decision. In the motion to set aside the award, he argued that the arbitration court exceeded the arbitration clause and violated several fundamental principles of the legal order of the Republic of Poland.

12.25. In the final judgement of 31 June 2017, case no. V ACa 129/17, the Regional Court in Katowice dismissed the defendant's motion to set aside the judgement. As of the day of adjudication in a case concerning a declaration of enforceability, the Debtor's cassation complaint against the judgement of 31 June 2017 was to be examined by the Supreme Court (*Sąd Najwyższy*).

12.26. In those circumstances, the Regional Court in Katowice in a decision of 27 September 2017, case no. V ACo 53/16, declared the enforceability of the arbitration court award. Subsequently, The debtor filed a complaint against this decision in which he requested the setting aside of the contested decision and referred the case back for reconsideration.

12.27. He advanced three main pleas. Firstly, he argued that the Court did not defer the case and did not suspend the proceedings until the examination of the cassation complaint.

12.28. As regards the second plea, the enforceability was declared despite the fact that the arbitration court exceeded the arbitration clause. In particular, the Debtor argued that the arbitration court took evidence from the agreement of 29 October 2014 despite the fact that in this document, the parties agreed not to use it as evidence in the arbitration proceedings.

12.29. Thirdly, the enforceability was declared despite the fact that the arbitration court's award violated several fundamental principles of the legal order of the Republic of Poland.

[Decision of the Regional Court in Katowice]:

12.30. The Regional Court in Katowice ruled in favour of the Creditor and dismissed the complaint. None of the pleas raised by the Debtor were founded.

12.31. The court found that there was no basis to defer the case, nor to suspend the proceedings. According to Art. 1216 § 1 k.p.c. [POL], the court with which a motion to declare the enforceability of the judgment has been filed may postpone the hearing of the case. After rendering a final decision on the motion, the postponement is not possible. Consequently, as of the date 31 June 2017, the court had no legal basis for the postponement.

12.32. Moreover, the possibility to set aside the decision regarding an arbitration court award does not constitute grounds to suspend the proceedings concerning a declaration of enforceability. The court may order a suspension only on a joint application by the parties. Such a motion was not filed with the court.

12.33. Regarding second and third matter raised by the Debtor in the complaint, the Regional Court stated that the exceeding of the arbitration clause and the violation of the fundamental principles of the legal order of the Republic of Poland was examined by the court in the judgement the of 31 June 2017.

12.34. According to Article 1217 k.p.c. [POL], the court does not investigate the admissibility of the arbitration clause and the compliance of the award with the public order clause if a motion to set aside a judgment of an arbitration court was finally dismissed. In other words, as long as the final judgement of 31 July 2017 is in force, it is not possible to adjudicate differently on the scope of the arbitration clause and the violation of the public order clause. in the proceedings to declare the enforcement, the court is bound by the abovementioned ruling regarding this issues.

12.35. In particular, it was decided in the proceedings to set aside the arbitration court award that the agreement of 29 October 2014 did not constitute any principles of the arbitration proceedings. According to § 8 par. 3 of the agreement of 29 October 2014 "the agreement may be revealed to the Arbitration Court to the necessary extent, but it cannot be used as evidence for the benefit of any of the parties. It cannot constitute the basis for the interpretation of the agreement".

12.36. The Regional Court was of the opinion that the parties agreed on the principles of the proceedings in § 8 of the agreement of 30 May 2011. These rules were confirmed in the procedural documents. Throughout the proceedings, the parties did not mention any other agreement of the parties regarding evidentiary proceedings. The prohibition to use the agreement as evidence was binding only on the parties. Agreements on the evidence are not known to Polish civil procedure. The Regional Court stated that the parties cannot exclude the application of the provisions regarding evidence prohibition in order to bind the court, unless exceptions are expressly provided by the law. The use of a document contrary to the parties' agreement should be considered as a violation loyalty, not a violation of the procedural principles by the arbitration court.

12.37. Furthermore, the use of the agreement of 29 October 2014 did not exceed the arbitration clause. The clause covered disputes relating to obligations under the agreement of 30 May 2011. The agreement of 29 October 2014 regarded the conclusion of the first agreement, therefore was within the scope of the arbitration clause.

12.38. Consequently, the Regional Court dismissed the Debtor's complaint. As a result, the declaration of the enforceability of the arbitration judgement remained in force.

| | |

Book Reviews

Czech (& Central European) Yearbook of Arbitration®

Oleg Skvortsov | Mikhail Savranskiy | Gleb Sevastianov | Tatyana Lunaeva

International Commercial Arbitration: Textbook

Moscow: Publishing House Statute, 956 pages (2018) ISBN: 978-5-8354-1452-9

The new Russian textbook "International Commercial Arbitration" is the most voluminous Russian-language textbook on international commercial arbitration, written by about 40 leading legal academics and practitioners from Russia and several other countries, including Austria, France, Sweden, Switzerland, and the Republic of Belarus. The editors of the book are three well-known Russian arbitration experts.

The book comprehensively reveals diverse aspects of international commercial arbitration. The authors refer to legislation, arbitration rules, numerous doctrinal sources and a significant practice of courts of various states.

As is known, current European lawyers are trained mainly by their national and Anglo-American textbooks on international arbitration. However, the reviewed textbook more fully and deeply reveals the peculiarities of resolving international commercial disputes that have a Russian dimension. In this regard, it should be recommended to students, lawyers and other professionals who are engaged in drafting cross-border contracts and/or the resolution of disputes involving parties from Russia.

The book touches upon theoretical issues of arbitration (including the detailed explanation of its legal nature through the prism of the author's theory of private procedural law) as well as numerous practical issues. It covers a number of complex and relevant topics of international arbitration, including the effect of an arbitration agreement on non-parties; succession under an arbitration agreement; supervision over the activities of arbitral institutions; status of experts in international arbitration; participation of public law entities in arbitral proceedings; the prejudicial effect of arbitration awards, the interrelation of arbitration and mediation procedures, and many others.

The authors took into account and interpreted the latest changes in the rules of the leading arbitral institutions.

It should be noted that in 2015—2017, the reform of arbitration legislation took place in Russia, the results of which mainly affected the establishment and operation of arbitral institutions. The rules governing the arbitration agreement and the arbitration procedure, however, also underwent certain changes. Serious innovations also appeared in the procedural legislation governing the assistance and control of state courts in the sphere of arbitration.

The legislative changes required amendments to the arbitration rules of leading Russian arbitral institutions, which include those with the two largest business associations of Russia — the International Commercial Arbitration Court and the Maritime Arbitration Commission at the Russian Chamber of Commerce and Industry, and the Arbitration Center at the Russian Union of Industrialists and Entrepreneurs.

These innovations, like the information and analysis traditionally contained in textbooks on international arbitration, are present in detail in this book.

At the same time, considerable attention is paid to the coverage of international arbitration treaties (the 1958 New York Convention) and the practice of their application in Russia, as well as to other documents of international origin used in this field. These mostly comprise of the texts of the United Nations Commission on International Trade Law (UNCITRAL): the UNCITRAL Arbitration Rules as revised in 2010 and the UNCITRAL Notes on Organizing Arbitral Proceedings (2016).

Documents of other reputable international organizations, both governmental (the Hague Conference) and non-governmental (International Law Association, International Bar Association, International Council for Commercial Arbitration, Chartered Institute of Arbitrators are also considered. They contain international standards and useful recommendations for regulation of international arbitration in addition to the provisions of the applicable law and the arbitration agreements.

Among other things, one can welcome the attempt to highlight in a comparative context, progressive international practices on topical issues of international arbitration, including a separate chapter on international arbitration in a number of leading jurisdictions and arbitration centers. It should be noted that the book also overviews international arbitration in many regions of the world, including the countries of the Commonwealth of Independent States.[1]

From the point of view of the depth of study and the range of topics considered, the book is interesting not only for students, but also for practicing lawyers.

The chapter on the history of international commercial arbitration deserves special mention: this subject is not often covered in such detail as in this book.

As is rightly noted in the final chapter of the book, the decisive factor in the use of international commercial arbitration remains its effectiveness. It seems that the practical advice and recommendations contained in the textbook can be useful for lawyers when organizing arbitral proceedings

---

[1]   With regard to international arbitration in the region of the Commonwealth of Independent States, a more detailed review is contained in the book "Law and Practice of International Arbitration in the CIS Region", edited by Kaj Hober, Yarik Kryvoi, Wolters Kluwer, 2017, published in English.

and participating in them as arbitrators or representatives, which in turn, will help to increase the efficiency of arbitration.

[*Dmitry Davydenko, PhD.*]

Chief Expert of the Center for Arbitration and Mediation of the Russian Chamber of Commerce and Industry, Director of the CIS Arbitration Forum

Lukáš Ryšavý

Nezávislost a nestrannost rozhodce

Praha: C. H. Beck, 224 pages (2018) ISBN : 978-80-7400-707-1

In October 2018 a monography by Lukáš Ryšavý entitled "Independence and Impartiality of the Arbitrator" was published by C. H. Beck. I consider this work to be very relevant as this issue is repeatedly addressed in both literature and jurisprudence as well as in the practically oriented areas (see e.g. the new version of IBA Guidelines on Conflicts of Interest in International Arbitration, 2014). The requirement of an independent and impartial arbitrator is present in all modern legislations of arbitration in some form, whether in national laws, international agreements or in rules of arbitration courts. Nonetheless, I tend to agree with the author that a comprehensive description of the issue of an arbitrator's independence and impartiality has been missing in Czech legal literature and therefore the work can be considered as a very important contribution in the field of (international) arbitration in the Czech Republic.

A comparison of Czech and German domestic legislations on arbitration was chosen for the analysis of the independence and impartiality of an arbitrator. This is an appropriate and logical method. On the one hand, Czech and German legislation stems from legal regimes that are historically and systemically very close. On the other hand, they differ in the area of arbitration in many ways. In addition, the method of comparison emphasizes the importance of arbitration in the international environment and consequently it can also positively influence the quality of domestic legislation. The author correctly notes that the German legislature incorporated the issue of arbitration into the Civil Procedure Code (Zivilprozessordnung) while a separate legal act was chosen for the Czech arbitration legislation. Additionally, the author also points out that the German legislature, unlike the Czech one, is almost a verbatim copy of the UNCITRAL Model Law on International Commercial Arbitration, containing only minor changes. I tend to agree with the author's opinion that despite the existing differences, the comparative approach illustrates the importance of a uniform approach to the application, interpretation of the concepts or the decision-making activity of the state judiciary regarding (international) arbitration.

The monography is divided into six chapters (including the introduction and conclusion) and can be characterized as possessing good and logical structure and systematics. In his work, the author has capably connected the theoretical and practical view from which he deduces possible conclusions and changes *de lege ferenda*.

In Chapter I, the author points out the general relevance and importance of arbitration as a truly equivalent alternative to the protection of rights and interests in proceedings before the national/state courts on the one hand and the relevance and importance of the arbitrator's independent and impartial decision-making (not forgetting to address the constitutional dimension of the issue) on the other hand. With specific examples, he illustrates the omnipresence of the issue of independence and impartiality in arbitration. Moreover, in the introductory chapter, the author presents the fundamental questions to which he desires to find the corresponding answers (How are, and how should the concepts of independence and impartiality in arbitration be interpreted and understood? Are there differences between a judge's independence and impartiality and the independence and impartiality of an arbitrator? Does the autonomy of parties create an obstacle to independent and impartial decision-making? etc.). Without revealing the conclusion, I can already state, that he has been able to find convincing answers to all the questions he stipulated formerly. On top of that, his findings are developed through well-crafted arguments and sufficiently supported by pertinent sources.

In Chapter II, the author provides a brief description of arbitration. He presents the basic advantages and disadvantages that are common but sometimes incorrectly associated with arbitration. The basic attributes of arbitration are presented by comparing arbitral proceedings with proceedings before State Courts. The Author mentions in more detail some categories of arbitration (international and national arbitration, and ad hoc and institutionalized arbitration) which are closely related to the issue of independence and impartiality. Additionally, he identifies party autonomy as one of the central, essential and typical characteristics of arbitration, which fundamentally distinguishes arbitration from proceedings before ordinary courts. He also correctly depicts its negative impacts and limits.

Chapter III is dedicated to the requirements of an arbitrator, respectively to the conditions under which a person may act as an arbitrator. The author precisely analyzes the individual legal conditions found in Czech and German legal regulations, among which fundamental differences might be found. I tend to agree with the author that while the German regulation stresses the principle of party autonomy, the Czech Arbitration Act provides (although minimally) in comparison with the German legislation rather protective conditions that might have a negative impact (e. g. the exclusion of judges from arbitration).

In Chapter IV, the author focuses on the content and terminology of the concepts of independence and impartiality, as well as on possible theoretical approaches to these concepts. Nonetheless, the author emphasizes not only those two concepts as he also analyzes other concepts which are related to independence and impartiality. In the given context, both Czech and German legislation as well as the relevant theories and case law apply the terms of bias and neutrality. The above-mentioned concepts are also thoroughly clarified by the author in terms of their meaning before the ordinary courts. Within this chapter, the reader will adequately learn about the historical genesis of the independence and impartiality in arbitration up to the status *de lege lata*. Moreover, I consider it important to draw attention to the section that is dedicated to the role of the Czech Civil Procedure Code, respectively the German Zivilprozessordnung in arbitration proceedings. The difference in the importance of these codes in the arbitration proceedings concerns the already mentioned different systemic classification of the regulation of the arbitration procedure into the Czech and German legal order.

The fifth chapter of the reviewed publication can be seen as the central one. After dealing with the definition of the arbitration proceedings as such and with the definition of the key concepts; the author chronologically presents various stages of the arbitration process in which the issue of independence and impartiality of the arbitrator may (more or less) arise. This is the most extensive chapter, divided into nine subchapters, and covers the issue of independence and impartiality from the constitution of the arbitral tribunal, through the course of arbitration proceedings, until end of the arbitration. Of course, even the stage after the end of the arbitration procedure is covered, which addresses the question of annulment, recognition and enforcement of an arbitral award. In view of the above, the author also deals with the different ways an arbitrator can be appointed (directly by parties, by a third party, by the arbitration tribunal, etc.) and focuses on the extent to which various methods of appointment of an arbitrator can affect his/her independence and impartiality. Besides the method of appointment of an arbitrator, the number of arbitrators is without a doubt also important. The author draws attention to a standard approach based on a three-member arbitration panel/tribunal, an issue of the relationship between the presiding arbitrator and the other members of the arbitration panel, and the question of the community of participants in the arbitration proceedings. One of the essential means of ensuring independent and impartial decision-making is through the arbitrator's duty of disclosure. Compliance with the duty to disclose is a prerequisite for the applicability of the grounds to challenge an arbitrator in the arbitration proceedings. The author focuses methodically on the extent of this duty, the moment of its occurrence and the consequences of its breach. In this chapter, attention is also drawn to the arbitrator´s duty to give instructions, including the question whether such a duty exists at all and/ or on what terms is it based. In this context, the author also outlines the problematic issues and risks associated with this duty. The legal means that can be used for the "removal" of the arbitrator and ensure the independence and impartiality of the decision is the challenge/disqualification of the arbitrator. This is also analyzed in detail in this chapter. Challenge/ disqualification of the arbitrator is used in the context of a state judge and a number of reasons are examined that will either, always, in some circumstances, or never lead to the disqualification of an arbitrator. In connection with the challenge/disqualification of an arbitrator, the author also discusses the procedural application of the grounds of bias, i.e. how it is possible to achieve that an arbitrator with a (justified) doubt as to his or her impartiality is disqualified from the hearing and the deciding of the case, respectively when such grounds for bias can (must) be applied. Consequently, the two final subchapters are devoted to the issues concerning recognition and enforcement of an arbitral award.

Chapter VI presents an overall summary of the current situation and of all the lessons learned. The author formulates the essential conclusions and shows the shortcomings of the existing regulations (especially the Czech one). However, he was not satisfied only with this simple statement. On the contrary, in addition to assessing the shortcomings of the current Czech legal regulation, the author provides concrete proposals for their removal *de lege ferenda*. This is highly appreciated.

Finally, it can be stated that Lukáš Ryšavý has processed the topic of independence and impartiality of the arbitrator in a factual yet readable way and his conclusions are based on extensive sources, both Czech and German, including several concrete examples and case law. The structure and system of the work is very logical and examines the issue of the independence and impartiality of the arbitrator in all stages of the arbitration proceedings. The author has done a very good job in pointing out the importance and practical implications of independence and impartiality for arbitration as well as the differences between arbitration and the proceedings before the national courts. I can strongly recommend this publication to all those who deal with or may encounter the issue of arbitration.

[*Dr. Vít Horáček*]

Advocate and Arbitrator, President of the International Arbitration Court of the Czech Commodity Exchange, Member of the ICC International Arbitration Court E-mail: vit.horacek@legalite.cz

News & Reports

News & Reports

Czech (& Central European) Yearbook of Arbitration®

On the Recognition and Enforcement of Awards of International Arbitration Courts: An Example from the International Arbitration Court at the BelCCI in the Territory of the Russian Federation

The implementation of the awards of the International Arbitration Court at the BelCCI in the territory of other States in comparison with the place of making awards presents a huge advantage due to the existence of the UN Convention on the Recognition and Enforcement of Foreign Arbitral Awards (New York Convention). More than 160 states participate in this Convention which was enacted in New York in 1958. However, despite the application by the participating States, one cannot fail to take into account national procedural legislation that adapts the provisions of the New York Convention within a particular jurisdiction. At the same time, the influence of the national procedural legislation on the interpretation of certain provisions of the New York Convention in a certain territory often turns out to be quite significant.

For a large number of Belarusian entities, the main foreign economic contractors are subjects to the law of the Russian Federation. In this regard, the number of external economic disputes between Belarusian and Russian subjects is also relatively large. This is in relation to other foreign economic disputes, not in absolute magnitude.

Thus, in the practice of the International Court of Arbitration at the BelCCI, disputes between Russian and Belarusian subjects are quite important.

Accordingly, a significant number of awards of the International Arbitration Court at the BelCCI are enforced in the territory of the Russian Federation. The specified enforcement is carried out on the basis of the provisions of the New York Convention, but taking into account the norms contained in the Arbitration Procedural Code (the APC) of the Russian Federation.

The proceedings on cases on the recognition and enforcement of foreign arbitral awards, which also include the decisions of the International Arbitration Court at the BelCCI, are regulated in the territory of the Russian Federation by Chapter 31 of the APC of the Russian Federation, which came into force on 1 September 2002.

According to paragraph 2 of Article 241 of the APC of the Russian Federation, the questions of recognition and enforcement of a foreign arbitral award are resolved on the basis of the relevant application of the party to the arbitration.

In accordance with paragraph 1 of Article 242 of the APC of the Russian Federation, this application is sent to the arbitration court of the subject of the Russian Federation at the location or place of residence of the debtor or, if the location or place of residence of the debtor is unknown, at the location of the debtor's property.

Based on the results of the consideration of the above-mentioned application, the competent arbitration court issues a ruling on the authorization to recognize and enforce a foreign arbitral award or refusal to do so.

Part 2 of Article 244 of the APC of the Russian Federation provides that the arbitration court refuses to recognize or enforce fully or in part a foreign arbitral award on the grounds provided for in paragraph 7 of part 1 of this Article and part 4 of Article 239 of the APC of the Russian Federation for refusal to issue an enforcement document to enforce the decision of international commercial arbitration, unless otherwise provided by an international treaty of the Russian Federation.

Part 4 of Article 239 of the APC of the Russian Federation prescribes that the arbitration court may refuse to issue the enforcement order for the enforcement of the decision of international commercial arbitration on the grounds provided for by the international treaty of the Russian Federation and the federal law on international commercial arbitration. According to subparagraph (b) of paragraph 1 of Article V of the New York Convention, recognition and enforcement of a foreign arbitral award may be refused at the request of the party against whom the decision was directed if it is presented with evidence of its inadequate notification of the appointment of an arbitrator or of arbitration.

Later in this article, a number of examples will be considered concerning the refusal to recognize and enforce the decisions of the International Arbitration Court at the BelCCI in the territory of the Russian Federation due, in the opinion of the arbitration courts of the Russian Federation, to inadequate notification of the respondent of the stages of the proceedings.

One of the problems associated with the proper notification of the respondent about arbitration proceedings is based on the determination of the address for sending correspondence on the case to the respondent. On 29 November 2006 the Arbitration Court of the Kaliningrad Region issued a ruling on the refusal to recognize and enforce the decision of the International Arbitration Court at the BelCCI of 12 May 2006, made on a dispute between a foreign enterprise A (Republic of Belarus) and a limited liability company B (Russian Federation).

The debtor, Limited Liability Company B, stated in the course of the proceedings for the recognition and enforcement of the decision that it had not been duly notified by the International Arbitration Court at the BelCCI about holding a hearing because the correspondence was not sent to the legal address of the debtor.

The Arbitration Court of the Kaliningrad Region found that the International Arbitration Court at the BelCCI used the address indicated on the debtor's letterhead forms, while the contract from which a dispute between the parties arose contained an indication of another address of the debtor, which was its legal address.

The debtor explained that his production premises were located at the address where the correspondence was sent by the International Arbitration Court at the BelCCI, while his office was located at the legal address. During the consideration of the case by the International Arbitration Court at the BelCCI, the debtor did not carry out production activities, and his staff consisted of only a director and an accountant. Among these persons there was no employee named K., who signed the receipt of correspondence sent to the debtor by the International Arbitration Court at the BelCCI.

In these circumstances, the Arbitration Court of the Kaliningrad Region concluded that the debtor was not properly notified of the arbitration. In the course of the proceedings the International Court of Arbitration at the BelCCI did not observe the procedure for notifying the party about the proceedings. Such a procedure is outlined in the Hague Convention on the Service Abroad of Judicial and Extrajudicial Documents in Civil or Commercial Matters of 1965.

In this regard, we note that the Hague Convention on the Delivery Abroad of Judicial and Extrajudicial Documents in Civil Cases of 1965 does not apply to the procedure for sending correspondence in the settlement of disputes by international arbitration courts.

Disagreeing with the findings of the Arbitration Court of the Kaliningrad region, the claimant sent a cassation appeal against the above ruling to the Federal Arbitration Court of the North-Western District. However, that court found no grounds for repealing the ruling of the Arbitration Court of the Kaliningrad Region.

In a ruling of 12 February 2007 it was stated that the debtor was not able to find out about the date and place of the proceedings, since the relevant correspondence was sent to him by the International Arbitration Court at the BelCCI at the address indicated on the company letterheads, and not at the legal address specified in the contract.

A similar scenario can be found in another case, considered by the International Arbitration Court at the BelCCI in the dispute arising between the unitary enterprise A (Republic of Belarus) and the limited liability company B (Russian Federation). In this case, notification of the initiation of the case, the statement of claim with the materials attached to it, the Rules of the International Arbitration Court at the BelCCI and the recommendation list of its arbitrators were forwarded to the respondent at the address indicated in the contract concluded by the parties.

On 13 March 2009, the Federal Arbitration Court of the North-Western District issued a resolution refusing to satisfy a cassation complaint, after considering the cassation appeal against the decision of the Arbitration Court of the Kaliningrad Region of 29 December 2008 about the refusal to recognize and enforce the above decision.

In this resolution it was stated that the previously named correspondence was handed to N., whose location in the debtor's office is denied. Only the notice of the time and place of the court hearing sent to the legal address of the debtor was received by them.

It should be noted that the debtor, who allegedly did not receive a statement of claim with the documents attached to it, did not consider it possible to inform the International Arbitration Court at the BelCCI.

Thus, in the above two examples, there is a clear tendency by the judicial authorities of the Russian Federation to recognize inadequate notification of the respondent, provided that correspondence is not sent to a legal address.

In connection with the above, we draw attention to the fact that the International Arbitration Court at the BelCCI sends correspondence to the respondent at the address specified in the statement of claim.

In one of the cases examined, the correspondence was sent to the postal address indicated on the defendant's letterhead, and in the second case to the postal address specified in the contract from which the dispute arose.

Sending correspondence to the defendant's postal address is allowed by the Rules of the International Arbitration Court at the BelCCI and the Law of the Republic of Belarus of 9 July 1999 'On the International Arbitration Court'. At the same time, sending correspondence at a legal address in comparison with the postal address has no advantages.

Thus, part one of Article 30 of the Law of the Republic of Belarus 'On the International Arbitration Court' and paragraph 3 of Article 20 of the Rules of the International Arbitration Court at the BelCCI contain the following provision: 'A written communication is deemed received if it is delivered to the recipient in person or at its permanent residence place, or at the location of his enterprise, or at his postal address, unless otherwise provided by agreement of the parties ... '. The above-mentioned norm provides for the equivalent use of the address as a permanent residence of the defendant, the location of his enterprise, and the postal address.

In the absence of any reference to the rule of law, it can be assumed that the conclusion of the Arbitration Court of the Kaliningrad Region and the Federal Arbitration Court of the Northwest District was based on the Article 122 of the APC of the Russian Federation, contained in Chapter 12, paragraph 1. This section contains a provision that a copy of the judicial act is sent by the arbitration court by registered mail with a notice of delivery or by delivery to the addressee directly in the arbitration court or at the address of the addressee.

The location of the organization in accordance with paragraph 4 of Article 121 of the APC of the Russian Federation is determined by the place of its State registration, unless otherwise stipulated in the constituent documents in accordance with the federal law.

However, in our opinion, it is disputable to disseminate the rules governing the procedure for sending court notices in the process of consideration of cases in arbitration courts of the Russian Federation, on the order of the correspondence direction. This is particularly true when the dispute is resolved by the International Arbitration Court at BelCCI. In this case the procedure is regulated not by the legislation of the Russian Federation, but by international law and Belarusian legislation in the field of international commercial arbitration, as well as by the Rules of the International Arbitrator Court at the BCCI.

In accordance with Article 12 of the Law of the Republic of Belarus 'On the International Arbitration Court', if the parties envisaged in the arbitration agreement the transfer of the dispute to the standing arbitral tribunal, then in the absence of agreement of the parties, they also agreed on the procedure for considering the dispute in accordance with its arbitration rules.

Consequently, the procedural rules for the consideration of disputes in all the above cases should be determined by the Rules of the International Arbitration Court of the BelCCI, including the instructions on the procedure for sending correspondence. Despite the correctness and validity of this conclusion one should not discount the nuances of law enforcement practice of Russian arbitration courts, in order to ensure the enforcement of the decisions of the International Arbitration Court at the BelCCI in the territory of the Russian Federation. Therefore, it is essential to indicate both the postal and legal address of the Respondent in the statement of claim for forwarding the correspondence in the territory of the Russian Federation. As another example of judicial practice on the issue under consideration in this article, we turn to the 'procedural continuation' of one of the previously cited cases.

The foreign enterprise A (the Republic of Belarus) applied to the Supreme Arbitration Court of the Russian Federation with a request to review, in the order of supervision, the earlier decision of the Federal Arbitration Court of the North-Western District on 12 February 2007.

In the ruling of the Supreme Arbitration Court of the Russian Federation of 8 May 2007, emphasis was again placed on the fact that the correspondence was not sent to the legal address of the debtor.

In addition, notices submitted by the postal institution at the request of the debtor were analyzed, from which it follows that the correspondence sent by the International Arbitration Court at BelCCI was handed to

Mr. K. The debtor presented the staffing table, the payroll for the social insurance fund and the calculation of advance payments for insurance contributions to compulsory pension insurance for persons making payments to others, indicating that an employee was named K and during the period of interest no one by that name had worked for the debtor. Likewise, services within the scope of the civil-law treaty had not been rendered. During the consideration of the case by the International Arbitration Court at the BelCCI, the debtor had not carried out production activities, and his staff consisted of only a director and an accountant.

On the basis of the foregoing, the Supreme Arbitration Court of the Russian Federation refused to transfer to the Presidium the case of the Arbitration Court of the Kaliningrad Region on revision in the order of supervision.

In order to arrive at the conclusion that the defendant was not properly notified of arbitration, it seems logical to find out why the postal institution has handed the correspondence to a person who is not related to the designated addressee. Is this the debtor's fault in this case? Did he properly organize his relations with the postal institution? Did he provide the post office information on persons authorized to receive correspondence on behalf of the debtor?

As a comparison we can look to the practice of the economic courts of the Republic of Belarus.

The respondent, objecting to the enforcement of the decision of the International Commercial Arbitration Court at the Ukrainian Chamber of Commerce and Industry on the territory of the Republic of Belarus, indicated that the legal address had been changed during the proceedings of the case. The International Commercial Arbitration Court at the Ukrainian Chamber of Commerce and Industry sent correspondence to the new address - 20, office 402. However, according to the constituent documents, the address is office 402-3. As a result, correspondence was received by the secretary of another legal entity.

The Economic Court noted that the office of debtor number three is in block 402 at house 20. According to the secretary who received the correspondence, she received all the correspondence that came to the addressee of block 402. After that, the correspondence was placed in a specially designated place, from where it was taken by the tenants. Such an order was agreed between everyone, there were no separate mailboxes, and coordination with the post office for personal receipt of correspondence was also absent.

In such circumstances, the Economic Court indicated that the notice of the time and place of the hearing was sent to the defendant and was not received by the latter because of improper organization of receipt of correspondence.

The courts have continued the theme of recognition and enforcement of the decisions of the International Arbitration Court at the BelCCI in the territory of the Russian Federation. Firstly, on 23 June 2009, the Moscow Arbitration Court issued a ruling on the recognition and enforcement of the decision of the International Arbitration Court at the BelCCI on 5 December 2008 on the suit of a joint venture (Republic of Belarus) to a limited liability company (Russian Federation). Secondly, on 27 March 2009 a decision was issued on recognition and enforcement of the decision of the International Arbitration Court at the BelCCI on 6 August 2008 on the suit of an open joint stock company (Republic of Belarus) to the limited liability company (Russian Federation).

Thirdly, on 24 November 2008, a decision was issued on recognition and enforcement of the decision of the International Arbitration Court at the BelCCI on 16 July 2008 on the suit of the limited liability company (Republic of Belarus) for a limited liability company (Russian Federation), which was left unchanged by a resolution of the Federal Arbitration Court of the Moscow District of 28 January 2009.

Nevertheless, there are circumstances that can serve as the basis for refusing to recognize and enforce these decisions. They also result from the failure to notify the defendant about the time and place of the hearing. For example, on 11 October 2007, the Arbitration Court of the Smolensk Region issued a ruling refusing to recognize and enforce the decision of the International Arbitration Court at the BelCCI on 10 August 2007 in case No. 605/40-06 on the suit of joint-stock company A (Republic of Belarus) to the entrepreneur B (Russian Federation).

The individual entrepreneur claimed that he was not properly notified of the time and place of the case and could not present his objections to the International Arbitration Court at the BelCCI.

The Arbitration Court of Smolensk region established that the International Arbitration Court attached to the BelCCI sent the defendant correspondence to the address Village N., 10, Smolensk Region, Russian Federation.

Exactly this address is indicated as the location of the individual entrepreneur B in the extract from the Unified State Register of Individual Entrepreneurs of the Russian Federation.

The notice of the time and place of the hearing of the International Arbitration Court at the BelCCI was sent by express courier mail, but was not received by the addressee because of his absence at the address indicated.

Having analyzed these circumstances, the Arbitration Court of the Smolensk region found that, without applying evidence of delivery of correspondence to the individual entrepreneur B, the letter of the express courier mail cannot confirm the fact of proper notification of the respondent.

The Federal Arbitration Court of the Central District, having considered the cassation appeal of joint-stock company A on the definition of the Arbitration Court of the Smolensk region, decided to leave this definition unchanged.

In the opinion of the cassation instance, the court of the first instance lawfully denied the application for recognition and enforcement of the decision of the International Arbitration Court at the BelCCI in connection with the lack of sufficient evidence to notify the defendant of the consideration of the dispute.

There are several important aspects of this decision.

The New York Convention establishes that the burden of proving the grounds for refusing to recognize and enforce foreign arbitral awards rests with the party against whom the award was made.

Thus, it was not the joint-stock company A that had to prove the proper notification of the respondent about the arbitration proceedings. Rather, the individual entrepreneur B was obliged not only to declare, but also to provide evidence of improper notice.

The International Arbitration Court at the BelCCI also has procedures for sending correspondence

First of all, in accordance with Article 12 of the Law of the Republic of Belarus 'On the International Arbitration Court', if the parties envisaged in the arbitration agreement to the transfer of the dispute to a permanent international arbitration court, then they also agreed on the procedure for considering the dispute in accordance with the arbitration rules, in the absence of another agreement.

Article 30 of the Law of the Republic of Belarus 'On the International Arbitration Court' provides that a written communication is deemed to be received if it has been delivered to the recipient personally or to the address of his permanent residence or location of his firm or his mailing address, unless otherwise provided by the agreement of the parties. When the place of delivery of a written communications cannot be determined upon a diligent inquiry, a written communication is considered to be received if it has been sent to the last known residence, location of the firm or mailing address by the registered mail or any other means which provide a record of the attempt to deliver such communication.

Paragraph 3 of Article 20 of the Rules of the International Arbitration Court of the BelCCI contains an order that a written communication is deemed to be received if it has been delivered to the recipient personally or to the address of his permanent residence or location of his firm or his mailing address, unless otherwise provided by the agreement of the parties. When the place of delivery of written communications cannot be determined upon diligent inquiry, a written communication is considered to be received if it has been sent to the last known address of the recipient. This is their permanent residence, location of their firm

Czech (& Central European) Yearbook of Arbitration®

or their mailing address as specified in the contract or in the letter head form of the firm received from the recipient during correspondence, and must be sent by the registered mail or any other means which provide a record of the attempt to deliver such communication. Herewith, the message is considered to be received on the day of its delivery or attempt to deliver or transfer to the recipient, as mentioned in paragraph 3 of this Article.

An analysis of the above norms allows us to make an unambiguous conclusion that in a number of cases, judicial correspondence that was not actually delivered to the addressee is nevertheless deemed to be properly delivered.

One of these cases occurs when the correspondence was sent to the last known address of the recipient, but was not received due to absence at the specified address.

At the same time, the place of delivery of the written message could not be established by diligent inquiry.

It follows from the case file No. 605/40-06, and this was reflected in the decision of the International Arbitration Court at the BelCCI that another address of the defendant was indicated in the contract signed by the parties. The correspondence sent to them included the statement of claim with attachments, the notice of the International Arbitration Court at the BelCCI on the initiation of the case, the Rules of the International Arbitration Court at the BelCCI and the Recommendation List of Its Arbitrators. It was not delivered to the addressee. On the envelope returned to the International Arbitration Court at the BelCCI, there was a postage stamp on the return of the letter saying 'unclaimed'.

The claimant, by means of diligent inquiry, established another address of the defendant in comparison with the one specified in the contract, which was listed in the Unified States Register of Individual Entrepreneurs of the Russian Federation. It was to this address that the claim was re-sent with attachments, including the notice of the International Arbitration Court at the BelCCI on the initiation of the case, the Rules of the International Arbitration Court at the BelCCI and the recommendation list of its arbitrators.

The defendant received the named correspondence on 29 November 2006, which is confirmed by an appropriate postal notification of delivery. In the notice of filing the case, the International Arbitration Court at the BelCCI suggested to the respondent to submit a response to the claim not later than 30 days after the receipt of the notification.

Thus, the defendant, having been duly notified of the procedure and deadlines for presenting their response to the statement of claim, did not submit any documents to the International Arbitration Court at the BelCCI. However, this did not prevent them from later successfully claiming that they did not have the possibility to present their explanations in the case No. 605/40-06 at the stage of consideration of the application for recognition and enforcement of the decision in this case.

Let us reiterate that the notice of the time and place of the court session was sent by an express courier mail to the defendant's address, which became known as a result of diligent inquiry, and was not received by the addressee because of his absence at this address.

We believe that the direction of the above-mentioned notification at the last known address of the respondent established through fair inquiry, fully meets the requirements of Article 30 of the Law of the Republic of Belarus 'On International Arbitration Court' and of paragraph 3 of Article 20 of the Rules of the International Arbitration Court of the BelCCI with regard to the appropriate notification of the party about the arbitration proceedings. It takes into account the receipt by the respondent of the judicial correspondence sent to the same address.

However, the Supreme Arbitration Court of the Russian Federation held a different opinion.

In the ruling No 3839/08 dated 28 April 2008 'On refusal to refer the case to the Presidium of the Supreme Arbitration Court of the Russian Federation', it is concluded that Article 20 of the Rules of the International Arbitration Court at the BelCCI provides for the obligation to send notices and other orders only by registered mail with the acknowledgment of receipt or by physically delivered against signature. Otherwise it is stipulated in cases when it is impossible to establish the address of the recipient of the correspondence.

The address of the individual entrepreneur however, was known to the International Arbitration Court at the BelCCI - it was in the village N., 10, Smolensk region, of the Russian Federation. The joint-stock company A did not provide any other proofs of the defendant's repeated notification of the time and place of consideration of the case.

Unfortunately, we cannot agree with the approach of the respected judicial organ of the Russian Federation. The International Arbitration Court at the BelCCI sent a notice of the time and place of the hearing to the respondent's address indicated in the Unified State Register of Individual Entrepreneurs of the Russian Federation and received a courier message that the addressee was not available at this address.

Following the arguments of the Presidium of the Supreme Arbitration Court of the Russian Federation, the International Arbitration Court at the BelCCI had to postpone the proceedings every time to send a notice of the time and place of the hearing to the same address until it was actually received by the respondent.

We are sure that this conclusion is based on the provision of paragraph 2 of Article 20 of the Rules of the International Arbitration Court at the BelCCI concerning the 'place of delivery of a written message', and not the address of the recipient of the correspondence.

It is difficult to imagine any other interpretation of this provision, especially considering that the address of the defendant's location is accessible establishes without any difficulties by means of applying to the authority where the State registration is made and information on the subjects included in the register.

The mechanism set forth in paragraph 2 of Article 20 of the Rules of the International Arbitration Court at the BelCCI comes into force if the place of delivery of a written message was not established by diligent inquiry, that is, the message was not actually delivered. The correspondence is considered received if it was sent to the defendant's last known address, but was not handed in due to the absence of the addressee at the address indicated, as there was written notice to the postal office.

It should be noted that paragraph 2 of Article 123 of the APC of the Russian Federation contains a very similar prescription stating that the persons participating in the case and other participants in the arbitration process are considered to be notified if a copy of the judicial act sent by the arbitration court at the last known court of the location of the organization, or place of residence of a citizen, was not handed in due to the absence of the addressee at the specified address, of which the communication body informed the arbitration court.

Unfortunately, the above approach was duplicated in yet another case, which was considered by the arbitration court of the Russian Federation. The Arbitration Court of the Stavropol Territory refused to recognize and enforce the decision of the International Arbitration Court at the BelCCI on 1 November 2004 on the suit of the foreign enterprise A (Republic of Belarus) to Limited Liability Company B (Russian Federation). In its ruling of 28 January 2005 the absence of documents confirming the proper notification of the respondent about the case at the International Arbitration Court at the BelCCI was indicated.

Having considered the cassation appeal against the above ruling, the Federal Arbitration Court of the North Caucasus Circuit refused to satisfy it on the grounds that the notice of the time and place of the trial sent by the courier's express mail was not handed to the respondent personally upon receipt as required by the Rules of the International arbitration court at BelCCI. By itself, an express courier mail without application of proof of delivery of correspondence cannot be sufficient evidence of this fact.

Before commenting on this example, let us pay attention to the fact that the letter of the express courier mail contained information about the receipt of the mail item on 5 August 2004, indicating the specific person who received it. Let us also recall that paragraph 2 of Article 20 of the Rules of the International Arbitration Court at the BelCCI establishes the procedure for the delivery of judicial correspondence by registered letters with the notice of delivery or delivery physically against signature. At the expense of the party, the delivery may be effected in a different rational way, upon its application or on the initiative of the court.

It seems that in the context of this article the wording 'physically delivered upon signature' implies personal, direct delivery of correspondence to the addressee, excluding such a link as the postal department.

A similar conclusion follows from Article 30 of the Law of the Republic of Belarus 'On the International Arbitration Court', which provides that a written communication is deemed received if it is delivered to the recipient in person, or at their permanent place of residence or at the location of their enterprise, or at their postal address, unless otherwise provided by agreement of the parties.

Evidence that refutes the fact of receiving the notice of the International Arbitration Court at the BelCCI by the individual entrepreneur B has not been presented.

There is also no evidence of a violation by the express courier mail of the rules regulating the procedure for the exercise of its functions in the delivery of correspondence.

Accordingly, in our opinion, there is no basis for concluding that the defendant was improperly notified of the consideration of the case by the International Arbitration Court at the BelCCI. In concluding this article, we note that for the party that lost the dispute, it is not enough to simply declare an inadequate notice of arbitration proceedings, but it is necessary to present the relevant evidence.

Transferring the burden of proving the fact of proper notification to the party that won the dispute does not correspond to the international obligations of both the Republic of Belarus and the Russian Federation, recorded in Article V of the New York Convention.

[Ian Iosifovich Funk, LL.D.]
is a Professor of BSU, Chairman of the International Arbitration Court at the BelCCI
E-mail: funk25@mail.ru

[Inna Vladimirovna Pererva, PhD.]
is the Head of Information and Consulting Center of the International Arbitration Court at the BelCCI
E-mail: iac@cci.by

Czech (& Central European) Yearbook of Arbitration®

News & Reports

Recognition and Enforcement of Arbitral Awards in Kazakhstan

I.   General Provisions

Arbitration as an alternative way to resolve commercial disputes in Kazakhstan has been used for more than twenty years. And in this relatively short time, it has undergone several stages in its development. Such stages have been completely diametrical, from the stage of formation and systematic development to the stage of the implicit and explicit destruction of arbitration courts, from the stage of passing the first arbitration laws to their consolidation.

On 31 October 2015, the new Civil Procedure Code of the Republic of Kazakhstan (hereinafter referred to as the CPC) was adopted.[1] It was followed by adoption on 8 April 2016, of Law No. 488-V "On Arbitration of the Republic of Kazakhstan" (hereinafter referred to as the Arbitration Law).[2] It combined two previously existing laws (On Arbitration Courts and On International Arbitration). According to Article 1 of the Arbitration Law, it applies to disputes arising out of civil law relations involving individuals and (or) legal entities, regardless of the place of residence or location of the disputed subjects within or outside the state, to be resolved by arbitration, unless otherwise established by the legislative acts of the Republic of Kazakhstan. Thus, the division of Kazakhstan's arbitration courts into internal arbitration courts and international arbitration in Kazakhstan was abolished.

The current CPC distinguishes the concepts of "arbitration" and "foreign arbitration". "Arbitration" means arbitration established and operating in the Republic of Kazakhstan (it can be both institutional arbitration and ad hoc arbitration). "Foreign arbitration" refers to both institutional and ad hoc arbitration established and operating outside the Republic of Kazakhstan.

Therefore, the provisions of Chapter 20 entitled Enforcement of Arbitral Award of the CPC (Articles 253 - 255) are devoted to the enforcement

---

[1]   Code # 377-V of 31 October 2015 of the Republic of Kazakhstan entitled Civil Procedure Code of the Republic of Kazakhstan // Kazakhstanskaya Pravda newspaper # 210 dated 3 November 2015 (28086).
[2]   The Law *On Arbitration* # 488-V of 8 April 2016 // Kazakhstanskaya Pravda newspaper # 67 dated 9 April 2016 (28193).

of an arbitral award rendered by Kazakhstani arbitration. And the provisions of Chapter 57 entitled Proceedings on Cases Involving Foreign Persons of the CPC (Articles 501, 503, 504) relate to the enforcement of an arbitral award rendered by foreign arbitration.

The decisions of foreign international commercial arbitration courts under the Convention on the Recognition and Enforcement of Foreign Arbitral Awards (New York, 10 June 1958, hereinafter referred to as the New York Convention) shall be recognized and enforced in the territory of the Republic of Kazakhstan in accordance with the Civil Procedural Code of the Republic of Kazakhstan. Kazakhstan has acceded to the Convention by Decree No. 2485 of 4 October 1995 of the President of the Republic of Kazakhstan On Accession of the Republic of Kazakhstan to the Convention on the Recognition and Enforcement of Foreign Arbitral Awards adopted in New York City on 10 June 1958.

Article 3 of the New York Convention stipulates the following provision: "Each Contracting State recognizes arbitral awards as binding and enforces them in accordance with the procedural rules of the territory where recognition and enforcement of such decisions is sought under conditions set forth in the following articles. The recognition and enforcement of arbitral awards to which this Convention applies shall not be subject to substantially more onerous terms or higher fees and duties than those that exist for the recognition and enforcement of domestic arbitral awards".

In accordance with paragraph 1 of Article 501 entitled Recognition and enforcement of decisions of foreign courts, arbitral awards of foreign arbitration of the Civil Procedure Code, the decisions, resolutions and rulings on the approval of settlement agreements, judicial orders of foreign courts as well as the arbitral awards of foreign arbitration courts shall be recognized and enforced by the courts of the Republic of Kazakhstan, if recognition and enforcement of such enactments are provided for by legislation and (or) an international treaty ratified by the Republic of Kazakhstan, or on the basis of reciprocity.

According to paragraph 1 of Article 4 of the Constitution of the Republic of Kazakhstan,[3] the applicable laws in the Republic of Kazakhstan are, inter alia, the norms of the regulatory resolutions of the Supreme Court of the Republic of Kazakhstan. In accordance with paragraph 3 of Article 5 of Law No. 480-V of 6 April 2016 "On enactments of the Republic of Kazakhstan" (hereinafter referred to as the Law on Enactments),[4] the regulatory resolution of the Supreme Court of the Republic of Kazakhstan contains explanations on the issues of judicial practice. In such case, according to paragraph 5 of Article 10 of the

---

[3]   Constitution of the Republic of Kazakhstan (approved in the republican referendum on 30 August 1995), available at: http://www.akorda.kz/ru/official_documents/constitution (accessed on 23 July 2018).

[4]   The Law "On Enactments" # 480-V of 6 April 2016 of the Republic of Kazakhstan, available at: https://online.zakon.kz/document/?doc_id=37312788 (accessed on 23 July 2018).

Law on Enactments, the regulatory resolutions of the Supreme Court of the Republic of Kazakhstan are outside the hierarchy of regulatory enactments established by Article 10 of the Law on Enactments.

Thus, in accordance with clause 30 of Regulatory Resolution No. 5 of 11 July 2003 "On Judgment" (hereinafter referred to as the Regulatory Resolution)[5] of the Supreme Court of the Republic of Kazakhstan, the awards of foreign courts and arbitrations, according to Article 501 of the CPC, may be subject to binding enforcement in the Republic of Kazakhstan within three years from the date when the decision enters into legal force, if provided for by law or by an international treaty of the Republic of Kazakhstan. Such award shall be enforced at the request of the interested party by a ruling of the court of the Republic of Kazakhstan in accordance with the rules on jurisdiction determined by the Civil Procedure Code at the place where an award shall be enforced.

The application is usually accompanied by:

- A duly certified copy of an award, the enforcement of which requires permission;
- An official document stating that the decision came into legal force if this circumstance does not result from the text of an award;
- Evidences confirming proper notification of the party or its representative, in case of procedural incapacity of the party against which an award is made, about the process;
- Enforcement document with a note on the partial enforcement of an award, if any;
- On matters of contractual jurisdiction, a document confirming the agreement of the parties on this issue.

It is noteworthy that this paragraph of the Regulatory Resolution has no delineation of the documents that are attached to the petition for the compulsory enforcement of the awards of foreign courts and the awards of foreign arbitrations. Meanwhile, as is well known, the New York Convention reduced the list of documents to be submitted for the recognition and enforcement of a foreign arbitral award, down to two documents, namely: the arbitral award itself (or its certified copy) and the original arbitration agreement (or its certified copy).[6]

In this regard, the expansion of the list of documents in the Regulatory Resolution does not comply with the requirements of the New York Convention, and therefore, in our view, it needs to be clarified. Currently, the provision is saved by the phrase in paragraph 30 of the Regulatory Resolution that the listed documents are attached to the application "as a rule", and not as requirements.

---

[5] Regulatory Resolution # 5 of 11 July 2003 of the Supreme Court of the Republic of Kazakhstan "On Court Awards", available at: http://adilet.zan.kz/rus/docs/P03000005S_ (accessed on 23 July 2018).

[6] International Commercial Arbitration. Saint-Petersburg: Editorial staff of Arbitration Court magazine; M.: Infotropic Media 40-42 (V.A. Mussina, O.Y.Skvortsova eds., 2012).

II.   Arbitral Award Enforcement Procedure

An arbitral award rendered by Kazakhstani arbitration shall be enforced in the procedure provided for in Articles 253-255 of the CPC.

An arbitral award made by a foreign arbitration shall be enforced in accordance with the procedure provided for in Articles 501, 503, 504 of the Civil Procedure Code.

In accordance with paragraph 1 of Article 503 of the CPC, in case the arbitral award is not enforced voluntarily within the time fixed therein, then the party to the arbitration in favor of which the arbitral award (the recoverer) was rendered is entitled to apply to the court for enforcement of the arbitral award at the place of arbitration or at the place of residence of the debtor or at the location of the legal entity; if the place of residence or location is unknown, then it will be at the location of the debtor's property.

According to paragraph 2 of Article 503 of the CPC, a duly certified arbitral award of a foreign arbitration or a duly certified copy is attached, and, if available, an original arbitration agreement or its duly certified copy shall be attached to the application for the issuance of the writ of enforcement for the enforcement of a foreign arbitral award. If these enactments or arbitration agreements are set out in a foreign language, then the party must submit a duly certified translation into Kazakh or Russian.

It should be noted that these provisions of the CPC fully meet the requirements of the New York Convention on the Recognition and Enforcement of Foreign Arbitral Awards with regard to the requirement to submit only two documents to the competent court, the decision itself and the arbitration clause.

What does a "duly certified" or "legalized" document mean? Legalization means an action through which a public official certifies the authenticity of a signature on an official or private document and the capacity of a signatory as well as, if required, the authenticity of a seal or stamp affixed on such enactment so that it can be considered true wherever it is presented. As is commonly known, there are two main legalization mechanisms: consular legalization and using an apostille (apostillization). An apostille is a special stamp to be affixed on official documents of a noncommercial nature issued by governmental authorities and institutions of countries that joined the Hague Convention of 5 October 1961 On Cancellation of Requirements for Legalization of Official Foreign Documents.[7] The apostille stamp affixed on a document does not require further legalization or certification of the document itself. Such document shall be recognized by official authorities and the institutions of all countries that joined the Hague Convention of 5 October 1961 and

---

[7]   The Republic of Kazakhstan joined the Hague Convention on 5 April 2000; the above Convention became effective for Kazakhstan on 30 January 2001.

has legal force in their territory.

Court practice initially chooses the most liberal path making foreign arbitral awards free from legalization. However, such approach did not prevail, and, in most cases, arbitration courts require a party to legalize such a document within the frames of proceedings for the recognition and enforcement of foreign arbitral awards.

In this case, the apostillization at the location of arbitration would be the most preferable legalization mechanism for a party (in terms of convenience and ease of implementation). However, according to the Hague Convention, which cancels the requirement to legalize foreign official documents, only official documents are subject to apostillization, which do not include the awards of nongovernmental authorities represented by international commercial arbitration.

How is the issue of the legalization (apostillization) of foreign arbitral awards solved in practice? The parties apply to a notary by choosing the appropriate notarial action (depending on the content of the national notarial law and the opportunities provided by it, i.e. a notary certifies a copy of an arbitral award (namely, they use such notarial actions as a certification of authenticity of a signature in an arbitral award or agreement). Further, the signature and notary's seal shall be subject to apostillization. Such mechanism of legalizing the decisions of foreign arbitration courts exists in most states.

Thus, in order to enforce in Kazakhstan an arbitral award rendered by the arbitrators of the Arbitration Institute of the Stockholm Chamber of Commerce in English, the party in favor of which an award was made shall arrange the translation of the award and arbitration agreement into Kazakh or Russian, and then it shall arrange notarial certification of the award and arbitration agreement in Stockholm. Then it shall arrange for apostillization of these documents and shall send them together with the application for arbitral award enforcement to a court at the place of the debtor's residence or at the location of the legal entity; if a place of residence or location is unknown, then it will be at the location of the debtor's property.

In accordance with paragraph 3 of Article 253 and paragraph 3 of Article 503 of the CPC, an application for the issue of the writ of execution can be filed no later than within three years from the date of expiration of the period for voluntary arbitral award enforcement.

An application for the issue of the writ of execution filed with a missed deadline and without an application for restoring the time limit and supporting documents shall be returned by the court without consideration, along with the relevant ruling. The ruling can be appealed and challenged at the court of appeals. The appellate court's decision shall be final.

The court is entitled to restore the time limit for filing an application for the issue of a writ of execution if it recognizes the reasons for missing the specified period of validity.

An application for issue of the writ of execution shall be examined by the judge alone within fifteen working days from the date of receipt of the application to the court (clause 6, Article 253 and clause 6, Article 503 of the CPC).

The court notifies the debtor of the received claim of the recoverer in arbitral award enforcement as well as of the place and time of its consideration in the court session. The recoverer is also notified of the place and time of consideration of his/her/its application. The failure of the debtor or the recoverer to appear in the court session is not an obstacle to consideration of the application if the debtor did not submit an application to postpone consideration of the application specifying valid reasons for his/her/its failure to appear in the court session.

An important rule is fixed in paragraph 8 of Article 503 of the CPC. It consists in the fact that when considering an application for the issue of an enforcement order for the enforcement of an arbitral award, the court has no right to review it on its merits.

Based on the results of a consideration of the application, the court makes a ruling on the issue of the writ of execution or on a refusal to issue it. The court ruling to issue the writ of execution is subject to immediate enforcement (Clause 9, Article 503 of the CPC).

III. Grounds for Waiver of Recognition or Enforcement of Arbitral Award

In accordance with Article 504 of the CPC, the waiver of issuance and issue of the writ of execution for foreign arbitral award enforcement are carried out according to the rules provided for by Chapter 20 of this Code. In such case, Article 504 refers to Article 255 of the CPC containing a full list of grounds for refusal to issue an enforcement order for arbitral award enforcement issued by the domestic Kazakhstani arbitration courts.

The grounds for refusal to recognize or enforce an arbitral award are provided in Article 57 of the Arbitration Law and Article 255 of the Civil Procedure Code.

So, according to Article 255 of the CPC:

"1. The court renders a ruling on refusal to issue a writ of execution for arbitral award enforcement if:

1) The party against whom the award was made will present evidence to the court that:

The arbitration agreement is invalid under the laws of the state to which the parties subordinated it and, in the absence of such indication, under the laws of the Republic of Kazakhstan;

The award is rendered in a dispute not provided for by the arbitration agreement or not subject to its terms or contains awards on the matters that go beyond the scope of the arbitration agreement as well as due to the lack of jurisdiction of the dispute to arbitration;

One of the parties to the arbitration agreement was recognized by the court as legally incompetent or partially incapacitated;

The party against whom the decision was rendered was not duly notified of the appointment of an arbitrator or of arbitration proceedings or could not submit its explanation to the arbitration court for other reasons recognized by the court as valid;

There is a court decision or arbitration award that entered into legal force made on the dispute between the same parties on the same subject matter and on the same grounds, or the ruling of the court or arbitration to terminate the proceedings in connection with the refusal of the plaintiff from the claim;

An arbitration award was made possible as a result of a criminal offense established by a court verdict that entered into legal force;

The arbitration panel or the arbitration procedure of the proceedings did not comply with the requirements of the law;

An award did not become binding on the parties or was cancelled, or its enforcement was suspended by the court of the country according to the law of which it was rendered;

2) The court shall establish that enforcement of such an arbitration award is contrary to the public order of the Republic of Kazakhstan or that the dispute in which an arbitration award was rendered cannot be the subject of arbitration in accordance with the law.

2. If the arbitration award in such matters that are covered by the arbitration agreement may be separated from awards in matters that are not covered by such agreement, then the issuance of the enforcement order for the enforcement of that part of the award that is covered by the arbitration agreement cannot be refused."

What problems arise in court practice after the enforcement of foreign arbitration awards in Kazakhstan? Let us consider this using an instance of the application of separate grounds for a waiver of recognition and enforcement provided for in Article 255 of the CPC.

III.1. Arbitration Agreement Is Invalid under the Laws of State to which the Parties Subordinated It, and If No Such Instruction Is Provided, under the Laws of the Republic Of Kazakhstan

The doctrine and national laws of the majority of states adhere to the principle of independence of the arbitration agreement (recognizing it as an independent agreement).

That is why the parties are entitled to independently choose the law applicable to the arbitration agreement. This law may differ from the law that the parties chose as applicable to the main agreement.

The question of the law applicable to the arbitration agreement arises when the question as to whether the arbitration agreement is valid or not is decided.

The validity of the arbitration agreement is determined by the law to which the parties subordinated it and, in the absence of such indication, under the law of the country where the award was rendered. This rule is contained in Article V(1)(a) of the New York Convention on the Recognition and Enforcement of Foreign Arbitration Awards, Article 34(2)(a)(i) of the UNCITRAL Model Law.

The European Convention in Article IX(1)(a) similarly settled the question of the law applicable to the arbitration agreement by specifying that the law chosen by the parties applies to the arbitration agreement, and in the absence thereof, the law of the country in which the decision is to be made shall apply. If, however, the parties did not specify the law applicable to the arbitration agreement and it is impossible to establish in which country the arbitration award should be rendered, the court must determine the applicable law on the basis of the conflict-of-law rule of the country in which the case is initiated.

In accordance with subparagraph 1) of paragraph 1 of Article 57 of the Law *On Arbitration*, subparagraph 1) of paragraph 1 of Article 255 of the CPC determines the validity of the arbitration agreement (in the absence of the parties indicating the law applicable to the arbitration agreement) under the laws of the Republic of Kazakhstan.

Since the Law *On Arbitration* regulates the operations of arbitration courts established and operating in the territory of the Republic of Kazakhstan, then the place of making a decision by such arbitration courts shall be the Republic of Kazakhstan.

Such provisions of the Law *On Arbitration* correspond to the globally accepted provisions on determining the validity of the arbitration agreement in respect of arbitration awards of domestic arbitration.

However, when it comes to enforcing a foreign arbitration award in the territory of the Republic of Kazakhstan, the provisions of this article regarding the validity of the arbitration agreement (in the absence of the parties indicating the law applicable to the arbitration agreement) contradict V(1)(a) of the New York Convention and Article IX(1)(a) of the European Convention.

The matter is that subparagraph 1), paragraph 1, Article 57 of the Law of the Republic of Kazakhstan and subparagraph 1), paragraph 1, Article 255 of the CPC refer to the application of the laws of the Republic of Kazakhstan, while the Conventions refer to the law of such country where the decision was made.

It is obvious that in this case the provisions of the Conventions must apply and the validity of the arbitration agreement must be determined under the law of such country where the foreign arbitration award was made but not under the Law of the Republic of Kazakhstan *On Arbitration,* which also provides an absolutely unreasonably expanded list of material terms of the arbitration agreement.[8]

So, according to paragraph 4 of Article 9 of the Law *On Arbitration,* the arbitration agreement must contain:

1) The intention of the parties to refer the dispute to arbitration;
2) An indication of the subject to be considered by the arbitration;
3) Specification of a particular arbitration;
4) The consent of the authorized body of the relevant branch or local executive body in the case provided for in paragraph 10, Article 8 of the Law *On Arbitration.*

The Research Institute of Private Law of Caspian University together with Kazakhstan International Arbitration prepared proposals for making amendments and supplements to the Law *On Arbitration* and the CPC at the request of the Arbitration Chamber of Kazakhstan in the spring of 2017.[9] Most of the proposals developed by us were approved and included in the draft Law of the Republic of Kazakhstan On Amendments and Supplements to Certain Enactments of the Republic of Kazakhstan On Enhancing Protection of Title and Arbitration (hereinafter referred to as the Draft Law) after discussion at the meetings of the General Meeting members of the Arbitration Chamber of Kazakhstan.[10]

The bill provides for bringing subparagraph 1) of paragraph 1 of Article 57 of the Law of the Republic of Kazakhstan and subparagraph 1) of paragraph 1 of Article 255 of the CPC in compliance with the provisions of Article V(1)(a) of the New York Convention on Recognition and Enforcement of Foreign Arbitration Awards and Article 34(2)(a)(i) of the UNCITRAL Model Law.

III.2. Arbitration Award That Was Rendered In The Dispute Either Not Provided For By The Arbitration Agreement Or Not Falling Within Its Conditions, or It Does Not Contain Resolutions On The Issues Arising Out Of The Arbitration Agreement

Most often, such a ground for refusal to enforce an arbitration award is

---

[8]   See, for example, M. K. Suleimenov, A.Y. Duisenova. Strong and weak points of the Law *On Arbitration,* available at: http://online.zakon.kz/Document/?doc_id=34860793 (accessed on 23 July 2018).

[9]   Proposals of the Research Institute of Private Law at Caspian University and Kazakhstan International Arbitration for amendments and supplements to the Law *On Arbitration* of the Republic of Kazakhstan and Civil Procedure Law of the Republic of Kazakhstan, available at: http://online.zakon.kz/Document/?doc_id=33142960 (accessed on 23 July 2018).

[10]   Available at: http://www.adilet.gov.kz/ru/articles/o-vnesenii-izmeneniy-i-dopolneniy-v-nekotorye-zakonodatelnye-akty-respubliki-kazakhstan-po-2 (accessed on 23 July 2018).

applied when there is an arbitration clause in the ancillary agreement but the main contract does not have such a clause. For example, a guarantee or collateral agreement (as an ancillary contract) has an arbitration clause but a loan agreement (as the main contract) does not have such a clause.

The arbitration court shall not be able to consider the dispute arising from the accessory contract as it will have to go beyond the arbitration agreement when examining the main contract in order to determine the occurrence of the circumstances and/or the fact of default on the main contract.

Based on the provisions of the second paragraph of subparagraph 1), paragraph 1, Article 57 of the Law *On Arbitration*, a court may also refuse to recognize and enforce such an award.

III.3. Grounds Contradicting the New York Convention

According to paragraph 1 of Article 57 of the Law *On Arbitration* (subparagraph 1), paragraph 1, Article 255 of the CPC, the court refuses to recognize and (or) enforce an arbitration award regardless of the country in which it was rendered, on the following grounds, if:

1) The party against whom the award was made would present the evidence to the court that:

There is a valid court decision or arbitration award made on the dispute between the same parties, on the same subject matter, and on the same grounds, or the ruling of the court or arbitration to terminate the proceedings in connection with the refusal of the plaintiff from the claim;

An arbitration award was made possible as a result of a criminal offense established by a court verdict that entered into legal force.

Such extension of the grounds contradicts the provisions of the New York Convention as well as the UNCITRAL Model Law on International Commercial Arbitration.

In practice, such contradiction may result in certain problems, primarily for state courts. There are no such grounds for refusing to recognize and (or) enforce an arbitration award not only in international documents but also in the domestic laws of other countries.

In view of the direct reference provided for in Article 504 of the CPC, the issue of the writ of execution for the enforcement of an arbitration award rendered by foreign arbitration courts can be refused on the grounds specified in Article 255 of the CPC.

In such case, in our opinion, the provisions of the New York Convention should apply. Otherwise, Kazakhstan will become an unfavorable jurisdiction for the enforcement of foreign arbitration awards, which will adversely affect the investment attractiveness of the country as a whole.

III.4. Arbitration Panel or Arbitration Procedure Did Not Meet the Legal Requirements

The basis for refusing to issue a writ of execution laid down in the eighth paragraph of subparagraph 1) of Article 255 of the CPC (paragraph nine of subparagraph 1), paragraph 1, Article 57 of the Arbitration Law), is narrower in its content than a similar basis provided for in the New York Convention.

According to the aforementioned norms of the CPC and the Law *On Arbitration*, the issue of the writ of execution may be refused in case the party against which the arbitration award was made would submit evidence to the court that the arbitration panel or the arbitration procedure of the proceedings did not meet the requirements of the law. While subparagraph o), paragraph 1, Article 5 of the New York Convention formulates such ground more broadly mentioning not only noncompliance with the legal requirements but first of all the discrepancy between the agreement of the parties: "the composition of the arbitration body or the arbitration proceeding did not comply with the agreement of the parties or, in the absence thereof, did not comply with the law of the country where Arbitration took place".

How is the same basis formulated in the UNCITRAL Model Law? Subparagraph (iv) of paragraph 1) of Article 36 of the Model Law reads as follows: "the arbitration panel or the arbitration proceeding did not comply with the agreement of the parties or, in the absence of such, did not comply with the law of the country where arbitration took place".

Both international documents describe, first of all, noncompliance with the agreement of the parties which fully corresponds to the nature of arbitration as an alternative way to settle civil disputes based on an agreement of the parties. And only provided there is no agreement of the parties, the requirements for the arbitration panel or arbitration proceeding must be determined in accordance with the law of such country where the arbitration took place.

In connection with such a careless formulation made in the eighth paragraph of subparagraph 1) of Article 255 of the CPC and the ninth paragraph of subparagraph 1), paragraph 1, Article 57 of the Law *On Arbitration*, a logical question arises: what law requirements are not met? Is it noncompliance with the requirements of the law of the Republic of Kazakhstan or the law of the country where the arbitration took place? This issue is of great practical importance for the recognition and enforcement of foreign arbitration awards.

With regard to arbitration awards rendered by Kazakhstan's arbitration courts in the territory of the Republic of Kazakhstan, it should apparently mean noncompliance with the requirements of the law of the Republic of Kazakhstan.

What about foreign arbitration awards? What law should there be in this case?

Let's suppose that the award was made by the London International Arbitration Court and is subject to recognition and enforcement in the territory of the Republic of Kazakhstan.

The unfair party against which the arbitration award was made, after having used such an ambiguous version of the eighth paragraph of subparagraph 1) of Article 255 of the CPC, will present evidence to the court that the arbitration panel or the arbitration proceeding did not meet the requirements of the Law of the Republic of Kazakhstan.

And it will be easy for such party to find such inconsistencies, since the award was rendered in the UK, where, of course, Kazakhstani Arbitration Law does not apply.

In such case, the court must apply the provisions of subparagraph 1), paragraph1, Article 5 of the New York Convention. The court must initially verify the consistency of the arbitration panel or arbitration procedure with the agreement of the parties and then, if the parties did not come to an agreement, verify compliance with the law of the country where arbitration took place (that is, the 1996 Arbitration Law of England, not of the Republic of Kazakhstan).

However, according to paragraph 1 of Article 501 of the CPC, arbitration awards of foreign arbitration courts are recognized and enforced by the courts of the Republic of Kazakhstan if the recognition and enforcement of such enactments are provided for by the laws and/or an international treaty ratified by the Republic of Kazakhstan, or on the basis of reciprocity.

The Draft Law provides for bringing the eighth paragraph of subparagraph 1) of Article 255 of the CPC in accordance with the provisions of subparagraph o), paragraph 1, Article 5 of the New York Convention.

III.5. Contradiction to the Ordre Public

Reservation to the public order is widespread in private international law. It is contained in different variations in the law of nearly all countries that have a codification under international private law; it was also contained in the laws of the Soviet Union and the Kazakh SSR.

The Law *On Arbitration* (subparagraph 1) of Article 2) determines the public order of the Republic of Kazakhstan as the basis of law and order fixed in the enactments of the Republic of Kazakhstan.

According to paragraph 1, Article 1090 of the Civil Code, foreign law does not apply in cases where its application would contradict the basis of the legal order of the Republic of Kazakhstan (public order of the Republic of Kazakhstan). In such cases, the law of the Republic of Kazakhstan applies.

However, refusal to apply foreign law cannot be based only on the difference between the political or economic systems of the corresponding foreign state from the political or economic systems of the Republic of Kazakhstan (see clause 2, Article 1090 of the Civil Code). The concept of public order (ordre public, public policy) is rather vague; it is applied based on the court's discretion.

A reservation regarding public order is called a "safety valve", a "rubber paragraph", etc.

Clarification is important in paragraph 2 of Article 1090 of the Civil Code that a reservation regarding public order cannot be used only on the basis of differences in political or economic systems.

A reservation in a public procedure can apply when the application of a foreign law would contradict the basis of the legal order of the Republic of Kazakhstan, its legal principles, and would produce consequences unacceptable from the point of view of Kazakhstani sense of justice.

Lawyers of different countries have tried to develop a list of all principles and provisions that would disclose the concept of the "public order". However, these attempts have been unsuccessful. This is understandable, because variability and flexibility are inherent in this institution.

The view was expressed in the literature that the concept of "the basis of law and order (public order)" includes four interrelated components:

a) Fundamental principles of the law of the given country, primarily constitutional as well as private law and civil procedure principles;

b) Generally accepted moral law which serves the basis for the public order;

c) The legitimate interests of citizens and legal entities, society and the state protection of which is the main task of the country's legal system;

d) Generally recognized principles and provisions of international law that are part of the legal system of the country, including international legal standards of human rights.

One thing is clear. The non-application of a foreign law on the basis of a violation of the public order is possible only in "exceptional cases".

Therefore, every such case must be seriously justified and may not be reduced to any violation, even if serious, of the provisions of the national law.

When applying such basis for cancellation of the arbitration award as a contradiction to the public order, it is necessary to warn against a very common misconception when a public order is identified with public interests. Contradiction to public interests cannot serve as a basis for cancelling an award.

An award may be cancelled, and enforcement may only be refused for previously agreed procedural violations. Based on the above, in the vast majority of the countries, arbitration awards are never verified by the competent state courts on their merits and are final.

Almost nowhere in the world does the court verify the legislative grounds for considering the dispute, because interpretation of the law can be different. This is because of a civil law dispute, and there are always different views on the law in a civil law dispute. This is the basis for the court system of any country, including Kazakhstan.

However, arbitration is not a part of the court system. The competent court can only review the procedural aspects.

If these principles are not respected, then such an organization called arbitration is, in fact, not arbitration. It turns into an appendage of the court system and is absolutely needless.

The rather inconsistent practice of applying such a ground for the abolition of arbitration awards as a contradiction to the public order began forming in Kazakhstan after the Arbitration Law was enacted in 2016.

There are two main aspects to this problem:

1) The non-prevailing party is unconscionable as a rule; if it fails to find any grounds for cancellation of the arbitration award, it often quite unreasonably refers to a contradiction to the public order;

2) Some courts have started cancelling arbitration awards while referring to a contradiction to the public order, which is often identified with the rule of law and which in principle is incorrect.

The concept of public order around the world is possible only in "exceptional cases". The Supreme Court of the Republic of Kazakhstan advised the following to the courts in the Recommendations of the Round Table on Application of the Arbitration Law:

"It should be noted that the application of the institution of public order is possible in exceptional cases when the enforcement of an arbitration award offends the basis of the public order of the Republic of Kazakhstan. In connection with the above, the courts, when cancelling the awards on this ground, should explain which specific public order is violated and how."[11]

III.6. A Dispute in which an Arbitration Award is Rendered May Not Be Subject to an Arbitration Proceeding in Accordance with the Law

According to paragraph 8 of Article 8 of the Arbitration Law, the following disputes are not subject to arbitration: 1) on which the interests

---

[11] Recommendations of the Round Table entitled Some Issues of Application of Law *On Arbitration* of the Republic of Kazakhstan (Astana, 30 July 2017): Published on the website of the Supreme Court of the Republic of Kazakhstan http://sud.gov.kz/rus/content/rekomendacii-kruglogo-stola-nekotorye-voprosy-primeneniya-zakona-respubliki-kazakhstan (accessed on 23 July 2018).

of minors are affected, 2) of persons recognized as legally incompetent or incapacitated, 3) of rehabilitation and bankruptcy, 4) between subjects of natural monopolies and their consumers, 5) between state bodies, 6) between subjects of the quasi-public sector.

In addition, according to paragraph 4 of Article 8 of the Arbitration Law, an arbitration agreement in a dispute settlement under a contract, the conditions of which are determined by one of the parties in the forms or other standard forms and could be accepted by the other party only by joining the proposed contract as a whole (agreement of accession), shall be valid if such agreement is made after the occurrence of grounds for filing a claim. Thus, the disputes arising from the accession agreement may be recognized as non-arbitrative if the arbitration clause was included in it upon entering into the contract. For example, a dispute arising from an energy supply contract (which is a contract of accession under Kazakh law) can be considered by the arbitration court only if the arbitration agreement was executed after the occurrence of the grounds for filing a claim.

In practice, a number of discussion questions arise regarding the jurisdiction of arbitration for certain categories of disputes. Let's consider a brief analysis of some of them.

III.6.1. Is Arbitration Court Entitled to Settle the Disputes Arising from Marriage Contracts or Not?

According to paragraph 1 of Article 39 of the Marriage and Family Code (hereinafter referred to as the MFC),[12] the marriage contract recognizes the agreement of persons entering into marriage or the spouses' agreement defining the property rights and duties of the spouses in marriage and (or) in the event of its dissolution.

All contracts based on equality, mediating property and related non-property relations, are civil law contracts. A marriage contract is also one of the above contracts.

If by virtue of direct legislative restriction of the competence of arbitration courts, they are not entitled to consider cases involving personal non-property relations and are not related to property relations, then the arbitration courts shall be entitled to resolve disputes arising from a marriage contract that is a civil contract governing property relations between spouses, subject to an arbitration agreement.

According to paragraph 2, Article 39 of the MFC, the marriage contract may provide for the property rights of children born or adopted in

---

[12] Code On Marriage and Family # 518-IV of December 26, 2011 of the Republic of Kazakhstan // Kazakhstanskaya Pravda newspaper # 6-7 of January 7, 2012 (26825-26826); Reports # 22 (2599), p. 174 of the Parliament of the Republic of Kazakhstan, December, 2011.

marriage. Therefore, if the interests of minors are affected in a dispute arising from marriage contract (for example, the property rights of children), then such disputes will not be subject to arbitration by virtue of sub-clause 1), paragraph 8 of Article 8 of the Arbitration Law.

III.6.2. Are Corporate Disputes Arbitrable or Not?

To answer the question of whether corporate disputes can be the subject of arbitration proceedings, two issues need to be resolved:

1) To determine the nature of corporate relations and their relationship to civil law relations,
2) To answer the question about the availability or lack of special jurisdiction of corporate disputes to state courts (paragraph 1, Article 27 of the CPC).

The corporate legal relations can be defined as intra-organizational (part of them) civil law relations related to participation in or management of corporate organizations, between:

1) Founders (participants) of a corporate organization, and
2) Between the corporate organization and its founders (participants).

The corporate relations are not obligations but are rather relative relations (property, non-property, organizational). Since corporate relations are civil and legal relations, then disputes arising from corporate relations can be subject to arbitration.

With regard to paragraph 1 of Article 27 of the Code of Civil Procedure, this clause containing the definition of corporate disputes, assigns jurisdiction of this category of civil cases to specialized inter-district economic courts (being members of the court system of the Republic of Kazakhstan).

Since arbitrations are not part of the system of state courts of the Republic of Kazakhstan, then the provisions of paragraph 27 of the CPC do not cover arbitration, and, accordingly, it is impossible to claim that corporate disputes cannot be arbitrable.

However, when considering certain categories of corporate disputes, the rights and interests of third parties may be affected. For example, this would include a corporate dispute related to the ownership of shares of a joint-stock company and exercise of the right to vote arising from it. A shareholder and the joint-stock company may enter into an arbitration agreement on submission of such dispute to arbitration. However, the question of whether a shareholder has the right to vote at a general meeting, or does not have such a right, directly affects the rights of other shareholders, since it changes the proportions of votes in a vote at general meeting. All other shareholders are interested in the consequences of resolving that dispute. However, if an agreement is executed without their participation, then they are deprived of the right to participate in arbitration.[13] In such case, the dispute obviously cannot be considered by an arbitration court.

Upon entering into an arbitration agreement as well as upon direct consideration of corporate disputes by arbitration courts, it is possible to advise the parties and arbitration institutes to be especially careful in regards to the issues of third parties.

[*Maidan Kuntuarovich Suleimenov*]
is the Director of the Research Institute of Private
Law of Caspian University, Chairman of Kazakhstani
International Arbitration, Academician of the National
Academy of Sciences of the Republic of Kazakhstan, Doctor
of Law, Professor.
E-mail: maidansuleimenov@gmail.com

[*Assel Duisenova*]
is a Leading Research Fellow of the Research Institute
of Private Law, Associate Professor of Adilet Higher
Law School of Caspian University, CEO of Kazakhstani
International Arbitration, Member of the Board of
Arbitration Chamber of Kazakhstan, Ph.D..
E-mail: aseld@mail.ru

Czech (& Central European) Yearbook of Arbitration®

---

[13]   Oleg Y. Skvortsov, Arbitration proceeding of business disputes in Russia: Problems, trends, prospects, Moscow: Wolters Kluwer, 408-409 (2005).

Bibliography, Current Events, CYIL & CYArb® Presentations, Important Web Sites

I.   Selected Bibliography for 2018

Opening Remarks:

This overview lists only works published in 2018. The individual chapters into which this overview is divided always cover both substantive and procedural issues.

Titles in translations are indicative.

I.1.   [CZE] – [CZECH REPUBLIC] – Titles published within the Czech Republic

I.1.1.   Monographs

ZDENĚK NOVÝ; KLÁRA DRLIČKOVÁ, ROLE VEŘEJNÉHO ZÁJMU V MEZINÁRODNÍ OBCHODNÍ A INVESTIČNÍ ARBITRÁŽI [Title in translation – ROLE OF PUBLIC INTEREST IN INTERNATIONAL COMMERCIAL AND INVESTMENT ARBITRATION], Prague: C. H. Beck (2018).[1]

LUKÁŠ RYŠAVÝ, NEZÁVISLOST A NESTRANNOST ROZHODCE [Title in translation – ARBITRATOR'S INDEPENDENCE AND IMPARTIALITY], Praha [Prague]: C. H. Beck (2018).

I.1.2.   Periodicals, Collections and Conference Proceedings

Bulletin advokacie [*Bulletin of the Czech Bar*], Prague: Česká advokátní komora] *Czech Bar Association*], 2018, ISSN: 1210-6348, Reg.No Ministry of Cultural Affairs Czech Republic E 6469[2]

Alexander J. Bělohlávek, *Notifikační povinnost rozhodců o svých vazbách na strany řízení ve světle mezinárodních standardů* [Title in translation – *Notification Duty of Arbitrators Regarding Their Connections to the Parties in the Light of International Standards*], No. 09, p. 36-39.

Martin Doleček, *Pravomoc soudů ve vztahu k rozhodčímu řízení* [Title in translation – *Court Jurisdiction in Relation to Arbitration*], No. 09, p. 40-42.

---

[1]   Published in Czech.
[2]   Papers published in Czech with abstracts in English and in German.

Pavel Horák, *Objektivní arbitrabilita – možnosti rozhodčího řízení* [Title in translation – *Objective Arbitrability – Courses of Action in Arbitration*], No. 09, p. 25-28.

Milan Kindl, *Na co nezapomínat při sjednávání rozhodčí smlouvy* [Title in translation – *Checklist for Negotiating an Arbitration Agreement*], No. 09, p. 29-32.

Martin Maisner, *Efektivita rozhodčího řízení* [Title in translation – *Effectiveness of Arbitration*], No. 09, p. 46-50.

Robert Němec; Viktor Glatz, *Rozhodčí řízení, jeho specifika a výhody* [Title in translation – *Arbitration, its Specifics and Advantages*], No. 09, p. 18-24.

David Řezníček, *Vykonatelnost a výkon rozhodčích nálezů* [Title in translation – *Enforceability and Enforcement of Arbitral Awards*], No. 09, p. 43-45.

Tomáš Sokol, *Konstituování rozhodčího fóra* [Title in translation – *Constitution of the Arbitration Forum*], No. 09, p. 32-35.

Obchodněprávní revue [Commercial Law Review], Prague: C.H.Beck, 2018, Vol. X, ISSN: 1211-0558[3]

Alexander J. Bělohlávek, *Rozhodčí řízení versus insolvenční řízení z pohledu práva EU – část 1* [Title in translation – *Arbitration versus Insolvency Proceedings from the Perspective of EU Law – Part 1*], Issue No. 6, p. 161-177.

Alexander J. Bělohlávek, *Rozhodčí řízení versus insolvenční řízení z pohledu práva EU – část 2* [Title in translation – *Arbitration versus Insolvency Proceedings from the Perspective of EU Law – Part 2*], Issue No. 7-8, p. 193-209.

The Lawyer Quarterly, Prague: Ústav státu a práva Akademie věd České republiky [Institute of State and Law of the Academy of Sciences of the Czech Republic], 2018, Vol. VIII, ISSN: 0231-6625[4]

Alexander J. Bělohlávek, *Anti-suit injunctions in arbitral and judicial procedures in the Czech Republic*, No. 4, p. 322-331.

---

[3] Papers published in Czech. Summary in German.

[4] A subsidiary title to the monthly periodical Právník [in translation – *The Lawyer*] which will be published by the Institute of State and Law of the Academy of Science of the Czech Republic in Czech. Papers published in *The Lawyer Quarterly* are primarily in English, exceptionally in other languages (such as German); abstracts are in English. For papers published in the periodical "*Právník*" [in translation – *The Lawyer*], issued monthly, see the separate excerpt from papers listed under the heading of the respective periodical.

Other publications

Alexander J. Bělohlávek, *Rozhodčí řízení v mezinárodním obchodním styku podle zákona č. 98/1963 Sb.* [Title in translation - *Arbitration in International Commercial Transactions pursuant to Act No. 98/1963 Coll.*], XI ENCYKLOPEDIE ČESKÝCH PRÁVNÍCH DĚJIN [ENCYCLOPEDIA OF CZECH LEGAL HISTORY / ENZYKLOPÄDIE DER TSCHECHISCHEN RECHTSGESCHICHTE], ŘÍZENÍ [PROCEEDINGS], PLZEŇ [PILSEN / CZECH REPUBLIC] / OSTRAVA [CZECH REPUBLIC]: ALEŠ ČENĚK / KEY PUBLISHING, ISBN: 978-80-7380-715-3 / ISBN: 978-80-7418-282-2, p. 615-620 (Karel Schelle; Jaromír Tauchen eds., 2018).[5]

Alexander J. Bělohlávek, *Interaction between international arbitration and cross-border insolvency – challenges faced by the arbitrators: Effects of Art 18 of the Regulation of the European Parliament and of the Council (EU) No. 2015/848* [Title in translation - *Interakce mezi mezinárodním rozhodčím řízením a přeshraniční insolvencí – výzvy rozhodcům: účinky čl. 18 nařízení Evropského parlamentu a Rady (EU) č. 2015/848*], RECENT DEVELOPMENTS IN PRIVATE INTERNATIONAL LAW CHIȘINĂU [CHISINAU – REPUBLIC MOLDOVA]: FACULTY OF LAW – MOLDOVA STATE UNIVERSITY [UNIV. DE STAT DIN MOLDOVA], ISBN: 978-9975-108-22-5 (print), p. 234-269 (Mihail Buruiană ed., 2018).[6]

I.2.   [POL] – [POLAND][7]

Monographs (incl. chapters in monographs) and Collections, Proceedings

GRZEGORZ SULIŃSKI, OSOBA TRZECIA W ARBITRAŻU HANDLOWYM [Title in translation - THIRD PARTY IN COMMERCIAL ARBITRATION], Warszawa: C.H. Beck S.A., ISSN 1897-4392 (2018).

ADR Arbitraż i Mediacja [*ADR Arbitration And Mediation*], Warszawa: C. H. Beck, 2018, ISSN: 1898-942X[8]

---

5   Published in Czech.
6   Published in English.
7   Polish bibliography concerning arbitration and ADR for 2018 compiled with the kind support of Kubas Kos Gałkowski - Adwokaci, Law firm (www.kkg.pl). Kubas Kos Gałkowski specialize (among others) in arbitration and ADR, in particular under the support of Agnieszka Pazdan, Agata Wojtczak and Kamil Zawicki.
8   Quarterly. Papers published in Polish and English.

Czech (& Central European) Yearbook of Arbitration®

Maciej Buczek, *Brexit a arbitraż w Wielkiej Brytanii* [Title in translation - *Brexit versus arbitration in the United Kingdom*].

Łukasz Chyla, *Legal effects of prejudicial awards in arbitral proceedings.*[9]

Joanna Mucha, *Ugodowe rozwiązywanie spraw rozpoznawanych w postępowaniach działowych – wybrane aspekty procesowe* [Title in translation - *Settlement of cases identified in departmental proceedings - selected procedural aspects*].

Krystian Mularczyk; Adam Majewski, *Sądownictwo polubowne i pozasądowe rozwiązywanie sporów konsumenckich w sektorze telekomunikacyjnym* [Title in translation - *Arbitration and extra-judicial resolution of consumer disputes in the telecommunications sector*].

Andrzej Olaś, *Dopuszczalność zrzeczenia się prawa do wniesienia skargi o uchylenie wyroku sądu polubownego w* świetle *art. 6 EKPCz – glosa do orzeczenia ETPCz z 1.3.2016 r. w sprawie Tabbane przeciwko Szwajcarii* [Title in translation - *Admissibility of waiving the right to bring a motion to set aside a judgment of an arbitration court under Article 6 ECHR - glossary to the ECtHR judgment of 1.3.2016 in Tabbane against Switzerland*].

Marcin Śledzikowski, *Związanie członka zarządu spółki z o.o. zapisem na sąd polubowny w procesie o naprawienie szkody na podstawie art. 293 KSH* [Title in translation - *Associating a member of the company's management board with an arbitration clause in an action for damages pursuant to Art. 293 of the Polish Companies Act*].

---

[9]   Paper published in English.

Mateusz Wiktor, *Wynagrodzenie mediatora w postępowaniu cywilnym* [Title in translation - *Remuneration of a mediator in civil proceedings*].

Łukasz Wydra, *Zasady słuszności jako zasady postępowania przed sądem polubownym* [Title in translation - *The principles of equity as the principles of arbitration proceedings*].

Karol Zawiślak, *Dopuszczalność stosowania instytucji kadłubowych zespołów orzekających – uwagi na tle polskiego prawa arbitrażowego* [Title in translation - *Admissibility of the use of hull institutions of adjudicating panels - comments against the background of the Polish arbitration law*].

Maciej Jarota, *Arbitraż społeczny – fakultatywna czy obligatoryjna metoda rozwiązywania sporów zbiorowych? Przyczynek do dyskusji o wykorzystaniu postępowania arbitrażowego w zbiorowych stosunkach pracy* [Title in translation - *Social arbitration - an optional or obligatory method of resolving industrial disputes? Contribution to the discussion on the use of arbitration in collective labour relations*].

<u>Glosa [Gloss], Warszawa: Wolters Kluwer Polska sp. z o.o., 2018, ISSN: 1233-4634.</u>

Witold Jurcewicz, *Potrącenie wierzytelności podlegającej właściwości sądu państwowego w postępowaniu arbitrażowym. Glosa do postanowienia Sądu Apelacyjnego w Krakowie z 22.11.2016 r. (I ACz 1997/16)* [Title in translation - *Deduction of a claim subject to the jurisdiction of a state court in arbitration proceedings. Gloss to the decision of the Court of Appeal in Kraków of 22 October 2016 (I ACz 1997/16)*].

<u>Iustitia [Iustitia], Warszawa: C.H. Beck S.A., 2018, ISSN: 1640-8365.</u>

Wiesława Kuberska; Alicja Wieczorek, *Skarga o uchylenie wyroku sądu polubownego w praktyce sądowej* [Title in translation - *Motion to set aside a judgment of an arbitration court in judicial practice*].

Polski Proces Cywilny [*Polish Civil Procedure*], Warszawa: Wolters Kluwer S.A., 2018, ISSN: 2082-1743.[10]

Joanna Derlatka, *Zasady mediacji w postępowaniu cywilnym – uwagi prakseologiczne i prawnoporównawcze* [Title in translation - *Principles of Mediation in Civil Proceedings - Praxeological and Comparative Legal Comments*].

Przegląd Prawa Handlowego [*Commercial Law Review*], Warszawa: Wolters Kluwer Polska Sp. z o. o., 2018, ISSN: 1230-2996[11]

Karol Wach, *Konstrukcja arbitrażu przymusowego* [Title in translation - *Structure of Mandatory Arbitration*].

Czech (& Central European) Yearbook of Arbitration®

---

[10] Quarterly. Papers publish in Polish, summaries in English.
[11] Monthly. Papers published in Polish, summaries in English.

II.   Current Events

Selected scientific conferences, seminars, academic lectures and other professional events and news in the development of arbitration and ADR in the particular countries[1]

II.1.   [CZE] – [CZECH REPUBLIC]

[CZE] PRAGUE, 26 February 2018
Prague Arbitration Day

[CZE] PRAGUE, 26 April 2018
Joint conference of the Judicial Academy of the Czech Republic and the Arbitration Court attached to the Economic Chamber of the Czech Republic and Agricultural Chamber of the Czech Republic on practical issues in arbitration. Speeches were presented by experienced judges of the Constitutional Court of the Czech Republic, Supreme Court of the Czech Republic, High Court in Prague, Municipal Court in Prague, Regional Court in Prague, District Court of Prague 1 and discussions were moderated by arbitrators.

[CZE] PRAGUE, 23 – 25 October 2018
8th Investment Treaty Arbitration Conference organised by the Minister of Finance of the Czech Republic aimed at sharing experience with treaty arbitration between senior government officials and top legal practitioners in the field. The event is organised under the auspices of the Ministry of Finance of the Czech Republic and hosted by the advisory firm KPMG Czech Republic.

The Prague BIT Conference, which took place on 25 October 2018, has started with a keynote speech by **George Kahale III**, Chairman, Curtis, Mallet-Prevost, Colt & Mosle, on **ISDS: Where to Go from Here.** The keynote address will be followed by four panel discussions on the following topics:

Set-aside Proceedings and/or Annulment Proceedings (chaired by Partner Paolo Di Rosa, Arnold & Porter Kaye Scholer)

---

[1]   Contributions mentioned herein represent a selection from papers related to arbitration. CYArb® editors hereby apologize to the lecturers for omitting some of them and their topics due to the limited space provided for this section. Editors referred especially to published and other accessible information. Readers are specifically warned that the information about papers presented at the individual conferences and other academic and scientific events is only a selection and definitely does not provide a full report on the entire proceedings and the academic scope of each particular event.

Recalcitrant Parties: Balancing Legitimacy and Due Process (chaired by Partner George von Mehren, Squire Patton Boggs)

Defining the Investment Protections with Precision (chaired by Partner Eduardo Silva Romero, Dechert)

Transparency in Investment Arbitration: Latest Developments? (chaired by Partner Dietmar W. Prager, Debevoise & Plimpton)

[CZE] PRAGUE, 14 December 2018
First Launch of Prague Rules
Session I - The History and the Spirit of the Prague Rules. Speakers: Alexander J. Bělohlávek and Vladimir Khvalei
Session II – Showing a sphinx face. Limits of the tribunal's role in the managing of arbitration proceedings. Speakers: Duarte Henriques, Hilary Heilbron QC, Beata Gessel-Kalinowska vel Kalisz, Klaus Peter Berger. Topics: Role of the Tribunal in Administering Arbitration Proceedings: the difference between Prague Rules and IBA Rules; Limits of Tribunal's role in managing arbitration; Is there a duty of tribunal to establish facts; The Proactive Facilitation of Settlement by International Arbitrators.
Session III – Let's not decide anything until we decide everything? In-house expectations on the outcome of arbitration and tribunal's role in the facilitation of settlement. Speakers: Michael McIlwrath, Dr. Clemens-August Heusch, Susanne Gropp-Stadler.
Session IV – Is the sky the only limit? Scope of discovery and e-discovery in arbitration. Speakers: Andrey Panov (moderator), Michael W. Bühler, Dorothy Murray. Topics: Discovery in Arbitration: Use and Abuse, Tribunal's Role in Document Disclosure, Civil Law vs. Common Law Approach.
Session V – Lie to me. Fact witnesses vs. documentary evidence: can documents lie? Speakers: José Rosell, Olena Perepelinska. Topics: Role of Witness Statements In Evidentiary Process, Tribunal's Role In Managing Witnesses, Weight of Witness Statements In Tribunal's Eyes, Can Witness Lie?

II.2.   [AUT] – [AUSTRIA]

[AUT] VIENNA, 24 - 25 January 2017
Vienna Arbitration Days 2017 as the leading arbitration conference in Austria.

[AUT] VIENNA, 7 June 2018
The University of Vienna and the Austrian Arbitration Association
(Arb|Aut) organised the "**Construction Disputes Before Arbitral
Tribunals and the State Courts**" forum. The panel discussion has
been animated by **Dr. Erhard Böhm** (Baier partners) and **Dr. Philipp
Duncker** (Hogan Lovells).

[AUT] VIENNA, 21 September 2018
This year's **Dreiländerkonferenz** was hosted in Vienna. After a get-
together at Gustl Kocht on 20 September 2018, the conference took
place at the Park Hyatt Vienna on 21 September 2018. Following the
tradition, the individual topics were discussed from the perspectives of
Austrian, Liechtenstein and Swiss arbitration law.

[AUT] VIENNA, 19 October 2018
After a hugely successful event in 2017, the 2nd annual GAR Live
Vienna took place on 19 October 2018. The event was co-chaired
by Stefan Riegler (Arb|Aut), Alice Fremuth-Wolf (VIAC) and Eliane
Fischer (YAAP) with a lunch-time keynote held by Jörg Risse on
"Poetic Prophecy: The Future of Arbitration". The programme
consisted of the following 4 sessions: **Session 1** dealt with Settlement
in Arbitration, **Session 2** was Question time on third party funding;
and M&A disputes, **Session 3** dealt with the future of investment
arbitration, **Session 4** was the famous GAR Live debate on the
following motto: "This house believes, in all but exceptional cases,
document production is a complete waste of time". Following the event,
a Lifetime award was presented to Prof Eric Bergsten with a laudatio
held by Daniel Girsberger and Stavros Brekoulakis.

II.3.   [BLR] – [BELARUS]

[BLR] MINSK, 20 - 21 September 2018
Eastern European Dispute Resolution Forum (EEDRF) organised by
leading law firms specialising in dispute resolution, Russian Arbitration
Association, UAA and International Law and Arbitration Association
(BILA).

II.4. [POL] – [POLAND] [2]

[POL] WARSAW, February – June 2018

Lewiatan Arbitration Moot 2018 organised by the Lewiatan Court of Arbitration at the Polish Confederation Lewiatan.

[POL] WARSAW, 14 – 16 February 2018

10th Warsaw Pre-moot for the Willem C. Vis International Commercial Arbitration Moot, organised by the Centre of Dispute and Conflict Resolution at the Faculty of Law and Administration of the University of Warsaw. The event included a conference entitled: "Should I Stay or Should I Go? Challenge of an Arbitrator".

[POL] WARSAW, 6 March 2018

Spring Meeting of the Young Arbitration Forum organised by the Young Arbitration Forum and the Court of Arbitration at the Polish Chamber of Commerce in cooperation with Linklaters. The topic of the meeting was "The Secretary's role in the international arbitration – practical aspects and everything you were afraid of asking".

[POL] WARSAW, 23 – 25 May 2018

Warsaw Arbitration & Mediation Days (WAMD) organised by the most important arbitration institutions in Poland: Polish National Committee of the ICC, Arbitration Court at the Polish Chamber of Commerce in Warsaw, Lewiatan Court of Arbitration, Polish Association of Engineers and Appraisers, University of Warsaw and SWPS University of Social Science and Humanities. The partners of the event were AIJA and ICC Paris.

The three-day conference offered presentations and lectures given by over 50 lawyers, experts, academics and practitioners from Poland, Germany, France, Great Britain, Czech Republic, Hungary, Georgia, Ukraine, Greece, Romania and even Brazil. There were over 20 panels devoted to key issues related to commercial and investment arbitration, mediation, financial aspects of alternative dispute resolution, as well as the role of psychology in this process.

---

[2] Compiled with kind support of Kubas Kos Gałkowski - Adwokaci, Law firm (www.kkg.pl). Kubas Kos Gałkowski are specialized (among others) in arbitration and ADR. Edited by Magdalena Matejczyk, associate, KKG Kubas Kos Gałkowski – Adwokaci.

Agnieszka Pazdan, Agata Wojtczak and Kamil Zawicki.

[POL] KRAKÓW, 7 June 2018

The 5th Allerhand Dispute Resolution, Mediation and Arbitration Summit organised by Krakow Bar Association and the Allerhand Institute. The purpose of the conference was to present the following topics: (1.) Arbitration in CEE, (2.) New issues of the ADR in CEE, (3.) Development of mediation in CEE.

[POL] NOWY TOMYŚL, 8 June 2018

Conference **Arbitration and Mediation in Theory and Practice.** This annual event has become one of the most important arbitration conferences in Poland and the CEE region, attended by arbitration and ADR academics as well as practitioners. The speakers of the 2018 Conference were Włodzimierz Brych, Andrzej Szumański, Flaga-Gieruszyńska, Magdalena Wasylkowska-Michór, Magdalena Skibińska, Grzegorz Lorych, Aurelia Puchała, Tomasz Antoszek, Stanisław Kaczmarek, Krystian Mularczyk, Aleksandra Włosińska, Włodzimierz Głodkowski, Jerzy Śliwa (all from Poland), Ergun Özsunay (Turkey), Joanna Kraus-Kolber (Belgium), Nikoloz Pitskhelauri (Georgia), Tatyana Gennadyevna Zakharchenko and Svitlana Maksymova (both from Ukraine), Piotr Nowaczyk (Poland), **Alexander Korsak** and Alexander Khrapoutski (**both from Belarus**), Patryk Kulig (Germany), Niyazi Mammadov (Azerbaijan).

[POL] WARSAW, 13 June 2018

Seminar **"Młody Arbitraż Mówi..." – „Young Arbitration Is Talking".** This seminar organised by the Court of Arbitration attached to the Polish Chamber of Commerce focused on organisational issues in arbitration.

[POL]WARSAW, 28 September 2018

Conference **"Arbitration – Standards, Tendencies and Perspectives".** Seminar organised by the Court of Arbitration attached to the Polish Chamber of Commerce together with, inter alia, the Faculty of Law and Public Administration of the Warsaw University.

Czech (& Central European) Yearbook of Arbitration ®

III.   Past CYIL and CYArb® Presentations in 2018

[CZE] PRAGUE, 14 December 2018

*First Launch of **Prague Rules**,* Prague [Czech Republic].
Session I - The History and the Spirit of the Prague Rules. Speakers:
Alexander J. Bělohlávek and Vladimir Khvalei
**Session II – Showing a sphinx face. Limits of the tribunal's role
in the managing of arbitration proceedings.** Speakers: Duarte
Henriques, Hilary Heilbron QC, Beata Gessel-Kalinowska vel Kalisz,
Klaus Peter Berger. Topics: Role of the Tribunal in Administering
Arbitration Proceedings: the difference between Prague Rules and IBA
Rules; Limits of Tribunal's role in managing arbitration; Is there a duty
of tribunal to establish facts; The Proactive Facilitation of Settlement by
International Arbitrators.
**Session III – Let's not decide anything until we decide everything?
In-house expectations on the outcome of arbitration and tribunal's
role in facilitation of settlement.** Speakers: Michael McIlwrath, Dr.
Clemens-August Heusch, Susanne Gropp-Stadler.
**Session IV – Is the sky the only limit? Scope of discovery and
e-discovery in arbitration.** Speakers: Andrey Panov (moderator),
Michael W. Bühler, Dorothy Murray. Topics: Discovery in Arbitration:
Use and Abuse, Tribunal's Role in Document Disclosure, Civil Law vs.
Common Law Approach.
**Session V – Lie to me. Fact witnesses vs. documentary evidence:
can documents lie?** Speakers: José Rosell, Olena Perepelinska. Topics:
Role of Witness Statements In Evidentiary Process, Tribunal's Role In
Managing Witnesses, Weight of Witness Statements In Tribunal's Eyes,
Can Witness Lie?

IV. Important Web Sites

http://www.czechyearbook.org; http://www.lexlata.pro

Czech Yearbook of International Law® and **Czech (& Central European) Yearbook of Arbitration®**
The website is currently available in sixteen languages: English, Bulgarian, Czech, Chinese, Japanese, Korean, Hungarian, German, Polish, Romanian, Russian, Portuguese, Slovenian, Spanish, Ukrainian, Vietnamese. This website allows access to the annotations of all core articles and to information about the authors of these articles as well as to the entire remaining contents (except core articles) of both yearbooks (CYIL and CYArb®).

IV.1. [CZE] – [CZECH REPUBLIC]

- http://www.cnb.cz. Česká národná banka (Czech National Bank as the Central bank of the Czech Republic).[1]
- http://www.compet.cz. Office for the protection of competition.[2]
- http://www.concourt.cz. The Constitutional Court of the Czech Republic.[3]
- http://www.csesp.cz. Czech Society for European and Comparative Law.[4]
- http://www.csmp-csil.org. The Czech Society Of International Law.[5]
- http://www.czech.cz. Portal „Hello Czech Republic". Basic information about the Czech Republic and news interesting for foreigners. Rather a promotional portal.[6]
- http://www.czso.cz. Czech Statistical Office.[7]
- http://dtjvcnsp.org. Česko-německý spolek právníků. [Czech-German Lawyers Association]. Deutsch-Tschechische Juristenvereinigung e.V.[8]
- http://ekf.vsb.cz. Faculty of Economics, VŠB Technical University

---

[1] Website available in English and Czech.
[2] Website available in English and Czech. Basic laws and regulations on the protection of competition in the Czech Republic are also available at the website, both in Czech and in English (unofficial translation).
[3] Website available in English and Czech. Part of the (significant) case law also available in English.
[4] Website available in English and Czech.
[5] Website available in Czech. In English only a brief summary of the webpages.
[6] Website available in English, Czech, French, German, Russian and Spanish.
[7] Website available in English and Czech.
[8] Website available in German.

of Ostrava.[9]

- http://ftp.pse.cz/Info.bas/Cz/Predpisy/brs_statut2.pdf. Statute of Burzovní rozhodčí soud při Burze cenných papírů Praha, a.s. [Exchange Court of Arbitration at the Prague Stock Exchange][10]

- http://www.hrad.cz.[11] Website of the Office of the President of the Czech Republic.

- http://www.icc-cr.cz. ICC National Committee Czech Republic.

- http://www.iir.cz. Institute Of International Relations Prague.[12]

- http://www.ilaw.cas.cz. Ústav státu a práva Akademie věd ČR, v.v.i. [Institute of State and Law of the Academy of Sciences of the Czech Republic][13]

- http://www.jednotaceskychpravniku.cz. Jednota českých právníků [Czech Lawyers Union]

- http://justice.cz. Czech justice portal including both courts and the Ministry of Justice, prosecution departments, Judicial Academy, Institute of Criminology and Social Prevention, as well as the Probation and Mediation Service and the Prison Service. [14]

- http://www.law.muni.cz. Faculty of Law, Masaryk University, Brno.[15]

- http://www.mzv.cz. Ministry of Foreign Affairs of the Czech Republic.[16]

- http://www.nsoud.cz. The Supreme Court of the Czech Republic.[17]

- http://www.nssoud.cz. The Supreme Administrative Court of the Czech Republic.[18]

- http://www.ochrance.cz. Public Defender of Rights (Ombudsman).[19]

- http://www.ok.cz/iksp/en/aboutus.html. Institute of Criminology and Social Prevention.[20]

- http://portal.gov.cz. Portal of the Public Administration.[21] This

---

[9] Website available in English and Czech. Some information (regarding post-graduate studies) also available in German. Department of Law see http://en.ekf.vsb.cz/information-about/departments/structure/departments/dept-119 (in English).

[10] The Statute is available in Czech. One of the three permanent arbitration courts established in the Czech Republic by law (statute), in compliance with Section 13 of Act No. 216/1994 Coll., on Arbitration and Enforcement of Arbitral Awards, as subsequently amended.

[11] Website available in English and Czech. This website also allows access to the personal webpage of the President of the Czech Republic.

[12] Website available in English and Czech. This Institute was founded by the Ministry of Foreign Affairs of the Czech Republic.

[13] Website available in English and Czech.

[14] Website available in Czech. The individual websites of the institutions covered by this portal also contain pages or summary information in English.

[15] Website available in English and Czech.

[16] Website available in Czech. Important information from this portal also available in English.

[17] Website available in Czech. Some basic information also in English and French.

[18] Website available in English and Czech.

[19] Website available in English and Czech.

[20] Website available in English and Czech.

[21] Website available in English and Czech.

website allows access to the websites of most supreme public administration authorities (including ministries).

- http://www.prf.cuni.cz. Faculty of Law, Charles University in Prague.[22]
- http://www.psp.cz. Parliament of the Czech Republic. Chamber of Deputies.[23]
- http://www.rozhodcisoud.cz. International Arbitration Court of the Czech Commodity Exchange.[24]
- http://www.senat.cz. Parliament of the Czech Republic. Senate.[25]
- http://www.society.cz/wordpress/#awp. Common Law Society.[26]
- http://www.soud.cz. Arbitration Court attached to the Economic Chamber of the Czech Republic and Agricultural Chamber of the Czech Republic.[27]
- http://www.umpod.cz. Office for International Legal Protection of Children.[28]
- http://www.upol.cz/fakulty/pf/. Faculty of Law. Palacký University, Olomouc.
- http://www.vse.cz. The University of Economics, Prague.[29]
- http://www.zcu.cz/fpr/. Faculty of Law, Western Bohemia University in Pilsen.[30]

IV.2. [SVK] – [SLOVAK REPUBLIC]

- http://www.concourt.sk. Constitutional Court of the Slovak Republic.[31]
- http://www.flaw.uniba.sk. Faculty of Law, Comenius University in Bratislava (SVK).[32]
- http://iuridica.truni.sk. Faculty of Law. Trnava University in Trnava

---

[22] Website available in Czech. Basic information available in English.
[23] Website available in English and Czech.
[24] Website available in English and Czech. Website of one of the three permanent arbitration courts established in the Czech Republic by law (statute), in compliance with Section 13 of Act No. 216/1994 Coll., on Arbitration and Enforcement of Arbitral Awards, as subsequently amended. This arbitration court was established by Act No. 229/1992 Coll., on Commodity Exchanges, as subsequently amended.
[25] Website available in English and Czech.
[26] Website available in Czech.
[27] Website available in English, Czech, German and Russian. Website of one of the three permanent arbitration courts established in the Czech Republic by law (statute), in compliance with Section 13 of Act No. 216/1994 Coll., on Arbitration and Enforcement of Arbitral Awards, as subsequently amended. This arbitration court was established by Section 19 of Act No. 301/1992 Coll., on the Economic Chamber of the Czech Republic and the Agricultural Chamber of the Czech Republic, as subsequently amended.
[28] The Office is the Central authority responsible for protection of children in civil matters having cross-border implications. Website available in English and Czech.
[29] Website available in English and Czech.
[30] Website available in Czech.
[31] Website available in English and Slovak.
[32] Website available in English and Slovak.

(SVK).³³

- http://www.justice.gov.sk. Ministry of Justice of the Slovak Republic.³⁴
- http://www.nbs.sk. Národná banka Slovenska (National Bank of Slovakia as the Central bank of Slovak Republic).³⁵
- http://www.nrsr.sk. National Council of the Slovak Republic (*Slovak Parliament*).³⁶
- http://www.prf.umb.sk. Faculty of Law. Matej Bel University, Banská Bystrica (SVK).
- http://www.prezident.sk. President of the Slovak Republic and Office of the President (SVK).³⁷
- http://www.test.sopk.sk. The Court of Arbitration of the Slovak Chamber of Commerce and Industry in Bratislava.³⁸
- http://www.uninova.sk/pf_bvsp/src_angl/index.php. Faculty of Law, Pan European University (SVK).³⁹
- http://www.upjs.sk/pravnicka-fakulta. Faculty of Law, Pavol Jozef Šafárik University in Košice (SVK).⁴⁰
- http://www.usap.sav.sk. Institute of State and Law, Slovak Academy of Science.⁴¹

IV.3.   [AUT] – [AUSTRIA]

- http://www.arbitration-austria.at. Österreichische Vereinigung für Schiedsgerichtsbarkeit. Austrian Arbitration Association (ArbAut).⁴²
- http://www.internationales-schiedsgericht.at/ and http://viac. eu Wiener Internationalen Schiedsgerichts (VIAC). Vienna International Arbitral Centre (VIAC).⁴³

IV.4.   [BLR] – [BELARUS]

- http://www.cci.by/ArbitrCourt/AboutCourt_en.aspx. International Arbitration Court attached to the Belarusian

---

³³ Website available in English and Slovak.
³⁴ Website available in English and Slovak. This website also allows access to the following portals: Courts, Slovak Agent before the European Court for Human Rights, Slovak Agent before the Court of Justice of the European Union, The Judicial Academy.
³⁵ Website available in English and Slovak.
³⁶ Website available in English, French, German and Slovak.
³⁷ Website available in English and Slovak.
³⁸ Website available in Slovak. Some basic information available in English.
³⁹ Website available in English, German and Slovak.
⁴⁰ Website available in English and Slovak.
⁴¹ Website available in Slovak.
⁴² Website available in English and German.
⁴³ Website available in English, Czech, German and Russian.

Chamber of Commerce and Industry.[44]

IV.5.   [BGR] – [BULGARIA]

- http://www.bcci.bg/arbitration/index.html. Arbitration Court at the Bulgarian Chamber of Commerce and Industry.
- http://www.lex.bg. Information server on Bulgarian law.

IV.6.   [EST] – [ESTONIA]

- http://www.koda.ee. Arbitration Court attached to the Estonian Chamber of Commerce and Industry.[45]

IV.7.   [HRV] – [CROATIA]

- http://www2.hgk.hr/en/about cce.asp?izbor=pac. The Permanent Arbitration Court at the Croatian Chamber of Commerce.[46]

IV.8.   [HUN] – [HUNGARY]

- http://www.mkik.hu/index.php?id=1406. Court of Arbitration attached to the Hungarian Chamber of Commerce and Industry.[47]
- http://www.mkik.hu/index.php?id=1409&print=1. Act LXXI [Hungary] of 1994 On arbitration. Nonofficial English translation published on the portal of the Hungarian Chamber of Commerce. [Law on arbitration].

IV.9.   [LVA] - [LATVIA]

- http://www.chamber.lv. The Arbitration Court of the Latvian Chamber of Commerce and Industry LCCI.[48]

IV.10.   [LTU] – [LITHUANIA]

- http://www3.lrs.lt/pls/inter3/dokpaieska.showdoc_l?p_id=56461. Law on Commercial Arbitration of The Republic of Lithuania

---

[44]   Website available in English and Russian.
[45]   Website available in English, Estonian and Russian.
[46]   Website available in Croatian. Basic information available in English. See the English presentation of the arbitration court at the website.
[47]   Website available in Hungarian. Basic information available in English.
[48]   Website available in English, Latvian and Russian.

No I-1274 as of 2 April 1996.[49] Official translation by Lietuvos Respulikos Seimas (on the portal of the Parliament of the Republic of Lithuania).

• http://www.arbitrazas.lt. Vilniaus komercinio arbitražo teismas. Vilnius Court of Commercial Arbitration.[50]

IV.11. [MKD] – [MACEDONIA]

• http://www.mchamber.org.mk/%28S%28crtmab45gznl ucyny5lvrv en%29%29/default.aspx?lId=2&mId=50&smId=0.[51] The Permanent Court of Arbitration attached to the Economic Chamber of Macedonia [Стопанската комора на Македонија].

IV.12. [MDA] – [MOLDOVA]

• http://www.arbitraj.chamber.md/index.php?id=93. Curtea de Arbitraj Comercial International pe linga Camera de Comert si Industrie a Republicii Moldova. The International Commercial Arbitration Court of the Chamber of Commerce and Industry of the Republic of Moldova.[52]

IV.13. [POL] – [POLAND][53]

• http://www.sakig.pl/. Sąd Arbitrażowy przy Krajowej Izbie Gospodarczej w Warszawie.[54] Court of Arbitration at the Polish Chamber of Commerce in Warsaw.
• http://www.iccpolska.pl/ Polski Komitet Narodowy Międzynarodowej Izby Handlowej. Polish ICC National Committee.
• http://oirp.bydgoszcz.pl/index.php?page=statut-2.
Sądu Polubowny przy Okręgowej Izbie Radców Prawnych w Bydgoszczy. Court of Arbitration attached to the Regional Chamber of Legal Advisors in Bydgoscz.[55]

---

[49] Published in: Parliamentary record, 1998-04-01, Nr. 4 (*Teisės aktą priėmė - Lietuvos Respublikos Seimas*).
[50] Website available in English, Lithuanian and Polish.
[51] Website available in English and Macedonian.
[52] Website available in English, Moldovan and Russian.
[53] Operation and accessibility of all websites were last checked on 17 November 2010.
[54] Website available in English, German, French, Polish and Russian.
[55] Website available in Polish.

- **http://www.gca.org.pl/x.php/1,392/Arbitraz.html.** Sąd Arbitrażowy przy Izbie Bawełny w Gdyni. **Arbitration Court attached to the Gdynia Cotton Association.**[56]
- http://oirp.gda.pl/portal-dla-przedsiebiorcow/sad-polubowny. Stały Sąd Arbitrażowy przy Okręgowej Izbie Radców Prawnych w Gdańsku. Permanent Court of Arbitration attached to the Regional Chamber of Legal Advisers in Gdańsk.[57]
- http://www.igg.pl/1/node/39. Sąd Arbitrażowy przy Izbie Gospodarczej Gazownictwa. Court of Arbitration attached to The Chamber of the Natural Gas Industry.[58]
- http://www.ihk.pl/index.html?id=1635. Sąd Arbitrażowy przy Polsko-Niemieckiej Izbie Przemysłowo-Handlowej. Court of Arbitration attached to the Polish – German Chamber of Commerce and Industry.[59]
- http://www.iph.krakow.pl/?a=page&id=31. Sąd Polubowny przy Izbie Przemysłowo-Handlowej w Krakowie. Court of Arbitration attached to the Chamber of Industry and Trade in Krakow.[60]
- http://www.iph.torun.pl/index.php?aid=113837484143da38b99 fb66. Sąd Polubowny przy Izbie Przemysłowo-Handlowej w Toruniu. Court of Arbitration attached to the Chamber of Industry and Trade in Torun.[61]
- http://isap.sejm.gov.pl. Legal information (laws and regulations) system on the portal of the Sejm [Parliament] of the Republic of Poland.[62]
- http://www.kigm.pl/index.php?option=com_content&task =view&id=60&Itemid=65&lang=p. **Międzynarodowy Sąd Arbitrażowy przy Krajowej Izbie Gospodarki Morskiej. International Court of Arbitration attached to the** Polish Chamber of Maritime Commerce in Gdynia.[63]
- http://www.knf.gov.pl/regulacje/Sad_Polubowny/index.html. Sąd Polubowny przy Komisji Nadzoru Finansowego. Court of Arbitration attached to the Polish Financial Supervision Authority.[64]

---

[56] Website available in English and Polish.
[57] Website available in English and Polish.
[58] Website available in Polish. Some basic information, especially about the Chamber, also available in English and German.
[59] Website available in German and Polish.
[60] Website available in Polish.
[61] Website available in Polish. The portal also offers English version which, however, was not available during our last visit [17 November 2010] (we cannot rule out technical problems but we could not verify that before handing over this manuscript to CYArb® for printing).
[62] Website available in Polish. See also http://sejm.gov.pl.
[63] Website available in Polish. Some basic information available in English.
[64] Website available in English and Polish.

- http://www.liph.com.pl/index.php?body=7. Polubowny Sąd Łódzkiej Izby Przemysłowo-Handlowej. Court of Arbitration attached to the Chamber of Industry and Trade in Łódz.[65]
- http://www.nig.org.pl/sa/pl1.html. Sąd Arbitrażowy przy Nowotomyskiej Izbie Gospodarczej w Nowym Tomyślu. Court of Arbitration attached to the Chamber of Economy in Nowym Tomyśl.[66]
- http://www.nsa.gov.pl/. Supreme Administrative Court.[67]
- http://oirp.olsztyn.pl/content/blogsection/23/73/. Stały Sąd Arbitrażowy przy Okręgowej Izbie Radców Prawnych w Olsztynie. Permanent Court of Arbitration attached to the Regional Chamber of Legal Advisors in Olsztyn.[68]
- http://www.piit.org.pl/piit2/index.jsp?layout=1&news_cat_id=62&place=Menu01. Sąd Polubowny ds. Domen Internetowych przy Polskiej Izbie Informatyki i Telekomunikacji w Warszawie. Arbitration Court for Internet Domains attached to **The Polish Chamber of Information Technology and Telecommunications**.[69]
- http://www.polubowny.org/index.html. Centrum Mediacyjne oraz Stały Sąd Polubowny przy Fundacji Adwokatury Polskiej i Ośrodku Badawczym Adwokatury im. adw. W. Bayera. Mediation Center and Permanent Court of Arbitration attached to the Donation of Polish Bar and Center for Bar Research of W. Bayer.[70]
- http://www.pssp.org.pl/index.htm. Polskie Stowarzyszenie Sądownictva Polubownego – Polish Arbitration Association.
- http://www.riph.com.pl/index.php/Company/sub32. Sąd Arbitrażowy przy Regionalnej Izbie Przemysłowo-Handlowej w Gliwicach. The Permanent Court of Arbitration at the Regional Chamber of Commerce & Industry in Gliwice.[71]
- http://www.sadarbitrazowy.org.pl/. Sąd Arbitrażowy przy Polskiej Konfederacji Pracodawców Prywatnych Lewiatan. Court of Arbitration at the Polish Confederation of Private Employers Lewiatan.[72]
- http://www.oirpwarszawa.pl/kategoria/pokaz/idk/612/ida/520/strona/. Stały Sąd Polubowny przy Okręgowej Izbie Radców Prawnych w Warszawie. Permanent Court of Arbitration Attached to the Regional Chamber of Legal Advisers in Warszawa.[73]

---

[65] Website available in Polish.
[66] Website available in Polish.
[67] Website available in Polish.
[68] Website available in Polish.
[69] Website available in English and Polish.
[70] Website available in Polish.
[71] Website available in Polish. Some basic information also available in English and German.
[72] Website available in English and Polish.
[73] Website available in Polish.

- http://www.rig.katowice.pl/default.aspx?docId=30. Sąd Arbitra-żowy przy Regionalnej Izbie Gospodarczej w Katowicach. Court of Arbitration attached to the Chamber of Economy in Katowice.[74]
- http://www.sa.dig.wroc.pl/sa/index.php?option=com_content&task=view&id=69&Itemid=28. Sąd Arbitrażowy przy Dolnośląskiej Izbie Gospodarczej we Wrocławiu. Court of Arbitration attached to the Lower Silesia Chamber of Economy in Wrocław.[75]
- http://www.sejm.gov.pl. Sejm Rzeczypospolitej Polskiej. Sejm [Parliament] of the Republic of Poland.[76]/[77]
- http://www.senat.gov.pl. Senat Rzeczypospolitej polskiej. The Senate of the Republic of Poland.[78]
- http://www.sn.pl/. Supreme Court of the Republic of Poland.[79]
- http://www.ssp.piph.pl/. Stały Sąd Polubowny przy Pomorskiej Izbie Przemysłowo-Handlowej w Gdańsku. Permanent Court of Arbitration attached to the See [Maritime] Chamber of Industry and Trade in Gdańsk.[80]
- http://www.trybunal.gov.pl. Constitutional Court.[81]
- http://www.wib.com.pl/index.php?idkat=11. Sąd Arbitrażowy przy Wielkopolskiej Izbie Budownictwa. Court of Arbitration attached to **The Wielkopolska Chamber of Construction.**[82]
- http://www.wiph.pl/content/view/69/53/. Sąd Arbitrażowy Izb i Organizacji Gospodarczych Wielkopolski. Arbitration Court attached to the All Polish Chamber of Industry and Trade.[83]
- http://www.zbp.pl/site.php?s=MGM0YzkzYWY1MTc3Nw. Sąd Polubowny przy Związku Banków Polskich. Court of Arbitration attached to the Polish Bank Association (ZBP).[84]
- http://www.ziph.pl/strona,19,polubowny-sad-gospodarczy. Polubowny Sąd Gospodarczy przy Zachodniej Izbie Przemysłowo-Handlowej w Gorzowie Wielkopolskim. Court of Arbitration attached to The Western Chamber of Industry and Commerce in Gorzow Wielkopolski.[85]

IV.14. [ROM] – [ROMANIA]

---

[74] Website available in Polish.
[75] Website available in Polish. Applicable Rules of proceedings available in English and German.
[76] Website available in English and Polish.
[77] See also http://isap.sejm.gov.pl – legal information system available through the portal of Sejm.
[78] Website available in English, French, German, Polish and Russian.
[79] Website available in English and Polish.
[80] Website available in Polish.
[81] Website available in English and Polish.
[82] Website available in Polish. Basic information, especially about the Chamber, available in English.
[83] Website available in Polish.
[84] Website available in English and Polish.
[85] Website available in Polish. Basic information and information about the Chamber also available in English, French, German and Russian.

- http://arbitration.ccir.ro. The Court of International Commercial Arbitration attached to The Chamber of Commerce and Industry of Romania.[86]

IV.15. [RUS] – [RUSSIAN FEDERATION]

- http://www.arbitrations.ru. Russian Arbitration Association.[87]
- http://www.iccwbo.ru. ICC National Committee Russian Federation
- http://www.spbcci.ru/engarbitaltribunal. The Arbitration tribunal at Saint-Petersburg Chamber of Commerce and Industry.[88]

IV.16. [SVN] – [SLOVENIA]

- http://www.sloarbitration.org. The Permanent Court of Arbitration, although attached to the Chamber of Commerce and Industry of Slovenia [CCIS].[89]
- http://www.sloarbitration.org/english/introduction/organization. html. Nonofficial English translations of Slovenian law on or related to arbitration published on the portal of the Permanent Court of Arbitration, although attached to the Chamber of Commerce and Industry of Slovenia. (i) Code of Civil Procedure of Slovenia.[90] (ii) Private International Law And Procedure Act.[91] [Law on arbitration].

---

[86] Website available in English and Romanian.
[87] Website available in English and Russian.
[88] Website available in English and Russian.
[89] Website available in English and Slovenian.
[90] Published in the: Official Gazette of the Republic of Slovenia, No. 26/99.
[91] Published in the: Official Gazette of the Republic of Slovenia, No. 56/99.

Index

A

achmea **4**/1; **10**/1, 2, 3, 4, 5, 6, 7, 11, 13, 16, 17, 21, 22, 26, 27, 29, 48, 49, 50, 54, 56, 57, 61

anationality **2**/8

annulled award **1**/1, 2, 3, 4, 6, 7, 9, 10, 13, 15, 17, 18, 19, 21, 22, 23, 24, 25, 26, 27, 28, 29; **3**/30, 33, 34, 35, 37, 53, 69; **4**/1, 2, 3, 7, 8, 9, 11, 12, 13, 14, 15, 16, 17, 19, 20, 21, 24, 25, 29, 30, 33, 34, 35, 36; **6**/3, 12; **8**/16, 21, 30, 41, 42; **11**/66, 67

arbitral award **1**/1, 2, 3, 4, 5, 6, 7, 8, 9, 10, 11, 12, 13, 14, 15, 16, 17, 18, 19, 20, 21, 22, 23, 24, 25, 26, 27, 28, 29; **2**/9, 19, 21, 22, 23, 24, 25, 26, 27, 32, 33, 34, 43, 73, 127, 130, 135; **3**/12, 42, 45, 51; **4**/1, 3, 5, 9, 11, 12, 13, 14, 15, 16, 17, 20, 23, 24, 26, 27, 28, 29, 30, 31, 33, 35, 36; **5**/1, 4,

5, 6, 7, 9, 12, 13, 14, 15, 17, 18, 20, 21, 22, 23, 24; **6**/1, 2, 3, 4, 9, 10, 11, 12, 14, 24, 25, 36, 41, 42, 46, 49, 54, 73, 74; **7**/1, 11, 12, 14, 15, 16, 17, 25, 30, 34, 36, 37, 40; **8**/1, 2, 3, 6, 15, 16, 17, 18, 19, 20, 21, 22, 23, 25, 26, 27, 28, 29, 30, 31, 32, 33, 35, 36, 37, 38, 40, 41, 42, 43, 44, 45; **9**/10, 12, 13, 14, 17, 18, 20, 21, 22, 23, 24, 25, 27, 28, 35, 36, 41, 42, 45, 46, 48, 49; **10**/7, 10, 11, 16, 17, 22, 24, 25, 26, 28, 47, 57, 58, 61; **11**/1, 2, 3, 4, 5, 6, 8, 9, 10, 11, 12, 13, 14, 15, 16, 17, 18, 19, 20, 21, 23, 24, 25, 26, 27, 28, 29, 30, 31, 32, 33, 34, 35, 36, 37, 38, 39, 40, 41, 42, 43, 44, 45, 46, 47, 48, 49, 50, 51, 52, 60, 61, 62, 63, 64, 65, 66, 67, 68, 69, 70, 71, 72, 73, 74, 75, 76, 77, 78, 79, 80, 83, 84, 86, 88, 91, 93, 94, 95, 96, 97, 99, 100, 101, 102, 104

arbitration **1**/1, 2, 4, 5, 6, 7, 8, 9, 10, 11, 12, 14, | 471

G

I

CALL FOR PAPERS FOR VOLUMES 2020/2021

Did you find the articles in the ninth volume of CYArb®
interesting?

Would you like to react to a current article
or contribute to future volumes?

We are seeking authors for both
the Czech Yearbook on International Law® and the
Czech (& Central European) Yearbook of Arbitration®.

The general topics for the 2020/2021 volumes are following:

CYIL 2020
*Human Rights, Humanity
and Sustainable Development
from the International Law
Perspective*

CYArb® 2020
*Arbitration and International
Treaties, Customs and
Standards*

CYIL 2021
Immunities and Privileges

CYArb® 2021
(Best) Practices in Arbitration

More general and contact information available at:

**www.czechyearbook.org
www.lexlata.pro**

CYIL – Czech Yearbook of International Law®, 2020
Human Rights, Humanity and Sustainable Development from the International Law Perspective

It is sometimes argued that human rights are an already settled and precisely defined category of imperative standards. Democratic states and international organisations have for decades now attempted to clarify and enforce, as much as possible, human rights and humanity standards, as well as human approaches, to the broadest possible extent. Nonetheless, the contents of even such crucial categories may be susceptible to various changes. The reason is that our present global world is completely different from the world in which the modern standards of human rights came into existence and developed. Globalisation and maximum exploitation of all resources lead the international public, with an ever-increasing urgency, to discuss and adopt measures which ought to secure sustainable development. However, what is the relationship between these measures and fundamental human rights and principles of humanity, and how much can the contents of the latter be influenced by the former? The procedural aspects are another important factor, namely whether the procedural mechanisms of protection and enforcement of human rights are affected as well, and whether perhaps the time has come for a change or, as the case may be, whether the implementation of such changes in our present international environment is possible at all.

CYArb® – Czech (& Central European) Yearbook of Arbitration®, 2020
Arbitration and International Treaties, Customs and Standards

Arbitration is a highly internationalised area. International practice has always influenced the legal development and practice in the individual countries. Conversely, national standards have influenced the creation of international standards and have also significantly influenced the creation and subsequent implementation of international agreements. The 2020 Volume will focus not only on the contents and interpretation of international agreements and international standards, but also on how they change in consequence of an extensive and fast globalisation, new information technologies, how the creation of regional groupings, various political and economic crises bear on or affect their application, etc. The editors wish to point out that fundamental multilateral international agreements are not the only important factors; the often unjustly ignored bilateral international treaties and international agreements limited to a particular region, such as legal assistance treaties, have played their role too as some of them also contain provisions concerning arbitration.

CYIL – Czech Yearbook of International Law®, 2021

Immunities and Privileges

The issues relating to immunities and privileges will be discussed from the public and private law point of view, addressing the immunity of a state, as well as personal and special immunities, their content, and manifestations. The needs of the globalized environment namely suggest that immunities often manifest in situations that international law was previously not concerned with at all, or only marginally. Attention will for example therefore be given to immunities from the perspective of how the Vienna Convention on Diplomatic Relations is applied in practice, immunities in the case of civil and criminal Court proceedings, but also immunities in special situations. Although privileges do not prime facie pose that significant of a question in international law, they cannot be ignored as they are a significant attribute of state representation, diplomatic employees, but also other representatives of the state in international relations.

CYArb® – Czech (& Central European) Yearbook of Arbitration®, 2021

(Best) Practices in Arbitration

Although we are talking about international standards of arbitration, the course of every arbitration is highly influenced by the place (seat) of arbitration. The so called denationalization of arbitration seems to be a debunked idea. Or is this not the case? In any event, despite a high degree of standardization of procedures in arbitration, the influence of national and regional standards cannot be ignored. The standardization of procedures is evident throughout the entire duration of arbitral proceeding. It is evident in commencement of proceedings, in the preparation for hearings, in the hearing themselves, in the burden of proof, as well as in the termination of proceedings. Every state and every region, same as every permanent arbitral institution, has its own "time-tested" procedures through which it influences the culture of arbitration.